Communications
in Computer and Information Science   2370

Series Editors

Gang Li, *School of Information Technology, Deakin University, Burwood, VIC, Australia*
Joaquim Filipe, *Polytechnic Institute of Setúbal, Setúbal, Portugal*
Zhiwei Xu, *Chinese Academy of Sciences, Beijing, Chir* ‾

Rationale

The CCIS series is devoted to the publication of proceedings of computer science conferences. Its aim is to efficiently disseminate original research results in informatics in printed and electronic form. While the focus is on publication of peer-reviewed full papers presenting mature work, inclusion of reviewed short papers reporting on work in progress is welcome, too. Besides globally relevant meetings with internationally representative program committees guaranteeing a strict peer-reviewing and paper selection process, conferences run by societies or of high regional or national relevance are also considered for publication.

Topics

The topical scope of CCIS spans the entire spectrum of informatics ranging from foundational topics in the theory of computing to information and communications science and technology and a broad variety of interdisciplinary application fields.

Information for Volume Editors and Authors

Publication in CCIS is free of charge. No royalties are paid, however, we offer registered conference participants temporary free access to the online version of the conference proceedings on SpringerLink (http://link.springer.com) by means of an http referrer from the conference website and/or a number of complimentary printed copies, as specified in the official acceptance email of the event.

CCIS proceedings can be published in time for distribution at conferences or as post-proceedings, and delivered in the form of printed books and/or electronically as USBs and/or e-content licenses for accessing proceedings at SpringerLink. Furthermore, CCIS proceedings are included in the CCIS electronic book series hosted in the SpringerLink digital library at http://link.springer.com/bookseries/7899. Conferences publishing in CCIS are allowed to use Online Conference Service (OCS) for managing the whole proceedings lifecycle (from submission and reviewing to preparing for publication) free of charge.

Publication process

The language of publication is exclusively English. Authors publishing in CCIS have to sign the Springer CCIS copyright transfer form, however, they are free to use their material published in CCIS for substantially changed, more elaborate subsequent publications elsewhere. For the preparation of the camera-ready papers/files, authors have to strictly adhere to the Springer CCIS Authors' Instructions and are strongly encouraged to use the CCIS LaTeX style files or templates.

Abstracting/Indexing

CCIS is abstracted/indexed in DBLP, Google Scholar, EI-Compendex, Mathematical Reviews, SCImago, Scopus. CCIS volumes are also submitted for the inclusion in ISI Proceedings.

How to start

To start the evaluation of your proposal for inclusion in the CCIS series, please send an e-mail to ccis@springer.com.

Hugo Plácido da Silva · Pietro Cipresso
Editors

Computer-Human Interaction Research and Applications

8th International Conference, CHIRA 2024
Porto, Portugal, November 21–22, 2024
Proceedings, Part I

 Springer

Editors
Hugo Plácido da Silva
IT - Instituto de Telecomunicações,
Instituto Superior Técnico
Lisbon, Portugal

Pietro Cipresso
University of Turin
Turin, Italy

ISSN 1865-0929   ISSN 1865-0937 (electronic)
Communications in Computer and Information Science
ISBN 978-3-031-82632-0   ISBN 978-3-031-82633-7 (eBook)
https://doi.org/10.1007/978-3-031-82633-7

This Springer imprint is published by the registered company Springer Nature Switzerland AG
The registered company address is: Gewerbestrasse 11, 6330 Cham, Switzerland

If disposing of this product, please recycle the paper.

Preface

This book contains the proceedings of the 8th International Conference on Computer-Human Interaction Research and Applications (CHIRA). This year, CHIRA was held in Porto, Portugal, on November 21–22, 2024. It was sponsored by the Institute for Systems and Technologies of Information, Control and Communication (INSTICC). CHIRA 2024 was also organized in cooperation with the ACM Special Interest Group on Management Information Systems (SIGMIS) and the European Society for Socially Embedded Technologies (EUSSET).

The purpose of CHIRA is to bring together professionals, academics and students who are interested in the advancement of research and practical applications in its field of interest, covering different aspects of Computer-Human Interaction, including Human Factors and Information Systems, Interactive Devices, Interaction Design and Adaptive and Intelligent Systems.

CHIRA 2024 received 76 paper submissions from 28 countries of which 16 were accepted and published as full papers and 45 were accepted and published as short papers. A double-blind paper review was performed for each submission, including papers submitted to the special sessions, by at least 2 but usually 3 or more members of the International Program Committee, which was composed of established researchers and domain experts.

The high quality of the CHIRA 2024 program was enhanced by the keynote lectures delivered by distinguished speakers who are renowned experts in their fields: Cathy Craig (Ulster University and CEO/Co-founder INCISIV Ltd., UK), Fabio Paternò (CNR-ISTI, Italy), and Laura Marchal-Crespo (TU Delft, Netherlands).

The conference was complemented by a Special Session on Pervasive Information Systems, chaired by Raoudha Ben Djemaa, and a Special Session on Interaction between Humans and Smart Spaces, chaired by Nuno Almeida and Ana Patrícia Rocha.

All presented papers will be submitted for indexation by DBLP, Google Scholar, EI-Compendex, INSPEC, Japanese Science and Technology Agency (JST), Norwegian Register for Scientific Journals and Series, Mathematical Reviews, SCImago, Scopus, zbMATH and Web of Science/Conference Proceedings Citation Index.

As recognition for the best contributions, several awards based on the combined marks of paper reviewing, as assessed by the Program Committee, and the quality of the presentation, as assessed by session chairs at the conference venue, were conferred at the closing session of the conference.

The program for this conference required the dedicated effort of many people. Firstly, we must thank the authors, whose research efforts are herewith recorded. Next, we thank the members of the Program Committee and the auxiliary reviewers for their diligent and professional reviewing. We would also like to deeply thank the invited speakers for their invaluable contribution and for taking the time to prepare their talks. Finally, a word of appreciation for the hard work of the INSTICC team; organizing a conference of this level is a task that can only be achieved by the collaborative effort of a dedicated and highly competent team.

We hope you all had an exciting and inspiring conference. We hope to have contributed to the development of our research community, and we look forward to having additional research results presented at the next edition of CHIRA, details of which are available at https://chira.scitevents.org.

November 2024

Hugo Plácido da Silva
Pietro Cipresso

Organization

Conference Chair

Pietro Cipresso   University of Turin, Italy

Program Chair

Hugo Plácido da Silva   IT - Instituto de Telecomunicações, Portugal

Program Committee

Iyad Abu Doush   American University of Kuwait, Kuwait
Nuno Almeida   University of Aveiro, Portugal
Josef Altmann   University of Applied Sciences Upper Austria,
                                     Austria
Michael Behringer   Universität Stuttgart, Germany
Fevzi Belli   Izmir Institute of Technology, Turkey
Cosimo Birtolo   Poste Italiane, Italy
Guido Borghi   Università di Bologna, Italy
Paolo Bottoni   Sapienza University of Rome, Italy
Chris Bowers   University of Worcester, UK
André Brandão   Universidade Federal do ABC, Brazil
John Brooke   Independent Researcher, UK
Giuseppe Caggianese   National Research Council of Italy, Italy
Valentín Cardeñoso Payo   Universidad de Valladolid, Spain
John W. Castro   University of Atacama, Chile
Stuart Charters   Lincoln University, New Zealand
Yang-Wai Chow   University of Wollongong, Australia
Cesar Collazos   Universidad del Cauca, Colombia
Lizette de Wet   University of the Free State, South Africa
Vincenzo Deufemia   Università di Salerno, Italy
Thomas Eskridge   Florida Institute of Technology, USA
Micaela Esteves   Independent Researcher, Portugal
Ahmed Farooq   University of Tampere, Finland
Alexandre Ferreira   Universidade Estadual de Campinas, Brazil

Francisco Rebelo	ITI/LARSys and CIAUD, University of Lisbon, Portugal
Jungpil Shin	University of Aizu, Japan
Markku Turunen	Tampere University, Finland
Frédéric Vanderhaegen	Université Polytechnique Hauts-de-France, France
Gregg Vesonder	Stevens Institute of Technology, USA
Nikolas Vidakis	Hellenic Mediterranean University, Greece
Spyros Vosinakis	University of the Aegean, Greece
Andreas Wendemuth	Otto von Guericke University, Germany
Marcus Winter	University of Brighton, UK
Ahmed Mohamed Fahmy Yousef	Fayoum University, Egypt
Floriano Zini	Free University of Bozen-Bolzano, Italy

Additional Reviewers

Nicolò Di Domenico	University of Bologna, Italy
Yi-Jheng Huang	Yuan Ze University, Taiwan, Republic of China
Hugo Plácido da Silva	IT - Instituto de Telecomunicações, Portugal

Invited Speakers

Cathy Craig	Ulster University/INCISIV Ltd., UK
Fabio Paternò	CNR-ISTI, Italy
Laura Marchal-Crespo	TU Delft, Netherlands

Invited Speakers

Virtual Reality: Taking Performance to the Next Level

Cathy Craig

Ulster University and CEO/Co-founder INCISIV Ltd., UK

Abstract. This talk will demonstrate how Virtual Reality (VR) can be used as a tool to understand and improve movement performance. The first part will show how rudimentary VR technology was used in the early 2000s to carefully control what the brain sees (perception), but also very accurately measure how the brain responds (action). The versatility of VR means it can be used to study human behaviour in many different sport and health applications. Examples from behavioural neuroscience will showcase how VR can help us understand decision-making in elite sport but also conditions such as freezing of gait in people with Parkinson's disease. The second part of the talk will highlight how the recent evolution of both VR hardware and software has opened exciting new possibilities to take research out of the lab so it can make a difference to people's lives. Examples will demonstrate how VR applications that are commercially available can enhance performance through the power of gameplay. This could be VR apps that train perceptuo-motor skills in the home or monitor changes in players' neural fitness that can occur because of injuries (e.g. concussions). The talk will conclude by sharing some thoughts on the future of VR technology and the Metaverse and highlight opportunities for researchers to take advantage of this technology.

Human Control in Daily Environment Automations

Fabio Paternò

Human Interfaces in Information Systems Laboratory, CNR-ISTI, Pisa, Italy

Abstract. How people interact with digital technologies is currently caught between the Internet of Things and Artificial Intelligence. Such technological trends provide great opportunities and new possibilities, but there are also risks and new problems. There can be intelligent services that eventually generate actions that do not match the real user needs. People may have difficulties understanding how to personalize the automatically generated automations. Thus, a fundamental challenge is how to provide tools that allow users to control and configure smart environments consisting of hundreds of interconnected devices, objects, and appliances. This means designing tools that allow people to obtain "humanations" (automations that users can understand and modify). This talk will discuss concepts and methods that can be useful to address the core challenges of human control over automations that can involve people, objects, devices, intelligent services, and robots. The goal is to identify innovative approaches to support end users, even without programming experience, to understand, create, or modify the automations in their daily environments, augmenting the human capacity to manage automations through effective interaction modalities, relevant analytics, understandable explanations, and intelligent recommendations. From this perspective, I will discuss how trigger-action programming can be a useful connection point between a wide variety of technologies and implementation languages and people without programming experience. However, it also presents nuances that may become apparent and critical in realistic cases, generating undesired effects. Aspects that should be considered carefully include temporal aspects of triggers and actions, configuring smart environments with multiple active automations, and security and privacy issues. I will also discuss current practises, some experiences in application domains, such as the smart home, the opportunities provided by interaction modalities such as conversational agents and mobile augmented reality, how to provide explanations to make the behaviour of the smart space more transparent, and possible future research directions.

Towards a Meaningful Robot-Assisted Neurorehabilitation Experience

Laura Marchal-Crespo

TU Delft, Netherlands

Abstract. Every year, millions of stroke survivors lose their functional autonomy due to paralysis, posing a tremendous societal and economic challenge. In the absence of a cure for stroke, clinical evidence suggests that patients should engage in personalized, task-specific, high-intensity training to maximize their recovery. In this talk, I put forward a new mindset to overcome many of the fundamental limitations of traditional approaches in stroke neurorehabilitation. I present the new trends in rehabilitation robotics and immersive virtual reality that leverage realistic interaction with tangible virtual objects and discuss how a better understanding of human skill acquisition can improve neurorehabilitation approaches. Laura Marchal-Crespo is an Associate Professor at the Department of Cognitive Robotics, Faculty of Mechanical Engineering, Delft University of Technology, the Netherlands. She is also associated with Erasmus Medical Center, Rotterdam, the Netherlands. Her research focuses on the general areas of human-machine interaction and biological learning and, in particular, the use of robotic devices and immersive virtual reality for the assessment and rehabilitation of patients with acquired brain injuries such as stroke.

Contents – Part I

Contents – Part II

Special Session on Pervasive Information Systems

Special Session on Interaction between Humans and Smart Spaces

Main Event

Systematic Integration of Design Prototypes into the LMS Moodle: Methods and Challenges in Practice

Thorleif Harder$^{(\boxtimes)}$ ⓘ, Gilbert Drzyzga ⓘ, Jan-Marco Bruhns,
and Anna-Lena Langhans

Institute for Interactive Systems, Technische Hochschule Lübeck, Lübeck, Germany
{thorleif.harder,gilbert.drzyzga,jan-marco.bruhns,
anna-lena.langhans}@th-luebeck.de

Abstract. Digitization has a central role to play in the ever-changing educational landscape, with learning management systems (LMS) such as Moodle becoming increasingly important. The integration of user-centered design prototypes into such systems is a significant challenge, particularly due to technical limitations and the need to maintain a high level of usability. This paper discusses a methodologically based approach, developed on the basis of a research project, to effectively transfer design prototypes into a functional Moodle plugin. Technical and design challenges are addressed through iterative development and the continuous involvement of students. The results show the various challenges of integrating design prototypes into the LMS Moodle, especially when adapting cascading style sheets (CSS) styling and structuring modular templates. It is also shown that the handling of dynamic content and visualization problems are crucial factors for effective implementation. Based on these findings, best practices were developed that emphasize the adaptation of design prototypes to technical environments and proactive adaptation to dynamic content. These practices provide valuable guidelines for developing LMS plugins that are not only technically functional, but also useable and adapted to specific learning needs.

Keywords: Learning management systems · User-Centered design · Moodle · Agile development · Best practices

1 Introduction

The advancing digitalization of education requires innovative solutions to improve the quality of online learning. While learning management systems (LMS) such as Moodle play a central role in the delivery of digital learning content [1], they often reveal limitations in terms of usability and individualization of the learning experience [2]. These challenges can sometimes impair learners' self-regulation - an important competence for effective studying in digital environments [3].

In this context, the importance of user-centered, intuitive design solutions, such as those developed in prototyping software, becomes apparent. These tools allow for

H. Plácido da Silva and P. Cipresso (Eds.): CHIRA 2024, CCIS 2370, pp. 3–20, 2025.
https://doi.org/10.1007/978-3-031-82633-7_1

the design of creative and usable user interfaces that can potentially increase learner engagement and self-regulation [4]. However, the integration of these design prototypes into the often rigid, technical structures of an LMS presents a substantial challenge. Although specific studies on the challenges of integrating design prototypes into LMSs are lacking, practical experiences from general software development point to similar difficulties, such as compatibility issues with different platforms and system versions, ensuring interoperability with other applications or plugins, and security and privacy issues [5]. The integration of general software solutions on LMS platforms is often not directly possible due to their specific structures and requirements. The targeted transfer from an interactive prototype to a fully functional Moodle plugin therefore requires careful consideration and integration of specific technical aspects, such as adapting to the Moodle architecture, ensuring data integrity and security and optimizing the user interface and experience [6].

To address these challenges, a structured approach based on a user-centered design process was employed. As demonstrated in a related design study [4], this approach involves iterative development and continuous user involvement to maintain the usability of the design throughout the development process. The design study outlined the following key steps:

1. **Needs Analysis and Expert Interviews.** Understanding the needs and preferences of users through semi-structured interviews and quantitative surveys [7].
2. **Prototype Development.** Creating flexible and interactive design prototypes using prototyping tools to facilitate quick iterations and early feedback [8].
3. **Evaluation and Iterative Adjustment.** Continuously improving the prototypes through various evaluation methods, such as eye-tracking studies and usability tests, to optimize the user interface and address cognitive challenges [9].

These steps conclude in the implementation phase, where the refined design prototypes are integrated into the LMS Moodle by translating design specifications into functional code. This ensures compatibility with the technical environment and maintains the user-friendliness achieved during the design process. Based on this background and the findings from the design study, this paper presents a structured methodology that addresses the technical challenges of integrating design prototypes into a functional Moodle plugin, such as adapting to Moodle's framework, ensuring seamless functionality, and optimizing user experience. The focus is on the integration of user-centered design elements to enhance the learning experience.

Through iterative development and continuous involvement of students, not only the technical implementation of the plugin is ensured, but also adaptation to specific user requirements is optimized. Additionally, best practices are presented to support future designers and developers in creating LMS plugins. These emphasize user-centered design, agile development, and effective collaboration, ensuring that future systems are both functional and user-intuitive.

1.1 Student-Centered Learner Dashboard (LD) to Enhance Self-regulation

As part of a research project involving a network of universities with over 4,000 digitally enrolled students, an LD was developed [4]. The primary goal of this project is the analysis of usage data from the LMS Moodle to analyze certain usage behaviors. The LD is to be integrated into the LMS Moodle as an optional plugin and will be available to online students, provided they give their consent. In addition, the dashboard is intended to motivate students to engage in critical self-reflection and self-organization through a visual display of their current learning progress and possible further development and to provide them with targeted recommendations for improvement [4].

The development of the LD was motivated by findings from previous qualitative and quantitative studies that identified the specific needs and preferences of online students [7]. The LD includes seven specific modules, also called "cards," designed to enhance learners' self-reflection and self-regulation. The creation of these cards is a response to learners' expressed desire for a flexible system [10]. Table 1 below summarizes the main cards of the LD.

Table 1. Summary of the main cards of the LD.

Functionality	Description
Planning assistant	The planning assistant provides an overview of upcoming web conferences, submission tasks, and other activities. Users can add new appointments and events directly in the dashboard, simplifying organization and planning
Learning progress	The speedometer visualizes learning progress and shows how far learners have progressed towards achieving their goals. It reflects progress based on task assessments and previous learning behavior, with color-coded areas indicating performance levels
Usage activity	The usage activity provides a detailed overview of the time spent on various activities in the LMS Moodle. This visualization helps users to quickly see how much time they spend on learning modules, discussion forums, tests, and other course components
Tasks overview	The "Tasks Overview" card lists all tasks in the course and shows their status. This helps students keep track of assignments and deadlines, ensuring effective workload management
Probability of task success	The "Probability of task success" card displays the likelihood of successfully completing submission tasks based on past performance and current progress. It shows the probability as a percentage
Learning goals	The "Learning Goals" card shows individual learning goals, categorized under tabs like "Today," "Tomorrow," "This Week," "This Month," and "Future." Completed goals can be marked and removed from the list under the "Completed" tab
Reading Progress Indicator	The "Reading Progress Indicator" lists all documents integrated into the course, such as PDFs, text documents, videos, or audio files, and shows the progress of reading these materials

There are also higher-level functionalities that are intended to make the LD customizable. These include an editing function that allows students to add, remove, and arrange the cards to address their individual needs. This flexibility in design supports the principles of user-centered design, which aim to adapt systems to meet the specific needs and preferences of end users [10]. In addition, the LD can be presented in three different views that display different information: Module View, Semester View, and Overall View. The module view provides a detailed overview of the specific content and activities of the current module. In the semester view, all modules taken in the current semester are displayed, and the overall view allows access to all modules and activities of the student's entire academic history. In this way, students can view all relevant information, even from previous semesters.

Figure 1 below provides a comprehensive visual summary of all seven cards of the LD. The numbers in the Fig. 1 correspond to the functionalities listed in Table 1, illustrating the integrated functionalities of the LD. The LD has also a header that provides various functions, including an edit/help function and a configuration menu. This Figure illustrates the integrated functionalities of the dashboard, showcasing how each card contributes to the overall goal of enhancing students' self-regulation and learning experience.

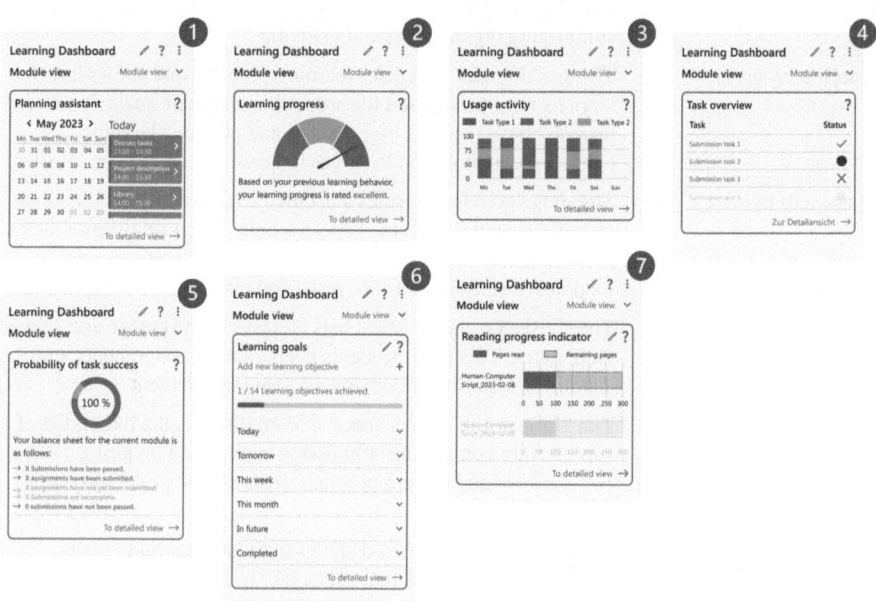

Fig. 1. Summary of the representation of the main cards in the LD.

These functions were systematically evaluated as part of the research project. For example, several eye-tracking studies identified cognitive challenges when interacting with the LD [9, 10]. These studies allowed close observation of users' eye movements to understand which areas of the LD can lead to cognitive overload. Furthermore, various traditional design methods were applied to identify challenges in both the accessibility of the system and the user experience. A participatory approach was taken to ensure the direct involvement of users in the development and optimization of the LD [11]. The user interface of the cards within the LD is carefully divided into two main views: a summary view and a detailed view.

Summary View. The summary view provides a reduced level of information density that allows students to initially gain an overview of the relevant content without being overwhelmed. This approach is based on cognitive load theory, which postulates that human information processing capacity is limited [12, 13]. By reducing irrelevant information, the cognitive capacity of learners is prevented from being overloaded by too many simultaneous inputs, leading to more efficient processing and better understanding of relevant content. In addition, this view supports information management by allowing students to selectively explore content that is most relevant to their learning goals and current needs. This strategic reduction and organization of information can thus enhance self-regulation and self-directed learning [10].

Detailed View. The detailed view provides a comprehensive density of information for students who want more in-depth information about the addressed card. This approach supports the concept of deep learning, which aims to help learners understand complex relationships and reflect critically on what they have learned [14]. By providing detailed information, students are encouraged to make connections between different areas of knowledge and enhance critical thinking. The detailed view allows learners to deepen their knowledge and analyze specific aspects of their learning material in detail, which can lead to a deeper and more lasting understanding. In addition, this view supports individual learning strategy by allowing students to learn at their own pace and according to their focus of interest, which is essential for effective educational processes.

Figure 2 below shows the basic structure of the LD and demonstrates the navigation options between the two views.

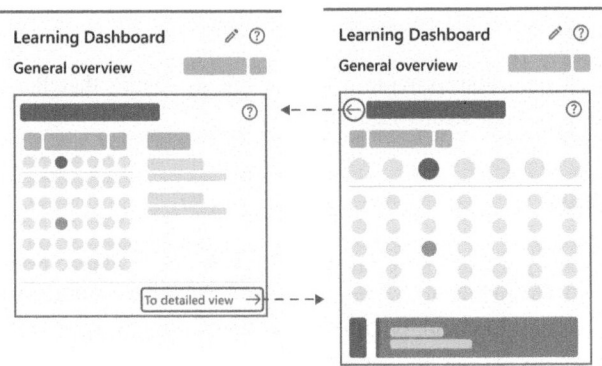

Fig. 2. Interaction between the summary- and detailed view [8].

Importance of the Research Project for the Integration of the Design Prototype into the LMS Moodle. The research project in which the LD was developed is particularly well suited to demonstrating the integration of design concepts into an operational

LMS such as Moodle, as it was designed from the scratch according to the principles of user-centered design. This approach places the needs and preferences of the user - in this case the students - at the center of the development process. By continuously involving the users in the design, from the first design prototypes to the final implementation in the Moodle system, it was possible to ensure that the final product is not only technically functional, but also usable and adapted to the specific learning needs.

This approach makes it possible to precisely achieve the goals defined in the project, such as enhancing students' self-regulation and organization through the dashboard. The application of the user-centered design process thus provides a solid basis for the presentation of the systematic integration and ensures that all developed features contribute effectively to supporting the learning process and can be used intuitively by users.

1.2   Objectives

The main objective of this paper is to present a methodologically based approach that enables design prototypes created with prototyping software to be systematically integrated into a Moodle plugin. Importance is attached to taking students' needs and preferences into account throughout the entire development process. Detailed documentation and evaluation of the development process will demonstrate how a usable design can be effectively implemented in a technical system.

Furthermore, the objective of the paper is to highlight challenges and solution strategies that arise during implementation. This provides practical insights and best practices for other developers working on the development of similar e-learning tools. The following research questions (RQ) guide the study:

1. How can design elements of a design prototype be effectively migrated to the technical architecture of the LMS Moodle?
2. What technical challenges are faced during the integration of a prototype into a Moodle plugin?

These research questions provide a framework to ensure that the paper is both theoretically sound and practically relevant.

2   Methodology

This section presents the LD development process, which is characterized by a structured user-centered design process according to [15]. The user-centered design approach covers all phases of development, but this article focuses specifically on the design and implementation phases. These are central to the integration of the LD into the LMS Moodle. Careful design conception, a 4-phase development model and interdisciplinary collaboration ensure the integration of design prototypes into technical Moodle plugins. By fostering a collaborative environment, the project leveraged diverse expertise to refine the LD. It also describes in detail how the various stakeholders are systematically supported to ensure effective integration into the final product. The complete methodology can be seen in Fig. 3 below.

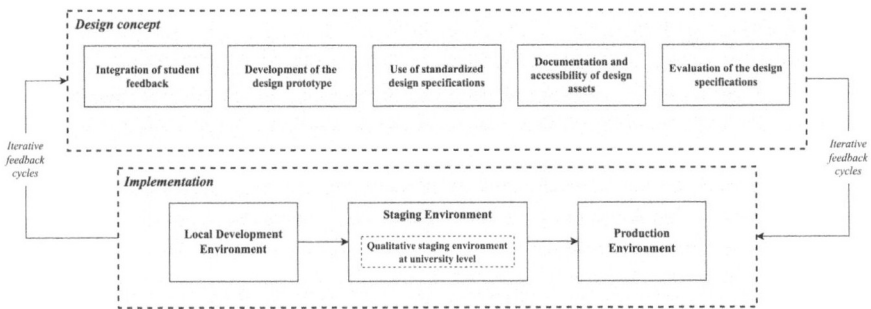

Fig. 3. Schematic representation of the methodical process for transferring design prototypes to the LMS Moodle.

2.1 Design Concept: Foundations for the Technical Integration into the LMS

As part of the user-centered design process, special focus was placed on the subsequent integration of the design prototypes into the LMS Moodle during the conception phase. This phase focused on creating a solid foundation for a smooth technical integration by applying specific design and development strategies from the beginning. The following sections address RQ1 and explain in detail the steps that were considered for an effective transfer:

Integration of Student Feedback. The design phase started with the creation of a paper prototype, which was informed by a thorough needs analysis based on semi-structured interviews and an in-depth quantitative survey of students [7]. The insights gained confirmed the need for an exclusively accessible LD and formed the basis for the development of initial design prototypes.

Development of the Design Prototype. Using the prototyping software Figma[1], flexible and interactive design prototypes were created. Figma allowed different design concepts to be iterated and adapted quickly, which was essential for obtaining early feedback. The prototypes included substantial visuals and interaction mechanisms designed to ensure an intuitive user experience within Moodle [8]. Additionally, various design iterations were tested in controlled environments to gather preliminary data on user interactions and preferences. These early tests were crucial for identifying potential usability issues before the full-scale implementation [4, 10, 11].

Use of Standardized Design Specifications. To facilitate later technical integration, standardized specifications for color schemes, typography, and layouts were used from the beginning. These specifications followed the established guidelines of the university network and served as a bridge between the designers and the developers. They ensured that design intentions could be realized without loss of clarity or quality and made it easier for developers to understand the desired final product [16].

Documentation and Accessibility of Design Assets. An accurate and comprehensive documentation of all design elements and assets was crucial to enable a seamless and

---

[1] https://www.figma.com/.

accurate integration of the designs into the technical implementation [17]. Figma's developer mode (dev mode)[2] was instrumental in providing developers with direct access to all necessary information such as color codes, fonts, interaction logics and code snippets. This comprehensive documentation enabled an exact replication of the visual and functional aspects of the prototype and ensured that the final product addressed the design specifications exactly. Additionally, all assets were stored in a centralized repository that was accessible to all stakeholders, further improving consistency and efficiency in the development process while simplifying the training of new team members.

Evaluation of the Design Specifications. The prototypes and associated documentation developed in this phase provided a solid foundation for the subsequent implementation phase. Close coordination between design and technical development ensured a coherent integration into the LMS that met both functional and aesthetic requirements. The design phase also included a comprehensive review of existing literature to ensure that the proposed solutions were grounded in current research and best practices. This literature review provided valuable insights into the common pitfalls and successful strategies in similar projects.

2.2 Structured Development Phases for Integration into the LMS

The structured development of the Moodle plugin was based on a 3-phase model that is oriented towards established software engineering practices and reflects modern approaches to systematic software development. This methodology is based on the principles of agile development, which emphasize flexibility and adaptive planning to ensure continuous improvement and high-quality software delivery [18].

An additional phase has been added to the process as a fourth element to address the specific requirements of higher education environments. This extension results in a 4-phase model that includes a qualitative staging system at the university level. This additional component allows for multiple university partners to be actively involved in the testing process, ensuring that the system is evaluated and validated from different academic perspectives. This helps to ensure that the LD meets the specific requirements and expectations of different university environments and enables a qualitative securing of the development process. The full process can be seen in Fig. 4 below:

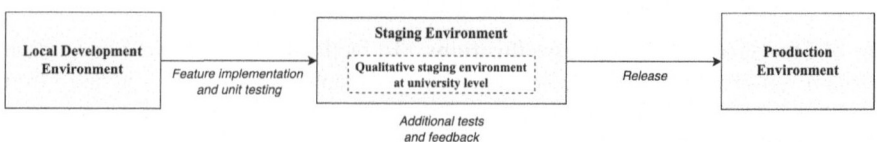

Fig. 4. Development Environments for Integrating Design-Prototype to LMS.

---

[2] Figma's developer mode (Dev Mode) is a special mode within the Figma design tool that gives developers direct access to design specifications. This feature facilitates the delivery of designs to developers by providing access to color codes, fonts, interaction logic, and code snippets.

Local Development System. The local development system is the first of the four-phase model and, as with the following environments, runs on Moodle 4.1. It is the primary working environment for developers, where new features and updates were first implemented and tested in an isolated environment, supported by regular reviews and adjustments to design decisions. The standardized design specifications from the design concept were used to ensure that the development remained consistent with the original user requirements and interface designs. The local environment also allowed developers to experiment and receive immediate feedback on code changes without compromising the stability of a live system. This enhances agile development practices and reduces the risk of incorrect code moving to more advanced stages [19].

Staging Environment. The second phase is the staging environment. This system closely mirrors the hardware and software configuration of the production system and served as a critical test stage before the final release [20]. For the test system in particular, constant feedback was maintained with the service provider of the university network so that new features of the production system were also aligned with the test system. In this environment in particular, all components and interactions were tested under real conditions to ensure that no unexpected errors or performance problems occurred. These tests were crucial to validate the quality and functionality of the LD and formed an essential basis for user acceptance testing, which ensures that the product meets user requirements [21].

User Acceptance Testing (UAT). The third phase involved an additional test system specifically set up as a User Acceptance Testing (UAT) environment. This test server instance was introduced to actively involve the other university partners in the testing process within the research project. In this way, the system could be viewed and evaluated from different academic perspectives, enabling a broader and deeper quality assurance.

Production Environment. The fourth and final phase of the model is the production system on which the finished LD was made available to users. This system must comply with the highest standards of security, stability and performance, as it runs in live operation. The integration from the staging environment to the production system only took place if all previous tests were successful and there were no more critical errors. The production system represents the final environment in which the LD is used, and its integrity is of paramount importance for the successful operation of the dashboard [22]. Within the research project in particular, the integration from the test system to the productive system was carried out by the technical service provider of the university network. Therefore, constant consultation was also held here so that the technical integration of the productive system was feasible.

This structured approach makes it possible to identify and rectify errors at an early stage. By separating the development and test phases from the production environment, it was ensured that no untested changes were transferred directly to the live system. This addresses the best practice approach of Continuous Integration/Continuous Deployment (CI/CD), which is widely used in software development to ensure software quality and minimize the risk of operational failures [21]. In addition, the risk of errors could be further minimized with the help of the additional test system at university level. By implementing this model, the reliability and user satisfaction of the learner dashboard was significantly increased.

2.3 Feedback and Adjustments in the Development Process

By analyzing logs over a period of three years, recurring challenges and problems in the development process were identified, especially during the integration from the prototyping tool Figma to the LMS Moodle. This comprehensive review highlighted key areas for improvement, particularly in terms of interface consistency and user experience optimization. This analysis provided insights into the causes of these problems and their impact on the process. Based on this, solutions were developed to avoid similar difficulties in the future and to continuously improve the development process. One important enhancement involved refining the coding standards and practices to ensure more robust and maintainable code. Regular code reviews and automated tests were introduced to identify problems at an early stage and optimize the development pipeline. Unit tests, integration tests and end-to-end tests were used. To carry out these tests, GitHub Actions for CI/CD was used, the configuration of which was specially adapted to the development of Moodle plugins. Reflecting on past experiences served to learn from them and increase the efficiency and quality of future projects. Moreover, these adjustments have led to the development of new best practices that are now integral to our workflow.

3 Results

The results show the various challenges involved in integrating design prototypes into the LMS Moodle. To this purpose, specific technical and design problems were considered, including the adaptation of Cascading Style Sheets (CSS) styling, the structuring of modular templates and the handling of dynamic content. In addition, the following results address RQ2 by highlighting the technical challenges involved in the integration of a design prototype as a plugin into a Moodle system. The findings underscore the importance of iterative testing and user feedback in refining the integration process.

3.1 Integration of Design and Functionality

The integration of design prototypes into the LMS presents both technical and design challenges that require specialized adaptation of the design elements. Challenges in the integration of CSS and styling became particularly clear during the technical implementation of the design in the Moodle system. Despite the use of Figma's developer mode (dev mode), which enabled the direct integration of design elements, it turned out that custom CSS styles were necessary for many components. This was mainly since certain elements were not adapted to the design by Moodle by default. The resulting mixture of standard Moodle elements and individually designed styles led to a confusing appearance.

It also showed that the CSS instructions proposed in Figma were usually not directly transferable. In practice, it often made more sense to analyze individually how the design elements could best be integrated into the Moodle environment. An example of this is the decision to use flexbox layouts instead of the absolute positioning proposed in the original design. Although these adjustments increased the technical implementation effort, they were necessary to ensure a consistent and functional user interface.

Another aspect that became apparent during the logical implementation of the design was the realization that some of the intended design elements were either redundant in practice or required additional elements. This often only became clear when the actual function of the elements was considered apart from their visual appearance and their practical implementation was planned. This observation emphasizes the importance of a flexible and iterative approach in the development process, which makes it possible to optimally coordinate and adapt design and functionality.

3.2 Template Structuring and Modularity

During the integration of the design prototype into Mustache templates [23], the structuring of the templates themselves and their modularity were significant challenges. This difficulty was partly since the design concepts in Figma had a high level of detail and complexity that could not be easily translated into the template syntax.

Another critical point was the transfer of the design into the features of HTML5 as well as native JavaScript and CSS. These technologies form the basis for the interactive and visual aspects of the LD. The challenge was to implement the modern and dynamic elements of the design prototype in such a way that they could be integrated into the LMS both functionally and aesthetically without compromising performance and user-friendliness.

In addition, the dynamic data originating from the programming language PHP: Hypertext Preprocessor (PHP) part of the application had to be effectively integrated into the templates. This required precise coordination between the back-end developers, who implemented the data logic, and the front-end developers, who integrated this data into the user interface. The seamless integration of this data was crucial for the functionality of the final product, especially for the display of real-time information.

Another problem was the structure of the templates themselves. The structure of the templates was not very modular and often confusing, which made maintenance and future extensions more difficult. The low modularity led to difficulties in the reuse of code and flexible adaptation to changing requirements. To meet these challenges, greater attention was paid to refactoring and modularizing the templates during the development process.

3.3 Dynamic Content and Visualization Problems

Handling dynamic content in Moodle presents developers with the task of visualizing data in a consistent and appealing way. A critical point here is the handling of dynamically generated content. Due to the nature of dynamically generated content, it was not always identical or even present, which meant that the code had to be flexible enough to deal with the lack of certain elements. This requirement increased the complexity of the development as precautions had to be taken to ensure that the absence of data did not affect the functionality of the application or lead to user errors.

Additionally, a problem arose from the content examples included in the prototype. These examples, which were used for demonstration purposes during the design phase, did not necessarily match the actual dynamic data generated by the system. This discrepancy between the design expectations and the actual data led to difficulties in matching the user interface and the backend logic. A balance had to be found between the representation of idealized content in the prototype and the realistic implementation of this content in the application.

Furthermore, the visualization of data through graphs posed an additional challenge due to the very limited Chart.js Application Programming Interface (API) that was used for the presentation in the context of Moodle. The limited customization capabilities of the API, paired with insufficient documentation, made it difficult to develop the highly interactive and informative graphs required for an effective visual representation of learning progress and activities. These limitations led to the consideration of alternative approaches and additional tools to meet the visualization requirements of the dashboard and ensure an engaging and functional representation.

3.4 Caching and System Integration

Integrating the LD into an existing system that uses various other plugins and dealing with caching issues were key challenges in the implementation process. Especially in the context of Moodle development, caching is an ongoing challenge that needs to be carefully addressed. In contrast to the JavaScript cache, disabling the CSS cache in the browser was more complex and required special "cache busting" techniques to ensure that users always loaded the latest versions of the stylesheets. While JavaScript caching accelerated development dynamics, CSS caching required precise measures to maintain the consistency and timeliness of the user interface without compromising system performance.

However, one of the biggest challenges was integrating the new LD into an environment that already contained other plugins. It was crucial that the existing functionalities, such as data export and consent to data usage, continued to function unaffected. This requirement necessitated extensive testing and coordination to ensure that the new software had no negative impact on the functionality of the existing system.

3.5 Version Management and Compatibility

Version management and the compatibility of software components in a rapidly evolving technological environment were fundamental challenges in the development of the LD. A central challenge in version management was understanding the functions of individual plugins. With a large number of plugins in the system, the question often was: "Which plugin does what?" This clarity was crucial in order to avoid overlaps and conflicts between the plugins and to facilitate the integration of new functions.

Another problem was dealing with different versions of the PHP and Moodle on the development and production systems. These inconsistencies led to difficulties in ensuring compatibility and functionality of the LD across different system environments. It was essential that the plugin ran stably on all systems, which required intensive testing and occasional adjustments.

Some of the existing documentation was from previous versions and had not been updated, which complicated development. In addition, the migration of the Moodle documentation to a new website was an external factor, which meant that important documents were temporarily unavailable. This situation required a high degree of flexibility and initiative from the development team to compensate for missing information and still move forward efficiently.

Older versions of Moodle used a lot of automation, which made it difficult to customize the modal dialogs. Newer versions of Moodle introduced a new mechanism for creating modals, which is generated by JavaScript functions and usually follows a simple scheme: Header, body and footer sections, which at best are only in text format. However, the modals within LD were more complex and required their own Mustache templates. Switching from the old to the new modals was a major challenge.

4 Best Practices

Based on the results, best practices were developed specifically for the integration of design prototypes into the Moodle LMS. These practices address the challenges and methodological approaches outlined above and aim to provide recommendations that effectively support the technical and design implementation of prototypes into functional learning environments. Implementing these practices can significantly enhance the efficiency and success of LMS integrations.

4.1 Best Practice 1: Adaptation of Design Prototypes to Technical Environments

Problem. The integration of user-centered, intuitive design solutions developed in prototyping software into the technically rigid structures of an LMS such as Moodle is a significant challenge. Specific to this project was the problem that the proposed CSS instructions from Figma were mostly not directly transferable, as the integration of the design elements into the existing Moodle themes required deeper customization. This mismatch between the flexible design prototypes and the technical implementation possibilities in Moodle led to increased complexity and additional work in the development phase.

Best Practice. To ensure seamless integration of the design prototypes into the LMS Moodle, it is advisable to use flexible layout systems such as CSS Flexbox or CSS Grid, which enable easier adaptation to different layout requirements. Frontend frameworks such as React or Vue, which can be securely integrated due to their component-based architecture and are compatible with Moodle, can also provide support [24]. It is important that technical limitations and the implementation possibilities of the target system are considered during the design process. Careful documentation of all design decisions and the resulting customizations is essential to give developers a deep understanding of the design intentions and facilitate implementation [25]. In addition, a clear guideline for the implementation of interactive elements should be established to ensure that the prototypes are correctly integrated into the Moodle environment. This strategic approach helps to overcome technical hurdles and supports the creation of a consistent and user-friendly learning experience.

4.2   Best Practice 2: Proactive Adaptation to Dynamic Content

Problem. During the implementation phase of the research project, it became clear that the dynamic content generated by the LMS often did not address the static content in the design prototypes. This discrepancy led to challenges in customizing the user interface, as content and layouts developed in Figma did not always directly match the actual data retrieved from the system. It was difficult to display the visualizations and interactive elements correctly when the real data was generated differently or in an unexpected format.

Best Practice. To ensure that the final products match the design prototypes both functionally and visually, it is crucial to conduct realistic tests early on using mock data that simulates the actual system data [26]. A continuous comparison between the data used in the prototypes and the real data provided by the LMS should be established. This includes obtaining regular feedback from users and conducting usability tests to ensure that the user interface remains intuitive and effective [9]. Furthermore, flexible adaptability should be embedded in the design strategy, allowing changes to be implemented quickly based on user feedback and real-world data. This proactive approach allows for early reaction to problems and ensures that the designs meet both user expectations and the technical requirements of the LMS [27].

4.3   Best Practice 3: Modularization of Templates

Problem. During the development of the project, it became clear that the original structure of the templates was not very modular and often unclear. This led to difficulties in maintenance and made future adjustments more difficult, as changes in one part of the system could have unintended effects on other parts. The lack of modularity impaired the flexibility and scalability of the overall system.

Best Practice. To improve maintainability and flexibility, it is advisable to implement a strictly modular architecture for templates. Each template should be designed in such a way that it fulfills a specific function and can function independently of other templates. This facilitates the testing of individual components and makes it possible to update or replace parts of the application independently of each other [28]. In terms of implementation, this means that each template only contains the data and logic required for its function and communicates with other templates via clearly defined interfaces. The use of template languages such as Mustache, which support a clear separation of logic and presentation, can be of great advantage here [23]. This methodical approach can increase the overall efficiency of the development process by allowing changes and bug fixes to be localized and implemented without extensive system disruptions.

4.4   Best Practice 4: Consistent Version Management for Technology Upgrades

Problem. The differences in versions of technologies such as PHP and the LMS Moodle between development and production systems were a significant risk to system compatibility and stability. Outdated or divergent documentation made the problem worse by making development and debugging more difficult.

Best Practice. It is crucial to introduce systematic version management that includes regular updates and compatibility tests. This should utilize a unified version management platform that spans all development and production environments [29]. This includes implementing automation tools to ensure that all environments are always synchronized while receiving the latest security and feature updates [21]. Documentation must be continuously updated and made available to all team members to ensure consistency and transparency of development. In addition, the documentation should contain clear instructions for migrating and testing new versions of technology to facilitate the transition between different versions of the system [30]. These measures can minimize the risk of compatibility problems and maximize the efficiency of the development process.

5 Discussion

This study focused on the challenges and methodological approaches to integrating design prototypes into the Moodle LMS. The two central research questions, RQ1 and RQ2, addressed the effectiveness of the integration of design elements into the technical structure of the LMS Moodle as well as the specific challenges involved. The findings highlight the importance of a user-centered design approach and continuous collaboration between designers and developers. The research results make it clear that successful integration requires comprehensive adaptation of the design and close technical coordination. Despite a systematic approach, there were challenges that had to be solved, particularly in the subsequent styling of elements or version management. A total of four best practices emerged during the entire development process: Adapting design prototypes to technical environments to ensure that designs can be effectively integrated into the LMS structures; proactively adapting to dynamic content, which requires constant alignment between design prototypes and real system data; and modularizing templates to improve flexibility and maintainability.

The research shows how essential thorough technical and design-oriented preparation is for the successful implementation of design prototypes in an LMS such as Moodle. In terms of RQ1, it shows that the effectiveness of the integration of design elements depends strongly on the adaptability of prototyping tools and the flexibility of development processes. This is supported by previous research showing that the integration of user-centered designs into technical systems requires significant adaptations and close collaboration between designers and developers [31, 32]. Challenges in styling or version management make it clear that the standard solutions of prototyping tools cannot always be directly integrated into existing LMS architectures. This underlines the need for an adapted approach in which technical restrictions and user requirements must be considered equally to effectively address the specific challenges addressed in RQ2.

The identified best practices reflect adaptive strategies that not only aim to facilitate integration, but also to ensure the quality and usability of the final product. By proactively adapting to dynamic content and modularizing templates, the flexibility of the system is increased, which contributes to improved adaptability to changing technological developments. These measures are crucial for closing the gap between the static design specifications of prototyping tools and the dynamic requirements of real usage scenarios [33]. They ensure that the developed learning environments meet both pedagogical and technical standards, which is a direct answer to research questions RQ1 and RQ2.

The study is specifically focused on the integration of design prototypes into the LMS Moodle, which limits the generalizability of the identified best practices to other LMS. The use of Figma as prototyping software could influence the generalizability of the results, as the specific features and limitations of this tool are not necessarily applicable to other design tools. Furthermore, the complexity of the technical adaptations that were necessary for the integration may vary in other LMS or with other tools. This could create additional challenges that were not fully captured in this study. These limitations have also been noted in other studies on design and development tools [34, 35].

6 Outlook

Future research could evaluate the applicability and flexibility of the developed best practices across different LMS and design tools. It would be informative to evaluate different prototyping software in terms of their impact on integration efficiency and develop strategies to improve collaboration between designers and developers. In addition, it would be valuable to explore the real-world application of these approaches in educational contexts to validate their pedagogical effectiveness and practical relevance. Additionally, investigating the integration of AI-driven design tools could further enhance the adaptability and efficiency of design integrations in LMS platforms, potentially leading to more dynamic and responsive educational environments. This exploration could also include user studies to assess the usability and effectiveness of the integrated designs from both an instructor's and a learner's perspective, thereby providing comprehensive insights into the educational impact of design innovations in digital learning spaces.

Acknowledgments. This work was funded by the German Federal Ministry of Education, grant No. 01PX21001B.

References

1. Ellis, R.K.: Learning Managament Systems. Alexandria, VI: American Society for Training & Development (ASTD) (2009)
2. Shaame, A., El Nabahany, U., Yunus, S., Kondo, T., Maro, W.: Personalisation of moodle learning management system for effective teaching and learning in higher learning institutions: a case of the State University of Zanzibar. Afr. J. Sci. Technol. Innov. Dev. **15**(7), 852–865 (2023). https://doi.org/10.1080/20421338.2023.2213597
3. Schumacher, C., Ifenthaler, D.: Investigating prompts for supporting students' self-regulation – a remaining challenge for learning analytics approaches? Internet High. Educ. **49**, 100791 (2021). https://doi.org/10.1016/j.iheduc.2020.100791
4. Drzyzga, G., Harder, T.: A three level design study approach to develop a student-centered learner dashboard. In: da Silva, H.P., Cipresso, P. (eds.) Computer-Human Interaction Research and Applications, pp. 262–281. Springer, Cham (2023)
5. Vaidyanathan, S., Lakshmi Priya, B.: Challenges in developing software in today's scenario: an analysis at developmental stage level. In: Misra, S., Arumugam, C., Jaganathan, S., Saraswathi S. (eds.) Advances in Digital Crime, Forensics, and Cyber Terrorism, pp. 199–222. IGI Global (2021). https://doi.org/10.4018/978-1-7998-4900-1.ch012

6. Riesener, M., et al.: A model for dependency-oriented prototyping in the agile development of complex technical systems. Procedia CIRP **84**, 1023–1028 (2019). https://doi.org/10.1016/j.procir.2019.04.196

7. Harder, T., Drzyzga, G.: Perzeption und Präferenzen von Online-Studierenden zu Lernenden-Dashboards: Designelemente, Akzeptanz und ML-basierte Lernfort-schrittsprognosen. In: Tagungsband der GMW2023: Integration und Ko-Kreation: Miteinander von Mensch und Maschine in Forschung und Bildung. Waxmann, Jena, Deutschland (2024)

8. Harder, T., Drzyzga, G.: Enhancing the user interaction of online students: analysis of an interaction concept for a learner dashboard. In: Proceedings of the 19th International Joint Conference on Computer Vision, Imaging and Computer Graphics Theory and Applications – HUCAPP, pp. 471–479. SciTePress (2024). https://doi.org/10.5220/0012374600003660

9. Drzyzga, G., Harder, T.: From low fidelity to high fidelity prototypes: how to integrate two eye tracking studies into an iterative design process for a better user experience. In: Proceedings of the 19th International Conference on Software Technologies, pp. 485–491. SCITEPRESS - Science and Technology Publications, Dijon (2024). https://doi.org/10.5220/0012854900003753

10. Drzyzga, G., Harder, T., Janneck, M.: Cognitive effort in interaction with software systems for self-regulation - an eye-tracking study. In: Harris, D., Li, W.-C. (eds.) HCII 2023. LNCS, vol. 14017, pp. 37–52. Springer, Cham (2023). https://doi.org/10.1007/978-3-031-35392-5_3

11. Drzyzga, G., Harder, T., Janneck, M.: Participative development of a learning dashboard for online students using traditional design concepts. In: da Silva, H.P., Cipresso, P. (eds.) Computer-Human Interaction Research and Applications, pp. 176–191. Springer, Cham (2023)

12. Sozio, G., Agostinho, S., Tindall-Ford, S., Paas, F.: Enhancing teaching strategies through cognitive load theory: process vs. product worked examples. Educ. Sci. 14(8), 813 (2024). https://doi.org/10.3390/educsci14080813

13. Sweller, J.: Cognitive load during problem solving: effects on learning. Cogn. Sci. **12**(2), 257–285 (1988). https://doi.org/10.1207/s15516709cog1202_4

14. Richardson, J.T.E.: Approaches to learning or levels of processing: what did Marton and Säljö (1976a) really say? The legacy of the work of the Göteborg Group in the 1970s. Interchange **46**(3), 239–269 (2015). https://doi.org/10.1007/s10780-015-9251-9

15. DIN EN ISO 9241-110:2020-10, Ergonomie der Mensch-System-Interaktion_- Teil_110: Interaktionsprinzipien (ISO_9241-110:2020). Deutsche Fassung EN_ISO_9241-110:2020 (2020). https://doi.org/10.31030/3147467

16. Pitale, A., Bhumgara, A.: Human computer interaction strategies—designing the user interface. In: 2019 International Conference on Smart Systems and Inventive Technology (ICSSIT), Tirunelveli, India, pp. 752–758. IEEE (2019). https://doi.org/10.1109/ICSSIT46314.2019.8987819

17. Mahamuni, R., Mantry, S., Jadhav, M.: Bridging the gap between service design specification and technical specification. In: Chakrabarti, A., Poovaiah, R., Bokil, P., Kant, V. (eds.) ICoRD 2021, vol. 222, pp. 79–90. Springer, Singapore (2021). https://doi.org/10.1007/978-981-16-0119-4_7

18. Hooda, S., Sood, V.M., Singh, Y., Dalal, S., Sood, M. (eds.): Agile Software Development: Trends, Challenges and Applications, 1st edn. Wiley (2023). https://doi.org/10.1002/9781119896838

19. Medeiros, J., Vasconcelos, A., Silva, C., Goulão, M.: Quality of software requirements speci-fication in agile projects: a cross-case analysis of six companies. J. Syst. Softw. **142**, 171–194 (2018). https://doi.org/10.1016/j.jss.2018.04.064

20. Sharma, A.: Test Environment Management. ITSM Press, Cambridge (2018)

21. Shahin, M., Ali Babar, M., Zhu, L.: Continuous integration, delivery and deployment: a systematic review on approaches, tools, challenges and practices. IEEE Access **5**, 3909–3943 (2017). https://doi.org/10.1109/ACCESS.2017.2685629

22. Kim, G., Debois, P., Willis, J., Humble, J., Allspaw, J.: The DevOps Handbook: How to Create World-Class Agility, Reliability, & Security in Technology Organizations, 1st edn. IT Revolution Press, LLC, Portland (2016)

23. Mustache, Mustache: logic-less templates (2014). http://mustache.github.io

24. Jingga, K., Sunindyo, W.: Component-based development using moodle as alternative for E-learning software development. In: 2020 12th International Conference on Information Technology and Electrical Engineering (ICITEE), pp. 125–130 (2020). https://doi.org/10.1109/ICITEE49829.2020.9271670

25. Meinel, C., Leifer, L. (eds.): Design Thinking Research: Investigating Design Team Performance, 1st edn. Springer, Cham (2020)

26. Nielsen, J.: Usability Engineering. Morgan Kaufmann Publishers Inc., San Francisco (1994)

27. Shneiderman, B., Plaisant, C., Cohen, M., Jacobs, S., Elmqvist, N.: Designing the User Interface: Strategies for Effective Human-Computer Interaction, 6th edn, Global edition. Pearson, Boston (2018)

28. Thaiya, M.S., Julia, K., Mbugua, S.: On software modular architecture: concepts, metrics and trends. IJCOT **12**(1), 3–10 (2022). https://doi.org/10.14445/22492593/IJCOT-V12I1P302

29. Kerzner, H.: Project Management: A Systems Approach to Planning, Scheduling, and Controlling, 13th edn. Wiley, Hoboken (2022)

30. Islam, M.A., Hasan, R., Eisty, N.U.: Documentation practices in agile software development: a systematic literature review. In: 2023 IEEE/ACIS 21st International Conference on Software Engineering Research, Management and Applications (SERA), Orlando, FL, USA, pp. 266–273. IEEE (2023). https://doi.org/10.1109/SERA57763.2023.10197828

31. Shania, M., Raharjo, T., Nur Fitriani, A.: Implementation user-centered design in agile software development: systematic literature review. IJOMS **2**(7), 2812–2831 (2023). https://doi.org/10.55324/ijoms.v2i7.480

32. Sohaib, O., Solanki, H., Dhaliwa, N., Hussain, W., Asif, M.: Integrating design thinking into extreme programming. J. Ambient Intell. Hum. Comput. **10**(6), 2485–2492 (2019). https://doi.org/10.1007/s12652-018-0932-y

33. Miraz, M.H., Ali, M., Excell, P.S.: Adaptive user interfaces and universal usability through plasticity of user interface design. Comput. Sci. Rev. **40**, 100363 (2021). https://doi.org/10.1016/j.cosrev.2021.100363

34. Muangbangyung, S., Srisawasdi, N.: Design and development of interactive moodle-based E-learning platform for competency training. In: IEEE ICEIB 2023, p. 11. MDPI (2023). https://doi.org/10.3390/engproc2023038011

35. Peramunugamage, A., Ratnayake, U.W., Karunanayaka, S.P., Jayawardena, C.L.: Design of Moodle-based collaborative learning activities to enhance student interactions. AAOUJ **19**(1), 37–54 (2024). https://doi.org/10.1108/AAOUJ-06-2023-0079

Towards Augmenting Human-Centred Design: Generative AI Tools for Interaction Research and Design

Tom Gross[(✉)] [iD]

Human-Computer Interaction Group, University of Bamberg, 96045 Bamberg, Germany
hci@uni-bamberg.de

Abstract. Generative AI tools are hailed as a motor for revolutionising our work and life. Recently, tools based on large language and foundation models, such as ChatGPT, have also become a hot topic in interaction research and interaction design. This paper contributes a discussion of whether and how Generative AI tools can be used to augment interaction research and interaction design throughout the whole process of Human-Centred Design for Interactive Systems as defined by the International Organization for Standardization. The paper compiles an extended, up-to-date version of the process model covering highly relevant additions of methods bridging the gap between interaction research and interaction design in each of the processes. It then suggests Generative AI tools to support those methods. Finally, it discusses vital aspects of interaction research and interaction design concerning the current design practice, the respective design situation, and the design circumstances at large.

Keywords: Human-Centred design · Generative AI · Process modelsm Methods · Interaction research · Interaction design

1 Introduction

Human-computer interaction is concerned with understanding users and their needs as well as technological opportunities to fulfil their needs, designing new and innovative ways of interaction between users and technology, and evaluating those new types of interactions to assess their quality [31].

The goals and methods of understanding, designing, and evaluating are distinct. The goal of understanding is to get insights into the users and their characteristics as well as their needs and requirements for future systems. Prominent examples of methods used for understanding users are interviews and experience sampling in the field [23] that inform personas that characterise groups of users and scenarios that provide a look into future interaction opportunities between users and systems [10]. Designing refers to envisioning new and better opportunities for users to reach their goals and fulfil their tasks with the help of inductive systems. Sketching is a central method for producing the first visual representations of a future system, typically with paper and pencil [6]. Those sketches

H. Plácido da Silva and P. Cipresso (Eds.): CHIRA 2024, CCIS 2370, pp. 21–38, 2025.
https://doi.org/10.1007/978-3-031-82633-7_2

can then be discussed with users and later used as a basis to develop early prototypes and final systems. Evaluating is critical to get feedback from diverse stakeholders involved—particularly the future users of the system. The methods here range from informal quick-and-dirty feedback on early sketches and prototypes to systematic empirical research on proper systems that is well planned, well executed, and thoroughly analysed and documented [41].

The origins of those methods are as broad and diverse as the backgrounds of the actors in HCI in academia and industry. They can be broadly clustered into interaction research and interaction design [22]. From an interaction research perspective, HCI has been defined as being at 'the intersection between the social and behavioural sciences on the one hand, and computer and information technology on the other' [8, p. 1]. Indeed, many actors in HCI have backgrounds in psychology, sociology, and anthropology, as well as computer science, information technology, and engineering. Concerning interaction design, designers contribute their backgrounds in visual design, product design, and industrial design to it.

The literature focusing on interaction research primarily covers methods for under-standing and evaluating but less for designing the above phenomena. HCI textbooks with thoughtful introductions to the field and broad chapters on methods are [7, 10, 13, 36, 38, 57]. In general, if they contain book chapters on designing, those textbooks look at the design from an 'engineering design' perspective where typically, design fol-lows a requirements phase and aims at generating solutions for relatively well-known and well-specified design challenges [59]. Research here often refers to empirical research—research that applies observation or experiments. Observation captures phenomena such as 'human thought, feeling, attitude, emotion, passion, sensation, reflection, expres-sion, sentiment, opinion, mood, outlook, manner, style, approach, strategy, and so on'. In contrast, experiments typically capture phenomena in a controlled setting where an independent variable influences a dependent variable [41, p. 130]. Observations are often used for understanding, and apply a qualitative research strategy, whereas con-trolled experiments are often performed for evaluation and apply a quantitative research strategy.

The literature with a primary focus on interaction design and a considerably smaller focus on understanding and evaluating are on the edge of HCI—that is, they are known and used by many academics and practitioners in HCI but are more dominant in study programmes of design and less in those explicitly on HCI [9]. Excellent textbooks are [3, 14, 18, 28, 34, 35, 47]. Those books often focus on designing the above phenomena from a perspective of 'creative design' that starts more openly where the definition of the design problem is part of the solution process and where the problem sometimes cannot easily be grasped and specified [59]. The design addresses different levels of human processing: the visceral level as the most immediate, with fast assessments and signals to muscles; the behavioural level relating to tasks and actions; and the reflective level as consciously judging over the visceral and behavioural levels [48].

Process models have been developed and applied to bridge the gap between inter-action research and interaction design by organising the overall process systematically into steps that often include the identification of the need for human-centred design; understanding and specification of the context of use; specification of the user and organisational requirements; production of the design solutions; and evaluation of the design against the requirements [31].

Despite HCI's user-centred process model's great merits concerning structuring and standardising the development of interactive systems, they have been criticised for narrowly focusing on an engineering design paradigm [39]. The basic assumption of engineering design is that at the outset of a project, we have a well-known design challenge that leads to clear requirements for the future system. This allows for a straightforward design and development process to find a solution for the future system. In contrast, the situation in a creative design paradigm is considered to be less clear. The design problem might be less known or not seen equally by all stakeholders. Different stakeholders might have contradictory requirements. Overall, in user-centred design, the engineering design perspective seems to dominate and emphasise the importance of the process [59].

The tremendous new opportunities of Generative Artificial Intelligence have the potential to play an essential role in HCI and to revolutionise many aspects of interaction research and design.

This paper contributes a discussion of whether and how Generative AI tools can be used to augment interaction research and interaction design throughout the whole process of Human-Centred Design for Interactive Systems as defined by the International Organization for Standardization. It first looks at related work concerning process models in HCI, Generative AI in interaction research and induction design, and user-centred practice. Then it compiles a process model based on Human-Centred Design for Interactive Systems with some extensions and details from more recent literature bridging the gap between interaction research and interaction design. It presents ways how Generative AI tools can be used to support the methods throughout the whole process model. It discusses the challenges of using those tools for the current design practice, the design situation, and the design at large.

2   Related Work

Our work builds on great inspirations from related work on process models to structure the overall research and design process, on using Generative AI tools for interaction research and interaction design, and on essential distinctions between engineering design and creative design.

2.1 Process Models in HCI

Process models aim to provide both novices and experts with guidance throughout the whole process. They make the process reliable and consistent. They are a basis for having repeated routines that can be achieved and offer a learning experience and documentation of the learnings. In larger projects, process models help the team maintain a shared understanding of the trajectory through the different steps in a project [20, 27, 44]. They suggest sequences of activities to reach a goal. They come in different flavours and have specific pros and cons.

In the engineering domain, the importance and reliability of a structured process are well-known [10]. Processes in HCI have been inspired by vital process models from software engineering [31]. Here, 'the systematic approach that is used in software engineering is sometimes called a software process. A software process is a sequence of activities that leads to the production of a software product.' [58, p. 9]. Process models are structured representations of process recommendations—'a software process model is a simplified representation of a software process. [...] These generic models ... are abstractions of the process that can be used to explain different approaches to software development.' [58, p. 28].

In HCI, the standard process model from the International Organization for Standardization is entitled 'Human-Centred Design of Interactive Systems' [31]. Its processes are identification of the need for human-centred design; understanding and specification of the context of use; specification of the user and organisational requirements; production of the design solutions; and evaluation of the design against the requirements. There are many process models, and they all have specifics regarding processes, sub-processes, and activities, as well as ways of documenting their activities. However, most of them cover the processes of the ISO model in one way or another [10, 19, 21, 24, 25, 27, 57].

2.2   Generative AI in Interaction Research and Interaction Design

In HCI and beyond, Generative Artificial Intelligence is an 'AI system that uses existing media to create new, plausible media' [46, p. 1]. Generative AI tools based on Large Language Models (LLMs) and Foundation Models (FMs) are increasingly widespread. Several of those tools, such as ChatGPT of OpenAI, are used in many domains for generating text, images, and source code. They prompt users for input, and users can assign roles to the tool, specify their roles, and ask for output [50]. ChatGPT can be used for general research, as well as for interaction research and interaction design.

Practical guides to the use of ChatGPT for research in general, suggest how to use the tool for writing research proposals, for data analysis, for literature reviewing, for grant writing, for modelling, for reviewing and critiquing, for learning complex topics, for title brainstorming, for presentation preparation, for writing improvements, and for generating literature review flow. Thereby, the user can instruct ChatGPT to take specific roles such as research assistant, senior researcher, peer reviewer, research librarian, journal editor, etc. [1].

Generative AI tools were suggested to be used for various types of HCI contributions in phases such as research planning, prototyping, data collection, analysis and synthesis, as well as dissemination and communication. For instance, in research planning they can be used to find relevant literature, to identify research gaps, and to help develop study designs and materials [16].

Overall, creativity support and tools to support creativity in HCI research have been a relevant topic in HCI, also before the widespread use of generative AI tools [53].

2.3   User-Centred Practices

In design research, the actual practices of designers during the design process are studied, analysed, and documented. User-centred practises of interaction research and interaction design have been characterised as partly engineering design and partly creative design process [59].

Design Research uses several criteria to distinguish research and design scenarios. Central criteria are the design goal, the steps towards the design goal, and the assessment of the results. Concerning the design goal, it is essential to distinguish the degree of formalisation—in other words, is the design goal clear and formalisable, or is it not? Consequently, the steps towards the goal can be more or less clear and more or less formalised at the outset. Moreover, with respect to assessing the result, it is important to distinguish if precise measurements can be applied [33].

User-centred design, seen and practised from an engineering design perspective, works well for situations with a high degree of structure, a low degree of complexity, and a low degree of dynamics [11]. Here, the requirements can be specified precisely at the outset, and then projects can be carried out step-by-step strictly according to the process model. No, or hardly any, improvisations and adaptations are required throughout the process.

User-centred design needs to be seen and practised from a creative design perspective if the situations have a low degree of structure, a high degree of complexity, and a high degree of dynamics. Such situations typically involve many stakeholders with diverse perspectives and priorities. Here, it can be necessary to develop many ideas in parallel and revisit basic assumptions during the project [59]. While having a clear plan here is necessary, it is equally important to be prepared for spontaneous improvisations and adaptations along the way.

3 Process Models and Methods

Process models are common in engineering and spread to software engineering. As we will see below, process models in software engineering provided an excellent basis for process models in HCI. HCI process models mainly include classical processes from the ISO norm but also come in more modern flavours. More recently, some works have suggested how to integrate generative AI into process models.

3.1 Lessons from Process Models in Software Engineering

Process models in engineering, particularly software engineering, have a long tradition and provide an excellent basis for modern process models in HCI. Early on, they targeted activities towards the analysis of the status quo and activities towards designing future systems. Several seminal models—especially the waterfall model and the spiral model—provide excellent references for organising processes until this day [61].

Process models in software engineering provide recommendations on how to organise individual processes and how to step through chains of processes. Often, their focus is on an abstract representation of the phases, leaving it to the respective teams to choose specific methods for individual activities in each process [58].

The classical waterfall model featured a sequence of steps to be followed in software engineering projects starting with system requirements, and moving on to software requirements, to analysis, to program design, to coding, to testing, and finally to operation [55]. The level of detail should increase through those different phases of analysis and design. Jumping a single step backwards or forwards for feedback or feedforward between steps was foreseen. However, significant iterations involving moving backwards and forwards between multiple steps were not part of the model.

The 'Spiral Model of Software Development and Enhancement' added such an iteration throughout the whole process. Each iteration throughout an entire cycle of the spiral started by identifying objectives concerning various parts of the project (e.g., the functionality or the performance of the project). It continued by designing alternatives for implementing those objectives. Various aspects of each alternative should be considered (e.g., schedule, cost), and risks should be minimised [5, p. 65]. Then, the scope was enlarged, and the next iteration could start.

In later models, the integration of users and consideration of users' needs became more explicit. The Unified Process, for instance, saw software development processes as a 'set of activities needed to transform a user's requirements into a software system' [32, p. 4]. Use cases drove it and thereby departed from users and their requirements for future functionality. It was software architecture-centred and focused on components and interfaces between them. In addition, it was iterative-incremental, which allowed to breakdown of the activities in all processes into smaller chunks that could be organised more efficiently. The Unified Modelling Language (UML) helped better structure software components and their interfaces [32, 61].

Overall, these and other process models in software engineering provided significant stimuli for process models in HCI. For instance, many process models in HCI up until today include use cases—often in HCI referred to as scenarios and storyboards. Likewise, many models function iteratively and incrementally, whereby it is essential to have the option to partly repeat some processes if necessary. However, at the same time, one should always keep an increment in mind in order not to run in a circle without making any progress.

3.2   The ISO Process Model in HCI

The process model of ISO entitled 'Human-Centred Design for Interactive Systems' is the most widespread process model in HCI and suggests six generic processes that should be part of all projects that develop interactive systems of software and hardware for human use [31].

This process model organises activities towards the development of interactive systems that users can interact with in an effective, efficient, and satisfactory way (cf. Fig. 1). Each project should start with a plan for the human-centred design process. Then, it is crucial to understand and specify the context of use and document it in a description of the context of use. Later, the user requirements are specified and documented in various papers, including the context of use specification, the user needs description, and the user requirements specification. Design solutions are developed that aim to meet these requirements. The design solutions are documented in a user interaction specification and a user interface specification, and the design solutions are then implemented. The design solutions then need to be evaluated against the previously specified requirements. The evaluation is documented in a conformance test documentation and long-term monitoring results.

The Human-Centred Design for Interactive Systems combines various essential principles. The process is analytic and addresses interaction research from the beginning, when users, their tasks, and their environment are analysed and specified, but also when design results are systematically evaluated. The process is design-oriented and addresses interaction design by multi-disciplinary teams. Finally, the process is participatory in that it involves users throughout the whole process, and it is iterative in that it iterates through the different activities until a satisfactory result has been found, which means the user requirements.

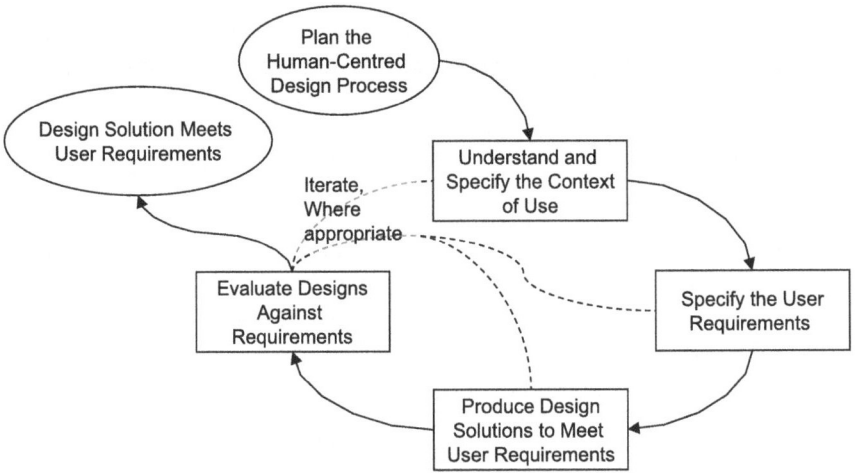

Fig. 1. ISO 9241–210:2019: Ergonomics of Human-System Interaction - Part 210: Human-Centred Design for Interactive Systems. Based on: [31].

3.3 Advanced Process Models in HCI

Two great advanced process models that have been widely used by academics and practitioners in interaction research and interaction design are the Wheel of UX Processes, Lifecycles, Methods, and Techniques, and the Goal-Directed Design Process. Here, I want to bring them together to benefit from the great details that both add to each process of the Human-Centred Design for Interactive Systems process model above.

The Wheel of UX Processes, Lifecycles, Methods, and Techniques has processes similar to those of Human-Centred Design for Interactive Systems and provides various levels of relevant details. It distinguishes Understand User Work and Needs (comparable to Understand and Specify the Context of Use above), Create Design Concepts (comparable to Specify the User Requirements above), Realise Design Alternatives (comparable to Produce Design Solutions above), and Verify and Refine Designs (comparable to Evaluate Designs) [27].

The Goal-Directed Design Process also provides relevant extensions. It foresees the processes Research (comparable to Understand and Specify the Context of Use above); Modelling, and Requirements Definition (both together comparable to Specify the User Requirements above); Design Framework, Design Refinement, and Design

Support (together comparable to Produce Design Solutions above, but also including Evaluate Designs in the Design Refinement process) [10].

Subsequently, we go through all processes of the Human-Centred Design for Interactive Systems process model and introduce relevant details and extensions provided by the two models mentioned above.

The process Understand and Specify the Context of Use involves considerable interaction research in a very broad sense to scope the project with its goals and schedule. It starts top down and looks at objectives, timelines, financial matters, markets, and branding opportunities. It also includes interaction with stakeholders and future users to understand their real goals and objectives for using a system. For this purpose, qualitative methods such as ethnographic studies and contextual inquiries provide valuable input [10]. In order to understand the future users as well as their tasks and their requirements and wishes for the future system, it is crucial to elicit data (e.g., in user interviews or user observations) and to analyse and document them [27].

The process of Specify the User Requirements provides further details by modelling future users and activities as well as specifying requirements. Users can be modelled in personas representing clusters of user groups based on highly relevant criteria concerning their motivation for using the future system. Personas come in various flavours—in this stage, it is advisable to use personas that not only characterise future users and their goals but also their behaviour towards reaching their goals. The requirements characterise the functionality and other aspects of the future system. Here, future usage scenarios are often created [10]. Here, it can also be relevant to model other aspects, such as user tasks in task models [27].

The process of Produce Design Solutions to Meet User Requirements is the stage at which the interaction research converges towards interaction design. It also starts top-down, where a design framework is typically created that characterises the overall intended user experience and user interaction with the future system. What follows after the design framework are typically interaction design patterns. The design is then refined stepwise. Refining here can have two different meanings: it can either mean adding details, or it can mean testing designs, getting feedback on designs, and revising and optimising designs [10]. Different design activities and outcomes exist: Generative design aims to ideate and sketch new ideas and produce low-fidelity prototypes of the future system. Conceptual design creates storyboards of the future interaction between the users and the system. Intermediate designs already specify and prototype the look and feel of the future system but typically leave out a lot of the final functionality [27].

The process of Evaluate Design against Requirements can be seen as the link between one iteration and the next iteration. In a narrow sense, it includes testing designs against established requirements. In a broader sense, it can have small iterative cycles that sometimes even short periods include activities evaluating a prototype, optimising a prototype, re-evaluating a prototype, and so forth [10]. Similar to the interaction research in the first process, it is essential to have a clear top-down strategy for the evaluation where the overall goals of the evaluation are specified, and metrics are defined accordingly. Also, the evaluation methods and techniques are chosen. It is also essential to adequately collect and analyse data and document and report the evaluation results [27].

Some design techniques are essential skills that can be useful throughout all processes. It should also be noted that the term design can be used in a narrower or broader sense. In a narrow sense, design and design techniques refer to innovation—to envision and produce new things. In a broader sense, the terms design and design techniques have been used to denote the overall process covered by the whole process model. In this latter sense, not all activities include crafting new things, but ultimately, they all contribute to the final design of the interactive system in one way or another. So, techniques for design in a broader sense include skills that help with interaction research, such as observing users and situations, abstracting the data captured, note-taking, and organising the data (e.g., in affinity diagrams, card sorting, or concept maps). Other skills that can be applied to interaction design are brainstorming, sketching, drawing, reasoning, and deducing. Having those skills for interaction research and interaction design and dynamically applying them when necessary (e.g., in case of internal or external changes to the project) contributes to an agile lifecycle. Doing it in small steps in an iterative, incremental process also contributes to agile working [27].

4 Process Models and Methods with Generative AI

Plenty of Generative AI tools can be used to support the process model, including all its processes and respective methods. Several Generative AI tools support the general design techniques. As we will see, they all have great potential to contribute to successful interaction research and design. This section presents an up-to-date compilation of interaction research and integration design methods as well as their support through Generative AI tools throughout all processes of the human-centred development of interactive systems process model.

4.1 Generative AI Tools Throughout All Processes of the Process Model

The multifarious Generative AI Tools have the potential to provide flexible support for all of the above process models' processes as well as their specific methods. Some guides are available but spread across the literature [16, 30, 56].

Table 1 below summarises the subsequent elaboration on processes, methods, and options for Generative AI tool support.

The process Understand and Specify the Context of Use involves considerable interaction research concerning the stakeholders and future users and their goals and objectives. The methods used here are of a qualitative nature and include ethnographic studies and contextual inquiries including user interviews and user observations. They are complemented with background research in the existing literature. The tools that I suggest for use here are: (1) ChatGPT or similar tools for supporting the search for literature and identifying the relevant literature. (2) ChatGPT can also help in planning ethnographic studies and contextual inquiries. (3) It can help interaction researchers analyse data by providing code for statistical analysis (e.g., in the statistics package R, or in the programming language Python). (4) Generative agents can simulate human behaviour and contribute to a better understanding of users and their behaviour [52].

Table 1. Summary of the processes, methods, and suggestions for Generative AI tools.

Process	Methods (Examples)	Generative AI Tools (Examples)
Plan the Human-Centred Design Process		
Understand and Specify the Context of Use	• Ethnographic studies and contextual inquiries, including user interviews and user observations • Background literature research	• ChatGPT for planning studies and inquiries • ChatGPT for searching and identifying relevant literature • ChatGPT with code for statistical analysis • Generative agents to simulate human behaviour
Specify the User Requirements	• Personas • Requirement specifications	• ChatGPT to generate personas • Generative agents to simulate dynamic personas • ChatGPT to perform helper roles such as research assistant, peer reviewer
Produce Design Solutions to Meet User Requirements	• Ideation • Sketching • Storyboarding • Low-fidelity prototyping	• ChatGPT to help brainstorming • Text-to-image models (e.g., DALL-E, Midjourney, Stable Diffusion) to generate sketches • ChatGPT to write storyboards • Combinations of Generative AI tools to foster divergent thinking
Evaluate Designs Against Requirements	• Planning the evaluation and choosing evaluation methods and techniques • Performing evaluation • Documenting the results	• ChatGPT to generate study designs • ChatGPT to suggest evaluation methods and techniques • GPT-3 to generate responses to questionnaires • ChatGPT with code for statistical analysis

The process Specify the User Requirements documents details on future users and their tasks as well as the functional and non-functional requirements for the future systems. The methods used here are personas and requirements specifications, amongst others. The tools that I suggest here are ChatGPT or similar tools, for instance, to generate personas. These personas can be dynamic—based on generative agents [52]—and allow researchers and designers to converse with them. The tools can thereby generate answers from diverse user groups, particularly those that researchers and designers do not have access to. Those tools can also be used as support when writing requirements documentation. ChatGPT can perform various roles that can be helpful when writing such documents—for instance, it can act as a research assistant, senior researcher, peer reviewer, or research librarian [1]. However, it should always be clear—even if ChatGPT mimics a senior role—that a human expert is absolutely required here who can judge the quality of the ChatGPT contributions.

The process Produce Design Solutions to Meet User Requirements is where interaction research converges towards interaction design and where the interaction is designed in a top-down manner. The methods used here are ideation and sketching, storyboarding, and low-fidelity prototyping. The tools that I suggest to be used here are ChatGPT or similar tools that can help with brainstorming (e.g., letting the tool generate some initial ideas). Text-to-image models can output images based on users' text inputs. They typically combine language models with generative image models. For instance, DALL-E [49], Midjourney [45], and Stable Diffusion [4] can generate sketches of future designs. ChatGPT can also write storyboards and sketch low-fidelity prototypes. Generative AI tools have been combined in order to foster divergent thinking. For instance, Midjourney was combined with Stable Diffusion to generate innovative product ideas [15]. Midjourney is a Generative AI tool; it was used to generate an image of an animal that is half elephant and half butterfly [45]. The result was then fed as prompts into Stable Diffusion, a deep-learning text-to-image model [4]. Stable Diffusion generated multifarious product ideas ranging from chairs to chocolate. In an analogous way, such a tool combination could be used to fuse separate parts of different designs into a new combined design.

The process Evaluate Design against Requirements assesses the effectiveness, efficiency, and satisfaction of the interaction between the users and the system. The methods used here are planning the evaluation and choosing evaluation methods and techniques as well as performing the evaluation and documenting the results. The tools I suggest to be used here are ChatGPT and similar tools that can support the creation of study designs. They can also suggest evaluation methods and techniques. The data can then be gathered empirically or generated automatically (e.g., generating responses to questionnaires with GPT-3 [26]). The tools can then help analyse the data as described above. They can support producing written evaluation reports and presentation material with evaluation results.

4.2   Generative AI Tools for General Design Techniques

As pointed out above, designers need special skills—design techniques—throughout all processes and stages. Augmenting human creativity can complement the skills of designers.

Augmenting human creativity aims to use Generative AI tools to improve and increase creativity by generating many ideas, identifying novel ideas, and improving the quality of ideas. Five ways can be suggested how Generative AI tools can do this.

Generative AI tools can: Promote divergent thinking by coming up with new connections between existing concepts; challenge expertise bias by coming up with uncommon ideas that are hard to imagine by human innovators, particularly in early design phases; assist in idea evaluation by assessing an idea's novelty, feasibility, specificity, impact, and workability; support idea refinement by handling large numbers of ideas resulting in new combinations; and facilitate collaboration with and among users by providing end users with generative AI tools, allowing them to specify their personalised versions. Furthermore, Generative AI tools can help designers who are suffering from design fixation. Design fixation refers to situations in which designers stick with ideas and consciously or unconsciously do not follow new ideas, even if they have the potential to be better than the existing ideas. Design fixation can be due to designers relying too much on existing design forms or consciously blocking new approaches. Depending on the feedback and input the designers wish, different Generative AI tools have been used in the literature (e.g., ChatGPT for text, Midjourney for images) [15, 60].

4.3 Evaluating Generative AI Tools for Interaction Research and Interaction Design

Generative AI tools have considerable potential for supporting and profoundly changing how interaction research and interaction design are done throughout all processes and methods. However, they require thorough evaluations.

Generative AI tools entail risks for individuals and society. For instance, they can create make up the contents of answers ('hallucinate'), and they run the risk of generating harmful and toxic answers. Therefore, responsible evaluation and auditing have been asked for—however, Generative AI tools are challenging to evaluate and audit for the following reasons. Previously, in AI and natural language processing (NLP), benchmarks could be used for automatic evaluations of models for machine translation, or text summarisation could be used. However, they do not work for large language models since they provide less validity and quality, which led to an 'evaluation crisis' [62].

Complementary to the preliminary evaluations and auditing required before the tools are disseminated, longitudinal studies should accompany the long-term use of Generative AI tools and the long-term effect on the creativity of individuals and society at large. So far, such longitudinal studies are missing [42, 43].

An interesting recent study that analysed the effect of the use of creativity support tools has, for instance, shown that their use led to homogenisation. The study compared the artefacts that were generated by participants with the help of an AI tool and by participants without. The group of participants without the tool produced a more diverse set of artefacts, whereas the group with the tool produced a more homogenous set [2].

Overall, Generative AI tools have been suggested and used in all processes and for supporting diverse methods. So, things look promising. However, systematic evaluation and auditing are missing, and first evaluation studies show that the creative output might be less diverse than expected. Recently, the role of the users—that is, the interaction researchers and interaction designers, but also the end-users—has been addressed. In the future, it will be necessary to understand better how those users adopt Generative AI tools to support creativity [51]. Likewise, a responsible integration of Generative AI tools into the everyday practice of interaction researchers and interaction designers will play an essential role towards the effect of Generative AI tools on individuals and society at large [37].

5 Discussion

Undoubtedly, Generative AI tools have great potential to contribute to the quality and quantity of the interaction research and interaction design outcomes of human-centred design processes. Currently, most guides on Generative AI tools in HCI and beyond focus on where and how those tools can be used, sometimes on a somewhat operational level with respect to perfectionising writing prompts. While this is very important and very helpful for both novice and expert users of Generative AI tools, questions remain with respect to the fit of the tools to the interaction research and interaction design practice, with respect to the complexity of the design situations, and with respect to the role of design on a global level.

5.1 Design Practice

The interaction research and interaction design practice in user-centred design needs to combine engineering design-like aspects of structured processes and methods with creative design-like aspects of an open and dynamic process of developing innovative solutions that have the potential to alter the original design problem. Here, different paradigms that seem incompatible at first sight need to be combined. On the one hand, a thorough process with a clear and discrete structure, as well as discrete activities and methods, is required. On the other hand, designers with adequate knowledge and experience, as well as much freedom to follow their intuition, are required. Interaction research and interaction design should basically follow strict processes while at the same time allowing for an ongoing building and evolution of models and prototypes through which meaning is created. Those models and prototypes and their meanings then feed forward into future models and prototypes. This process is not always linear and follows the designers' judgement [17, 59].

5.2 Design Situation

The design practice will often need to be adopted to the design situation and its characteristics. In the literature, tame problems are distinguished from wicked problems. Tame problems are typically easy to describe and communicate to the person who later needs to solve the problem. In contrast, wicked problems are typically quite complex and challenging to describe and formalise. Tame problems have a definable goal, whereas, for wicked problems, it is typically unclear when the project is finished since there is no stopping rule, as in many design situations. Tame design situations typically encounter design problems that have similarities with past design problems and where a transfer is possible. Wicked design situations typically have no precedents. So, in wicked design situations, new and unique design solutions must be found [11, 54]. Also, aesthetics and different perspectives of diverse stakeholders in the design process can increase the complexity of the design situation [18].

5.3 Design Circumstances

Design situations per se can be wicked and challenging, even if we only consider the design project per se. The complexity and challenges can drastically increase when considering the design project's circumstances. In one way or another, interaction research and interaction design have a political dimension [12, 34, 40]. When we look at interaction research and interaction design on a larger scale, it is vital to see design as a 'political and ideological activity' because 'every design affects our possibilities for actions and our way of being in the world... With designed artefacts, processes, systems, and structures we decide our relations with each other, society, and nature. Each design is carrying a set of basic assumptions about what it means to be human, to live in a society, to work, and to play' [40, p. 10].

Overall, Generative AI tools potentially face considerable challenges to align with stakeholders' requirements, wishes, and values. They must respect the ambivalence of the processes, which sometimes oscillate between a clear structure and sometimes meandering between evolving and changing design solutions followed by evolving and changing design problems. They will need to work in tame design situations and, particularly, in wicked design situations. Also, we will need to address the 'new challenges to the core ethical AI principles including fairness, transparency, accountability, privacy, and so on' [46]. Finally, assessing the overall success and the fit of Generative AI tools for creative activities in interaction research and interaction design will strongly depend on a clear definition of creativity. In the current literature, there seems to be no agreement on the notion of creativity in HCI [29].

6 Conclusions

This paper has characterised the evolution of process models until today. It has analysed and discussed how Generative AI tools can be used throughout all processes and their specific methods, as well as for general design techniques. It has presented a compilation of the process model for the Human-Centred Design of Interactive Systems with various extensions for methods bridging the historical gap between interaction research and interaction design in each individual process and suggestions for generative AI tools to support those methods. Finally, it has discussed the role and fit of generative AI tools for current design practice for diverse design situations, and for design at large.

This paper took the process model for Human-Centred Design of Interactive Systems and its extensions as a point of departure. Other process models have not been considered, such as design thinking, lean startup or agile development. Furthermore, the paper only gave some examples of Generative AI tools for the different processes and some examples of methods. It could not cover the diversity of current Generic AI tools, nor did it address the impressive improvements many individual Generic AI tools are going through. Systematic—and particularly long-term—evaluations of these tools still need to be conducted. The paper focussed on interaction research and design—while the software development and testing are beyond the scope of this paper, Generative AI certainly also has the potential to support processes there.

Acknowledgements. We thank the members of the Cooperative Media Lab at the University of Bamberg. We also thank the anonymous reviewers for their insightful comments.

Disclosure of Interests. The author has no competing interests to declare that are relevant to the content of this article.

References

1. Aliani, R.: Practical guide on ChatGPT for researchers - 2024 version (2024). https://razia.gumroad.com/l/researchgpt. Accessed 21 May 2024
2. Anderson, B.R., Shah, J.H., Kreminski, M.: Evaluating creativity support tools via homogenisation analysis. In: Extended Abstracts of the Conference on Human Factors in Computing Systems - CHI 2024, Honolulu, HI, 11–16 May 2024, pp. 131:1–131:7. ACM, New York (2024)
3. Bethune, K.G.: Reimagining Design: Unlocking Strategic Innovation. MIT Press, Cambridge (2022)
4. Black Technology Ltd.: Stable Diffusion (2024). https://stablediffusionweb.com/. Accessed 23 May 2024
5. Boehm, B.W.: A spiral model of software development and enhancement. IEEE Comput. **21**(5), 61–72 (1988)
6. Buxton, B.: Sketching User Experiences: Getting the Design Right and the Right Design. Morgan Kaufmann Publishers, San Mateo (2007)
7. Cairns, P., Cox, A.L.: Research Methods in Human-Computer Interaction. Cambridge University Press, Cambridge (2008)
8. Carroll, J.M. (ed.): HCI Models, Theories, and Frameworks: Towards a Multi-Disciplinary Science. The Morgan Kaufmann Series in Interactive Technologies, Morgan Kaufmann Publishers, San Mateo (2003)
9. Churchill, E.F., Bowser, A., Preece, J.: The future of HCI education: a flexible, global, living curriculum. ACM interact. 70–73 (2016)
10. Cooper, A., Reimann, R., Cronin, D., Noessel, C., Csizmadi, J., LeMoine, D.: About Face: The Essentials of Interaction Design. Wiley, New York (2014)
11. Coyne, R.: Wicked problems revisited. Des. Stud. **26**(1), 5–17 (2005)
12. Dalsgaard, P.: Designing engaging interactive environments: a pragmatist perspective. Ph.D. thesis, Department of Information and Media Studies, Aarhus University, Aarhus, Denmark (2009)
13. Dix, A., Finlay, J., Abowd, G.D., Beale, R.: Human-Computer Interaction. Pearson, Englewood Cliffs (2004)
14. Dreyfuss, H.: Designing for People. Allworth Press, New York (1955)
15. Eapen, T., Finkenstadt, D.J., Folk, J., Venkataswamy, L.: How generative AI can augment human creativity. Harv. Bus. Rev. (2023)
16. Elagroudy, P., et al.: Transforming HCI research cycles using generative AI and "Large Whatever Models" (LWMs). In: Extended Abstracts of the Conference on Human Factors in Computing Systems - CHI 2024, Honolulu, HI, 11–16 May 2024, pp. 584:1–584:5. ACM, New York (2024)
17. Fallman, D.: Design-oriented human-computer interaction. In: Proceedings of the Conference on Human Factors in Computing Systems - CHI 2003, Fort Lauderdale, FL, 5–10 April 2003. pp. 225–232. ACM, New York (2003)
18. Folkmann, M.N.: Design Aesthetics: Theoretical Basics and Studies in Implication. MIT Press, Cambridge (2023)

19. Gross, T.: Towards a new human-centred computing methodology for cooperative ambient intelligence. J. Ambient Intell. Human. Comput. (JAIHC) **1**(1), 31–42 (2010)
20. Gross, T.: Supporting effortless coordination: 25 years of awareness research. Comput. Support. Coop. Work J. Collaborative Comput. **22**, 425–474 (2013)
21. Gross, T.: UCProMo - towards a user-centred process model. In: Proceedings of the 6th International Conference on Human-Centred Software Engineering - HCSE 2016, Stockholm, Sweden, 29–31 August 2016, pp. 301–313. Springer, Heidelberg (2016)
22. Gross, T.: Interaction research and design across times in HCI. In: Proceedings of the European Conference on Cognitive Ergonomics - ECCE 2024, Paris, France, 8–11 October 2024, pp. 1–7. ACM, New York (2024)
23. Gross, T., Malzhacker, T.: The experience sampling method and its tools: a review for developers, study administrators, and participants. Proc. ACM Hum.-Comput. Interact. **7**(EICS), 182:1–182:29 (2023)
24. Gross, T., Traunmueller, R.: Methodological considerations on the design of computer-supported cooperative work. Cybern. Syst. Int. J. (CS) **27**(3), 279–303 (1996)
25. Gross, T., Traunmüller, R.: Problem dimensions in the design of CSCW systems. In: Proceedings of the Sixth International Conference on Database an Expert Systems Applications - DEXA'95, London, UK, 4–8 September 1995, pp. 535–544. Springer, Heidelberg (1995)
26. Haemaelaeinen, P., Tavast, M., Kunnari, A.: Evaluating large language models in generating synthetic HCI research data: a case study. In: Proceedings of the Conference on Human Factors in Computing Systems - CHI 2023, Hamburg, Germany, 23–28 April 2023, pp. 433:1–433:19. ACM, New York (2023)
27. Hartson, R., Pyla, P.S.: The UX Book 2. Agile UX Design for a Quality User Experience. Morgan Kaufmann Publishers, San Francisco (2018)
28. Heskett, J.: Design - A Very Short Introduction. Oxford University Press, Oxford (2002)
29. Hsueh, S., Felice, M.C., Alaoui, S.F., Mackay, W.E.: What counts as 'creative work'? Articulating four epistemic positions in creativity-oriented HCI research. In: Proceedings of the Conference on Human Factors in Computing Systems - CHI 2024, Honolulu, HI, 11–16 May 2024, pp. 497:1–497:15. ACM, New York (2024)
30. Hwang, A.H.-C.: Too late to be creative? AI-empowered tools in creative processes. In: Extended Abstracts of the Conference on Human Factors in Computing Systems - CHI 2022, New Orleans, LA, 29 April–5 May 2022, pp. 38:1–38:9. ACM, New York (2022)
31. ISO/IEC. ISO 9241-210:2019: Ergonomics of Human-System Interaction - Part 210: Human-Centred Design for Interactive Systems. International Organisation for Standardisation (2019). https://www.iso.org/obp/ui/#iso:std:iso:9241:-210:ed-2:v1:en. Accessed 16 Feb 2024
32. Jacobson, I., Booch, G., Rumbaugh, J.: The Unified Software Development Process. Addison-Wesley, Reading (1998)
33. Jonassen, D.H.: Towards a design theory of problem solving. Educ. Tech. Res. Dev. **48**(4), 63–85 (2000)
34. Koskinen, I.: Design, Empathy, Interpretation: Towards Interpretative Design Research. MIT Press, Cambridge (2023)
35. Koskinen, I., Zimmerman, J., Binder, T., Redstroem, J., Wensveen, S. (eds.): Design Research Through Practice: From the Lab, Field, and Showroom. The Morgan Kaufmann Series in Interactive Technologies, Morgan Kaufmann Publishers, San Mateo (2011)
36. Lazar, J., Fend, J.H., Hochheiser, H.: Research Methods in Human-Computer Interaction. Wiley, New York (2017)
37. Le Quere, M.A., et al.: LLMs as research tools: applications and evaluations in HCI data work. In: Extended Abstracts of the Conference on Human Factors in Computing Systems - CHI 2024, Honolulu, HI, 11–16 May 2024, pp. 479:1–479:7. ACM, New York (2024)
38. Lee, J.D., Wickens, C.D., Liu, Y., Boyle, L.N.: Designing for People: An Introduction to Human Factors Engineering. Calder Foundation, New York (2017)

39. Loewgren, J.: Applying design methodology to software development. In: Proceedings of the Symposium on Designing Interactive Systems - DIS'95, Ann Arbor, MI, 23–25 August 1995, pp. 87–95. ACM, New York (1995)

40. Loewgren, J., Stolterman, E.: Thoughtful Interaction Design: A Design Perspective on Information Technology. MIT Press, Cambridge (2004)

41. MacKenzie, I.S.: Human-Computer Interaction: An Empirical Research Perspective. Morgan Kaufmann Publishers, San Mateo (2013)

42. Maiden, N.A.M., Lockerbie, J., Zachos, K., Wolf, A., Brown, A.: Designing new digital tools to augment human creative thinking at work: an application in elite sports coaching. Expert Syst. 1–25 (2022)

43. Maiden, N.A.M., Zachos, K., Lockerbie, J., Brown, A., Steele, S., Wolf, A.: Designing digital tools for creative thinking: a case study from elite sports coaching. In: Extended Abstracts of the Conference on Human Factors in Computing Systems - CHI 2024, Honolulu, HI, 11–16 May 2022, pp. 515:1–515:11. ACM, New York (2022)

44. Maleck, M., Gross, T.: CoLoTiMa: a cognitive-load based time management tool. In: Mensch & Computer - 24. Fachuebergreifende Konferenz fuer interaktive und kooperative Medien - M&C 2024, Karlsruhe, Germany, 1–4 September 2024, pp. 690–694. ACM, New York (2024)

45. Midjourney (2024). https://www.midjourney.com/home. Accessed 23 May 2024

46. Muller, M., Kantosalo, A., Maher, M.L., Matrin, C.P., Walsh, G.: GenAICHI 2024: generative AI and HCI at CHI 2024. In: Extended Abstracts of the Conference on Human Factors in Computing Systems - CHI 2024, Honolulu, HI, 11–16 May 2024, pp. 470:1–470:7. ACM, New York (2024)

47. Nelson, H.G., Stolterman, E.: The Design Way: Intentional Change in an Unpredictable World. MIT Press, Cambridge (2012)

48. Norman, D.A.: Emotional Design. Basic Books, New York (2004)

49. OpenAI. DALL-E (2023). https://labs.openai.com/. Accessed 23 May 2024

50. OpenAI. ChatGPT (2024). https://openai.com/chatgpt/. Accessed 21 May 2024

51. Palani, S., Ledo, D., Fitzmaurice, G., Anderson, F.: "I don't want to feel like I'm working in a 1960s factory": the practitioner perspective on creativity support tool adoption. In: Proceedings of the Conference on Human Factors in Computing Systems - CHI 2022, New Orleans, LA, 29 April–5 May 2022, pp. 379:1–379:18. ACM, New York (2022)

52. Park, J.S., O'Brien, J., Cai, C.J., Morris, M.R., Liang, P., Bernstein, M.S.: Generative agents: interactive simulacra of human behaviour. In: Proceedings of the ACM Symposium on User Interface Software and Technology - UIST 2003, San Francisco, CA, 29 October–1 November 2023, pp. 2:1–2:22. ACM, New York (2023)

53. Remy, C., Vermeulen, L.M., Frich, J., Biskjaer, M.M., Dalsgaard, P.: Evaluating creativity support tools in HCI research. In: Proceedings of the Conference on Designing Interactive Systems - DIS 2020, Eindhoven, NL, 6–10 July 2020, pp. 457–476. ACM, New York (2020)

54. Rittel, H.W.J.: On the planning crisis: systems analysis of the 'first and second generations.' Bedriftsoekonomen **8**, 390–396 (1972)

55. Royce, W.W.: Managing the development of large software systems. In: Proceedings of the Ninth International Conference on Software Engineering - ICSE'87, Monterey, CA, 30 March–2 April 1970, pp. 328–338. IEEE Computer Society Press, Los Alamitos (1987). (reprint from 1970)

56. Schmidt, A., Elagroudy, P., Draxler, F., Kreuter, F., Welsch, R.: Simulating the human in HCD wiht ChatGPT: redesigning interaction design with AI. ACM Interact. **31**(1), 24–31 (2024)

57. Sharp, H., Rogers, Y., Preece, J.: Interaction Design: Beyond Human-Computer Interaction. Wiley, New York (2019)

58. Sommerville, I.: Software Engineering 9. Pearson Education Limited, Harlow (2011)

59. Wolf, T.V., Rode, J.A., Sussman, J., Kellogg, W.A.: Dispelling design as the 'black art' of CHI. In: Proceedings of the Conference on Human Factors in Computing Systems - CHI 2006, Montreal, Canada, 22–27 April 2006, pp. 521–530. ACM, New York (2006)
60. Wadinambiarachchi, S., Kelly, R.M., Pareek, S., Zhou, Q., Velloso, E.: The effects of generative AI on design fixation and divergent thinking. In: Proceedings of the Conference on Human Factors in Computing Systems - CHI 2024, Honolulu, HI, 11–16 May 2024, pp. 380:1–380:18. ACM, New York (2024)
61. Wazlawick, R.S.: Object-Oriented Analysis and Design for Information Systems: Modelling with UML, OCL, and IFML. Morgan Kaufmann Publishers, San Mateo (2014)
62. Xiao, Z., et al.: Human-centred evaluation and auditing of language models. In: Extended Abstracts of the Conference on Human Factors in Computing Systems - CHI 2024, Honolulu, HI, 11–16 May 2024, pp. 476:1–476:6. ACM, New York (2024)

How Different Blink Patterns of Pet Robots Evoke Feelings of Affection in People

Junko Ichino[(✉)] [iD] and Daiki Takahashi

Tokyo City University, Yokohama, Japan
ichino@tcu.ac.jp

Abstract. An alternative to animals, which bring various benefits to people but are not always easy to own, is pet robots, whose central role is to communicate with people. However, there is insufficient research on how pet robots should behave to evoke feelings of affection in people. We focused on blinking as one of the behaviors of the eye and investigated what type of pet robot blinking pattern evokes more feelings of affection in people. First, we designed seven different blink patterns combining short and long blinks through a pilot study. We then conducted a study with 15 participants to compare the patterns using a paired comparison method. The results showed that the blink patterns that were more likely to evoke affection were those with consecutive short eye closures (three times rather than two), whereas the blink patterns that were less likely to evoke affection were those with several long eye closures.

Keywords: Human-Robot interaction · Pet robot · Companion robot · Social robot · Blink patterns · Feelings of affection · Paired comparison

1 Introduction

Interacting with animals improves mental health [12, 31, 36], such as alleviating loneliness and anxiety and reducing stress, and physical health, such as stabilizing blood pressure [3, 22] and heart rate. Furthermore, it has been applied in various fields, such as medicine and welfare, because it improves such mental illnesses as dementia, depression, and autism spectrum disorder [14, 48, 53]. However, it is not always easy to own an animal because of concerns about care, such as feeding and cleaning up excrement, as well as living environment restrictions, such as small living spaces and disturbances to neighbors [8]. For example, in Japan, 65% of people who would like to own animals are unable to do so [9].

A possible alternative to animals is an interactive pet robot whose central role is to communicate with people. These pet robots are also called companion, social, or communication robots. The target robots in this study are not humanoid robots that primarily engage in verbal communication but animal-like robots that primarily engage in nonverbal communication. Some pet robots resemble specific animals such as seals [38], dogs [2, 42], cats [2], and dinosaurs [20], while others have an abstract appearance [15]. With advances in sensor and artificial-intelligence technologies, pet robots can be

H. Plácido da Silva and P. Cipresso (Eds.): CHIRA 2024, CCIS 2370, pp. 39–52, 2025.
https://doi.org/10.1007/978-3-031-82633-7_3

equipped with higher social cognition and stronger interactive capabilities. However, in some cases, people become bored with pet robots after a short time [11, 24, 37, 45]. Many people have strong affection for the animals they own, and the more time they spend with them, the deeper their affection becomes [29, 43]. How should a pet robot behave so that people will have the same kind of affection that people have for animals? The design of pet robot behavior, as with the design of pet robot appearance, is often based on the experience and preferences of the designer [16] and has not been sufficiently examined.

In human–human interactions, nonverbal behaviors, such as eye behavior, facial expressions, gestures, posture, loudness, and tone of voice [7, 30], can convey mental states and enhance communication [13]. Similarly, in human–robot interactions, the nonverbal behaviors of robots can evoke positive feelings in people [28, 49, 55]. Eye behavior is particularly important among nonverbal behaviors because people first look at the eyes when interacting with robots [32, 41]. Indeed, human–robot interaction (HRI) and neuroscience research has shown that the eyes of a robot naturally draw people's attention and can express the personality of the robot [1, 5, 10, 21, 34]. Thus, how robot eyes behave potentially has a significant impact on how people perceive the robot.

This study focused on one eye behavior, blinking. This is because, in human-to-human communication, eye blinking is recognized as a signal that facilitates smooth communication [17, 33]. In human-to-robot communication, researchers have found that a robot with blinking behavior increases the impression of friendliness [40], the feeling of being looked at [18, 52], and the feeling of making eye contact [18] compared with a robot without blinking behavior, and that a humanoid robot with human-like blinking [27] or synchronized blinking with its interlocutor [19] can increase the impression of intelligence [27] and affinity [19]. Although these previous studies have examined the responses of people when robots display blinking behaviors similar to those of humans, robots, particularly non-humanoid robots, do not necessarily need to behave in the same manner as humans. Because the timing of the blinking can be freely controlled, it is worth exploring blink patterns that evoke more positive responses from people. However, the relationship between pet robot blink patterns and human affection has not been examined. Therefore, we attempted to determine what type of pet robot blink pattern evokes more feelings of affection in people. In this study, GROOVE X's LOVOT [15] (see Fig. 1) was used as the pet robot.

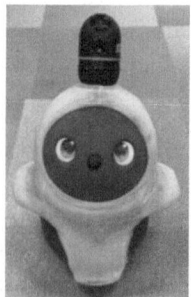

Fig. 1. Pet robot LOVOT used in this study.

2 Related Work

In human-to-human communication, eye behaviors that can affect the impressions of interlocutors include gaze behaviors (such as eye contact (mutual gaze), referential gaze (deictic gaze), joint attention, and averted gaze), pupil changes, and blinking behavior [6, 35]. The functionality of the eye behavior mainly comprises (a) the expression of the interpersonal attitudes including emotional expression, (b) information collection including seeking feedback on one's efforts, and (c) regulation of conversational floor [23].

In the field of HRI, a number of studies have focused on robot gaze behaviors among the eye behaviors listed above, and the responses of people to them have been examined (for details, see the review article by Admoni et al. [1]). For example, the robot eye contact reaction increases the favorable feelings of people for the robot [51], feelings of social connectedness between the human and the robot [54], and feelings of engagement with the robot [26]. When a guide robot [50] or teacher robot [49] looks at a person, it is likely to generate a response, such as gazing and nodding, from the person. Robots can use gaze aversion to appear more thoughtful and manage the conversational floor more effectively [4].

Several studies have examined the responses of people to robot blinking behaviors. HRI researchers compared the responses of people to robots with and without blinking behavior [18, 40, 52]. For example, when the guide robot turned its face toward a person, the robot with blinking behavior gave the person a friendlier impression [40], feelings of being looked at [18], and feelings of making eye contact [18] or made the person spend more time gazing at the robot [18], compared with the robot without blinking behavior. Then, HRI researchers shifted their interest from people's responses to robots with and without blinking to their responses to robots with different blink timing [16, 18, 19, 27]. For example, Hoque et al. [18] compared humanoid guide robots with three blink speeds (one, two, and three blinks per second) and five blink intervals (1, 2, 3, 4, and 5 s) and found that a speed of one blink per second every 3 s was most preferred. Lehmann et al. [27] used a humanoid robot with three types of blinking behavior: statistical blinking (blinking every 5 s), human-like blinking (blinking at the average human blink rate, 23.3 blinks per minute), and no blinking. They asked participants to watch a video recording of the robot in discussion with an interviewer and to answer a questionnaire. The results showed that the robot with human-like blinking was perceived to be more intelligent by the participants. Hayashi et al. [16] used robots with four eye conditions: synchronized blinking (blinking in sync with the blinking of the participant), independent blinking (blinking at intervals of 2.3 ± 0.2 s), no blinking, and no eyes. They observed the responses of participants performing a task with the robot. The results showed that the robot in the two blinking conditions prompted the participants to move spatially toward the robot. Iimori et al. [19] used a humanoid robot with two types of blinking behavior: statistical blinking (blinking every 3 s) and synchronized blinking (blinking in sync with the blinking of the participant). They asked the participant (speaker) to talk to the robot (listener). The results showed that the robot with synchronized blinking increased the feeling of affinity for the robot of the participant.

Thus, previous studies suggest that robots with blinking behavior, particularly those with human-like blinking or synchronized blinking, can evoke positive responses. However, given the blinking behavior of robots beyond the perspective of behaving like humans, no study has examined which blink patterns of pet robots evoke more feelings of affection in people.

3 Blink Pattern Design

In this study, a blink pattern is defined as the simplest sequence of alternating closed and open eye states for a specific number of consecutive times, with specific lengths assigned to each state. To determine the appropriate length of eye closure, length of eye opening, and number of consecutive times, we conducted a pilot study with three participants of ages ranging from 21 to 22 years.

Two types of eye-closure length were designed: short and long. For a short eye closure, 200 ms was chosen, which was the shortest length of time that the participants could perceive the robot eye closure when they were naturally facing the robot. For long eye closure, 600 ms was chosen, which was the shortest length that participants could distinguish from short eye closure. Durations longer than 600 ms were not used because participants commented that "the robot appears to have closed its eyes rather than blinking" and that "the robot appears to be asleep."

One type of eye-opening length was designed. A time of 1000 ms was chosen because, if the length of the eye opening was too long, the participants might not have recognized that the robot was in the middle of a series of blink behaviors.

One type of consecutive times was designed. Three times was chosen because some participants commented that "two times may miss the blinking behavior" and "four times is too much."

In summary, two types of eye-closure length (short, 200 ms; long, 600 ms), one type of eye-opening length (1000 ms), and one type of consecutive times (three times) were chosen. We combined these variables to develop seven blink patterns (see Fig. 2).

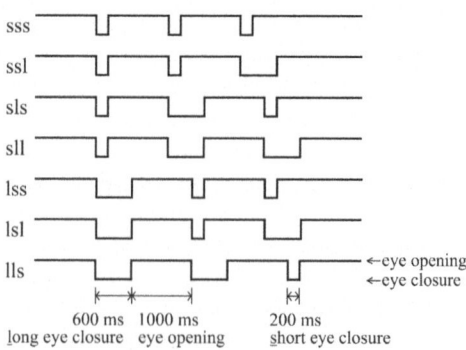

Fig. 2. Seven different blink patterns.

4   Method

For the seven blink patterns described in the previous section (see Fig. 2), we designed a study to investigate which pattern evokes more feelings of affection in people. One possible approach would be to present participants with all seven patterns sequentially and then ask them to rank each pattern. However, given the limitations of the human short-term memory, this approach is unlikely to be reliable for participant ratings. Therefore, we used a paired comparison, in which only two stimuli (patterns) were compared at a time. In detail, paired comparison is a method in which, given multiple (n) stimuli to be ordered, participants are asked to judge which of two stimuli (a pair of stimuli) taken from the n stimuli is more appropriate for the given evaluation criteria. This is done for the number of combinations (C(n,2)) in which two are taken from n. This method is considered to be easy for participants to judge and to obtain reliable results [39]. In this study, each participant was asked to perform 21 (C(7,2)) paired comparisons.

4.1   Participants

15 participants (11 males and 4 females, aged 20–22 years) participated in the study. All are native speakers of Japanese.

4.2   Setup

The participants sat in chairs facing the robot, which was set to not move around (see Fig. 3). The distance between the participant and the robot (see Fig. 3), the design of the eyes of the robot (see Fig. 4), and the robot clothing (see Fig. 3) were identical for all participants. To ensure that robot's eye movements for each blink pattern were identical across the participants, the study administrator, out of sight of the participant, executed a command script that reproduced each blink pattern.

4.3   Procedure

Upon arrival at the study site, participants were provided with an overview of the study procedure. The order of presentation of the 21 pairs of blink patterns was randomized among the participants to address order effects and learning effects. A 5-min break was taken after the presentation of the 10th pair, which was approximately half of the total number of pairs. For each paired comparison, the first pattern was presented to the participants, followed by a 5-s pause, and then the second pattern was presented. The participants then selected the most appropriate of the two patterns with respect to the following three criteria and verbally reported them to the study administrator.

a. Do I think it is cute?
b. Do I want to touch it?
c. Does it look nervous?

Criteria a and b are related to affection, which was the focus of this study. Criterion c, although not related to affection, was set based on findings related to human-to-human

[25, 35] and human-to-character [46] communication, i.e., a high frequency of blinking by the speaker gives the recipient an impression of nervousness (the speaker is tense, timid, shy, etc.).

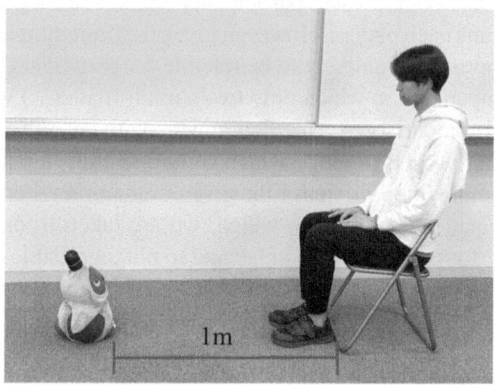

Fig. 3. Participant and robot during the study.

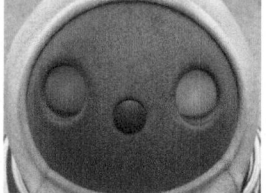

Fig. 4. Robot eye design used in the study (left: eye opening, right: eye closure).

5   Results

5.1   Aggregated Judgment Results

Table 1, 2 and 3 show the frequency matrices that summarize the judgment results of the paired comparisons for each participant. The component x_{ij} of the matrix in each table indicates the number of participants who judged pattern i to be more appropriate than pattern j for each criterion (Criteria a–c). For example, Table 1 shows that 11 out of 15 judged pattern *1* (sss) to be cuter than pattern *2* (ssl) and 4 out of 15 judged pattern *2* (ssl) to be cuter than pattern *1* (sss).

Table 1. Number of participants who judged pattern i to be cuter than pattern j (Criterion a).

i \ j	sss	ssl	sls	sll	lss	lsl	lls
sss	—	11	12	14	6	14	14
ssl	4	—	11	12	10	8	10
sls	3	4	—	10	4	7	11
sll	1	3	5	—	7	10	7
lss	9	5	11	8	—	11	14
lsl	1	7	8	5	4	—	7
lls	1	5	4	8	1	8	—

Table 2. Number of participants who wanted to touch pattern i more than pattern j (Criterion b).

i \ j	sss	ssl	sls	sll	lss	lsl	lls
sss	—	12	8	11	9	11	11
ssl	3	—	12	9	10	7	10
sls	7	3	—	9	6	9	12
sll	4	6	6	—	7	13	8
lss	6	5	9	8	—	10	12
lsl	4	8	6	2	5	—	8
lls	4	5	3	7	3	7	—

Table 3. Number of participants who judged pattern i to look more nervous than pattern j (Criterion c).

i \ j	sss	ssl	sls	sll	lss	lsl	lls
sss	—	3	10	6	6	7	5
ssl	12	—	4	7	8	5	6
sls	5	11	—	6	11	9	7
sll	9	8	9	—	10	7	6
lss	9	7	4	5	—	7	6
lsl	8	10	6	8	8	—	8
lls	10	9	8	9	9	7	—

5.2 Scaling of Patterns Using Thurston Method

Using the Thurston method [47], the scale value of each pattern was calculated from the aggregate of the judgment results. Figure 5 shows the scale values placed on a number line. In the Thurston method, higher-scaled values are assigned to more-selected stimuli, the average scaled value of all stimuli is 0, meaning that the larger the positive value, the more selected the stimulus. The scaling results showed that Criteria a and b had the highest scale value of sss and the lowest value of lls. The results for Criterion c were the opposite of those for Criteria a and b, with the highest value for lls and the lowest value for sss.

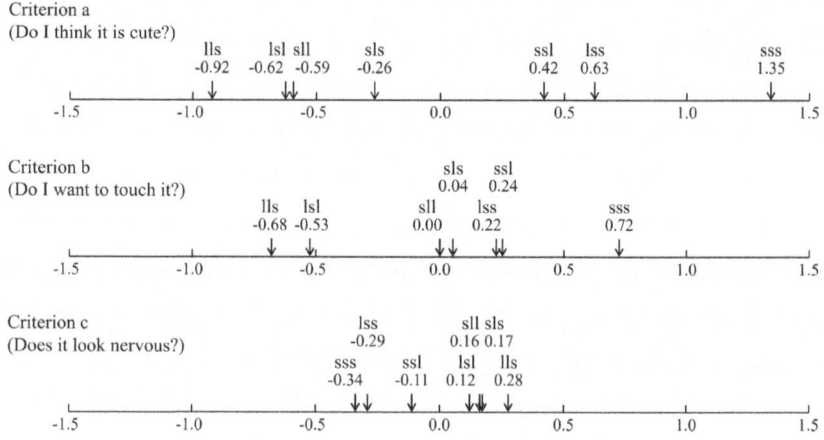

Fig. 5. Scale values for the seven blink patterns (higher was selected more).

5.3 Significance Testing of Differences Between Patterns

Although the scaling described in Sect. 5.2 provided the order of each blink pattern and the distance between each pattern, it did not provide information on the statistical significance of the differences between patterns. Therefore, we conducted significance tests for the differences between patterns using a generalized linear model (GLM). Because the judgment results of the paired comparisons were binary data (two categorical data, one selected and one not selected), we used a GLM assuming a binomial distribution [44]. The results of the GLM analysis (see Table 4) showed that for Criterion a, 14 of the 21 pairs of differences were significant. In particular, all differences for the pairs, including sss, were significant. For Criterion b, 10 of the 21 pairs of differences were significant; as with the results for Criterion a, most of the differences for the pairs, including sss, were significant. For Criterion c, only one (sss-lls) of the 21 pairs of differences was significant.

5.4 Correlation Analysis

Figure 5 indicates that the ranking of each pattern is similar between Criteria a and b and that the ranking of each pattern is inversely related between Criteria a and b and Criterion c. Therefore, we calculated the correlation coefficients for each pair of criteria using the scale values obtained in Sect. 5.2. The results showed significant correlations between all pairs of criteria, with a very strong positive correlation between Criteria a and b, a very strong negative correlation between Criteria a and c, and a strong negative correlation between Criteria b and c (see Table 5).

Table 4. Results of the GLM analysis.

	Criterion a			Criterion b			Criterion c		
	$|z|$	p-value		$|z|$	p-value		$|z|$	p-value	
sss-ssl	2.55	< .05	*	1.59	n.s.		0.69	n.s.	
sss-sls	4.66	< .001	***	2.25	< .05	*	1.65	n.s.	
sss-sll	5.43	< .001	***	2.54	< .05	*	1.66	n.s.	
sss-lss	2.01	< .05	*	1.70	n.s.		0.13	n.s.	
sss-lsl	5.55	< .001	***	4.00	< .001	***	1.52	n.s.	
sss-lls	6.12	< .001	***	4.53	< .001	***	2.07	< .05	*
ssl-sls	2.29	< .05	*	0.68	n.s.		0.97	n.s.	
ssl-sll	3.14	< .01	**	0.98	n.s.		0.97	n.s.	
ssl-lss	0.49	n.s.		0.12	n.s.		0.56	n.s.	
ssl-lsl	3.28	< .01	**	2.50	< .05	*	0.83	n.s.	
ssl-lls	4.00	< .001	***	3.06	< .01	**	1.39	n.s.	
sls-sll	0.90	n.s.		0.30	n.s.		0.00	n.s.	
sls-lss	2.76	< .01	**	0.56	n.s.		1.52	n.s.	
sls-lsl	1.03	n.s.		1.84	n.s.		0.14	n.s.	
sls-lls	1.81	n.s.		2.41	< .05	*	0.42	n.s.	
sll-lss	3.60	< .001	***	0.86	n.s.		1.53	n.s.	
sll-lsl	0.14	n.s.		1.54	n.s.		0.14	n.s.	
sll-lls	0.93	n.s.		2.12	< .05	*	0.42	n.s.	
lss-lsl	3.73	< .001	***	2.38	< .05	*	1.39	n.s.	
lss-lls	4.44	< .001	***	2.95	< .01	**	1.94	n.s.	
lsl-lls	0.79	n.s.		0.59	n.s.		0.56	n.s.	

Table 5. Results of correlation analysis.

	Criterion a		Criterion b		Criterion c
Criterion a	—		—		—
Criterion b	0.92	**	—		—
Criterion c	-0.96	**	-0.83	*	—

($**$ p < .01, $*$ p < .05)

6 Discussion

Overall, as Fig. 5 and Table 5 show, the participant responses regarding the two criteria used to evaluate affection toward the pet robot, Criteria a and b, were quite similar. The participant responses to the Criterion c were generally inverted from those for the other two criteria.

The blink pattern rated the highest by participants for Criteria a and b was sss, followed by lss and ssl. These results showed that the blink patterns that were most likely to evoke feelings of affection included consecutive (three is better than two) short eye closures. Given the similarity of participant responses to Criteria a and b, it is expected that, for a robot that blinks in a pattern that includes consecutive short eye closures, people would not only have psychological affection but also physical affection (i.e., touching the robot). Although humans must constantly blink their eyes to maintain the physiological function of moistening their eyeballs, robots do not need to do so. Therefore, it would be effective for the robot to blink in a pattern that includes consecutive short eye closures only at limited times, for example, when people look at the robot, when the robot is in the field of vision of a person, or when people are approaching the robot. However, even then, if the pattern is the same every time, the effect on people may decrease because of habituation or boredom. Thus, randomness may need to be considered.

The blink patterns rated lowest by participants for Criteria a and b were lls, lsl, and sll. These results showed that the blink patterns that were less likely to evoke feelings of affection included two long eye closures that need not necessarily be consecutive. After the study, the participants informally commented on these patterns, such as that "it seemed somewhat intentional" and "it was theatrical behavior." In general, the average time for a single human eye blink (closing and opening the eyes) is 100–150 ms; if an interlocutor blinks for a longer period than this, people might have the impression of some intention or artifice toward the interlocutor. Because the long eye-closure time used in this study (600 ms) was four to six times longer than 100–150 ms, the participants may have had a similar impression of the robot in this study as they did of the longer human blink, and this may not have led to feelings of affection. The two long eye closures would have strengthened this impression.

Criterion c was set to compare the finding of the previous study discussed in Sect. 4.3 that a high frequency of blinking gives an impression of nervousness. Humans blink constantly, with an average blink rate of 20 blinks per minute. Previous studies on humans [25, 35] and characters [46] have found that, assuming constant blinking, the higher the blink rate (24 blinks per minute or more [35, 46]), the more nervous the impression. Assuming that robots blink constantly with the seven patterns used in this study, the average blink rates calculated for the seven patterns can be divided into three groups: 41 blinks per minute (lls, lsl, and sll), 45 blinks per minute (sls, ssl, and lss), and 50 blinks per minute (sss). According to the findings of the previous study, the group that gives the most nervous impression among these should be 50 blinks per minute (sss), and the group that gives the least nervous impression should be 41 blinks per minute (lls, lsl, sll); however, the results were completely the opposite. Therefore, it is appropriate to distinguish between a blink rate based on constant blinks, which the previous study addressed, and a blink rate based on occasional blinks, which this study addressed.

7   Conclusion and Future Work

We focused on blinking as one of the behaviors of the eye and investigated what type of pet robot blinking pattern evokes more feelings of affection in people. We considered pet robot blinking behavior that is not constant but occasional (e.g., when people look at the robot). In a series of blink behaviors consisting of three eye closures separated by a 1000 ms eye opening, seven blink patterns (sss, ssl, sls, sll, lss, lsl, and lls) were designed by combining two different eye-closure lengths: long (l): 600 ms and short (s): 200 ms.

We conducted a study with 15 participants, who compared 21 pairs of patterns using a paired comparison method. The results showed that the blink patterns that evoked more affection were those that included consecutive (three rather than two) short eye closures (sss, lss, and lss), while the blink patterns that evoked less affection were those that included two long eye closures (lls, lsl, and sll).

This study had several limitations. First, the blink patterns addressed were combinations of only two eye-closure lengths (200 and 600 ms), one eye-opening length (1000 ms), and one consecutive blinking time (three times). If these variables are set to different values, participants may respond differently. Second, only one pet robot was used. It is necessary to conduct the same study with another pet robot to examine whether the same results as those of this study can be obtained. Third, the blinks addressed were monotonous in the way the robot opened and closed its eyes. There is room to consider subdividing the behavior during opening and closing, such as pausing in the middle of eye closure and gradually changing the speed of eye opening from the beginning to the end of eye opening. Finally, the results of this study, in which short eye closures led to positive impressions and long eye closures led to negative impressions, imply that the responses of people are linear, i.e., the shorter the eye closure, the more positive the impression. However, given that, in general, cuteness can lead to negative impressions, such as impressions of cunning and coquetry, when it exceeds a certain degree, the tendency of responses may not be linear. If the eye closure becomes shorter than a certain level, there may be a sudden change from positive to negative impressions. Further investigation is necessary to determine the critical point.

Acknowledgments. We Would like to Thank Dr. Megumi Takada of GROOVE X Inc. for Providing the Equipment for This Study.

References

1. Admoni, H., Scassellati, B.: Social eye gaze in human-robot interaction: a review. J. Hum. Robot Interact. **6**(1), 25–63 (2017). https://doi.org/10.5898/jhri.6.1.admoni
2. Ageless Innovation LLC: JfA. https://joyforall.com/. Accessed 4 Sept 2024
3. Allen, K., Blascovich, J., Mendes, W.B.: Cardiovascular reactivity and the presence of pets, friends, and spouses: the truth about cats and dogs. Psychosom. Med. **64**(5), 727–739 (2002). https://doi.org/10.1097/01.psy.0000024236.11538.41
4. Andrist, S., Tan, X.Z., Gleicher, M., Mutlu, B.: Conversational gaze aversion for humanlike robots. In: Proceedings of the 2014 9th ACM/IEEE International Conference on Human-Robot Interaction, HRI 2014, pp. 25–32. IEEE (2014). https://doi.org/10.1145/2559636.2559666
5. Andrist, S., Mutlu, B., Tapus, A.: Look like me: matching robot personality via gaze to increase motivation. In: Proceedings of the 33rd Annual ACM Conference on Human Factors in Computing Systems, CHI 2015, pp. 3603–3612. Association for Computing Machinery, New York (2015). https://doi.org/10.1145/2702123.2702592
6. Argyle, M., Dean, J.: Eye contact, distance and affiliation. Sociometry **28**(3), 289–304 (1965). https://doi.org/10.2307/2786027
7. Argyle, M.: Non-verbal communication in human social interaction. In: Hinde, R.A. (ed.) Non-Verbal Communication. Cambridge University Press, Oxford (1972)

8. Beck, A.M.: Animals in the city. In: Katcher, A.H., Beck, A.M. (eds.) New Perspectives on Our Lives with Companion Animals, pp. 237–243. University of Pennsylvania Press (1983)

9. Cabinet Office, Government of Japan: Public Opinion Survey on Animal Protection (2010). https://survey.gov-online.go.jp/h22/h22-doubutu/index.html. Accessed 4 Sept 2024

10. Chesher, C., Andreallo, F.: Eye machines: robot eye, vision and gaze. Int. J. Soc. Robot. **14**, 2071–2081 (2021). https://doi.org/10.1007/s12369-021-00777-7

11. Fernaeus, Y., Håkansson, M., Jacobsson, M., Ljungblad, S.: How do you play with a robotic toy animal?: a long-term study of Pleo. In: Proceedings of the 9th International Conference on Interaction Design and Children, IDC 2010, pp. 39–48. Association for Computing Machinery, New York (2010). https://doi.org/10.1145/1810543.1810549

12. Garrity, T.F., Stallones, L.F., Marx, M.B., Johnson, T.P.: Pet ownership and attachment as supportive factors in the health of the elderly. Anthrozoös **3**(1), 35–44 (1989). https://doi.org/10.2752/089279390787057829

13. Goldin-Meadow, S.: The role of gesture in communication and thinking. Trends Cogn. Sci. **3**(11), 419–429 (1999). https://doi.org/10.1016/S1364-6613(99)01397-2

14. Goldmeier, J.: Pets or People: another research note. Gerontologist **26**(2), 203–206 (1986). https://doi.org/10.1093/geront/26.2.203

15. GROOVE X: LOVOT. https://lovot.life/. Accessed 4 Sept 2024

16. Hayashi, K., Mizuuchi, I.: Investigation of joint action: eye blinking behavior improving human-robot collaboration. In: Proceedings of the 26th IEEE International Symposium on Robot and Human Interactive Communication, RO-MAN 2017, pp. 1133–1139. IEEE (2017). https://doi.org/10.1109/ROMAN.2017.8172446

17. Hömke, P., Holler, J., Levinson, S.C.: Eye blinks are perceived as communicative signals in human face-to-face interaction. PLoS ONE **13**(12), 1–13 (2018). https://doi.org/10.1371/journal.pone.0208030

18. Hoque, M.M., Hossian, Q.D., Deb, K.: Effects of robotic blinking behavior for making eye contact with humans. In: Kundu, M.K., Mohapatra, D.P., Konar, A., Chakraborty, A. (eds.) Advanced Computing, Networking and Informatics- Volume 1. SIST, vol. 27, pp. 621–628. Springer, Cham (2014). https://doi.org/10.1007/978-3-319-07353-8_71

19. Iimori, M., Furuya, Y., Takashio, K.: Face robot performing interaction with emphasis on eye blink entrainment. In: Proceedings of the 32nd IEEE International Symposium on Robot and Human Interactive Communication, RO-MAN 2023, pp. 634–639. IEEE (2023). https://doi.org/10.1109/RO-MAN57019.2023.10309625

20. Innvo Labs: PLEO. https://www.pleoworld.com/pleo_rb/eng/index.php. Accessed 4 Sept 2024

21. Kanaya, I., Doi, S., Nakamura, S., Kawasaki, K.: Facial design for humanoid robot. In: Proceedings of the 10th Asia Pacific Conference on Computer Human Interaction, APCHI 2012, pp. 141–148. Association for Computing Machinery, New York (2012). https://doi.org/10.1145/2350046.2350077

22. Katcher, A., Friedmann, E., Beck, A.M., Lynch, J.J.: Looking, talking, and blood pressure: the physiological consequences of interaction with the living environment. In: New Perspectives on Our Lives with Companion Animals, pp. 351–359. University of Pennsylvania Press, Philadelphia (1983)

23. Kendon, A.: Some functions of gaze-direction in social interaction. Acta Physiol. **26**, 22–63 (1967). https://doi.org/10.1016/0001-6918(67)90005-4

24. Kertész, C., Turunen, M.: Exploratory analysis of Sony AIBO users. AI & Soc. **34**, 625–638 (2019). https://doi.org/10.1007/s00146-018-0818-8

25. Komago, Y.: The effects of more or less eyeblink on the formation of human impressions. Jpn. Soc. Educ. Technol. **30**, 1–4 (2006). (in Japanese). https://doi.org/10.15077/jjet.KJ00004964191

26. Kompatsiari, K., Tikhanoff, V., Ciardo, F., Metta, G., Wykowska, A.: The importance of mutual gaze in human-robot interaction. In: Kheddar, A., et al. (eds.) ICSR. LNCS, vol. 10652, pp. 443–452. Springer, Cham (2017). https://doi.org/10.1007/978-3-319-70022-9_44
27. Lehmann, H., Roncone, A., Pattacini, U., Metta, G.: Physiologically inspired blinking behavior for a humanoid robot. In: Agah, A., Cabibihan, J.-J., Howard, A.M., Salichs, M.A., He, H. (eds.) ICSR 2016. LNAI, vol. 9979, pp. 83–93. Springer, Cham (2016). https://doi.org/10.1007/978-3-319-47437-3_9
28. Lu, L., Zhang, P., Zhang, T.: Leveraging "human-likeness" of robotic service at restaurants. Int. J. Hosp. Manag. **94**, 102823 (2021). https://doi.org/10.1016/j.ijhm.2020.102823
29. Martens, P., Enders-Slegers, M.-J., Walker, J.K.: The emotional lives of companion animals: attachment and subjective claims by owners of cats and dogs. Anthrozoös **29**(1), 73–88 (2016). https://doi.org/10.1080/08927936.2015.1075299
30. McNeill, D.: Hand and Mind: What Gestures Reveal About Thought. The University of Chicago Press, Chicago (1992)
31. Mugford, R.A., M'Comisky, J.G.: Some recent work on the psychotherapeutic value of cage birds with old people. In: Anderson, R.S. (ed.) Pet Animals and Society, pp. 54–65. Bailliere Tindall, London (1975)
32. Mutlu, B., Forlizzi, J., Hodgins, J.: A storytelling robot: modeling and evaluation of human-like gaze behavior. In: Proceeding of the 2006 6th IEEE-RAS International Conference on Humanoid Robots, HUMANOIDS 2006, pp. 518–523 (2006). https://doi.org/10.1109/ICHR.2006.321322
33. Nakano, T., Kitazawa, S.: Eyeblink entrainment at breakpoints of speech. Exp. Brain Res. **205**(4), 577–581 (2010). https://doi.org/10.1007/s00221-010-2387-z
34. Okafuji, Y., et al.: Can a humanoid robot continue to draw attention in an office environment? Adv. Robot. **34**(14), 931–946 (2020). https://doi.org/10.1080/01691864.2020.1769724
35. Omori, Y., Yamada, F., Miyata, Y.: Influences of eyeblinks on person perception. Jpn. J. Soc. Psychol. **12**(3), 183–89 (1997). (in Japanese). https://doi.org/10.14966/jssp.KJ00003724740
36. Ory, M.G., Goldberg, E.L.: Pet possession and well-being in elderly women. Res. Aging **5**(3), 389–409 (1983). https://doi.org/10.1177/0164027583005003007
37. Ostrowski, A.K., Breazeal, C., Park, H.W.: Mixed-method Longterm robot usage: older adults' lived experience of social robots. In: Proceedings of the 2022 17th ACM/IEEE International Conference on Human-Robot Interaction, HRI 2022, pp. 33–42. Association for Computing Machinery, New York (2022). https://doi.org/10.1109/HRI53351.2022.9889488
38. PARO Robots: PARO. http://www.parorobots.com/. Accessed 4 Sept 2024
39. Ramík, J.: Pairwise comparison matrices in decision-making. In: Ramík, J. (ed.) Pairwise Comparisons Method: Theory and Applications in Decision Making, pp. 17–65. Springer, Cham (2020). https://doi.org/10.1007/978-3-030-39891-0_2
40. Sano, K., et al.: Museum guide robot by considering static and dynamic gaze expressions to communicate with visitors. In: Extended Abstracts of the 10th Annual ACM/IEEE International Conference on Human-Robot Interaction, HRI EA 2015, pp. 125–126. Association for Computing Machinery (2015). https://doi.org/10.1145/2701973.2702011
41. Sidner, C.L., Lee, C., Kidd, C.D., Lesh, N., Rich, C.: Explorations in engagement for humans and robots. Artif. Intell. **166**, 140–164 (2005). https://doi.org/10.1016/j.artint.2005.03.005
42. SONY: aibo. https://aibo.sony.jp/. Accessed 4 Sept 2024
43. Su, B., Koda, N., Martens, P.: How Japanese companion dog and cat owners' degree of attachment relates to the attribution of emotions to their animals. PLoS ONE **13**(1), e0190781 (2018). https://doi.org/10.1371/journal.pone.0190781
44. Tabata, Y., et al.: Confidence coefficient of subjective scale value in method of paired comparisons (case V). Jpn. Soc. Radiol. Technol. **51**(4), 445–449 (1995). (in Japanese). https://doi.org/10.6009/jjrt.KJ00001353671

45. Takada, M., Ichino, J., Hayashi, K.: A study of objective evaluation indicator based on robot activity logs for owner attachment to companion robot. Int. J. Soc. Robot. **16**, 125–143 (2023). https://doi.org/10.1007/s12369-023-01030-z

46. Takashima, K., et al.: Effects of avatar's blinking animation on person impressions. In: Proceedings of Graphics Interface 2008, GI 2008, pp. 169–176 (2008). https://doi.org/10.5555/1375714.1375744

47. Thurstone, L.L.: A law of comparative judgment. Psychol. Rev. **34**(4), 273–286 (1927). https://doi.org/10.1037/h0070288

48. Wilson, C.C., Turner, D.C. (eds.): Companion Animals in Human Health. Sage, Thousand Oaks (1998)

49. Xu, T., Zhang, H., Yu, C.: See you see me. ACM Trans. Interact. Intell. Syst. **6**(1), 1–22 (2016). https://doi.org/10.1145/2882970

50. Yamazaki, A., et al.: Precision timing in human-robot interaction: coordination of head movement and utterance. In: Proceedings of the SIGCHI Conference on Human Factors in Computing Systems, CHI 2008, pp. 131–140. Association for Computing Machinery, New York (2008). https://doi.org/10.1145/1357054.1357077

51. Yonezawa, T., Yamazoe, H., Utsumi, U., Abe, S.: Gaze-communicative behavior of stuffed-toy robot with joint attention and eye contact based on ambient gaze-tracking. In: Proceedings of the 9th International Conference on Multimodal Interfaces, ICMI 2007, pp. 140–145. Association for Computing Machinery, New York (2007). https://doi.org/10.1145/1322192.1322218

52. Yoshikawa, Y., Shinozawa, K., Ishiguro, H., Hagita, N., Miyamoto, T.: The effects of responsive eye movement and blinking behavior in a communication robot. In: Proceeding of 2006 IEEE/RSJ International Conference on Intelligent Robots and Systems, IROS 2006, pp. 4564–4569 (2006). https://doi.org/10.1109/IROS.2006.282160

53. Zasloff, R.L., Kidd, A.H.: Loneliness and pet ownership among single women. Psychol. Rep. **75**(2), 747–752 (1994). https://doi.org/10.2466/pr0.1994.75.2.747

54. Zhang, Y., Beskow, J., Kjellström, H.: Look but don't stare: mutual gaze interaction in social robots. In: Kheddar, A., et al. (eds.) Social Robotics. LNAI, vol. 10652, pp. 556–566. Springer, Cham (2017). https://doi.org/10.1007/978-3-319-70022-9_55

55. Zinina, A., Zaidelman, L., Arinkin, N., Kotov, A.: Nonverbal behavior of the robot companion: a contribution to the likeability. Procedia Comput. Sci. **169**, 800–806 (2020). https://doi.org/10.1016/j.procs.2020.02.160

Arm in Motion: How Motion Modality and Erratic Behavior of a Robotic Arm Shape User Perception

E. Liberman-Pincu$^{(\boxtimes)}$ ⓘ and T. Oron-Gilad ⓘ

Ben-Gurion University of the Negev, 84105 Beer-Sheva, Israel
elapin@post.bgu.ac.il

Abstract. This study examines the impact of motion design on user perceptions and interactions with robotic arms, which are expanding from industrial applications to supporting daily human tasks. The research investigates how different motion components influence user perceptions and preferences. Employing an online questionnaire, we analyze participants' responses to videos of robotic arms performing laundry sorting tasks, revealing significant relationships between motion modalities, erratic behavior, and characteristic attribution. The findings contribute to the design of robotic arm movements to effectively communicate and engage with users, enhancing human-robot interaction in both industrial and social contexts.

Keywords: Motion design · Robotic arm · Human-Robot interaction · Human-Robot relationship

1 Introduction

Robotics research is a dynamic and ever-evolving field, with robotic arms being a cornerstone since their introduction in the 1960s. Traditionally utilized in manufacturing, robotic arms are expanding into daily human tasks, yet in-depth studies on their interaction with humans outside industrial settings remain scarce. The drive to integrate robotic arms into both industrial and social spheres hinges on enhancing human-robot interaction, a key factor in the field's growth. Our previous studies explored the effect of visual qualities (e.g., color, structure) and design manipulations on users' perceptions, behaviors, and attitudes [1, 2] and suggested that visual qualities, along with non-verbal communication such as LED indicators, graphic user interface components, and motion design, shape the human-robot relationship [3].

In Human-Robot Interaction, robots exhibit two primary motion types: locomotion, the robot's movement from one location to another, and configuration, which involves movements of the robot's parts without changing its location [4].

Recent findings reveal that body language, which is mildly anthropomorphic or zoomorphic, allows users to have a more intuitive understanding [5]. This insight is pivotal as we aim to investigate how different motion components of a robotic arm—such as speed, acceleration, and erratic behavior, affect user perception.

© The Author(s), under exclusive license to Springer Nature Switzerland AG 2025
H. Plácido da Silva and P. Cipresso (Eds.): CHIRA 2024, CCIS 2370, pp. 53–62, 2025.
https://doi.org/10.1007/978-3-031-82633-7_4

Previous studies investigated the effect of different motion components on users' perceptions and behaviors and found significant relations between these variables. Saerbeck and Bartneck [6] examined the relationship between robot motion characteristics (acceleration and curvature) and perceived affect. Their results highlight a strong link between motion parameters and affect attribution; furthermore, they found that acceleration levels can predict perceived arousal. Participants in a study conducted by Kashi and Levy-Tzedek showed a preference for smooth movements when interacting with the robotic arm, finding it more flowing and human-like [7].

In a study conducted by Shi et al. [8], the effect of robot speed on task performance quality was explored within a human environment. The researchers emphasized the significance of human feelings of safety and comfort. Notably, they discovered a direct correlation between robot speed and the human's sense of security. Bortot et al. [9] explored how robot movement speed affects interactions with humans in an industrial factory environment. The robot in question featured a stationary articulated arm. Participants circled the robot at an average distance of half a meter. Interestingly, when the robot arm's movement speed increased, the participants also responded with increased speed.

Our research seeks to explore the intricacies of motion components within robotic arms and their influence on user perception. We achieve this by deconstructing robotic motion elements and subsequently creating new motion modalities. By exploring these motion modalities, we can uncover how they shape perceptions of reliability, professionalism, and innovation, thereby informing the design of robotic arms that can effectively communicate and engage with users through their movements.

2 Method and Study Design

2.1 Deconstruction of Motion Components

We systematically deconstructed the robotic motion into seven distinct parameters based on the literature review. Each parameter plays a crucial role in shaping the behavior of robotic systems. The following parameters were identified:

Speed: The rate of movement of the robot.
Acceleration: The change in speed over time.
Proximity: The distance between the robot and its surroundings.
Motion Mode: The specific type of motion (e.g., linear, rotational).
Direction Changes Amount: The frequency of changes in direction.
Direction Changes Pace: The rate at which direction changes occur.
Pre-calculation Time: The time taken for planning and decision-making before executing a motion.

For each parameter, we assigned distinct values, as illustrated in Fig. 1.

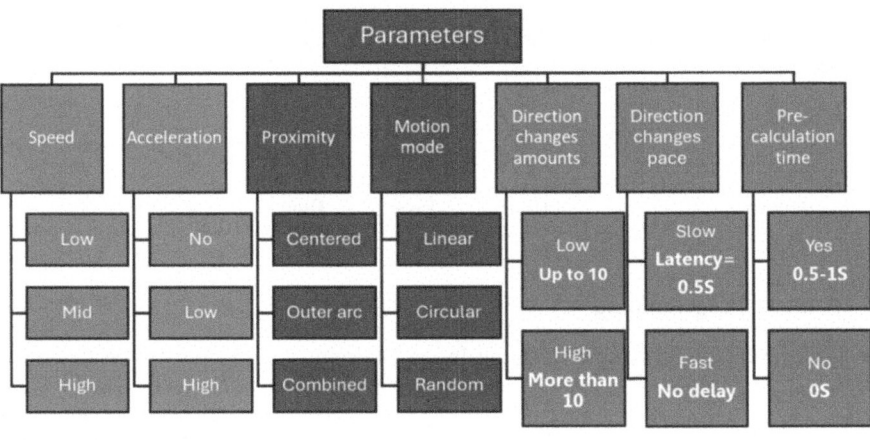

System data with non-numeric values
Data derived from the literature survey with non-numeric values
Numerically valuable data

Fig. 1. Deconstruction of motion component (actual values were set in accordance with the specific robotic arm capabilities; we used the Sawyer robotic arm from Rethink Robotics).

2.2 Defining Robot Behavior Profiles

We used the motion components to create two distinct groups of robotic motion: **Motion Modality** and **Erratic Behavior**.

Motion Modality encompasses:

- **Steady State (SS):** Defined by a low speed, absence of acceleration, central proximity, and linear motion.
- **Orbital Flow (OF):** Characterized by medium speed, minimal acceleration, peripheral proximity, and circular motion.
- **Dynamic Flux (DF):** Marked by high speed, significant acceleration, a mix of central and peripheral proximity, and unpredictable motion patterns, including both linear and circular movements.

Erratic Behavior is classified into:

- **Low Level:** Exhibiting infrequent direction changes, slow pace of direction changes, and a pre-action calculation period.
- **High Level:** Featuring frequent direction changes, rapid pace of direction changes, and an absence of pre-action calculation time.

We developed six distinct robotic profiles by integrating these parameters, each representing a unique combination of the aforementioned groups, as detailed in Table 1.

Table 1. Six distinct robotic arm motion profiles programmed for this study.

	Robot number					
	1	2	3	4	5	6
Motion Modality	SS	SS	OF	OF	DF	DF
Erratic Behavior	Low	High	Low	High	Low	High

2.3 Robotic Programming

We used the Sawyer robotic arm in the Intera environment, specifically designed for this robot. We systematically programmed the robot's six characteristics based on the predetermined parameters and levels. Each characteristic was captured in a video from various angles to create the final videos. The edited video length ranges from 30 s to one minute. Figure 2 presents a screenshot of the experimental setup, showcasing the robot and the laundry sorting environment.

Fig. 2. A screenshot of the experimental setup showcasing the Sawyer arm robot and the laundry sorting environment. Garment items were placed on a table for the robot to sort and place into the laundry bin.

2.4 Online Questionnaire

In this study, we employed an online questionnaire to investigate participants' perceptions of robots engaged in laundry sorting tasks. Initially, participants were asked to provide personal details, including demographic information, attitudes towards robots (measured by NARS [10]), and their prior experience with robots. Following, participants were presented with a series of six videos, each featuring a robot performing the sorting process. After viewing each video, participants were asked to select characteristics out of a list of descriptive terms according to their impressions of the robot's performance. These terms ranged from positive descriptors such as "friendly" and "professional" to potentially negative ones like "threatening".

Furthermore, participants were queried regarding their perception of the robot arm's motion, specifically evaluating its smoothness and pre-planned nature. For each category, they provided rankings on a scale of 1 to 7. Additionally, respondents were prompted to characterize the motion flow as either mechanical or organic.

3 Results

Fifty-two participants aged 18–61 (average = 30.65, SD = 9.7) took part in this online experiment: 27 males, 24 females, and one who chose not to specify their gender. The respondents' NARS scores followed a normal distribution (average 176.55, SD = 44.9). We found a positive correlation between age and NARS scores, indicating that negative emotions tend to rise as age increases. No significant differences were observed in NARS scores between males and females.

Thirty respondents (58%) own a domestic robot; compared to the respondents who don't own a robot, they tended to perceive the robots as *reliable* (28% compared to 23%, X^2 (1, $N = 312$) = 5.9, $p = .015$), *friendly* (17% compared to 11%, X^2 (1, $N = 312$) = 4.66, $p = .031$), *innovative* (38% compared to 29%, X^2 (1, $N = 312$) = 23.48, $p < .001$), and *intelligent* (29% compared to 14%, X^2 (1, $N = 312$) = 9.93, $p = .002$) regardless of the robot's motion profile.

We analyzed the data to evaluate the effect of motion modalities and erratic behavior on characteristics attribution and motion perception. Our findings are detailed below.

3.1 The Effect of Motion Modality and Erratic Behavior on Characteristics Attribution

Each characteristic's dependent variable is binary. A score of 0 was given when a character was not marked, and a score of 1 was given when it was marked. The binomial logit model was analyzed within the generalized estimation equations (GEE) framework, including the fixed effects for modality (SS, OF, and DF) and erraticness (low/high) and two random effects, which accounted for the individual differences among participants and the differences among the robots (1–6). We found significant relations (at $p < .05$) between the motion modality and the participants' perceptions of the robots as intelligent, professional, friendly, threatening, operational, and industrial. The erratic behavior level was found to affect the perception of the robot as reliable and friendly at $p < .1$. The significant relations are detailed in Table 2; the following paragraphs elaborate on these effects.

The **Steady State** profile was perceived as more *professional*; 53% of the participants selected to ascribe this character to the SS robots, compared to 25% and 44% ascribed to OF and DF, respectively. It was also perceived as *friendlier* (22% compared to 11% for both OF and DF), *less threatening* (only 4% compared to 16% (OF) and 24% (DF)),

Table 2. The Effect of Motion Modality and Errattic Behavior on Characteristics Attribution.

	Motion Modality		Erratic Behavior	
Intelligent	X^2 (2, $N = 312$) = 10.5, $p = .005$	SS >> DF > OF	Not significant	
Professional	X^2 (2, $N = 312$) = 16.8, $p < .001$	SS > DF >> OF	Not significant	
Reliable	Not significant		*X^2 (1, $N = 312$) = 3.7, $p = .055$	High > Low
Friendly	X^2 (2, $N = 312$) = 7.26, $p = .027$	SS > OF = DF	*X^2 (1, $N = 312$) = 3.1, $p = .076$	High > Low
Threatening	X^2 (2, $N = 312$) = 13.8, $p < .001$	DF > OF >> SS	Not significant	
Innovative	Not significant		Not significant	
Clumsy	Not significant		Not significant	
Operational	X^2 (2, $N = 312$) = 17.2, $p < .001$	OF > SS >> DF	Not significant	
Industrial	X^2 (2, $N = 312$) = 13.7, $p = .001$	OF >> SS > DF	Not significant	

> signifies $p < .1$, >> signifies $p < .01$

and more ***intelligent*** (34% compared to 15% and 19%). In addition, it was perceived as a little more ***reliable***; 32% of the participants selected this character to describe these robots, compared to 19% and 27% for OF and DF. However, these relations were not significant.

The **Orbital Flow** profile was seen as more ***operational*** (56% compared to 49% (SS) and 28% (DF)) and ***industrial*** (53% compared to 37% (SS) and 28% (DF)). However, it was also perceived significantly as ***less professional***; only 25% selected this character to describe OF robots, compared to 53% (SS) and 44% (DF), and ***less intelligent*** (15% compared to 34% and 19%). In addition, it was perceived as ***clumsier*** and ***less reliable.*** However, these relations were not significant.

The **Dynamic Flux** profile was considered significantly more ***threatening***; 24% ascribed this character to DF robots, compared to 16% and 4% for OF and SS, respectively. In addition, it was perceived significantly as ***less operational*** and ***industrial***. On the other hand, respondents showed a tendency to ascribe ***innovative*** to DF robots (40% compared to 31% for both SS and OF). However, these relations were not significant.

Low-level erratic behavior was associated with ***innovation***; 37% selected the word innovative to describe these robots, compared to 31% who selected the word to describe robots exhibiting high levels of erratic behavior. However, these relations were not significant.

Robots exhibiting **high-level erratic behavior** were perceived as ***friendlier*** (18% compared to 11%) and more ***reliable*** (31% compared to 21%). These associations were statistically significant at a significance level of $p < 0.1$. Additionally, these robots were perceived as slightly more *intelligent* (25% compared to 21%), although these differences were not statistically significant. Figure 3 illustrates the participants" selections of characteristics by motion modality (left) and erratic behavior level (right).

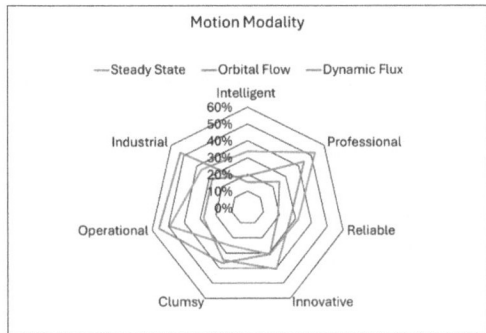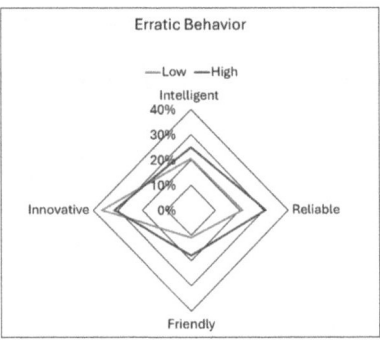

Fig. 3. The participants" selections of characteristics by motion modality (left) and erratic behavior level (right).

3.2   The Effect of Motion Modality and Erratic Behavior on Motion Perception

In this section, participants were asked about their perception of the motion in two categories: *smoothness* and *motion planning*. For each category, they were asked to rank their agreement on a scale of 1–7. Since the dependent variable is ordinal, the cumulative logit model was analyzed within the generalized estimation equations (GEE) framework, including the fixed effects for modality (SS, OF, and DF) and erratic-ness (low/high) and two random effects, which accounted for the individual differences among participants and the differences among the robots (1–6).

The motion modality significantly influenced the perception of smooth and continuous movement (X^2 (2, $N = 312$) = 7.08, $p = .028$). The respondents perceived the OF profile as less smooth compared to the SS and DF profiles; the average rank for OF was 4.1 out of 7, while SS and DF received ranks of 4.7 and 4.56, respectively. The level of erratic behavior did not significantly influence participants' perception of smoothness.

Motion planning perception (the robot plans ahead its path) was mainly affected by the motion modality (X^2 (2, $N = 312$) = 7.58, $p = .023$). However, the erratic behavior level was found to affect at $p < .1$ (X^2 (1, $N = 312$) = 3.63, $p = .067$). The respondents ranked the SS profile highest, with a score of 4.85 out of 7. In contrast, the DF profile was perceived as less planned, receiving a rank of 4.17. The OF profile fell in between, with a rank of 4.42. High erratic behavior was perceived as more planned, with an average rank of 4.6 out of 7, compared to 4.3 for low erratic behavior.

Furthermore, the respondents were asked to characterize the motion flow as either mechanical or organic. The impact of **motion modality** on the perception of *motion flow* was significant (X^2 (2, $N = 312$) = 25.78, $p < .001$). Specifically, the DF profile was perceived as organic (59%), while both the SS and OF profiles were associated with mechanical characteristics. The level of erratic behavior did not significantly influenceparticipants" perception of motion flow. Figure 4 illustrates the respondents' perception of motion flow by motion modality.

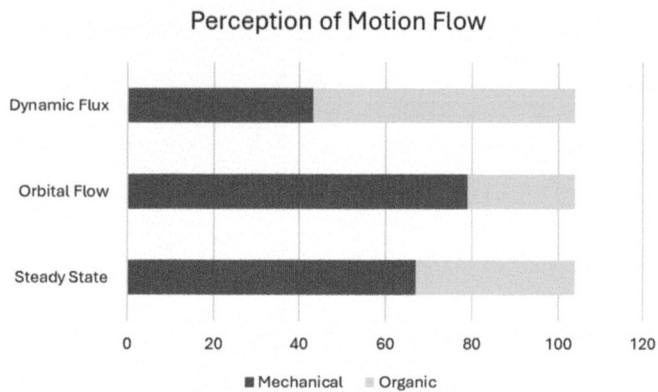

Fig. 4. The respondents' perception of motion flow by motion modality.

4 Discussion, Conclusions, and Future Work

This study investigated the impact of motion components on user perception of robotic arms in non-industrial settings. Our systematic deconstruction of motion into seven parameters—speed, acceleration, proximity, motion mode, direction change amount, direction change speed, and pre-calculation time—has allowed us to create distinct robotic behavior profiles that can be used to inform the design of SARs.

We have gained valuable insights into how speed, acceleration, proximity, and erratic behavior influence perceptions of robotic characteristics. Our findings suggest that motion modality significantly affects the attribution of characteristics such as intelligence and friendliness, while erratic behavior levels impact the perception of reliability. In addition, we found these different modalities affect the users' perception of the motion flow and nature.

The steady-state profile garnered positive perceptions from participants. It was regarded as professional, friendly, and intelligent. This motion mode likely conveyed a sense of stability and precision, instilling confidence in the robot's capabilities. Its motion was perceived as smooth and planned ahead and was considered more mechanical.

The Orbital Flow profile was seen as mechanical and less smooth; the respondents perceived it as more operational and industrial, but it also carried a sense of clumsiness. Users associated this motion modality with practical functionality, perhaps due to its operational connotations. However, the perceived clumsiness might indicate that it lacked finesse.

The Dynamic Flux profile was perceived as more innovative, but it was also deemed more threatening. The respondents describe its flow as more organic and less planned ahead. Participants recognized its uniqueness but expressed reservations about its suitability for operational and industrial contexts.

These findings highlight the importance of considering motion design when aiming to integrate robotic arms into social environments where user comfort and acceptance are crucial.

Moreover, the perception of **erratic behavior** as more reliable and friendly at higher levels is an intriguing result that warrants further investigation. It could imply that a certain degree of unpredictability in robot motion may contribute positively to human-robot interaction, perhaps by making the robot seem more lifelike or engaging.

The study also opens up new avenues for exploring how motion modalities can be optimized for different applications, ensuring that SARs are not only functional but also well-received by users. Future research could delve into the nuances of how these motion components interact with other design elements, such as visual and auditory cues, to create a holistic user experience.

Acknowledgment. This research was supported by the Ministry of Innovation, Science and Technology, Israel (grant 3-15625), and by Ben-Gurion University of the Negev through the Helmsley Charitable Trust, the Agricultural, Biological and Cognitive Robotics Initiative, the W. Gunther Plaut Chair in Manufacturing Engineering and by the George Shrut Chair in Human Performance Management. We wish to acknowledge the contribution of our undergraduate students, Roi Zimerman and Ahal Widman, to the generation of robotic movement profiles.

Disclosure of Interests. The authors have no competing interests to declare that are relevant to the content of this article.

Appendix

Robot number	Video
Robot 1	https://youtu.be/3W8G8xxy9Ks
Robot 2	https://youtu.be/g89xXzJMJPQ
Robot 3	https://youtu.be/gc6FH9PHkaQ
Robot 4	https://youtu.be/1ScWsB4Qzn8
Robot 5	https://youtu.be/unhYd4fBmEo
Robot 6	https://youtu.be/bouhR-gXZM4

References

1. Liberman-Pincu, E., Parmet, Y., Oron-Gilad, T.: Judging a socially assistive robot by its cover: the effect of body structure, outline, and color on users' perception. ACM Trans. Hum.-Robot. Interact. **12**, 1–26 (2023). https://doi.org/10.1145/3571717
2. Liberman-Pincu, E., David, A., Sarne-Fleischmann, V., et al.: Comply with me: using design manipulations to affect human-robot interaction in a COVID-19 officer robot use case. Multimodal Technol. Interact. **5**, 71 (2021). https://doi.org/10.3390/mti5110071

3. Liberman-Pincu, E., Van Grondelle, E.D., Oron-Gilad, T.: Designing robots with relationships in mind: suggesting two models of human-socially assistive robot (SAR) relationship. In: ACM/IEEE International Conference on Human-Robot Interaction (2021)
4. Schulz, T., Torresen, J., Herstad, J.: Animation techniques in human-robot interaction user studies. ACM Trans. Hum.-Robot. Interact. **8**, 1–22 (2019). https://doi.org/10.1145/3317325
5. Chatterjee, S., Parmet, Y., Oron-Gilad, T.: Body language for personal robot arm assistant. Int. J. Soc. Robot. **14**, 15–37 (2022). https://doi.org/10.1007/s12369-021-00748-y
6. Saerbeck, M., Bartneck, C.: Perception of affect elicited by robot motion. In: 5th ACM/IEEE International Conference on Human-Robot Interaction, HRI 2010, pp. 53–60 (2010)
7. Kashi, S., Levy-Tzedek, S.: Smooth leader or sharp follower? Playing the mirror game with a robot. Restor. Neurol. Neurosci. **36**, 147–159 (2018). https://doi.org/10.3233/RNN-170756
8. Shi, D., Collins, E.G., Donate, A., et al.: Human-aware robot motion planning with velocity constraints. In: 2008 International Symposium on Collaborative Technologies and Systems, CTS'08 (2008)
9. Bortot, D., Ding, H., Antonopolous, A., Bengler, K.: Human motion behavior while interacting with an industrial robot. Work **41**, 1699–1707 (2012)
10. Nomura, T., Suzuki, T., Kanda, T., Kato, K.: Measurement of negative attitudes toward robots (2006)

An Examination of Pre-school Children's Usage Behavior of Augmented Reality: Traditional vs. AR-Assisted LEGO® Building

Enes Yigitbas(✉) and Alessio Dell'Aquila

Paderborn University, Zukunftsmeile 2, 33102 Paderborn, Germany
{enes.yigitbas,alessio.dellaquila}@upb.de

Abstract. Many children are introduced to LEGO® bricks for the first time at a young age. LEGO® models are usually built according to a set of building instructions, each instruction step being printed onto paper as an orthographic projection. However, as children's spatial reasoning skills are yet to be fully developed, they tend to misinterpret positions and shapes from these types of instructions, resulting in suboptimal performance in LEGO® construction tasks. With Augmented Reality (AR), users can perceive and interact with three-dimensional, virtual content as if it was present in the real world, eliminating the need to convert two-dimensional instructions into three-dimensional models. In this work, an **AR-A**ssisted **LEGO® B**uilding **I**nstruction (ARALBI) application was developed, providing three-dimensional reference LEGO® models. ARALBI was specifically designed to be used by preschool children, with them constructing the real model step by step next to the virtual model. It was tested against typical paper-building instructions in a user study based on the General Assembly Task Model (GATM). Using AR instructions, preschool children performed better in terms of effectiveness (i.e. made fewer mistakes) but not efficiency (i.e. required more time to finish assembling the model) when compared to paper instructions. The results of this study indicated that preschool children, who never used AR technology before, enjoyed the use of the AR application and preferred it over paper-building instructions.

Keywords: AR · Children · LEGO® · Modeling · Assistance · Usability

1 Introduction

The LEGO® system, a globally renowned construction toy developed by the LEGO Group, has captivated the imaginations of children and adults alike for decades[1]. Founded on the fundamental principle of interlocking plastic bricks, the LEGO® system enables the creation of intricate models through a step-by-step assembly process using a set of instructions. Similar to other types of technical drawings, these instructions, often presented in orthographic projection, play a pivotal role in transforming two-dimensional depictions into a finalized, three-dimensional model.

---

[1] LEGO is a trademark of the LEGO Group of companies which does not sponsor, authorize or endorse this work.

© The Author(s), under exclusive license to Springer Nature Switzerland AG 2025
H. Plácido da Silva and P. Cipresso (Eds.): CHIRA 2024, CCIS 2370, pp. 63–81, 2025.
https://doi.org/10.1007/978-3-031-82633-7_5

The construction process of LEGO® models relies heavily on the comprehensibility of the accompanying instructions. Spatial reasoning skills, defined as the "ability to generate, retain, retrieve, and transform well-structured visual images" [10, p. 267], therefore play a critical role in the construction of such models.

During a short and informal pre-study, used to evaluate children's assembly skills, ten preschool children aged four to five were tasked with assembling a LEGO® model of a turtle, consisting of fifteen bricks and eight instruction steps. Using paper instructions featuring orthographic depictions of the instruction steps, the study revealed the following main issues: Firstly, similar-shaped bricks, such as the beak and tail of the turtle, were frequently interchanged despite slight color differences. Green 2 × 3 and 2 × 4 bricks also caused confusion, which was resolved after asking the children to count the connection points on top of the bricks. Furthermore, the children struggled with correctly positioning bricks. They specifically tended to misplace bricks that were partially obstructed by other parts of the model. Finally, bricks were not fully connected by the children, resulting in incomplete brick connections and thus unstable models.

Based on these observations we derived two main issues with traditional paper instructions from these results: First, the shape and color of LEGO® bricks are difficult to read from the paper instructions. Especially bricks that are similar in both shape and color are susceptible to being interchanged. Additionally, interpreting the correct position for attaching a brick is difficult. In particular, bricks that are (partially) obscured by other bricks in the instructions tend to be misplaced more often.

These issues go along with the results of a study that have shown that using orthographic (or isometric) images in assembly tasks requires a higher cognitive load than using a reference object. Participants who used orthographic images as a reference made more errors, had less correctly assembled models, and took longer to complete the task. Providing a reference model that children could compare their in-progress model against might therefore help in counteracting these issues. However, the researchers did not utilize any of the advanced technologies available to us nowadays but instead worked with physical reference models [13].

As technology becomes increasingly intertwined with play and education, the potential impact of augmented reality (AR) on children's block assembly skills becomes an interesting subject for exploration and analysis. Since children constitute the primary target audience for LEGO® products, this paper dives into the topic of supporting children in LEGO® construction tasks with the help of AR by providing them with a holographic reference model that is assembled step by step in conjunction with the real model. As a first step in determining whether preschool children benefit from AR-building instructions, we, therefore, wanted to answer the following research question (RQ): *Do preschool children complete LEGO® construction tasks more efficiently or effectively using AR instructions, as opposed to traditional paper instructions?*

To answer this research question, we first introduce an **AR-A**ssisted **LEGO®** **B**uilding **I**nstruction (ARALBI) application that displays a three-dimensional reference model to replace two-dimensional depictions of the model in paper instructions. This application was developed for Microsoft's HoloLens 2, an AR head-mounted display (HMD), and is able to load generic LEGO® models/instructions provided in LDraw™ file format. The AR application was evaluated in terms of efficiency (time required to assemble a model), effectiveness (amount of errors during the assembly process), and cognitive workload and compared directly against traditional paper instructions in a user study. We hypothesized that effectiveness would increase at the cost of efficiency. Additionally, we determined whether the children preferred ARALBI or paper instructions.

The rest of this paper is structured in the following way: In Sect. 2, we present and discuss previous research related to this paper. Section 3 describes the concept and implementation of ARALBI, which was developed to be compared against paper instructions. In Sect. 4, the planning and execution of the user study as well as its results are outlined and discussed. Lastly, the paper is concluded in Sect. 5.

2 Background and Related Work

In recent years Augmented Reality (AR) and Virtual Reality (VR) have been a topic of intense research. While VR interfaces support the interaction in an immersive computer-generated 3D world and have been used in different application domains of education (e.g., [24,25,31,32]), AR enables the augmentation of real-world physical objects with virtual elements and has been also applied in various application domains such as training [28], construction planning [29], robot programming (e.g., [7,27]), or for realizing smart interfaces (e.g., [6,26,30]).

In the following, we especially focus on and present related approaches that deal with the combination of child education, AR, and Lego as en enabler for children's spatial reasoning skills Several studies have highlighted the positive impact of engaging in construction activities with LEGO® bricks and similar toys on children's spatial reasoning skills. These skills play a crucial role in various aspects of everyday life and are often associated with fostering proficiency in STEM-related (science, technology, engineering, and mathematics) fields [20].

In the following, related work focusing on AR LEGO® assembly is presented.

2.1 AR LEGO® Assembly

One of the earliest approaches to evaluating the effectiveness of AR assembly tasks was conducted in 2003 by measuring efficiency (time) and effectiveness (number of errors). They examined two different approaches to displaying the instructions in AR: (1) Displaying orthographic instructions in the user's field of view, which was reported to interfere with workspace visibility. (2) Indicating brick positions using virtual arrows on the real model. The results of their study showed that AR has the potential for improving performance in assembly tasks but limitations of AR technology at that time rendered it inapplicable for practical uses [17].

To standardize the evaluation of the efficiency and effectiveness of interactive AR assembly tasks like building LEGO® models, Funk et al. proposed the General Assembly Task Model (GATM). The model splits each assembly step into four phases ($t_{locate\_part}, t_{pick}, t_{locate\_pos}, t_{assemble_x}$), the durations of which are measured independently. They further provided a benchmark based on the GATM, taking into account the number of errors made during assembly and the cognitive load [4].

Following their proposal of the GATM, they examined four different types of instructions. These included (1) regular paper instructions, (2) instructions displayed digitally on a tablet, (3) orthographic AR instructions for an HMD displayed in the user's field of view, and (4) in-situ instructions projecting light at brick positions using a top-mounted depth sensor and projector. Their study indicated that in-situ instructions performed the best whilst the AR instructions performed the worst with participants stating that the instructions blocked part of their sight [5].

Based on the previous study, a similar study was conducted with in-situ AR instructions displayed using both a smartphone and an AR HMD. For each step, a corresponding bin containing the required brick was highlighted with a crosshair icon. Participants of their study stated that the smartphone oftentimes interfered with the assembly process. Furthermore, the limited field of view of the HoloLens was presumed to be a reason for a high cognitive demand [2].

The application *HoloLego* was developed for the Microsoft HoloLens to visualize LEGO® models in AR. The application displayed the model on a baseplate using markers to increase accuracy. However, the application was restricted in terms of model interchangeability and construction direction. Additionally, the limiting field of view of the first generation of HoloLens was negatively annotated by the participants [18].

Another study compared three different assembly conditions for LEGO® models, two of which used an AR HMD whilst the third one used regular paper instructions. Results of this study have shown that rotating the model helped in identifying a brick's assembly position more efficiently [1].

Further research efforts have compared paper instructions to hand-held AR instructions. An animated 3D model was registered using a marker and displayed on a tablet. Participants of their study stated that being able to look at the model from different angles was helpful and that the animations helped in figuring out the correct position of a brick [23].

A recent application named *BRICKxAR* similarly allowed users of hand-held devices to assemble LEGO® models with the help of AR. This application projects the virtual instructions onto the real model while it is being built. At the same time, parts of the virtual model obstructed by the user's arm or hand were hidden to achieve a high level of realism. However, it was explicitly stated that the application has not been tested with AR glasses/HMDs [22].

2.2   Discussion

Interestingly, despite children being and staying the LEGO Group's main target group [9], none of the AR LEGO® instruction approaches discovered during the literature research included children in their studies. Generally, not many studies on how AR should be used with preschool children have been conducted before, but their results indicated that children seem interested in this technology.

The identified AR LEGO® instruction approaches did imply that adults benefit from AR instructions in terms of effectiveness. We therefore wanted to research whether children benefit from AR building instructions as well.

The results of this literature review imply that AR applications for preschool children are still a widely researchable topic and that the approach taken in this paper, including both ARALBI and its evaluation, is a novel contribution to this research field.

3 Methodology

To answer the introduced research question RQ, we first developed our custom AR building instructions application. The technical background of this application is presented in Sect. 3.1. Afterward, we conducted a user study aimed at assessing the usability of ARALBI and identifying the preferred instruction type among participants. The design and procedure of this study are shown in Sects. 3.2 and 3.3, respectively. Finally, the collected data and its analysis are explained in Sect. 3.4.

3.1 Concept and Implementation

The literature discovered on the topic of AR LEGO® instructions offered quite diverse implementations and gave insight into different aspects of how building instruction applications could be implemented. In general, three different approaches for displaying step-by-step LEGO® instructions were discovered:

1. Regular orthographic images are printed onto paper, displayed on a mobile or PC screen, or presented in a user's field of view using an HMD.
2. Virtual 3D models that function as a rotatable, scalable, translatable, and sometimes animated reference model which is rendered next to the physical model either on a mobile or PC screen or in a user's field of view using an HMD.
3. In-situ instructions align the instructions with the physical model either by projecting them onto the model using light or by registering the virtual model in AR and rendering (and sometimes animating) new bricks at the positions they should be placed.

Since approach one is covered by traditional paper instructions, we opted for approach two for our ARALBI application for the following reasons: First, this maintained comparability between our AR-based instructions and paper instructions, as this ensured that models would be built by reference using both AR and paper instructions. Second, it could be questioned whether reducing the amount of errors (and subsequently learning opportunities) for children is actually desirable. We would argue that by choosing approach two, children are still allowed to make mistakes and may recognize or correct them by comparing the physical model the reference model without any further indication that a brick was misplaced. This could not be guaranteed using in-situ instructions because the physical and reference model would misalign, resulting in an obvious indication of an error.

We developed our application for Microsoft's HoloLens 2. Compared to hand-held AR devices, it has the advantage that users can still use both of their hands to assemble the LEGO® Model.

Unity Engine (Unity) [19] was chosen as the basis for our application as it provides a full-featured 3D graphics and sound engine, which were the main features required for our application. For communication between Unity and HoloLens, Microsoft's Mixed Reality Toolkit (MRTK) [11] was utilized. ARALBI was implemented using version 2020.3.42f1 of the Unity engine, as version 2020.3 was Microsoft's recommended version for developing AR applications for HoloLens 2.

Figure 1 depicts an architectural overview of our application, its main components, and their interactions. Apart from the *User* and the *AR Device*, which were summarized as the *AR User*, all other components were implemented purely in software. These will be briefly described in the following sections.

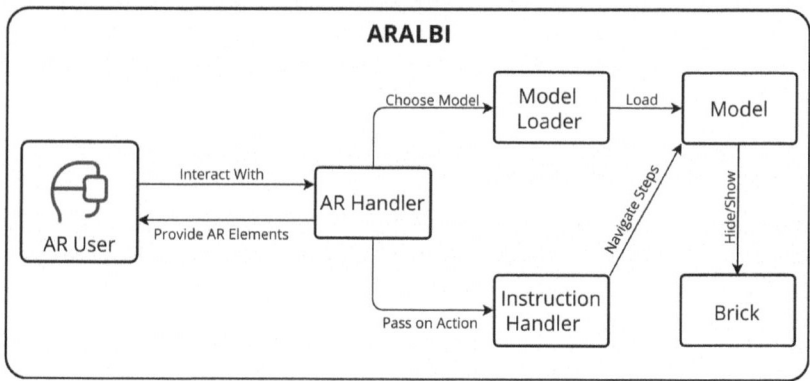

Fig. 1. Architectural overview.

AR Handler. The *AR Handler* manages interactions between the *AR User* and AR content, serving as a communication layer between the user and all other components. It is used to choose a *Model*, which is then supplied to the *Model Loader* and passes on any navigational actions to the *Instruction Handler*.

The AR interface provides simple buttons for navigating back and forth, with icons instead of text indicating their functionality, making them understandable to preschool children. An additional button is supplied to repeat a step's animations, functioning as a shortcut to going to the previous step and back to the current one. To not overload children with too much user interface, other user interface elements like labels showing the current step or the total number of steps have been avoided.

The application allows users to position and fixate the *Model* at a desired location. During the construction process, users can freely move around the *Model* to inspect it from various angles. We opted for this approach, as additional buttons, sliders or other input options for rotating the *Model* could make the children lose focus on the task. This also incorporates the benefits mentioned in previous studies [1,23].

Figure 2 shows the user interface of the application with the LEGO® *Bricks* required to construct the loaded *Model* being positioned on a table close by.

Model Loader. A setback in most AR building instruction applications discovered during our literature research was their lack of functionality to easily swap out the constructed LEGO® model. The *Model Loader* component is therefore responsible for

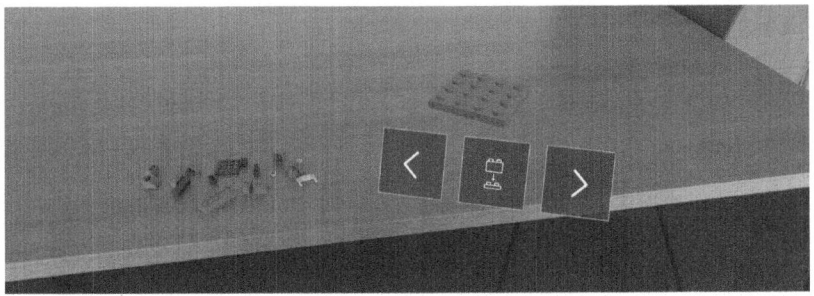

Fig. 2. The AR user interface of ARALBI.

parsing LDraw™ files, extracting essential information from the LDraw™ commands provided in those files, and constructing a LEGO® *Model* based on these commands within the application. It implements a file parser capable of interpreting LDraw™ files and extracting relevant data for model construction. LEGO® models are broken down into discrete instruction steps as specified via the commands. The construction of the 3D models adheres to the parsed information, which ensures an accurate representation of the model. The component maintains the order and structure of instruction steps for logical progression throughout the instructions (moving back and forth in the list of steps). We did not choose any existing implementation of such a file parser in order to maintain flexibility when construction the virtual model.

Instruction Handler. The *Instruction Handler* responds to user inputs, updating the active step of the LEGO® *Model* for navigating the instructions. The initial active step is always the first step of the entire *Model*. It further implements essential navigation functions such as moving to the next step, going back to the previous step, and jumping to a specific step. However, as it was unclear whether the step count of sub-models should count towards the step count of the whole *Model*, it is only possible to jump to the steps of the main *Model*. Sub-models within the main *Model* are managed by preserving a reference to the active sub-model during the construction process. As sub-models are basically standalone models themselves, they are assembled step-by-step just like the main *Model*. After a sub-model is completed it is attached as a whole to the main *Model*. To support users in identifying correct *Brick* positions, *Bricks'* appearances are animated after step transitions to highlight positions for new *Bricks*. As official LEGO® models support multiple *Bricks* per step as well, if a step includes more than one *Brick*, all *Bricks* are added to an animation queue and the animation is applied to each *Brick* one after another. We chose a simple fly-in animation because color highlights could hinder the correct identification of a *Brick's* color. This further adheres to the arrows used in official LEGO® instructions which indicate the correct attachment positions. Whenever an animation ends, i.e. a *Brick* is attached, a click sound is played to emulate the similar sounds of attaching real LEGO® *Bricks* to each other. Additionally, a success sound is played after the final *Brick* of the *Model* was attached to indicate that no further steps will follow. Figure 3 depicts a *Brick* while being animated and after being attached to the *Model*.

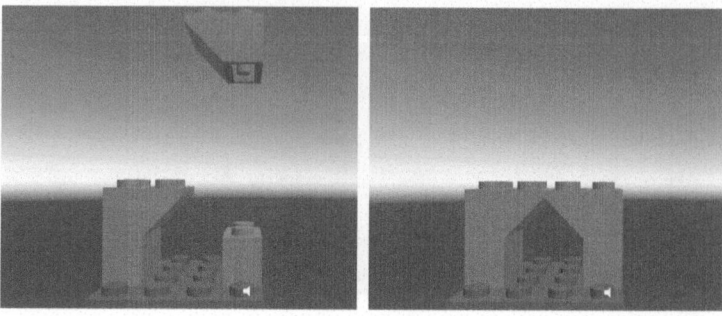

Fig. 3. A LEGO® brick during animation (left) and after being attached to the model (right) in the Unity Editor.

Model & Brick. The *Model* consists of one or multiple steps, which in return consist of one or multiple *Bricks*. Based on its active step, the *Model* hides all *Bricks* from the following steps. Although the LDraw™ file format specification allows for directly creating 3D model meshes, in order to reduce the required time for implementing our application, a different solution was chosen for adding 3D models of LEGO® *Bricks* to ARALBI. Blender is an open-source 3D modeling tool, supporting not only modeling but also rigging, animation, simulation, and more [3]. Similar to Unity, Blender's functionality can be extended using plugins. A plugin to import LDraw™ files into Blender and export them into Unity-compatible 3D model file formats like .fbx files [12] was used to export LDraw™ *Brick* models into Unity to be used by ARALBI.

3.2 Study Design

As we wanted to compare AR instructions against paper instructions, each participant had to complete one task for each instruction type. Each task used a different LEGO® model to prevent the participants from remembering how a model is constructed. For the paper instruction task, each instruction step was printed onto a separate page.

To counterbalance biases in the study's results, we opted for an alternating task order. Half of the participants started with the first task, and the remaining half started with the second task. Similarly, the order of instruction types alternated to ensure an equal distribution across tasks.

As the study involved preschool children, the research was conducted in a familiar environment, namely, the kindergarten they attend. To minimize interruptions and maintain a controlled setting, participants were placed in a separate room with a supervising kindergarten teacher always nearby. The room was equipped with child-sized furniture and devoid of potentially distracting elements like other toys. Figure 4 shows a participant of our user study during the completion of the assigned tasks using both the paper instructions and the AR instructions.

3.3 Study Procedure

We were granted permission by a local kindergarten to recruit children for our study. Upon informing the parents of the study procedure and the technology we utilized

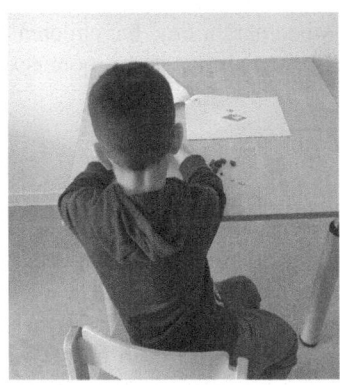 

Fig. 4. A participant assembling a LEGO® model using paper instructions (left) and AR instructions (right).

(specifically Microsoft HoloLens 2), ten children, aged four to six, were randomly selected as participants. Once the parents signed the consent form, the children were allowed to partake in the study.

The study took place over two days in February 2023, specifically on February 14 and February 15. On that day, the participating children were taken to a separate room in their kindergarten one after another. The researchers were waiting for them and greeted them upon arrival. Afterward, the children were briefed about the study procedure and were informed that they could interrupt or quit participation at any point in time. Additionally, the children were asked after each task, whether they wanted to continue.

All children had to complete the same tasks (i.e. assemble a model once using paper instructions and once using AR instructions), only the order in which they were given the tasks differed. Based on the predetermined task order, participants were either given access to review all pages of the paper instructions or had the AR HMD placed on them, allowing them to familiarize themselves with the HoloLens' functionality. Once they indicated that they would like to start, they were handed the LEGO® parts required to construct the model. Time measurements were taken as soon as the first brick was picked up. After finishing a task, the instruction type was swapped out and this process was repeated.

Upon completion of both tasks, participants were presented with the usability questionnaires. As the participants were neither able to read nor proficient in the English language, the questions were read to them in German. We began by asking the questions of our custom questionnaire, followed by the SUS questionnaire, and concluded with the NASA-TLX questionnaire. Although the last two questionnaires could be considered too complex for children to understand, we still included them in the study because, firstly, they are widely established and, secondly, versions adapted for children are available.

Once the final question was answered, the formal part of the study concluded, and the participating child was thanked for their involvement. Subsequently, the child exited the room, and the study proceeded with the next participant.

Since our study was conducted during a normal kindergarten day, the children's parents were not around. However, a kindergarten teacher was always in the room next door.

3.4 Data Collection and Analysis

To ensure meaningful study results, certain metrics were established based on the GATM and its follow-up research [5]. These metrics included efficiency, effectiveness, perceived workload (NASA-TLX questionnaire), general usability (SUS questionnaire), and custom questions on the preferred instruction type. Efficiency was measured by stopping the full assembly time and sub-measurements for each instruction step (t_{pick} and $t_{assemble}$), while effectiveness was evaluated by counting errors in brick placement, orientation, color, shape, and identifying missing or redundant bricks. Critical errors were those undetected after task completion.

The children's perceived workload was measured using an adapted NASA-TLX questionnaire, placing visual indicators (Emojis) at the extremes of each question. General usability was similarly measured using an adapted SUS questionnaire, also with visual indicators. Custom questions were used to measure the preferred instruction type and enjoyment as well as get general feedback on ARALBI. Additionally, emotional responses during task completion were observed. All data collected during our study was stored anonymized and securely, being only accessible to the researchers.

4 Evaluation

This section provides a presentation and discussion about the evaluation results, their implications as well as threats to validity.

4.1 Results

Demographics. In total, 10 preschool children participated in the user study. 8 of the participants were male with only 2 being female. All participants were between the ages of 4 and 6 ($Mdn = 5, M = 4.8, SD = 0.6$). Based on gender, the mean age for male preschool children was 4.875 ($SD = 0.6$), compared to a mean of 4.5 ($SD = 0.5$) for female preschool children.

As this study focused on evaluating different instruction types for LEGO® building tasks, the participants of the study were also asked about their prior experience with LEGO® bricks and instructions. All the participants stated that they had played with LEGO® bricks and built LEGO® models following step-by-step paper instructions before. When asked about the participants' experience with mixed reality technology, of all participants only 2 stated that they had previously used VR HMDs, both of which were male. The other participants did neither come in contact with VR nor AR technology before. Interestingly, those with VR experience immediately tried pressing the virtual buttons of the AR application, whereas all other participants were more hesitant to interact with AR content.

Efficiency. Efficiency was measured per task for each user by stopping the time they took to complete a task. Independent of the task order, all participants required more time to complete the task using AR instructions than using paper instructions. The mean task completion time for paper instructions was 03:51.08 min with a standard deviation of 00:48.72 min (in seconds: $M = 231.08$, $SD = 48.716$) whilst the mean task completion time for AR instructions was 05:33.19 min with a standard deviation of 01:37.52 min (in seconds: $M = 333.19$, $SD = 97.516$). The resulting task completion times are depicted in Fig. 5.

In general, between all participants, the completion time for paper instructions varied less than the completion time for AR instructions, as is identifiable in the box plot in Fig. 5. Paper instruction completion time span from around 03:00 min to around 04:00 min, with one exception taking almost 06:00 min, whilst AR instruction completion time span from around 04:00 min to almost 09:00 min.

On average, the t_{pick} phase (Paper: $M = 130.31$, $SD = 34.47$; AR: $M = 211.10$, $SD = 66.863$) took longer than the $t_{assemble}$ phase (Paper: $M = 100.77$, $SD = 22.73$; AR: $M = 122.09$, $SD = 35.295$), independent of the used instruction type. However, for paper instructions, t_{pick} took 1.3 times as long as $t_{assemble}$, whereas for AR instructions, t_{pick} took 1.7 times as long as $t_{assemble}$.

To perform a significance test, it had to be determined whether the data belonged to a normal distribution, as the t-test can only be used with normally distributed data. Otherwise, the Wilcoxon Signed-Rank test may be used.

To determine whether the data is normally distributed, the Shapiro-Wilk test was used. For $\alpha = .05$, this test reported a $p = .823$ for the paper instruction completion times and a $p = .749$ for the AR instruction completion times. Therefore, neither of the data sets could be considered normally distributed.

Subsequently, as the sample size is too small to be approximated via the normal distribution, the Wilcoxon Signed-Rank test reported a $W = 0 < 10 = W_{critical}$ for $\alpha = .05$, indicating that AR instructions had statistically significantly longer task completion times than paper instructions.

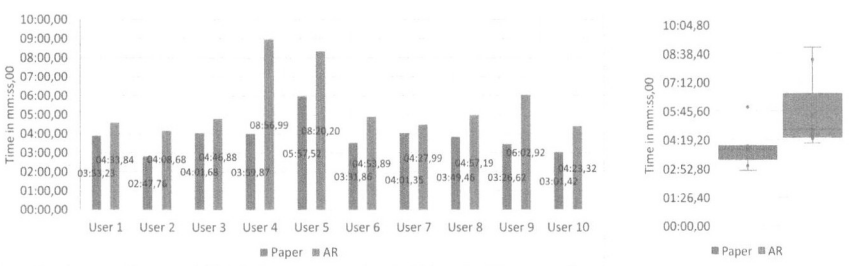

Fig. 5. The total time each user needed to complete the paper instruction and AR instruction tasks.

Effectiveness. In the user study, effectiveness was measured by counting the total amount of errors a participant made while completing a task. Besides the types of errors listed in Sect. 3.2, no additional types of errors were detected during the execution of the study (as dropping a LEGO® brick was not considered an error). Figure 6 depicts the total amount of errors per user during task execution. User 7 did not make any mistakes during their task.

The most commonly observed errors for both types of instructions were positional errors, followed by orientation errors for paper instructions and shape errors for AR instructions. All but one participant had a lower total amount of errors using AR instructions ($M = 1.3, SD = 1.418$) when compared to paper instructions ($M = 2.2, SD = 1.4$).

Similar to efficiency, the Shapiro-Wilk test resulted in a $p = .051$ for the paper instructions and $p = .101$ for the AR instructions, indicating that both data sets do not belong to a normal distribution.

Subsequently, as the sample size is once again too small to be approximated via the normal distribution, the Wilcoxon Signed-Rank test reported a $W = 3.5 < 10 = W_{critical}$ for $\alpha = .05$, which indicated that using AR instructions required statistically significantly fewer errors to assemble a LEGO® model than using paper instructions.

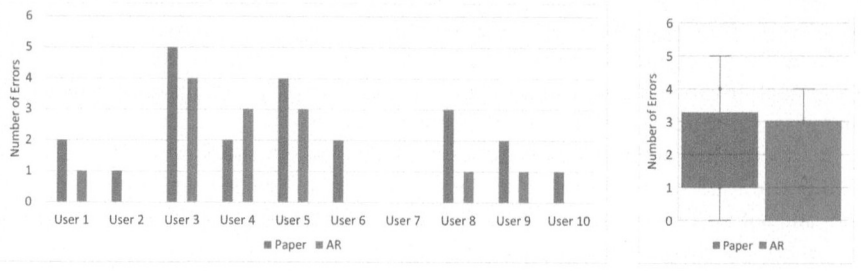

Fig. 6. The total amount of errors each user made while completing the paper instruction and AR instruction tasks.

Workload. The participants' perceived workload while using the AR instructions was measured based on an adapted version of the NASA-TLX questionnaire suitable for children [8]. All six subscales of the questionnaire were included in the participant survey, with each of them ranging from 0 to 20.

Instead of using the weighted TLX score, the raw TLX score was measured, as this kept the number of questions to a minimum and ensured that the children's attention span was not exceeded. In fact, it was argued that the weighted TLX score provides only little additional value compared to the raw TLX score [21]. The raw TLX score of each question was calculated by averaging the values provided by the participants and multiplying them by 5. The same applied to the raw TLX score per participant. The total raw TLX score was the average of these calculated values.

The raw TLX score per question, per participant, and the overall score are shown in Table 1. With an average raw TLX score of 23.67, the tasks completed using ARALBI would require a medium amount of mental workload [14].

Table 1. The results of the NASA-TLX questionnaire for AR instructions.

Question	P1	P2	P3	P4	P5	P6	P7	P8	P9	P10	Raw TLX Score by Question
					Response by Participant						
Mental Demand	9	20	20	0	20	10	0	0	20	20	59.5
Temporal Demand	0	0	0	10	0	0	0	3	0	0	6.5
Physical Demand	10	11	10	20	0	0	7	0	20	0	39
Performance	0	0	0	0	0	0	0	0	4	0	2
Effort	2	6	10	0	20	0	6	0	10	0	27
Frustration	0	0	0	0	6	0	0	0	10	0	8
Raw TLX Score by Participant	17.5	30.83	33.33	25	38.33	8.33	10.83	2.5	53.33	16.67	∅ Raw TLX Score: 23.67

Usability. Similar to the perceived workload, ARALBI's usability was measured based on an adapted version of the SUS questionnaire adjusted specifically for children [15]. Included in the participant survey were all ten questions that are typically asked in the SUS questionnaire, with each question ranging from 0 to 4. The SUS scores per question and participant were calculated similarly to how the NASA-TLX scores were calculated, but instead of multiplying by 5, the values were multiplied by 20.

In general, with an average SUS score of 76.75, the usability of our application could be rated as good with potentially improvable aspects.

The SUS score per question, per participant, and the overall score are shown in Table 2.

Table 2. The results of the SUS questionnaire for AR instructions.

Question	P1	P2	P3	P4	P5	P6	P7	P8	P9	P10	SUS Score by Question
					Response by Participant						
Would you like to play with the AR glasses a lot more?	4	3	0	3	3	4	4	3	0	4	70
Was it hard to play with the AR glasses?	2	1	4	1	1	3	3	3	2	4	60
Did you think the AR glasses were easy to use?	4	4	1	3	4	2	4	3	2	3	75
Would you need help to play with the AR glasses a lot more?	4	4	4	3	4	4	4	3	2	4	90
Did you know what to do next, when playing with the AR glasses?	3	2	4	1	4	4	3	4	4	3	80
Did some things with the AR glasses make no sense?	4	2	4	4	4	3	4	4	2	3	85
Would it be easy for your friends to learn how to play with the AR glasses?	0	4	2	4	4	3	2	3	3	1	65
Did you have to do weird things to play with the AR glasses?	4	2	4	1	4	3	2	2	2	3	67.5
Were you proud of how you played with the AR glasses?	4	4	4	4	4	4	4	4	3	4	97.5
Did you have to learn a lot to play with the AR glasses?	4	2	3	1	3	4	4	4	3	3	77.5
SUS Score by Participant	82.5	70	75	62.5	87.5	85	85	82.5	57.5	80	∅ SUS Score: 76.75

Custom Questions. The custom questions, the participants of the study were asked after completing their tasks, included general ratings of their experience with ARALBI.

The first question asked was about the participants' preferred instruction type. In general, 7 of 10 participants preferred the AR instructions, whereas 3 of 10 participants preferred the paper instructions. Interestingly, all female participants preferred the paper instructions. Of the male participants, only 1 of 8 preferred the paper instructions, with all others preferring the AR instructions.

Afterward, the participants were asked to give a general rating of the fun they had whilst using our AR application. The answer was given on a Likert-type scale with values ranging from 0 to 4. The average fun rating among all participants was 3.6 ($SD = 0.663$). Male participants rated the fun slightly higher ($M = 3.75, SD = 0.433$) with the worst rating being a 3, whilst female participants rated it slightly lower ($M = 3, SD = 1$), with the worst rating being a 2.

It was further asked what feature the participants liked the most. Of all participants, only 5 gave an answer to this question. 3 of those participants stated that being able to walk around the LEGO® model and look at it from different angles was the most liked feature. The other 2 liked that the LEGO® bricks were attached to the virtual model using an animation.

Lastly, the children were asked if they had any suggestions for improving the AR instruction application. This question was answered by just 2 participants. The first suggestion was removing the pointer that is displayed on the index finger when the HoloLens detects the user's hand. The second suggestion was using different LEGO® models, as that participant found the used models of animals strange.

4.2 Discussion

Efficiency. Participants required more time to complete their task with AR instructions than paper instructions, aligning with related studies [2,5,18].

Our observations revealed possible reasons for the longer assembly time:

1. Children moved around the 3D model to inspect from multiple angles where a brick needed to be attached.
2. The children frequently dropped LEGO® bricks due to their motor skills not yet being fully developed. The process of retrieving the bricks was more cautious while they were wearing the AR HMD.
3. Some children found the HoloLens' pointer irritating, which is displayed at the fingertips to keep track of the hand's position in AR space. This contributed to a slightly longer assembly time.
4. As HoloLens' hand-tracking feature is designed for adults, it occasionally failed for children, increasing the time for going to the next step. Pulling up their sleeves improved hand-tracking but did not fully resolve the issue.

Although the first reason outlines a positive aspect of ARALBI, especially the latter three reasons might indicate that our application or even AR technology as a whole is not yet suitable for children. Both software and hardware of AR devices need to be improved and adapted for children in order to reduce physical and mental strain, which in return could improve efficiency.

Effectiveness. Continuing, AR instructions significantly enhanced participants' LEGO® model assembly accuracy, aligning with prior research findings that highlighted reduced errors compared to paper instructions [2,17].

Participants, on average, made nearly twice as many errors with paper instructions than with AR instructions. The 3D reference model and animations played a pivotal role in accurately determining brick positions. Notably, no participant committed orientation errors with AR instructions; instead, they looked around the AR model to correctly identify brick orientations.

Regarding critical errors, i.e. errors that were not detected by a participant before completing the task, only one participant made such an error using paper instructions. Using AR instructions, errors were most often detected during the next step and quickly corrected.

Workload. The *Temporal Demand*, *Performance*, and *Frustration* categories received low workload ratings (ranging from 2 to 8). This aligns with our observations, as participants expressed no signs of rush or frustration during the AR instruction task. However, one participant was particularly frustrated with incorrectly functioning hand-tracking, contributing to a higher *Frustration* rating.

The remaining three questions, *Mental Demand*, *Physical Demand*, and *Effort*, received ratings between 27 and 59.5, indicating a medium to high workload. A higher rating in *Mental Demand* may be attributed to children's unfamiliarity with AR technology. Increased ratings for *Physical Demand* and *Effort* could be linked to the additional weight on the children's heads, similar to how the participants of other studies reported the weight of the HoloLens to be uncomfortable [18]. As already mentioned in Sect. 4.2, adapting AR devices for children could improve these ratings.

Due to the order in which the questionnaires were presented and the nature of the chosen visual indicators for the six subscales, the results of the NASA-TLX questionnaire might not fully reflect participants' perceived workload. Similar studies reported higher NASA-TLX scores, suggesting potential inaccuracies [2,5,17]. However, as their studies were targeted at adults, more research on the perceived mental workload of children in AR scenarios is needed to draw meaningful conclusions on the accuracy of our results.

Usability. The usability evaluation results indicate that children easily managed the interaction with the AR instruction application. They mentioned feeling confident and stated they wouldn't need additional help with ARALBI in the future. This was confirmed during an informal subsequent visit to the kindergarten when children from the study revisited the AR instructions without any problems. However, the application got a low rating for complexity, with participants indirectly suggesting it was unnecessarily complicated. Although they did not further specify, it's likely that children included the time given to familiarize themselves with AR technology in their rating. Participants also expressed concerns about others potentially struggling with the AR application. However, this perception might be influenced by the tendency of children to overestimate their own abilities while accurately estimating others' performance [16]. During our study, participants might have underestimated the performance of others, given that all participants performed well.

Custom Questions. Notably, none of the female participants favored AR instructions over paper instructions. However, due to the low number of female participants compared to male participants (and the low number of participants in general), no generalizable conclusion can be drawn about gender differences in the preferred instruction type.

In terms of enjoyment, almost all children had fun using AR instructions for building LEGO® models. One girl rated her enjoyment a 2, the lowest among all participants. This participant also gave the lowest ratings in both NASA-TLX and SUS questionnaires, which was likely influenced by technical difficulties (hand-tracking issues), leading to frustration during the study.

Regarding the suggestions provided by the participants, removing the index finger pointer could complicate spatial identification, but this could be addressed with realistic hand occlusion, as seen in other applications [22]. The second suggestion, offering a wider range of models, is worth considering in future studies. As our application allows for easily exchanging models, only ensuring similar difficulty levels needs to be considered.

4.3   Implications

Despite the (for our participants' age) large age gap of two years, we could not identify any meaningful differences between their results. The study's results and the children's feedback implied that not only is ARALBI still open to improvements, but AR technology as a whole can be improved upon with children in mind, for example by removing hand-tracking problems with children's hands (or small hands in general). Overall, we hypothesized that AR LEGO® instructions would improve children's effectiveness, but at the same time expected their efficiency to decrease. Both these hypotheses held true, indicating that the accuracy of constructing LEGO® models using a 3D reference model increases at the cost of needing more time to construct the model. This goes along with the results of the related research regarding AR instructions for adults.

4.4   Threats to Validity

As we did not have permission to film the children during the execution of their tasks, the measurements taken for efficiency might not be fully accurate. Efficiency was measured using a stopwatch, which may have resulted in the measurements for t_{pick} and $t_{assemble}$ differing by a few milliseconds from the actual time the participants required for each of those steps. Furthermore, the time measurements for both t_{pick} and $t_{assemble}$ might be inaccurate as children tended to pick all bricks of a step at a time. This could have been avoided by only using one brick per step but would have reduced realism, as original LEGO® models often require multiple bricks to be assembled per step as well.

Furthermore, usability evaluation with preschool children turned out to be more difficult than expected. Despite the questions of both SUS and NASA-TLX questionnaires having been adapted for evaluating usability with children, they sometimes seemed to not understand the questions they were asked. This was especially the case for the NASA-TLX questionnaire, as this was the last questionnaire asked and the children appeared to be exhausted. They also tended to choose the extremes of this questionnaire more often than values in between, as this was where the visual indicators were placed.

Finally, the low number of participants complicates the derivation of generalizable results.

5 Conclusion and Future Work

In this paper, we have investigated the potential of AR technology to improve children's spatial reasoning skills. In this context, we have analyzed whether preschool children would perform better in assembling LEGO® models using an AR reference model compared to orthographic paper instructions. For this purpose, we have developed an AR application for displaying 3D LEGO® instructions, specifically developed for preschool children as the main target group.

In a user study, this application was subsequently tested in terms of efficiency and effectiveness against traditional paper instructions for LEGO® models. The results of this study suggest that preschool children not only enjoy the use of AR technology, but AR building instructions also increased their effectiveness (i.e. reduced the number of errors during assembly) at the cost of worse efficiency (i.e. they needed more time to finish assembling the models). Furthermore, we discovered that the hand-tracking capabilities of HoloLens 2 are not yet fully compatible with the small hands of children.

In future work, we plan to evaluate our AR application with a wider range of participants comparing the instruction approach used in our study to different types of instruction approaches. Furthermore, our application could be extended with additional features, which would further help in determining brick positions.

References

1. Baldassi, S., Cheng, G.T., Chan, J., Tian, M., Christie, T., Short, M.T.: Exploring immersive AR instructions for procedural tasks: the role of depth, motion, and volumetric representations. In: ISMAR-Adjunct, pp. 300–305 (2016)
2. Blattgerste, J., Strenge, B., Renner, P., Pfeiffer, T., Essig, K.: Comparing conventional and augmented reality instructions for manual assembly tasks. In: Proceedings of the 10th International Conference on PErvasive Technologies Related to Assistive Environments, PETRA '17, pp. 75–82. ACM (2017)
3. Blender Foundation: Blender (2023). https://www.blender.org/. Accessed 7 Mar 2023
4. Funk, M., Kosch, T., Greenwald, S.W., Schmidt, A.: A benchmark for interactive augmented reality instructions for assembly tasks. In: Proceedings of the 14th International Conference on Mobile and Ubiquitous Multimedia, MUM '15, pp. 253–257. ACM (2015)
5. Funk, M., Kosch, T., Schmidt, A.: Interactive worker assistance: comparing the effects of in-situ projection, head-mounted displays, tablet, and paper instructions. In: Proceedings of the 2016 ACM International Joint Conference on Pervasive and Ubiquitous Computing, UbiComp '16, pp. 934–939. ACM (2016)

6. Krings, S., Yigitbas, E., Jovanovikj, I., Sauer, S., Engels, G.: Development framework for context-aware augmented reality applications. In: EICS '20, pp. 9:1–9:6. ACM (2020)
7. Krings, S.C., Yigitbas, E., Biermeier, K., Engels, G.: Design and evaluation of AR-assisted end-user robot path planning strategies. In: EICS '22, pp. 14–18. ACM (2022)
8. Laurie-Rose, C., Frey, M., Ennis, A., Zamary, A.: Measuring perceived mental workload in children. Am. J. Psychol. **127**(1), 107–125 (2014)
9. LEGO Group: Erfolgreiches Geschäftsjahr 2019 für die LEGO GmbH: Jedes zweite Kind in Deutschland hat im Jahr 2019 mindestens ein neues LEGO® Produkt bekommen. LEGO Newsroom (2020). https://www.legonewsroom.de/?p=8037. Accessed 19 Nov 2022
10. McGee, M.G.: Human spatial abilities: psychometric studies and environmental, genetic, hormonal, and neurological influences. Psychol. Bull. **86**(5), 889–918 (1979)
11. Microsoft: What is Mixed Reality Toolkit 2? (2022). https://learn.microsoft.com/en-us/windows/mixed-reality/mrtk-unity/mrtk2/?view=mrtkunity-2022-05. Accessed 7 Mar 2023
12. Morrison, M.: ExportLDraw (2023). https://github.com/cuddlyogre/ExportLdraw. Accessed 27 Jan 2023
13. Pillay, H.: Cognitive processes and strategies employed by children to learn spatial representations. Learn. Instr. **8**(1), 1–18 (1998)
14. Prabaswari, A., Basumerda, C., Utomo, B.: The mental workload analysis of staff in study program of private educational organization. IOP Conf. Ser. Mater. Sci. Eng. **528**, 012018 (2019). https://doi.org/10.1088/1757-899X/528/1/012018
15. Putnam, C., Puthenmadom, M., Cuerdo, M.A., Wang, W., Paul, N.: Adaptation of the system usability scale for user testing with children. In: Extended Abstracts of the 2020 CHI Conference on Human Factors in Computing Systems, pp. 1–7. Association for Computing Machinery, New York (2020)
16. Schneider, W.: Performance prediction in young children: effects of skill, metacognition and wishful thinking. Dev. Sci. **1**(2), 291–297 (1998)
17. Tang, A., Owen, C., Biocca, F., Mou, W.: Comparative effectiveness of augmented reality in object assembly. In: CHI, CHI '03, pp. 73–80. ACM (2003)
18. Thies, D.: Entwicklung eines augmentierten Montageszenarios mit Lego-Bausteinen für die Microsoft HoloLens (2017)
19. Unity Technologies: Unity Real-Time Development Platform (2023). https://unity.com/. Accessed 21 Jan 2023
20. Wai, J., Lubinski, D., Benbow, C.: Spatial ability for STEM domains: aligning over 50 years of cumulative psychological knowledge solidifies its importance. J. Educ. Psychol. (2009)
21. Wiebe, E.N., Roberts, E., Behrend, T.S.: An examination of two mental workload measurement approaches to understanding multimedia learning. Comput. Hum. Behav. **26**(3), 474–481 (2010). https://doi.org/10.1016/j.chb.2009.12.006
22. Yan, W.: Augmented reality instructions for construction toys enabled by accurate model registration and realistic object/hand occlusions. Virtual Reality **26**(2), 465–478 (2021)
23. Yang, Y., Karreman, J., de Jong, M.: Comparing the effects of paper and mobile augmented reality instructions to guide assembly tasks. In: IEEE International Professional Communication Conference (ProComm), pp. 96–104 (2020)
24. Yigitbas, E., Gorissen, S., Weidmann, N., Engels, G.: Collaborative software modeling in virtual reality. In: 24th International Conference on Model Driven Engineering Languages and Systems, pp. 261–272. IEEE (2021)
25. Yigitbas, E., Gorissen, S., Weidmann, N., Engels, G.: Design and evaluation of a collaborative UML modeling environment in virtual reality. Softw. Syst. Model. **22**(5), 1397–1425 (2023)
26. Yigitbas, E., Grün, S., Sauer, S., Engels, G.: Model-driven context management for self-adaptive user interfaces. In: UCAmI 2017. LNCS, vol. 10586, pp. 624–635. Springer (2017)

27. Yigitbas, E., Jovanovikj, I., Engels, G.: Simplifying robot programming using augmented reality and end-user development. In: Human-Computer Interaction - INTERACT. LNCS, vol. 12932, pp. 631–651. Springer (2021)
28. Yigitbas, E., Krois, S., Renzelmann, T., Engels, G.: Comparative evaluation of AR-based, VR-based, and traditional basic life support training. In: SeGAH 2022, pp. 1–8. IEEE (2022)
29. Yigitbas, E., Nowosad, A., Engels, G.: Supporting construction and architectural visualization through BIM and AR/VR: a systematic literature review. In: INTERACT 2023. LNCS, vol. 14143, pp. 145–166. Springer (2023)
30. Yigitbas, E., Sauer, S.: Engineering context-adaptive UIS for task-continuous cross-channel applications. In: HCSE 2016 and HESSD 2016. LNCS, vol. 9856, pp. 281–300. Springer (2016)
31. Yigitbas, E., Schmidt, M., Bucchiarone, A., Gottschalk, S., Engels, G.: Gamification-based UML learning environment in virtual reality. In: MODELS 2022, pp. 27–31. ACM (2022)
32. Yigitbas, E., Tejedor, C.B., Engels, G.: Experiencing and programming the ENIAC in VR. In: Mensch und Computer 2020, pp. 505–506. ACM (2020)

Interviewing ChatGPT-Generated Personas to Inform Design Decisions

Jemily Rime(✉)

StoryLab, Anglia Ruskin University, Cambridge, UK
`jemily.rime@aru.ac.uk`

Abstract. This paper uses the example of the development of a new podcast production tool to pinpoint some of the successes and limitations of relying on Large Language Models (LLMs) to assist software developers in User-centred design (UCD) methods. We ask ChatGPT to create 16 personas of podcast creators and answer in character to a set of questions that was asked to 16 human creators to gather design feedback, in order to make a new podcasting tool. From this comparison, we discover that the personas generated are credible, but expose some data-privacy issues, and confirm the skewed, incomplete, nature of ChatGPT's training dataset. We find a correlation between a generated persona and its answers, and that its role-playing could be valuable but lacks the more extreme, or clear-cut opinions, often most helpful when gathering user opinions for development. From the lessons learned through this comparative exercise, we share recommendations regarding the possible uses of LLMs in UCD.

Keywords: User-centred design · Participatory design · AI tools for design

1 Introduction

The benefits of user involvement for software development have been outlined by many researchers. Kujala [18] shows that user involvement has positive effects on system success and user satisfaction, and Kuhn [17] says collecting target users' design requirements can guarantee a user-informed design process, and therefore contribute to the end product. This has solidified the practice of User-centred design (UCD) in the past decades [1], through techniques like Agile Software Development (ASD), Participatory Design (PD) or Iterative Software Development (ISD). Involving users in software design can take various forms: Lane et al. [21] distinguishes three main ways to agglomerate people's perspectives in this context: *surveys*, *prototyping*, and *open-ended interviews*. Regardless of the way feedback is gathered, there is an emphasis on establishing and maintaining an open dialogue between the designer and user.

Since the public release of OpenAI's ChatGPT,[1] there have been a series of news articles and opinion pieces about being ushered into an age where human effort is swiftly replaced by the computational power of artificial intelligence[2,3]. Language

---

[1] https://chat.openai.com/chat.

[2] https://www.theguardian.com/commentisfree/2023/mar/04/misplaced-fears-of-an-evil-chatgpt-obscure-the-real-harm-being-done.

[3] https://www.nytimes.com/2023/03/08/opinion/noam-chomsky-chatgpt-ai.html.

© The Author(s), under exclusive license to Springer Nature Switzerland AG 2025
H. Plácido da Silva and P. Cipresso (Eds.): CHIRA 2024, CCIS 2370, pp. 82–97, 2025.
https://doi.org/10.1007/978-3-031-82633-7_6

models like ChatGPT are being integrated within our traditional workflows and have displayed the ability to perform tasks on our behalf, whether that is writing an unpleasant email, summarising an article, or producing documentation for a class in code. At the forefront of important, contemporary, and borderline philosophical discussions, are the nature of AI understanding [25], and the potential issues brought on by relying on models that use logical "shortcuts" [23].

The ability to converse with a Large Language Model (LLM) that has been trained on substantial dataset, like ChatGPT, opens doors for research practices, particularly, the possibility to emulate human behaviours and reactions. In the case of software development, the conversational nature of a PD process means users could be emulated by a model, offering fictional opinions on real-world problems. But although this approach might solve some of the inherent issues with RG [6], do these benefits outweigh the risks and costs [3] of using AI for such tasks?

This study focuses on the application of such methods to a specific use case, the development of a podcasting tool, to draw some hypotheses on how generative AI could be used to assist designers and developers. After a brief overview of relevant literature and of the method used in this comparative work, we discuss the results and form recommendations regarding the use of LLMs like ChatGPT for UCD.

2   Related Work

2.1   User-Centred Design

UCD is "a broad term to describe design processes in which end-users influence how a design takes shape" [1]. Software developers are routinely taught to consider the end-user when designing projects [9]. Multiple methods aim to connect designer and user, and hybrid solutions that mix and match approaches are becoming more common. For example, Ferrario [11] describes a framework that melds together elements of ASD, PD and ISD, where ASD is itself a manifesto that comprises different methods that have in common the "unforgiving honesty of working code and the effectiveness of people working together with goodwill" [13], and ISD fundamentally includes conversation and feedback [3].

Kautz [14, p.216, L.26] lists the benefits of using PD as follows:

> "(1) Improving the knowledge on which information systems are built. (2) Enabling people to develop realistic expectations, and reducing resistance to change. (3) Increasing workplace democracy by giving the members of an organization the right to participate in decisions that are likely to affect their work"

PD is not often criticised; its implementation almost falls under common sense. However, it can sometimes be complicated to implement, because of time or monetary constraints, as it is a complex process involving large groups of stakeholders. Similarly, ASD requires planning and complex organisation strategies to avoid delays [19]. The next section outlines some of the limited criticism RG receives.

2.2   Requirements Gathering

Gathering the opinions of stakeholders is a key aspect of all the design techniques that fall under UCD [24]. Design requirements are necessary to inform the various methods that utilise PD. Through requirements gathering (RG), a designer can *"capture infor-mation through the use of multidisciplinary views. Such views express what is to be built.'* [6, p. 34, 1.19]. This design roadmap can be created using *ethnographic anec-dotes, expert verification, usability testing* or *semi-structured interviews* [32]. The com-mon denominator of these procedures is communication [21].

Requirements can be drawn from these procedures. ISO/IEC/IEEE 29148 [12] defines the characteristics of individual requirements: *necessary, implementation free, unambiguous, consistent, complete, singular, feasible, traceable,* and *verifiable.*

Because RG does not come with strong methodological constraints, Kuhn [17] argues that one of its main drawbacks is that there can be no scientific analysis of the data gathered, and hence no scientific grounding for design decisions made from these requirements. This can be mitigated by applying qualitative analysis methods like thematic analysis [7] to transcripts of conversations or tests, offering a justification for otherwise informal impressions. This analysis can sometimes be aided by automated, procedural, or AI-driven tools [24].

2.3   User Personas

Personas are fictitious, specific, concrete representations of target users [28, p.11]. Per-sonas are often based on data collected through ethnographic study and observation, (see "Cooperian Personas" [9]), and help designers visualise their archetypal users and their needs. Personas are mostly utilised in role-playing, but they can have other pur-poses, like focusing on issues, meeting maintenance, empathy, clarification or approxi-mation [10]. In role-playing, designers will often "put-on" these characters, pretending to interact with a prototype or give feedback on an idea. This reinforces the storytelling aspect of persona use, as described by Pruitt and Grudin [28]. Personas are not just typ-ical users, they are also characters, Pruitt and Grudin [28] even use the term "method acting".

The effectiveness of personas is determined by the quality of the personas created. Jones et al. [13] lists four textbook examples of bad personas: *Promotional personas* (created to promote the designer's assumption), *Elastic personas* (could be anybody), *Twin personas* (superficially different but very similar with respect to particular dimen-sions of the design), *"My Mother" personas* (based on a known individual). We can use these examples of bad personas to evaluate the quality of personas created or generated.

2.4   Conversational LLMs: A Short Introduction to ChatGPT

LLMs are self-supervised deep neural networks trained on very broad datasets [2], and although they are not necessarily linked to generative pre-trained transformer models (GPTs), they are often associated with them, in part because of the very public and popular OpenAI model, ChatGPT. More recent publicly available models, like Google Gemini, were not yet available at the time this study was conducted. The version of

ChatGPT used in this article is based on GPT-3.5, which shows prowess in both natural language understanding (NLU), and text generation. Until the release of GPT-4, GPT-3.5 achieved state-of-the-art results in some NLU tasks [4]. Its outputs are tightly linked to the prompts it is given. Bavarian, et al. [4] found changes in input prompts have a significant impact on results using GPT-3.5.

Because of this source of variability, researchers have begun looking into prompt engineering, a field that focuses on determining the best prompts to carry out a specific task [5]. Bommarito et al. [5] lists advice for picking prompts for generating images from texts, including the importance of keywords in comparison to connecting words, and iteratively constructing prompts by looking at what a model could generate from specified seeds. Looking at the effect of prompt engineering on problem-solving, modifying prompts leads to generating successful solutions more reliably.

Researchers like Moritz [25] or Korzynski et al. [16] describe the process of metaprompts, where a model is asked to engineer more efficient prompts based on initial prompts given by the user.

Although the use of LLMs isn't a common practice within the field of design, it is being explored as a tool to help teach and create [11]. In software engineering, some ultra-specific chatbots were developed to answer developers' coding queries [27].

3 Case Study: The Development of a New Podcast Production Tool via Participatory Design

3.1 Procedure

We take the opportunity of developing a new editing software for podcasting to compare the output of semi-structured interviews conducted with real target users, and ChatGPT-generated personas. We use ChatGPT's ability to remember conversations in order to carry out "realistic" interviews with personas it generated. By asking ChatGPT to answer questions in the shoes of the personas it generated, we hope to collect a range of feedback and requirements that could in turn inform design decisions.

The software being developed is designed in collaboration with a group of podcast creators, and focuses on making podcasts more immersive and personalised. For this purpose, 16 podcast creators were interviewed. They were recruited through internal BBC channels and via a public advertisement on a specialist podcasting news website, and took part in semi-structured interviews to talk about their current practices and expectations for the future of podcasting. We used these conversations as a way to begin gathering requirements for such software to be developed. The results of these conversations can be found in previously published work [30,31], and although the contents of the interviews are essential to this case study, the design goal of a podcast production tool should be seen as a placeholder for other software.

In order to evaluate the quality of the personas generated by ChatGPT as well as the credibility of its answers to questions when "in character", we ask ChatGPT to create 16 personas of podcast creators (from then on, referred to as AI-Ps), then to role-play as these personas, and answer a subsection of questions that were asked to the human participants (from then on, referred to as HPs). We choose to only generate and analyse 16 personas to establish a one-to-one comparison with the human dataset, and to highlight the differences between the two approaches when collecting an equivalent amount of data.

Previous literature looked at ways to use ChatGPT as a virtual assistant to designers, but only evaluated "appropriateness" of the answers with respect to expected behaviour [15]. In contrast, this study compares ChatGPT's output to real human answers. By doing so, we can evaluate the pertinence of the personas created and gauge the validity of basing design decisions on AI-generated feedback. Rather than building another argument supporting the obsolescence of human effort, we hypothesise that the wide range of responses given by humans cannot be equally matched by virtual personas, but that there could be value in carrying out informative fictitious interviews using a conversational LLM to consolidate decisions and inform future conversations with users.

The nature of this specific comparison should enable us to build hypotheses surrounding the use of AI tools such as ChatGPT to facilitate UCD, and be used as a possible justification for larger-scale research to be undertaken. The evolving risks, costs, and potential ethical issues arising from using such models should be updated and factored in further reflection.

3.2   Interview Questions and Prompt Engineering

In order to build the questions that comprised the interviews, we used a focus group consisting of a senior podcast producer, software engineer, and academic researcher. There was a list of six questions as well as a task that required participants to react to a series of videos demonstrating new technologies [30,31]. We focus this study on three specific questions, which give an overview of the expectations of participants in semi-structured interviews:

1. What tools are necessary for your work?
2. What attributes make for good podcasting tools?
3. What is your opinion on using AI voice synthesis for podcast production?

In Question 1., participants were expected to expand on the software and hardware they regularly used; in Question 2., participants could express the features that influenced them to use particular tools. Question 3. was part of the task presented to participants. A 45-second video introducing the concept and potential uses of AI voice synthesis was shown, and participants' reactions were recorded.

To improve the quality of the answers provided by ChatGPT, we adapt these questions by trial and error. Asking *"What tools are necessary for your work?"*, we find that ChatGPT is a bit too broad in its answers, talking about microphones, headphones, a nameless digital audio recorder, a digital audio workstation, a computer, social media, and an internet connection. Although these are all indeed necessary for the production of a podcast, narrowing down the field covered by this prompt enables us to more closely compare answers. The focus is brought on audio editing software especially, as we had a complete dataset from our HPs talking about their preferred audio editing software.

Table 1. Prompts given to ChatGPT.

Prompt 1	Could you make up the persona of a fictional podcast creator, listing the following information: name, age, gender, years of experience, job title, genre of podcast created, programming skills?
Prompt 2	Answer the following question as this podcast creator: What audio editing software do you use?
Prompt 3	Answer the following question as this podcast creator: What attributes make a good podcasting tool?
Prompt 4	Answer the following question as this podcast creator: What is your opinion on using AI voice synthesis for podcast production?

Question 2. and 3. produce expected results, but in order to prevent any confusion on ChatGPT's part, we preface all three questions by the segment: *"Answer the following question as this podcast creator"*, which makes sure it continues role-playing as the persona it generated. The prompts used can be seen in Table 1, and an archive of the ChatGPT responses is publicly available.[4]

To generate the personas, we ask: *"Could you make up the persona of a fictional podcast creator, listing the following information: name, age, gender, years of experience, job title, genre of podcast created, programming skills ?"*. Prior iterations of this prompt include *"Could you give me the profile of a random fictional podcast host?"*, which led to inconsistent format in answer, and lacked the specific intentions behind the word "persona". Using the word "persona" instead of profile did give out consistent formatting, but the information relayed by the user-persona-sheet generated did not always cover all the information we could compare to our HPs' data.

3.3 Data Analysis

A thematic analysis was carried out on the transcripts of the interviews with podcast creators, using [7]'s approach to thematic analysis. Questions were analysed separately, but the transcripts were also fully analysed to minimise bias and make sure no overarching themes were missed by this parsimonious approach to thematic analysis. A similar method is applied to ChatGPT's output, looking at codes and groupings of codes as sub-themes, and themes, subsequently going back to the data to ensure the accuracy of the themes chosen. Detailed examples for the thematic analysis carried out on both HPs' and AI-Ps' answers can be found in anonymised research artefacts[5]. We use these analyses to yield quantitative results and draw comparisons between the two groups [26].

---

[4] Transcripts can be accessed: https://bit.ly/3Y9TMjM.
[5] https://bit.ly/3Y9TMjM.

> **Name:** Maya Singh **Age:** 28 **Gender:** Female **Years of experience:** 3 **Job title:** Producer and Host **Genre of podcast created:** True Crime **Programming skills:** Advanced
>
> Maya Singh is a rising star in the world of podcasting, known for her gripping and immersive true crime podcasts. With a background in journalism and a keen eye for storytelling, Maya has quickly made a name for herself in the industry, earning critical acclaim and a growing audience of devoted listeners.
>
> As both a producer and host, Maya has a deep understanding of the entire podcast production process, from researching and writing compelling scripts, to recording and editing high-quality audio. Her advanced programming skills allow her to manipulate sound and music to create a truly immersive experience for her listeners.
>
> Maya's true crime podcasts are known for their attention to detail and their ability to transport listeners directly into the heart of the story. She is skilled at balancing the need for accurate reporting with the desire to create a compelling narrative that keeps listeners engaged and coming back for more.
>
> With three years of experience in the podcasting world, Maya is just getting started and has big plans for the future of her true crime empire.

Fig. 1. Profile sheet of a persona generated by ChatGPT from Prompt 1 *"Could you make up the persona of a fictional podcast creator, listing the following information: name, age, gender, years of experience, job title, genre of podcast created, programming skills?"*

4   Evaluating the Quality of the AI-Generated Personas

4.1   AI Generated Personas vs. Human Participants

An example AI-P can be seen in Fig. 1. The "average" (or mode, for nominal data) profile of the AI-Ps and HPs are different from one another. The average AI-P is a 25–34-year-old female producer of a true crime podcast, with a basic understanding of programming, while the average HP is a 35–50-year-old male producer who creates lifestyle podcasts and has no experience with programming.

When looking at gender, the AI-Ps are a much more diverse group (mostly female, and with a non-negligible -19%- non-binary representation), but in terms of age, we lose the extremities of the distribution of the HPs. AI-Ps only fit into two definite age groups (25–34 and 35–50), as opposed to four for the HPs (18–24, 25–34, 35–50 and 50–65). This "narrowing" trend will be relevant to other aspects of this case study. For instance, AI-Ps only answered having three different jobs (multiple roles can be combined per respondent), "producer" (94%), "host" (31%), and "executive producer" (19%), as opposed to HPs, who reported eight different professions: "producer" (75%), "jack of all trades" (31%), "host" (25%), "sound engineer" (25%), "advisor" (19%), "executive producer" (19%), "developing innovative podcasts" (19%), and "researcher" (13%).

This might be due to the ChatGPT's understanding of what a "creator" is (e.g., it might not include audio editors/sound engineers under the banner of "creators"), or constitute further evidence of a narrower distribution across answers. The AI-Ps were more likely to be producers than hosts, and hosts more likely than executive producers.

A similar statement can be made of the HPs. We will explore whether these trends are representative of the podcasting industry in Sect. 4.2.

There was a disproportionate representation of true crime creators in the AI-Ps (69%), when compared to HPs (13%). If we put aside the humorous theory that Chat-GPT might simply have a particular passion for gore, it could be the result of the nature of the dataset ChatGPT is based upon: true crime has very active fanbases online [33,35], and therefore might be overly represented in the dataset.

Conversely, this discrepancy, as well as the ones mentioned beforehand, could be due not to the skewed nature of the dataset on which ChatGPT was trained, but rather due to the accuracy of representation in the participant group. The greatly unbalanced gender ratio in the HPs' group could support this hypothesis.

4.2   AI Generated Personas vs. the Realities of the Podcasting Industry

A study looking at 617 active podcast creators in the US found that only 29% of pod-casters identified as female, and 2% as Non-Binary or Other [8]. This distribution is closer to the one observed in the HPs' group than the AI-Ps'. There is no data available regarding the coding proficiency of podcast creators, but a survey of a thousand US students aged 16–23 showed that 45% of students could code or were learning how to [20]. This particular demographic does not translate well to the podcasting industry, but it is a valid benchmark to nuance the data presented here. Fourty-four percent of HPs reported being able to program, while 81% of AI-Ps were proficient in at least one coding language – the former proportion (of HPs being able to code) seems a bit more realistic.

AI-Ps were most likely to be involved with true crime programs. According to Edison research, in Q4-2021 to Q2-2022, the top genres of podcasts in the US were Comedy, Society and Culture, News, True Crime (following Apple's API categories, which do not include Spotify's "Lifestyle & Health") [29]. This confirms the presence of a bias linked to ChatGPT's training dataset, as mentioned by Lund et al. [22].

4.3   AI Generated Personas vs. "bad Personas"

We introduced the "bad personas" of Jones et al. [13]. We compare ChatGPT's output to these four archetypes to evaluate their "badness".

Promotional Personas are created to reinforce the designer's preconceptions of what the design should be. In the case of ChatGPT, it is interesting to distinguish in what ways our prompts communicate what our end goal, and consequently end-user, are expected to be. Although ChatGPT isn't explicitly told our goal is to create an audio production tool that uses AI and other new technologies to facilitate production, requiring the AI-Ps' coding skills to be disclosed could have hinted at this and skewed the output towards a more technologically savvy group of fictional users. This speaks to the great influence of prompt engineering on such tasks, where disclosing information like the desired output format can greatly influence the content.

Elastic Personas are sufficiently non-descript that they could be stretched to any person. ChatGPT created credible personas that have tangible opinions on the questions they are asked. This might be in part thanks to the wealth of information about podcasting available online - would it be the same for a field not as well documented on the internet?

Twin Personas are possibly most at risk of occurring when relying on a machine. Indeed, although our prompt specified that "random personas" should be created, there is no such thing as true randomness in computer science. We see evidence of this skewed "randomness" in the disproportionate representation of true crime in the genres of podcasts on which personas worked. The need for randomness is restricted to the persona generation task; the answers given by each persona should be influenced by their personality and background rather than a result of randomness in order to fulfil the goal of communicating user-specific requirements. From the answers given by the AI-Ps to Prompt 2 (*What audio editing software do you use?*), we conclude that there is a correlation between the persona generated and their answer: the least experienced personas used Audacity, and the most experienced used Pro Tools, which is a practice we could verify with the HPs' group. HPs who reported using Logic Pro both had an interest or background in music, which is also the case of the one AI-P that mentioned Logic Pro.

My Mother Personas are based on real human beings. This might seem like an unlikely occurrence in this scenario – ChatGPT doesn't have a mother, or a family, but it does have a training dataset. After a Google search of the names of the podcasters generated, we find that 7 of the 16 names are associated with a podcast project within the first page of search results. Other attributes rarely match (e.g., none were involved in true crime podcasts), except in the case of one persona: a 25–35-year-old journalist who focuses their work and hosts podcasts on LGBTQ+ issues. Sharing a patronym as well as a profile seems to indicate ChatGPT was influenced directly by a LinkedIn profile. But beyond the issue of creating a "bad persona", there could be real data privacy and copyright issues stemming from publishing research and generated personas without screening for any potential "real world" matches. This could support the idea that an algorithm evaluating the uniqueness of data output by an LLM is necessary to make ethical use of these tools.

4.4   Comparing AI-Generated Personas' and Human Participants' Answers to Semi-Structured Interview Questions

AI-Ps are most keen on using Adobe Audition (81% mentioning it in their answer to Prompt 2: *"What audio editing software do you use?"*). They mention three other software: Pro Tools (19%), Audacity (13%), and Logic Pro (6%). HPs also prefer Adobe Audition (41% mentioning it in their answer to the same question), but also mention fourteen other software: Protools (25%), SADiE (19%), Hindenburg (13%), Logic (13%), Audacity (13%), Powair (6%), Ableton (6%), Descript (6%), Reaper (6%), Wavelab (6%), RX Advanced (6%), Garage Band (6%), Sony Vegas (6%), and Levelator (6%). The takeaways from both sets of answers contradict one another. In the case of HP's interviews, we could conclude that although there are preferences and customs for specific software, the representation of fifteen different software across all interviewees' answers highlights the independent nature of podcast production, and makes it complicated to narrow down to a single audio editing software upon which to base any further tool. For the AI-Ps, we could come to the erroneous conclusion that any tool compatible with Adobe Audition and Pro Tools would be acceptable for almost all users.

We generate 5 more personas including the keyword "BBC" in the prompt. This generated output is also available publicly. This addition drastically changes the answers given to Question 1. Although Adobe Audition is still mentioned, other editing software are often preferred by the personas, like Pro Tools, Logic Pro, or even Hindenburg. There is no mention of the software SADiE, a DAW that is used across many teams at BBC, which is a helpful reminder that if a connection between question A and answer α is not made online, it cannot be included in ChatGPT's output. This is particularly problematic when emulating human behaviour, because existing correlations might not always be disclosed online. The AI-Ps lose the breadth and specificities of human answers, and it would be interesting to investigate whether the more personas answer these questions, the less diverse the set of answers recorded becomes. This task also reinforces the importance and accompanying limitations of prompt-engineering to the results presented in this case-study.

The analysis of the answers to Prompt 3 (*What attributes make good podcasting tool?*) suggests that the HPs and AI-Ps agree on the most important features that make for a good podcasting tool, with similar focuses on "Efficiency" "Usefulness" and "Compatibility", although the AI-Ps thoroughness in its answers (see Fig. 2a) leads to these themes being over-represented across different interviews. Some of the themes expressed are unique to the AI-Ps, like needing "technical support", "documentation", or a tool that "allows for automation". All of these are valid design concerns, which could lead the designers to further reflect on these issues, and had these answers been generated prior to the human interviews, could have informed a new avenue for conversation.

In Prompt 4, *"What is your opinion on using AI voice synthesis for podcast production?"*, AI-Ps and HPs share their concerns for using AI voice synthesis in podcast production. If three HPs are enthusiastic about the technology, none of the AI-Ps match this enthusiasm. Overall, AI-Ps have much more nuanced answers, discussing both the benefits and risks of the technology regardless of their overall opinion. This points towards the in-built necessity of ChatGPT to be thorough. Unlike humans, it appears to systematically formulate its answers in the dialectical method, following a "thesis, antithesis, synthesis" pattern (see Fig. 2b). This makes it harder to gather straightforward answers, as personas with quirks and clear-cut opinions are much easier to extract requirements from Jones et al. [13].

We also notice repeated speech patterns that don't carry meaning but give an impression of sameness from one answer to the next across all four prompts (see Fig. 2a). Some of the most noticeable phrases were: "overall" (16 AI-Ps) "ultimately" (9 AI-Ps), "appreciate" (6 AI-Ps), "additionally" (6 AI-Ps) "first and foremost" (4 AI-Ps).

5   Reflections

5.1   Potential Uses and Recommendations

If a designer is looking for a wide range of definite, clear-cut, opinions on a topic or as a reaction to a prototype, HPs provide a breadth of answers unmatched by ChatGPT's

> "In my opinion, a good podcasting tool should have several key attributes. Firstly, it should be user-friendly and easy to navigate, even for those who are new to podcasting. Secondly, it should have robust audio editing features that allow for precise editing and enhancement of audio quality. Thirdly, it should have a range of export options to ensure that the final product can be distributed on multiple platforms. Fourthly, it should allow for collaboration between team members, with the ability to share files and collaborate on a single project. Fifthly, it should have a support system that is easily accessible and responsive to any issues that may arise. Finally, a good podcasting tool should be affordable, with pricing plans that suit the needs and budgets of different podcasters. Overall, a good podcasting tool should make the production process more efficient and effective, allowing podcasters to focus on creating great content."

(a) Response of "Maxine", a 28 y.o True Crime podcast producer, to Prompt 3 "What attributes make a good podcasting tool?". Structural words denoting ChatGPT's thoroughness are highlighted in purple,

Thesis As a podcast producer with years of experience in the industry, I have mixed feelings about using AI voice synthesis for podcast production. On one hand, I can see the potential benefits of using AI voice synthesis to create realistic-sounding voices for narration, character dialogue, and other aspects of podcast production. This technology could potentially save time and money by eliminating the need to hire voice actors or record and edit audio.

Anti-thesis However, I also believe that there are significant risks and drawbacks to using AI voice synthesis for podcast production. For one, the technology is not yet perfect and can often produce unnatural or robotic-sounding voices that may detract from the overall quality and appeal of a podcast. Additionally, the use of AI voice synthesis raises ethical and moral concerns around the potential for the technology to be misused or abused, such as creating deepfake content or impersonating real people. [...]

Synthesis In summary, while AI voice synthesis has the potential to offer some benefits in podcast production, I believe that the risks and drawbacks outweigh these benefits. As a podcast producer, I would prefer to focus on creating content that is authentic, engaging, and reflective of the unique voices and perspectives of individuals."

(b) Response of "Max", a 38 y.o. Technology and Business podcast to Prompt 4 "What is your opinion on using AI voice synthesis for podcast production.", highlighted to showcase the dialectical method followed.

Fig. 2. Responses of AI-Ps that highlight the commonalities of language used by ChatGPT.

attempts. The data gathered from the interviews with ChatGPT-generated personas does match the one gathered from the participants in many ways, but it does not represent the more extreme views found in human transcripts, instead painting a large-scale picture of possible requirements archetypal users might have of the software being designed.

A simple way to integrate ChatGPT into forms of UCD could be to use it to help design interviews with real users. On this occasion, we relied on a focus group, but this might not be an available option to all designers. Relying on a tool like ChatGPT to build open-ended interview questions could be a useful alternative to more time-consuming, resource-intensive preparation processes.

If this use-case focused on role-playing using AI-generated personas, one could easily imagine a scenario where personas created traditionally, via ethnographic observations or studies, would be given to a model in order to be brought to life. This could circumvent privacy issues exposed throughout this case study. The ability of ChatGPT to remain "in character" and stay consistent with the role it is playing is apparent throughout this evaluation and could be used for the designer's benefit – making it so designers don't have to act out scenes with fictional users, but more importantly, allowing for larger sets of data to be collected, potentially automatically.

Carrying out this comparison also kick-started a reflection on how representative the participant group was of the target industry, which enabled us to confirm or challenge some assumptions about our target user.

5.2   Limitations

This case-study gives insight not only into how designers can use ChatGPT for their benefit, but also into how and what data are processed and used by the model. A deep neural network is often compared to a "black box", but by figuring out what we can use the box for, we can get hints as to what it is made out of. For instance, the knowledge that some of the personas created were inferred from real people, using websites like LinkedIn as a source of information, reveals that the output does not necessarily transform the training data.

This realisation also leads us to a final recommendation, and first limitation: LLMs can be used to help with UCD methods, but designers should be particularly wary of disclosing or sharing output data from generated personas without having determined how original the output is. We can easily imagine scenarios where this "shortcut" taken by ChatGPT would constitute a serious data privacy or copyright issue. This small-scale exploratory study should be seen as a cautionary tale in terms of data privacy.

Both sets of transcripts were analysed by the same researcher, which could have led to implicit bias, because the researcher knew what codes and themes to expect from the answers given by the personas. Conducting a similar study including multiple groups of annotators could help determine whether the results presented here are replicable. The replicability of the results is also dependent on the prompts used. We have explored the effect of modifying slightly the prompt given to ChatGPT, and a single keyword seems to skew an entire set of results (cf. Section 4.4). This could have greatly influenced the diversity and scope of the results gathered. If Prompt 1 contained direction to create a group of personas "representative of podcasters", would the results have significantly differed? The influence of varying prompts (via, for instance, metaprompting [25]) should therefore be further explored in a tangential, larger scale case-study.

Mitchell and Krakauer [23] question the nature of understanding in LLMs, hypothesising that the understanding displayed by such models is distinct to human understanding and has specific uses: problems that demand large datasets are particularly well suited for LLMs and their "spurious" correlations and "shortcuts", but problems that require specific, limited knowledge and a deep understanding of causality are best suited to humans. This theory brings nuance to the findings of his study: some software development will benefit from the specificity and intricacy of human thought; meanwhile, some projects could benefit from the large-scale data amalgamation occurring in LLMs.

We should also address the issue of ethics in using LLMs. In the case of ChatGPT, the training dataset is based on the internet. Two questions arise: How ethical is the internet? And, how ethical is it to use scraped data? Humans are influenced by the online content they consume daily, and their decisions, conversations, and creations are tightly linked to their media and cultural intake. Yin et al. [36] argue for an evaluation system that judges the originality of AI-generated output. Over a certain threshold, the authors claim we can no longer distinguish any of the input data in the output produced, and this makes it fall within the acceptable confines of inspiration, rather than theft. However, and particularly in the case of creative models, a distinction could be made, stemming from the fundamental difference in the nature of machine understanding and human understanding, as highlighted above. The case of the "stolen persona" revealed in this study shows the extent of data privacy dangers when the training data and output of a model are left unchecked.

In terms of how ethical the training data is itself, an article published in Time magazine discusses at length the practices of filtering controversial data by labeling the furthest confines of the internet.[6] Can we justify using LLMs if they are trained in manners that could be deemed "unethical", if real lives are affected by a tool that simply assists us in tasks we can perform on our own?

Perhaps, smaller custom models trained on particular user types, with data sourced and processed in unequivocally ethical ways, could provide more transparency and control for researchers, designers, and users alike.

5.3 Future Work

A portion of this paper evaluates the quality of the personas generated by ChatGPT – if these are adequate for this case-study's purposes, conducting further investigation into how well ChatGPT remains in character using existing personas would allow making further recommendations for designers looking to expand their design-method toolbox.

The recommendations made in Sect. 5.1 are theoretical, and based solely on the lessons learned from this case study. Designing a mock tool using AI to assist in the UCD process could help see how feasible and successful the recommendations made in this paper are, and answer the following questions: Can we find a plus value sufficient to justify its integration into existing workflows? Are the assumptions of cost-cutting and time-saving valid? In practice, are designers comfortable with holding conversations with fictional users via AI chatbots?

This simple experiment also brings to light some of ChatGPT's recurrent behaviour, which aside from repeating some turn of phrases, also repeats answer structures regardless of the persona it is pretending to be, and sometimes, breaks character. These behaviours could be further analysed to understand more about the training data and processing occurring in this model. It would also enable us to make conclusions about how the model interplays with the personas and their answers.

As technologies have evolved since conducting this case-study, new AI-assistants have emerged. Comparing their different outputs from similar prompts within the context of design could provide new insights into the AI-chatbot market, its applications, and the unique issues associated to each system [34].

Overall, conducting research going beyond the scope and particularities of this particular case study would help solidify the results presented.

---

[6] https://time.com/6247678/openai-chatgpt-kenya-workers/.

6 Conclusion

In this case-study, we compared the answers of 16 human podcast creators to personas generated by ChatGPT to establish whether conversational LLMs could be used to assist in UCD methods. We found that the personas generated are credible, but they revealed important data privacy issues, and highlighted the skewed or incomplete nature of Chat-GPT's training dataset. By looking at the correlation between answer and persona, we confirmed that the answers given by ChatGPT when in character weren't just random, but given in relation to the user portrayed. The answers of these fictional users were comparable to the ones of participants, but did not display as wide a range of opinions. The thematic analysis conducted highlights the similarity in speech patterns that occur independently of the persona ChatGPT pretends to be. These issues might hinder iterative design tasks, as clear-cut opinions are often preferred to mild or average reactions. Finally, we share three recommendations regarding the possible uses of tools like ChatGPT in UCD: 1) as a way to help put together semi-structured interviews, 2) as a control group to better gauge whether the partcipants' interviewed are representative of the target user, 3) for its role-playing functionalities, asking it to bring to life personas created by the designers. Overall, these AI tools can be seen as ways to complement and assist designers in human-focused design methods. It would be oxymoronic to take the user out of UCD, but we can learn to best use these new technologies to facilitate research or development projects. More importantly, this case-study brings to light the necessity for more research in the fast-changing field of LLMs and their application to design practices, in order to confirm or refute the conclusions formulated.

References

1. Abras, C., Maloney-Krichmar, D., Preece, J., et al.: User-centered design. In: Bainbridge, W. (ed.) Encyclopedia of Human-Computer Interaction, vol. 37, no. 4, pp. 445–456. Sage Publications, Thousand Oaks (2004)
2. et al., R.B.: On the opportunities and risks of foundation models (2022)
3. Bahrini, A., et al.: Chatgpt: applications, opportunities, and threats. In: 2023 Systems and Information Engineering Design Symposium (SIEDS), pp. 274–279. IEEE (2023)
4. Bavarian, M., et al.: Efficient training of language models to fill in the middle (2022). http://arxiv.org/abs/2207.14255
5. Bommarito II, M., Katz, D.M.: GPT Takes the Bar Exam (2022). http://arxiv.org/abs/2212.14402
6. Christel, M., Kang, K.: Issues in requirements elicitation. Technical report CMU/SEI-92-TR-012, Software Engineering Institute, Carnegie Mellon University, Pittsburgh, PA (1992). http://resources.sei.cmu.edu/library/assct-view.cfm?AssetID=12553
7. Clarke, V., Braun, V., Hayfield, N.: Thematic analysis. Qual. Psychol. Pract. Guide Res. Methods 3, 222–248 (2015)
8. Devlin, P.: It's Time to Tune In to Women Podcasters (2022). https://www.thepodcasthost.com/business-of-podcasting/women-podcasters/
9. Floyd, Ingbert r., C.J.M., Twidale, M.B.: Resolving incommensurable debates: a preliminary identification of persona kinds, attributes, and characteristics 2, 12–26 (2008)
10. Friess, E.: Personas and decision making in the design process: an ethnographic case study. In: Proceedings of the SIGCHI Conference on Human Factors in Computing Systems, pp. 1209–1218. CHI 2012, Association for Computing Machinery, New York, NY, USA (2012)

11. Fuchs, K.: Exploring the opportunities and challenges of NLP models in higher education: is chat GPT a blessing or a curse? In: Frontiers in Education, vol. 8, p. 1166682. Frontiers Media SA (2023)
12. ISO/IEC/IEEE: 29148 (2011). https://standards.ieee.org
13. Jones, M.C., Floyd, I.R., Twidale, M.B.: Teaching Design with Personas (2008)
14. Kautz, K.: Investigating the design process: participatory design in agile software development. Inf. Technol. People **24**(3), 217–235 (2011)
15. Kocaballi, A.B.: Conversational AI-powered design: ChatGPT as designer, user, and product (2023). http://arxiv.org/abs/2302.07406
16. Korzynski, P., Mazurek, G., Krzypkowska, P., Kurasinski, A.: Artificial intelligence prompt engineering as a new digital competence: analysis of generative AI technologies such as chatgpt. Entrepreneurial Bus. Econ. Rev. **11**(3), 25–37 (2023)
17. Kuhn, K.: Problems and benefits of requirements gathering with focus groups: a case study. Int. J. Hum. Comput. Interact. **12**(3–4), 309–325 (2000)
18. Kujala, S.: User involvement: a review of the benefits and challenges. Behav. Inf. Technol. **22**(1), 1–16 (2003)
19. Kula, E., van Deursen, A., Gousios, G.: Modeling team dynamics for the characterization and prediction of delays in user stories. In: Proceedings of the 36th IEEE/ACM International Conference on Automated Software Engineering, pp. 991–1002. ASE 2021, IEEE Press (2022). https://doi.org/10.1109/ASE51524.2021.9678939
20. Kuykendall, B.K.: 03/11/22: over half of students surveyed see coding skills as vital but over a third lack learning access - (2022). https://thejournal.com/articles/2022/03/11/over-half-of-students-surveyed-see-coding-skills-as-vital-but-over-a-third-lack-learning-access.aspx
21. Lane, S., O'Raghallaigh, P., Sammon, D.: Requirements gathering: the journey. Commun. ACM **38**(5), 31–32 (1995)
22. Lund, B.D., Wang, T.: Chatting about chatgpt: how may AI and GPT impact academia and libraries? Library Hi Tech News (2023)
23. Mitchell, M., Krakauer, D.C.: The debate over understanding in AI's large language models. Proc. Natl. Acad. Sci. **120**(13), e2215907120 (2023)
24. Moore, J.M., Shipman III, F.M.: A comparison of questionnaire-based and GUI-based requirements gathering. In: Proceedings of the 15th IEEE International Conference on Automated Software Engineering, p. 35. ASE 2000, IEEE Computer Society, USA (2000)
25. Moritz, E.: Chatting with chat (gpt-4): Quid est understanding. Centre for Digital Philosophy at Western University, London, Canada (2024)
26. Nyumba, O.T., Wilson, K., Derrick, C.J., Mukherjee, N.: The use of focus group discussion methodology: insights from two decades of application in conservation. Methods Ecol. Evol. **9**(1), 20–32 (2018)
27. Poldrack, R.A., Lu, T., Beguš, G.: Ai-assisted coding: Experiments with gpt-4. arXiv preprint arXiv:2304.13187 (2023)
28. Pruitt, J., Grudin, J.: Personas: practice and theory. In: Proceedings of the 2003 Conference on Designing for User Experiences, pp. 1–15. DUX 2003, Association for Computing Machinery, New York, NY, USA (2003)
29. Research, E.: Weekly Insights 1.11.2023 - Top Podcast Genres in the U.S. Q3 2022 (2023). https://www.edisonresearch.com/weekly-insights-1-11-2023-top-podcast-genres-in-the-u-s-q3-2022/, section: Featured
30. Rime, J., Archer-Boyd, A., Collins, T.: How will you pod? Implications of creators' perspectives for designing innovative podcasting tools. ACM Trans. Multimed. Comput. Commun. Appl. **20**(3), 1–25 (2023)
31. Rime, J., Francombe, J., Collins, T.: How do you pod? A study revealing the archetypal podcast production workflow. In: Proceedings of the 2022 ACM International Conference on Interactive Media Experiences, pp. 11–18 (2022)

32. Salminen, J., Wenyun Guan, K., Jung, S.G., Jansen, B.: Use cases for design personas: a systematic review and new frontiers. In: Proceedings of the 2022 CHI Conference on Human Factors in Computing Systems, pp. 1–21. CHI 2022. Association for Computing Machinery, New York, NY, USA (2022)
33. Sherrill, L.A.: The "Serial Effect" and the true crime podcast ecosystem. Journalism Pract. **16**(7), 1473–1494 (2022)
34. Singh, S.K., Kumar, S., Mehra, P.S.: Chat gpt & google bard AI: a review. In: 2023 International Conference on IoT, Communication and Automation Technology (ICICAT), pp. 1–6. IEEE (2023)
35. Traylor, C.M.: Serialized killing : usability and user experience in the true crime genre (2019)
36. Yin, Z., Reuben, F., Stepney, S., Collins, T.: "A good algorithm does not steal – it imitates": the originality report as a means of measuring when a music generation algorithm copies too much. In: Romero, J., Martins, T., Rodríguez-Fernández, N. (eds.) EvoMUSART 2021. LNCS, vol. 12693, pp. 360–375. Springer, Cham (2021). https://doi.org/10.1007/978-3-030-72914-1_24

An Experiment to Investigate Changes in Physiological Signals During Subtle Wind and Scent Presentation for Designing Subtle Notifications

Masaki Omata$^{(\boxtimes)}$ ⓘ and Takumi Shioda ⓘ

University of Yamanashi, Kofu, Yamanashi, Japan
{omata,shio22}@hci.media.yamanashi.ac.jp

Abstract. Notifications for visual and auditory modalities from smart phone have some problems. For the visual modality, the user needs to actively control his or her viewpoint toward the phone. For the auditory modality, the user may not hear the notification sound because it is drowned out by surrounding sound. As a solution to the problems, we have proposed a subtle notification system that uses wind and scent to notify users of less important notifications and identify the user's awareness of the notification based on changes in the user's physiological signals. In this paper, we conducted an experiment to measure and analyze physiological signals when subtle wind and scent stimuli were presented to participants performing a reading task, in order to design the proposed system. The results show that the wind stimulus caused a change in skin conductance and the scent stimulus caused a change in the amplitude of respiratory movement. This suggest that even such weak and invisible stimuli are noticed by a user performing a task and are reflected in the user's physiological responses.

Keywords: Notification · Physiological signal · Wind · Scent · Subtle

1 Introduction

In recent years, many IoT (Internet of Things) devices have been spreading around us, and we interact with the devices in various ways. Visual and/or auditory modalities are often used as notification modalities to inform the users of status and conditions of the devices [1, 2]. Notifications from visual modality allow the users to receive a large amount of information at a time. The examples include illumination of a screen of a smartphone when a message is received and a pop-up window on a desktop of a computer. On the other hand, notifications by auditory modality are more likely to be noticed by the users. The examples include a ringtone of a smartphone or a sound of a home appliance operating.

However, the notification modalities have some problems. For the visual modality, the user must actively control his or her viewpoint, since there is only one point of gaze at which a person can focus his or her attention [3]. Although a user can respond with peripheral vision except at the point of concentration, direct light stimulation is required. For the auditory modality, the user may not hear the notification sound because it is drowned out by surrounding sound, or conversely, the notification sound may be heard by other people and become a nuisance. Furthermore, as more and more IoT devices are expected to be used in the future, users may not be able to recognize which device is emitting notification and what it means. The problems may cause annoyance and stress for users who receive notifications.

As a solution to the problems, we have proposed a subtle notification system that uses wind and scent. The system uses light and sound to notify users of important notifications, and wind and scent to notify users of less important notifications. Compared to visual and auditory information, wind and scent are less likely to be noticed by the user and are rarely used as a notification modality [3]. On the other hand, they can provide information to users without interfering with visual and auditory modalities. We believe that realization of the notification system using wind and scent will reduce the number of notifications that are only for visual and auditory modalities, thereby reducing annoyance caused by notifications. In addition, we have proposed that the system can identify the user's awareness of a notification based on changes in the user's physiological signals. The system will only re-send the notification when it determines that the user is unaware of the notification, thus reducing the number of re-notifications and the annoyance of re-notifications after the user notices.

In this paper, we conducted an experiment to measure and analyze physiological signals when wind and scent stimuli are presented to participants in order to realize the proposed system. We compared the physiological signals when wind and scent stimuli were not presented to the participants with the physiological signals immediately after wind or scent stimulus was presented, and derived useful changes in physiological signals when the stimuli were presented.

The contributions of this paper are as follows.

- Most participants performing a reading task can notice subtle winds and scents.
- Wind stimuli have the potential to induce changes in skin conductance and scent stimuli have the potential to induce changes in the amplitude of respiratory movements.

2 Related Work

This section introduces previous research on various modalities in notifications from information equipment such as smartphones, especially for subtle notifications, and discusses the position of our research.

Raudanjoki et al. designed ShadowSparrow that carries information through functional lights and shadows [1]. The concept uses illustrative bird images and other relevant visuals (e.g., dishwasher and e-mail icons) cast on the surroundings for ambient information visualizations and notifications. Chuang applied animation principles to design the expressivity with LED lights and speakers commonly embedded in electronic devices [2]. They explored set of individual and group light behaviors that can provide intuitive communications on expressing specific behaviors of an IoT system. Hansson et al. discussed some of problems with auditory and tactile notifications because users are interrupted by auditory cues and tactile is typically not very visible to other people [4]. They, therefore, developed The Reminder Bracelet which conveys visual notifications. It was clear that the users felt the concept of subtle and public notification. Mashhadi et al. explored how mobile notifications were regarded as increasing number of applications were adopting notification services [5]. They found that users like to associate vibration and sound to important notifications and that light is typically preferred for low priority notifications and also in social contexts where the user does not want to disturb others. Silva et al. proposed the construction of a context-aware notification system with the identification of opportune and inopportune moments for the interruption of drivers, in order to mitigate the effects of disruptive notifications delivered to a person in a driving situation [6]. The system obtained a general accuracy of 88% in identifying the opportune and inopportune moments.

Based on the findings of the previous studies, we have proposed a new notification system in which notifications of high importance are notified by clear light and/or sound, and notifications of low importance are notified by subtle wind and/or scent. In addition, we have proposed a new method to reduce the number of re-notifications by detecting the user's awareness of notifications based on changes in the user's physiological signals. We assume, for example, business e-mails and visitor notifications as examples of highly important notifications, and conversely, advertisement e-mails from shopping sites and responses to temperature settings of an air conditioner as examples of less important notifications.

In our proposed system, we focused on wind and scent, which are rarely used in previous studies, as subtle notification modalities for less important information. Wind is a stimulus that acts on the sense of pressure in the skin and deep tissues [7]. The pressure sense is a part of the tactile sense and is a cutaneous sensation that perceives pressure caused by mechanical deformation of the skin, including body hair. Scent is a stimulus that affects the sense of smell among the special senses [7]. It is perceived by olfactory cells located at the back of a nasal cavity, and the electrical signals reach the brain, which perceives the odor. Maggioni et al. validated effectiveness of smell as notification modality and presented findings on the performance of smell in conveying information [8]. They demonstrated that olfactory notifications improve users' confidence and performance in identifying the urgency level of a message. On the other hand, our study is different from theirs in that it assumes a subtle presentation and also uses physiological signals as indexes of the user's response.

3   Experiment

The main objective of this experiment is to demonstrate that a response to a subtle stimulus can be estimated from physiological signals by investigating how participants' physiological signals change when a wind or scent stimulus is subtly presented to the participants. The secondary objectives are to determine whether the participants noticed the subtle stimuli and, if so, the degree of annoyance of the stimuli, based on the questionnaire survey about the presented stimuli. Participants were not told that they would be presented with wind and scents, but only that the experiment was to measure physiological signals during a reading task.

3.1 Task

The experimental task was to read a book on basic knowledge about user interfaces [9] for 5 min. After the five minutes, the participants answered a quiz about what they had read. After the reading task in the two conditions of wind and scent presentation, the participants were asked to answer a questionnaire about the presented stimuli.

The reasons for choosing the reading task were to maintain the participant's state of concentration and to minimize any responses other than physiological responses to the wind or scent stimulus to the participant. We considered that reading was a task that did not involve physical activity and was easy to concentrate on. On the other hand, we considered that watching movies or working on a computer would also allow concentration, but we were concerned that gazing at a screen would cause screen apnea [10] and affect physiological signals.

In the post-reading quiz, about 20 questions were asked, including fill-in-the-blanks and description questions related to the book's contents. No questions were asked about the contents other than those described in the book and about applications of the descriptions.

In the post-task questionnaire, participants were asked whether they noticed the wind and aroma stimuli, if so, how often the wind was presented and what type of scent, whether they were able to concentrate on reading, and whether they were interested in the book content. Five-point Likert scales were used for the degree questions. For the type of aroma, participants were asked to choose one of five options: floral, spicy, fruity, herbal, and animalic aromas. Table 1 shows the main questions of the questionnaire and their response alternatives.

Table 1. Main questions of the questionnaire at the end of the task.

Modality	Question	Alternatives
Wind	How much did you notice wind while you were reading the book?	Not at all, Not much, Neither, Somewhat, Definitely
	How many times did you notice the wind?	
	Did the wind interfere with your reading?	Not at all, Not much, Neither, Somewhat, Very much
Scent	How much did you notice scents while you were reading the book?	Not at all, Not much, Neither, Somewhat, Definitely
	How many different scents did you notice?	
	Did the scents interfere with your reading?	Not at all, Not much, Neither, Somewhat, Very much

In the questionnaire survey at the end of the experiment, participants were asked to rank the five notification methods in order of their suitability for this experimental condition: smartphone light stimulus, smartphone ringtone, smartphone vibration, wind in this experiment, and fragrance in this experiment, without overlapping rankings.

3.2 Experimental Environment

Figure 1 shows the experimental environment and a participant. The participant was seated in a chair. The experimenter was seated behind the participant to the left in order to operate a laptop computer for the measurement of physiological signals during the task execution. The scent presentation device (Aroma Shooter, Aromajoin Co.) was placed 60 cm in front of the participant, hidden inside a camera stand for capturing facial images of the participant. The stand had a mesh structure that did not interfere with the emission of a scent. The wind presentation device (Yuzuki, F019) was placed 80 cm behind the participant, at the same height as the back of the participant's head. To measure physiological signals, a blood volume pulse (BVP) sensor (SA9308M, Thought Technology Ltd.) was placed on the middle finger of the participant's non-dominant hand, a skin conductance sensor (SA9309M, Thought Technology Ltd.) between the index and ring fingers of the non-dominant hand (see Fig. 2 left), and a respiratory movement sensor (SA9311M, Thought Technology Ltd.) was placed on the participant's abdomen (see Fig. 2 right).

Fig. 1. Experimental environment and a participant.

Fig. 2. Sensors for physiological signal measurement.

To prevent ambient noise from interfering with the participants' task, they were asked to wear ear muffs (Peltor Optime III, 3M) and soundproofing boards were placed on the windows. Because masks were required due to the COVID-19, participants were asked to wear uniform non-woven masks to prevent individual differences in perception of the scents. The room temperature was kept constant at 24 °C by an air conditioner.

3.3 Stimulus

Low (1.1 m/s) and medium (1.7 m/s) fan wind speeds were used as wind stimuli. Both were only faintly perceptible in the hair swinging at the back of the head or at the neck. During the 5-min reading task, each participant was presented with each wind speed five times (10 times in total) in a random timing and order. Each presentation lasted 5 s.

Orange and lavender scents were used for the scent stimuli. Orange is known to refresh and relieve tension and stress, while lavender is known to calm the heart rate [11]. The first type of scent was presented 60 s after the start of the reading task, and the second type of scent was presented 180 s after the start. The influence of residual scents was reduced by allowing the two-minute interval between the first and second presentation. The order in which the scents were presented was set so that half of the participants received orange for the first type and half received lavender for the first type, in order to counterbalance the order effect.

3.4 Physiological Signal

Blood volume pulse (BVP), skin conductance (SC), and respiratory movement (RM) were measured as physiological signals. The amplitude of each pulse was derived from the BVP wave and RM. The BVP wave is the propagation of pressure waves in the arterial system, produced by the pumping action of the heart [12]. It is measured from the amount of light reflected by infrared light directed from the sensor to the skin surface. It is known that the BVP varies with mental and physical load. The SC is the electrical change caused by skin perspiration [12]. It is measured by the potential difference between a pair of electrodes. The value increases as sweating increases due to sweat gland activity caused by mental excitement or anxiety under sympathetic nerve innervation. The RM increase or decrease the value depending on the stretching or contraction of the chest or abdomen [12]. Deep and slow breathing occurs in the resting state, and shallow and fast breathing occurs with exercise or mental workload.

The physiological indexes were analyzed to determine whether there was a significant increase or decrease in their values before or after the stimulus presentation. In the analysis, we tested for significant differences between the resting mean and the mean of the 20 s after the stimulus when changes occurred for BVP and SC, and between the resting mean and the mean of the 30 s after the stimulus when changes occurred for RM.

3.5 Procedure and Participant

First, informed consent was obtained from each participant. Participants were not informed that they would be presented with wind or scents but were told that the experiment was to measure physiological signals during a reading task and that they would be given a quiz on the content of the book after the reading. To obtain basic data for calculating the amount of change in physiological signals during the task, the patient's resting physiological signals before the experimental task were recorded for a minute.

Each participant participated in the experiment one at a time, and each participant performed two trials. To avoid the influence of residual scent, the reading task with wind presentation was performed on the first trial, and the reading task with scent presentation was performed on the second trial. After each trial, participants answered a quiz about what they had read.

After the wind presentation on the first trial, the experimenter informed the participant that he had been presented with wind from behind during the reading task, and the participant responded to a questionnaire asking if he had been aware of the wind presentation, how many times, and how annoying the wind presentation was compared to the light presentation, ring tones, or vibration. Similarly, after the second scent presentation, the experimenter told the participant that scents were presented, and the participant responded to a questionnaire asking how many different scents he perceived, what kind, and how annoying the scents were compared to light, sound, and vibration.

Six undergraduate students (all male, mean 22.0 years, standard deviation 1.41 years) from the faculty of engineering participated in the experiment.

3.6 Result

As an overall result, Table 2 and 3 show the number of responses for each physiological index, the questionnaire survey, and the quiz for each participant. The symbols in the physiological indexes mean that "++" indicates a significant change was observed two or more times, " +" indicates a change was observed once, and "O" indicates little change was observed. The order of the participants in the tables is in the order of concentration in the right-most column. The order of concentration means that the first place means that the participant was more concentrated on the reading task. The highest total score of the responses to the questionnaire, the number of correct answers to the quiz, and the time to answer the quiz was scored, and the highest total score was ranked first.

Table 2. List of each participant's reaction to the wind presentation in the order of concentration.

Participant No	SC	RM	BVP	RM ampl	BVP ampl	Num. of times noticed	Quiz score	Quiz answer time (s)	Deg. of Noticing	Concentration rank
1	O	O	O	++	+	3	16	251	Middle	1
2	O	O	O	+	O	5	16	286	Middle	2
3	++	+	O	++	++	1	12	277	Low	3
4	++	O	O	O	++	3	16	310	Middle	4
5	++	O	++	+	+	3	15	241	Middle	5
6	++	O	O	O	++	6	8	423	High	6

Table 3. List of each participant's reaction to the sent presentation in the order of concentration.

ParticipantNo	SC	RM	BVP	RM ampl	BVP ampl	Num. of times noticed	Quiz score	Quiz answer time (s)	Deg. of Noticing	Concentration rank
2	O	O	O	+	+	2	12	116	High	1
6	O	O	O	++	+	1	7	140	Middle	2
1	+	+	O	+	O	1	10	254	Middle	3
5	+	O	O	O	+	2	11	168	High	4
3	O	O	O	+	O	2	5	134	High	5
4	++	O	O	O	O	0	6	155	Low	6

Table 2 shows that the four participants with the lowest concentration showed a significant change in SC due to wind stimulus. In addition, four participants showed a change in amplitude of RM, and five participants showed a change in amplitude of BVP. Furthermore, participants with lower concentration tended to be more aware of the wind stimulus. The raw RM data and BVP data did not change for most of the participants. In the questionnaire, the average number of times the participants reported noticing the wind stimulus was 3.5 times, with the standard deviation of 1.6 times. The mean percentage of correct answers to the quiz on the book content was 66%, with the standard deviation of 14%.

Table 3 shows that the scent stimuli caused a change in the amplitude of the RM of the participants with the highest concentration. In addition, the participants who showed a change in the amplitude of their RM also showed a higher degree of noticing the scent stimuli. In Table 3, as in Table 2, the raw data of RM and BVP did not change for most of the participants. The mean percentage of correct answers to the quiz about the book content in the scent experiment was 53%, with the standard deviation of 16%.

In the questionnaire survey, the participants were asked to rank conventional light, sound, and vibration modalities and the wind and scent modalities in our experiment in order of their suitability as notification modalities, and the results were analyzed using normalized rank method. The results shows that there are no significant differences among the modalities.

3.7 Detailed Analysis

Based on the results in Table 2, we observed the raw data of the SC of each of the six participants, as the wind stimulus caused a change in SC. Figures (a) to (f) in Fig. 3 show the raw SC data for each participant and the time of wind stimulation (red: medium wind, yellow: weak wind), with the horizontal axis representing the time course and the vertical axis representing micro siemens. The dashed ovals in this figure show that SC increased rapidly during or after the wind stimulus for four of the six participants. The degree of increase was greater in the medium wind condition than in the weak wind condition. For the four participants, there is a significant difference (t-test, $p < 0.05$) when comparing the mean SC value during the 20 s after stimulus presentation, when the responses were observed, to the mean SC value during the 60 s after the task started.

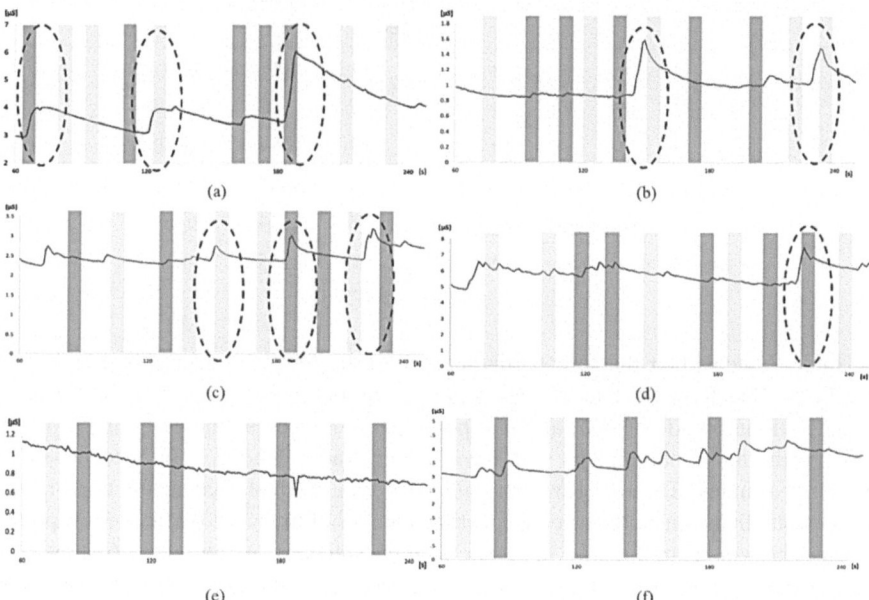

Fig. 3. Raw data of skin conductance of each participant in wind stimulus presentation. (Color figure online)

The results in Table 3 indicate that the amplitude of RM was changed by the scent stimulus, so we observed the amplitude of the RM of each of the six participants. Figures (a) to (f) in Fig. 4 show the amplitude of the RM of each participant and the time of presentation of the scent stimulus (red bands), with the horizontal axis representing the time course and the vertical axis representing the amplitude. The amplitude here refers to the value calculated as a relative measure of the amplitude of each respiration. The dashed ovals in the figure show that the amplitude increased rapidly after the scent presentation in four of the six participants, and that the increases were particularly pronounced after the second scent presentation. For the four participants, there is a significant difference (t-test, $p < 0.05$) when comparing the mean RM values during the 30 s after stimulus presentation, when the responses were observed, to the mean RM values during the 60 s after the task started.

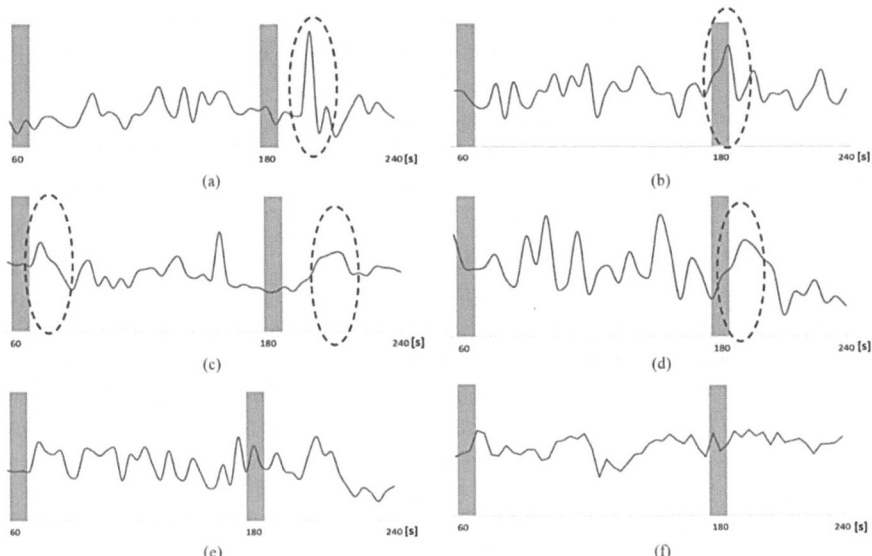

Fig. 4. Raw data of the amplitude of each participant's respiratory movement in scent stimulus presentation. (Color figure online)

3.8 Discussion

The experimental results show that the SC was significantly changed by the wind presentation and the amplitude of RM was significantly changed by the scent presentation. The detailed analysis suggests that the wind presentation caused an increase in SC due to mental perspiration caused by the unexpected wind hitting the back of the head. In the condition of the scent presentation, the RM was activated by the behavior of trying to smell more of the perceived scent. The reason why the changes in SC to wind stimuli were more pronounced in participants who were less concentrated on the reading task may be that they were more likely to notice other information and to notice the wind stimuli that had not been previously instructed to them, because they were less concentrated on the task.

Although there was no correlation between the presence or absence of changes in the amplitude of RM and high or low concentration, two of the four participants who showed changes in amplitude correctly identified the two types of scents, and the remaining two participants also noticed the one type of scent, suggesting that changes in the amplitude of RM are more likely to occur when participants are aware of the scents.

For future research, we need to increase the number of participants and generalize the results of the experiment in this paper. At that time, we plan to recruit an equal ratio of male to female participants, although all participants in this paper were male. With regard to olfaction, many previous studies have reported that women have a higher olfactory sensitivity than men [13]. With regard to airflow stimuli, Miura et al. reported that women tended to give higher coldness scores, and men tended to give lower coldness scores [14]. In addition, the analysis of physiological signals in this paper was focused on graph observation, but we plan to proceed with statistical and numerical calculations and waveform analysis in the future. Furthermore, as a limitation of the experiment in this paper, it was conducted under conditions without other odors or wind, but if practical implementation is to be considered, it will be necessary to design an experiment that also takes other odors and wind into consideration.

4 Conclusion

In order to design the notification system that selects a notification modality according to the importance of the notification and estimates the user's awareness of the notification based on changes in physiological signals, we conducted an experiment to verify changes in physiological signals during wind and scent presentation.

The results of the experiment showed that the wind stimulus caused a change in skin conductance (SC) and the scent stimulus caused a change in the amplitude of respiratory movement (RM). Therefore, it can be said that even such weak and invisible stimuli are noticed by the user performing a main task and are reflected in the user's physiological responses. This suggests the possibility of using wind and scent to present less important notifications, the possibility of using physiological signals that can be acquired without the user's intention or manipulation to identify awareness, and the possibility of using the physiological signals to automatically determine the user's awareness of a notification in a design of the system in which notification modalities are selected according to importance of notifications.

For future implementation of the proposed system, it is necessary to quantitatively evaluate whether or not the proposed system interferes with the user's work and concentration. Since the importance of information is highly subjective to each user, it is necessary to design a system that allows each user to customize importance of notifications.

Acknowledgments. This work was supported by JSPS KAKENHI Grant Number 23K11181.

References

1. Raudanjoki, Ö., Genç, Ç., Hurtig K., Häkkilä, J.: ShadowSparrow: an ambient display for information visualization and notification. In: Proceedings of the 19th International Conference on Mobile and Ubiquitous Multimedia (MUM '20), pp. 351–353. Association for Computing Machinery, New York, NY, USA (2020)
2. Chuang, Y.: Designing the expressivity of multiple smart things for intuitive and unobtrusive interactions. In: Proceedings of the 2020 ACM Designing Interactive Systems Conference (DIS 2020), pp. 2007–2019. Association for Computing Machinery, New York, NY, USA (2020)
3. Minakuchi, M.: Representation of peripheral information by wind for assistance in watching content. In: DBSI Letters, vol. 6, no. 1, pp. 1–4 (2007)
4. Hansson, R., Peter, L., Johan, R.: Subtle and public notification cues for mobile devices. In: Ubicomp 2001: Ubiquitous Computing, pp. 240–246 (2001)

5. Mashhadi, A., Mathur, A., Kawsar, F.: The myth of subtle notifications. In: Proceedings of the 2014 ACM International Joint Conference on Pervasive and Ubiquitous Computing: Adjunct Publication (UbiComp 2014 Adjunct), pp. 111–114. Association for Computing Machinery, New York, NY, USA (2014)
6. Silva, A.V.D., Borges, L., Vieira, V.: CDNA: a context-aware notification system for driver interruption. In: Proceedings of the 17th Brazilian Symposium on Human Factors in Computing Systems (IHC 2018), Article 11, pp. 1–8. Association for Computing Machinery, New York, NY, USA (2018)
7. Uchikawa, K.: Auditory, Tactile and Vestibular Sensations. 224. Asakura Shoten, Japan (2008)
8. Maggioni, E., Cobden, R., Dmitrenko, D., Obrist, M.: Smell-O-Message: integration of olfactory notifications into a messaging application to improve users' performance. In: Proceedings of the 20th ACM International Conference on Multimodal Interaction (ICMI 2018), pp. 45–54. Association for Computing Machinery, New York, NY, USA (2018)
9. Koga, N.: Fundamentals of User Interface Design, Gijutsu-Hyoron, Japan (2010)
10. Kure Kyosai Hospital, Electronic Screen Syndrome (2022). https://www.kure-kyosai.jp/user/news/322/cipnzn6wlos8s8870rvprqf6s-vyq9_0.pdf. Accessed 8 Oct 2023
11. Sellar, W.: The Directory of Essential Oils. C W Danie (1992)
12. Miyata, Y., Fujisawa, K., Kakigi S., Yamazaki, K.: New Physiological Psychology Volume I: Fundamentals of Physiological Psychology. Kitaohji Shobo, Japan (1998)
13. Uchikawa, K., Shinomori, K.: Gustatory Sense, Olfactory Sense. Asakura Publishing, Japan (2008)
14. Miura, K., Ishikawa, T., Itoigawa, T., Mitsui, M., Nozawa, A.: Psychological and physiological responses to airflow stimuli: differences in responses based on sex and targeted body site. Int. J. Industr. Ergonomics **68**, 176–185 (2018)

Towards Multi-stakeholder Evaluation of ML Models: A Crowdsourcing Study on Metric Preferences in Job-Matching System

Takuya Yokota[✉][iD] and Yuri Nakao[iD]

Fujitsu Limited, Kawasaki, Japan
{yokota-takuya,nakao.yuri}@fujitsu.com

Abstract. While machine learning (ML) technology affects diverse stakeholders, there is no one-size-fits-all metric to evaluate the quality of outputs, including performance and fairness. Using predetermined metrics without soliciting stakeholder opinions is problematic because it leads to an unfair disregard for stakeholders in the ML pipeline. In this study, to establish practical ways to incorporate diverse stakeholder opinions into the selection of metrics for ML, we investigate participants' preferences for different metrics by using crowdsourcing. We ask 837 participants to choose a better model from two hypothetical ML models in a hypothetical job-matching system twenty times and calculate their utility values for seven metrics. To examine the participants' feedback in detail, we divide them into five clusters based on their utility values and analyze the tendencies of each cluster, including their preferences for metrics and common attributes. Based on the results, we discuss the points that should be considered when selecting appropriate metrics and evaluating ML models with multiple stakeholders.

Keywords: Machine learning · Multi-stakeholder · Fairness · Crowdsourcing · Job-matching system

1 Introduction

As machine learning (ML) technologies have impacts on a diverse range of stakeholders, there have been ongoing efforts to improve the transparency of ML systems by including a variety of stakeholders in the evaluation of ML models [8, 18, 27, 29, 30]. To evaluate ML models, various performance metrics (e.g., accuracy, and precision), and fairness metrics (e.g., disparate impact [7] and counterfactual fairness [20]) are used. Those metrics are used to evaluate how well an ML system meets business or social goals [17, 34]. On the other hand, it is difficult to determine which metrics should be chosen and prioritized to what extent a priori. Hence, it is necessary to investigate how people related to the decisions, i.e., stakeholders, perceive the importance of each metric to achieve the goals. Therefore, some studies have aimed to incorporate stakeholders in selecting these metrics and determining their weights [1, 30, 43]. For example, one approach is to have stakeholders directly adjust the parameters of the ML model themselves [29], while another is to survey their preferences for each metric [43].

H. Plácido da Silva and P. Cipresso (Eds.): CHIRA 2024, CCIS 2370, pp. 110–130, 2025.
https://doi.org/10.1007/978-3-031-82633-7_8

On the other hand, it is difficult to fairly aggregate stakeholders' perspectives on the ML model evaluation. While some studies pre-defined the stakeholder groups to collect feedback from the stakeholder groups' points of view [6,30], different opinions exist within the same stakeholder group [30,31], and there has been a concern that even in a stakeholder group, a minority opinion in the group can be ignored [10,11]. Then, How should stakeholder feedback on ML models be collected? How should stakeholder groups be determined?

To address these questions, as a first step toward evaluating ML models including diverse stakeholders, we propose a method for examining what metrics people tend to prefer, how these tendencies can be grouped, and what attributes people are likely to include in each group. In this study, we used crowdsourcing to assign 837 participants residing in the U.S. the task of showing two outputs from hypothetical ML models for job-matching and choosing the model they thought was better. Based on the results of this task, we determined people's preferred metrics and clustered them based on their preferences. Furthermore, we analyzed what attributes people tended to include in each cluster, i.e., stakeholder groups. In this study, we address the following two-fold research questions:

RQ1. How are participants' preferences for ML performance metrics clustered?
RQ2. What demographic attributes have a significant effect on the preferences clustered with our method?

The contributions of our study are as follows:

– A new method to analyze the characteristics of stakeholders who evaluate ML models in similar ways.
– The analysis of what tendencies in attributes people who make a particular evaluation of ML models share in the domain of job-matching.
– Implication toward fair multi-stakeholder evaluation of ML models based on the results.

2 Related Work

2.1 Evaluation Metrics for Machine Learning Models

Existing studies have emphasized that evaluating ML models involves carefully choosing metrics, such as performance and fairness, tailored to specific situations. While general metrics like Accuracy, Precision, and Recall are broadly applicable across a range of domains [35], Sokolova and Lapalme [38] discussed the relevance of these metrics can vary depending on the application. Additionally, beyond performance measures, fairness metrics, such as Disparate Impact [7], are gaining importance. ML model operators need to carefully choose which of these various metrics to use based on their purpose and ethical considerations.

Moreover, people's priorities for these metrics differ based on the context and stakes of decision-making [3,13,15,39]. For example, for high-stake decision-making situations, e.g., cancer-detection predictions, people prioritize accuracy over fairness compared with a flu-symptom-severity prediction (low-stake situations) [39]. Harrison et al.

found that people see a model as biased when it has disparate false-positive rates that disadvantage African American defendants in a recidivism risk-assessment system [13]. Furthermore, the perception of metrics changes on the basis of people's education level [41] and characteristics of the tasks [13]. Previous studies quantified the change or difference in participants' attitudes toward ML systems [3,39]. They used explanations about the mechanisms of algorithms or performance metrics that express the behavior of an ML system as proxies.

In this study, we selected Accuracy, Specificity, Sensitivity (Recall), and Precision as evaluation metrics to understand stakeholder preferences in the context of a job-matching system. Additionally, as fairness metrics, we pick up Disparate Impact (DI) [7], Equalized Odds (EO) [12], and Counterfactual Fairness (CF) [20] as evaluation metrics to collect the preferences relate to fairness as well. This allows for a comprehensive exploration of how stakeholders evaluate the performance and fairness of the job-matching system. Additionally, this study extends the existing studies about people's perception of the metrics by including the viewpoint that they are stakeholders who are potentially affected by the system rather than just the general public. This approach is selected to gather diverse insights on modeling user preferences for metrics.

2.2 Stakeholder Models in Multi-Stakeholder Machine Learning Systems

Not only the human factors in the choice of ML metrics but the importance of considering a diverse range of stakeholders in the development and implementation of business applications has been emphasized. Mitchell et al. [28] and Lee et al. [23] emphasized the importance of acknowledging the stakeholders of ML systems. In business applications, the identification of key stakeholders is crucial. Preece et al. [36] mention including decision-makers, end users, and those impacted by decision-support systems. Golbin et al. [9] specify including data scientists, developers, business sponsors, and regulators as pivotal stakeholders.

There have also been existing studies to include stakeholders' viewpoints in the operation and development of machine learning and other artificial intelligence systems. Burke et al. [5] designed a method to incorporate stakeholders' preferences into ML models for recommender systems, emphasizing the need to balance benefits among predefined stakeholders like item providers, receivers, and system owners. Similarly, Zheng and Toribio [44] advocated for balancing multiple stakeholders' needs in recommender systems, proposing a model that enhances transparency by explaining key parameters affecting stakeholders' utility. In a recidivism prediction system, Narayanan [32] highlighted how various stakeholders of a recidivism prediction system prioritize different performance metrics. Extending this approach, Yokota and Nakao [43] employed a utility-based method to extract crowdsourcing workers' preferences for ML model evaluation metrics (i.e., performance metrics and fairness metrics) in a virtual scenario of a system to assess the recidivism risks of defendants.

On the other hand, stakeholder identification should be able to be tailored to each system so that we can appropriately consider all relevant stakeholders in the development and implementation process, not only by predetermining the stakeholder groups. In our crowdsourcing study, we analyze how stakeholders' demographic attributes influence their preferences for performance and fairness metrics used to evaluate ML models. We specifically focus on metrics such as accuracy and fairness (e.g., disparate impact [7]), excluding other types of evaluations like usability measures. Through this study, we aim to clarify the need to include the demographic and domain-specific attributes of the stakeholders to understand their needs and preferences in more detail.

3   Method

Our research is a crowdsourcing study that explores which demographic attributes of participants affect their preferences for ML model evaluation metrics. First, we presented participants with a hypothetical job-matching scenario and asked them to select their preferred model output through a series of discrete choice tasks. This approach allowed us to capture their preferences as a balance of seven performance and fairness metrics using a utility funtion. Then, to address RQ1 "How are participants' preferences for ML performance metrics clustered?," we clustered their preference patterns and identified the characteristics of each cluster based on the seven metrics. After that, to answer RQ2 "What demographic attributes have a significant effect on the preferences clustered with our method?," we examined the relationship between the participants' demographic attributes and their clustered preferences using association analysis.

3.1   Procedure

We conducted our crowdsourcing research using Amazon Mechanical Turk (MTurk) with the following procedure. After consenting to the form, participants were shown the scenario. In the scenario, we described the current state of AI use in job-matching, presenting a hypothetical use case, as follows:

> In the United States, many employers and job seekers use job-matching websites. Currently, Artificial Intelligence (AI) systems support employers' decisions by showing an optimized list of candidates. An AI system uses applicants' resumes and CVs as training data to calculate its AI model to predict the possibility of matching. The training data for the AI model includes several attributes, such as applicants' education, job history, and skills. The AI system calculates the applicants' expertise based on the training data and predicts the likelihood of successful matching as "Likely to be hired" or "Not likely to be hired."

Participants were then asked to select one AI model from two options and repeated this process 20 times to accurately capture their preferences. During each selection task, participants were shown the 10 applicants' race, expertise, actual matching results, and prediction results from two ML models. We note that we used hypothetical ML model results, generated randomly, in the selection task instead of actual models trained with data. We used these hypothetical results to efficiently elicit participants' preferences.

We elaborate on this main task in 3.3. After completing the main task, we collected demographic information from the participants. This demographic data was used to investigate the relationship between stakeholders' attributes and their preferences, as detailed in Sect. 3.5.

To check whether participants paid appropriate attention, we inserted two attention-check questions: one after explaining the scenario and another after participants completed 10 out of the 20 main tasks. The first question asked, "We care about the quality of our survey data. For us to get the most accurate measures of your opinions, it is important that you provide thoughtful answers to each question in this survey. Do you commit to providing thoughtful answers to the questions in this survey?" Participants who answered "No" were excluded from the analysis. The second question asked, "Please click on one of the options such as Disagree. We want to test your attention, so please click on the answer Agree." Participants who missed this instruction were more likely to choose a wrong option, i.e., "Disagree." We excluded data from participants who answered these attention-check questions incorrectly (i.e., chose "disagree").

3.2 Participants

The participants are recruited through MTurk. We limit participants who live in the U.S. MTurk allows participants to complete tasks called 'Human Intelligence Tasks' (HITs). HITs are posted by providers who want to ask participants to help complete the tasks. Participants are paid once their work is approved. To ensure response quality, participants in our study had to complete at least 500 HITs with a 95% approval rate. The 500 HIT threshold was chosen based on prior research showing that participants with over 500 HITs tend to provide higher-quality responses than those with fewer [33]. The 95% approval rate is regarded as a standard for ensuring high-quality responses in MTurk studies [21,26,33]. Our study was conducted from 20th to 23rd December 2022. We compensated the participants US$2.42 for their time. This amount is based on the estimated average time to complete the survey, which was 20 min according to a pilot study. Using the U.S. minimum wage of US$7.25 per hour, we calculated the compensation proportionally for the estimated 20 min, which resulted in US$2.42. After the experiment, the actual average time to complete the survey was 18.2 min (*standard deviation (SD)* = 34.50), meaning the participants were paid slightly more than the minimum wage. This approach is consistent with other studies that also use the U.S. minimum wage as a baseline [21,42]. 1100 people responded to the survey. We omitted 263 participants in total, leaving 837 valid entries. These omissions included participants who did not finish the survey ($N = 14$) and those whose reCAPTCHA scores[1], which range from 0 to 1, were under 0.5, suggesting potential bot responses ($N = 22$). The median reCAPTCHA score was 1.0, and only 12 participants in valid entries had scores under 0.8, indicating that the vast majority of participants were likely human. We also omitted participants who gave contradictory answers to multiple choice questions ($N = 38$) and those who failed the attention-check questions ($N = 189$).

Next, we show the demographic information of participants as follows. The largest age group was 25–34 years old (62.1%), and the second largest was 35–44 years old (20.3%). For other age groups, 18–24 was 3.3%, 45–54 was 8.2%, 55–64 was 5.4%, 65+ was 0.6%. Those identifying themselves as female were 33.2%, and as male were

---

[1] reCAPTCHA is an optional function of Qualtrics, an online service used to create and distribute the survey. See the documents on reCAPTCHA Enterprise for details about the reCAPTCHA score. https://cloud.google.com/recaptcha-enterprise.

66.8%. No one identified themselves as 'gender non-binary' or 'others not listed.' For the ethnic group, 89.0% were White, 3.1% were African American, 2.0% were Asian, 1.7% were Hispanic, 4.2% were Native American or Alaska Native, and there were no Native Hawaiians or Pacific Islanders. Regarding income, 6.3% earned 'less than $25,000,' 28.2% earned '$25,000 to $49,999,' 32.7% earned '$50,000 to $74,999,' 25.2% earned '$75,000 to $99,999,' 6.0% earned '$100,000 to $149,999,' and 1.6% earned '$150,000 or more.' The demographic attributes obtained are adapted from the questionnaire used in the previous studies [21, 22, 43].

Additionally, we asked the information on the participants possibly related to our scenario. First, for the participants' work situations, all the participants were employed: 96.3% had a full-time job, 2.9% had a part-time job, and 0.8% were students with full-time jobs. Their occupations were dominated by a few categories: 36.9% were professional, 34.2% were managerial, and 18.8% were self-employed. Regarding education level, most had a '4-year degree' (66.2%), and the second largest group had a 'professional degree' (14.2%). Other groups were 'high school graduates' (12.1%), 'less than high school' (2.2%), 'some college' (3.8%), and '2-year degree' (1.6%). Thus, 82.0% of the participants were above '2-year degree,' which means they were well educated. Regarding political affiliation, 39.5% of the participants were Republicans, 49.0% were Democrats, and 11.4% were Independent.

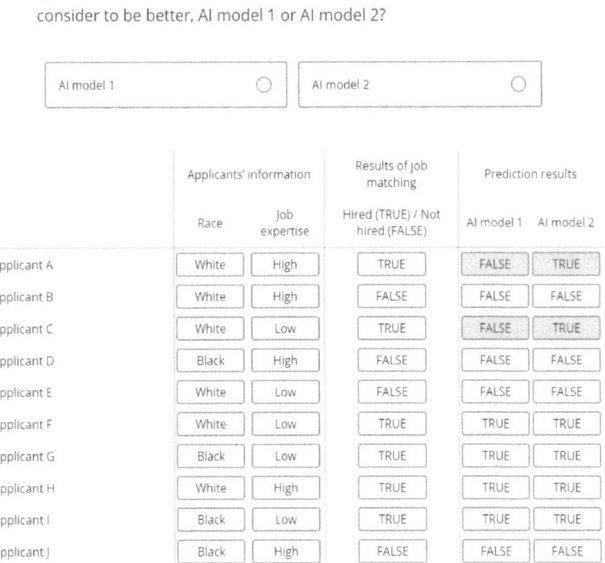

Fig. 1. Discrete choice task: ten job applicants' information, race as Black or White, expertise as high or low, and actual results of matching as hired (true) or not hired (false), with the prediction results of two hypothetical ML models. Only two rows had different sets (with a yellow background for emphasis) to reduce cognitive overload. Both rows and values were randomized in each task. (Color figure online)

3.3   Main Task

For the main task, we showed participants information about ten job applicants along with the prediction results of two hypothetical ML models. We then asked them to choose the better of the two models. Participants made this choice twenty times, each time with a different combination of ML models. This allowed us to calculate each participant's preference using a utility function based on the discrete choice model while also avoiding cognitive overload. Figure 1 shows a question presented to the participants in this task. In the question, applicants' race, job expertise, results of job-matching, and prediction results from hypothetical ML models 1 and 2 are shown. For "race," there were two values, i.e., Black and White. For "job expertise," there were also two values, i.e., "high", which indicates the applicant was qualified for the job in terms of job experience and certifications, and "low", which means the applicant was less qualified for the job. For "results of job-matching," there were two values, i.e., TRUE and FALSE, which are based on the actual results of past job-matching. TRUE means the applicant was hired, and FALSE means they were not hired. Finally, the "Prediction results" from the two ML models (ML model 1 and ML model 2) were shown. These models predict the job-matching results using applicants' race, education, job experience, job history, and skills. The prediction results were shown as TRUE (likely to be hired) or FALSE (not likely to be hired).

In our setting, participants were asked to compare two AI models and choose the one with better results. However, these two models do not actually exist. Instead, we created the questions by randomly selecting two out of ten applicants and making their prediction results differ between "AI model 1" and "AI model 2." The true or false values for these predictions were determined randomly. The remaining eight rows were consistent with the "Results of job-matching" column. This setup allowed us to observe participants' reactions to the differing results and calculate their preferences using a utility function.

3.4   Utility Function

Performance Metrics. On the basis of the responses to the questionnaire, we calculated the participants' preferences as the set of preference values for ML metrics. The metrics are categorized into performance metrics and fairness metrics. As performance metrics, we use accuracy, specificity (or true-negative rates), sensitivity (or recall), and precision. As fairness metrics, we used disparate impact (DI), equality of opportunity (EO), and counterfactual fairness (CF). We give details of these seven metrics as follows:

Accuracy: Accuracy is a metric that indicates how well the overall prediction results match the true values. In this study, accuracy is calculated as the sum of the applicants who were correctly predicted divided by the total number of applicants. There are two types of correct prediction; where an applicant was predicted as 'TRUE (likely to be hired)', i.e., true positive, and where an applicant was predicted as 'FALSE (NOT likely to be hired)', i.e., true negative.

Specificity (or True Negative Rates): Specificity is a metric that expresses the percentage of cases predicted to be negative among true negative cases. In this study, specificity is calculated as the ratio of the number of applicants correctly predicted as FALSE to the total number of applicants who actually were NOT hired (FALSE).

Sensitivity (or Recall, True Positive Rate): Sensitivity is a metric that expresses the percentage of cases predicted to be positive among true positive cases. In this study, sensitivity is calculated as the ratio of the number of applicants correctly predicted as TRUE to the total number of applicants who actually were hired (TRUE).

Precision: Precision is a metric that expresses the ratio of true positive cases among the predicted positive cases. In this study, precision is calculated as the ratio of the number of applicants correctly predicted as TRUE to the total number of applicants who were predicted as TRUE.

DI: DI is a group fairness metric that evaluates whether the probability of being judged as a positive case is not unfairly low for people in protected groups. In this study, DI is calculated as the ratio of the proportion of Black applicants (regarded as an underprivileged group) who obtained a favorable outcome (TRUE prediction) to the proportion of White applicants (regarded as a privileged group) who obtained a favorable outcome [7]. When we denote the protected attributes as r (where $r = b$ for Black and $r = w$ for White), DI is as follows:

$$DI = \frac{P(\hat{y} = 1 | r = b)}{P(\hat{y} = 1 | r = w)} \tag{1}$$

Here, $\hat{y} = 1$ denotes the predicted label indicating a favorable outcome. When $DI = 1$, the model is thought of as completely fair with respect to the protected attribute.

EO: EO is a group fairness metric that evaluates whether the probability of being judged as a positive case is not unreasonably low among people with positive labels and in protected groups. In this study, EO is calculated as the ratio of the probability of Black applicants (underprivileged group) correctly predicted as TRUE in the total number of Black applicants who actually were hired to the probability of White applicants (privileged group) of correctly predicted as TRUE in the total number of White applicants who actually were hired [12]. When we denote the protected attributes as r, EO is as follows:

$$EO = \frac{P(\hat{y} = 1 | r = b, y = 1)}{P(\hat{y} = 1 | r = w, y = 1)} \tag{2}$$

Here, $y = 1$ represents the actual label if the applicant is hired (TRUE). When $EO = 1$, the model is thought of as completely fair with respect to the protected attribute.

CF: CF is an individual fairness metric that evaluates whether similar individuals receive similar outcomes. In our study, CF is defined as the ratio of applicants whose job expertise is high and predicted as TRUE to the total number of applicants. This is because, in the concept of individual fairness, an ML model is fair if it gives similar predictions to similar individuals [20]. The applicants should be determined only by their job expertise, not by their demographic attributes. Therefore, if "Job expertise"="High", then the prediction of the model $\hat{y}$ should be 1.

Here, we pick group fairness metrics, i.e., DI and EO, because it is possible that there are differences in the awareness of employees' interests between direct recipients of the decisions, i.e., employees and employers. For example, while employees might prioritize these fairness metrics, employers do not prioritize them to the same extent. Additionally, the individual fairness metric, CF, is chosen because it is assumed that highly skilled participants might prioritize occupational suitability and believe that fairness should be determined solely on the basis of job competence.

Additionally, please note that there are trade-offs between some metrics while others overlap. For instance, specificity and sensitivity (recall) are in trade-off relations [12,37]. Recall (sensitivity) and precision are also in trade-off relations. However, accuracy may increase when specificity (true negative rates), sensitivity (recall), or precision increases. We used the essential metrics for both performance and fairness to determine a participant's nuanced preferences.

Discrete Choice Model. To calculate the participants' preferences, we used the discrete choice model [19,24] to calculate the preferences to maximize the utility for each participant on the basis of their choices of models. When participant i chooses model j, the utility function U_{ij} should satisfy the following inequality:

$$U_{ij} > U_{ik} \quad \forall j \neq k \tag{3}$$

In the discrete choice model U_{ij} is expressed as follows:

$$U_{ij} = V_{ij} + \epsilon_{ij} \tag{4}$$

where V_{ij} is the deterministic (observed) part and ϵ_{ij} is the random (unobserved) part. In this study, V_{ij} was a function of observed variables x_{ij} (accuracy as Acc, specificity as Spe, sensitivity as Sen, precision as Pre, and DI, EO, CF):

$$V_{ij} = \alpha + \beta_{Acc_i} x_{Acc_{ij}} + \beta_{Spe_i} x_{Spe_{ij}} + \beta_{Sen_i} x_{Sen_{ij}}$$
$$+ \beta_{Pre_i} x_{Pre_{ij}} + \beta_{DI_i} x_{DI_{ij}} + \beta_{EO_i} x_{EO_{ij}} + \beta_{CF_i} x_{CF_{ij}} \tag{5}$$

The parameters β are the preference values of the seven metrics and the same for all models within each individual, and x_{ij} are the metric values of the jth model that participant i selects. For example, when there are only two models, ML model 1 and ML model 2, the likelihood of participant i choosing ML model 1, L_{i1}, is as follows:

$$L_{i1} = Prob.[U_{i1}] = \frac{\exp\{U_{i1}\}}{\sum_{k=1}^{2} \exp\{U_{ik}\}}, \tag{6}$$

The log-likelihood L_i of participant i after the lth tasks ($l = 1, \ldots, 20$) is defined as the product of the likelihood of single selection L_{ij}, which we denote as

$$L_i = \log \prod_{l=1}^{20} L_{ij} \tag{7}$$

Estimation of the discrete choice model is based on a maximum likelihood procedure to find the parameters of β, the preference values of the seven metrics, that maximize L_i.

3.5   Data Analysis

K–Means Cluster Analysis. To investigate the patterns in participants' preferences, we clustered the preferences with k-means clustering [14]. In k-means clustering, k points are first selected as initial centroids in the feature space. As the feature space, we set the 7-dimensional space consisting of the preferences for seven performance ML metrics, i.e., the preferences for accuracy, specificity, sensitivity, precision, DI, EO, and CF. The k clusters are then formed by assigning each data point to its closest centroid. In this study, the data points were the preferences of the participants ($N = 837$). The centroid of each cluster is next moved to the center of the points that belong to each centroid. Forming clusters and computing centroids are then repeated until the positions of centroids stop moving. Through the clusters resulting from k-means clustering, we analyzed the patterns of preferences for performance metrics. Using the patterns, we analyzed the distinctive demographic attributes of participants when the preferences were divided into clusters.

In k-means clustering, we initially have to set the number of clusters k. We use the elbow method to determine k [4]. With this method, the ideal number of groups is determined as the number at which, if more groups are added, there is no significant difference in the reduction of variance within groups. We used the Python scikit-learn library with the default setting to apply the k-means clustering algorithm and elbow method[2]. With the library, we identified that $k = 5$ is the ideal number of clusters.

Association Analysis. In this study, we use association analysis to explore the relationships between participants' demographic attributes and clusters. Association analysis is a data mining technique that is used to discover relationships between items within a dataset [16,25]. Out of this technique, we used lift values as our evaluation metric. Lift values provide a measure of how strongly two items are associated. In our case, we investigate how one value in the demographic attributes is associated with a specific cluster to analyze the relationship between participants' demographic attributes and clusters. In other words, we consider a value in participants' demographic attributes and a specific cluster as two different items.

The formula for calculating the lift value is as follows:

$$\text{Lift}(A, B) = \frac{P(A \cap B)}{P(A)P(B)} \tag{8}$$

where $P(A \cap B)$ is the probability of both A and B occurring together, $P(A)$ is the probability of A occurring, and $P(B)$ is the probability of B occurring [25]. If the lift value is greater than 1, it suggests that items A and B have a positive association with each other [16]. Conversely, a lift value less than 1 indicates a negative association

---

[2] https://www.scikit-yb.org/en/latest/api/cluster/elbow.html.

between the items. By using the lift value as a measure, we can quantify the strength of the relationship between a specific value in participants' demographic attributes and a cluster, leading to a more structured analysis.

It is important to note that there is no universal benchmark that indicates a significant "high" or "low" lift value. In our analysis, we set threshold values at 0.750 for low lift value and 1.250 for high lift value for interpreting lift values, aiming to identify strong and weak associations between demographic attributes and clusters. These thresholds were chosen to capture attributes that deviate by at least 25% from a lift value of 1, which would indicate no association. This approach allows for a comprehensive interpretation of the data, particularly when considering the influence of smaller cluster sizes. In this study, a high lift value indicates that a particular attribute increases the likelihood of being in that cluster by a factor corresponding to the lift value. For example, a lift value of 2 would mean that the attribute doubles the probability of a participant belonging to that cluster.

4   Results

We first summarize the clustering results and then examine the demographic differences between clusters using the association analysis.

4.1   K–Means Cluster Analysis

As a result of k-means clustering, we obtained five clusters, A-E, as shown in Fig. 2. Cluster A had the most participants ($N = 377$), and the second largest cluster was cluster B ($N = 368$). Clusters C, D, and E had 41, 29, and 22 participants, respectively. Each bar in the figure represents each cluster. The horizontal axis shows the names of clusters. The vertical axis shows the normalized preference values. The preference value of a participant for each performance metric was normalized by dividing preference values by the maximum absolute value of the preference and setting the maximum absolute value of the preference to 1. The preference value of each cluster was calculated as the average preference value for each performance metric of participants who were assigned to each cluster. In Fig. 2, for example, almost all the participants in cluster B prioritized precision.

In the clustering result, there are two prominent patterns. As the first pattern, the participants in the largest two clusters, A and B, did not show any specific tendencies for fairness metrics, i.e., DI, EO, and CF. The participants in A and B did not prioritize nor trivialize fairness metrics. On the other hand, the two clusters had opposite tendencies for the other performance metrics, i.e., accuracy, specificity, sensitivity, and precision. The participants in cluster A prioritized specificity and trivialized precision. In contrast, participants in cluster B prioritized precision and trivialized specificity.

As the second pattern, the participants in clusters C, D, and E had specific tendencies for the fairness metrics. The participants in cluster C prioritized EO and CF and trivialized DI. In contrast, the participants in cluster D trivialized CF and EO, while they did not seem to have a specific tendency in preference for DI. The participants in cluster E trivialized EO, prioritized DI, and did not have a strong tendency toward CF.

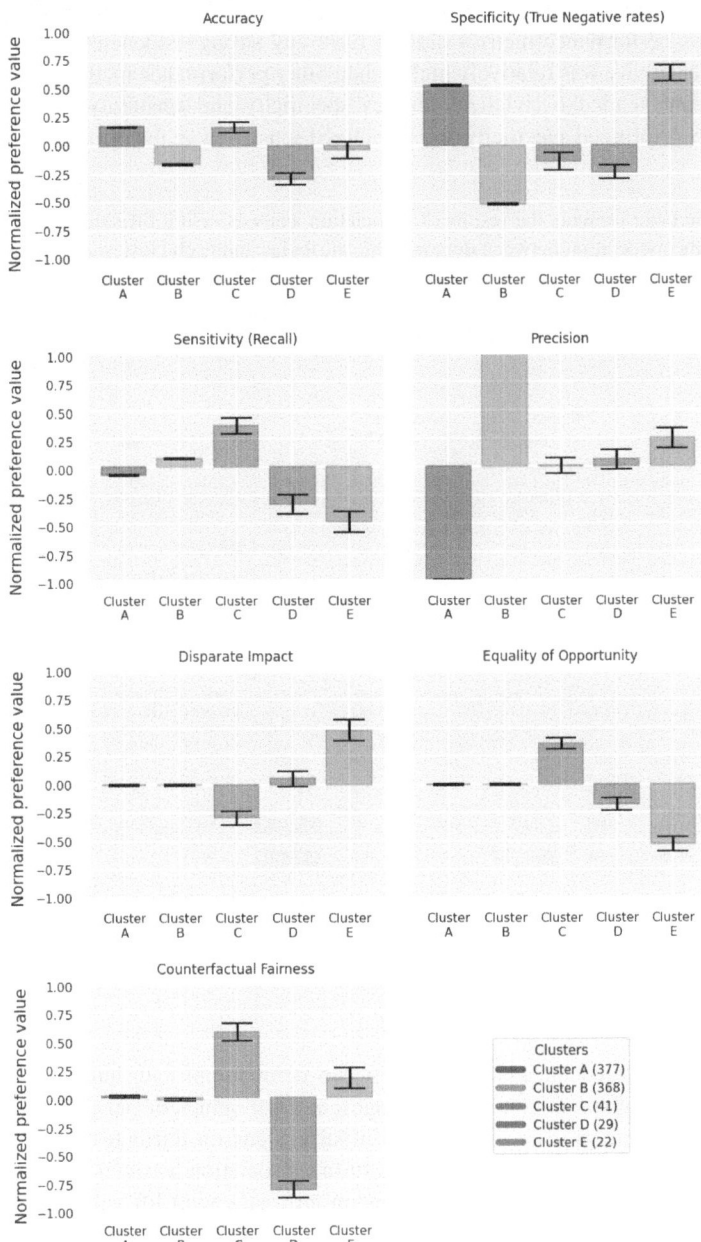

Fig. 2. Result of k-means clustering. Each color represents the average preference value of participants assigned to each cluster. The vertical axis represents preference values that have been normalized to a range of −1 to 1. Error bars indicate standard error.

These three clusters were also different in their preference values for other performance metrics. In cluster C, although the participants' preference values for almost all of the non-fairness performance metrics did not have any strong tendencies, the preference value for sensitivity was relatively higher than other performance metrics. In cluster D, the participants tended to trivialize accuracy, specificity, and sensitivity. In cluster E, the participants prioritized specificity and trivialized sensitivity at the same level as EO.

Table 1. The table presents the results of association analysis, using lift values to quantify the strength of the association between demographic attributes and each cluster. A lift value greater than 1 indicates a positive association between the attribute and the cluster, while a value smaller than 1 indicates a negative association. Cells with lift values below 0.750 are highlighted in light gray, and cells with lift values greater than 1.250 are highlighted in dark gray with white text for emphasis.

Clusters		Work status		Education level		Programming years		Income	
		Employee	Employer	2 years or less	4 years or more	5 years or less	More than 5 years	High	Low
A (N=377)	count (%)	168 (44.6%)	209 (55.4%)	77 (20.4%)	300 (79.6%)	246 (65.3%)	131 (34.7%)	113 (30%)	264 (70%)
	lift value	0.947	1.047	1.042	0.990	1.011	0.979	0.916	1.041
B (N=368)	count (%)	179 (48.6%)	189 (51.4%)	72 (19.6%)	296 (80.4%)	246 (66.8%)	122 (33.2%)	122 (33.2%)	246 (66.8%)
	lift value	1.033	0.970	0.999	1.000	1.036	0.934	1.013	0.994
C (N=41)	count (%)	18 (43.9%)	23 (56.1%)	4 (9.8%)	37 (90.2%)	18 (43.9%)	23 (56.1%)	13 (31.7%)	28 (68.3%)
	lift value	0.933	1.060	0.498	1.122	0.680	1.581	0.969	1.015
D (N=29)	count (%)	15 (51.7%)	14 (48.3%)	4 (13.8%)	25 (86.2%)	16 (55.2%)	13 (44.8%)	12 (41.4%)	17 (58.6%)
	lift value	1.099	0.912	0.704	1.072	0.855	1.263	1.264	0.872
E (N=22)	count (%)	14 (63.6%)	8 (36.4%)	7 (31.8%)	15 (68.2%)	14 (63.6%)	8 (36.4%)	14 (63.6%)	8 (36.4%)
	lift value	1.352	0.687	1.624	0.848	0.986	1.025	1.944	0.541
Total (N=837)	count (%)	394 (47.1%)	443 (52.9%)	164 (19.6%)	673 (80.4%)	540 (64.5%)	297 (35.5%)	274 (32.7%)	563 (67.3%)

Clusters		Age		Gender		Race		Political affiliation		
		18 to 44	45 or more	Female	Male	Non-White	White	Democrat	Republican	Other
A (N=377)	count (%)	319 (84.6%)	58 (15.4%)	120 (31.8%)	257 (68.2%)	43 (11.4%)	334 (88.6%)	180 (47.7%)	153 (40.6%)	44 (11.7%)
	lift value	0.986	1.082	0.958	1.021	1.038	0.995	0.975	1.026	1.018
B (N=368)	count (%)	323 (87.8%)	45 (12.2%)	130 (35.3%)	238 (64.7%)	34 (9.2%)	334 (90.8%)	184 (50%)	143 (38.9%)	41 (11.1%)
	lift value	1.023	0.860	1.064	0.968	0.841	1.020	1.021	0.971	
C (N=41)	count (%)	36 (87.8%)	5 (12.2%)	14 (34.1%)	27 (65.9%)	5 (12.2%)	36 (87.8%)	23 (56.1%)	14 (34.1%)	4 (9.8%)
	lift value	1.024	0.858	1.028	0.986	1.109	0.986	1.145	0.863	0.851
D (N=29)	count (%)	24 (82.8%)	5 (17.2%)	8 (27.6%)	21 (72.4%)	6 (20.7%)	23 (79.3%)	12 (41.4%)	13 (44.8%)	4 (13.8%)
	lift value	0.965	1.213	0.831	1.084	1.882	0.891	0.845	1.134	1.203
E (N=22)	count (%)	16 (72.7%)	6 (27.3%)	6 (27.3%)	16 (72.7%)	4 (18.2%)	18 (81.8%)	11 (50%)	8 (36.4%)	3 (13.6%)
	lift value	0.848	1.918	0.821	1.089	1.654	0.919	1.021	0.920	1.189
Total (N=837)	count (%)	718 (85.8%)	119 (14.2%)	278 (33.2%)	559 (66.8%)	92 (11%)	745 (89%)	410 (49%)	331 (39.5%)	96 (11.5%)

4.2   Association Analysis by Lift Value

Our analysis explored the association between demographic attributes and the clusters. Table 1 shows the numbers, percentages, and lift values of participants who had each attribute value in each cluster. We initially focus on attributes with lift values greater than 1.250 because these indicate a strong association between the demographic attributes and the clusters. Then, we focus on attributes with lift values below 0.750 to identify negative associations with the clusters. Note that except for the work status, there were imbalances in the distribution of participants across attributes. Political affiliation and gender did not show a positive or negative association with any of the clusters.

Although most attributes in clusters A and B had lift values close to 1, indicating a weak association, clusters C, D, and E showed various tendencies in lift values. Cluster

C was associated with more programming years (lift value of 1.581). On the negative side, cluster C had a low lift value of 0.498 for participants with "2 years or less" of education and 0.680 for fewer programming years, suggesting a negative association with these attributes. Cluster D had an association with more programming years (1.263) and high income (1.264). The cluster also had a strong association with a non-white racial background (1.882). On the other hand, it had a low lift value of 0.704 for participants with "2 years or less" of education, suggesting a negative association. Cluster E was diverse in its associations. It had positive lift values for being an employee in work status (1.352). Also, low educational level (1.624), high income (1.944), older age (1.918), and non-white (1.654) are related to the cluster. On the negative side, cluster E showed a lift value of 0.541 for participants with low income and 0.687 for those who are employers.

5 Discussion

We discuss our results from the perspectives of our research questions. We then discuss the implications and limitations of our study.

5.1 Preferences for Metrics

To address RQ1, we clustered participants' preferences with k-means clustering (Fig. 2). The graphs of clusters A and B were seemingly in contrast. The participants in cluster A trivialized precision and prioritized specificity and accuracy, while those in cluster B showed the opposite tendency. While clusters C and E did not indicate a clear difference in pattern compared to clusters A and B, clusters C and E seemed to be in contrast to the preferences for sensitivity, DI, and EO. Cluster D, however, did not show a contrasting pattern from the others, yet it trivialized CF the most among all clusters.

Some of these tendencies are based on the relationship among the seven performance metrics. The relationships between sensitivity (or recall) and specificity are in a trade-off relation. If sensitivity increases, specificity decreases, and vice versa. This suggests that there are similarities in the tendencies of clusters A and E, i.e., relatively high preference values for specificity and relatively low preference values for sensitivity, and clusters B, and C, i.e., the opposite tendency to clusters A and E for the preferences for specificity and sensitivity. Note that EO is a measure of the demographic parity of sensitivity. Therefore, a participant can prioritize sensitivity and EO simultaneously. This suggests that it is natural that, in all clusters, the preferences for sensitivity and EO are similar. Therefore, it was difficult to determine whether the participants prioritized or trivialized sensitivity or EO on the basis of only this analysis.

Overall, the participants' preferences for metrics were divided into recognizable patterns. The main pattern was whether the participants had specific preferences for the fairness metrics (clusters, C, D, and E), or not (clusters A and B). The majority of the participants were in the clusters A and B. In the clusters in which the participants had specific preferences for fairness metrics, different clusters had different preferences for each fairness metric. Clusters C and D had opposite tendencies, especially toward CF. Additionally, despite DI being one of the most well-known fairness metrics [2], only the participants in cluster E tended to prioritize DI. It is also notable that the participants in the clusters without any specific preference for fairness had opposite tendencies to precision and specificity.

5.2 Demographic Attributes

To address RQ2, we compared the differences in demographic attributes between clusters using association analysis. We analyzed the relationship between demographic attributes and clusters, as detailed in Table 1. Clusters C, D, and E are particularly noteworthy because they showed distinct patterns in both fairness metrics and demographic attributes.

Our analysis shows that educational attributes influence membership in cluster C. Specifically, having a lower education level reduces the likelihood of being in cluster C by half (lift value of 0.498). Similarly, having fewer programming years decreases the likelihood by over 25% (lift value of 0.680). On the other side, more programming years increase the likelihood of being in cluster C by more than 1.5 times (lift value of 1.581). This suggests that cluster C is associated with educational and programming experience. Most participants in this cluster prioritize CF and are experienced programmers. This trend suggests that individuals who believe that job expertise should determine hiring are actually skilled. Additionally, this cluster also prioritizes sensitivity, along with the EO, which aims to reduce false negatives. This shows the idea of making fewer errors to ensure that qualified candidates get hired. The trivialization of DI by this cluster suggests that the cluster does not place emphasis on racial disparities in the likelihood of being predicted to be hired.

Regarding cluster D, having lower education levels reduces the likelihood of belonging to cluster D by over 25% (lift value of 0.704). On the other hand, being a non-white individual increases the likelihood of belonging in this cluster by more than 1.8 times (lift value of 1.882). Participants in cluster D tend to trivialize CF and EO, and they did not show a clear preference for DI. This suggests that people in this cluster may not believe that higher job expertise should be the only reason for getting hired. Similarly, the trivialization of EO suggests they may not be concerned with reducing false negatives. They also trivialize specificity. This suggests they are not focused on minimizing false positives. Since they do not clearly prefer any other metrics, there is room for interpretation. For instance, they might believe that hiring decisions should not be based solely on attributes like race and expertise.

Participants in cluster E prioritize DI, trivialize EO, and show a relatively small trend for CF while also prioritizing specificity. The preference for DI suggests they are concerned about racial disparities in the likelihood of being hired. The trivialization of EO indicates they are not aiming to reduce false positives. On the other hand, prioritizing specificity implies they want to minimize the risk of hiring unsuitable candidates. Demographic attributes positively associated with this cluster include being an employee (lift value of 1.352), having a lower level of education (1.624), higher income (1.944), older age (1.918), and being non-white (1.654). Being low-income halves the likelihood of belonging to this cluster (0.541), and being an employer reduces it to 0.687. The prioritization of specificity suggests they may be seeking a beneficial state for employers by reducing the risk of false positives. The high lift values for higher income and older age indicate that they might hold higher job responsibilities. However, these lift values should be interpreted cautiously, especially considering the small size of cluster E, which has only 22 participants.

5.3   Minority Group

In this study, we emphasize examining preferences within both majority and minority groups because the focus of this study is to give due consideration to minority opinions. Utilitarian methods, such as averaging preferences, may be sufficient for calculating the total utility of all stakeholders. However, in the context of fairness, it is critical to focus on demographic minorities and explore ways to secure their interests. Utilitarian approaches to aggregating preferences could inadvertently marginalize minority groups if the majority does not consider fairness metrics.

We observed clear differences among majority and minority groups in their preferences for metrics and tendencies in demographic attributes. Clusters A and B, the majority clusters, consist of 89% of the participants, and they show interest only in performance metrics. Cluster A prioritizes precision and trivializes specificity, while cluster B does the opposite. Both clusters aim to reduce false positives but differ in whether they want to increase true positives or true negatives. On the other hand, minority groups, represented by clusters C, D, and E, are generally concerned with fairness. Related to the tendencies in demographic attributes, cluster C correlates with education level and programming years, possibly explaining a preference for individual fairness CF. Additionally, cluster D is associated with education level, programming years, and race, and cluster E is associated with work status, educational level, income, age, and race. These tendencies in demographic attributes clarify that it is effective to pay attention to demographic attributes when characterizing minority clusters. On the other hand, it should also be noted that the smaller size of minority groups poses challenges for detailed quantitative analysis.

5.4   Implications Towards Multi-Stakeholder ML Evaluation

Checking Attributes That Represent Minorities in ML Model Evaluation. When evaluating ML models with multiple stakeholders, it should be checked if there are specific attributes that represent the minority group in the sense that their evaluation of the ML model differs from others. This is because the results of this study indicate that stakeholder preferences can be clustered and that general demographic attributes and domain-specific attributes such as work status are associated with the tendencies in minority clusters.

Explain to the Group That Gives Different Evaluations to the ML Model to Make Them Aware of the Different Values. When it is necessary to balance the trade-offs between each cluster's preferences, different explanations should be provided in a way that balances preferences. Our results indicate that many people are generally more interested in performance than fairness metrics. To ensure group or individual fairness, we may need to explain the importance of improving fairness metrics to such people.

There also may be different attributes among those who have specific preferences for fairness metrics.

Recruit a Diverse Group of People When Evaluating ML Models. The diversity of the people who evaluate ML models relates directly to the output of the evaluation. And to ensure the diversity of those who evaluate models leads to a fair model evaluation process. In the domain of job-matching, it is important to recruit diverse evaluators regarding programming years or income, as revealed in our experiment. For example, the results of this study indicate that those who prioritize applicants with higher skills tend to be those with more programming years, while those who prioritize group fairness tend to be those with higher incomes. The former, in particular, aligns with the commonly observed tendency to favor people with attributes similar to one's own. Based on this results, because it is difficult for people to ignore their own interests, diverse people should participate in the model evaluation.

5.5 Limitations and Future Work

Although our results indicate associations between clusters and demographic attributes, they do not clarify a causal relationship. We need to conduct a qualitative analysis to understand the reasons behind the participants' choices. This will help us interpret the reasons for the patterns of metric prioritization that we found.

This study did not comprehensively investigate all demographic attributes or all stakeholders. For example, we did not consider recruitment agents who use job-matching systems. Despite that, we successfully revealed that the relationship between clustering outcomes and demographic attributes involves not only work status (employee/employer), which is determined easily in the scenario of job-matching, but also other attributes, such as education level and programming years.

In our study, there was an imbalance in the age distribution of participants, with over 60% being in the 25–34 age group. In real-world job-matching systems, the proportion of older individuals would be larger [40]. This difference in age distribution could affect the clustering results. Therefore, it is important to consider the age distribution bias when generalizing the results of this study.

We found that 94.8% of participants had experience in developing one or more ML models. However, in real-world systems, it is likely that a larger proportion of individuals have limited knowledge of ML. Therefore, the clustering results or demographic biases within clusters could change if tested with a more representative sample.

We acknowledge that participants recruited via MTurk may have been motivated by financial compensation. This motivation might have led some participants to rush through the experiment by skipping the instructions or answering questions carelessly. As a result, this could introduce noise into the experiment results. To mitigate this issue, we included attention-check questions.

This study employed a scenario-based approach using hypothetical job-matching system. However, the motivation of participants in such a controlled environment may differ from that of individuals with real-world experience and interests in a job-matching system. In future work, we could target individuals such as employers and job seekers who are actively using job-matching services in order to confirm our the results of this study.

Next, this study was limited to collecting only basic demographic information. To identify the crucial demographic attributes for clustering participants, we need to carefully consider the appropriate attributes that ensure diversity among the participants. Similarly, the small sample size in minority clusters poses challenges for cross-validating these attributes, indicating a need for more robust methods to discover inter-attribute relationships. Future research should aim to include a larger and more diverse sample to validate these findings.

Finally, when considering the generalizability of the procedure and study results, one limitation is that the current procedure focuses only on two features (race and job expertise) with two values each. Real-world scenarios often involve multiple features with varying values. Applying our method to an ML model used for the classification task for three or more classes would require transforming the classification results into binary or significantly increasing the number of preference-extraction tasks to determine accurate individual preferences. For this purpose, it is crucial to consider how to transform the classification results into binary and how to address the cognitive load imposed by these modifications.

6 Conclusion

Toward evaluating ML systems, including the values of multiple stakeholders, we proposed a crowdsourcing method to investigate how the stakeholders' preferences for the metrics are clustered and with what attributes stakeholders in each cluster have. We conducted an experiment in the context of job-matching and obtained empirical results from 837 participants, clustered them with their preferences, and analyzed the tendencies in the participants' demographic attributes in each cluster. We found that there are clusters of the majority of people who have clear tendencies on the performance metrics, such as specificity or precision, and clusters of minority people who have characteristics of preference for the fairness metrics. To make multi-stakeholder evaluation more practical, it is crucial to develop the model of stakeholders based on their preferences for the metrics and the stakeholder groups based on their demographic attributes.

References

1. Ahn, Y., Lin, Y.R.: FairSight: visual analytics for fairness in decision making. IEEE Trans. Visual Comput. Graph. **26**(1), 1086–1095 (2020). https://doi.org/10.1109/TVCG.2019.2934262
2. Barocas, S., Selbst, A.D.: Big data's disparate impact. Calif. Law Rev. 671–732 (2016)
3. van Berkel, N., Goncalves, J., Russo, D., Hosio, S., Skov, M.B.: Effect of information presentation on fairness perceptions of machine learning predictors. In: Proceedings of the 2021 CHI Conference on Human Factors in Computing Systems. CHI 2021, Association for Computing Machinery, New York, NY, USA (2021). https://doi.org/10.1145/3411764.3445365
4. Bholowalia, P., Kumar, A.: EBK-Means: a clustering technique based on elbow method and k-means in WSN. Int. J. Comput. Appl. **105**(9) (2014)

5. Burke, R.D., Abdollahpouri, H., Mobasher, B., Gupta, T.: Towards multi-stakeholder util-ity evaluation of recommender systems. In: Cena, F., Desmarais, M.C., Dicheva, D. (eds.) UMAP (Extended Proceedings). CEUR Workshop Proceedings, vol. 1618. CEUR-WS.org (2016). http://ceur-ws.org/Vol-1618/SOAP_paper2.pdf
6. Cheng, H.F., et al.: Soliciting stakeholders' fairness notions in child maltreatment predic-tive systems. In: Proceedings of the 2021 CHI Conference on Human Factors in Computing Systems. CHI 2021, Association for Computing Machinery, New York, NY, USA (2021). https://doi.org/10.1145/3411764.3445308
7. Chouldechova, A.: Fair prediction with disparate impact: a study of bias in recidivism pre-diction instruments (2017)
8. Delecraz, S., Eltarr, L., Becuwe, M., Bouxin, H., Boutin, N., Oullier, O.: Responsible artifi-cial intelligence in human resources technology: an innovative inclusive and fair by design matching algorithm for job recruitment purposes. J. Responsible Technol. **11**, 100041 (2022)
9. Golbin, I., Lim, K.K., Galla, D.: Curating explanations of machine learning models for busi-ness stakeholders. In: 2019 Second International Conference on Artificial Intelligence for Industries (AI4I), pp. 44–49 (2019). https://doi.org/10.1109/AI4I46381.2019.00019
10. Greenwood, M., Anderson, E.: 'i used to be an employee but now i am a stakeholder': impli-cations of labelling employees as stakeholders. Asia Pac. J. Hum. Resour. **47**(2), 186–200 (2009). https://doi.org/10.1177/1038411109105441
11. Greenwood, M.R.: Community as a stakeholder: Focusing on corporate social and environ-mental reporting. J. Corp. Citzsh. **4**, 31–45 (2001). http://www.jstor.org/stable/jcorpciti.4. 31
12. Hardt, M., Price, E., Price, E., Srebro, N.: Equality of opportunity in supervised learning. In: Lee, D., Sugiyama, M., Luxburg, U., Guyon, I., Garnett, R. (eds.) Advances in Neural Infor-mation Processing Systems. vol. 29. Curran Associates, Inc. (2016). https://proceedings. neurips.cc/paper/2016/file/9d2682367c3935defcb1f9e247a97c0d-Paper.pdf
13. Harrison, G., Hanson, J., Jacinto, C., Ramirez, J., Ur, B.: An empirical study on the perceived fairness of realistic, imperfect machine learning models. In: Proceedings of the 2020 Confer-ence on Fairness, Accountability, and Transparency, pp. 392–402. FAT* 2020, Association for Computing Machinery, New York, NY, USA (2020). https://doi.org/10.1145/3351095. 3372831
14. Hartigan, J.A., Wong, M.A.: Algorithm as 136: a k-means clustering algorithm. J. Roy. Stat. Soc. Ser. C (Appl. Stat.) **28**(1), 100–108 (1979)
15. Holstein, K., Wortman Vaughan, J., Daumé, H., Dudik, M., Wallach, H.: Improving fair-ness in machine learning systems: what do industry practitioners need? In: Proceedings of the 2019 CHI Conference on Human Factors in Computing Systems, pp. 1–16. CHI 2019, Association for Computing Machinery, New York, NY, USA (2019). https://doi.org/10.1145/ 3290605.3300830
16. Hussein, N., Alashqur, A., Sowan, B.: Using the interestingness measure lift to generate association rules. J. Adv. Comput. Sci. Technol. **4**(1), 156 (2015)
17. Jordan, M.I., Mitchell, T.M.: Machine learning: trends, perspectives, and prospects. Science **349**(6245), 255–260 (2015)
18. Kim, M., Kim, S., Kim, J., Kim, Y.: Do stakeholder needs differ? - designing stakeholder-tailored explainable artificial intelligence (XAI) interfaces. Int. J. Hum. Comput. Stud. 103160 (2023). https://doi.org/10.1016/j.ijhcs.2023.103160, https://www.sciencedirect.com/ science/article/pii/S1071581923001696
19. Kjaer, T.: A review of the discrete choice experiment-with emphasis on its application in health care. Syddansk Universitet Denmark (2005)
20. Kusner, M.J., Loftus, J., Russell, C., Silva, R.: Counterfactual fairness. In: Advances in Neu-ral Information Processing Systems, vol. 30 (2017)

21. Lee, M.K.: Understanding perception of algorithmic decisions: fairness, trust, and emotion in response to algorithmic management. Big Data Soc. **5**(1), 2053951718756684 (2018)
22. Lee, M.K., Jain, A., Cha, H.J., Ojha, S., Kusbit, D.: Procedural justice in algorithmic fairness: leveraging transparency and outcome control for fair algorithmic mediation. Proc. ACM Hum.-Comput. Interact. **3**(CSCW) (2019). https://doi.org/10.1145/3359284
23. Lee, M.K., et al.: Webuildai: participatory framework for algorithmic governance. Proc. ACM Hum.-Comput. Interact. **3**(CSCW) (2019). https://doi.org/10.1145/3359283
24. McFadden, D.: Conditional logit analysis of qualitative choice behavior. Front. Econometrics (1974)
25. McNicholas, P., Murphy, T., O'Regan, M.: Standardising the lift of an association rule. Comput. Stat. Data Anal. **52**(10), 4712–4721 (2008)
26. Meyers, E.A., Walker, A.C., Fugelsang, J.A., Koehler, D.J.: Reducing the number of non-naïve participants in mechanical turk samples. Methods Psychol. **3**, 100032 (2020)
27. Miller, G.J.: Stakeholder roles in artificial intelligence projects. Project Leadersh. Soc. **3**, 100068 (2022)
28. Mitchell, M., et al.: Model cards for model reporting. In: Proceedings of the Conference on Fairness, Accountability, and Transparency, pp. 220–229. FAT* 2019, Association for Computing Machinery, New York, NY, USA (2019). https://doi.org/10.1145/3287560.3287596
29. Nakao, Y.: Toward human-in-the-loop AI fairness with crowdsourcing: effects of crowdworkers' characteristics and fairness metrics on AI fairness perception. In: The Tenth AAAI Conference on Human Computation and Crowdsourcing (HCOMP 2022) (Work-in-Progress) (2022). https://www.humancomputation.com/assets/wips_demos/HCOMP_2022_paper_2733.pdf
30. Nakao, Y., Strappelli, L., Stumpf, S., Naseer, A., Regoli, D., Gamba, G.D.: Towards responsible AI: a design space exploration of human-centered artificial intelligence user interfaces to investigate fairness. Int. J. Hum. Comput. Interact. **39**(9), 1762–1788 (2023)
31. Nakao, Y., Stumpf, S., Ahmed, S., Naseer, A., Strappelli, L.: Toward involving end-users in interactive human-in-the-loop AI fairness. ACM Trans. Interact. Intell. Syst. **12**(3) (2022). https://doi.org/10.1145/3514258
32. Narayanan, A.: Tutorial: 21 fairness definitions and their politics - youtube (2018). https://www.youtube.com/watch?v=jIXIuYdnyyk&list=WL&index=3&t=1633s. Accessed 02 Dec 2021
33. Peer, E., Vosgerau, J., Acquisti, A.: Reputation as a sufficient condition for data quality on amazon mechanical Turk. Behav. Res. Methods **46**, 1023–1031 (2014)
34. Pessach, D., Shmueli, E.: A review on fairness in machine learning. ACM Comput. Surv. **55**(3) (2022). https://doi.org/10.1145/3494672
35. Powers, D.M.: Evaluation: from precision, recall and f-measure to roc, informedness, markedness and correlation. arXiv preprint arXiv:2010.16061 (2020)
36. Preece, A.D., Harborne, D., Braines, D., Tomsett, R., Chakraborty, S.: Stakeholders in explainable AI. CoRR **abs/1810.00184** (2018). http://arxiv.org/abs/1810.00184
37. Rodolfa, K.T., Lamba, H., Ghani, R.: Empirical observation of negligible fairness-accuracy trade-offs in machine learning for public policy. Nat. Mach. Intell. **3**(10), 896–904 (2021)
38. Sokolova, M., Lapalme, G.: A systematic analysis of performance measures for classification tasks. Inf. Process. Manage. **45**(4), 427–437 (2009)
39. Srivastava, M., Heidari, H., Krause, A.: Mathematical notions vs. human perception of fairness: a descriptive approach to fairness for machine learning. In: Proceedings of the 25th ACM SIGKDD International Conference on Knowledge Discovery & Data Mining, pp. 2459–2468. KDD 2019, Association for Computing Machinery, New York, NY, USA (2019). https://doi.org/10.1145/3292500.3330664

40. United States Department of Labor: Percent distribution of the labor force by age and sex. https://www.dol.gov/agencies/wb/data/annual-data/percent-distribution-laborforce-age-sex. Accessed 13 Sept 2024

41. Wang, R., Harper, F.M., Zhu, H.: Factors influencing perceived fairness in algorithmic decision-making: algorithm outcomes, development procedures, and individual differences. In: Proceedings of the 2020 CHI Conference on Human Factors in Computing Systems, pp. 1–14. CHI 2020, Association for Computing Machinery, New York, NY, USA (2020). https://doi.org/10.1145/3313831.3376813

42. Whiting, M.E., Hugh, G., Bernstein, M.S.: Fair work: crowd work minimum wage with one line of code. In: Proceedings of the AAAI Conference on Human Computation and Crowdsourcing, vol. 7, pp. 197–206 (2019)

43. Yokota, T., Nakao, Y.: Toward a decision process of the best machine learning model for multi-stakeholders: a crowdsourcing survey method. In: Adjunct Proceedings of the 30th ACM Conference on User Modeling, Adaptation and Personalization, pp. 245–254. UMAP 2022 Adjunct, Association for Computing Machinery, New York, NY, USA (2022). https://doi.org/10.1145/3511047.3538033

44. Zheng, Y., Ghane, N., Sabouri, M.: Personalized educational learning with multi-stakeholder optimizations. In: Adjunct Publication of the 27th Conference on User Modeling, Adaptation and Personalization, pp. 283–289. UMAP 2019 Adjunct, Association for Computing Machinery, New York, NY, USA (2019). https://doi.org/10.1145/3314183.3323843

Current Design Practices in Applied Augmented Reality Research: A Methodological Review

Lukas D. Teutenberg$^{(\boxtimes)}$ (ID), Lukas R. G. Fitz (ID), and Jochen Scheeg

Department of Business and Management, Brandenburg University of Applied Sciences, Magdeburger Str. 50, 14770 Brandenburg an der Havel, Germany
{teutenbe,fitz,scheeg}@th-brandenburg.de

Abstract. Successful Augmented Reality (AR) solutions require high technology acceptance and desire among users. Applying appropriate design methodologies can enhance the development of desirable AR systems and help to streamline design research projects. This article presents a methodological literature review of 58 pertinent articles, exploring the representation of methodological design frameworks in currently applied AR research practice. In result, User-Centered Design was identified most frequently by a large margin. Though, it could be observed that most articles from the field of applied AR only marginally describe any design processes. Moreover, Human-Centered Design, Participatory Design and Value Sensitive Design were only scantily represented; less than half of the papers followed a Design Science Research or Action Design Research approach. Several implications for applied research and practice are derived from these findings and discussed together with future research opportunities. Overall, this study contributes to the refinement of methodological design practice in the field of applied AR research.

Keywords: Augmented reality · Design methods · Applied science · Literature review

1 Introduction

The rapid development of digital technologies has paved the way for groundbreaking innovations in multiple domains. One of these innovations is Augmented Reality (AR). By integrating computer-generated content onto the real world, AR offers remarkable possibilities. It has become widely applicable across multiple sectors, including education, health, entertainment, and manufacturing, and is continuously transforming the way people interact with both digital and physical environments [1]. Also from a business perspective, AR is becoming more relevant across various industries [2]. What is more, the number of users and revenue figures are forecasted to increase significantly within the next four years [3], indicating growing business potential. This growth can be interpreted as a general excitement and curiosity for the technology and as such underlines the relevance of scientific studies on AR. Previous research found that technology acceptance factors such as usability, usefulness, fun and productivity are essentially relevant for the success of AR solutions [4]. Individual and organizational readiness in

H. Plácido da Silva and P. Cipresso (Eds.): CHIRA 2024, CCIS 2370, pp. 131–146, 2025.
https://doi.org/10.1007/978-3-031-82633-7_9

the context of user-centric success factors were also highlighted for industrial AR use cases [5]. Thus, the successful deployment of AR systems hinges on the quality of the fit between users and technology, which therefore must be considered a fundamental requirement in AR system design processes [6]. Seeing that the development of new AR solutions is an ongoing research trend [7, 8] and that hyped topics like the metaverse are boosting AR as a bridge technology even more [9], appropriate design practices are set to play a crucial role for the future of the whole field. The research question (RQ) that motivates this research paper is: "What methodological design frameworks are currently employed in applied AR research?".

To tackle the RQ, this paper focuses on seven selected methodological design frameworks and presents a methodological literature review that synthesizes the representation of these frameworks in AR publications. By considering applied AR specifically, this study concretely addresses the tangible practice of AR artifact development described in research. The overall aim is to contribute to the continued refinement of AR system design practices, prospectively enhancing human experiences in a digitalized world.

2 Methodologies and Frameworks

To allow for an effective generation of value through design processes, specific techniques are required. The creation and research of such techniques is called "methodology" in the field of philosophy [10]. In the Information Systems (IS) field, "methodology" is rather understood as the outcome of technique-creation, hence, techniques are ready for IS researchers to be employed by choosing methodologies. In this sense, methodologies are often described using "frameworks", and, as the definitions are similar, the terms are often used synonymously [11].

The approach, also known as the principle, describes the philosophical mindset brought to the concept of design [12]. It describes the assumptions, values, and working practices taken by designers when deciding what frameworks to use or how to design them. An example for an approach would be the general mindset of integrating users into a design process. Frameworks set boundaries for the approach and formulate a general structure in which the philosophical fundamentals can be set into action [11]. They also determine rules and methods that can be applied to appropriately achieve the desired outcomes. This includes both methods and phases. Phases included in a framework usually determine the sequence of methods applied. Each phase is filled with different methods. Methods are systematic, predefined, and orderly sets of actions aimed at achieving specific subgoals that contribute to value generation [11]. They can be differentiated by various factors, such as being deterministic or nondeterministic, diverging or converging. To operationalize a method, different techniques are combined, culminating in a procedure. Such procedures serve as guidelines, indicating which techniques are to be applied to achieve a method's objective [11]. Techniques fundamentally generate a measurable outcome that is shaped and processed during the further phases and procedure [13]. It is important to acknowledge that not every approach requires a framework. If a designer is knowledgeable about the subject at hand, appropriate methods can be chosen without restrictions. In favor of clarity, the combined term "methodological design framework" (MDFW) is used in this paper to describe the idea of setting context-specific boundaries and workflows for a design process. However, the ontology will serve as a guideline for the methodological review in this paper when searching for indications of individual techniques, procedures, methods and frameworks in the body of literature.

3   Framework Selection

For this study, common MDFWs applied in IS research shall be included. To narrow the scope, they are considered common if the search string "MDFW name" AND "augmented reality" reaches more than 10,000 hits on Google Scholar. The following results were obtained (September 3rd (2023)):

- Design Thinking (DT); 15,600 hits
- User-Centered Design (UCD); 11,800 hits
- Participatory Design (PD); 11,000 hits

After the first three MDFW had been selected, they were used for orientation to include more frameworks that are compatible with the topic of AR and well-distinguishable from the former three. Implicitly, the following MDFW were additionally selected:

- Human-Centered Design (HCD); 7,200 hits
- Value Sensitive Design (VSD); 1.020 hits
- Design Science Research (DSR); 3,180 hits
- Action Design Research (ADR); 409 hits

Table 1 summarizes key characteristics of each MDFW and refers to fundamental literature behind each entity. In brief, DT requires an experimental, collaborative and human-centered mindset, as solutions are created iteratively in an error-friendly environment with human users as a main source of information in so-called needfinding phases that are embedded in thorough desk research, empirical investigations, findings synthesis, co-ideation and prototyping. Hence, DT attempts to methodologically boost human creativity capabilities and to foster the creation of innovative and desirable solutions UCD, on the other hand, prioritizes the needs, preferences, and feedback of users to create products and experiences that are intuitive, efficient, and enjoyable for them. HCD is closely related to both DT and UCD. But, while UCD is limited to users with specific roles in an organization or process, HCD takes fundamental human factors into account, such as personality traits, individual background, opinions or beliefs.

Highlighting human-centered aspects even more, VSD focuses on design that is compliant with moral values and ethics in a society and strives for a holistic understanding of the impact that design has on values and vice versa. DSR and ADR are exceptional MDFWs in this selection, as they both represent research frameworks with a clear purpose to guideline research projects. Therein, DSR proposes a scientific approach to design that strictly involves theoretical knowledge and rigor to create new design artifacts and extend design knowledge. On top of that, ADR combines research and practice utility, as it suggests designers to iteratively build, put into action and evaluate artifacts and implications for both design researchers and practitioners.

Table 1. Summary of MDFW concepts.

MDFW	Approach	Framework / Model	Techniques	Ref
ADR	Emphasizing theory-informed, generalizable solutions, reciprocal shaping, and constant, authentic evaluation throughout a collaborative and organically emergent design process	Four major phases which can be repeated iteratively: problem formulation, building-intervention-evaluation, reflection and learning, and formalization of learning	No specific techniques, but scientific rigor is premised; similar to DSR	[14]
DSR	Highlights artifact creation, relevant problem-solving, thorough artifact evaluation, verifiable research contributions, methodological rigor, design as solution-seeking, and clear research communication to diverse audiences	Entails identifying a problem from the body of knowledge and with scientific rigor, setting solution objectives, designing an artifact, demonstrating functionality, evaluating effectiveness, and communicating findings, with a continual, flexible approach to research and design phases	Commonly employs techniques such as qualitative artifact comparison, satisfaction surveys, and simulations, mathematical models and simulations	[15–17]
DT	Emphasis is put on iterative design with a strong focus on user integration, creativity, empathy, early errors and expanding expected possibilities	Many different frameworks exist, but in general: focus on identification of the problem, user/human-centered needfinding, synthesis into problem statements, ideation, solution prototyping and testing	No boundaries or limitations, but mainly user-oriented, enhancing creative thinking/ ideation and strong group work	[18–20]
HCD	Six principles: flexibility, interplay between technology and social expectations, prioritizing human needs, balancing technical and social aspects, acknowledging varied user knowledge, and intertwining planning and implementation	Balances socio-technological aspects through two iterative cycles: the first cycle focuses on stakeholder collaboration, while the second cycle targets consensus on system goals, planning, and implementing changes with designated stakeholders	No specified but with an emphasis on human-centered investigation techniques such as open or semi-structured interviews, personas, mutual brainstorming, dotmocracy, stakeholder analysis	[21, 22]
PD	Also known as Scandinavian approach or Co-Design; focuses on democratization of design and innovation with stakeholders by integrating them into all design-phases	Four scenarios are outlined: "Probe" for participant identification, "Prime" to deepen problem domain immersion, "Understanding" to enhance stakeholder insight, and "Generate" to devise ideas and concepts with future relevance	Includes open interviews, participant observations, scenarios, mock-ups, workshops, design games, case-cased and cooperative prototyping	[23, 24]
UCD	Aims to create a robust and intuitive solution for users based on their wants; no clear distinction between wants and needs; the solution should guide the user and have set boundaries to limit errors	Three phases: discovery, design and development; has a dual characteristic: it can be applied in both linear and iterative ways, depending on time constraints or practitioner preferences	Key techniques are field studies, usability evaluations, focus groups, user interviews and surveys	[25, 26]

(*continued*)

Table 1. (*continued*)

MDFW	Approach	Framework / Model	Techniques	Ref
VSD	Very strong emphasis on moral and ethics; twelve exemplary values are suggested to be considered in every artifact-review, with different severity-levels determined by the designers	Conceptual, empirical and technical investigation; each phase focuses on either redefining / re-estimating values, evaluating both technical and value measurements of the design, and lastly the analysis of conflicting technical issues	Six suggested techniques: emphasizing, identifying stakeholder values, stakeholder analysis, value scenarios, and value-oriented strategy development	[27–29]

4   Literature Review

In response to the RQ, a literature review is conducted to synthesize what components of the described MDFWs are present in IS research centered around AR system development. First, the search for literature will be described as well as decisions made along the journey. Afterwards, the extracted literature will be analyzed in regards of indications for applied MDFWs in the collected articles. The descriptive outcome is synthesized in a concept matrix [30], represented by Table 2 in this section.

4.1   Search Process

Initially, the following search string was defined for the literature search:

("augmented reality" OR "AR") AND ("development" OR "design" OR "implementation" OR "prototype") AND ("hardware" OR "software" OR "device" OR "system" OR "application")

In acknowledgement of pros and cons [31, 32], both IEEE Xplore (IEEEX) and Google Scholar (GS) were used as source databases for the literature search. This search strategy consciously aimed at a broad and interdisciplinary coverage of applied AR research projects from international AR scholars publishing in both conference proceedings and journal papers. All search results were filtered for English language and publication years 2018–2023. The search string and filters combined led to 3,570 total hits in IEEEX and 1,420,000 in GS (September 10th, 2023). To narrow the search in GS, the search string was optimized by adding 'AND ("real-world" OR "practical application")', which led to an outcome of 11,600 articles. Sorted by relevance, the first 5% (rounded) of hits, 180 IEEEX and 600 in GS, were manually processed as visualized in Fig. 1. 112 IEEEX and 510 GS articles were excluded, mainly because of titles and/or abstracts pointing at theoretical contributions such as "comparative analysis", "review", "theory building", "framework creation", "software architecture" or "approach to AR".

From the remaining articles, contents were screened for design process descriptions. Remarkably, another 23 IEEEX papers and 42 GS papers were excluded in this step, predominantly because they only detailed a static AR system "assembly" or "architecture" in system design sections or, minorly, because they still yielded entirely theoretical contributions such as method or framework development. Moreover, one duplicate was found and removed, leaving 45 and 47 GS papers to continue with. In the last step, besides

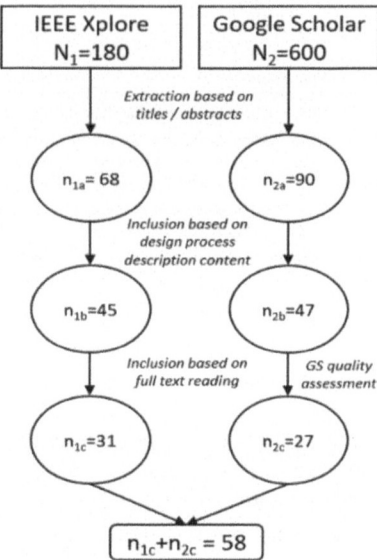

Fig. 1. Literature extraction process.

reading the so-far-included papers in full, the following quality criteria for handling GS-indexed papers in literature reviews [32] were applied: Can the document source be traced?; Is the document produced by an university/research institute, lab/scientific society/international organization?; Have the authors published elsewhere?; Can the results be reproduced? Finally, 31 IEEEX and 27 GS papers remained.

4.2 Results

Table 2 provides an overview of the 58 articles analyzed regarding MDFW indications. The articles were read again and the concept matrix was created following a mutual synthesis process involving three researchers. They identified some major indications for MDFW, that is, articles explicitly naming a framework and/or strictly following respective guidelines. Mostly however, minor MDFW indications were found, referring to articles that apply certain methods or techniques typical for certain MDFW but without naming or embedding them into a systematic design approach. As these articles still hold relevancy to this review, the researchers faced the challenge of how to integrate these minor findings whilst still differentiating them from the aforementioned major indications or mentions. To overcome this, a differentiation between major and minor indications of MDFWs in the articles was established. Three different symbols were integrated in the concept matrix, which describe the following:

X major MDFW indication
O minor MDFW indication based on indiv. Methods/techniques applied
– MDFW not indicated

Within the 58 articles, a total of 124 indications of MDFWs could be identified. 33 of these were identified as major and 91 as minor indications. Figure 2 shows the distribution of major and minor indications. With 56 markings, UCD is most strongly represented by a large margin. A frequent overlap between UCD and DT can be observed, often based on the use of techniques like user stories or user-centric interviewing. The fewest representations were found regarding PD and VSD with 7 and 8 indications respectively. HCD is similarly absent with 9 indications in the collected articles. Regarding design research frameworks, in spite of absences in two third of the articles, DSR was represented more often with 17 indications, compared to ADR with 9 markings.

In general, the full text analyses showed that most authors only designate a minimal amount of space to the description of design processes and tend to preferably focus on technical details such as hard-/software components, tools and assembly. The overall goal to "put together" AR systems seems to receive priority over systematically deriving design requirements or principles towards desirable solutions for human users.

5 Discussion

To start with a general remark about the reviewed literature, most authors do not focus on thoroughly describing their design process in AR development. Instead, they rather introduce the finished AR solution as a given, previously engineered artifact. Nevertheless, a large majority evaluates the technical capabilities of their AR solutions and involves prospective users in functional tests, leading to minor UCD indications. Given that AR is always used in specific contexts and by specific user groups, frequent UCD indications in the literature seem reasonable. On the other hand, ideation techniques, albeit seldomly applied, were often oriented to what users themselves described as necessary to solve a given problem.

Considering core reasons for choosing more human-centered approaches, this practice can be criticized for potentially leading to wrongful interpretations and missing out underlying user problems and needs. In the present review, some studies revolved around sensitive topics such pandemic control AR warning systems or supporting mentally disordered and visually-impaired users through AR – nevertheless, user-centered requirements were rather assumed than derived or inquired by integrating users. Involving a distinctive empathizing and needfinding phase, DT and HCD provide helpful techniques to complement such UCD approaches, which is also reflected by co-occurrences among UCD and DT in the present results.

Another noteworthy observation concerns the low utilization of ADR as a research framework. Although finding case organizations for prototypical design implementations is never a trivial task in applied sciences, which might explain the slight preference for DSR in the present results, the scientific evaluation of real-world usability and usefulness can be considered a crucial success factor that has yet been under-leveraged. ADR is a relatively new approach compared to the other MDFW examined, however, an important selling point for ADR is that whole research branches profit from useful insights generated out of each iteration. After all, the formalization of learning about problems and solutions derived from design-and-interventional experience may help to advance the entire AR research domain.

Table 2. Concept matrix of literature review findings (X - major MDFW indication; O - minor MDFW indication).

Ref	ADR	DSR	DT	HCD	PD	UCD	VSD
[33]	-	-	O	O	-	X	-
[34]	O	-	-	-	-	O	-
[35]	-	-	O	-	X	O	-
[36]	-	-	O	-	-	X	-
[37]	O	O	O	-	-	X	-
[38]	-	O	-	-	-	X	-
[39]	-	O	-	-	-	O	-
[40]	-	-	O	-	-	X	-
[41]	-	-	O	-	X	O	-
[42]	-	-	-	-	-	O	O
[43]	-	-	O	-	O	O	-
[44]	O	-	O	-	-	O	-
[45]	-	-	X	-	-	O	-
[46]	-	-	O	-	-	O	-
[47]	O	O	O	-	-	O	-
[48]	O	O	O	-	-	O	-
[49]	-	O	-	-	O	O	-
[50]	-	O	O	-	-	O	-
[51]	-	-	O	X	-	O	-
[52]	-	-	-	O	-	O	-
[53]	-	X	O	-	-	O	-
[54]	-	-	O	-	-	O	-
[55]	-	X	-	-	-	-	-
[56]	O	-	-	-	-	O	-
[57]	-	-	O	-	-	X	-
[58]	-	-	-	-	-	O	-
[59]	-	O	-	-	-	O	-
[60]	O	O	-	-	-	X	-
[61]	-	-	-	-	-	X	-
[62]	-	-	-	-	-	O	-
[63]	-	-	-	O	-	O	-

(*continued*)

Table 2. (*continued*)

Ref	ADR	DSR	DT	HCD	PD	UCD	VSD
[64]	-	-	-	-	-	O	-
[65]	-	-	X	X	O	X	O
[66]	-	-	-	-	-	X	-
[67]	-	-	-	-	-	O	-
[68]	-	-	-	-	-	O	-
[69]	-	-	-	-	-	O	-
[70]	-	-	-	-	-	O	O
[71]	-	-	-	-	-	O	-
[72]	-	-	-	-	-	O	-
[73]	-	-	-	-	X	X	-
[74]	-	-	-	-	-	X	O
[75]	O	-	-	X	O	O	-
[76]	-	-	-	X	-	X	O
[77]	-	-	-	X	-	X	X
[78]	-	X	-	-	-	X	-
[79]	-	-	-	-	-	O	-
[80]	-	-	-	-	-	X	O
[81]	-	O	-	-	-	O	-
[82]	-	-	-	-	-	X	-
[83]	-	O	-	-	-	-	-
[84]	-	-	-	-	-	X	-
[85]	-	O	-	-	-	O	-
[86]	-	-	-	-	-	O	-
[87]	-	-	-	-	-	X	-
[88]	-	O	-	-	-	O	-
[89]	-	O	O	O	-	O	O
[90]	-	-	-	-	-	O	-
Count	8	17	19	9	7	56	8

The pronounced absence of VSD yields more ground for discussion. While weaknesses of applying VSD specifically as a MWFD are evident [91], it can be argued that the general idea of integrating ethical considerations in AR design is still relevant. Especially with increased synergies emerging from modern-day advanced technologies such as artificial intelligence and metaverses, the ethical implementation of AR systems seems important for a sustainable and resilient future of the field. As mentioned before,

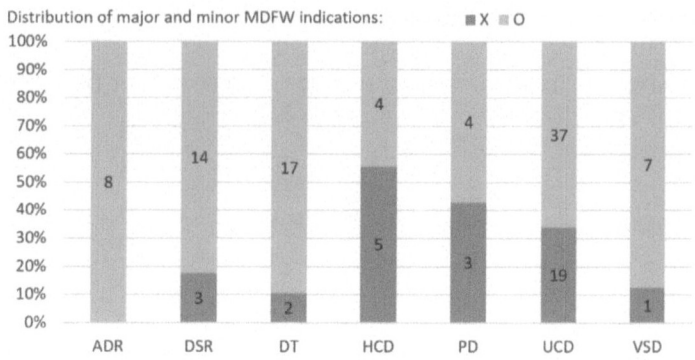

Fig. 2. Distribution of major and minor MDFW indications in reviewed articles

AR devices and applications are always connected to human users and may thereby, for instance, process sensitive data or pose threats to the environment – risks that could precautiously be assessed throughout VSD inquiries. Regarding the little representation of PD, one explanation might be the marginal interest in including non-experts in the development of a solution that involves a relatively new technology such as AR. PD is known to be challenging if participants are unaware of possibilities or technical restrictions, hence, coming up with viable ideas could become a guessing game for laymen. Nevertheless, PD supporters may argue that stakeholders with conceptual or strategic knowledge on AR implementation could contribute to PD projects with valuable insights generated from interdisciplinary exchange [92].

All in all, the exact reasons for the low representation of MDFWs in AR development can only be hypothesized so far. Decisions in favor of the systematic use of either of the examined frameworks will find supporting arguments, as discussed in this section. Future empirical work could further develop and investigate research questions regarding (non-)use of MDFWs in this area.

6   Conclusion

This work has been driven by the motivation to understand and provide an overview of MDFWs represented in literature on applied AR development. The review revealed a lack of design process descriptions in a large majority of the considered literature. Still, the RQ can be partially answered by summarizing the most remarkable findings. With a large representation among the reviewed papers, UCD was preferably applied to understand the users' wants and to derive a possible solution design, as well as to validate yet-designed solutions by involving a target audience. UCD has one of the easiest design cycles and, despite its age, provides a viable entry point for new researchers and practitioners, which might be one reason for its popularity. DT could often be found in co-occurrence with UCD, introducing more iterative and feedback-driven design work to the applied AR research examples. However, DT itself was barely mentioned in the papers; individual techniques indicated minor representations. Furthermore, HCD, PD, and VSD were seldomly represented in the sampled literature. Multiple reasons for this may be discussed, for instance, the complex design cycles and reliance on philosophical elements, and the design being heavily reliant on outputs from external stakeholder groups. Another aspect to further investigate in future research are AR-ADR and -DSR projects, as these are complete method frameworks. These FW differ in the way they might be identified and how they are applied, as well as the impact these complete FW have upon design results and implementation rigor. In summary, a strong disconnection between the current applied development of AR systems and the use of MDFWs can be objected, drawing on the here performed review. As a consequence, applied AR research seems to be prone to rendering final AR solutions as a mere product of possibility – "It can be done", but not desirability – "It should be done".

In regards of limitations, the here presented results could be enhanced by integrating more open search strings and widening the searched databases. Furthermore, despite working together as a team of researchers, the influence of individual biases can never be ruled out. On the other hand, this explorative work yields many starting points for future research on applied AR design, especially concerning the proposed research gaps in regards of human-centered, value-sensitive or participatory AR design and the critical assessment of actual added-value in such MDFWs for applied AR research projects. Moreover, the merit of conducting literature reviews in the field of AR is underlined and future contributions reviewing these meta-layers are strongly commended to sustainably shape successful and knowledge-based AR solution designs in future research and practice.

References

1. Evangelista, A., Ardito, L., Boccaccio, A., Fiorentino, M., Messeni Petruzzelli, A., Uva, A.E.: Unveiling the technological trends of augmented reality: a patent analysis. Comput. Ind. **118**, 103221 (2020)
2. Kaplan, A.D., Cruit, J., Endsley, M., Beers, S.M., Sawyer, B.D., Hancock, P.A.: The effects of virtual reality, augmented reality, and mixed reality as training enhancement methods: a meta-analysis. Hum. Factors **63**(4), 706–726 (2021)
3. Statista: Statistics report on augmented reality (AR). https://www.statista.com/study/38227/augmented-reality-ar-statista-dossier/. Accessed 24 Nov 2023
4. Van Kleef, N., Noltes, J., van der Spoel, S.: Success factors for augmented reality business models. Study tour Pixel (2010)
5. Masood, T., Egger, J.: Augmented reality in support of Industry 4.0—Implementation challenges and success factors. Robot. Comput. Integr. Manuf. **58**, 181–195 (2019)
6. Krauß, V., Boden, A., Oppermann, L., Reiners, R.: Current practices, challenges, and design implications for collaborative AR/VR application development. In: Proceedings of the 2021 CHI Conference on Human Factors in Computing Systems, ACM (2021)
7. Tezer, M., Yıldız, E.P., Masalimova, A.R., Fatkhutdinova, A.M., Zheltukhina, M.R., Khairullina, E.R.: Trends of augmented reality applications and research throughout the world: meta-analysis of theses, articles and papers between 2001–2019 years. Int. J. Emerg. Technol. Learn. **14**(22), 154–174 (2019)
8. Borgohain, D.J., Bhanage, D.A., Verma, M.K., Pawar, A.V.: Global research trends in augmented reality: scientometric mapping based on Scopus database. Inf. Discovery Delivery **50**(4), 387–403 (2022)

9. Abbate, S., Centobelli, P., Cerchione, R., Oropallo, E., Riccio, E.: A first bibliometric literature review on Metaverse. In: 2022 IEEE Technology and Engineering Management Conference (TEMSCON EUROPE), pp. 254–260 (2022)

10. Herrman, C.S.: Fundamentals of Methodology - Part I: Definitions and First Principles. SSRN J. (2009)

11. Andiappan, V., Wan, Y.K.: Distinguishing approach, methodology, method, procedure and technique in process systems engineering. Clean Techn Environ Policy 22(3), 547–555 (2020)

12. Schallmo, D., Williams, C.A., Lang, K.: An integrated design thinking approach – literature review, basic principles and roadmap for design thinking. In: Proceedings of the XXIX ISPIM Innovation Conference (2018)

13. Burnham, J.: Approach, method, technique: making distinctions and creating connections. J. Syst. Consultation Manage. 3(1), 3–26 (1992)

14. Sein, M.K., Henfridsson, O., Purao, S., Rossi, M., Lindgren, R.: Action design research. MIS Quarterly 35(1) (2011)

15. Hevner, A.R., March, S.T., Park, J.: Design research in information systems research. MIS Q. 28(1), 75–105 (2004)

16. Peffers, K., Tuunanen, T., Gengler, C.E., Rossi, M., Hui, W.: The design science research process: a model for producing and presenting information systems research. In: Proceedings of the 2006 Design Science Research in Information Systems and Technology (DESRIST) Conference (2006)

17. Peffers, K., Tuunanen, T., Rothenberger, M.A., Chatterjee, S.: A design science research methodology for information systems research. J. Manag. Inf. Syst. 24(3), 45–77 (2007)

18. Brown, T.: Design Thinking. Harvard Business Review (2008)

19. Plattner, H., Meinel, C., Weinberg, U.: Design Thinking: Understand - Improve - Apply. Münchner Verlagsgruppe GmbH (2009)

20. Uebernickel, F., Brenner, W.: Design thinking. In: Hoffmann, C.P., Lennerts, S., Schmitz, C., Stölzle, W., Uebernickel, F. (eds.) Business Innovation: Das St. Galler Modell, pp. 243–265. Springer Fachmedien, Wiesbaden (2016)

21. Gasson, S.: Human-centered vs. user-centered approaches to information system design. J. Inf. Technol. Theory Appl. 5(2), 29–46 (2003)

22. Cooley, M.: Human-centered design. In: Robertson, E.J. (ed.) Information Design, pp. 59–81. MIT Press (1999)

23. Kensing, F., Blomberg, J.: Participatory design: issues and concerns. Comput. Support. Coop. Work 7(3–4), 167–185 (1998)

24. Sanders, E.B.N., Brandt, E., Binder, T.: A framework for organizing the tools and techniques of participatory design. In: Proceedings of the PDC 2010: The 11th Biennial Participatory Design Conference, pp. 195–198 (2010)

25. Abras, C., Maloney-Krichmar, D., Preece, J.: User-centered design. In: Bainbridge, W. (ed.) Encyclopedia of Human-Computer Interaction, Sage Publications (2004)

26. Norman, D.A.: The psychology of everyday things. Basic Books (1988)

27. Hendry, D.G., Friedman, B., Ballard, S.: Value sensitive design as a formative framework. Ethics Inf. Technol. 23(1), 39–44 (2021)

28. Flanagan, M., Howe, D.C., Nissenbaum, H.: Embodying values in technology: theory and practice. In: Van Den Hoven, J., Weckert, J. (eds.) Information Technology and Moral Philosophy, pp. 322–353. Cambridge University Press (2008)

29. Cummings, M.L.: Integrating ethics in design through the value-sensitive design approach. Sci. Eng. Ethics 12(4), 701–715 (2006)

30. Webster, J., Watson, R.T.: Analyzing the past to prepare for the future: writing a literature review. MIS Q. 26(2), xiii–xxiii (2002)

31. Halevi, G., Moed, H., Bar-Ilan, J.: Suitability of Google Scholar as a source of scientific information and as a source of data for scientific evaluation—Review of the Literature. J. Informet. **11**(3), 823–834 (2017)
32. Yasin, A., Fatima, R., Wen, L., Afzal, W., Azhar, M., Torkar, R.: On using grey literature and google scholar in systematic literature reviews in software engineering. IEEE Access **8**, 36226–36243 (2020)
33. Abdul Razak, M.R., Anwar, R., Ahmad Najamuddin, N.: Real estate augmented reality marketing media strategy: formgiving architectural design. E-BPJ **7**(SI9), 563–568 (2022)
34. Agati, S.S., Bauer, R.D., Hounsell, M.D.S., Paterno, A.S.: Augmented reality for manual assembly in Industry 4.0: gathering guidelines. In: Proceedings of the 22nd Symposium on Virtual and Augmented Reality (SVR), pp. 179–188 (2020)
35. Alhumaidan, H., Lo, K.P.Y., Selby, A.: Co-designing with children a collaborative augmented reality book based on a primary school textbook. Int. J. Child-Comput. Interact. **15**, 24–36 (2018)
36. Anuwar bin Ahmad Najamuddin, N.: Augmented reality design: the study of property development marketing tools. i-SPiKE, pp. 761–764 (2021)
37. Berkemeier, L., Zobel, B., Werning, S., Ickerott, I., Thomas, O.: Engineering of augmented reality-based information systems: design and implementation for intralogistics services. Bus. Inf. Syst. Eng. **61**(1), 67–89 (2019)
38. Brata, K.C., Liang, D.: An effective approach to develop location-based augmented reality information support. IJECE **9**(4), 3060 (2019)
39. Daineko, Y., Tsoy, D., Seitnur, A., Ipalakova, M.: Development of a mobile e-learning platform on physics using augmented reality technology. Int. J. Interact. Mob. Technol. **16**(05), 4–18 (2022)
40. Grandi, J.G., Cao, Z., Ogren, M., Kopper, R.: Design and simulation of next-generation augmented reality user interfaces in virtual reality. In: Proceedings of the 2021 IEEE Conference on Virtual Reality and 3D User Interfaces Abstracts and Workshops (VRW), pp. 23–29 (2021)
41. Han, D.-I.D., Abreu E Silva, S.G., Schröder, K., Melissen, F., Haggis-Burridge, M.: Designing immersive sustainable food experiences in augmented reality: a consumer participatory co-creation approach. Foods **11**(22), 3646 (2022)
42. Irshad, S., Rambli, D.R.A., Sulaiman, S.: Design and implementation of user experience model for augmented reality systems. In: Proceedings of the MoMM 2020: The 18th International Conference on Advances in Mobile Computing and Multimedia, pp. 48–57 (2020)
43. Kerr, J., Lawson, G.: Augmented reality in design education: landscape architecture studies as ar experience. Int. J. Art Design Ed. **39**(1), 6–21 (2020)
44. Khambari, M.N.M., Rofie, F.S.M.: Augmented reality mobile application co-design experience: delineating the nuances from the lens of a system developer. ASS **17**(11), 198 (2021)
45. Korn, O., Buchweitz, L., Rees, A., Bieber, G., Werner, C., Hauer, K.: Using augmented reality and gamification to empower rehabilitation activities and elderly persons. a study applying design thinking. In: Proceedings of the AHFE 2018: Advances in Intelligent Systems and Computing 787, pp. 219–229, Springer, Cham (2019)
46. Lu, J.: Mobile augmented reality technology for design and implementation of library document push system. J. Real-Time Image Proc. **18**(2), 283–293 (2021)
47. Ludwig, T., Hoffmann, S., Jasche, F., Ruhrmann, M.: VacuumCleanAR: augmented reality-based self-explanatory physical artifacts. In: Proceedings of the MuC'20: Mensch und Computer 2020, pp. 291–302 (2020)
48. Paliokas, I., et al.: A gamified augmented reality application for digital heritage and tourism. Appl. Sci. **10**(21) (2020)

49. Pieterse, A.D., Hierck, B.P., De Jong, P.G.M., Kroese, J., Willems, L.N.A., Reinders, M.E.J.: Design and implementation of "AugMedicine: lung cases", an augmented reality application for the medical curriculum on the presentation of Dyspnea. Front. Virtual Real. **1**, 534–577 (2020)
50. Raith, A., Kamp, C., Stoiber, C., Jakl, A., Wagner, M.: augmented reality in radiology for education and training—a design study. Healthcare **10**(4) (2022)
51. Ricci, M., Scarcelli, A., D'Introno, A., Strippoli, V., Cariati, S., Fiorentino, M.: A human-centred design approach for designing augmented reality enabled interactive systems: a kitchen machine case study. In: Gerbino, S., Lanzotti, A., Martorelli, M., Mirálbes Buil, R., Rizzi, C., Roucoules, L. (eds.) Advances on Mechanics, Design Engineering and Manufacturing IV, pp. 1413–1425. Springer International Publishing (2023)
52. Romero, M.R., Harari, I., Diaz, J., Macas, E.: Hoope project: user-centered design process applied in the implementation of augmented reality for children with ASD. In: HCII 2022. Lecture Notes in Computer Science 13309, pp. 277–290. Springer, Cham (2022)
53. Saragih, R.E., Suyoto: development of interactive mobile application with augmented reality for tourism sites in Batam. In: Proceedings of the 2020 Fourth World Conference on Smart Trends in Systems Security and Sustainablity (WorldS4), pp. 512–517 (2020)
54. Tsai, W.-T., Chen, C.-H.: The use of augmented reality to represent gamification theory in user story training. In: Proceedings of the 3rd International Conference on Education and Multimedia Technology, pp. 265–268 (2019)
55. Vasilevski, N., Birt, J.: Human-centered design science research evaluation for gamified augmented reality. Front. Virtual Real. **2**, 713–718 (2021)
56. Volante, J.W.: Augmented reality technician assistance program. In: Proceedings of the Research and Scholarship Symposium, Cedarville University (2018)
57. Williams, M., Yao, K.K.K., Nurse, J.R.C.: Developing an augmented reality tourism app through user-centred design (extended version). In: Proceedings of the 31st British Human Computer Interaction Conference (2020)
58. Yang, W., Xiao, Q., Zhang, Y.: HAR^2bot: a human-centered augmented reality robot programming method with the awareness of cognitive load. J. Intell. Manuf. (2023)
59. Zhao, Q.: The application of augmented reality visual communication in network teaching. Int. J. Emerg. Technol. Learn. **13**(07) (2018)
60. Bork, F., Lehner, A., Kugelmann, D., Eck, U., Waschke, J., Navab, N.: VesARlius: an augmented reality system for large-group co-located anatomy learning. In: Proceedings of the 2019 IEEE International Symposium on Mixed and Augmented Reality Adjunct (ISMAR-Adjunct), pp. 122–123 (2019)
61. Fan, X., Li, X., Song, L., Zhang, Y., Liu, M., Miao, Q.: Usability evaluation of AR human-machine interface based on user experience. In: Proceedings of the 2022 International Conference on Virtual Reality, Human-Computer Interaction and Artificial Intelligence (VRHCIAI), pp. 23–29 (2022)
62. Knopp, S., Klimant, P., Allmacher, C.: Industrial use case - AR guidance using hololens for assembly and disassembly of a modular mold, with live streaming for collaborative support. In: Proceedings of the 2019 IEEE International Symposium on Mixed and Augmented Reality Adjunct (ISMAR-Adjunct), pp. 134–135 (2019)
63. Gao, J., Wu, B., Sato, K.: A wearable warning system design for mask recognition via AR smart glasses. In: Proceedings of the 2021 IEEE Intl Conference on Dependable, Autonomic and Secure Computing, Intl Conference on Pervasive Intelligence and Computing, Intl Conference on Cloud and Big Data Computing, Intl Conference on Cyber Science and Technology Congress (DASC/PiCom/CBDCom/CyberSciTech), pp. 896–900 (2021)
64. Matsumoto, T., Kosaka, T., Sakurada, T., Nakajima, Y., Tano, S.: Picking work using AR instructions in warehouses. In: Proceedings of the IEEE 8th Global Conference on Consumer Electronics (GCCE), pp. 31–34 (2019)

65. Hiererra, S.E., Meyliana, Ramadhan, A., Purnomo, F.: Prototype UX design: mobile augmented reality application based on gamification for cultural heritage tourism. In: Proceedings of the 8th International HCI and UX Conference in Indonesia (CHIuXiD), pp. 30–35 (2022)
66. Cheng, K., Koda, K., Masuko, S.: Reimagining the stadium spectator experience using augmented reality and visual positioning system. In: Proceedings of the 2022 IEEE International Symposium on Mixed and Augmented Reality Adjunct (ISMAR-Adjunct), pp. 786–787 (2022)
67. Alejos, J.C.T., Cruzado, R.J.P., Cabanillas-Carbonell, M., Salazar, J.L.H.: Mobile application with augmented reality for the learning of the cell. In: Proceedings of the 2020 IEEE Congreso Bienal de Argentina (ARGENCON), pp. 1–4 (2020)
68. Cai, M., Amrizal, M.A., Abe, T., Suganuma, T.: Design and implementation of AR-supported system for piano learning. In: Proceedings of the IEEE 8th Global Conference on Consumer Electronics (GCCE), pp. 49–50 (2019)
69. Cai, M., Amrizal, M.A., Abe, T., Suganuma, T.: Design of an AR-based system for group piano learning. In: Proceedings of the IEEE International Symposium on Mixed and Augmented Reality Adjunct (ISMAR-Adjunct), pp. 20–21 (2019)
70. Cruz, D.R.D., Sevilla, J.S.A., Gabriel, J.W.D.S., Cruz, A.J.P.D., Caselis, E.J.S.: Design and development of augmented reality (AR) mobile application for malolos' Kameztizuhan (Malolos Heritage Town, Philippines). In: Proceedings of the 2018 IEEE Games, Entertainment, Media Conference (GEM), pp. 1–9 (2018)
71. Ariff, M.I.M., Rohaizi, M.L.H., Salleh, K.A., Wahab, J.A., Adam, N.L., Arshad, N.I.: Augmented reality application for solar system learning: a research in progress. In: Proceedings of the 2021 IEEE Region 10 Symposium (TENSYMP), pp. 1–4 (2021)
72. Hamidane, R., L. H, M., Bellarbi, A., R, M.: Implementation of a preventive maintenance system based on augmented reality. In: Proceedings of the 3rd International Conference on Pattern Analysis and Intelligent Systems (PAIS), pp. 1–6 (2018)
73. Hertel, J., Gabel, J., Kruse, L., Wollborn, M., Steinicke, F.: Co-design of an augmented reality maintenance tool for gas pressure regulation stations. In: Proceedings of the 2022 IEEE International Symposium on Mixed and Augmented Reality Adjunct (ISMAR-Adjunct), pp. 720–724 (2022)
74. Hidayat, W.N., Hakiki, M.A., Nashrullah, M.F., Elmunsyah, H., Sutikno, T.A.: Development of mobile learning application based on augmented reality with index card match method. In: Proceedings of the 4th International Conference on Vocational Education and Training (ICOVET), pp. 304–309 (2020)
75. Kalmpourtzis, G., Ketsiakidis, G., Vrysis, L., Xi, T., Wang, X.L., Dimoulas, C.: Eliciting educators' needs on the design and application of augmented reality educational board games on cultural heritage: the case of CHARMap. In: Proceedings of the 2021 IEEE Global Engineering Education Conference (EDUCON), pp. 1282–1286 (2021)
76. Li, X.Z., Kang, X.: Intangible cultural heritage based augmented reality mobile learning: application development and heuristics evaluation. In: Proceedings of the 2023 Joint International Conference on Digital Arts, Media and Technology with ECTI Northern Section Conference on Electrical, Electronics, Computer and Telecommunications Engineering (ECTI DAMT & NCON), pp. 26–30 (2023)
77. Malouta, A., Chrysanthi, A., Kasapakis, V.: Herstory: an AR storytelling application presenting women's heroic lives in public space. In: Proceedings of the 2022 International Conf. on Interactive Media, Smart Systems and Emerging Technologies (IMET), pp. 01–04 (2022)
78. Maringka, J.F., Pambuko, R.H., Widianto, M.H.: Development of educational application about mental disorders with augmented reality for android. In: Proceedings of the 2022 International Conference on Informatics, Multimedia, Cyber and Information System (ICIMCIS), pp. 390–394 (2022)

79. Mambu, J.Y., Anderson, E., Wahyudi, A., Keyeh, G., Dajoh, B.: Blind reader: an object iden-
    tification mobile- based application for the blind using augmented reality detection. In: Pro-
    ceedings of the 1st International Conference on Cybernetics and Intelligent System (ICORIS),
    pp. 138–141 (2019)
80. Maulana, F.I., Wijaya, I.B.A., Azis, B., Harjo, A.A., Suwondo, L., Livianty, V.: Evaluation
    of user experience on the augmented reality Glovic cafe and bakery Jember application to
    maximize user experience. In: Proceedings of the 8th International Conference on Education
    and Technology (ICET), pp. 270–274 (2022)
81. Ng, X.H., Lim, W.N.: Design of a mobile augmented reality-based indoor navigation sys-
    tem. In: Proceedings of the 4th International Symposium on Multidisciplinary Studies and
    Innovative Technologies (ISMSIT), pp. 1–6 (2020)
82. Nasir, S., Zahid, M.N., Khan, T.A., Kadir, K., Khan, S.: Augmented reality application for
    architects and interior designers: Interno a cost effective solution. In: Proceedings of the
    IEEE 5th International Conference on Smart Instrumentation, Measurement and Application
    (ICSIMA), pp. 1–6 (2018)
83. Permanasari, A.E., Hidayah, I., Priyowibowo, F.M., Hidayat, M.A., Prayoga, F.B., Sakkinah,
    I.S.: An augmented reality application for animal learning media at alian butterfly park. In:
    Proceedings of the 6th International Conference on Science and Technology (ICST), pp. 1–5
    (2020)
84. Permanasari, A.E., Liman, J., Sakkinah, I.S., Maulana, Y.: An educational mobile application
    development with AR-based as a promotion media alian butterfly park. In: Proceedings of
    the 5th International Conf. on Science and Technology (ICST), pp. 1–4 (2019)
85. Salazar, J.L.H., Pacheco-Quispe, R., Cabeza, J.D., Salazar, M.J.H., Cruzado, J.P.: Augmented
    reality for solar system learning. In: Proceedings of the IEEE ANDESCON, pp. 1–4 (2020)
86. Schiavi, B., Gechter, F., Gechter, C., Rizzo, A.: Teach me a story: an augmented reality appli-
    cation for teaching history in middle school. In: Proceedings of the 2018 IEEE Conference
    on Virtual Reality and 3D User Interfaces (VR), pp. 679–680 (2018)
87. Shi, G., et al.: Design of cockpit ergonomic evaluation simulation system based on augmented
    reality. In: Proceedings of the 11th International Conference on Intelligent Human-Machine
    Systems and Cybernetics (IHMSC), pp. 33–36 (2019)
88. Velaora, M., Roy, R.V., Guéna, F.: ARtect, an augmented reality educational prototype for
    architectural design. In: Proceedings of the Fourth World Conference on Smart Trends in
    Systems, Security and Sustainability (WorldS4), pp. 110–115 (2020)
89. Vergari, M., Kojic, T., Bertges, N.S., Vona, F., Möller, S., Voigt-Antons, J.N.: Exploring users'
    sense of safety in public using an augmented reality application. In: Proceedings of the 15th
    International Conf. on Quality of Multimedia Experience (QoMEX), pp. 193–196 (2023)
90. Tsoukalos, D., Triantfyllou, V., Kotsopoulos, K.I., Tsolis, D.: Aitoloakarnania fortifications:
    an AR application for the promotion of the fortifications of Aitoloakarnania. In: Proceedings
    of the 13th International Conference on Information, Intelligence, Systems & Applications
    (IISA), pp. 1–6 (2022)
91. Winkler, T., Spiekermann, S.: Twenty years of value sensitive design: a review of method-
    ological practices in VSD projects. Ethics Inf. Technol. 23(1), 17–21 (2021)
92. Robertson, T., Simonsen, J.: Challenges and opportunities in contemporary participatory
    design. Des. Issues 28(3), 3–9 (2012)

Emotion-Aware Interfaces: Empirical Methods for Adaptive User Interface

Syrine Haddad[1,3]([✉]), Olfa Daassi[2,3], and Safya Belghith[1,3]

[1] National Engineering School of Tunis, University of Tunis El Manar, Tunis, Tunisia
[2] National Engineering School of Carthage, University of Carthage, Carthage, Tunisia
[3] Laboratory of Robotics, Informatics, and Complex Systems (LR-RISC-ENIT), Tunis, Tunisia
{syrine.haddad,safya.belghith}@enit.utm.tn

Abstract. Designing User Interfaces (UIs) that can interpret and respond to user emotions has evolved from a passing trend to a core tenet of design philosophy. As technology advances, it becomes increasingly important to predict users' emotional states during interface interactions. This paper proposes a cutting-edge deep learning model designed to predict a wide range of emotions in users, such as Happiness, Anger, Calmness, and Surprise. The research started with a thorough survey, gathering feedback from 72 users regarding UI designs tailored to various emotions. Using these insights, interfaces were developed to address different emotional states. Following the design phase, a user interaction study was conducted involving 29 participants interacting with these interfaces while their facial expressions were recorded. Subsequently, a predictive model for user emotions was developed, achieving an accuracy of 83%, showcasing its robustness and reliability in discerning and predicting user emotions based on interactions with UIs. This model was seamlessly integrated into a proposed real-time adaptive UI system. Notably, existing literature has traditionally relied on pre-existing software for emotion detection in adaptive systems. Our contribution is to demonstrate an Emotional Interface Adaptation System that uses a trained model in real-world circumstances to provide a dynamic and responsive user experience that adapts in real-time to users' emotional cues.

Keywords: Emotion-driven GUI design · Facial expression analysis · Emotion adaptive systems

1 Introduction

User Interfaces (UIs) significantly shape user experiences across digital platforms, including mobile apps, web interfaces, and desktop software [2,12,15,23]. Traditionally, UI design focused on functionality, usability, and aesthetics [3,6,10,11]. However, recognizing the role of emotions in user interaction has led to a shift towards emotion-driven design [4,5,8,23], which can enhance usability, engagement, and satisfaction [7,9,16]. Emotion-driven design allows for more personalized interfaces that dynamically adapt to users' emotional states, improving experiences in fields like entertainment and healthcare. We hypothesize that UIs evoke emotional responses based on content

H. Plácido da Silva and P. Cipresso (Eds.): CHIRA 2024, CCIS 2370, pp. 147–165, 2025.
https://doi.org/10.1007/978-3-031-82633-7_10

and aesthetics. To test this, we recorded users' facial expressions while interacting with a movie website featuring different designs. Our study begins with a survey on users' preferences for emotion-tailored UI designs, leading to the creation of interfaces that evoke emotions such as Happiness, Calmness, Surprise, and Anger. We validated these interfaces through user interaction studies, analyzing facial expressions in real-time to assess emotional responses. Using deep learning, we developed a model to predict emotions based on user interactions with 83% accuracy, integrating it into an Emotional Interface Adaptation system. In sum, this paper makes the following contributions:

1. We introduce an approach to UI design centred around incorporating user emotions as a primary design factor, leading to the creation of interfaces tailored to evoke specific emotional responses. (Section 3)
2. We conduct a controlled experiment to capture facial emotion responses to validate the emotion-driven interfaces. (Section 4)
3. We develop a computational model for facial emotional recognition (Sect. 5) and integrate the trained emotion prediction model into an Emotional Interface Adaptation system.

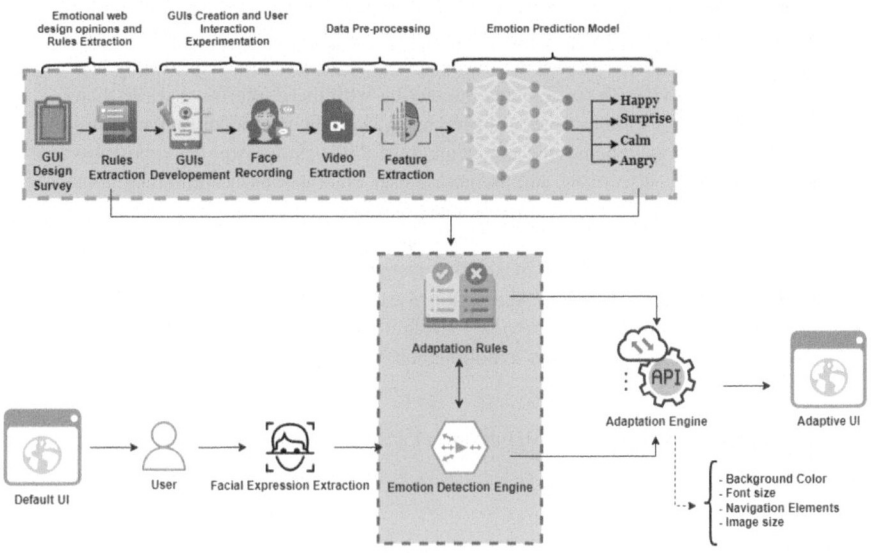

Fig. 1. Architecture of the proposed Emotional Interface Adaptation System.

2   Related Work

Our research is based on two domains of expertise: affective evaluation of UI design, and the adaptation of user interfaces based on emotions. Therefore, in this section, we discuss previous work on these domains.

2.1   Affective Evaluation of UI Design

Predicting affective responses in UI designs using physiological and peripheral signals is scarce.

Lockner et al. [19] combined screen records, face recognition, and galvanic skin response with SAM and GEW, concluding that facial expressions and electrodermal activity were unreliable for emotion detection, though SAM and GEW helped differentiate emotions despite limitations.

Standardized questionnaires like PANAS [21] are commonly used for emotion evaluation. Plass et al. [20] found that round shapes with warm colors increased positive emotions in multimedia learning.

Wang et al. [22] used the SEAT tool to assess emotions on visual interfaces, achieving semantic emotion discrimination. Mori et al. [23] tested web designs with 40 participants, identifying design elements that evoke emotions like fun, anxiety, and love, offering guidelines for emotionally engaging interfaces.

2.2   Emotion-Driven User Interface Adaptation

Considering approaches that study interactive system adaptation regarding emotions, adaptations can be triggered either on the functional part of the application [25] - e.g. for changing the content - or on the User Interface (UI) part - e.g. for adapting the design or the interaction modality.

In this paper [27], the authors introduced the concept of an intelligent mirror system called iMirror, which incorporates facial expression recognition and color emotion adaptation. The system consists of four main modules: face image acquisition, expression recognition, light feedback, and power. Facial expressions are identified using the Extreme Learning Machine, and color lights are adjusted based on color emotion psychology. Experimental results demonstrated an average recognition accuracy of 80% for various facial expressions, with most participants agreeing to the use of colorful lights that adapt to their emotions.

Another adaptive system proposed in [33] called Adaptive User-Interface Based on User's Emotion (AUBUE). The AUBUE system can detect a user's emotions based on interactions with the keyboard and modify the interface's color accordingly. The system combines Human-Computer Interaction (HCI) and affective computing to create emotionally intelligent user interfaces that can adapt to the user's emotional state. By using the Ortony, Clore, and Collins (OCC) model of emotions, the system focuses on three emotions: joy, distress, and Anger, and maps these emotions to a mood space for color selection. The AUBUE system consists of keyboard interpretation, event interpretation, mood update, and color selection components to accurately map the user's emotions and adapt the interface color accordingly.

Galindo et al. in [29] focused on utilizing user emotions to trigger UI adaptation for maintaining user experience during the interaction, with emotions categorized based on user's age, gender, and UI dimensions such as aesthetics and usability. An experiment was conducted where participants interacted with different versions of a travel website, with emotions detected every 10 s to identify emotions indicating usability and aesthetic problems at runtime. This paper discuss also the integration of these findings into a prototype called Perso2U, designed to dynamically adapt UIs to user emotions. Overall, the results indicate that emotions can play a crucial role in UI design and adaptation to enhance user satisfaction and engagement.

There are other adaptive user interface systems that focus solely on the emotional aspects of the user, as proposed by [26, 28].

A common limitation of these systems is that they rely on existing software to recognize emotions. This dependency can be problematic because a single software solution may not adequately recognize the user's emotions. This constraint frequently involves the use of many software components to achieve more precise emotion prediction. However, this method can be time-consuming, costly, and complicated. To the best of our knowledge, no approach has yet been proposed that creates a deep learning model based on data collected from users interacting with a GUI.

3   A Survey: Collecting Opinions About Emotional Web Design

Seventy-two users completed an online questionnaire. The questionnaire comprised two sections: 1) personal information, 2) Web design and basic emotion. The first part aimed to collect personal information from the users and their experience with the web. In the second part, users have to answer some questions related to 4 emotions (Happiness, Surprise, Calmness, and Anger) and their relevant web design criteria.

3.1   Participants

The participants were 72 (41 females and 31 males) aged between 18 and 46 years ($M =22.21$, $SD = 6.6$, $Mdn = 34.5$). 41 users are under-graduated in their 5th year, 21 are under-graduated in their 3rd and 4th year, 6 participants were in their 1st and 2nd year, while 3 users had a master's degree and one participant had a PhD. The participants are used to internet browsing (67 users surf the internet daily, while 5 navigate several times a week). The experiment considered both skilled and unskilled users in web development (54 had a background related to web programming, while 18 did not). Also, 43 users were familiar with UI design, whereas 29 had no background related to it.

3.2   Procedure

The experiment was announced virtually by sending an email to university students. In each section of the questionnaire, the user has to answer ten questions for each emotion (Happiness, Surprise, Calmness, and Anger).

The choice of questions and the given answers were based on previous studies that examined color-emotion relations [17, 18] and design criteria for web applications [23]. Their answers were generated in a sheet file.

3.3   Results

The results presented are derived from responses that exceed the 50% threshold. In cases where responses falls below this threshold, we prioritize the options with the

Table 1. Colors for each emotion.

Emotion	Main Colors (Shades)	Hex Code
Happiness	Red (Red Ribbon)	#e9083f
Anger	Red (Hot Cuba), Black (Coarse Wool)	#bc0032, #1c1a26
Calmness	Red (Rose Frost), Gray (Haze)	#ffebe9, #f1eff9
Surprise	Blue (Pink OCD)	#563cf9

highest number of votes to determine our results. The relationship between color and emotion is closely tied to color preferences. The first part of the questionnaire asked the users to associate one color or more (we have used the Node.js Extended Color Palette) with each emotion. For the colors and their shades' names, we have used the website icolorpalette (https://icolorpalette.com/). Table 1 summarizes the results.

The next parts of the questionnaire asked the users for suggestions regarding specific associations between each emotion and design feature criteria. Firstly, the users had to choose between the following groups related to data insertion and website structure 1) few or many pages, 2) short or long text, 3) textbox (to insert short data) or textarea (to insert long information). Table 2 summarizes the results. Based on the page structure results, we observe for the emotions (happiness, Surprise, and Calmness) that the page structure can be the same as we expected. So we added another question related to interface overload content based on Scapin and Bastien criteria [13]. The users had to choose between: 1) bright and flashy colors, 2) busy or cluttered layouts, 3) excessive use of animations, 4) intrusive pop-ups or ads, and 5) None of these. Table 3 summarizes the results. Then we investigated the emotional impact of multimedia element style. Users were asked to choose one element from each group: 1) the presence of video, animations, images, no multimedia, 2) small, medium, and large sizes of images, 3) blurred or clear images. Table 4 summarizes the results.

Table 2. Page Structure for each emotion.

Emotion	Page Structure
Happiness	few pages, short text, textbox
Anger	many pages, long text, textarea
Calmness	few pages, short text, textbox
Surprise	few pages, short text, textbox

Table 3. Overload Content for each emotion.

Emotion	Overload Content
Happiness	bright or flashy colors
Anger	busy or cluttered layouts, excessive use of animations
Calmness	none of these
Surprise	bright or flashy colors, intrusive pop-ups and ads

Finally, the questionnaire also aimed to collect users' opinions about the navigation elements where the user had to choose one element from each group: 1) links, standard or graphic buttons, 2) static (fixed elements) or dynamic elements. Table 5 summarizes the results.

Table 4. Multimedia elements for each emotion.

Emotion	Multimedia elements
Happiness	animations/images, clear-medium images
Anger	videos/animations, large-blurred images
Calmness	no multimedia/images, clear-medium images
Surprise	animations, clear-medium images

Table 5. Navigation elements for each emotion.

Emotion	Navigation elements
Happiness	graphic buttons, dynamic elements
Anger	links, dynamic elements
Calmness	standard buttons, static elements
Surprise	graphic buttons, dynamic elements

4   A User Study: Applying the Emotion-Based Design

Based on the findings of the previous study, we created four web interfaces incorporating the gathered web design principles. Each interface aimed to evoke one of the four emotions on the scale. Each web interface showcased identical content but with distinct design styles. We selected movies as the focal point of our emotion-based application. Specifically, the interfaces included movie suggestions, trailers, and descriptions accessible by clicking on each movie. Additionally, there was a contact form for inquiries or to report any issues related to the movies. Furthermore, an "About" page was included to delineate the purpose of the movie website. Ultimately, we enlisted 29 distinct users who had not previously participated in the study. These users were tasked with evaluating the four web interfaces through interactive assignments. Following this, they were asked to assess the effectiveness of the web design in evoking a particular emotion via a questionnaire. Participants were not informed about the specific objective of the study, which was to evaluate their facial reactions to UIs.

4.1   Participants

We recruited 29 participants ($M = 21.06$, $SD = 2.3$, $Mdn = 18$) who were between the ages of 18 and 66 years and had not previously participated in the first study. There were 15 females and 14 males in this group. The greatest level of qualification held by 24 individuals is a bachelor's degree; 2 have graduated, 2 have PhDs, and 1 has a master's degree. The majority of the study's participants come from various academic backgrounds, such as architecture, urban planning, engineering, and marketing. Only 2 of these individuals have taken lessons specifically on UI design, whereas the remaining 27 have not. This distribution highlights the varied levels of experience with UI design within the participant pool, encompassing both those with formal training in the area and those without.

4.2 Stimuli

We created and implemented the Emotional Movie System, an interactive online platform that allows users to choose an emotion and engage with the associated web design. To accommodate a wide range of emotional experiences, we deliberately designed four separate interfaces, each customized to elicit and engage specific emotions: Happiness, Calmness, Surprise, and Anger. These interfaces were created to provide immersive experiences that correspond to the selected emotion, increasing user engagement and investigating the effect of interface design on emotional responses.

The designed pages are presented in Fig. 2 as follows:

- Each interface has a "Home" page for movie suggestions (Fig. 2).
- An "About" page with a website description (Fig. 2).
- Another page for the "Contact Form" to report issues or request that movies be updated (Fig. 2).
- Finally a movie description page along with a button to watch its trailer on YouTube or IMDb (Fig. 2 and Fig. 2).

All interfaces have the same movie content, but they differ in terms of design. The design criteria applied consider the primary aspects of Web design, such as colors and visual elements, clear or blurry text, the size of images and videos, page structures, content distribution, the presence and type of multimedia elements, the elements for navigation and interaction, and text insertion elements.

4.3 Procedure

The entire experiment was performed in a room on a laptop. Participants were introduced to the test procedure by a coordinator, and signed a consent form that we were allowed to record the test and participants' faces via the webcam. Participants were asked to interact with four different movie websites. We did not mention the purpose of the study or the reason behind recording their facial reactions. Each website was specifically designed to elicit a particular emotion: Happiness, Surprise, Calmness, and Anger. After interacting with each website, participants were asked to fill out a questionnaire. The questionnaire was structured into different groups, each focusing on specific aspects of the website and the participant's emotional response. The entire experiment was directed by a coordinator who was available for questions and observed task completion. A warm-up session was conducted to explain the experiment procedures. We recorded audio, screen, and the face of every participant. The video files were exported in mp4 format. When the experiment was finished, participants filled out a demographic questionnaire.

4.4 Tasks

We asked the participants to complete the following tasks:

- Scroll through each page and evaluate its design.
- Fill out a contact form on the movie website to request a movie or make an inquiry (Fig. 7).
- Visit the description of a movie of their choice (Fig. 6 and Fig. 3).
- Finally, respond to a questionnaire about the design related to each emotion.

This process was repeated for each emotion.

4.5 Results

The collected data, including responses on usability, design, emotional response, and functionality, was structured into a dataset. An ANOVA test revealed a significant effect of emotions on aesthetics perception (F-$stat$ = 5.736, $p \leq 0.05$), showing that emotions significantly influence how users perceive UI aesthetics. A Kruskal-Wallis test further confirmed a link between emotions and color perception (H = 19.584, $p \leq 0.05$).

For the "Happiness" interface, 22 participants suggested changing the color from "Red" (associated with danger) to alternatives like "Blue," "Yellow," or "Pastel Pink," aligning with prior studies [17, 18]. Additionally, participants showed nervous behaviors during the contact form task, prompting changes for later participants, and verbal expressions of frustration occurred due to excessive pop-ups (Fig. 5).

5   Emotion Prediction Model

For the construction of an emotion prediction model, certain steps warrant consideration. This section outlines the data preprocessing, the implementation of the deep learning model on the gathered data, and the resulting outcomes.

5.1 Data Preprocessing

From the camera footage captured during the experiment, we extracted videos in which the participants were interacting with the website. Each participant had 4 videos of 4 min, totaling 116 video files (29 participants * 4 videos). We extracted frames for every 200 milliseconds. The total number of frames was 10,748 files split into 80-10-10 (80% for training, 10% for validation, and 10% for testing). We ensured that each video frame contained only the participants' face, using the OpenCV library for video processing and the pre-trained Haar Cascade classifier [24] for face detection. This classifier is based on the principle of boosting, which is formed by collecting several weak classifiers to have a system with high capacity. The frames were converted to grayscale, to make our model invariant to color and lighting conditions.

5.2 Computational Model

To predict the user's affective reactions while interacting with websites. We used the Convolutional Neural Network (CNN) model designed to recognize affective responses from audio-visual inputs proposed by [14]. We took the part that worked with video inputs and fine-tuned the model hyperparameters to suit our data. We also excluded the multi-layer perceptron (MLP) component for our model. In the following, we describe the final architecture illustrated in Fig. 3. The model expects a 3-channel input, following the convention used in deep learning frameworks like PyTorch where even grayscale images are represented as RGB images with three channels. The first convolutional layer (Conv1) takes this 3-channel input and applies 32 filters of size 5×5, followed by Max-pooling and Dropout. The second (Conv2) and third (Conv3) layers increase the filter count to 64 and 128, respectively, using 3×3 filters each. After each convolution, ReLU activation is applied. The fully connected layers begin with FC1, which takes the output from the last convolutional layer and flattens it to a vector. This layer has (128*30*62) input features and outputs 120 features, using Xavier initialization. The subsequent layers (FC2 and FC3) further reduce the feature dimensions to 84 and finally 4, representing the output classes of the model.

All fully connected layers use ReLU activation except for the last layer, which employs a Softmax function for classification. The model also includes an adaptive average pooling layer (AvgPool) to ensure consistent input size to the fully connected layers regardless of the input image size.

Prior to feeding the images into the model, we resize the detected faces in each frame to a uniform size of 62×62 px. We also apply random horizontal flipping and rotation (up to 30 °) as data augmentation techniques, to increase the model's robustness. We split the data into 80% for training, 10% for validation, and 10% for testing. We used cross-entropy loss and the Adam optimizer with a learning rate of 0.0001, momentums $\beta_1 = \beta_1 = 0.9$, and a weight decay of 0.0001. The model is trained for 30 epochs using early stopping with patience of 5 epochs.

5.3 Results

To better understand the collected data, we trained a CNN model with activation hooks attached to specific layers to capture hierarchical features. After generating predictions, we extracted activation maps from Conv1, Conv2, and Conv3 (see Fig. 4), which highlight important regions in the images that influence the model's predictions [34]. These maps visually represent the spatial distribution of features the model considers critical for classification, such as facial expressions. Conv1 captures low-level details like edges and textures, while deeper layers (Conv2 and Conv3) identify more abstract features. Visualizing activation maps helps diagnose model behavior, ensuring it focuses on key elements for accurate, generalizable predictions. Overall, activation maps are an effective tool for visualizing and understanding the inner workings of CNNs, providing insight into the model's feature extraction and decision-making processes. Figure 4 shows the visualization of the activation maps alongside the original input face images. We observed clear differences between the visual representations of the last layer (Conv3) when participants were interacting with the different UI designs. Following

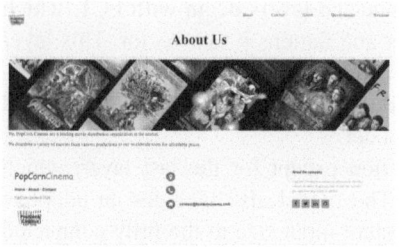

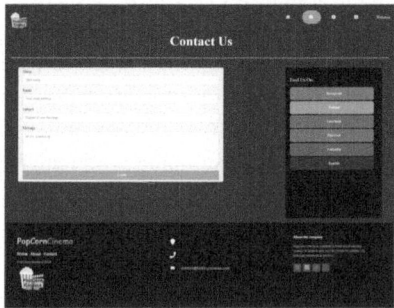

Fig. 2. Examples of the designed UIs eliciting specific emotions.

these observations, we computed ANOVA results for Conv2 and Conv3, as well as Tukey's Honestly Significant Difference (HSD) post-hoc test results for both layers. These statistical tests were conducted to analyze the differences in mean activation values among different emotional states as captured by the Conv2 and Conv3 layers of the neural network. For the second convolutional layer (Conv2), The *F-statistic* is significant ($t = 7.328$) with a P-value of $p < .01^{**}$, indicating significant differences among the group means. Whereas for the third convolutional layer (Conv3) The *F-statistic* is highly significant ($t = 985.826$) with a P-value of $p < .01^{**}$, indicating extremely significant differences among the group means. Tukey's HSD post-hoc test was used to

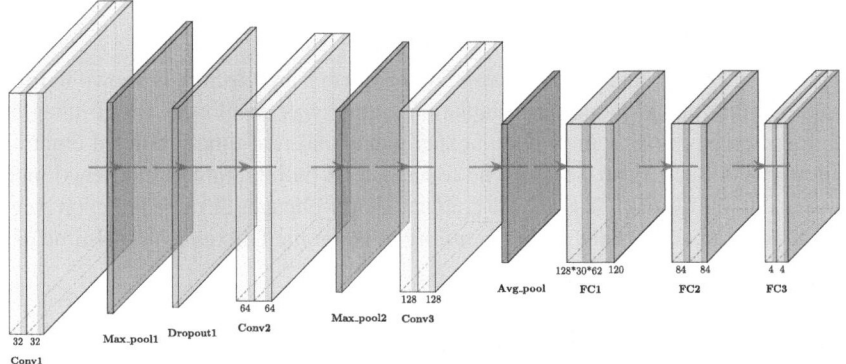

128*30*62 120   84 84   4 4
Avg_pool   FC1   FC2   FC3

64 64
128 128
Max_pool2 Conv3
Max_pool1 Dropout1 Conv2
32 32
Conv1

Fig. 3. Convolutional Neural Network Model for Facial Emotion Detection.

compare pairs of emotions after ANOVA to identify significant differences in mean activation values. For the second convolutional layer (Conv2), "Surprise" showed significant differences with "Anger," "Calmness," and "Happiness." In the third convolutional layer (Conv3), significant differences were found between all emotion pairs, except for "Calmness" vs. "Happiness." In summary, both ANOVA and Tukey's HSD post-hoc tests indicate significant differences in mean activation among the emotions for Conv2 and Conv3 layers. These results provide statistical evidence that the activation patterns differ significantly across different emotional states, as captured by the neural network layers.

Furthermore, we have computed the confusion matrix in Fig. 5, which summarizes the outcomes of these tests and visually represents the classification accuracy of the neural network model across the four emotional categories, has reached an accuracy of 83% on the test set, a significant improvement over previous studies that claimed facial expressions in HCI were not relevant [1].

Additionally, we seamlessly integrated the trained model to predict real-time emotions. This process is clearly shown in Fig. 6. This integration represents an important achievement in that it facilitates instant emotion analysis and improves the practical applicability of the model in a variety of situations. This real-time ability is essential for applications that require quick answers, such as adaptive user interfaces, interactive gaming, mental health monitoring, and customer service interactions. By implementing a real-time emotion recognition algorithm, we ensured that the model could cope with live data inputs, such as video streams or webcam feeds, and generate predictions in real-time. This required enhancing the model's performance to handle continuous data flow effectively while maintaining accuracy.

Overall, the ability to seamlessly integrate and use the trained model for real-time emotion prediction demonstrates the strength and versatility of our technique, paving the way for its application in a variety of real-world situations.

6 Emotional Interface Adaptation System

The proposed Emotional Interface Adaptation System's architecture is shown in Fig. 1. To validate the trained model, an adaptation engine was developed, which integrates rules for each emotion from previous experiments and real-time predicted emotions, as discussed in Sect. 3 and Sect. 4. The focus here is on integrating the trained model and rules into the system. Testing was conducted on webpages designed to elicit *Anger*, allowing an evaluation of the system's ability to adapt the UI based on real-time emotional cues.

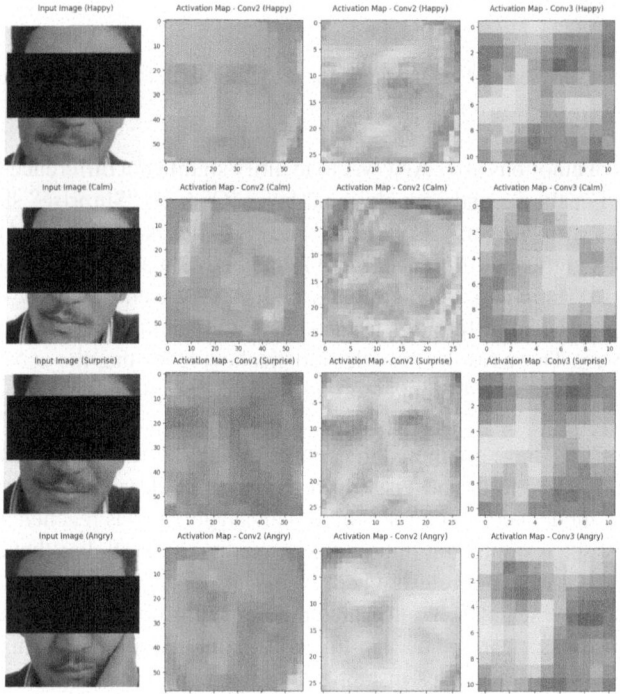

Fig. 4. Visualizing the activation maps of one participant while interacting with UI designs.

Figure 7 illustrates the user interface adaptation process. When a user opens the UI, the integrated webcam captures real-time facial images every 5 s Fig. 8). These images are displayed interactively on a canvas within the UI. The captured frames are then processed by the emotion detection model Sect. 5, predicting emotions like "Happiness," "Anger," "Surprise," and "Calmness," along with confidence levels. Based on these predictions, the UI adapts its design in real-time, following the guidelines derived from the study in Sect. 3. This ensures the UI dynamically responds to the user's emotional state, enhancing user experience and engagement.

In the example presented in Fig. 8, when the user opens the UI as a first step like illustrated in Fig. 8a, the model did not receive yet any frames of the user's facial expressions. Once the *angry* emotion is detected, the UI elements such as the background color, font size, navigation elements, and image size, get updated from the UI characteristics that provoke the *Anger* emotion to the design rules that elicit *Calmness* as illustrated in Fig. 8b.

Sequentially, when the system detected *Happiness* emotion, the rules related to *Happiness* have been applied to the UI (Fig. 8c).

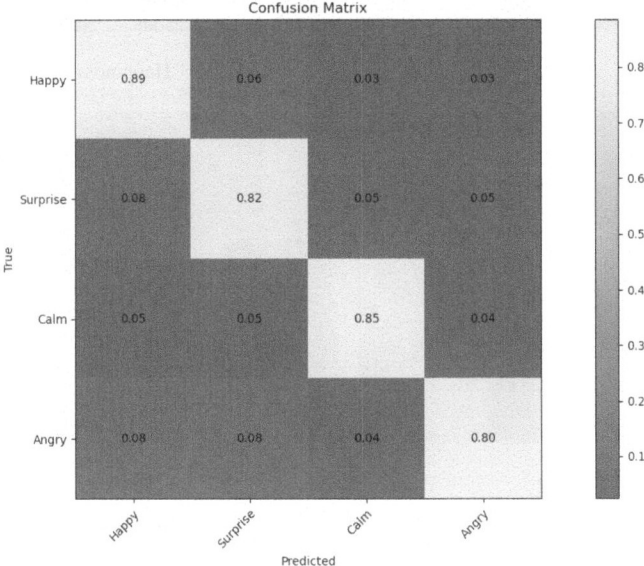

Fig. 5. Confusion Matrix for emotion classification using facial expressions.

In another example illustrated in Fig. 9 to validate the efficiency of our model, when the user wasn't engaged with the UI, the model was accurate in predicting *undefined emotion*.

7   Discussion

In this paper, we conducted an online survey to collect user opinions about UI designs related to each emotion (Happiness, Calmness, Anger, and Surprise). We have applied the collected data and developed four designs of a movie website, one design for each emotion, but the website's content remains the same. We conducted a second experiment in which we collected user affective reactions to the developed UIs design by recording their facial expressions. We have created a deep-learning model to predict the

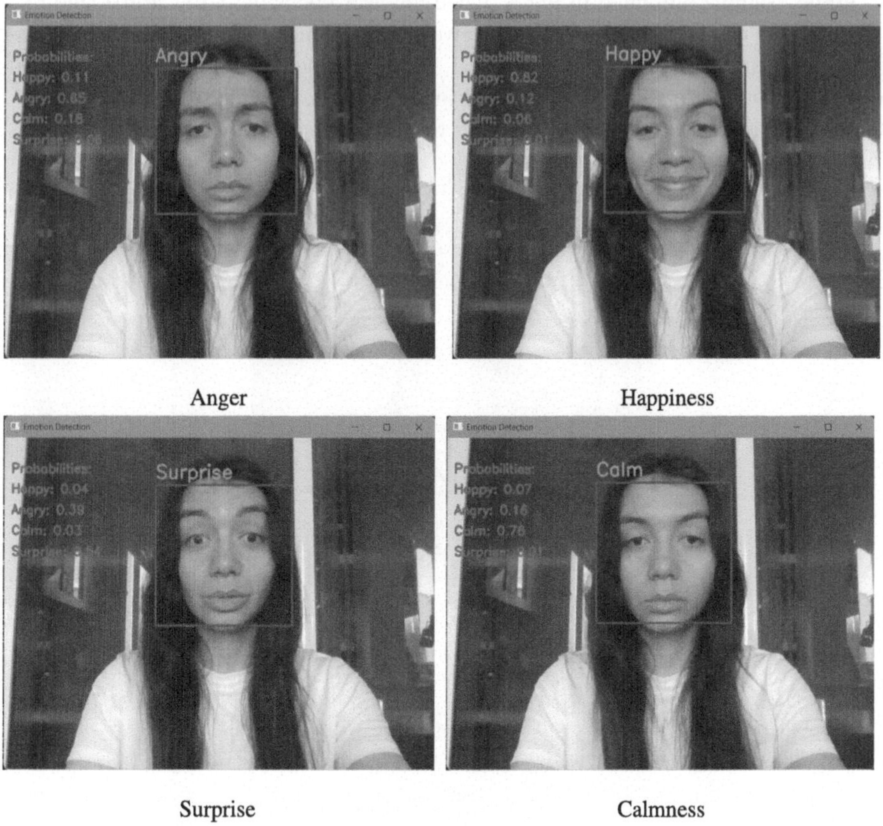

Anger

Happiness

Surprise

Calmness

Fig. 6. Realtime Emotion Detection.

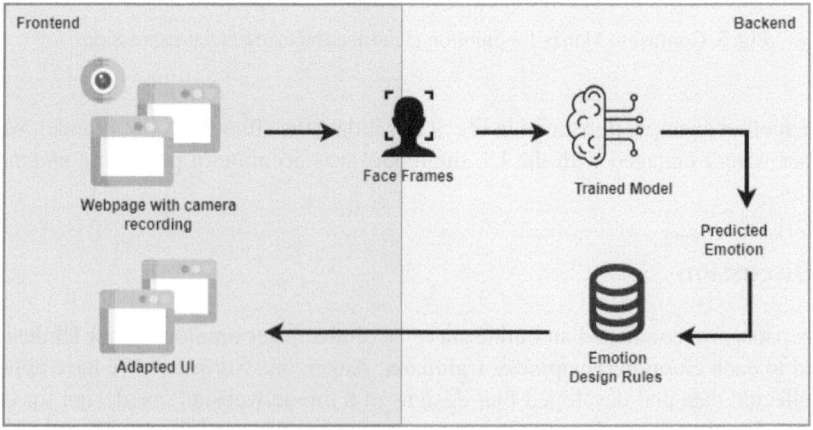

Fig. 7. Architecture of the Adaptation Engine.

(a) Start Point (no emotion detected).

(b) Adapted UI after "Anger" emotion detected.

(c) Adapted UI after "Happiness" emotion detected.

Fig. 8. Views during the UI adaptation.

user's emotional state with the collected data. We have integrated this computational model into an emotional interface adaptive system to evaluate its efficiency in real-world scenarios. We have applied the collected design rules for each emotion for the adaptation engine. We have addressed the challenging task of predicting user emotion from facial expressions in the context of HCI. Although prior work [1] found that facial expressions are not a reliable source in HCI due to the user's expressionless way of interacting with the interface, our computational model for facial expressions achieved good results with an accuracy of 83% to predict the emotional state of users.

Our approach diverges from conventional methods that lean on readily available tools for emotion detection [30–32], primarily because these tools are often trained on actors in controlled settings. Additionally, effective prediction often requires multiple software programs due to their inability to capture user emotions in the context of HCI.

Fig. 9. Example of a user disengagement to UI.

This results in the complex and cumbersome use of multiple software simultaneously. This distinction forms the cornerstone of our strategy. By departing from these standard practices, we aim to create a more nuanced and adaptable framework to capture real-world emotional nuances and variations better. This approach acknowledges the complexity and diversity of emotional expressions in natural human interactions, which is crucial for enhancing the accuracy and relevance of our emotion detection system. One of the limitations of our work is that we relied on one source to detect the emotional state. Nevertheless, for future work, we will try to integrate Eye Tracking (ET) and Electroencephalogram (EEG) to have a better understanding of the user's emotions. Currently, our prototype proposes simple adaptations (color, font size, navigation elements, image size) to emotions without referring to relevant work in psychology concerning preferences, or ergonomics and designers concerning user experience (UX). Coupling this existing knowledge with our system would allow us to provide a more relevant adaptation system.

8 Conclusion

We have extracted design rules for specific emotions such as Happiness, Surprise, Anger, and Calmness. We have developed a computational model to recognize users' emotional states through facial expressions during their interactions with UI designs in a free-viewing task. We have integrated this model into an emotional adaptive interface system to evaluate its efficiency in real-world scenarios.

Our research offers a new, efficient, and implicit method for UI affective evaluation, providing valuable insights for researchers and designers and paving the way for advancements in emotional assessment in software design.

Disclosure of Interests. The authors declare no disclosure of Interests.

References

1. Lockner, D., Bonnardel, N.: Emotion and interface design: how to measure interface design emotional effect? (2014)
2. Deshmukh, P. S., Date, S. S., Mahalle, P. N., Barot, J.: Automated GUI testing for enhancing user experience (UX): a survey of the state of the art. In: International Conference on ICT for Sustainable Development, pp. 619–628. Springer (2023)
3. Hartmann, J., Sutcliffe, A., Angeli, A.D.: Towards a theory of user judgment of aesthetics and user interface quality. ACM Trans. Comput. Hum. Interact. (TOCHI) 15(4), 1–30 (2008)
4. Demirbilek, O.: Evolution of emotion driven design. In: Emotions and Affect in Human Factors and Human-Computer Interaction, pp. 341–357. Elsevier (2017)
5. Galindo, J. A., Dupuy-Chessa, S., Mandran, N., Céret, E.: Using user emotions to trigger UI adaptation. In: 2018 12th International Conference on Research Challenges in Information Science (RCIS), pp. 1–11. IEEE (2018)
6. Sutcliffe, A.: Designing for User Engagement: Aesthetic and Attractive User Interfaces. Springer, Cham (2022)
7. Shakoor, A.: The Impact of Emotional Design in UX
8. Medjden, S., Ahmed, N., Lataifeh, M.: Adaptive user interface design and analysis using emotion recognition through facial expressions and body posture from an RGB-D sensor. PLoS ONE 15(7), 1–37 (2020). https://doi.org/10.1371/journal.pone.0235908
9. Lottridge, D., Chignell, M., Jovicic, A.: Affective interaction: understanding, evaluating, and designing for human emotion. Rev. Hum. Factors Ergonomics 7(1), 197–217 (2011)
10. Reinecke, K., Bernstein, A.: Improving performance, perceived usability, and aesthetics with culturally adaptive user interfaces. ACM Trans. Comput. Hum. Interact. (TOCHI) 18(2), 1–29 (2011)
11. Zen, M., Vanderdonckt, J.: Towards an evaluation of graphical user interfaces aesthetics based on metrics. In: 2014 IEEE Eighth International Conference on Research Challenges in Information Science (RCIS), pp. 1–12. IEEE (2014)
12. Kropp, M., Morales, P.: Automated GUI testing on the Android platform. Test. Softw. Syst. 67 (2010)
13. Bastien, C., Scapin, D.: Ergonomic criteria for the evaluation of human-computer interfaces. Dissertation, Inria (1993)
14. Details withheld to preserve blind review, 2023
15. Lan, M., Liao, J., Yao, Q.: The smartphone GUI design research based on the user experience. In: 2013 Fourth International Conference on Digital Manufacturing & Automation, pp. 1556–1560. IEEE (2013)

16. Engelmann, J.B., Hare, T.A., Fox, A.S., Lapate, R.C., Shackman, A.J., Davidson, R.J.: Emotions can Bias Decision-making Processes by Promoting Specific Behavioral Tendencies. Oxford University Press, Oxford (2018)

17. Kaya, N., Epps, H.H.: Relationship between color and emotion: a study of college students. Coll. Stud. J. **38**(3), 396–405 (2004)

18. Feng, H., Lesot, M.-J., Detyniecki, M.: Using association rules to discover color-emotion relationships based on social tagging. In: Knowledge-Based and Intelligent Information and Engineering Systems, pp. 544–553. Springer, Cham (2010). https://doi.org/10.10007/1234567890

19. Lockner, D., Bonnardel, N.: Towards the evaluation of emotional interfaces. In: Kurosu, M. (ed.) HCI 2015. LNCS, vol. 9169, pp. 500–511. Springer, Cham (2015). https://doi.org/10.1007/978-3-319-20901-2_47

20. Plass, J.L., Heidig, S., Hayward, E.O., Homer, B.D., Um, E.: Emotional design in multimedia learning: effects of shape and color on affect and learning. Learn. Instr. **29**, 128–140 (2014). https://doi.org/10.1016/j.learninstruc.2013.02.006

21. Watson, D., Clark, L.A., Tellegen, A.: Development and validation of brief measures of positive and negative affect: the PANAS scales. J. Pers. Soc. Psychol. **54**(6), 1063–1070 (1988). https://www.proquest.com/scholarly-journals/development-validation-brief-measures-positive/docview/614309965/se-2

22. Wang, J., Liu, Y., Wang, Y., Mao, J., Yue, T., You, F.: SAET: the non-verbal measurement tool in user emotional experience. Appl. Sci. **11**(16), 7532 (2021). https://doi.org/10.3390/app11167532

23. Mori, G., Paternò, F., Furci, F.: Design criteria for stimulating emotions in web applications. In: Abascal, J., Barbosa, S., Fetter, M., Gross, T., Palanque, P., Winckler, M. (eds.) INTERACT 2015. LNCS, vol. 9296, pp. 165–182. Springer, Cham (2015). https://doi.org/10.1007/978-3-319-22701-6_12

24. Viola, P., Jones, M.: Rapid object detection using a boosted cascade of simple features. In: Computer Vision and Pattern Recognition, 2001. In: CVPR 2001. Proceedings of the 2001 IEEE Computer Society Conference on, vol. 1, pp. I–511. IEEE (2001)

25. Janssen, J.H., Van Den Broek, E.L., Westerink, J.H.: Tune in to your emotions: a robust personalized affective music player. User Model. User-Adap. Inter. **22**(3), 255–279 (2012)

26. Medjden, S., Ahmed, N., Lataifeh, M.: Design and analysis of an automatic UI adaptation framework from multimodal emotion recognition using an RGB-D sensor. Proc. Comput. Sci. **170**, 82–89 (2020). https://doi.org/10.1016/j.procs.2020.03.011

27. Yang, R.-P., Liu, Z.-T., Zheng, L.-D., Wu, J.-P., Hu, C.-C.: Intelligent mirror system based on facial expression recognition and color emotion adaptation - iMirror. In: 2018 37th Chinese Control Conference (CCC), pp. 3227–3232 (2018). https://doi.org/10.23919/ChiCC.2018.8483540

28. Märtin, C., Herdin, C., Engel, J.: Model-based user-interface adaptation by exploiting situations, emotions and software patterns. In: International Conference on Computer-Human Interaction Research and Applications (2017)

29. Galindo, J.A., Dupuy-Chessa, S., Mandran, N., Céret, É.: Using user emotions to trigger UI adaptation. In: 12th International Conference on Research Challenges in Information Science (RCIS18), pp. 340–350 (2018). https://doi.org/10.1109/RCIS.2018.8406661

30. McDuff, D., Mahmoud, A., Mavadati, M., Amr, M., Turcot, J., Kaliouby, R., et al.: AFFDEX SDK: a cross-platform real-time multi-face expression recognition toolkit. In: Proceedings of the 2016 CHI Conference Extended Abstracts on Human Factors in Computing Systems, pp. 3723–3726. ACM (2016)

31. Microsoft.com: Microsoft Emotion API. https://www.microsoft.com/cognitive-services/en-us/emotion-api (n.d.)

32. Loijens, L., Krips, O.: FaceReader methodology (2008)
33. Dalvand, K., Kazemifard, M.: An Adaptive user-interface based on user's emotion. In: 2nd International eConference on Computer and Knowledge Engineering (ICCKE), October 18–19 (2012)
34. Zhou, B., Khosla, A., Lapedriza, A., Oliva, A., Torralba, A.: Proceedings of the IEEE Conference on Computer Vision and Pattern Recognition (CVPR), pp. 2921–2929 (2016)

Bridging Medical Genetics, Genetic Counselling, and Patients: Proposing an Immersive, Interactive, and Holographic Health Information Platform with Evaluation Methods for Personalized Patient Education

S. Chan-Bormei[1]([✉]), C. Srisukajorn[2], P. Teekakirikul[3,4], and H. Miri[5] [ORCID]

[1] AI and Computer Engineering, CMKL University, Bangkok, Thailand
csuy@cmkl.ac.th
[2] International Medical Program, Faculty of Medicine, Chulalongkorn University, Bangkok, Thailand
chalisa@docchula.com
[3] Preventive Genomics Clinic, Bumrungrad Genomic Medicine Institute and Department of Medicine, Bumrungrad International Hospital, Bangkok, Thailand
[4] Heart Institute and Department of Cardiovascular Medicine, Bumrungrad International Hospital, Bangkok, Thailand
polakit@bumrungrad.com
[5] International School of Engineering, Chulalongkorn University, Bangkok, Thailand
hossein.m@chula.ac.th

Abstract. This paper proposes the use of a personalized and interactive health information platform, dubbed HoloGrad, to explore the intersection of medical genetics and patient engagement. HoloGrad is an immersive and user-centered health information system, using virtual and holographic visualization for 3D interactions in medical genetics. This enables clear and comprehensible presentation and delivery of specialized information to patients. We posit that our approach to individualized genetic counselling can enhance information comprehension, increase retention, improve doctor-patient communication, and reduce genetic counseling time. This is achieved by presenting 3D visualizations on mixed-reality headsets, such as HoloLens and MetaQuest. Patients can see in 3D what a medical geneticist or genetic counselor is demonstrating through holograms and virtual simulations. This makes it easier to view, manipulate, and understand complex genetic structures and procedures. HoloGrad also boasts an interactive Pedigree Tree feature – a fully editable graphical tool for visualizing genealogical relationships and assessing disease risk by tracking family health history. To our knowledge, HoloGrad is the first platform to integrate a fully-fledged Pedigree Tree feature that allows medical professionals and patients to create a comprehensive overview of familial health, aiding in identifying potential genetic predispositions and empowering informed decision-making regarding preventative measures, monitoring plans, and treatment options. The evaluation methods and assessment strategies outlined in this paper offer valuable insights and guidelines, serving as a pivotal resource for those engaged in the exploration of virtual and holographic technologies and visualization tools.

H. Plácido da Silva and P. Cipresso (Eds.): CHIRA 2024, CCIS 2370, pp. 166–176, 2025.
https://doi.org/10.1007/978-3-031-82633-7_11

Keywords: Interactive devices · Immersive experiences · Mixed reality ·
Holographic visualization · Gesture-Based interaction · Design and Evaluation

1 Introduction

Throughout history, humanity has undergone a significant evolution in *communication and visualization methods* from cave paintings to complex languages. In the digital age, marked by exponential data growth and data-driven decisions, there arises a need for a medium to effectively and efficiently represent, analyze, and interpret vast amounts of data and information. While traditional 2D visualization has long served this purpose, the innate 3D nature of human perception and motion (as evidenced by our binocular vision and depth perception capabilities, e.g., [1] as well as numerous studies, e.g., [2]) calls for *immersive three-dimensional visualization*. These visualizations offer enhanced depth and facilitate intuitive, interactive, and dynamic representations beyond the confines of physical space, addressing some of the evolving demands of data exploration, information comprehension, and insights delivery (e.g., [3] and [4]).

One of the fields where such visualizations are making a significant impact is *personalized healthcare*. The advent of cutting-edge technologies is transforming personalized healthcare platforms, offering new avenues for innovation. Individualized and user-centered health information systems are, in fact, indispensable in healthcare: (1) they provide customized medical information and advice that can positively influence individual treatment or therapy success; (2) they can improve doctor-patient communication towards enhanced patient comprehension and increased information retention. Among the advancements in personalized healthcare is the emergence of *virtual and holographic health information systems*, revolutionizing medical information delivery in interactive and immersive 3D formats.

2 Background

Holographic and mixed reality technologies cater to diverse user groups. Experts, such as professionals in telecommunications, spatial navigation, and training, leverage these technologies for advanced applications such as holographic communication, virtual environments for training, and spatial data processing. The general public also benefits from these innovations through enhanced education with interactive learning experiences, immersive entertainment, innovative marketing strategies, and captivating live performances.

Interactive virtual and holographic technologies hold immense potential to transform healthcare (e.g., [4] and [5]). These tools are being explored for enhancing medical image analysis, surgical planning and execution, biomedical research, and remote patient monitoring. Furthermore, they are revolutionizing medical education and training by providing immersive learning experiences. A critical aspect is their ability to *improve communication between healthcare providers and patients*, leading to better understanding, decision-making, and overall patient care.

A major challenge during doctor-patient discussions is the *communication and visualization of information, procedures, events, or outcomes*. This is typically achieved through conversations, videos, slides, or simply drawing on paper. The abundance of 2D information sources (e.g., brochures, books, websites, slides, etc.) and diverse medical topics (e.g., symptoms, treatments, family implications, inheritance, order of screening procedures and testing events, etc.) often overwhelm patients, particularly in medical genetics and genetic counseling. This complexity results in a high intrinsic cognitive load, as outlined in the Cognitive Load Theory [6].

Patients lacking genetics knowledge often rely on *heuristics and cognitive biases* when processing complex genetic information, potentially resulting in confusion and communication challenges. Therefore, in medical genetics and genetic counseling, immersive 3D visualizations could greatly assist in informing and educating patients. They could also convey personalized medical information more easily and more effectively than mere 2D imagery, helping patients better understand their situations and complex genetic information, leading to improved support in pre- and post-counseling sessions. Such impactful outcomes also have *pedagogical* implications for educational practices, as the need for individualizing knowledge and information transmission to patients is aptly applicable to education too.

3   Review of Platforms, Tools, and Solutions

In a previous publication [4] we have presented a *literature review* of existing platforms and tools, beginning with user categories since innovative holographic and mixed reality technologies cater to professionals seeking expert solutions as well as the general public as end-users. We have also explored *research and applications* of interactive virtual and holographic technology in medicine, highlighting their potential to revolutionize medical practices. Additionally, we have reviewed some *related work* on various virtual and holographic applications and platforms. To avoid redundancy, we will not repeat this information in the current paper.

Moreover, we have previously unveiled HoloGrad [7] as a pioneering personalized health information platform designed to revolutionize the way medical professionals, medical translators, and patients engage with genetic data and information. This innovative holographic system allows users to immerse themselves in a dynamic 3D environment, enabling exploration through intuitive hand gestures, voice commands, hand-controllers, and gesture-controlled keyboard holograms. HoloGrad also offers an interactive feature known as the Pedigree Tree – a fully editable graphical tool incorporated into the platform that assists in visualizing genealogical relationships and assessing disease risk by tracking the health history of family members. As far as we are aware, the integration of such an advanced Pedigree Tree feature within HoloGrad marks a new step in the realm of interactive and customizable virtual and holographic genetic visualization tools and health information systems (Fig. 1).

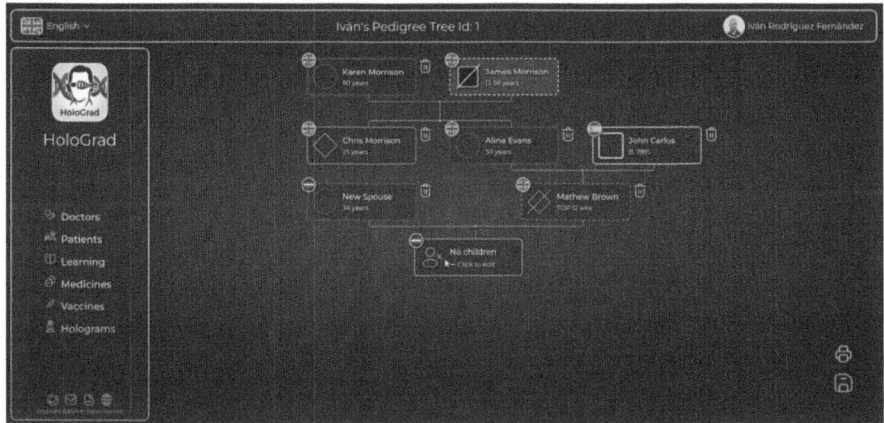

Fig. 1. A simple View of a Patient's Pedigree Tree.

4 Technological Foundation

The technological foundation of the HoloGrad platform (also unveiled previously [7]) is built upon hardware and software components designed to offer an immersive and interactive mixed reality experience. At the forefront stands HoloLens – a self-contained holographic computer and mixed reality headset, leveraging the Windows Holographic OS. Equipped with depth-sensing capabilities, gesture recognition, and real-time hologram adjustments, it delivers an immersive and interactive environment for users. Complementing this is MetaQuest – boasting high-resolution passthrough mode for seamless integration of real-world surroundings with digital content, making it ideal for immersive mixed reality experiences and enhanced training simulations. This headset comes with hand-controllers that facilitate easier selection and manipulation of holograms and other virtual content, surpassing reliance solely on hand gestures, a feature distinct from that of the HoloLens' (Fig. 2).

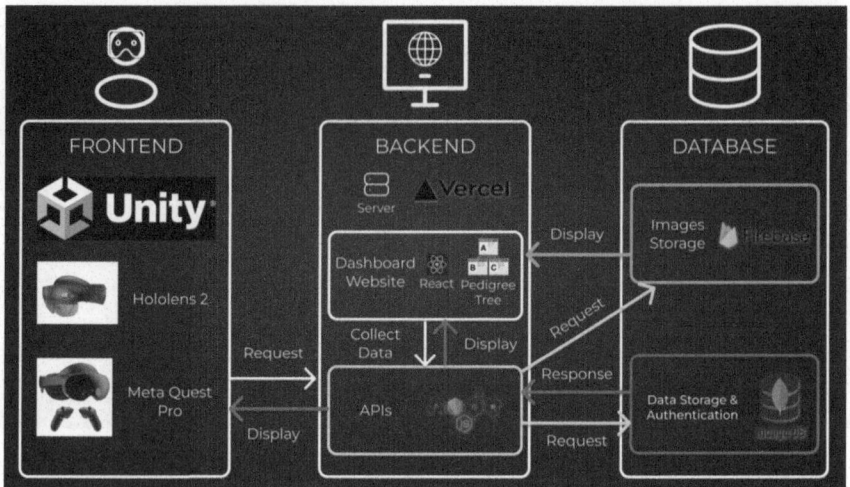

Fig. 2. A System Architecture Diagram: System Components, Data Flow, and Integration.

Driving the backend infrastructure is a combination of Vercel and Netlify platforms, each serving distinct purposes. Vercel hosts the backend dashboard, facilitating educational content management and offering automated visual analytics for medical professionals and patients. Netlify powers the content creation and management aspect of the dashboard, ensuring scalability and efficiency. The frontend interface of the application used by the doctors and hospital staff is developed using ReactJS, providing interactivity and responsiveness, while Firebase and MongoDB handle backend functionalities such as real-time database management, storage and user authentication (Figs. 3 and 4).

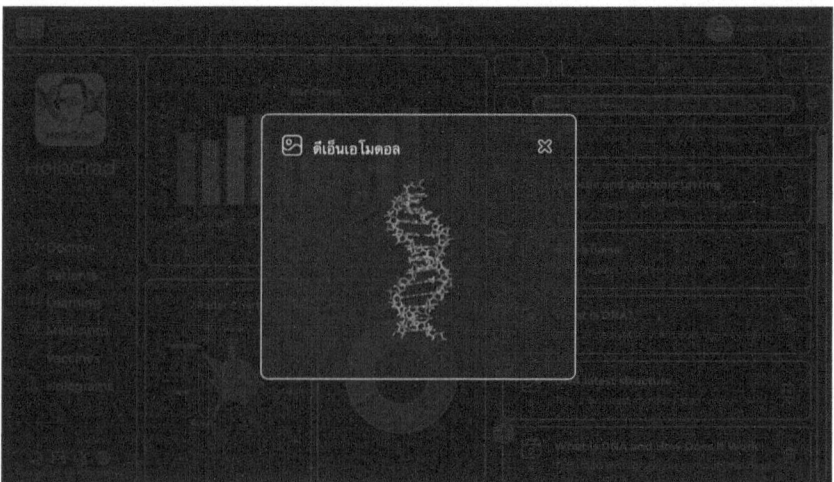

Fig. 3. Interactive Features within HoloGrad – DNA Structure Viewing in 3D.

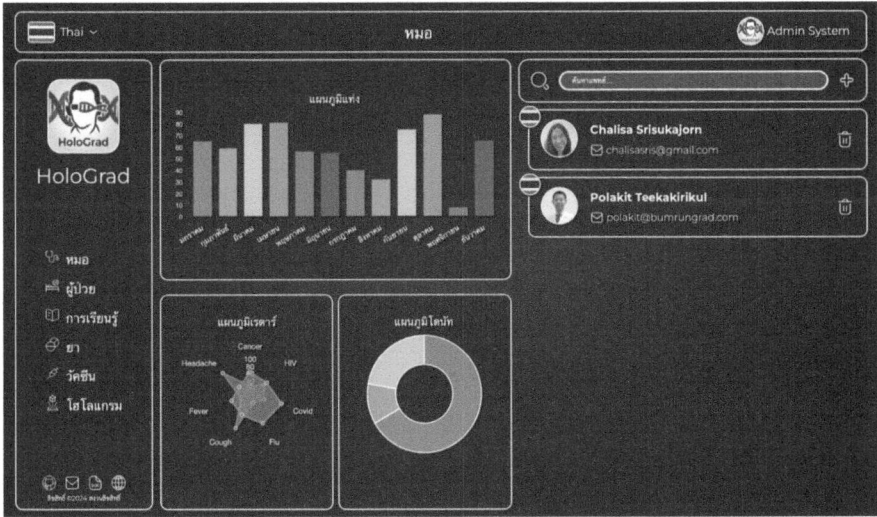

Fig. 4. A Simple View of Administrator Interface and Visualization Dashboard.

Central to the HoloGrad system is its comprehensive user management system, catering to hospital administrators, doctors, medical translators, and patients – each with specific privileges and access levels. The platform's diverse functionalities include *patient profile management*, *educational content dissemination*, *personalized genetic data visualization*, and *real-time interaction through mixed reality headsets*. Notably, the inclusion of the Pedigree Tree feature within the backend dashboard offers geneticists and genetic counsellors a powerful tool for visualizing and analyzing genealogical relationships, enabling a deeper understanding of hereditary diseases and facilitating informed decision-making for both healthcare professionals and patients.

5 Hypothesis

Our hypothesis is that patients who receive genetic information and counselling through the HoloGrad platform will have *a higher level of comprehension*, *increased information retention*, and *improved communication* with geneticists and genetic counsellors (as well as genetic nurses and medical translators) compared to patients receiving traditional methods of information delivery. HoloGrad comprises a visualization cockpit, currently integrated into HoloLens and MetaQuest headsets (and into the Apple Vision Pro in due course) creating a flexible and interactive virtual and holographic display as a visual aid to convey personalized genetic information to users. It has been designed, developed, and implemented as a mixed reality platform that can support 3D visualizations and interactions within the fields of medical genetics and genetic counseling that involve presenting background genetic information and displaying complex genetic structures as well as guiding patients through genetic procedures, thus contributing to patient education in a clear and effective manner (Fig. 5).

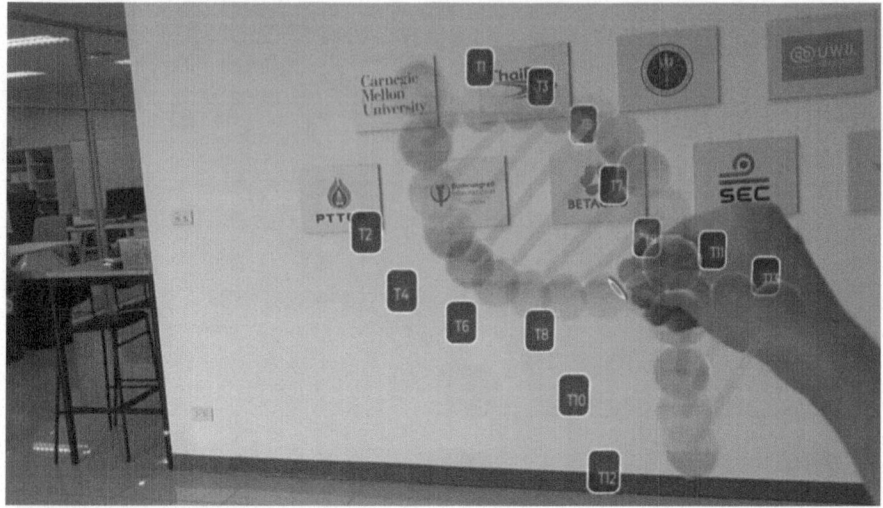

Fig. 5. An Interactive 3D Visualization of DNA Structure in HoloGrad.

We, therefore, propose the use of HoloGrad to explore the intersection of medical genetics, genetic counseling, and patient engagement. We believe that such an individualized health information system can ensure that patients are not overwhelmed, considering their information needs. Providing personalized information units for which the patient is excited and ready to see and learn, reduces the intrinsic cognitive load to a low level and constitutes a solid basis for an enjoyable flow [8]. For example, patients will be able to circle and examine virtual DNAs, see a preview of the steps involved in genetic screening and testing procedures, and myriad other forms of educational content prepared by the medical professionals. This will lead to improved patient education and result in consultation and counseling sessions becoming more effective and individualized, and thus shorter.

6   Proposed Evaluations

The HoloGrad design and implementation will be assessed through (1) *qualitative user-studies;* (2) *formative and summative assessments;* (3) *holistic qualitative evaluation with users;* (4) *global evaluation in the form of structured and semi-structured interviews with users;* (5) *Cognitive Walk-Through (CWT) evaluation;* and (6) *Forced Choice evaluation.* In other words, we will evaluate the HoloGrad system through qualitative user-studies as well as formatively and summatively using cognitive task assessments, patient surveys and questionnaires, in addition to a series of tests and physiological measures, followed by extending the evaluations to measure personal commitment to follow the prescribed course of treatment or therapy, and ascertaining if the knowledge-behavior gap [9] has been closed (Fig. 6).

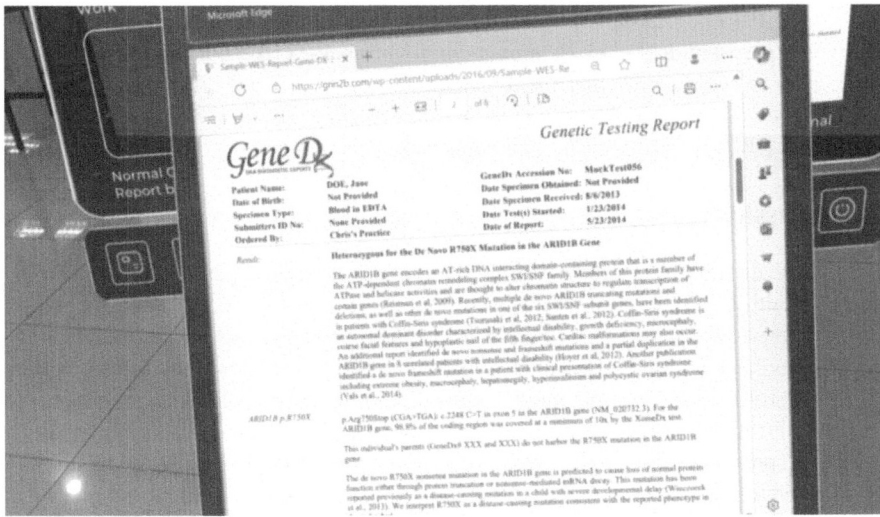

Fig. 6. A Visualization of Genetic Testing Report.

We will also use a holistic qualitative evaluation of HoloGrad with clinicians and patients (identifying specific usages and advantages that our approach offers users to accomplish tasks, and assessing the quality of takeaway experiences by gauging how it inspires a memorable experience that enhances information comprehension and increases information retention) as well as a global evaluation in the form of structured and semi-structured interviews with clinicians and patients (enabling targeted inquiries about users' opinions of the system, such as usefulness, appeal, and ease of use). Furthermore, we will perform CWT evaluation where system users are given pre-defined tasks to explore the system (for assessing the intuitiveness of the system and how quickly the content can be accessed, navigated, and grasped). Moreover, we will conduct Forced Choice evaluation where system users make choices between specified components, in order to get an overview of the system usability, develop a general understanding of patient satisfaction and ease of navigation.

In addition to these proposed evaluation methods, we will incorporate considerations inspired by [10] on *human–computer integration* and the *sense of agency*. This will involve examining how HoloGrad influences users' sense of agency, particularly regarding their perception of *control and influence* over the system's outcomes. Also, we will assess users' experiences in terms of their perceived *autonomy* and the extent to which they attribute actions and outcomes to themselves versus the system (i.e., Holo-Grad). This augmented evaluation framework aims to provide deeper insights into the implications of HoloGrad's integration within the context of human–computer interaction and interactive devices, emphasizing the importance of users' sense of agency and control in shaping their overall experience with the system. We, therefore, propose the following additional assessment strategies: (7) *User Studies to measure the sense of agency that users feel when interacting with HoloGrad;* (8) *Agency Delegation Assessment to evaluate how well HoloGrad balances agency delegation between the user and*

the system; (9) Integration Type Evaluation to analyze whether HoloGrad's integra-
tion type aligns with users' expectations and preferences; (10) Outcome Augmentation
Assessment to evaluate whether the augmentation of outcomes by HoloGrad enhances
users' sense of agency; and finally *(11) Sense-of-Agency considerations in the planned*
interviews, CWT and Forced Choice Evaluations.

7 Discussion

HoloGrad is driven by the ambition to create a novel, interactive, personalized, and holographic health information platform, incorporating a *genetic visualization tool* as well
as a *pedigree tree visualization tool*, where medical professionals, medical translators,
and patients can perceive and examine genetic data and procedures, and visually explore
3D perspectives using intuitive hand gestures, voice commands, hand-controllers, and
gesture-controlled keyboard holograms. The HoloGrad platform facilitates the visualization and presentation of incorporated *educational content* and *individualized medical*
information to the patient, while enabling *natural interactions* with diagnostic data and
3D visualizations through virtual and holographic interfaces.

The HoloGrad testbed containing various learning content is currently under evaluation by medical geneticists, genetic counsellors, genetic nurses and medical translators
through the numerous assessments proposed in section six. Following this phase, patient
trials will be conducted once (1) appropriate ethical and regulatory approvals have been
obtained, (2) safety and efficacy protocols have been established, and (3) data analysis
from the initial evaluation phase has been thoroughly reviewed. Doctors (e.g., medical
geneticists and genetic counsellors) should be able to plan and choose what information
and which method of presentation will be used for displaying to patients. Patients will
see, hear, and interact with the educational content that doctors have planned and chosen
for them in advance. Medical translators will possess the capability to observe and listen
to the materials that patients will encounter, enabling them to anticipate what requires
translation in advance. After examining the patient, a medical professional may wish to
upload or save their findings in the electronic medical records which can be securely
stored on the hospital servers (Fig. 7).

We have contended in [4] and [7] that the adoption of virtual and holographic
health information systems such as HoloGrad holds several potential implications for
personalized healthcare, including the following:

A) *Enhanced Patient Engagement.* Their displays and interactive interfaces empower
   patients to actively participate in their healthcare journey, leading to improved
   treatment adherence.
B) *Improved Communication.* They can enhance communication between healthcare
   providers and patients, promoting shared decision-making and ensuring a better
   understanding of presented medical information.
C) *Precision Medicine.* Providing therapies tailored to each patient is the vision of Precision Medicine, particularly in medical genetics and genetic counseling, where each
   individual's genetic makeup is inherently unique and vital for personalized healthcare. HoloGrad can leverage individualized data and analytics to support Precision
   Medicine, delivering targeted interventions and therapies tailored to individuals'
   unique characteristics.

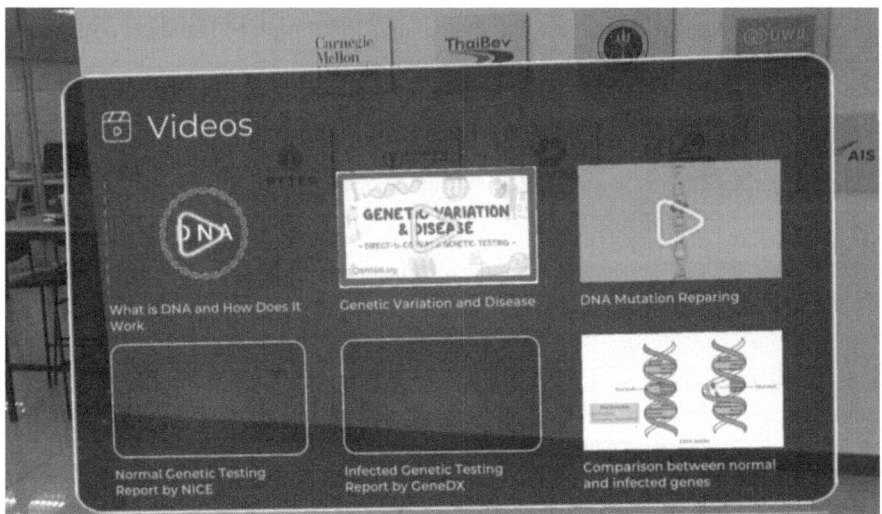

Fig. 7. Patient Education through Video Integration in HoloGrad.

8 Conclusion and Future Work

By leveraging advanced technologies, particularly immersive virtual and holographic tools and experiences, HoloGrad aims to revolutionize personalized medical genetics and genetic counseling. This innovative endeavor propels us towards the forefront of Precision Medicine, where tailored medical solutions based on individual genetic profiles re-define the future of healthcare. The platform is currently under evaluation by medical geneticists, genetic counselors, genetic nurses, and medical translators. Following this phase, patient trials will be conducted to ensure safety and efficacy. Medical professionals will be able to plan and choose the information and methods of presentation for patients, while medical translators can prepare for translation needs in advance.

Through upcoming case studies and user feedback in the next phase of the research, we will examine the efficacy and impact of this approach in bridging medical genetics, genetic counselling, and patients. The findings and initial feedback we have received so far from medical geneticists, genetic counselors, genetic nurses, and medical translators at the partner hospital, highlight the platform's significant potential and ease of use to enhance comprehension and decision-making in the realm of personalized genetics healthcare. This led us to propose a conceptual framework for the use of HoloGrad, with the evaluation methods and assessment strategies outlined in this paper, offering valuable insights and guidelines for researchers, developers, and healthcare professionals exploring virtual and holographic technologies and visualization tools.

This research contributes to the ongoing discourse on innovative strategies, interactive devices, and advanced technology-enabled interventions for improving healthcare delivery as well as patient studies and outcomes in medical genetics and genetic counselling. Furthermore, the assessment strategies and evaluation methods proposed in this paper constitute a valuable resource for researchers, developers, and medical professionals interested in leveraging virtual and holographic technologies to create interactive and personalized health information platforms, ultimately enhancing healthcare practices.

Acknowledgments. The HoloGrad R&D project is sponsored by Thailand's PMU-C which is a research funding unit that manages research and innovation funds aimed at enhancing the national competitiveness by creating innovations that enable industries to develop high-value goods and services to enter the global market, facilitating collaboration between the public and private sectors in Thailand and from abroad, and encouraging joint investment from firms, ranging from SMEs to large corporates. Grant Number: C05F660157.

Disclosure of Interests. The last author (Principal Investigator of the HoloGrad project) has received a research grant from PMU-C that includes a matching funds contribution from the Bumrungrad International Hospital. The research grant has been used to design and develop the HoloGrad platform, which stands poised for deployment at the hospital pending successful user tests and patient trials, subject to authorization and approval from hospital executives and managements.

References

1. Ware, C.: Visual Thinking for Information Age (3rd Ed) Morgan Kaufmann Publishers (2019)
2. Ginosar, G., Karpas, E.D., Weitzner, I., et al.: Dissociating two aspects of human 3D spatial perception by studying fighter pilots. Sci. Rep. **13**, 11265 (2023)
3. Qu, Z., Lau, C.W., Simoff, S.J., Kennedy, P.J., Nguyen, Q.V., Catchpoole, D.R.: Review of innovative immersive technologies for healthcare applications. Innovations Digit. Health, Diagn. Biomarkers **2**(2022), 27–39 (2022)
4. YongQi, Z., Chan-Bormei, S., Miri, H.: Transforming healthcare with immersive visualization: an analysis of virtual and holographic health information platforms. Manuscript (ICHVR 2023) Beihai, China. In: Proceedings of 2023 International Conference on Haptics and Virtual Reality. Su, J. & Qiao, X. (Eds.) Advances in Haptics & Virtual Reality – Learning & Analytics in Intelligent Systems, vol. 37, pp. 81–104. Springer, Switzerland (2024)
5. Kouijzer, M.M.T.E., Kip, H., Bouman, Y.H.A., Kelders, S.M.: Implementation of virtual reality in healthcare: a scoping review on the implementation process of virtual reality in various healthcare settings. Implementation Sci. Commun. **4**(1), 67 (2023)
6. Sweller, J.: Implications of Cognitive Load Theory for Multimedia Learning. In: Mayer, R.E. (ed.) The Cambridge Handbook of Multimedia Learning, pp. 19–30. Cambridge University Press (2005)
7. Chan-Bormei, S., Miri, H.: HoloGrad – A holographic health information platform for patient education: delivering personalized genetic information and counseling to users. Manuscript (ICVARS 2024) Melbourne, Australia. In: Proceedings of the 8th International Conference on Virtual and Augmented Reality Simulations, pp. 67–78. ACM, New York, USA (2024)
8. Schiefele, U., Raabe, A.: Skills-demands compatibility as a determinant of flow experience in an inductive reasoning task. Psychol. Rep. **109**(2), 428–444 (2011)
9. Stibe, A., Krüger, N., Behne, A.: Knowledge behavior gap model: an application for technology acceptance. In: International Conference on Mobile Web Information Systems, pp. 3–17 (2022)
10. Cornelio, P., Haggard, P., Hornbaek, K., et al.: The sense of agency in emerging technologies for human-computer integration: a review. Front. Neurosci.Neurosci. **16**, 949138 (2022)

Why Do(n't) You Trust Us? Highlighting the Importance of Trust and Transparency for Designing B2B Platforms in Electronics Manufacturing

Rafael Vrecar[1,2(✉)] 📷, Astrid Weiss[1] 📷, Wilfried Lepuschitz[3] 📷, Aaron Wedral[1,5] 📷, and Michaela Gaea Čolakovová[1,4] 📷

[1] Human-Computer Interaction Group, Institute of Visual Computing and Human-Centered Technology, TU Wien, Argentinierstraße 8, 1040 Vienna, Austria
{rafael.vrecar,astrid.weiss}@tuwien.ac.at
[2] Paris Lodron Universität Salzburg, Jakob-Haringer-Str. 8/Techno 5, 5020 Salzburg, Austria
rafael.vrecar@plus.ac.at
[3] bee produced GmbH, Julius-Tandler-Platz 7/11, 1090 Vienna, Austria
wilfried.lepuschitz@beeproduced.com
[4] Faculty of Biomedical Engineering, Department of Information and Communication Technologies in Medicine, Czech Technical University in Prague, Prague, Czech Republic
michaela-gaea.colakovova@fbmi.cvut.cz
[5] Independent Researcher, Vienna, Austria

Abstract. As online platforms have become increasingly important in the last decade, it also makes sense to conduct B2B (Business to Business) operations on online platforms. This paper deals with the aspects of trust and transparency in a B2B context, specifically in the development (and operation) of a platform where microelectronics manufacturers are connected with customers who want to produce a certain (part of a) product and find the best company to do so. The methods used were workshops with different stakeholder groups and expert reviews of the user interfaces of the platform under development. Our findings include that transparency and the power/freedom to do and undo actions within such a platform are essential for potential users as well as the care for their intellectual property. Additionally, we identified pitfalls in the current design which could reduce trust, e.g., as in our context, inconsistency regarding error messages.

Keywords: User trust · Online Platform Transparency · B2B platforms · Electronics manufacturing services · Data collection · Data handling

1 Introduction

In the last decade, online platforms evolved as vital means for fostering the relationship between service providers and customers [11]. These platforms and their respective companies are collecting vast amounts of data, which are not always collected and exploited appropriately and fairly, as, e.g., outlined in [5]. The tendency is that platforms prefer to acquire as much data as possible to be able to extract more insights and, in this way, adapt their services and attract more customers [4].

When looking at different kinds of such platforms, the users' needs for privacy, trust, and data protection might be quite different [8]. For example, when shopping on online platforms as a private individual, the protection of orders and visited products (i.e., the *user/customer data*) might be of high importance to the user, potentially contradicting the interest of the company to find links in customer data in order to provide the user with personalized offers. The developments regarding user-targeting ads and, in contrast to that, the privacy concerns of different stakeholders regarding the handling of their data are contents of current discussions, as can be seen in, e.g., [3]. Compared to that, in the context of a B2B (*Business to Business*) platform for microelectronics production, the protection of intellectual property has a very high priority for customers, as leaks could not only damage but ruin a whole business.

This paper explicitly deals with the B2B platform context. More specifically, we accompanied the process of a small start-up initiative to develop such a platform from an Human-Computer Interaction (HCI) research perspective. Including the HCI perspective aimed to help the platform to develop their features putting the user in the center of their product. This goal was articulated in the funding proposal which supported this research (see @refacknowledgements). Therefore, in this context, we asked *"What does (not) influence trust when handling user data in a B2B platform context?"* as our main question. In order to explore this, we aimed to involve three different stakeholder perspectives: *A)* **customers** who want to produce their ideas, *B)* **manufacturers** who want to receive orders, and *C)* **developers/operators** of the corresponding B2B platforms connecting the former two stakeholders.

Our concrete use case was that we worked closely together with a B2B platform developer who plans on operating a platform for electronics manufacturing services, i.e., connecting customers who want to produce, e.g., their custom circuit boards for their product with manufacturers who are best suited for the task based on parameters like locality, price, environmental friendliness, certifications, etc. The current state of development, more details on the platform we worked with, and the concrete flow of operation are described in Sect. 3.

We ran workshops with all three pre-defined stakeholder groups, in order to understand user requirements, expectations and concerns. All workshop participants had knowledge of the platform at hand and its context-of-use. Additionally, some of them already had seen extensive previews of the it. Moreover, we conducted an expert review of the current stage of the user interfaces of the platform and the already developed functionalities especially focusing on aspects of trust and transparency. We used the results to structurally list common pitfalls and potential solutions, based on the insights of both approaches, especially relevant in a B2B context.

2   Related Work

Shree et al. [12] analyzed how B2B platforms increased in amount over the last decade. However, they also state that the research in this context is not yet as extensive as in other fields. In their analysis, they underlined that there are various factors whether a

B2B platform succeeds or fails. Moreover, it is interesting to see why B2B digital platforms are often unable to exploit their possibilities and have higher failure rates compared to B2C (*Business to Customers*) platforms. Important in this context are *technological, organizational*, and *legal* factors. Riemensperger and Falk [10] second the different pace/success rate of B2B platforms compared to B2C platforms. In this context, they state that in the setting of manufacturing, as in our case, e.g., microelectronics parts, an equivalent "winner-takes-it-all effect" does not exist (yet) and that "key competitiveness" depends on "data-driven operation of the physical world".

Zhou et al. [13] highlight different points. *A*) they suggest a connection between B2B platform usage and increased performance outcomes of the business buyers using said platform. *B*) Using B2B platforms, according to their investigation, leads to lower transaction cost and *higher trust* towards the platforms compared to traditional supply chain methods. This outcome can be interpreted as B2B platforms offering features/mechanisms to create more efficient and secure transactions, i.e., reducing costs (e.g., for monitoring and negotiation) while, at the same time, enhancing *trust* among parties. *C*) The transaction frequency is a "cheerful moderator", meaning platform usage affects transaction costs and buyers' trust. This suggests a relation between transactions conducted and the advantages of lower transaction costs and higher trust (increase simultaneously). Regular platform use could lead to better familiarity with the platform's features, greater efficiency when conducting transactions, and stronger relationships between business partners, reducing costs while enhancing trust even further.

Moreover, in this context, Hein et al. [6] emphasized the importance of value co-creation, meaning that for the success of a B2B platform it is essential that values for the different stakeholders are created at the same time in a collaborative process. Anderson et al. [2] back up the importance of value creation, however, in contrast, in a between B2B and B2C markets context. In addition, it should be mentioned that the relationship between usability and trust is also a topic of interest, as seen in, e.g., [1].

What this literature review clearly indicates is the importance of *trust* and *value creation* for the success of a B2B platform. Additionally, it indicates that there are still unknowns with regard to how to approach designing platforms specifically for a B2B context, i.e., how to best incorporate stakeholder requirements into the design process and how said requirements differ from the requirements from platforms designed for private customers.

3   Use Case and Platform Description

3.1   State of Development and Scale of the Platform

The platform we worked with was at the time of conducting the studies (Q3 and Q4 of 2023) still in development and not in active operation. However, at that time, the launch was eagerly anticipated for within the next year. Therefore, the platform already was in a later stage of its development, near feature completion, and entering an extensive testing phase additionally to preliminary tests and previewing sessions with stakeholders.

Regarding the future scale of the platform, it has to be stated that this cannot be defined yet. However, the architecture should not negatively influence scalability as it is accounted for making the addition of new partners easy. Moreover, the data for the production of electronics artifacts in that scale is rather easily manageable, e.g., compared to storing lots of videos.

3.2   Flow of Interaction When Using the Platform

The following overview – as graphically shown in Fig. 1 – should briefly outline in which steps the interaction with the platform is divided. Please note that each step requires the completion of the prior step and that the platform enforces this.

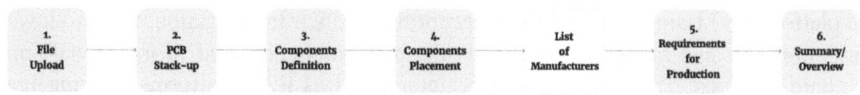

Fig. 1. Flow of Interaction.

The interaction we reviewed consists of the following six steps (in operation, there will be seven steps).

1. **File Upload:** In this step, the necessary files are uploaded and can be further edited to meet all requirements set by the platform. The whole process happens in the browser window.
2. **PCB[1] Stack-up:** Here, the PCB is further configured and specified: thickness, number of layers, and other parameters are set.
3. **Components Definition:** This step specifies, which components will be used and to what quantity. Furthermore, it can be decided if a specific component needs to provided by the customer or will be required from the manufacturer.
4. **Components Placement:** In this step, the placement of the components can be decided within a live preview which constantly refreshes to account for changes.
5. **Requirements for Production:** If there are specific certifications and other requirements necessary, they may be defined in this step.
6. **Summary/Overview:** Before requesting an offer or ordering, the whole input can be reviewed and edited if necessary.

The "7th" step will be between Step 5 and 6 and will show the overview of the potential manufacturers. However, when we conducted our study, this overview was not yet finished and we did not have any real-world data and therefore decided to leave it out.

Note that for the future, it is also planned that the mentioned *7th step* will include recommendations based on Machine Learning. Therefore, this issue already has been incorporated into our exploration.

---

[1] *Printable Circuit Board.*

3.3 Degree of HCI Researchers' Involvement in Platform Development

The HCI researchers who planned and ran the workshops and the expert review neither were nor had been actively involved in any development of the platform. However, the development of the in Sect. 4 described materials closely involved developers and future operators of the start-up initiative developing the platform. Therefore, the platform owners were involved in shaping the research but the direction and final decisions have always been made by the researchers independent form the platform owners (although they had the option of a veto). Moreover, the analysis, interpretation and write up of the results happened independently from the platform owners. As all results are completely anonymized, the platform owners did not request any restrictions in publishing the results.

4 Methods

We approached the topic with two core methods: workshops and an expert review of the prototypical state of the software. Those methods have been applied independently from each other and also with different aims for investigation. This approach was intentionally chosen in order to achieve a broader perspective. Therefore, the results are not directly comparable to each other but rather complement each other. The workshops were held with different *invited participants*, one at a time. Therefore, each workshop's size was smaller than, e.g., focus groups.

4.1 Workshops

In order to gain the desired insights, our workshops have been conceptualized so that each workshop consisted of a semi-structured interview, where different predefined questions were asked. Additionally, they had an embedded discussion in order to provide space for remarks beyond the answers to the questions.

Each workshop consisted of at least one HCI researcher, one future platform operator and one *invited participant*, i.e., not the HCI researcher(s) and not the future platform operator(s), but potential customers or manufacturers using or partnering up with the platform.

The invited participants had no access to the concrete contents prior to the actual workshop. However, all of them had knowledge of the platform and some of them had been given previews in advance.

In order to tailor the contents of the workshops towards each stakeholder group, different questions have been asked in each case. Moreover, as the workshop should also deal with the topics of transparency and trust on a broader scale, a common base of questions/discussion points has also been identified. Additionally, to obtain context of the corresponding invited participant "representing" a stakeholder group, a few demographic data points have been surveyed as well.

Questions and Discussion Points. The workshop contents have been developed in two sessions between the B2B platform developers and the researchers. For that, the different stakeholder groups (customers, manufacturers, platform operators/developers) have been identified first, in order to align the questions to their needs and perspective. Afterwards, we took the perspective of one stakeholder at a time and thought about the potential concerns and questions they might have. Based on that, we created a first draft of the questions to be asked. Building on this draft, the second discussion session rephrased a few questions slightly in order to frame them within a broader perspective. Out of this, the following workshop contents resulted.

Demographic Data: Stakeholder group (customer, manufacturer, platform developer) • Position and field of responsibilities • Years of experience in said position/field • Age • Education • General (personal) Approach/Preference regarding data collection (opt-in vs. opt-out)

Questions/Discussion Points for all Groups: What data do you expect to be collected in such an ordering process? Which of these data are stored permanently?[2] • To what extent do a) anonymization and b) explainability of the stored data and the storing circumstances and processing have an influence on your handling of such a system? • To what extent do you believe that the system "learns" or "learns wrong things" when you are interacting with it? Are you concerned about this? If so, why? To what extent does explainability play a role in this context? • Do you have any other questions/comments?

Customers Questions/Discussion Points: To what extent does knowledge about data retention influence your order placement? • To what extent are you willing to make your data available for improving the system in exchange for a discount on your order? How significant would this discount need to be? • To what extent and why is the security of your intellectual property important to you? What must be taken care of in the handling of your data?

Manufacturers Questions/Discussion Points: To what extent does data storage influence your pricing, if at all? • What is your general opinion of systems that use Machine Learning to make a selection? How important is the transparency of this selection to you? Why or what is or is not important to you?

Platform Developers Questions/Discussion Points: How can you ensure that the system does not learn fundamentally "wrong things"? Can you? • Assume that the system has learned to unfairly disadvantage a manufacturing company. How do you address this issue? Can you even address this? • How do you ensure that the system's "learning" does not inadvertently result in company secrets of the clients being leaked? • What problems do you see with such an intermediary system? How can you counteract them?

---

[2] Note that we did not ask specifically about GDPR, as the company must be GDPR compliant based on where it operates.

Procedure. Eight online workshop sessions have been conducted with audio and video being recorded. Five representative customers have participated as well as two manufacturers, and one workshop was conducted with platform developers and operators. The duration of the workshop has been 15 min on average[3] for the customers. The workshop with the manufacturers took $\approx$ 10 and $\approx$ 20 min. In each workshop, every question/point could be discussed.

Each workshop started with a brief introduction of the project and the platform in development. Afterwards, we explained the structure of the workshop and outlined the different groups of discussion points. Moreover, after the contents group with the points for all stakeholder groups, and at the very end of the workshop, the invited participant has been given space to add personal thoughts and remarks.

For working with the platform developers, we have taken a different approach as we hold a meeting together with the CEO, two lead developers, and two HCI researchers, where we discussed all the listed questions together and in parallel interacted with the platform in order to get a better understanding of the whole interaction and development process.

Analysis. For data analysis, we used a content analysis procedure as described below.

For each Recording

1. Prepare a form based on the questionnaire which leaves space after each question/point to fill it with notes.
2. Listen to the recording and take notes based on the points the invited participants make or issues/questions they raise.
3. Structure the notes and identify keywords/headlines for each issue.
4. Listen to the recording again and add notes if necessary.

Merging the Results

1. Merge the notes per question of all invited participants.
2. For each question:
   (a) Summarize connected issues to a meta issue.
   (b) Count for each meta issue how often it has been raised (and by whom).

4.2 Expert Review

Additionally to the workshops, two HCI experts with a finished Master's degree in Computer Science with strong focus on Human-Computer Interaction and aiming on pursuing a PhD in this field conducted an expert review of the user interface that was already developed when we began our collaboration with the B2B platform. We focused on identifying issues that could undermine trust in the platform or result in opaque interactions for users.

The expert review was conducted by independently doing a walk-through of the whole platform at hand (with test data) and then, directly after each step, discussing and merging the results.

---

[3] $2x \approx 12$ min; $1x \approx 13$ min; $2x \approx 17$ min.

After collecting our findings, we clustered them into *general issues* which were present in multiple steps or were independent from the actual activity and issues specific to individual steps of the ordering process.

5   Results

5.1   Workshops

Demographic Data. All invited participants were in leadership positions, namely owner, manager, head of IT, co-founder, lead electronics developer, head of purchasing, and managing partner. All respondents had been in their position for two years or more, with a minimum of two years and a maximum of almost twenty years. Their ages ranged from 31 to 56, with a median of 42 and an average age of $\approx$ 42.1. The respondents' education ranged from PhD at technical universities to completed apprenticeships, all related to computer science, electronics, or machinery.

Regarding their preferences for data collection, cookie banners, etc., there was a consensus that they were somewhat annoying and inconvenient, but that they still did not "accept everything". However, most of the invited participants emphasized that the degree of restriction depends strongly on the effort required to achieve these restrictions (i.e., if websites make it easy to reject cookies, they do so, if not, they do not bother too much). Private browsing was mentioned as a workaround, since all cookies are deleted after a session anyway. They also stated that their willingness to share data depends on the level of trust they have in the site in the first place.

Questions for All Groups. Regarding the data that invited participants expect to be temporarily or permanently stored for such an ordering process, they expected different data (groups):

– Project/product data (parameters, parts lists, schematics, size, quantity, Gerber[4] files, article code)
– Company data (name, contact details, tax and compliance details, address, responsible person)
– Additional data, e.g., shipping tracking, IP address

In addition, all invited participants expected that some data would need to be stored permanently for compliance reasons, e.g., company, order amount, project metadata. However, most of them expected that project-specific intellectual property would be kept only as long as necessary, i.e., for reordering parts. In addition, most of them expected that they could request the deletion of their data (GDPR) and that some of the data would be used for service improvement through Machine Learning.

Regarding the questions whether *anonymity* and *explainability* are important to them, most of them mentioned that anonymization and transparency regarding the stored data is important to them. However, explainability was not considered as important, with arguments of not caring or simply not understanding what is happening anyway, i.e., AI/Machine Learning. However, it was also pointed out that people already

---

[4] Gerber Format Specification: https://www.ucamco.com/en/gerber, accessed March 5, 2025.

visit the platform with the intention of ordering something and therefore already expect that some data will be stored later anyway. Some also made a distinction between visiting sites as a company, i.e., using the company's internet connection and device, and visiting sites in a private context. In addition, underlying regulations and protection of intellectual property were mentioned, i.e., transparency in this respect.

Assuming that the system used operates on the collected data with Machine Learning and uses this workflow to improve results, user experience, etc., the invited participants were asked whether they were afraid that the system would "learn" from their interaction in general or even "learn wrong things". The majority were not afraid of the system learning in general or learning wrong things because it was argued that if the results lead to a disadvantage for their own company, they would stop using the platform anyway. Moreover, it was also stated that it is to be expected (simply based on statistics) that a system might learn "wrong things", but that – if the positives outweigh the negatives – they would still use the platform. In addition, it was argued that one should expect that *a human entity* would monitor the results on a regular basis anyway, and that incorrect learning would be corrected that way.

When asked for additional comments, most invited participants did not have any. Regarding NDAs (*Non-Disclosure Agreement*), it was noted that in many cases the fear of losing a good reputation is enough to work with larger partners; however, when working with smaller, less well-known companies, NDAs are part of the daily business. One invited participant emphasized that they strongly believe that the attitude towards data collection is a very subjective matter and therefore a high degree of flexibility, i.e., fine-granular settings, regarding the degree of data collection is most important. An additional comment was made about the trade-off between privacy/data protection and convenience/ease of use (i.e., pre-filled forms when reordering, etc.).

Customers-Specific Questions. Regarding the question of whether knowledge of data collection/storage influences procurement, invited participants' answers show that it depends on the context, i.e., how valuable the intellectual property is, how important data protection is to potential sub-customers, whether it is a "core technology" or just an ordinary part. Some invited participants said that it was rather irrelevant, but that the platform itself had to be trustworthy. A discount could be an incentive to share more data, but again it depends on the context. *Ten percent* were mentioned as a starting point. In contrast, one invited participant stated that they would not consider a discount to be trustworthy and would only begin to question the legitimacy of the partner. These insights support what we know from the literature, namely that institutional trust plays a crucial role in B2B platforms, especially online marketplaces. It influences inter-organizational relationships and transaction success [9]. However, this type of trust is mainly developed through mechanisms such as legal bonds and cooperative norms, but it can also be impacted through design regarding accreditation and feedback mechanisms [7].

De facto, all invited participants agreed that intellectual property protection is very important to them, not only financially but also legally. In addition, it was mentioned that a data leak, even if after a court case it is agreed that the company has suffered damage, the time when the leaked data is already out there is much more damaging, even if one gets compensation afterwards. Because once the data is out there, companies can change a few things to make it untraceable and therefore not protected by patents, etc.

Manufacturer-Specific Questions. Manufacturers were asked if knowledge of data collection/storage affected their asking price.

Both agreed that it does not influence their pricing, but that a) it might be important in building trust and b) it might be interesting to know what asking price a bid in the past had.

Regarding their view on Machine Learning systems that select the most suitable business partner or similar, they answered that it would be interesting to see how the selection process works, but rather on a general level (e.g., 5 pages of white paper vs. 250 pages). One invited participant mentioned that progress is a good thing, that they generally have a positive view on Machine Learning technologies.

Developer-Specific Questions The session with developers confirmed the expected data collection by customers and vendors. However, it was also explained that, for now, the recommendations will not be based on Machine Learning, but on a custom algorithm that takes into account various parameters in a deterministic way. In addition, the recommendations will be verified by humans.

5.2 Expert Review

This section briefly describes the issues identified by the expert review. Within Sect. 6, we discuss why some issues are rather "obvious" and not specific to the application context at hand, compared to some *specific*, and from our perspective, *highly relevant* ones to the specified B2B context.

Issues marked with X have been removed from consideration as explained directly following the list.

General Issues:

G.1 Incomplete, inconsistent error messages X
G.2 No start-over/delete all option
G.3 Unexpected behavior in some paths X
G.4 Maintaining control at every stage is difficult, a step reset option is missing

Step I *File Upload* Issues:

I.1 File deletion visibility on small screens X
I.2 Inconsistent minimum screen width X
I.3 Potential confusion between Gerber file and Gerber layout file
I.4 No "Undo" for deletion
I.5 Confusing iconography (e.g., trash can looks like a cooking pot) X

Step II *PCB Stack-up* Issues:

II.1 Thickness adjustment defaults to zero X
II.2 Tool-tip clarity
II.3 Stacking view alignment
II.4 Preview is not clustered
II.5 Inconsistent brushing and linking
II.6 Filename visibility X

Step III *Components Definition* **Issues:**

III.1 Sometimes "dead end" after deleting a component X
III.2 Ambiguity in locating the edit option X

Step IV *Components Placement* **Issues:**

IV.1 SVG rendering anomalies X
IV.2 Table import without "Undo" functionality
IV.3 Cross-hair symbol appears misleading X
IV.4 Over-engineered file import

Step V *Requirements for Production* **Issues:**

V.1 Initial error message X
V.2 Unusual selection process
V.3 Ambiguity in mandatory fields
V.4 Complicated certification selection
V.5 Small size of comments field X
V.6 Billing address and shipping address linkage
V.7 Inconsistency in error message display
V.8 Inadequate address validation

Step VI *Summary/Overview* **Issues:** None.

The following issues (marked with X) have been removed from consideration for this paper: $G.1$, $G.3$, $I.1$, $I.2$, $I.5$, $II.1$, $II.6$, $III.1$, $III.2$, $IV.1$, $IV.3$, $V.1$, and $V.5$. We removed these issues because being unable to conduct some actions on smaller screens without reasoning/explanation is a bad habit in all software projects, the same goes for the scaling of elements based on screen width as the same rules should apply for elements of the same kind. Iconography should enhance the experience and not confuse people (e.g., one cannot cook a circuit board by pressing on a button [cooking pot], one would much rather want to see a distinct trash can). Moreover, a "dead end" should never happen, even less so if you just conduct an arbitrary action. SVG rendering bugs have to be fixed independently from the context in which the SVG file is embedded. Having an error message showing up by default should also never be an intended behavior. In our case, users were greeted with an error message stating "this field is required," before they even had the chance to fill it in.

Note that we argue that all above mentioned and below discussed issues are relevant in relation to trust as they might strongly influence how users *perceive/experience* the interaction with the platform. For example, when they do not have control to change or delete data immediately, they might *already feel* insecure about using the platform.

6 Discussion

Based on the results of the workshops and review of the interfaces, we derived a set of important points which should not only improve the design of the evaluated platform, but are relevant for B2B platforms in general. These discussion points were carefully derived from the results of the aforementioned analysis process. All involved researchers participated in the discussions, ensuring that the points were examined from multiple perspectives.

The following discussion points have been mainly derived from the results of the workshops. This has been done based on "Merging the Results – (2)(a)" in 4.1. For that, the identified meta issues have been rephrased to be imperatives, if necessary (e.g., *Transparency* has been rephrased to *Be transparent.*)

Additionally, the identified discussion points also have been checked against the results from the review of the interfaces and held up, i.e., did not contradict them in any way but rather seconded why the issues of the interfaces we identified are relevant. We identified five key points:

1. **Be Transparent.** Explain to *customers* who upload their intellectual property *which* data is being collected and for *what* reasons. The same applies for *manufacturers* when starting a partnership with your platform.
2. **Give Users Power.** If *customers* are uncomfortable sharing certain data, allow them to opt out, even beyond the requirements of GDPR. The same applies to *manufacturers*, although they should clearly know that their data might influence how often or strongly they can be recommended.
3. **Make It Easy for *customers* to stay in control.** Do not use *Dark Patterns* to make it difficult, time-consuming, or cumbersome to opt out of data collection/processing. The same applies for *manufacturers* but their data appears to be in general less protected than intellectual property, e.g., pricing is often even publicly available.
4. **Communicate Care.** *Customers* and *manufacturers* should not only know what happens to their data, but also that your platform cares about them and their data. You want to work with them in a symbiotic, win-win relationship, not an exploitative one.
5. **Make Separation Easy.** Do not try to keep *customers* as well as *manufacturers* by force. If they are happy with your services, they will continue to work with you. Sometimes a job is simply done and your services are no longer needed. Think of this as a successful relationship with a successful ending, not a failure.

While those points do not aim to be a complete set in order to ensure that a platform is definitely transparent and trustworthy, they should much rather be a common discussion starting point for platform developers and operators in order to aim towards maximizing transparency and trustworthiness of a platform in this application context.

Following up on those general discussion points, we list rather software-specific/implementation-specific points based on the issues we identified in the review of the interfaces. Those issues we considered to be important for or specific towards B2B platforms, especially in the electronics manufacturing context. Out of those, we identified the following discussion points[5].

1. **"Start-over" or "Delete all" Feature.** This should allow users to easily *granularly* reset their progress. It should enhance trust by giving users more control over their actions within the system.
2. **Clear Options and Feedback at Every Step.** This should allow users to understand and control what is happening by enhancing user interface elements to make navigation and decision-making more intuitive.
3. **Resets for Each Step.** A reset feature for individual steps, allowing users to revert changes in a specific part of the process without affecting others, as users might require the ability to reset each step individually once they are satisfied with the preceding step, should be considered. Additionally, in our project context, deleting files cannot be undone, posing a risk of accidental data loss or – more likely – a necessity for re-uploading the file. This could be mitigated by introducing an undo feature or a temporary file recovery system, such as a *trash* function, which could mitigate this issue.
4. **Clear and Consistent Terminology – Especially for Domain-Specific Terms.** In our project context, users might get confused over the distinction between Gerber files and Gerber layout files, as the indicator states that no Gerber file is provided, even though a Gerber *layout* file is provided.
5. **Using tool-tips carefully and consistently.** If one does not place tool tips visibly and consistently, this might lead to potential misunderstanding or missed information. One should also consider the timing of their appearance and positioning on the screen.
6. **Alignment in a PCB Stack-up View.** While a stack-up view might be helpful in a configuration process, its alignment must be optimal for practical use. Therefore, one should adjust the alignment of the stacking view to enhance its functionality and usefulness while ensuring it aligns sensibly with other UI elements, especially table lines with corresponding stack-up layers.
7. **Not Separating Without Reason.** In our case, the previews are on the left and right side of the page, unnecessarily separating similar UI elements, allowing for similar interactions. Developers should, therefore, consider the feasibility of arranging previews next to each other to aid users in visualizing changes or selections more effectively.
8. **Allowing Consistent Selection of Elements.** In our case, the implementation of the *brushing and linking* does not allow for the selection of links. This makes it impossible, for instance, to explore selected layers in a *vertical view* and, afterwards, in a *XY preview* without it changing back to the default selection in between.
9. **Carefully Elaborating Which Edit Options Should Be Provided Within the Tool and Which Requirements an Imported File Already Must Have.** E.g., our table import feature allows changes but lacks an "Undo" option, which can lead to irreversible actions. Therefore, implementing an "Undo" feature for the table import

---

[5] Please note again that those discussion points do not aim to be complete or finished but rather show a work in progress state which could be further elaborated on in future work.

function to allow users to revert changes would help. Additionally, the file import feature might be seen as overly complicated or over-engineered. Therefore, simplifying the file import process, focusing on user-friendliness, and removing unnecessary complexities to streamline user interaction would be welcome, i.e., it is better not to allow editing of tables within the interface but rather guide the users towards doing that on their local system in advance.

10. **Have a Powerful Undo Functionality.** Aligning with the prior issue, the general absence of an "Undo" function across the process can lead to mistakes and decrease user confidence in the system. Integrating a comprehensive "Undo" functionality throughout the software to allow users to quickly correct mistakes and feel more secure/confident in their actions might be appreciated by them.

11. **Allowing to Go Back the Way One Came.** In our case, once a selection is made, users cannot revert to a default "choose" option without using a specific "X" button. Improve the selection mechanism to allow easier reverting to the default option.

12. **Explaining, *why* Fields Are Mandatory.** In our case, whether certain fields are mandatory is unclear, causing user uncertainty while selecting.

13. **Troubles with Certification.** In our case, selecting the necessary certifications for the manufactured artifacts was non-intuitive. Simplifying the certification selection process and making it more user-friendly and intuitive will clarify to users which certifications they need. Creating relations of certifications, e.g., having shown which certification already is a super-set of others, based on its requirements, might help in this process.

6.1 Limitations and Future Work

First and foremost, our work on trust and transparency design for B2B platforms, is based only on one use case – electronics manufacturing. In order to better understand the interrelation of topics specific to B2B platforms and HCI issues, future work is needed, e.g., it would be interesting to explore the ecological validity of our identified factors with big institutionalized B2B solutions, such as Alibaba, Amazon Business, and ThomasNet, as our work revealed the importance of institutional trust for manufacturers and customers.

Additionally, to the narrow use case, the small number of participants and their limited availability are also a clear limitation, as we were not able to really follow up on the results and ask questions when something was unclear during the analysis phase. Moreover, it has to be stated that the stakeholders we worked with all were potential customers or business partners for the platform at hand. Therefore, there was a trade-off between mentioning and discussing all concerns while avoiding to raise doubts about the concrete platform in development in order to not negatively effect their business relations. This was a specific requirement by the cooperation partner to conduct the study. In order to comply with this requirement, we took a more general approach of formulating potential issues or transparency aspects.

From the project perspective, a follow-up to revisit the platform again with the same stakeholders once in operation is a relevant future research activity. Additionally to similar workshops, future research can work with logging and usage data which will give us novel insights.

7   Conclusion

To summarize, we conducted a series of workshops with three different stakeholder groups and run an expert review of a B2B platform in the electronics manufacturing context from an HCI perspective. Several critical factors have been pinpointed regarding transparency and trust within the current state of the platform. These aspects are also intended to be extrapolated into the broader context of B2B interface design. Similar to [13], we identified the relevance of trust and that it mainly was interpreted as institutional trust by our stakeholders.

On a more individual level, transparency was a key concern for users, as well as having "power" within the platform, i.e., changing one's actions or reverting them quickly. As users are concerned about their data, especially their economically crucial intellectual property, providers should act with care and communicate this.

Moreover, users want to avoid entangling relations with much effort once they decide to leave a service for whatever reason. When designing software for an ordering process of the described kind, different issues might get overlooked at first. While one might want to make data curating easy within the software, whether this complexity is appropriate has to be decided, as users might already have preferred tools to curate their data locally. For transparency, it would be desirable to provide users with clear guidance on which format the uploaded files should have instead of allowing to edit them online. Additionally, ordering can be a complex process. It might need iterations, changes, and corrections. Allowing control in each step and creating "checkpoints" to not have to redo everything once a specific step does not turn out as expected, is much appreciated.

To conclude, the development team is currently evaluating all points mentioned in Sect. 5. They will be considered when defining the user stories for further software development. While the discussion points provide precise recommendations for integration into the software, the five key points are more general and thus require more effort to be turned into concise tasks.

Acknowledgements. We gratefully acknowledge the funding provided by "Roadmaps Digitaler Humanismus Wirtschaftsagentur Wien und WWTF."

AI-supported tools (DeepL, Grammerly) have only been used for proofreading and clarifying the writing, and therefore strictly *not* for generating text of any kind.

References

1. Acemyan, C.Z., Kortum, P.: The relationship between trust and usability in systems. Proc. Human Fact. Ergon. Soc. Annual Meet. **56**(1), 1842–1846 (2012). https://doi.org/10.1177/1071181312561371
2. Anderson, E.G., Lopez, J., Parker, G.G.: Leveraging value creation to drive the growth of B2B platforms. Prod. Oper. Manag. **31**(12), 4501–4514 (2022). https://doi.org/10.1111/poms.13866
3. Cooper, D.A., Yalcin, T., Nistor, C., Macrini, M., Pehlivan, E.: Privacy considerations for online advertising: a stakeholder's perspective to programmatic advertising. J. Consum. Mark. **40**(2), 235–247 (2023). https://doi.org/10.1108/JCM-04-2021-4577
4. Duan, Y., Ge, Y., Feng, Y.: Pricing and personal data collection strategies of online platforms in the face of privacy concerns. Electron. Commer. Res., 1–21 (2020). https://doi.org/10.1007/s10660-020-09439-8
5. Gawer, A.R., Srnicek, N.: Online platforms: Economic and societal effects. Report PE 656.336, Panel for the Future of Science and Technology (STOA), European Parliament, Brussels (2021). https://doi.org/10.2861/844602
6. Hein, A., Weking, J., Schreieck, M., Wiesche, M., Böhm, M., Krcmar, H.: Value co-creation practices in business-to-business platform ecosystems. Electron. Mark. **29**(3), 503–518 (2019). https://doi.org/10.1007/s12525-019-00337-y
7. Kuttainen, C.: The role of trust in B2B electronic commerce: evidence from two e-marketplaces. Ph.D. thesis, Luleå tekniska universitet (2005). https://urn.kb.se/resolve?urn=urn:nbn:se:ltu:diva-26551. Accessed 29 Jan 2025
8. Morimoto, M.: Privacy concerns about personalized advertising across multiple social media platforms in Japan: the relationship with information control and persuasion knowledge. Int. J. Advert. **40**(3), 431–451 (2021). https://doi.org/10.1080/02650487.2020.1796322
9. Pavlou, P.A.: Institution-based trust in interorganizational exchange relationships: the role of online b2b marketplaces on trust formation. J. Strateg. Inf. Syst. **11**(3–4), 215–243 (2002). https://doi.org/10.1016/S0963-8687(02)00017-3
10. Riemensperger, F., Falk, S.: How to capture the B2B platform opportunity. Electron. Mark. **30**(1), 61–63 (2020). https://doi.org/10.1007/s12525-019-00390-7
11. Rivares, A.B., Gal, P., Millot, V., Sorbe, S.: Like it or not? the impact of online platforms on the productivity of incumbent service providers. OECD Economics Department Working Papers **17**(1548) (2019). https://doi.org/10.1787/080a17ce-en
12. Shree, D., Kumar Singh, R., Paul, J., Hao, A., Xu, S.: Digital platforms for business-to-business markets: a systematic review and future research agenda. J. Bus. Res. **137**, 354–365 (2021). https://doi.org/10.1016/j.jbusres.2021.08.031
13. Zhou, L., Mao, H., Zhao, T., Wang, V.L., Wang, X., Zuo, P.: How B2B platform improves buyers' performance: insights into platform's substitution effect. J. Bus. Res. **143**, 72–80 (2022). https://doi.org/10.1016/j.jbusres.2022.01.060

Enriched with Behaviour Theory Topic Guide Template for Digital Behaviour Change Interventions

Farhat-ul-Ain$^{(\boxtimes)}$, Kelly Toom, and Vladimir Tomberg

Tallinn University, Tallinn, Estonia
farhat23@tlu.ee

Abstract. Interviews and focus groups are interaction design user research methods that aim to understand user needs and goals regarding the potential use of digital products. In the case of designing Digital Behaviour Change Interventions (DBCIs) for health, these methods need to be adjusted to allow explicit focus on understanding determinants that possibly influence individual health-related behaviours (for example, beliefs, motivations, social pressure). Behaviour change theories and models help to identify these determinants of influencing behaviours. However, interaction designers are not competent in having knowledge of behaviour change theories, which makes it difficult to integrate this knowledge into interaction design user research. It can limit the design for theory-based DBCIs. The current study proposed and evaluated a generic topic guide template for interaction design user research enriched with a behaviour change theory. The paper proposes guidelines for adapting and analysing the data. The proposed topic guide template was adapted to understand the needs and age-related differences of children with type I diabetes. Focus groups were conducted with parents and medical professionals. Results indicated various behaviour change-related needs of the children and highlighted age-related differences in children's skills, independence, and motivation to manage diabetes. Various behaviour change theory-based design implications for interaction design were derived. The results highlight the importance of enriching the user research methods with behaviour change theories and models for designing DBCIs for health.

Keywords: Interaction design · User research · Behaviour change theory

1 Problem Statement

Digital Behaviour Change Interventions (DBCIs) for health can support forming, altering or maintaining health-related behaviours [1–3]. Designing DBCIs for health requires contributions from multidisciplinary fields, including interaction design [4] and intervention design [5]. Intervention design involves understanding individuals' factors or determinants that influence health-related behaviours, such as beliefs, motivation, and social or peer pressure, which are based on various behaviour change theories and models [6]. This further involves the selection of appropriate behaviour change techniques (for

H. Plácido da Silva and P. Cipresso (Eds.): CHIRA 2024, CCIS 2370, pp. 193–212, 2025.
https://doi.org/10.1007/978-3-031-82633-7_13

example, prompts and cues, rewards, and self-monitoring) [5, 7] that potentially influence determinants of behaviour to facilitate change in health behaviours. It is recommended to design behaviour change theories based DBCIs [8–11].

Interaction design primarily focuses on the structure and interactive behaviour of the digital product [4, 12, 13]. Interaction design approaches, such as User-Centered Design, focus on involving the user throughout the design process. Goal-Directed Design is an extension of User-Centered Design and provides a detailed process of designing digital products to ensure the achievement of specific user goals [4, 14, 15]. User research is conducted in the initial phases of User-Centered Design and Goal-Directed Design [4, 14, 15]. The user research methods, such as observations, interviews, and focus groups, help to understand user needs, goals, behaviours, attitudes, aptitudes, motivations (what motivates people to use products), environments (e.g., the context of technology usage), decision-making process, problems and frustrations that are caused by the current product or a comparable system for designing digital systems important for designing digital products. The user research methods address the different types of users and their needs, their behavioural patterns (e.g., frequency, desires, motivation), the user's technical expertise, and domain-related expertise (subject area-related expertise) [4]. Insights from the User Research phase inform the overall design processes by identifying different types of users and design-related requirements regarding potential digital products [4, 13].

Interaction designers use focus groups and interviews to explore when, why, and how the product fits into users' lives or work processes [4, 13], and provide an understanding of the topic in terms of the general agreement [16]. The researcher determines how and why specific points and ideas are accepted, and others are rejected based on the different viewpoints of the focus group participants. In the case of DBCIs, these methods need to be adjusted to allow explicit focus on the behavioural change-related needs of the users. It can help designers understand specific determinants influencing behaviours, which can further lead to the selection of appropriate behaviour change techniques. However, the integration of behaviour change theories is often missed in the interaction design process [17, 18]. Frameworks for designing DBCIs suggest designing theory-based interventions, but they do not provide enough guidance on the integration of this theoretical knowledge into interaction design methods [19]. It makes the results of user research less useful for DBCI than they might be because the resulting data provides fewer BC-related insights.

Qualitative methods of data collection, such as interviews and focus groups, are often conducted using tailored in-advance topic guides that supply the topics and questions related to the study themes [20, 21]. In the interaction design, topic guides are used to elicit rich and in-depth responses from participants by encouraging open-ended dialogue and exploration of ideas. The topic guides per se are more generative and, in the case of design for DBCI, are rarely theory-based [22]. In contrast, the intervention designers conduct qualitative studies based on behaviour change theories to understand determinants influencing behaviours. Intervention designers commonly develop interviews or focus group topic guides that are based on relevant behaviour change theories and models and ensure that the data collection is aligned with the theoretical concepts of the selected theory [23–25].

Designing a theory-based topic guide for DBCI requires an understanding of behaviour change theories and models. Due to the availability of various behaviour change theories, it is difficult for interaction designers to select one specific behaviour change theory or model to design a topic guide for user research [26]. In the current work, we aimed to propose a generic topic guide template for interaction design user research that can help to elicit the users' behaviour change-specific needs. We hypothesised that enriching the user research topic guide for qualitative studies (focus groups, interviews) based on behaviour change theories can help understand user determinants of behaviour and elicit design implications for DBCIs for health. The research question for the current study is: How can behaviour change theories be integrated into a topic guide for inter-action designers to understand users' behaviour change-related needs when conducting user research for designing DBCIs?

2   Review of Topic Guides for Designing DBCIs for Health

In this section, both theory- and non-theory-based topic guides used to design DBCIs were reviewed. Most studies used qualitative approaches to understand user needs. Relatively few studies have published topic guides for interviews or focus groups.

The findings suggested that non-theory-based studies' topic guides attempted to explore user goals and preferred features of DBCIs [27–32]. For example, features for healthy eating, features for social support (private messages, online support groups), information presented in simple terms, options for situational eating, email reminders, tracking features, automated chatbots, etc. However, results generated from the analysis do not help to understand specific determinants of behaviour (e.g., motivation, emotions, beliefs, skills, etc.) required to design DBCIs. This primarily limits the designing of theory-based DBICs and the selection of appropriate behaviour change techniques.

Overall, the questions in non-theory-based topic guides were focused on broader behavioural goals such as weight reduction and could be adaptable to other contexts or conditions. For example, the sample question in Fig. 1 (Sample Question: Qc & Qd) can be easily adapted to understand the needs of designing DBCIs in other healthcare contexts.

The theory-based topic guides help to identify various psychological determinants of behaviours [33–37]. The results of the interviews or focus groups are used to identify determinants of behaviour and selection of appropriate behaviour change techniques. Schnall et al. (2023) aimed to design an application for tobacco cessation based on the Health Belief Model and Fogg's functional model [35]. The topic guide itself was not directly based on the Health Belief Model (only two out of five questions covered two domains of the health belief model), and the author linked the results of the interview with the domains of the health belief model. The interview results were also linked to the two domains included in the topic guide (perceived barriers and perceived benefits). This suggests that it is important to design topic guides that are directly based on behaviour change theory to cover all major domains of theory; otherwise, important domains worth exploring might be neglected during research. Dack et al. (2019) conducted interviews to understand the needs of patients with Type II diabetes. The topic guide was based on Normalisation Process Theory and Corbin and Strauss' model). The findings were also linked with the theories, but the authors have not published the topic guide [36].

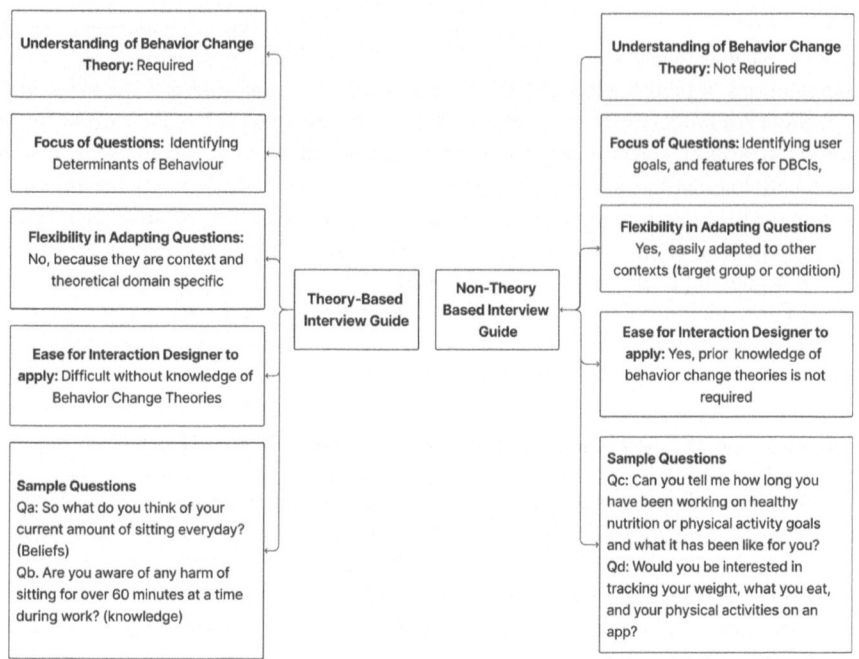

Fig. 1. Comparison of Theory and Non-Theory-Based Topic Guides.

Adapting and implanting a theory-based topic guide is difficult because questions are based on the theoretical domains or constructs of the theory and are very specific according to target behaviour. For example, questions such as "Are you aware of any harm of sitting for over 60 min at a time during work?" are very specific according to target behaviour and require answers related to particular target behaviour It limits the applicability and adaptability of such questions in other contexts. As non-theory-based topic guides focused on identifying features of DBCIs, the features implemented in DBCIs are not directly linked with behaviour change techniques. In contrast, behaviour change techniques are selected before selecting features and thus linked with behaviour change theory and techniques.

Based on the literature review, we can conclude that non-theory-based topic guides are useful for providing user goals and preferred features for DBCIs but cannot be directly linked with individual determinants of behaviour change techniques. Meanwhile, theory-based interview topic guides provide better support for identifying determinants of behaviour and selecting behaviour change techniques according to those determinants. Designing a theory-based topic guide requires an understanding of behaviour change theories. It is important to note that no structured topic is typically used to understand individual needs. Intervention designers already know and understand behaviour change theories and intervention design processes, so it is easy for them to select a particular theory and use it to understand behaviour determinants. However, it is challenging for interaction designers to know various behaviour change theories, to select and apply them for supporting the behaviour needs of the users.

The purpose of the current study is to provide a generic behaviour change theory topic guide template that could be easily applicable and adaptable to various contexts.

3 Theory-Based Topic Guide Template for User Research

This section provides a brief overview of behaviour change theories, a comprehensive theory-enriched topic guide template for eliciting rich, relevant data needed to design DBCIs.

3.1 Behaviour Change Theories and Intervention Design Research

Behaviour change theories are founded on the idea that individual, social, and environmental factors will dynamically change and interact to influence behaviour [1], and up to 83 behaviour change theories have been proposed in the field of behaviour change [6]. For example, the theory of planned behaviour emphasises the role of individuals' positive or negative attitudes towards health-related behaviour, social norms (social expectations, peer influences, social support) and individual perceived control for determining individuals' behaviours [38]. Some theories study behaviour change as people's gradual progression through discrete stages of change, such as the transtheoretical Model [39] and the Precaution Adoption Process Model [40].

It is challenging for designers to select one specific behaviour change theory from the range of behaviour change theories [41]. Michie et al. [42] proposed the COM-B (Capability, Opportunity and Motivation -Behaviour model) model, which combined various theories of behaviour change, making it more useful for interaction designers to apply when designing DCBIs for health. We aimed to use the COM-B model to design a theory-based topic guide template for interaction designers [42]. COM-B helps to consider various determinants of behaviour (for example, physical skills, knowledge, resilience, memory, availability of time and resources, motivation, and emotional beliefs) compared to other theories, such as the theory of planned behaviour (which only focuses on attitude, social norms and perceived behaviour control) [43]. More details about the COM-B model are presented below.

COM-B Model. Cane et al. [44] combined thirty-three theories of health behaviour change (twenty-eight determinants of behaviours) into fourteen domains publiased as Theoretical Domain Framework (TDF). Later, these fourteen domains were further classified into three key components [42]: Capability (C), Opportunity (O), and Motivation (M), referred to as the COM-B model. Each component is further divided into two subcategories encapsulating the fourteen domains of the TDF (Table 1). For example, the knowledge domain in TDF is the part of "psychological capability" in COM-B along with other TDF domains such as memory, decision-making process, etc.

Table 1. Description of COM-B Components.

COM-B Components	Description
Capability	• **Physical capability** refers to an individual's physical skills and abilities to perform a behaviour (TDF domains: physical skills) • **Psychological capability** encompasses cognitive resources, knowledge, and understanding necessary to perform a behaviour (TDF domains: knowledge, memory, attention and decision-making processes, behavioural regulation)
Opportunity	• **Social opportunity** pertains to the external influences and social norms that facilitate or hinder behaviour (TDF domains: social influences, e.g. norms, social pressures) • **Physical opportunity** involves environmental factors and resources that enable behaviour enactment (TDF domains: environmental context and resources, e.g., time and money)
Motivation	• **Reflective motivation** represents conscious intentions, goals, and belief about abilities and consequences that drive behaviour (TDF domains: Belief about capability, belief about consequences, roles and identity, intention to perform behaviour, goals, optimism) • **Automatic motivation** involves automatic responses, emotions, and habits and routines that influence behaviour (TDF domains: emotions, reinforcement)

Michie et al. [7] proposed three stages for developing behaviour change interventions. The first stage *(understanding the target behaviour)* involves conducting qualitative studies to identify determinants influencing behaviours based on the COM-B model. The Intervention Design begins with an in-depth understanding of individual needs, focusing specifically on exploring the determinants that influence behaviours. We assume that interaction design experts can adopt a similar approach when conducting user research by leveraging the knowledge of behaviour change theories. To support this goal, the study aimed to develop a comprehensive topic guide template based on the COM-B model for interaction design. The guide template is intended to help designers understand the determinants influencing behaviour and design DBCIs.

The second stage *(identifying intervention options)* is based on selecting appropriate intervention functions, i.e., broad categories by which an intervention can change behaviour (e.g., education, persuasion, training, etc.). The third stage *(identifying behaviour change techniques, content and implementation options)* focuses on selecting appropriate behaviour change techniques that can support the behaviour change process. Michie et al. [45] Developed the taxonomy of ninety-three behavioural change techniques, which can be selected according to the appropriate psychological needs of the users. These behaviour change techniques are later strategised into DBCIs to support behaviour change. Another advantage of selecting the COM-B model is that results can be directly linked with the selection of behaviour change techniques [43] following the second and third stages.

3.2 Enriching Interaction Design User Research Topic Guide with COM-B Model

COM-B model was introduced in the topic guide for conducting focus groups or interviews (Table 2). Literature on user research, psychology, and behaviour change provided the foundational knowledge required to design questions for the topic guide template [46]. Relevant previous literature is consulted to design a generic topic guide template for the current study [7, 33, 34, 47]. The questions for the topic guide were developed through an iterative process involving multiple rounds of drafting and refinement. Consultations with experts in intervention design and interaction design were integral to this process.

Each question is directly relevant to the COM-B components, sub-components and related TDF domains. For instance, psychological capability-related questions will help elicit responses that will directly guide and help understand the psychological capability-related needs of the users. Identified needs will further help in deriving design implications (these implications suggest how design decisions need to be made to address identified needs, challenges, or opportunities) corresponding to each COM component. It is intended to allow designers to understand user behaviour change-related needs more holistically (understanding various theory guide determinants that can influence behaviours) and structurally (eliciting responses that relate to COM-B components).

The questions are designed to be flexible and adaptable to fit different health behaviours. For example, questions such as: What kind of mental skills are required, e.g., the ability to resist urges, keep things in mind (nor forget) and make appropriate decisions to [perform specific behaviour]? can be easily adapted to fit various health-related behaviours (going for a walk, eating healthy food, counting calories).

The proposed questions in the topic guide template can be used as a base and adapted for different target populations. For example, questions directed at parents or healthcare professionals to help understand their children's or patients' needs can be adapted as "Do your children or patients have the knowledge required to [perform specific behaviour]?". Similarly, the questions can be adapted to compare user needs of different groups, such as differences in age groups (such as the difference in knowledge of children, adolescents and adults) and employment status (needs of working, non-working and freelancers, etc.).

Questions can be adapted according to literacy level (providing examples and more explanation of the questions, if needed) and cultural background. It is recommended that the adapted topic guide be pilot-tested with a small sample of users to identify any issues or areas for improvement. If needed, refine the wording, structure, and flow of the questions. Interaction designers can include probing questions and follow-up prompts to delve deeper into specific areas of interest or concern identified during the interview.

Table 2. Theory Enriched Topic Guide Template for Interaction Designers.

COM-B -Based Questions	Purpose
Physical Capability • What are the different physical skills or abilities (physical strength, stamina) required to perform [perform specific behaviour]? Do you have those skills? • Are there any physical health conditions or limitations that affect your ability to perform certain tasks related to [perform specific behaviour]?	Intended to support an understanding of physical limitations and capabilities that can influence behaviour.
Psychological Capability • What kind of knowledge is required to [perform specific behaviour]? Do you have the knowledge required to [perform specific behaviour]? • What kind of mental skills are required, such as., the ability to resist urges, keep things in mind (nor forget) and make appropriate decisions to [perform specific behaviour]? Do you have those mental skills to [perform specific behaviour]? The interviewer can break down questions into sub-questions focusing on one mental skill in one question.	Intended to support understanding of current knowledge, memory, attention, and decision-making processes that can influence behaviour.
Social Opportunity • Can you describe any social norms or expectations that impact [performing specific behaviour]? • Are there any social support systems or networks that could help you [perform specific behaviour] more effectively?	Intended to support understanding of social influences, norms, and social pressures that can influence behaviour.
Physical Opportunity • Are there any physical barriers or constraints in your environment that impact [performing specific behaviour]?? • To what extent do resources such as time, money, and accessibility of health services facilitate/ hinder [performing specific behaviour]??	Intended to support understanding of the availability and accessibility of resources, such as time and money, that can influence behaviour.
Reflective Motivation • How do you perceive the consequences of [performing specific behaviour]? • Can you describe any beliefs or attitudes that influence your decision-making regarding [performing specific behaviour]? • Do you intend to change your behaviour? • Are you optimistic about changing your behaviour? • Do you have specific goals for changing your behaviour? • To what extent is this behaviour accepted by your society (friends, family, employment)?	Intended to support understanding of beliefs about capability, consequences, intention to perform behaviour, goals, optimism, and identity that can influence behaviour.
Automatic Motivation • What are your current habits and routines related to the [behaviour]? • To what extent will [performing specific behaviour] make you happy or feel?	Intended to support understanding of emotions, habits, and reinforcement factors that can influence behaviour.

(*continued*)

Table 2. (*continued*)

	• Are there any incentives or rewards that can motivate you to perform [specific behaviour]?	
	Additional Questions: • What are your expectations from the potential mobile application? • What are the most important things the diabetes application should contain to improve dietary adherence?	Intended to support understanding of user expectations from technology

3.3 Analyzing Data Gathered with Enriched Topic Guide

The qualitative data needs to be interpreted using a deductive framework approach [48], in which themes and sub-themes are structured within the theoretical framework. Overall, the analysis needs to be divided into three stages, as shown in Fig. 2.

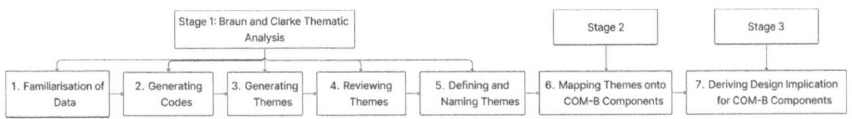

Fig. 2. Proposed Methodological Process for Data Analysis.

In the first stage of data analysis, thematic analysis using five Braun and Clarke's [49] approach needs to be conducted. Several themes and sub-themes indicating various determinants of behaviour will be identified. Firstly, the data has to be familiarised with double-reading transcriptions and noting initial ideas in the data set (Familiarisation with data). Secondly, initial codes need to be generated across the entire data set (Generating code). Thirdly, themes need to be generated concerning the codes created before for the entire data set (Generating themes). Fourth, themes must be reviewed against the data again, and improvements need to be made if needed (Reviewing themes). Lastly, each theme needs to be defined and named (Defining and naming themes). The process also included selecting data items to use as conversation extracts.

In the second stage, themes need to be mapped onto COM-B components using the framework approach [48]. It will help to organise themes according to COM-B components. For example, forgetting to take medications can be linked with psychological capability.

In the third stage, design implications needs to be derived for each thematic category that emerged under the COM-B component. Design implications are the insights or considerations derived from research findings and can guide the development or improvement of a product. These implications suggest how design decisions should be made to address identified needs, challenges, or opportunities. These design implications are refined in subsequent phases of the design, such as user persona and eliciting user requirements.

4   Evaluation of Topic Guide Template: Case Study

It is important to note that the theory-enriched topic study template was designed by experts in Interaction Design and Intervention Design who have knowledge of both Interaction and Intervention Design practices. It was important to evaluate the proposed topic guide template's effectiveness in generating data that could potentially be helpful for designing DBCIs for health and to what extent it could be easily adaptable. The pilot study was conducted by an expert in the field of interaction design who had already been introduced to the COM-B model.

For this purpose, we have conducted a pilot study to understand age-related differences in the management of diabetes of smaller children (7–11) and adolescents (11–18 years of age) and various determinants that influence children's behaviours towards adherence to treatment regimes. Children with Type I Diabetes (T1DM) have to follow complex treatment recommendations, such as physical activity, carbohydrate calculation, and insulin intake. Studies indicate that adherence to treatment recommendations declines significantly during the transition from parental care to self-care and puberty periods, which could be due to the different psychological needs of the children [50, 51].

Six focus groups were conducted with parents of children diagnosed with T1DM and general physicians. Table 3 includes adapted COM-B questions for parents and general physicians. Questions in the proposed topic guide template were carefully adapted to avoid missing any sub-components of the COM-B model and related TDF domains while making it more contextualised to understand the needs of children with T1DM. Various probing questions were also included to understand children's needs in more detail.

Each focus group had 3–6 participants. The focus groups were recorded and transcribed using Sonix's online transcription service (https://sonix.ai/), resulting in textual data. The authors reviewed and checked the transcriptions, and corrections were made. The qualitative data was analysed according to the guide provided in Sect. 4.1. The results of the thematic analysis are presented in the following sections.

Table 3. Adapted Theory-Based Topic Guide for Conducting User Research.

COM B Components	Description
Capability	• **Physical capability**: *What difference exists in the physical abilities* (physical strength, stamina) *of children of various age groups regarding following treatment regimes?* • **Psychological capability:** *What is the difference in children's* knowledge, mental skills, and mental strength (e.g., develop resilience against temptation/urges, memory, decision-making plan) *of various age groups to follow treatment regimens at different ages?* Several sub-questions focused on one psychological capability in one question (as mentioned in Table 2).
Opportunity	• **Social opportunity:** *To what extent do social influences* (social pressures, norms, etc., from parents, teachers, and kids) *facilitate/ hinder adherence? Has gender any role in social influences?* (Probe: social influences, norms, social pressures) • **Physical opportunity:** *To what extent do such* resources as time, money, and accessibility of health services facilitate/ *hinder adherence?* (Probe: Availability and accessibility of resources, e.g., time and money) Several sub-questions were made focusing on exploring one domain, such as time, in one question (as mentioned in Table 2)
Motivation	• **Reflective motivation:** *What difference exists in* perceived consequences of non-adherence *in children of various age groups? What is the difference in children's* beliefs and attitudes towards diabetes management at different ages? *What is the difference in children's* intention to perform diabetes management-related skills *at different ages?* (Probe: Belief about capability, consequences, intention to perform behaviour, goals, optimism, identity) • **Automatic motivation:** *To what extent do children* feel happy, and what motivates them to follow treatment guidelines? (Probe: emotions, habits, reinforcement) Several sub-questions were made focusing on exploring one domain in one question (as mentioned in Table 2)
Additional Questions	• What are your expectations from the potential mobile application? • What are the most important things the diabetes application should contain to improve dietary adherence?

4.1 Themes, Sub-themes and Design Implications Related to Capability

The results related to physical capability (individual's physical skills and abilities to perform a behaviour) indicated that children's diabetes-related skills, such as using the pump, calculating carbohydrates, and measuring glycemic levels, improve with age and independence improve with age (Fig. 3). As mentioned by one of the parent's participants: – "He became more independent at about the age of five by operating his pump, and let us say he could operate it himself at six." Similarly, another participant mentioned improvement in skills: – "He has become independent with the pump, with everything, even measuring from the tip of the finger; it comes out better and better with age."

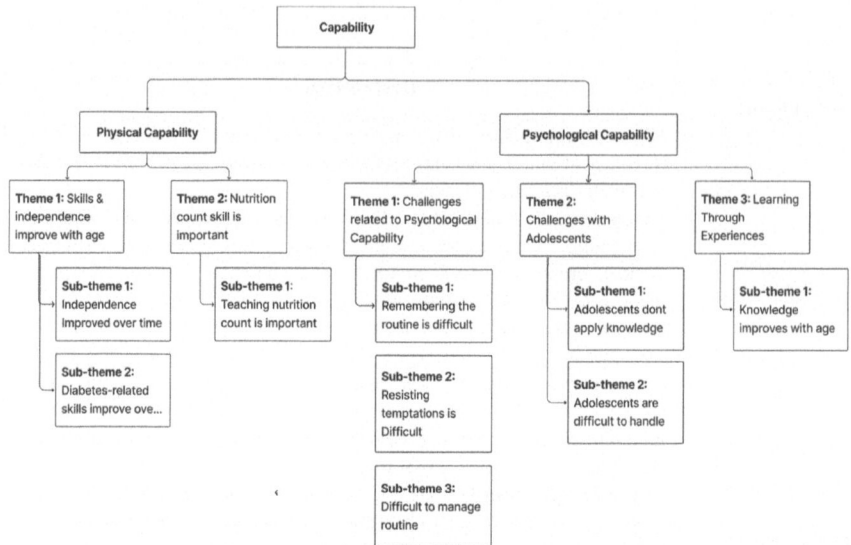

Fig. 3. Themes, Sub-themes and Design Implications Related to Capability.

Children start to show independence at a young age (e.g. wanting to check sugar and inject on their own), but their treatment adherence at a young age is more dependent on their parents. Teaching nutrition counts is important for children, as highlighted by the participant: – "Nutrition teaching is definitely needed."

Results indicated (Fig. 3) various needs of children with T1DM and age-related differences in children and adolescents related to psychological capability (cognitive resources, knowledge, and understanding necessary to perform a behaviour). Parents and medical staff highlighted issues related to remembering and forgetfulness of tasks needed for disease management (e.g., injecting insulin), specifically in adolescents, as highlighted by participants: – "forgets that he has to do it every time." The results suggested that children face difficulty resisting temptations.

The current study has highlighted that adolescents are difficult to handle and do not apply knowledge to practice, as indicated by the participant: – "And, this is the time to get out of parental control. That this is actually a very difficult time for the family." Another participant mentioned: – "At the age of adolescence, their theoretical knowledge can be very good, but then questions arise in practice, just do not apply this knowledge." This highlights the age-related differences in the psychological capability of children and adolescents.

Based on the results, various design implications for designers can be derived to enhance physical capability and psychological capability in children with T1DM, such as consideration of age-related differences in skills and independence for diabetes management, interactive simulations or boards to help children learn and gain experience, virtual peer mentorship, game features to enhance knowledge and nutrition counting skills, reminders to manage routine, real-time monitoring of behaviour and just-in-time intervention, and features to support goal setting and provide age-appropriate feedback.

4.2 Themes, Sub-themes and Design Implications Related to Opportunity

Various themes related to physical opportunity (external influences and social norms that facilitate or hinder behaviour) have emerged from the collected data, as shown in Fig. 4. For example, changes in schedule, especially during weekends, influence treatment adherence, as indicated by the participant: – "At the weekend, yes, the rhythm goes out of place again; he sleeps longer, and then there are more outdoor activities and other things." Participants also mentioned issues related to having limited time. No age-related differences were found for physical opportunity.

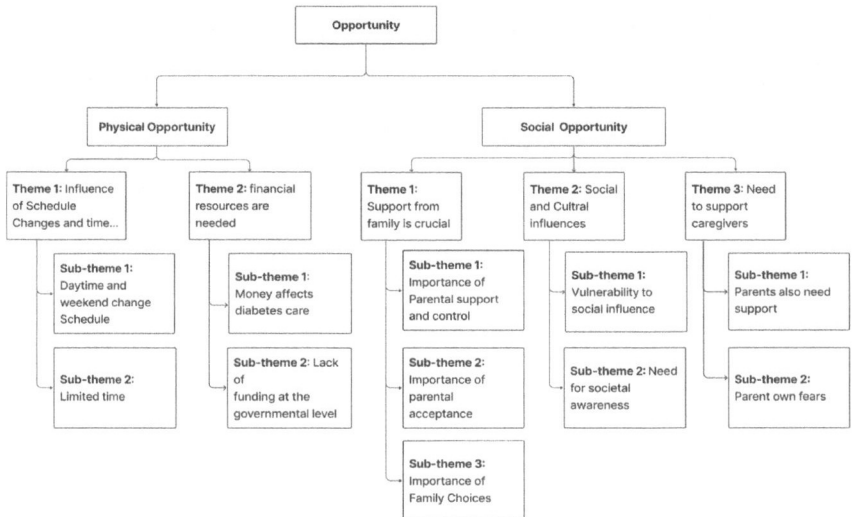

Fig. 4. Themes, Sub-Themes and Design Implications Related to Opportunity.

Various themes related to social opportunity (environmental factors and resources that enable behaviour enactment) have emerged, as shown in Fig. 4. Results have highlighted the importance of family support and parental acceptance in managing diabetes, as reported by the participant: – "A child of any age is a child; in fact, a small person in particular needs parental help. But you can't say that these bigger teens need it when they say they're independent, but you need control". Results indicated that social pressure also influences overall treatment adherence.

Based on the results, various design implications for designers can be derived to maximise physical and psychological opportunities for children with T1DM, such as flexible reminders and alerts to allow adjustments on weekends, provision of developing emergency plans in case unexpected schedule changes Specific weekend plan tools, just-in-time support in high-risk situations, a digital co-communication platform for children and parents, a shared calendar and task tracker, family goal-setting Tools to set diabetes management goals together, and digital tools for tracking parents' emotions (e.g., stress) and delivering personalised support to parents.

4.3   Themes, Sub-Themes and Design Implications Related to Motivation

The results indicated the difference in reflective motivation (conscious intentions, goals, and beliefs about abilities and consequences) in young children and adolescents (Fig. 5). Findings suggest that children are conscious but do not perceive future consequences and severity of the disease, as mentioned by the participant: – "He does not think that he feels bad after an hour." However, adolescents know the consequences of the disease but do not intend to follow guidelines: – "Sometimes, pre-teens, teenagers, when they don't want to do anything…" The results indicated that maintaining motivation is challenging in the long term.

Findings related to automatic motivation (emotions, habits, and routines) indicated in Fig. 5 suggest that children experience many negative emotions mentioned by parents: – "Life with Diabetes is a great stress for her. Because these are tears, disappointments, rejection, and resentment." Children also experience fear and feelings of fatigue, as highlighted by the participants: – "Sometimes there is the fear of coping and also the fact that one does not dare to admit it all…".

Results also indicated different factors influencing children's motivation, For example, rewards and incentives, medical reports and visiting doctors: – "When they come for a visit …many are inspired by the fact that if they have had this bad figure, it has gotten better now that it really motivates or who keep their reading as permanent as well, optimal."

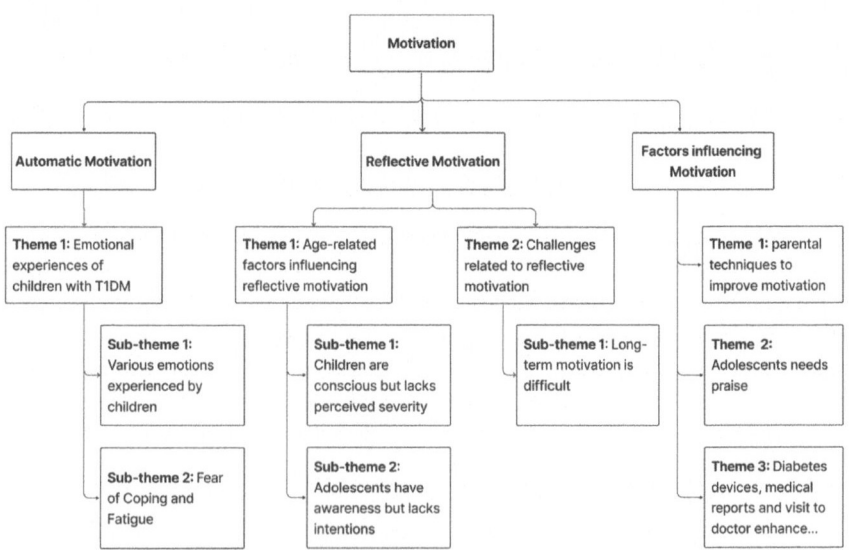

Fig. 5. Themes, Sub-Themes and Design Implications Related to Motivation.

Various design implications for designers were derived to enhance reflective and automatic motivation in children with T1DM, such as age-appropriate design, game features (taking care of an avatar with T1DM and informing of the consequences if it falls ill), features that can support intention formation for adolescents (In-app goal setting, visualising goals achieved, and in-app incentives or rewards), real-time monitoring of children motivation and emotions and just in time support, online support groups, persuasive messages, features to support online consultation with medical professionals, advanced chatbots or conversational agents, and features like point scoring.

4.4 Summary of Age-Related Differences Among Small Children and Adolescents

Designers need to consider age-related differences and needs when designing DBCIs for health to help children achieve their behavioural goals. Figure 6 presents a brief overview of these differences in the form of a timeline that designers can consider when designing DBCIs for children diagnosed with T1DM to promote treatment adherence.

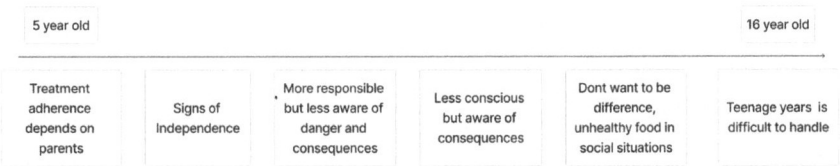

Fig. 6. Age-related Difference in Adherence to Diabetes Management.

Age-related differences highlight the importance of tailored and personalised support for parents, children, and adolescents according to their needs. By considering these differences, more effective and inclusive solutions can be designed and developed to meet the diverse needs of children and adolescents with T1DM.

4.5 Additional Significant Findings

Some suggestions for design emerged directly from parents and medical professionals. For example, parents preferred to use digital mode over paper formats to record data and expressed the need to save data by date. They expressed the need to access children's health-related data to have control and notifications to observe their children. Medical professionals suggested having an app that can make carb calculation easy (e.g., can capture the image and inform about carbs), supports communication, helps organise meetings, and provides education through mobile applications about the factors that can influence diabetes.

5 Conclusion

The current study explored the provision of an enriching topic guide for interaction design user research methods (focus groups and interviews) with behaviour change theory. We proposed a generic theory-based topic guide template for interaction designers that can help them understand the users' behaviour change-related needs. The proposed theory-based topic guide aimed to help interaction designers integrate behaviour change theory from the beginning of the design process and provided a structured approach for deriving design implications aligned with understanding user behaviour change-specific needs. It is important to note that although insights from intervention design research could be valuable for interaction designers, it is still important for them to understand the theoretical components of behaviour change theories and derive design implications aligned with user behaviour change-related needs. The generic topic guide aims to help designers use behaviour change theory while designing DBCIs for health.

The evaluation indicated that the proposed theory-based topic guide template was easy to adapt according to target behaviour (treatment adherence), and it was possible to tailor questions to address parents and medical professionals without losing the theoretical foundations. The result indicated that the theoretical basis of the proposed topic guide template ensured in-depth data collection, providing insights into user needs and clear design implications. The results provided a structured (aligned with theoretical components of the COM-B model) and holistic understanding of the behaviour change-related needs and age-related differences of children with T1DM, which was otherwise not possible using a non-theory-based topic guide.

Several design implications related to improving the capability of children with T1DM were elicited, such as consideration of age-related differences in children's levels of independence and skills, interactive simulations or games to enhance children's skills and independence. The results indicated challenges in managing routines (especially on weekends), peer influences and the importance of parental support. Many design implications can be used to maximise children's opportunities to engage in adherence-related activities. The results indicated different motivational factors, such as visiting the doctor and parental support, that could be supported by the integration of various design features, for example, online consultations and shared calendars with parents to enhance children's motivation to perform adherence-related behaviours. Adolescents need more support in intention formation than smaller children and lack the motivation to engage in diabetes management-related behaviour.

Overall, the results indicate differences in perceived consequences, the severity of the diseases, cognitive abilities, levels of independence and skills among children and adolescents. This means that the design of DBCIs needs to be tailored according to these differences. Hence, a one-size-fits-all approach for designing DBCIs is not appropriate considering these differences. The design implications derived for each thematic category can be theoretically linked with the resulting behaviour change techniques [45], such as reminders and notifications related to prompts and cues. Notably, these design implications can be directly linked with the theory-based determinants of behaviour, which were not likely to be identified using non-theory-based topic guides. Similarly, tracking behaviours is related to feedback and monitoring-related techniques. These design implications can be refined using the taxonomy of behaviour change techniques. For example, the taxonomy lists many types of goal-setting techniques, such as goal setting (behaviour), problem-solving, goal setting (outcome), behavioural contract and commitment, that can be selected.

The proposed generic topic guide template's adaptability and theoretical base would allow the integration of theory from the beginning of the interaction design process. This generic topic guide can be easily contextualised to explore specific problems. Although using the proposed topic guide template would still require a basic understanding of

COM-B components, it will reduce designers' time in extensively reviewing the literature on behaviour change theories. The COM-B-based topic guide template will ensure comprehensive coverage of various determinants of behaviours, enabling designers to gather targeted insights about users and further select appropriate behaviour change techniques. The results can be used in further design phases, such as user personas and generating user requirements for designing DBCIs.

Future studies can adapt the proposed theory-based topic guide template for designing DBCIs and highlight the benefits and limitations of integration of theory interaction design user research.

Acknowledgements. Grant TF/1323, Supporting Design for Digital Health Behaviour Change, funded by TLU Research Fund.

Disclosure of Interests. The authors declare that there is no conflict of interests.

References

1. Hekler, E.B., et al.: Advancing models and theories for digital behavior change interventions. Am. J. Prev. Med. **51**, 825–832 (2016). https://doi.org/10.1016/J.AMEPRE.2016.06.013
2. Yardley, L., Choudhury, T., Patrick, K., Michie, S.: Current issues and future directions for research into digital behavior change interventions. Am. J. Prev. Med. **51**, 814–815 (2016). https://doi.org/10.1016/j.amepre.2016.07.019
3. Oinas-Kukkonen, H., Win, K.T., Chatterjee, S.: Introduction to health behavior change support systems (HBCSS) minitrack. In: Proceedings of the Annual Hawaii International Conference on System Sciences. 2016-March, vol. 3073 (2016). https://doi.org/10.1109/HICSS.2016.386
4. Cooper, A., Reimann, R., Cronin, D., Noessel, C., Csizmadi, J., Lemoine, D.: About Face The Essentials of Interaction Design, 4th edn. John Wiley & Sons, Inc., Hoboken (2014)
5. Skivington, K., et al.: A new framework for developing and evaluating complex interventions: update of Medical Research Council guidance. BMJ **374** (2021). https://doi.org/10.1136/BMJ.N2061
6. Michie, S., West, R., Campbell, R., Brown, J., Gainforth, H.: ABC of Behaviour Change theories. Silverback Publishing, Sutton (2014)
7. Michie, S., Atkins, L., West, R.: The Behaviour Change Wheel: A Guide to Designing Interventions. Silverback Publishing, Sutton (2014)
8. Hekler, E.B., Klasnja, P., Froehlich, J.E., Buman, M.P.: Mind the theoretical gap: interpreting, using, and developing behavioral theory in HCI research. Presented at the (2013)
9. Yardley, L., et al.: Understanding and promoting effective engagement with digital behavior change interventions. Am. J. Prev. Med. **51**, 833–842 (2016). https://doi.org/10.1016/J.AMEPRE.2016.06.015
10. Sucala, M., et al.: Behavior science in the evolving world of digital health: considerations on anticipated opportunities and challenges. Transl Behav Med. **11**, 495–503 (2021). https://doi.org/10.1093/TBM/IBAA034
11. Walsh, J.C., Groarke, J.M.: Integrating behavioral science with mobile (mhealth) technology to optimize health behavior change interventions. Eur. Psychol. **24**, 38–48 (2019). https://doi.org/10.1027/1016-9040/A000351
12. Jones, M., Marsden, G.: Mobile Interaction Design. John Wiley & Sons, Inc., Hoboken (2006)
13. Sharp, H., Rogers, Y., Preece, J.: Interaction Design: Beyond Human-Computer Interaction. John Wiley & Sons, Inc., Hoboken (2019)

14. Wei, C., Xing, F.: The comparison of user-centered design and goal-directed design. In: 2010 IEEE 11th International Conference on Computer-Aided Industrial Design and Conceptual Design, CAID and CD'2010, vol. 1, pp. 359–360 (2010). https://doi.org/10.1109/CAIDCD. 2010.5681336

15. Williams, A.: User-centered design, activity-centered design, and goal-directed design: a review of three methods for designing web applications. In: SIGDOC'09 - Proceedings of the 27th ACM International Conference on Design of Communication, pp. 1–8 (2009). https:// doi.org/10.1145/1621995.1621997

16. Stewart, D.W., Shamdasani, P.N., Rook, D.W.: Focus Groups: Theory and Practice, 2nd edn. Sage Publications, Inc., Thousands Oaks (2007). https://doi.org/10.4135/9781412991841

17. Blake, H., Roberts, A., Stanulewicz, N.: Telemedicine and mHealth interventions for children and young people with type one diabetes (T1DM). J Endocrinol Diab. Res. 1, 100104 (2015)

18. Kwon, B.C., Hur, I., Yi, J.S.: A review of web-based dietary interventions: from the human–computer interaction practitioners' perspective. Hum. Fact. Ergon. Manuf. Serv. Ind. 24, 241–261 (2014). https://doi.org/10.1002/HFM.20371

19. Farhat-Ul-Ain, T.V.: Mapping design frameworks for digital behaviour change interventions to goal-directed design. In: 2023 10th International Conference on Behavioural and Social Computing (BESC), pp. 1–7 (2023). https://doi.org/10.1109/BESC59560.2023.10386260

20. Krueger, R.A., Casey, M.A.: Focus groups: a practical guide for applied research (2014)

21. Roberts, R.E.: Qualitative interview questions: guidance for novice researchers. Qual. Rep. 25, 3185–3203 (2020). https://doi.org/10.46743/2160-3715/2020.4640

22. Sanders, E.B.N., Stappers, P.J.: Probes, toolkits and prototypes: three approaches to making in codesigning. CoDesign 10, 5–14 (2014). https://doi.org/10.1080/15710882.2014.888183

23. Vincenzo, J.L., Patton, S.K., Lefler, L.L., McElfish, P.A., Wei, J., Curran, G.M.: A qualitative study of older adults' facilitators, barriers, and cues to action to engage in falls prevention using health belief model constructs. Arch. Gerontol. Geriatr. 99, 104610 (2022). https://doi. org/10.1016/J.ARCHGER.2021.104610

24. Nasution, A., Yusuf, A., Keng, S.L., Rasudin, N.S., Iskandar, Y.H.P., Ab Hadi, I.S.: Development of mobile app for breast examination awareness using health belief model: a qualitative study. Asian Pac J Cancer Prev. 22, 3151 (2021). https://doi.org/ https://doi.org/10.31557/ APJCP.2021.22.10.3151

25. Atkins, L., et al.: A guide to using the theoretical domains framework of behaviour change to investigate implementation problems. Implement. Sci. 12, 1–18 (2017). https://doi.org/10. 1186/s13012-017-0605-9

26. Voorheis, P., Bhuiya, A.R., Kuluski, K., Pham, Q., Petch, J.: Making sense of theories, models, and frameworks in digital health behavior change design: qualitative descriptive study. J. Med. Internet Res. 25, e45095 (2023). https://doi.org/10.2196/45095

27. Rivera, J., et al.: User-centered design of a mobile app for weight and health management in adolescents with complex health needs: qualitative study. JMIR Form Res. 2, e7 (2018). https://doi.org/10.2196/formative.8248

28. Dening, J., George, E.S., Ball, K., Islam, S.M.S.: User-centered development of a digitally-delivered dietary intervention for adults with type 2 diabetes: the T2Diet study. Internet Interv. 28, 100505 (2022). https://doi.org/10.1016/J.INVENT.2022.100505

29. Duan, H., et al.: Using goal-directed design to create a mobile health app to improve patient compliance with hypertension self-management: Development and deployment. JMIR Mhealth Uhealth 8, e14466 (2020). https://doi.org/10.2196/14466

30. Zhang, Y., Li, X., Luo, S., Liu, C., Liu, F., Zhou, Z.: Exploration of users' perspectives and needs and design of a type 1 diabetes management mobile app: mixed-methods study. JMIR Mhealth Uhealth 6, e11400 (2018). https://doi.org/10.2196/11400

31. van Beurden, S.B., Simmons, S.I., Tang, J.C.H., Mewse, A.J., Abraham, C., Greaves, C.J.: Informing the development of online weight management interventions: a qualitative investigation of primary care patient perceptions. BMC Obes. **5**, 1–10 (2018). https://doi.org/10.1186/s40608-018-0184-6

32. Weerasekara, M., Smedberg, Å.B.: Exploration of user needs and design requirements of a digital stress management intervention for software employees in Sri Lanka: a qualitative study. BMC Public Health **23**, 1–13 (2023). https://doi.org/10.1186/s12889-023-15480-7

33. Huang, Y., Benford, S., Price, D., Patel, R., Li, B., Ivanov, A., Blake, H.: Using internet of things to reduce office workers' sedentary behavior: intervention development applying the behavior change wheel and human-centered design approach. JMIR Mhealth Uhealth. **8** (2020). https://doi.org/10.2196/17914

34. Curtis, K.E., Lahiri, S., Brown, K.E.: Targeting parents for childhood weight management: development of a theory-driven and user-centered healthy eating app. JMIR Mhealth Uhealth **3**, e69 (2015). https://doi.org/10.2196/mhealth.3857

35. Schnall, R., et al.: Theoretically guided iterative design of the Sense2Quit app for tobacco cessation in persons living with HIV. Int. J. Environ. Res. Public Health **20**, 4219 (2023). https://doi.org/10.3390/IJERPH20054219/S1

36. Dack, C., et al.: A digital self-management intervention for adults with type 2 diabetes: combining theory, data and participatory design to develop HeLP-Diabetes. Internet Interv. **17**, 100241 (2019). https://doi.org/10.1016/J.INVENT.2019.100241

37. Jones, S.E., Hamilton, S., Bell, R., Araújo-Soares, V., White, M.: Acceptability of a cessation intervention for pregnant smokers: a qualitative study guided by Normalization Process Theory. BMC Public Health **20**, 1 (2020). https://doi.org/10.1186/s12889-020-09608-2

38. Ajzen, I.: The theory of planned behavior. Organ. Behav. Hum. Decis. Process. **50**, 179–211 (1991). https://doi.org/10.1016/0749-5978(91)90020-T

39. Prochaska, J.O., DiClemente, C.C.: Stages and processes of self-change of smoking: toward an integrative model of change. J. Consult. Clin. Psychol. **51**, 390–395 (1983). https://doi.org/10.1037/0022-006X.51.3.390

40. Weinstein, N.D., Sandman, P.M., Blalock, S.J.: The precaution adoption process model. Wiley Encycl. Health Psychol., 495–506 (2020). https://doi.org/10.1002/9781119057840.CH100

41. Konstanti, C., Karapanos, E., Markopoulos, P.: The behavior change design cards: a design support tool for theoretically-grounded design of behavior change technologies. Int. J. Hum. Comput. Interact. **38**, 1238–1254 (2022). https://doi.org/10.1080/10447318.2021.1990519

42. Michie, S., van Stralen, M.M., West, R.: The behaviour change wheel: a new method for characterising and designing behaviour change interventions. Implement. Sci. **6**, 1–12 (2011). https://doi.org/10.1186/1748-5908-6-42

43. McDonagh, L.K., et al.: Application of the COM-B model to barriers and facilitators to chlamydia testing in general practice for young people and primary care practitioners: a systematic review. Implement. Sci. **13**, 1–19 (2018). https://doi.org/10.1186/s13012-018-0821-y

44. Cane, J., O'Connor, D., Michie, S.: Validation of the theoretical domains framework for use in behaviour change and implementation research. Implement Sci. **7** (2012). https://doi.org/10.1186/1748-5908-7-37

45. Michie, S., et al.: The behavior change technique taxonomy (v1) of 93 hierarchically clustered techniques: building an international consensus for the reporting of behavior change interventions. Ann. Behav. Med. **46**, 81–95 (2013). https://doi.org/10.1007/S12160-013-9486-6

46. Kallio, H., Pietilä, A.M., Johnson, M., Kangasniemi, M.: Systematic methodological review: developing a framework for a qualitative semi-structured interview guide. J. Adv. Nurs. **72**, 2954–2965 (2016). https://doi.org/10.1111/JAN.13031

47. French, S.D., et al.: Developing theory-informed behaviour change interventions to implement evidence into practice: a systematic approach using the Theoretical Domains Framework. Implement. Sci. **7**, 38 (2012). https://doi.org/10.1186/1748-5908-7-38

48. Gale, N.K., Heath, G., Cameron, E., Rashid, S., Redwood, S.: Using the framework method for the analysis of qualitative data in multi-disciplinary health research. BMC Med. Res. Methodol. **13**, 1–8 (2013). https://doi.org/10.1186/1471-2288-13-117/PEER-REVIEW

49. Braun, V., Clarke, V.: Using thematic analysis in psychology. Qual. Res. Psychol. **3**, 77–101 (2006). https://doi.org/10.1191/1478088706QP063OA

50. Gandhi, K., Vu, B.-M.K., Eshtehardi, S.S., Wasserman, R.M., Hilliard, M.E.: Adherence in adolescents with Type 1 diabetes: strategies and considerations for assessment in research and practice. Diab. Manag. **5**, 485–498 (2015). https://doi.org/10.2217/dmt.15.41

51. Lyons, S.K., Libman, I.M., Sperling, M.A.: Diabetes in the adolescent: transitional issues. J. Clin. Endocrinol. Metab. **98**, 4639–4645 (2013). https://doi.org/10.1210/jc.2013-2890

Evaluating Remote Communication Applications Using Student Usability Reviews

Alecsandru Grigoriu[✉]

Faculty of Computer Science, Alexandru Ioan Cuza University, General Henri Mathias Berthelot 16, 700483 Iasi, Romania
secretariat@info.uaic.ro
https://www.info.uaic.ro/

Abstract. The paper investigates and assesses the user interface design of well-known remote communication applications (e.g., Zoom, Microsoft Teams, Google Meet) for improved user experience and interaction. University students evaluate the applications as part of a series of creative challenges, covering important HCI (Human-Computer Interaction) aspects such as existing affordances, visual variables, or interaction flows. The study contributes to an already-established literature review of the uses and effects of video-conferencing tools during and after the COVID-19 pandemic. With volunteer students as participants, they offer a new perspective for the research by acting both as users and evaluators. The study consisted of two connected experiments between early 2023 and 2024, learning and improving with each iteration transitioning from an ad-hoc qualitative-focus approach to a well-defined quantitative-centered tactic. The results for the first experiment showed that the participants preferred Zoom, Discord, and Webex as the top three choices out of nine distinct alternatives. The second experiment positioned Discord as the most advantageous of the final three-the application dominated with a Mean SUS (System Usability Scale) score of 77.42, and ranked first in six out of eight criteria (and one tie) using a custom rating scale.

Keywords: Usability study · Student reviews · Remote communication applications · Zoom · Discord · Webex · System Usability Scale · Qualitative research · Quantitative research

1 Introduction

With the increasing need for remote communication applications, there is a demand for effective and user-friendly designs especially amongst scholars and practitioners alike [11]. This paper aims to investigate the design and evaluation of remote communication applications for improved user experience and interaction. The evaluation *per se* is done by final-year undergraduate university students as part of a creative challenge during a HCI (Human-Computer Interaction) class. The evaluations focus on experimentation through a predetermined design criteria. The challenge aims to explore and improve well-known remote applications (on Desktop, Web or Mobile) such as Zoom, Discord, WebEx.

© The Author(s), under exclusive license to Springer Nature Switzerland AG 2025
H. Plácido da Silva and P. Cipresso (Eds.): CHIRA 2024, CCIS 2370, pp. 213–229, 2025.
https://doi.org/10.1007/978-3-031-82633-7_14

The research centers students as participants in the study mainly because they fit in terms of audience and use case – the students are familiar with various remote communication applications for learning and attending online classes, and collaborating remotely within a team. The experiments presented in this paper cover several important HCI topics (existing affordances, visual variables, and interaction flow, visual metaphors and idioms, cognitive overload [12], empiric laws of Fitts' [10], Hick's [9], and Steering [8]) while critical goals of this research include:

- Review and analyze the different student solutions and evaluations.
- Evaluate each solution in terms of usability, user experience, effectiveness, innovation, and feasibility.
- Identify common topics and best practices across the different solutions.
- Make recommendations for improvement based on the evaluation.
- Iterate each experiment based on the quality of responses and evaluations achieved by the volunteer students.

Details about the conducted studies are presented in Sect. 3.

2   Related Work

This paper is inspired by previous research on remote communication application design and usability, focusing specifically on evaluating the student solutions to the remote communication application challenges. It draws on existing literature and best practices in usability testing and evaluation.

Previous studies have compared applications such as Google Meet, Microsoft Teams, Zoom, Skype, or Discord (to name a few) [17,20,22] as popular software tools used during COVID-19 for different use cases and purposes. The impact has reached global levels, with studies from diverse regions [14,15] exploring the fast adoption, effectiveness, and productivity of remote communication tools. For example, Zoom [23] [27] gains an advantage in education and learning with low hardware requirements and five critical features for educators: Learning Management System (LMS) integration, breakout rooms, polling, recordings, and in-conference chat. However, Zoom users may face more security vulnerabilities. Overall, Zoom is considered a better choice for educational purposes [1].

Other studies focus on the impact of remote communication applications on virtual teams, highlighting the collaboration [3] and performance [5] challenges experienced by the teams and existing mitigation strategies. Recent literature reviews focus on vital features and obstacles users experience when interacting with virtual conferencing technologies (identified from 60 related open-source journal articles from 5 digital library repositories) [6]. Another recent paper presents a statistical analysis of user preferences regarding the usability of Web teleconferencing interactive systems [13].

Moreover, the overall scope of remote communication tools has diversified in various directions, from using Zoom to collect qualitative interview data in the medical healthcare sector [18] to using Discord as a teaching support platform for software engineering students [25].

Recent studies on usability and user experience evaluation have focused on applying the System Usability Scale (SUS) [24] or User Experience Questionnaire (UEQ) [19] to gain insights. In contrast, others monitor the Quality of Experience (QoE) [16, 21, 26] by measuring the quality of audio/video connections, internet bandwidth, CPU speed, or resolution.

This paper extends the literature review by combining usability evaluation techniques and allowing Computer Science students to perform reviews as both users and evaluators.

3   Methodology

The research methodology centers around two connected experiments rolled between early 2023 and 2024:

- The first study consisted of a custom assignment the students had to accomplish. The assignment focused on them evaluating their two favorite remote communication applications of choice based on a predefined list of HCI-related criteria: existing affordances, visual variables, interaction flows, visual metaphors, idioms, and CLI (Command Line Interface) alternative representations, cognitive overload, empiric laws (Fitts', Hick's, Steering), UX/UI improvements and new features.
- Based on the insights gained and the quality of responses from the first experiment, the second evaluation tackled a more structured and quantitative design. Students had to evaluate the top three selected apps from the previous test using the System Usability Scale. Moreover, for each application, the participants had to evaluate the previous mentioned criteria using a custom rating scale (*1—lowest to 5—highest*). The second experiment concluded with students listing UX/UI improvements and new features.

The following sections (4, 5) will describe each experiment in detail, covering the structure, results, and lessons learned. A preview is presented in Fig. 1.

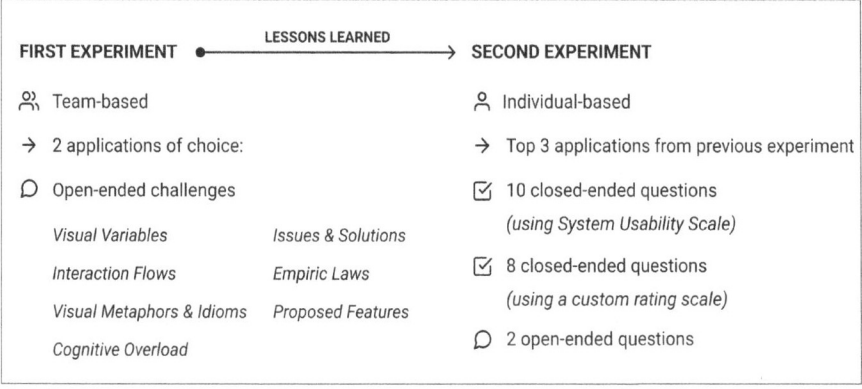

Fig. 1. A preview of the overall research methodology consisting of two connected experiments.

4 First Student Evaluation Experiment

4.1 Structure

For the first experiment, students had to complete an assessment that evaluated remote communication applications using different criteria. Specific rules were set for the students who participated. The final form received by the participants is listed below:

Choose two of your favorite remote communication applications (e.g., Zoom, Google Meet, Slack, Microsoft Teams) and complete the following:

- *Observe the existing affordances, visual variables and interaction flows for a given use case – for example, delivering an academic presentation or attending a specific meeting at late hours – and propose better approaches (if any).*
- *Compare the visual metaphors and idioms and suggest the similar ones for a text-only interaction (CLI – Command Line Interface). Discuss the cognitive overload in special conditions/contexts.*
- *List minimum three improvements that can be made to optimize these applications from the point of view of the main audience on at least two platforms – for instance, Web and mobile native, desktop native and mobile native. Each improvement will be listed in pairs: UI/UX problem identified and solution suggested.*
- *How the empiric laws (Fitts', Hick's, Steering) might be reconsidered/adapted in the context of multi-device interaction?*
- *List three new features that can be added to improve the experience and sketch those new features on paper and/or digitally.*

4.2 Results

The expected outcome of this first experiment is a comprehensive qualitative evaluation of the student solutions to the remote communication application challenge, including a summary of strengths and weaknesses, common themes and best practices, and recommendations for improvement.

After the deadline, **24** teams send **47** solutions. Out of the top chosen applications, Zoom came in first, continuing the popularity trend identified by previously mentioned studies (with 16 evaluations, **34.04 %**), followed by Discord and Webex (9 evaluations, **19.15 %**). Overall, a total of **nine distinct applications** have been evaluated. The complete list is provided by Table 1.

Since the questions were open-ended, a qualitative interpretation of the data collected was needed. Ideation techniques inspired by the Affinity Diagram Tactic [7] such as grouping recurrent themes into clusters and writing statements for each cluster added. Where the statistical data allowed it, quantitative insights concluded: for example, the number of recurrent themes found. In the following sub-sections, the paper covers all the major insights gathered from each of the requirements previously listed.

Table 1. Final list of remote communication applications analyzed by students.

Application name	Student Reviews	Ratio
Zoom	16	34.04%
Discord	9	19.15%
Webex	9	19.15%
Google Meet	4	8.51%
Microsoft Teams	3	6.38%
Skype	3	6.38%
TeamSpeak	1	2.13%
Facebook Messenger	1	2.13%
Slack	1	2.13%

Existing Affordances. Affordance [2] represents the hints and clues pointing to how a person interacts with an object. For example, in the case of user interfaces, designers can add affordance to an interface by adding a button with a clear label attached. **All teams** associated affordance for their remote applications with features they saw before their eyes. This led to students also adding buttons and labels as affordance tactics. Only **seven** of the 24 teams went into detail and presented other aspects, such as icons, tabs, and the use of color to highlight possible affordances. For example, on Discord, a team stated that icons in communication channels indicate whether the channel is intended for voice or text communication, providing clarity and reducing confusion. In the Skype's case, another team highlighted using mute/unmute microphone or turn on/off camera positioned bottom left, next to each other.

Visual Variables. Looking at students' interpretation of visual variables, most students relied on pointing the features in front of their eyes and how they affect or are being mapped out in the application's interface. Fifteen out of 24 (**62.5 %**) chose to do so, while **nine** of the teams went into details and explored how icons, color, orientation, size, shape, contrast, motion, or texture can impact the user's experience with the interface. Below is a list of fragments how the students analyzed, taking into account a detailed stack of visual variables. Discord is popular among the gaming community, but other types of users benefit from its features as well. For example during and after the COVID-19, schools have started to use Discord as a remote online learning platform. The increase of usage has determined the company behind the application to make several changes in favor of new learning opportunities[1].

– Discord uses a variety of colors to differentiate different channels, users, roles, and statuses. The UI includes various shapes, such as rectangular text boxes, circular avatars, and square buttons.

---

[1] How to use Discord for your classroom – https://discord.com/blog/how-to-use-discord-for-your-classroom (Accessed on June 15, 2024).

– Discord utilizes size to indicate the relative importance of different elements. Larger fonts are added for headings and channel names, while smaller fonts are used for individual messages. Motion and animations provide feedback and create a sense of interactivity. For example, when users join a voice chat, their avatar will move to the chat room to visually indicate their presence.

Interaction Flows. In terms of interaction flows, the students mapped out the steps to achieve specific tasks based on three use cases:

– A general approach: students tested out the main features of the applications (25 out of 47 evaluations – **53.2 %**);
– Attending a virtual class taught by a teaching assistant (16 out of 47 assessments – **34 %**);
– Giving a virtual presentation (6 out of 47 evaluations – **12.8 %**);
– Participating in a virtual job interview (only **one** evaluation).

The students managed to depict the cases listed above. Below is an example of how students described attending a class flow via Breakout Rooms[2] in Zoom:

– Teachers select the "Breakout rooms" button and choose the number of rooms and how the students are assigned manually, automatically, or by choice;
– After the teacher creates the breakout rooms, students can access and enter only the assigned space or choose one.

Visual Metaphors and Idioms. **A third** of the teams detailed metaphors and idioms highlighting features. As recurrent themes, the students considered as metaphors the following:

– Enabling the microphone on/off (real-life audio device icon);
– Accessing settings (gear or cog icon);
– Raising a hand to ask a question or intervene (hand icon).

Regarding idioms, the students mentioned the following features:

– Opening the gallery view (a nine-point grid icon);
– Sharing the screen (a rectangle with an up arrow inside the icon);
– Accessing more details or options (a group of three dots as icon);

A safe assumption is that students perceive metaphors based on what objects they previously interacted with, while for idioms, they associate them when encountering new groups of icons made of simple shapes (arrows, lines, dots).

Surprisingly, **21 out of the 24 teams** converted the metaphors and idioms directly into command line interface (CLI) commands. From simple tasks to detailed instructions, I list below examples of CLI commands the students suggested as alternatives for a text-only interaction – see Tables 2. Although, none of the teams that chose Discord mentioned its official commands feature[3].

---

[2] Zoom Breakout Rooms – https://www.zoom.com/en/products/virtual-meetings/features/brea kout-rooms/ (Accessed on June 15, 2024).

[3] Discord Application Commands – https://discord.com/developers/docs/interactions/applicati on-commands.

Table 2. Substituting action's metaphors/idioms with commands (Discord).

Action	Commands
Listing servers	`ls servers`
Changing a server	`cd <server>`
Listing channels from server	`ls <server>`
Changing a channel	`cd <#channel>`
Read a message	`read <message>`
Write a message	`write <message>`
Listing friends	`ls friends`
Accessing a friend	`cd <@friendName>`
Read message from a friend	`read <@friendName>`
Write a message to a friend	`write <message> <@friendName>`

Cognitive Overload. While analyzing the teams' interpretation of cognitive overload – meaning exceeding the maximum amount of information the user's working memory can process [4], we observed the following aspects and shared insights:

- Participating student teams perceive cognitive overload when the applications display too much information; for example, when many attendees are in the meeting.
- An interesting observation is that students considered the sharing screen feature overwhelming due to the multiple clicks required and displaying many screen options at the time (e.g., Zoom, Webex, Discord mentioned).
- On Discord, there may be a situation where a user needs to join a voice channel for a class, but he/she does not have the required role to see that channel. With numerous voice and text channels, it can be difficult for the user to determine which class it takes place in.
- Zoom meetings often involve video conferencing, screen sharing, and chatting, which can lead to cognitive overload when focusing on multiple things simultaneously.

Issues and Solutions. The recurrent issues identified by the teams venture around the interfaces being cluttered, overwhelming, and inconsistent, especially from one platform to the other. We list below three examples where students detail the negative aspects of interactivity.

- On Web and mobile native platforms, too much clutter on the Discord's UI leads to cognitive overload for users. As solutions, students recommend simplifying the interface by reducing the UI clutter and adopting a visual hierarchy to guide users' attention to important information – separate sections with whitespace and contrasting colors to make the interface easier to navigate. In addition, users can hide or collapse sections they do not need.

- Zoom's gallery view can overwhelm many participants, making it difficult to see everyone on the call. As a solution, students suggest a feature to dynamically resize video feeds based on the number of participants, allowing users to see everyone on the call without scrolling or toggling between views. Moreover, AI-based video processing can focus on active speakers and minimize distractions from other participants.
- The user experience on Microsoft Teams can differ significantly between Web and mobile versions. As solutions, the students suggested ensuring a consistent design across both platforms (Web and Mobile) for easy recognition. More precisely, to implement responsive design principles[4] that adapt to different screen sizes and other device's properties.

Empiric Laws. This challenge presented the most inconclusive results regarding the use of Fitts', Hicks', and Steering laws. The recurrent approach for the teams was to present each law as it is without going into detail about how the rules might be reconsidered/adapted in the context of multi-device interaction. There were some exceptions, but other than those, the students failed to explore more. For example, a team made the following remarks for Zoom:

- In the context of multi-device interaction, Fitts' Law may need to be adapted to account for different devices with varying input methods, such as touchscreens or trackpads. The UI should provide consistent sizing and positioning of buttons and targets across all devices to minimize cognitive load and reduce the need for adaptation between devices. Users can customize controls and target sizes for their preferred device and input method.
- Hick's Law may need to be adapted to take account for the increased complexity of navigating between multiple devices and screens. The UI should use consistent navigation patterns across all devices and screens to minimize cognitive load and reduce the need for adaptation between devices. Also, the application should provide clear feedback to help users understand the consequences of their actions and navigate between screens and devices.
- Steering Law may need to be adapted for different input methods and devices. In addition, Zoom offers customizable input methods that allow users to select their preferred mode of interaction on each device.

Proposed Features. The students did not hesitate to propose various new features ranging from virtual handshakes to AI-powered assistants. Moreover, the groups either came with new proposals or, interestingly, migrated features from one application to the other. Below is a comprehensive description of several features proposed:

Discord

- Add interactive screen sharing where users can manipulate the screen;

---

[4] Responsive Design – https://www.interaction-design.org/literature/topics/responsive-design.

- Include virtual backgrounds where users can select from 3D environments;
- Incorporate a collaborative whiteboard where users can draw their ideas;
- Integrate external calendar applications for specific events;
- Send individual voice messages;
- Display system information such as CPU/GPU speed, and current FPS (Frames Per Second);

Facebook Messenger

- Include mini-games for users to play in private or group messages;
- Have a dedicated on-boarding flow so users understand and know all the platform's features.

Google Meet

- Have breakout rooms like Zoom;
- Include meeting Q&As, polls, online tests, and homeworks;
- Control via voice commands specific meeting features;
- Integrate with Google Docs or Github Co-Pilot;
- Download the attendance list or other types of content as CSV (Comma Separated Values) files.

Microsoft Teams

- Have a dedicated "camera-bot" assistant to monitor online meetings and ensure all participants have their cameras turned on. Once it is activated, the bot detects any participant who does not have the camera on and performs various actions (e.g., sending an alert, removing the user from the meeting);
- Include a voice modifier to add playfulness to the meeting;
- Attendees could change the visibility status to "I am away" when they leave.

Skype

- Add interactive screen sharing where users can manipulate the screen;
- Integrate external calendar applications for specific events;
- Include "smart" notifications to filter messages with various levels of priority.

Slack

- Include the possibility of adding tasks and managing them;
- Have collaborative document editing;
- Integrate virtual events and calendar applications;
- Simulate Augmented Reality (AR) for a shared physical space during remote collaboration.

TeamSpeak

- Include voice-to-text as a means to send messages;
- Add the possibility to drag and drop files while sharing;
- Change the UI theme based on color preferences.

Webex

- Include a virtual handshake as a greeting action;
- Have a student catalog to set up before a meeting;
- AI-based summarization of existing chats;
- Quickly preview files before sharing;
- Add new custom themes for personalization.

Zoom

- Have mood indicators to highlight how a specific attendee feels;
- Play collaborative mini-games during meetings;
- Filter participants based on if the microphone is on or off;
- Join multiple conference meetings at once;
- Participate in a Virtual Reality meeting using a dedicated headset;
- Modify the participant's voice by applying several filters;
- Change volume levels for users in the meeting room;

4.3 Lessons Learned

Although the information gathered was staggering, the tools set for this first experiment support different use cases (without focusing on group of tasks or user objectives), making the final results difficult to compare. This approach provided only an outline based on user reviews and focused mainly on qualitative data, providing specific insights but not a general unified overview. Moreover, having a wide range of applications selected but not distributed evenly made it even harder to extract patterns and conclusions. From this point, it became apparent that a new design is needed for a well-defined study that combines the results meaningfully. This was the basis when organizing the second experiment.

5 Second Student Evaluation Experiment

5.1 Structure

For the second experiment, the experience of the first try represented the basis. We selected and focused only on the three most preferred remote communication applications: Zoom, Discord, and Webex (revisit Table 1). Moreover, the scope and use cases were narrowed down. Individual new participants would perform the tests this time by interacting and reviewing only the selected applications (Web/Desktop versions) and their main features. At choice, the participants could organize an external call if it helped them in their review (all three applications were available for use). After their analysis, they had to complete a new questionnaire organized into four parts:

– A set of 10 (quantitative) questions part of the System Usability Scale;
– A set of 8 (quantitative) questions using a custom rating scale to grade the following criteria: affordance, visual variables, interaction (user) flows, metaphors/idioms, Fitts' Law, Hick's Law, Steering Law, and cognitive overload;
– An optional open-ended question collecting opinions regarding issues, solutions, and improvements for each platform;
– An optional open-ended question collecting new feature proposals for each platform;

Participants had to complete the experiment in 30 min. Overall, **66 students** enrolled for the second experiment. Each participant is a senior year student at a Computer Science Faculty between 20 and 24 years old (64% Male, 36% Female). 22 out of the 66 participants have or had previous work experience (up to three years) in IT-related fields.

5.2 Results

SUS Score. The first part of the questionnaire followed the 10 criteria provided by the System Usability Scale (with answers rated from 1 - Strongly Disagree to 5 - Strongly Agree):

– *I think that I would like to use this system frequently.*
– *I found the system unnecessarily complex;.*
– *I thought the system was easy to use.*
– *I think that I would need the support of a technical person to be able to use the system.*
– *I found the various functions in this system were well integrated.*
– *I thought there was too much inconsistency in this system.*
– *I would imagine that most people would learn to use this system very quickly.*
– *I found the system very cumbersome to use;*
– *I felt very confident using the system.*
– *I needed to learn a lot of things before I could get going with this system.*

For the System Usability Scale, the research collected 65 valid entries out of 66. Afterwards the SUS for each entry for each application is calculated. Finally, the Mean SUS for each application is compared (See Table 3). Discord achieved the highest value with a mean score of **77.42**, followed by Zoom with **73.46**, while Webex reached **66.27**. If the *Curved Grading Scale* rating system is applied, Discord would be rated the Mean Grade B+, Zoom a B and Webex a C. Compared to similar research studies [24] where Microsoft Teams (Mean SUS: 48) and Skype (Mean SUS: 44.28) had a Mean Grade of F, the SUS scores obtained in the second experiment of this research paper are significant higher. Although different applications were tested, the higher scores could be the result of various factors: a safe assumption is that the participants had previous experience interacting with such tools (especially in the context of COVID-19); moreover, if we take the average scores for the 4th (*I think that I would need the support of a technical person to be able to use the system* from 1.26 to 1.42 on average) and 9th question individually (*I needed to learn a lot of things before I could get going with this system* from 1.48 to 1.98 on average), the participants felt confident to know, handle, and use the system on their own.

Table 3. Mean System Usability Scale Results for Zoom, Discord and Webex.

Application	Participants	Mean SUS Score
Zoom	65	73.46
Discord	65	77.42
Webex	65	66.72

PART II   *NAME:*

Rate the applications based on the following criteria (1 - Very low score... 5 - Very high score):
Questionnaire refers to Zoom, Discord and Webex on Web/Desktop.

The application's use of *visual variables:*

Color, Size, Shape, Texture, Typography, Spacing, Orientation, Opacity, and Transparency.

	1	2	3	4	5
Zoom	O	O	O	O	O
Discord	O	O	O	O	O
Webex	O	O	O	O	O

Fig. 2. A sample of the custom questionnaire where participants graded different criteria using the custom rating scale – in this example, the application's visual variables.

Custom Rating Scales. For the ratings, 61 entries out of 66 were valid. The participants had to choose a value *(1—lowest to 5—highest)* for each of the criteria explained to ensure the volunteers understood the concepts (see Fig. 2).

Compared with Zoom and Webex, Discord dominated the scores (six categories out of eight and one tie). Table 4 summarizes the average scores for each category for Zoom, Discord, and Webex. A comparison view can be explored in Fig. 3. Discord registered the highest score for affordance (3.9), visual variables (4.2), interaction (user) flows (4.1), metaphors/idioms (4.2), Fitts' Law (3.6), and Hick's Law (3.5). Regarding Steering Law, it has a tie with Zoom (3.4). Regarding cognitive overload, Discord obtained the highest rating of the three (3.6), resulting in an interpretation of a high level exceeding the maximum amount of information the user's working memory can process. The participants perceived this as a negative particularity for Discord, while Zoom (with a cognitive overload rating of 2.8) was greeted positive. At the opposite pole, Webex scored the lowest in four categories and two ties with Zoom.

If a leaderboard existed, Discord would be first, Zoom would be second, and Webex would be third. This classification would coincide with the order of the Mean SUS scores.

Table 4. Average score based on Rating Scale entries.

Criteria	Zoom	Discord	Webex
Affordance	3.5	**3.9**	3.4
Visual Variables	3.4	**4.2**	3.4
Interaction Flows	3.7	**4.1**	3.6
Metaphors/Idioms	3.8	**4.2**	3.6
Fitts' Law	3.4	**3.6**	3.4
Hick's Law	3.2	**3.5**	3.4
Steering Law	**3.4**	**3.4**	3.3
Cognitive Overload	**2.8**	3.6	3.1

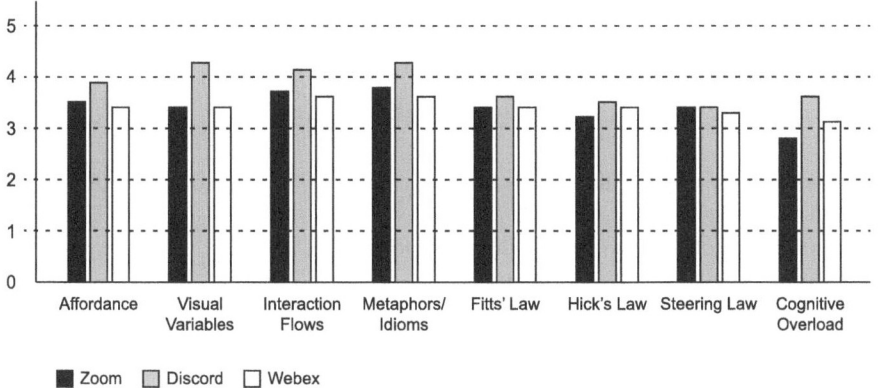

Fig. 3. A comparison view of the average custom rating scores (Zoom, Discord, and Webex) for each criteria.

Improvements. The participants' suggestions were at the same level of diversity as the first experiment, with shared ideas resurfacing. Below is a short list of the most requested improvements for each of the three applications:

Zoom

- Not having the ability to freely customize the layout and positioning of the participants' video in a meeting;
- Cannot quickly switch between private and public (everyone) chat conversations and do not have the chat history available after a meeting ends;
- De-cluttering the bottom navigation by minimizing the number of buttons and rethinking their size.

Discord

- Too much information, too crowded screen, all over the place, over-complicated navigation;

- Complex settings which require getting used to it or having a demanding learning curve;
- More customization is needed, allowing diverse themes even in the free subscription plan.

Webex

- Difficult to find or change settings;
- Just like Zoom, not having the ability to freely customize the layout and positioning of the participants' video in a meeting; also, de-cluttering the bottom navigation;
- Several participants stated that Webex has frequent connection issues.

New Features. For new features, the participants kept the trend of the first experiment and proposed either new capabilities for the applications or borrowing from one to the other. Below is a short list of the top new features the volunteers proposed:

Zoom

- Connecting a mixed-reality headset and participating in a meeting benefiting from an AR/VR view;
- Sharing multiple screens at once during a video call;
- Splitting the chat into public and private;

Discord

- Have breakout rooms when joining a server call;
- Have custom themes available, at least a limited number in the free unpaid version;
- Again, splitting the chat into public and private;

Webex

- To be able to customize the layout, especially in the video call (the participants' video panels);
- Same as Zoom, sharing multiple screens at once during a video call;
- The ability to apply different filters on the video stream during a meeting.

One crucial aspect worth mentioning is that the volunteers also proposed that the applications should have an AI-based conversational agent available for either note-taking or support. With the rise of Generative AI tools [29], it is no surprise that the volunteers (in their 20 s) would include this option.

5.3   Lessons Learned

When compared, the second experiment provided more precise data and insights, contributing to the foundation the first created. Using SUS and custom ratings offered the right amount of traction the participants needed to complete the tests. Even with this progress, the open-ended part (improvements and features) can be improved further. Although these questions were optional, the answers proved challenging to analyze and ideate, as many varied in form, while some volunteers skipped this part entirely. As a future improvement, the open-ended part can be converted to be more quantitative, focusing on rating or marking true/false the top insights already found in the two experiments.

6   Conclusion and Further Work

The research paper first presented an extensive literature review of remote communication applications during and after COVID-19, highlighting different use cases. It continued with a contribution to the education area with two experiments in which student volunteers reviewed and evaluated their preferred choice of tools. While the first experiment focused on gaining qualitative data insights, the second experiment narrowed the focus to a more quantitative interpretation. Zoom, Discord, and Webex were the finalists from a comprehensive list of preferred solutions. Discord proved the most advantageous based on the volunteers' evaluations, which included customs criteria and well-known tactics like the System Usability Scale (Discord - 77.42, Zoom - 73.46, Webex - 66.72).

Choosing to implement two separate experiments has proven to be an inspiring tactic. Learning from the first tests paved the way for a more structured and strategic approach for the second try. In doing so, the results and insights gathered made the research a success, leaving room for improvement and continuation. A third experiment is in concept phase with a new batch of volunteers. New evaluation methods are also considered: for example, the User Evaluation Questionnaire (UEQ) [28] gains traction in evaluating remote communication applications with results also positioning Discord on top of Zoom or Microsoft Teams [19]. Moreover, Google Meet is being added to the shortlist of tools being assessed as it settles among user preferences [16]. Nevertheless, combining industry-standard evaluations with custom assessments based on HCI-related topics sparks motivation to develop this research in the future. The paper could also be a valuable resource to stakeholders who want to integrate remote communication applications into their educational environment while discovering new insights into improving the experience.

Acknowledgements. The study was possible with the contribution of the participants who volunteered. Gratitude and appreciation are in order. A special mention also goes to Prof. Dr. habil. *Sabin-Corneliu Buraga* for his support while making this paper.

References

1. Ahmad, S., Siddiqui, K.: Comparative study of alternative teaching and learning tools: google meet, microsoft teams, and zoom during COVID-19. In: Teaching in the Pandemic Era in Saudi Arabia, pp. 120–129 (2022). https://doi.org/10.1163/9789004521674_008
2. Norman, D.: The Psychology of Everyday Things. Basic Books, New York (1988)
3. Morrison-Smith, S., Ruiz, J.: Challenges and barriers in virtual teams: a literature review. SN Appl. Sci. **2**(6), 1–33 (2020). https://doi.org/10.1007/s42452-020-2801-5
4. Sweller, J.: Cognitive load theory, learning difficulty, and instructional design. Learn. Instr. **4**, 295–312 (1994). https://doi.org/10.1016/0959-4752(94)90003-5
5. Garro-Abarca, V., Palos-Sanchez, P., Aguayo-Camacho, M.: Virtual teams in times of pandemic: factors that influence performance. Front. Psychol. **12**, 624–637 (2021). https://doi.org/10.3389/fpsyg.2021.624637
6. Hurst, W., Withington, A., Kolivand, H.: Virtual conference design: features and obstacles. Multimedia Tools Appl. **81**, 16901–16919 (2022). https://doi.org/10.1007/s11042-022-12402-4
7. Lucero, A.: Using affinity diagrams to evaluate interactive prototypes. In: Human-Computer Interaction-INTERACT 2015, vol. 9297 (2015). https://doi.org/10.1007/978-3-319-22668-2_19
8. Accot, J., Zhai, S.: Performance evaluation of input devices in trajectory-based tasks: an application of the steering law. In: Proceedings Of ACM CHI 1999 Conference on Human Factors In Computing Systems, pp. 466–472 (1999). https://doi.org/10.1145/302979.303133
9. Hick, W.: On the rate of gain of information. Q. J. Exp. Psychol. **4**, 11–26 (1952). https://doi.org/10.1080/17470215208416600
10. Fitts, P.: The information capacity of the human motor system in controlling the amplitude of movement. J. Exp. Psychol. **47**, 381–391 (1954). https://doi.org/10.1037/0096-3445.121.3.262
11. Allen, T., Golden, T., Shockley, K.: How effective is telecommuting? assessing the status of our scientific findings. Psychol. Sci. Public Interest **16**, 40–68 (2015). https://doi.org/10.1177/1529100615593273
12. Lee, Y.Y., Martin, K.I.: The flipped classroom in ESL teacher education: an example from CALL. Educ. Inf. Technol. **25**(4), 2605–2633 (2019). https://doi.org/10.1007/s10639-019-10082-6
13. Gumasing, M., Belizario, D., Reyes, M., Pacunayen, H., Piamonte, J.: Factors affecting preferences of web conferencing sites: a system usability study. In: Proceedings of the 2023 14th International Conference on E-Education, E-Business, E-Management and E-Learning, pp. 94–99 (2023). https://doi.org/10.1145/3588243.3588251
14. Bhardawaj, A., Bhardwaj, R., Chaudhary, A.: A study on the effects of various video conferencing tools and apps for remote working during the COVID-19 pandemic. J. Remote Work **97**, 1–10 (2023)
15. Mahyoob, M.: Online learning effectiveness during the COVID-19 pandemic: a case study of Saudi universities. Int. J. Inf. Commun. Technol. Educ. Off. Publ. Inf. Res. Manag. Assoc. **17**, 1–14 (2021). https://doi.org/10.4018/IJICTE.20211001.oa7
16. Chang, H., Varvello, M., Hao, F., Mukherjee, S.: A tale of three videoconferencing applications: zoom, webex, and meet. IEEE/ACM Trans. Network. **30**(5), 2343–2358 (2022). https://doi.org/10.1109/TNET.2022.3171467
17. Cóndor-Herrera, O., Jadán-Guerrero, J., Ramos, C.: Analysis of video conferencing platforms for online teaching during the Covid-19 pandemic. In: Proceedings of the 14th International Conference on Applied Human Factors and Ergonomics (AHFE 2022) (2022). https://doi.org/10.54941/ahfe1002378

18. Archibald, M., Ambagtsheer, R., Casey, M., Lawless, M.: Using zoom videoconferencing for qualitative data collection: perceptions and experiences of researchers and participants. Int. J. Qual. Methods **18**, 160940691987459 (2019). https://doi.org/10.1177/1609406919874596

19. Mora-Jimenez, L., Ramírez-Benavides, K., Quesada, L., López, G., Guerrero, L.: User experience in communication and collaboration platforms: a comparative study including discord, microsoft teams, and zoom. In: Advances in Human Factors in Communication and Collaboration, pp. 52–61 (2022). https://doi.org/10.1007/978-3-030-96293-7_6

20. Parasian, N., Yuliati, R.: Video conference as a mode of communication in the pandemic era. In: Proceedings of the 6th International Conference on Social and Political Sciences (ICOSAPS 2020), pp. 9–17 (2020). https://doi.org/10.2991/assehr.k.201219.002

21. Matulin, M., Mrvelj, Š., Abramović, B., Šoštarić, T., Čejvan, M.: User quality of experience comparison between skype, microsoft teams and zoom videoconferencing tools. In: Proceedings of the International Conference on Communication Technologies and Applications (ICCTA 2021) (2021). https://doi.org/10.1007/978-3-030-78459-1_22

22. Rio-Chillcce, A.D., Jara-Monge, L., Andrade-Arenas, L.: Analysis of the use of videoconferencing in the learning process during the pandemic at a University in Lima. Int. J. Adv. Comput. Sci. Appl. **12**(5) (2021). https://doi.org/10.14569/IJACSA.2021.01205102

23. Karl, K.A., Peluchette, J.V., Aghakhani, N.: Virtual Work Meetings During the COVID-19 pandemic: the good, bad, and ugly. Small Group Res. **53**(3), 343–365 (2022). https://doi.org/10.1177/10464964211015286

24. Flame, R.R.F., Prasetyo, Y.T., Nadlifatin, R., Ayuwati, I.D., Persada, S.F., Chuenyindee, T.: Usability evaluation of communication tools used as remote support in machine service industry: a comparison between microsoft teams and skype. In: Proceedings of the 2023 6th International Conference on Computers in Management and Business (ICCMB '23), pp. 117–121 (2023). https://doi.org/10.1145/3584816.3584834

25. Bridson, K., Atkinson, J., Fleming, S.D.: Delivering round-the-clock help to software engineering students using discord: an experience report. In: Proceedings of the 53rd ACM Technical Symposium on Computer Science Education, vol. 1 (SIGCSE 2022), pp. 759–765 (2022). https://doi.org/10.1145/3478431.3499385

26. Cuijpers, J., et al.: An empirical evaluation of video conferencing systems used in industry, academia, and entertainment. In: Companion of the ACM/SPEC International Conference on Performance Engineering (ICPE '21), pp. 171–174 (2021). https://doi.org/10.1145/3447545.3451174

27. Balogova, K., Brumby, D.: How do you zoom?: a survey study of how users configure videoconference tools for online meetings. In: Proceedings of the 1st Annual Meeting of the Symposium on Human-Computer Interaction for Work (CHIWORK '22), Article No. 5, pp. 1–7 (2022). https://doi.org/10.1145/3533406.3533408

28. Schrepp, M., Hinderks, A., Thomaschewski, J.: Applying the user experience questionnaire (UEQ) in different evaluation scenarios. In: Proceedings of the International Conference on Design, User Experience, and Usability, pp. 383–392 (2014). https://doi.org/10.1007/978-3-319-07668-3_37

29. Vargas-Murillo, A.R., Pari-Bedoya, I.N.M.D.L.A., Guevara-Soto, F.D.J.: The Ethics of AI assisted learning: a systematic literature review on the impacts of ChatGPT usage in education. In: Proceedings of the 2023 8th International Conference on Distance Education and Learning (ICDEL 2023), pp. 8–13. Association for Computing Machinery, New York (2023). https://doi.org/10.1145/3606094.3606101

Enhancing EEG-Based User Verification with a Normalized Neural Network Ensemble Approach

Roberto Saia[(⊠)][iD], Riccardo Balia[iD], Alessandro Sebastian Podda[iD],
Livio Pompianu[iD], Salvatore Carta[iD], and Alessia Pisu[iD]

Department of Mathematics and Computer Science, University of Cagliari,
Palazzo delle Scienze, Via Ospedale 72, 09124 Cagliari, Italy
{roberto.saia,riccardo.balia,sebastianpodda,livio.pompianu,
salvatore,alessia.pisu96}@unica.it

Abstract. The development of user identity verification approaches using biometric systems based on EEG data holds significant promise across various domains. However, the inherent complexity and variability of this data make designing reliable solutions challenging. In response to these challenges, this work introduces a Normalized Neural Network Ensemble (NNNE) approach for EEG-based user verification. It leverages neural networks to enhance the current state-of-the-art performance, aiming to overcome the problems associated with EEG data by capturing spatial and temporal patterns in EEG signals more effectively. In detail, the proposed approach relies on an architecture centered around an ensemble of Multi-Layer Perceptron artificial neural networks regulated by a soft voting criterion. As part of the preprocessing steps, the input data is normalized by transforming features based on quantile information. Additionally, the MLP hyperparameters and the number of MLP evaluators in the ensemble are automatically optimized. Considering the high heterogeneity of the state-of-the-art works in this field, which are characterized by a wide variability in the choices of components, approaches, and strategies, making comparisons between their performances difficult and sometimes impossible, this paper exploits the opportunity offered by the Biometric EEG Dataset (BED), which provides benchmark values that facilitate comparisons within the context of widely adopted approaches in literature in terms of stimuli and feature extraction techniques. The experimental results show that the proposed NNNE approach improves the performance of the state-of-the-art one (Hidden Markov Model) used by the authors of the dataset to define the reference values, significantly.

Keywords: AI security · Access control · Biometrics · Verification · EEG · Stimuli

1 Introduction

The rapid growth in technology and the ever-increasing need for biometric systems to perform user identification tasks have led to development efforts focused on enhancing the performance of these systems. In such a research field, EEG-based approaches

H. Plácido da Silva and P. Cipresso (Eds.): CHIRA 2024, CCIS 2370, pp. 230–248, 2025.
https://doi.org/10.1007/978-3-031-82633-7_15

represent a powerful opportunity thanks to their potential to offer a unique and reliable user identification based on their brain activity patterns. This is an opportunity related to the possibility of detecting brain activity using easy-to-use, small-sized, and low-cost devices and sensors, which is a relatively recent scenario that has opened up new perspectives in many fields of scientific research. In other words, these devices are able to perform an *Electroencephalogram* (EEG) through the measurement of the brain's electrical activity using electrodes positioned on the scalp. The exponential increase in systems/services requiring a reliable user authentication process needs robust biometric systems to perform such a task, leading many researchers toward developing effective systems. Within this dynamic research context, researchers consider EEG-based approaches a great opportunity due to their reliance on unique patterns of user brain activity. The main advantage of these approaches is their potential to provide a reliable means of user identification.

One of the strengths of EEG-based biometric systems is their capability to capture and analyze complex brain activity patterns by considering the variations in individuals' electroencephalograms (EEGs) finding distinctive patterns that characterize each user. The inherent variability in an individual's brain activity gives uniqueness to the brain patterns, enabling the definition of personalized and secure approaches for user identification. For these reasons, the modern scenario can benefit from the advent of easy-to-use, compact, and cost-effective EEG devices and sensors because they open up new possibilities for widespread application. The ease of acquiring EEG data through a few electrodes placed on the scalp renders the technology accessible across diverse scenarios, both in controlled and real-world ones. The potential versatility of EEG-based biometric systems can play a crucial role across various domains, e.g., in healthcare, where these systems can help the patient identification process, granting the confidentiality of medical records. In the realm of cybersecurity, their potential adds an extra layer of protection against unauthorized access.

The combination of advanced EEG technologies with the accessibility of user-friendly and low-cost devices makes their use possible in numerous domains, from healthcare to cybersecurity, offering new opportunities to design secure and personalized identification approaches. Based on the challenges in the EEG-based biometric systems research area highlighted by the literature [16, 18] and inspired by different ensemble learning approaches [5, 12, 15], we defined the proposed Normalized Neural Network Ensemble (NNNE) approach for EEG-based personal verification. It leverages an architecture based on an ensemble of Multi-Layer Perceptron (MLP) Artificial Neural Networks (ANNs) governed by a soft voting criterion that considers the output class's predicted probability, allowing us to better capture spatial and temporal patterns in EEG data. As a preliminary step, the input data is normalized according to a quantile approach that transforms the data features based on the quantile information, together with automatic optimization of the MLP hyperparameters and the number of them in the ensemble.

The validation process adopted to evaluate the proposed approach uses a publicly available dataset named BED [3] that contains a collection of EEG signals recorded from several users, providing a test environment similar to the real-world scenario. Notably, the dataset authors provide baseline results for performance comparison by employing the robust approach based on *Hidden Markov Model* (HMM) proposed in [11], except for the use of regular models, which led to better results, instead of *left-right* ones. To the best of our knowledge, at the time of writing, these results represent the state-of-the-art performance achieved on the BED dataset, and we consider them in the remainder of this work for comparison (we both refer to them as *HMM* results or *baseline* results). The proposed approach aims to address the issues that most canonical methods face in managing the complex patterns associated with EEG signals, providing the following main scientific contributions:

(i) formalization of a Novel Normalized Neural Network Ensemble (NNNE) approach for EEG-Based personal verification: we provide a comprehensive formalization of the entire NNNE architecture. This formalization encompasses determining the optimal number and hyperparameters for the Multi-Layer Perceptron (MLP) artificial neural networks utilized in the ensemble strategy and the optimal rule used for the class predictions;

(ii) definition of a preprocessing step aimed to optimize EEG Data: in conjunction with the formalization of the NNNE approach, we introduce a preprocessing step specifically designed to optimize the neural network input data. This involves implementing a quantile-based approach to normalize input data, where the features are transformed by quantile information;

(iii) evaluation of the NNNE approach on datasets related to different state-of-the-art data preprocessing techniques and different stimuli to users during EEG acquisition: to assess the effectiveness of the proposed NNNE approach, we conduct an extensive evaluation on datasets defined through different state-of-the-art data preprocessing techniques for feature extraction, and different stimuli applied to users during EEG acquisition.

2 Background and Related Work

The literature of recent years relating to the use of EEG data for the definition of biometric systems for user identification tasks [17, 18] indicates a growing interest in this research area, proposing ever more efficient strategies and implementations [2], as well as taking into account transversal aspects [20].

The human brain consists of billions of neurons, and each of them has the potential to establish communication channels with thousands of others through weak electric signals (microvolts). Such electrical activities create brain waves that can be categorized into five groups based on their frequency (ranging from 4 to 100 Hz). Each group is identified using a Greek letter: the *Delta* wave (less than 4 Hz), the *Theta* wave (4 to 8 Hz), the *Alpha* wave (8 to 12 Hz), the *Beta* wave (13 to 30 Hz), and the *Gamma* wave (greater than 30 Hz). It should be noted that different brain regions exhibit various wave frequencies that can occur simultaneously. An EEG device can record the brain's electrical activity through sensors on the scalp, measuring voltage fluctuations that typically range from 10 to 100 millivolts in adults. The positioning of the electrodes on the scalp follows the *International 10–20 System*, as illustrated in Fig. 1. This placement considers the correlation between electrode locations and the corresponding areas of the cerebral cortex, providing a guide for the correct electrode placement, where each position is identified by a letter (that denotes the lobe) and a number/letter (that indicates the hemisphere location).

Some representative recent works in this field are: the work in [22], where the authors propose a viable method (with respect to acquisition time and using an affordable EEG device) for biometric user identification employing the Eyes Closed (EC) and visual stimulation protocols; the approach proposed in [8], where the authors utilize single-trial familiar-name AEPs, using two frontal EEG electrodes for the EEG data collection; the study in [24], which proposes a system framework for Visual Evoked Potential (VEP) based biometrics, comparing the effectiveness of three types of VEP signals in user identification task; in [9], the authors instead propose an approach for biometric user identification based on EEG data using a benchmark dataset composed by EEG data collected under diverse visual and non-visual stimuli through an inexpensive EEG device.

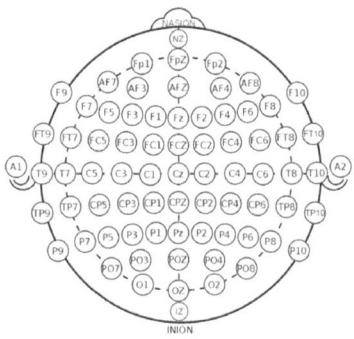

Fig. 1. International 10–20 System.

2.1   Evoked Potentials

A crucial challenge in this field of research lies in the differences found in the EEG signals of diverse subjects, due to which it is necessary to define a new evaluation model for each subject, which presents a substantial computational load. In addition, the analysis of EEG signals poses significant challenges due to its low signal-to-noise ratio and non-stationary nature. The literature demonstrates a significant use of techniques and strategies to achieve temporal repeatability of acquired patterns, an essential requirement for such systems. Some of them utilize different external stimuli to enhance the distinctiveness of brainwave patterns and, consequently, improve their stability and the reliability of the user identification process over time.

More formally, these techniques are defined *Evoked Potentials* (EPs), indicating the electrical responses recorded within a specific part of the nervous system, primarily in the brain, triggered by external stimuli. However, it should be noted that these stimulation techniques often lack practicality as authentication mechanisms due to extended detection times and expensive equipment.

Table 1. Low/Medium-cost EEG Devices.

Device		Specifications		Electrodes
Brand	Product Name	Data Resolution (bits)	Bandwidth Range (Hz)	Number of Electrodes
Emotiv	Insight	14	0.50–43	05
Emotiv	Epoch X	14/16	0.16–43	14
Emotiv	**Epoch +**	**14/16**	**0.16–43**	**14**
Emotiv	Epoch Flex	14	0.20–45	32
InteraXon	Muse-2	12	0.20–45	04
InteraXon	Muse S	12	0.20–45	04
Neurowsky	MindWave Mobile 2	12	3.00–100	01
OpenBCI	Cyton Biosensing Board	24	1.00–50	08

2.2   Feature Extraction

In the context of EEG data, the most widely used techniques for feature extraction are the: *Mel-Frequency Cepstral Coefficients* (MFCC), which is a technique [1] largely used in speech and audio processing. In EEG data analysis, it is exploited to represent and classify features. In more detail, the EEG signal is divided into short time frames, a spectrum is computed for each frame, the Mel filterbank is applied to the power spectrum to mimic the human ear's frequency response, the logarithm of filterbank energies is computed, followed by the application of the Discrete Cosine Transform (DCT) to obtain coefficients. The representation of EEG signals in terms of MFCC allows us to capture the relevant features while discarding irrelevant information; *Autoregressive Reflection Coefficients (ARRC)*, which is derived from an autoregressive model fitted to the EEG signal, providing a model for temporal dependencies [10]. The EEG signal is modeled as an autoregressive process, expressing each value as a linear combination of its previous values, and the coefficients of this autoregressive model are the ARR coefficients, which offer a compact representation of the temporal dynamics in EEG data; *Spectral Features (SPEC)*, which is a technique [7] that involves the analysis of the frequency content of the EEG signal, providing insights into power distribution across frequency bands. The EEG signals are transformed into the frequency domain using techniques such as Fourier or Wavelet transform, and then the power spectral density or other frequency-domain features are computed.

2.3   Open Problems

The literature indicates that the primary focus in this research domain lies in designing systems that optimize performance concerning user-friendliness, affordable hardware, and identification performance, showing efforts made to mitigate known issues through advanced protocols and methodologies. In this context, two primary challenges emerge: the first pertains to the nature of the data, and the second relates to the data acquisition process. In more detail, the first challenge is associated with the instability of EEG patterns over time. The data's complexity, non-linearity, and non-stationarity hinder the direct extraction of meaningful information from these signals in the time domain [21]. Numerous works in the literature underscore this challenge, emphasizing the necessary efforts to leverage EEG data for biometric purposes. It is worth noting that stimulating users, for example, through evoked potentials techniques during EEG data acquisition, aims to mitigate this problem. As highlighted by various studies, the introduction of external stimuli during EEG data acquisition exhibits better repeatability than EEG data acquired without such stimuli.

The second challenge revolves around factors such as user heterogeneity in terms of EEG waves and the need to perform system calibration during acquisition/stimulation. This aspect is explicitly or implicitly addressed in many literature works, where several proposed approaches are often unsuitable for real-world biometric user identification due to this issue [8]. Examples include works using expensive and large EEG equipment with a high number of electrodes, requiring time-consuming application and the use of conductive paste, unlike the dry EEG electrodes prevalent in low-cost devices. This implies that a widely applicable biometric user identification system should use hardware that does not necessitate complex preparation/calibration operations, enabling users to operate it independently, similar to other widely-used biometric systems.

The literature provides numerous examples of effective approaches. For instance, in [14], stable EEG response characteristics are demonstrated across multiple sessions using a stimulation technique. In [13], the authors show improved EEG signal stability over time with a visual stimulation approach, and in [23], a test of the EEG system stability over a 30-day period is performed, whereas in [19], wavelet packet decomposition is employed to extract more permanent patterns. In any case, the practical use of EEG signals in biometrics faces an extra challenge due to interference from unwanted artifacts related to various sources such as muscle, ocular, respiratory, and cardiac activities. Consequently, the adoption of preprocessing techniques is necessary to minimize these influences.

2.4 EEG Devices

Table 1 shows brief information about the most popular low to medium-cost EEG devices that have revolutionized many research areas since these devices offer the opportunity to conduct experiments based on EEG data, which in the past were only possible using expensive hardware (the device used to collect EEG data for the dataset used in this work is highlighted in bold).

3 Approach Implementation

This section provides details about the proposed NNNE approach. In brief, EEG data is preprocessed, and the subsequent steps involve optimizing hyperparameters, determining the optimal number of MLP evaluators in the ensemble, and finally, verifying the user, as detailed in the following.

3.1 Input Data

The system's input is represented by the Biometric EEG Dataset (BED) [3], which has been designed to enable the verification of biometric approaches based on EEG data acquired using low-cost acquisition devices, such as the *Emotiv Epoc+* used in this case. In more detail, the EEG data were collected by 14-channel EEG signals at a sampling frequency of 256 Hz using the Emotiv wireless EEG headset. It includes data related to different state-of-the-art preprocessing techniques for feature extraction, different stimuli to users during EEG acquisition, and different disjointed data acquisition sessions, as detailed in Sect. 4.1.

Considering that are involved three different processing techniques for feature extraction (MFCC, ARRC, SPEC), twelve stimuli (AS, MC, RC, RO, VC3, VC5, VC7, VC10, VF3, VF5, VF7, VF10), and three sessions (1, 2, 3), this leads to $(3 \times 12 \times 3) = 108$ different datasets.

3.2   EEG Data Preprocessing

The EEG data is then preprocessed through a Quantile Normalization (QN), which ensure that data have the same distribution, making them comparable across different samples. The process involves the following steps:

1. Sort the values in each column (feature) of the dataset in ascending order.
2. Assign ranks to the sorted values, with ties receiving the average rank.
3. Calculate the average value for each rank across all columns, resulting in the quantile values.
4. Replace the original values with their corresponding quantile ones.

More formally, let X be the original dataset with n rows (samples) and m columns (features). For each column j, let X_{ij} represent the value of the i-th row. The normalized value Y_{ij} is calculated as shown in Eq. 1: More formally, let X be the original dataset with n rows (samples) and m columns (features). For each column j, let X_{ij} represent the value of the i-th row. The normalized value Y_{ij} is calculated as shown in Eq. 1, where k iterates over all rows in column j. This process ensures that each column has the same distribution of values, making it suitable for cross-sample comparisons.

$$Y_{ij} = \text{Quantile\_Value}(X_{ij}) = \frac{1}{n} \sum_{k=1}^{n} X_{kj} \qquad (1)$$

3.3   MLP Hyperparameters Optimization

In this step, the most significant hyperparameters of the Multi-Layer Perceptron (MLP) neural network (reported in Table 2) are automatically optimized based on the training data. This is done to identify the most effective configuration for later use in the ensemble classification approach. In more detail, the hyperparameters *activation*, *hidden_layer_sizes*, *learning_rate_init*, *alpha*, and *max_iter* are tested in all their combinations of values using a Grid Search approach validated through the k-fold cross-validation criterion with k=5.

The selection of these parameters is based on the Equal Error Rate (EER) metric. Given that this is an automatic process, the optimal configuration is determined dynamically based on the characteristics of the input data. Therefore, the specifics of parameter values are not explicitly provided as they depend on the processed data.

Table 2. MLP Classifier Involved Hyperparameters.

Hyperparameter	Description
activation	Activation function for the hidden layer. It determines the output of each neuron. Common options include 'identity', 'logistic', 'tanh', and 'relu'
hidden_layer_sizes	Number of neurons in each hidden layer. It allows defining the architecture of the neural network
learning_rate_init	Initial learning rate. It influences the step size in updating the weights during training
alpha	L2 regularization term. A penalty added to the loss function to prevent overfitting
max_iter	Maximum number of iterations. The number of times the entire training dataset is passed forward and backward through the neural network

3.4 MLP Ensemble Optimization

After identifying the best combination of MLP hyperparameters, this step involves determining the optimal number of MLP classifiers to use in the ensemble approach. In this context, it is important to note that while the hyperparameters of MLP classifiers within the ensemble are the same to maximize their individual performance, each MLP classifier is initialized differently through the random_state parameter to maximize ensemble performance. The process can be formalized through the Eq. 2, where N_o indicates the optimal number of MLP classifiers in the ensemble, $Ensemble\,(N)$ represents the ensemble of N MLP classifiers, and $EER\,(Ensemble\,(N))$ is the Equal Error Rate (EER) metric computed on the performance of the ensemble with N classifiers.

$$N_o = \arg\min_N \text{EER}\,(\text{Ensemble}\,(N)) \tag{2}$$

In this formalization, the objective is to find the optimal number of MLP classifiers (N_o) that minimizes the EER metric when using an ensemble of N MLP classifiers with the identified best combination of hyperparameters. The random initialization of each MLP classifier, controlled by the random_state parameter, introduces diversity into the ensemble, aiming to maximize its overall performance. The selection of the optimal number of classifiers is crucial for achieving the best trade-off between model complexity and performance. The minimization process is based on the EER metric, which is commonly used in binary classification problems and is suitable for evaluating the overall performance of the ensemble.

3.5 MLP Ensemble Classification

In this step, the ensemble approach based on previously defined and optimized MLP classifiers is used to perform user verification tasks in the test sets. The classification adopts a multiclass Soft Voting criterion, considering the evaluation of each individual MLP classifier in the ensemble in terms of the probability of a user belonging to possible target classes. In addition, for the validation of the proposed approach, its performance is evaluated in terms of Area Under the Curve (AUC) and Equal Error Rate (EER).

More formally, the ensemble approach regulated through a Soft Voting criterion is shown in Eq. 3, where $\hat{y}$ is the predicted class, N is the number of classifiers, and P_{ij} is the probability predicted by the i-th classifier for the j-th class.

$$\hat{y} = \text{argmax}_j \left(\frac{1}{N} \sum_{i=1}^{N} P_{ij} \right) \tag{3}$$

The adoption of a Soft Voting criterion in the context of User Verification based on EEG data, particularly within an ensemble approach, is motivated by its ability to provide more probabilistic decision-making. In Soft Voting, instead of relying only on the majority decision, the algorithm considers the confidence levels or probabilities assigned by each individual classifier. This approach leads toward a more sophisticated aggregation of decisions, taking into account the uncertainty associated with each classifier's prediction. In the domain of EEG-based User Verification, the inherent complexity and variability of brain signals make it challenging to achieve perfect consensus among classifiers. By incorporating Soft Voting, the ensemble model gains flexibility in capturing the subtle nuances present in the data. This is especially crucial when dealing with scenarios where individual classifiers may exhibit varying degrees of certainty or ambiguity in their predictions.

3.6   User Verification

The output of the entire process will be the classification of each input user into a specific class. In this context, the term class refers to the identity of the user being verified through this system. Each user's input is categorized into a particular class, representing the confirmed identity as determined by the verification system. It should be noted that although the proposed approach seems to perform user identification due to its validation using the BED dataset, its practical application is user verification. In real-world scenarios, where the input data come from actual users, the system verifies whether the provided EEG data matches the stored data of the claimed user, ensuring the system's ability to authenticate users.

Algorithm Definition. Based on the previous steps, the Algorithm 1 implements the proposed NNNE approach to classify the new EEG data: as input it requires the training set T, the unclassified EEG data U, the classification approach A (i.e., MLP), and the value to use for the initialization of the random number generator seed, providing as output the classification of the EEG data in the set U.

Asymptotic Time Complexity Analysis. Algorithm 1 involves several processes with varying time complexities, analyzed as follows:

1. **Data Normalization (Quantile Normalization):** The complexity of processing each element in the training set (T) and unclassified EEG data (U) is $O(m \cdot d + u \cdot d)$, where m is the training set size, d is the data dimensionality, and u is the unclassified data size.
2. **Optimal Hyperparameters and Classifiers Number:** Finding the optimal MLP hyperparameters (H) and the number of ensemble MLP classifiers (N) has a complexity of $O(k)$, where k represents the complexity of these operations.
3. **Ensemble Model Training (MLP Training):** Training N ensemble classifiers, with each classifier having a training complexity of α, results in a total complexity of $O(N \cdot \alpha)$.
4. **Unclassified EEG Data Processing:** Processing unclassified EEG data of size u with complexity β has a total complexity of $O(u \cdot \beta)$.

5. **Ensemble Classification:** Combining predictions from N MLP models with complexity γ results in a total complexity of $O(N \cdot \gamma)$.

The overall computational complexity of the algorithm is $O(m \cdot d + u \cdot d + k + N \cdot \alpha + u \cdot \beta + N \cdot \gamma)$. The term with the highest growth rate determines the maximum complexity:

- If N dominates, the maximum complexity is $O(N \cdot \alpha + N \cdot \gamma)$.
- If m and u dominate, the maximum complexity is $O(m \cdot d + u \cdot d)$.
- If k dominates, the maximum complexity is $O(k)$.

Parallelization can be employed to reduce computation times. Many processes in the NNNE algorithm, such as data normalization, ensemble model training, and ensemble classification, can be parallelized using multi-core processors or distributed computing resources. For instance, frameworks like TensorFlow or PyTorch enable concurrent training of MLP models on GPUs, and libraries like Dask and Joblib facilitate task parallelization in distributed environments. They can be exploited to reduce computation time in real-world scenarios where time efficiency is crucial.

Algorithm 1. NNNE Approach.

Require: T=Training set, U=Unclassified EEG data, A=Classification approach , rnd=Random number generator seed initialization value
Ensure: R=Classification of the U data
1: **procedure** NNNE(T, U, A, rnd)
2:      $T \leftarrow dataNormalization\,(T)$ ▷ Training set data normalization
3:      $U \leftarrow dataNormalization\,(U)$ ▷ Unclassified EEG data normalization
4:      $H \leftarrow getHyperparameters\,(T, A)$ ▷ Get optimal classifier hyperparameters
5:      $N \leftarrow getClassifierNumber\,(T, A\,(H))$ ▷ Get optimal number of ensemble classifiers
6:      **for each** $n \in N$ **do**   ▷ Trains the ensemble classifier models
7:          rnd = rnd + 1   ▷ Differentiates the initialization of the random number generator seed
8:          $m \leftarrow trainModel\,(A\,(H)\,, rnd)$ ▷ Trains evaluation model
9:          $M.add\,(m)$ ▷ Store model
10:      **end for**
11:      **for each** $u \in U$ **do**   ▷ Unclassified EEG data processing
12:          $r \leftarrow getEnsembleCalssification\,(u, M)$ ▷ Perform ensemble classification
13:          $R.add\,(r)$ ▷ Store classification
14:      **end for**
15:      **return** R ▷ Returns classification of U EEG data
16: **end procedure**

---

4 Experiments

The experimental setup utilized a machine running on the Linux operating system with Kernel version 6.1.0-12-amd64 x86_64. The hardware specifications of the machine include 32 gigabytes of RAM and an Intel® Core™ i7-6700 CPU @ 3.40 GHz with 8 cores. The code was developed using the Python programming language and the scikit-learn library[1]. Additionally, we initialized the pseudo-random number generator seed to 1 to ensure experiment reproducibility.

---

[1] http://scikit-learn.org.

4.1 Dataset

The Biometric EEG dataset (BED) used is publicly available upon request on the zen-odo.org website[2]. It includes various sets of data, among them those used to establish the baselines (obtained using the Hidden Markov Model state-of-the-art approach) against which we compared to validate the proposed NNNE approach. Specifically, the *Verification* folder contains three Matlab files, *ARRC.mat*, *MFCC.mat*, and *SPEC.mat*, corresponding to the same EEG data from 21 users collected during 3 distinct and chronologically separated sessions (spaced a week). To eliminate artifacts, such as those related to muscle activity, jaw clenching, or eyes blinking, the EEGLAB toolbox [6] was used to preprocess the EEG signals using the PREP pipeline [4], which involves the following steps: (i) it applies a filter to eliminate line noise; (ii) it refers the signal to an approximation of the actual average reference; (iii) it identifies and fills the data gaps for problematic channels in relation to the reference.

The dataset involves EEG data from 21 users, acquired across three temporally separate sessions. Throughout these sessions, 12 different stimuli were applied, and the data were processed with the Autoregression Reflection Coefficients (ARRC), Mel-Frequency Cepstral Coefficients (MFCC), and Spectral Features (SPEC) techniques to extract the features. In more detail, the dataset folder *Verification* contains 3 different files, each of them composed by a different set of features extracted, and the involved features are sequential in time when they refer to the same stimulus. Each file is structured as follows: *data* (time-series features); *y* (user identifier); *stimuli* (stimulus identifier); *session* (session identifier); *INFO* (additional details). The *Emotiv Epoc+* device was used for data acquisition, and the EEG data acquisition sessions were conducted in a controlled environment to minimize environmental factors in the recordings. Each used stimulus refers to a specific activity or mental state that users were subjected to during the EEG data acquisition. A brief explanation of each stimulus is reported in Table 3 (more details can be found in the reference paper [3]).

We strategically chose the BED database rather than opting for alternative databases or defining new ones, since it is shaped to be much broader and more comprehensive than the others in literature (as described in Sect. 3.1, it involves 3 different processing techniques for feature extraction, 12 different stimuli, and 3 distinct and chronologically separated sessions, thus providing 108 different datasets). Hence, by aligning with the objectives of the BED dataset creators, who stress the importance of consistency in stimuli and feature extraction for meaningful comparisons, we believe that such a decision favored the generalizability of our findings.

4.2 Metrics

The evaluation of the proposed NNNE approach's performance was conducted using the same metrics as those employed for the baselines reported in the reference paper [3]. These are two metrics widely used in this domain to assess user identification/verification systems: AUC and EER.

---

[2] https://zenodo.org/records/4309472.

Table 3. Stimuli Description.

Acronym	Stimulus	Description
AS	image	Likely involves the presentation of visual images or stimuli to elicit specific cognitive responses
MC	cognitive	Cognitive tasks generally involve higher-level mental processes such as memory, attention, problem-solving, or decision-making
RC	rest_closed	Represents a period of rest with participants keeping their eyes closed, EEG recordings capture the brain's activity during a resting state without external visual input
RO	rest_open	Similar to "rest_closed," this stimulus represents a resting state but with participants keeping their eyes open
VC3	vepc3	Visual evoked potential at 3 Hz, standard checker-board pattern with pattern reversal
VC5	vepc5	Visual evoked potential at 5 Hz, standard checker-board pattern with pattern reversal
VC7	vepc7	Visual evoked potential at 7 Hz, standard checker-board pattern with pattern reversal
VC10	vepc10	Visual evoked potential at 10 Hz, standard checker-board pattern with pattern reversal
VF3	vep3	Visual evoked potential at 3 Hz, flashing with a plain color set as black
VF5	vep5	Visual evoked potential at 5 Hz, flashing with a plain color set as black
VF7	vep7	Visual evoked potential at 7 Hz, flashing with a plain color set as black
VF10	vep10	Visual evoked potential at 10 Hz, flashing with a plain color set as black

Area Under the Curve. The Area Under the Curve (AUC) is a popular metric for assessing the quality of binary classifiers. It measures the area under the Receiver Operating Characteristic (ROC) curve, which plots the true positive rate against the false positive rate at various classification thresholds. The AUC score ranges between 0 and 1, with higher values indicating better classifier performance, then an ideal classifier achieves an AUC score of 1, whereas random guessing results lead toward a score of 0.5. Formally, the ROC curve is a graphical representation of the trade-off between true positive rate (sensitivity) and false positive rate (1 - specificity) at various threshold settings. AUC is a summary measure of the ROC curve and it is defined as shown in Eq. 4, where Sensitivity is the true positive rate, and Specificity is the true negative rate.

$$\text{AUC} = \int_0^1 \text{Sensitivity}(\text{specificity}^{-1}(t)) \, dt \tag{4}$$

Equal Error Rate. The Equal Error Rate (EER) is another commonly used metric in biometric systems, where the trade-off between False Acceptance Rate (FAR) formalized in Eq. 5 and False Rejection Rate (FRR) formalized in Eq. 6 is crucial, and EER is the point at which the FAR equals the FRR. It represents a balanced performance point, indicating the point at which both error rates are equal.

$$\text{FAR} = \frac{\text{False Acceptances}}{\text{Total Number of Impostor Attempts}} \tag{5}$$

$$\text{FRR} = \frac{\text{False Rejections}}{\text{Total Number of Genuine Attempts}} \tag{6}$$

4.3 Strategy

The experiments were conducted using session 1 as training set for the selection of the optimal hyperparameters, as well as the optimal number of MLP neural networks to use within the ensemble classifier, and separately, the session 2 and 3 as test sets for the validation of the proposed approach according to the AUC and EER metrics. The obtained results are reported in Table 4 and Table 5, where the last two columns report the comparison results between the baseline HMM values provided in the reference paper [3] and the values of the proposed NNNE approach, indicating with + when NNNE achieves better values, with − when it gets worse values, and, if applicable, with = in the case of equal values.

Table 4. NNNE Approach Trained With Session 1 and Tested With Session 2.

Dataset	Stimulation	HMM AUC	HMM EER	NNNE AUC	NNNE EER	Comparison AUC	Comparison EER
ARRC	AS	0.7320	0.2911	0.7265	0.3105	−	−
ARRC	MC	0.7034	0.3180	0.7335	0.3254	+	−
ARRC	RC	0.7285	0.2961	0.6579	0.3749	−	−
ARRC	RO	0.6765	0.3355	0.5792	0.4313	−	−
ARRC	VC3	0.5420	0.4594	0.5105	0.4921	−	−
ARRC	VC5	0.6611	0.3282	0.5146	0.4870	−	−
ARRC	VC7	0.6714	0.3409	0.6284	0.3890	−	−
ARRC	VC10	0.5725	0.4234	0.5260	0.4894	−	−
ARRC	VF3	0.6425	0.3604	0.5633	0.4645	−	−
ARRC	VF5	0.6813	0.3314	0.5667	0.4509	−	−
ARRC	VF7	0.7478	0.2865	0.6104	0.4158	−	−
ARRC	VF10	0.7479	0.2733	0.6217	0.4208	−	−
MFCC	AS	0.7699	0.2633	0.8629	0.1921	+	+
MFCC	MC	0.6917	0.3085	0.8279	0.2364	+	+
MFCC	RC	0.7567	0.2792	0.7713	0.2592	+	+
MFCC	RO	0.6617	0.3601	0.7354	0.3035	+	+
MFCC	VC3	0.6099	0.4092	0.6225	0.4087	+	+
MFCC	VC5	0.6846	0.3315	0.7215	0.3160	+	+
MFCC	VC7	0.6476	0.3643	0.7185	0.3132	+	+
MFCC	VC10	0.6250	0.3886	0.7451	0.2895	+	+
MFCC	VF3	0.6602	0.3503	0.7622	0.2742	+	+
MFCC	VF5	0.6632	0.3573	0.6808	0.3403	+	+
MFCC	VF7	0.7017	0.3183	0.7215	0.3171	+	+
MFCC	VF10	0.7431	0.2826	0.7619	0.2758	+	+
SPEC	AS	0.7465	0.2880	0.7993	0.2558	+	+
SPEC	MC	0.7035	0.3135	0.7790	0.2734	+	+
SPEC	RC	0.7192	0.3164	0.7210	0.3015	+	+
SPEC	RO	0.6528	0.3660	0.6148	0.3950	−	−
SPEC	VC3	0.5934	0.4209	0.5214	0.5012	−	−
SPEC	VC5	0.7567	0.2669	0.6576	0.3720	−	−
SPEC	VC7	0.6771	0.3392	0.6210	0.4048	−	−
SPEC	VC10	0.6424	0.3729	0.5729	0.4328	−	−
SPEC	VF3	0.6687	0.3593	0.6783	0.3593	+	=
SPEC	VF5	0.6606	0.3667	0.6020	0.4212	−	−
SPEC	VF7	0.7380	0.2837	0.7051	0.3409	−	−
SPEC	VF10	0.7551	0.2622	0.6973	0.3424	−	−

5   Discussion

In this study, we explored the performance of a novel multiclass approach (NNNE) for user identification in EEG datasets processed according to different feature extraction methods: Mel-Frequency Cepstral Coefficients (MFCC), Autoregression Reflection Coefficients (ARRC), and Spectral Features (SPEC). In addition, the EEG data were acquired under various stimuli (AS, MC, RC, RO, VC3, VC5, VC7, VC10, VF3, VF5, VF7, and VF10), the description of which is shown in the Table 3. Our evaluation compares the baseline HMM (HMM AUC and HMM EER columns) with the novel approach (NNNE AUC and NNNE EER columns) in terms of Area Under the Curve (AUC) and Equal Error Rate (EER).

Table 5. NNNE Approach Trained With Session 1 and Tested With Session 3.

Dataset	Stimulation	HMM AUC	HMM EER	NNNE AUC	NNNE EER	Comparison AUC	Comparison EER
ARRC	AS	0.6487	0.3587	0.7173	0.3258	+	+
ARRC	MC	0.6668	0.3348	0.6934	0.3504	+	−
ARRC	RC	0.7643	0.2567	0.6642	0.3655	−	−
ARRC	RO	0.6797	0.3354	0.6604	0.3635	−	−
ARRC	VC3	0.5932	0.3959	0.5711	0.4315	−	−
ARRC	VC5	0.7251	0.2922	0.6464	0.3942	−	−
ARRC	VC7	0.6069	0.3860	0.6255	0.3996	+	−
ARRC	VC10	0.6059	0.3874	0.5285	0.4732	−	−
ARRC	VF3	0.5905	0.4008	0.5487	0.4599	−	−
ARRC	VF5	0.7061	0.2997	0.6920	0.3356	−	−
ARRC	VF7	0.6514	0.3582	0.5667	0.4521	−	−
ARRC	VF10	0.6636	0.3454	0.6002	0.4232	−	−
MFCC	AS	0.7109	0.3113	0.7808	0.2691	+	+
MFCC	MC	0.6706	0.3389	0.7899	0.2664	+	+
MFCC	RC	0.7030	0.3190	0.8081	0.2245	+	+
MFCC	RO	0.7321	0.2963	0.7407	0.2982	+	-
MFCC	VC3	0.6505	0.3574	0.7109	0.3164	+	+
MFCC	VC5	0.7070	0.3172	0.7281	0.2871	+	+
MFCC	VC7	0.6514	0.3616	0.7103	0.3102	+	+
MFCC	VC10	0.5539	0.4386	0.6237	0.4025	+	+
MFCC	VF3	0.6044	0.4010	0.6743	0.3394	+	+
MFCC	VF5	0.7575	0.2642	0.7928	0.2397	+	+
MFCC	VF7	0.6870	0.3209	0.6800	0.3439	-	-
MFCC	VF10	0.6493	0.3728	0.7590	0.2729	+	+
SPEC	AS	0.6385	0.3821	0.7406	0.3146	+	+
SPEC	MC	0.6204	0.3847	0.7617	0.2878	+	+
SPEC	RC	0.6922	0.3357	0.7437	0.2853	+	+
SPEC	RO	0.7122	0.3152	0.6702	0.3465	−	−
SPEC	VC3	0.6322	0.3776	0.6144	0.3965	−	−
SPEC	VC5	0.6958	0.3322	0.7120	0.3160	+	+
SPEC	VC7	0.6579	0.3637	0.6049	0.4023	-	−
SPEC	VC10	0.5569	0.4445	0.5511	0.4606	−	−
SPEC	VF3	0.6356	0.3495	0.5415	0.4696	-	−
SPEC	VF5	0.6756	0.3278	0.7238	0.3068	+	+
SPEC	VF7	0.6803	0.3337	0.6251	0.3986	−	−
SPEC	VF10	0.6255	0.3842	0.6503	0.3749	+	+

5.1 Overview

In light of the results obtained by validating the NNNE approach in sessions 2 (Table 4) and 3 (Table 5) separately, we can start to make the following considerations:

– For the ARRC dataset in the test session 2, the NNNE approach demonstrated competitive results. Notably, in stimuli such as AS and MC, the achieved values were comparable to or even exceeded the corresponding Baseline HMM AUC values. The EER values showed slight increases, indicating a trade-off between AUC and EER.

– Similarly, in test session 3, the ARRC dataset displayed consistent performance patterns. For instance, in stimuli like AS and MC, the NNNE AUC values remained robust, showcasing the potential of the proposed approach. The EER values, though slightly higher, demonstrated the method's ability to maintain competitive identification performance.
– For the MFCC dataset, test session 2 shows promising outcomes. Across various stimuli, the achieved NNNE values consistently outperform the Baseline HMM AUC values, indicating the effectiveness of the proposed approach. On the other hand, the EER values indicated favourable trade-offs, improving user identification capabilities.
– In test session 3 for the MFCC dataset, a similar trend was observed. Stimuli such as AS and MC showcased the strengths of the novel approach, with higher NNNE AUC values and marginally increased EER values, reinforcing its potential for user identification tasks.
– Lastly, for the SPEC dataset, both the test sessions 2 and 3 show encouraging results. The NNNE values consistently outperform the Baseline HMM AUC values in stimuli like AS and MC. Although some stimuli showed slight increases in EER values, the overall performance highlighted the viability of the proposed approach.

5.2 In-Depth Analysis

Concerning the baseline HMM values, the optimal combination of feature extraction technique and stimulation during training session 1 and test session 2 is AUC=0.7699 and EER=0.2633 (i.e., dataset MFCC with stimulation AS), whereas for the NNNE approach, it is AUC=0.8629 and EER=0.1921 (using the same dataset and stimulation). Considering instead the optimal combination of feature extraction technique and stimulation during training session 1 and test session 3 the baseline HMM values are AUC=0.7643 and EER=0.2567 (dataset ARRC, stimulation RC), whereas, for the NNNE approach, they are AUC=0.8081 and EER=0.2245 (dataset MFCC, stimulation RC).

Based on the outcomes mentioned above, the proposed NNNE approach outperforms the baseline HMM performance, significantly improving the performance of the EEG-based biometric verification system. This is also because the NNNE approach achieves the best results in both test sessions using the same feature extraction technique (MFCC), unlike the reference baselines where the best results are related to different feature extraction techniques, showing an inconsistency that makes its practical use difficult. Last but not least, both stimulation methods (AS and RC) that give us the best results with the MFCC feature extraction technique (Fig. 2 and Fig. 3) are compatible and suitable for use in user verification biometric systems.

In conclusion, the performed experiments demonstrate that the proposed method, based on a conventional use of an ensemble strategy with MLP neural networks, can outperform the reference performance. This is achieved when supported by quantile input data normalization and real-time optimization of involved hyperparameters. It proves to be effective in enhancing the performance of biometric systems based on EEG data.

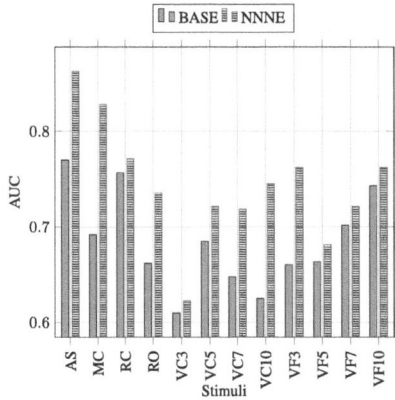

Fig. 2. MFCC Comparison by AUC.

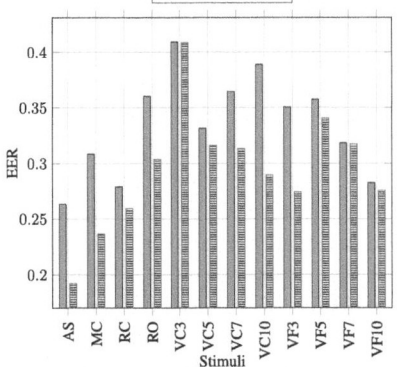

Fig. 3. MFCC Comparison by EER.

5.3   Final Remarks

Regarding the limited improvements in certain datasets, the adoption of an ensemble of neural network models, the introduction of computational complexity due to the ensemble strategy, and the use of a single dataset, it is appropriate to make the following clarifications:

– The limited improvement in datasets processed with Spectral Features (SPEC) and the few improvements in EEG datasets processed with Autoregression Reflection Coefficients (ARRC) indicates the inability of the NNNE approach to effectively leverage the spectral and autoregressive features, respectively. This consideration suggests further experiments aimed at understanding the challenges associated with the SPEC and ARRC preprocessing techniques and analyzing the characteristics of features extracted through these techniques. The results will be useful to improve the NNNE architecture to handle the transformed data better.
– In the context of EEG data analysis for user verification tasks, adopting an ensemble of MLPs offers several advantages over a single larger MLP or different ANN architectures. The ensemble strategy improves generalization by capturing diverse patterns in the data and averaging out predictions, thereby reducing the impact of noise and variability. This approach also improves robustness and stability in predictions. Additionally, the modularity of ensembles allows for easier training and tuning because each MLP can be trained independently and replaced without affecting the overall system. Compared to single larger models or more complex architectures like CNNs or RNNs, ensembles provide a better balance between bias and variance, making them more efficient and effective for handling the noisy and variable nature of EEG data.
– The adoption of an ensemble of neural network models in the proposed solution, specifically considering the Equal Error Rate (EER) metric, was aimed to enhance the overall performance. It is acknowledged that combining diverse neural network models introduces a notable training overhead. However, it's crucial to highlight

that preliminary experimentation has revealed that increased training costs are not directly correlated with improved performance. In the context of ensemble methods, the greater training cost associated with combining different neural network models is mitigated by the parallelization of processes within the utilized implementation.

– The deploying of the proposed NNNE method in real-world scenarios for EEG-based user verification presents the common challenges that affect this kind of device since while the adopted hardware allows us a user-friendly, low-cost, and large-scale use, it presents a greater complexity than other biometric systems. However, this is destined to reduce over time thanks to technological advancements, a trend in recent years oriented to balance performance and ease of use (e.g., problems related to the correct sensor placement, external factors variability, etc.).

– The decision to benchmark our approach against the BED dataset, as opposed to a broader set of works from the literature, was made due to the high level of heterogeneity that characterize the state-of-the-art solutions, where the diverse choices in preprocessing techniques, stimuli, and evaluation metrics across different works do not allow us a meaningful comparison. Consequently, the BED dataset serves as a standardized reference point, offering a more controlled and consistent evaluation of the proposed approach.

6   Conclusion and Future Work

The growing number of research works focused on defining biometric systems based on EEG data contrasts with the lack of public reference values that allow researchers to compare and validate their novel approaches. In this context, the recent release of the BED dataset in the literature, together with the paper [3] that describes its creation based on widely adopted EEG feature extraction and external stimuli techniques, along with reporting reference values for each combination of these techniques, defined using the state-of-the-art Hidden Markov Model (HMM) approach, provides a powerful tool to evaluate the performance of the new approaches.

Exploiting this opportunity, this work proposes the Normalized Neural Network Ensemble (NNNE) approach to enhance the performance of biometric systems based on EEG data for user identification tasks. It employs an ensemble of Multi-Layer Perceptron artificial neural networks governed by a soft voting criterion that considers the predicted probability of each output class. Combining it with a preliminary process aimed to normalize the input data based on quantile information, and optimize the hyperparameters involved with the MLP neural networks and the ensemble structure. The results in terms of AUC and EER highlight the effectiveness of employing a conventional ensemble strategy based on MLP neural networks combined with the quantile normalization of input data and the real-time optimization of the involved hyperparameters, which proves to be effective in modeling spatial and temporal patterns in EEG data. This demonstrates its efficacy in enhancing biometric performance, showing its versatility to improve existing biometric approaches and create novel ones, which can be exploited across a broad range of real-world scenarios.

As future work, we will extend the experiments to include additional EEG datasets. This extension aims to investigate the factors contributing to the varying performance of the NNNE approach across different conditions and datasets.

Acknowledgment. We acknowledge financial support under the National Recovery and Resilience Plan (NRRP), Mission 4 Component 2 Investment 1.5 - Call for tender No.3277 published on December 30, 2021 by the Italian Ministry of University and Research (MUR) funded by the European Union - NextGenerationEU. Project Code ECS0000038 - Project Title eINS Ecosystem of Innovation for Next Generation Sardinia - CUP F53C22000430001- Grant Assignment Decree No. 1056 adopted on June 23, 2022 by the Italian Ministry of University and Research (MUR).

References

1. Abdul, Z.K., Al-Talabani, A.K.: Mel frequency cepstral coefficient and its applications: a review. IEEE Access **10**, 122136–122158 (2022)
2. Al Alkeem, E., et al.: An enhanced electrocardiogram biometric authentication system using machine learning. IEEE Access **7**, 123069–123075 (2019)
3. Arnau-González, P., Katsigiannis, S., Arevalillo-Herráez, M., Ramzan, N.: Bed: a new data set for eeg-based biometrics. IEEE Internet Things J. **8**(15), 12219–12230 (2021)
4. Bigdely-Shamlo, N., Mullen, T., Kothe, C., Su, K.M., Robbins, K.A.: The prep pipeline: standardized preprocessing for large-scale eeg analysis. Front. Neuroinform. **9**, 16 (2015)
5. Carta, S.M., Consoli, S., Podda, A.S., Recupero, D.R., Stanciu, M.M.: Ensembling and dynamic asset selection for risk-controlled statistical arbitrage. IEEE Access **9**, 29942–29959 (2021)
6. Delorme, A., Makeig, S.: Eeglab: an open source toolbox for analysis of single-trial eeg dynamics including independent component analysis. J. Neurosci. Methods **134**(1), 9–21 (2004)
7. Islam, M.K., Rastegarnia, A., Yang, Z.: Methods for artifact detection and removal from scalp eeg: a review. Neurophysiologie Clinique/Clin. Neurophysiol. **46**(4–5), 287–305 (2016)
8. Jijomon, C., Vinod, A.: Person-identification using familiar-name auditory evoked potentials from frontal eeg electrodes. Biomed. Signal Process. Control **68**, 102739 (2021)
9. Katsigiannis, S., Arnau-González, P., Arevalillo-Herráez, M., Ramzan, N.: Single-channel eeg-based subject identification using visual stimuli. In: 2021 IEEE EMBS International Conference on Biomedical and Health Informatics (BHI), pp. 1–4. IEEE (2021)
10. Lawhern, V., Hairston, W.D., McDowell, K., Westerfield, M., Robbins, K.: Detection and classification of subject-generated artifacts in eeg signals using autoregressive models. J. Neurosci. Methods **208**(2), 181–189 (2012)
11. Maiorana, E., Campisi, P.: Longitudinal evaluation of eeg-based biometric recognition. IEEE Trans. Inf. Forensics Secur. **13**(5), 1123–1138 (2018). https://doi.org/10.1109/TIFS.2017.2778010
12. Massaoudi, M., Refaat, S.S., Chihi, I., Trabelsi, M., Oueslati, F.S., Abu-Rub, H.: A novel stacked generalization ensemble-based hybrid lgbm-xgb-mlp model for short-term load forecasting. Energy **214**, 118874 (2021)
13. Mu, Z., Yin, J., Hu, J.: Application of a brain-computer interface for person authentication using eeg responses to photo stimuli. J. Integr. Neurosci. **17**(1), 113–124 (2018)
14. Piciucco, E., Maiorana, E., Falzon, O., Camilleri, K.P., Campisi, P.: Steady-state visual evoked potentials for eeg-based biometric identification. In: 2017 International Conference of the Biometrics Special Interest Group (BIOSIG), pp. 1–5. IEEE (2017)
15. Rezaeipanah, A., Syah, R., Wulandari, S., Arbansyah, A.: Design of ensemble classifier model based on mlp neural network for breast cancer diagnosis. Intel. Artif. **24**(67), 147–156 (2021)

16. Saia, R., Carta, S., Fenu, G., Pompianu, L.: Brain waves and evoked potentials as biometric user identification strategy: an affordable low-cost approach. In: SECRYPT, pp. 614–619. SCITEPRESS (2022)
17. Saia, R., Carta, S., Fenu, G., Pompianu, L.: Brain waves combined with evoked potentials as biometric approach for user identification: a survey. In: Proceedings of SAI Intelligent Systems Conference, pp. 718–734. Springer, Heidelberg (2023). https://doi.org/10.1007/978-3-031-47724-9_47
18. Saia, R., Carta, S., Fenu, G., Pompianu, L.: Influencing brain waves by evoked potentials as biometric approach: taking stock of the last six years of research. Neural Comput. Appl., 1–27 (2023)
19. Seha, S.N.A., Hatzinakos, D.: A new approach for eeg-based biometric authentication using auditory stimulation. In: 2019 International Conference on Biometrics (ICB), pp. 1–6. IEEE (2019)
20. Srivastva, R., Singh, Y.N., Singh, A.: Statistical independence of ecg for biometric authentication. Pattern Recogn. **127**, 108640 (2022)
21. Subha, D.P., Joseph, P.K., Acharya, U.R., Lim, C.M., et al.: Eeg signal analysis: a survey. J. Med. Syst. **34**(2), 195–212 (2010)
22. Yap, H.Y., Choo, Y.H., Mohd Yusoh, Z.I., Khoh, W.H.: Person authentication based on eye-closed and visual stimulation using eeg signals. Brain Inf. **8**(1), 1–13 (2021)
23. Zeng, Y., Wu, Q., Yang, K., Tong, L., Yan, B., Shu, J., Yao, D.: Eeg-based identity authentication framework using face rapid serial visual presentation with optimized channels. Sensors **19**(1), 6 (2019)
24. Zhao, H., Chen, Y., Pei, W., Chen, H., Wang, Y.: Towards online applications of eeg biometrics using visual evoked potentials. Expert Syst. Appl. **177**, 114961 (2021)

Systematic Literature Review of Gamification Design in Higher Education Programming Courses: Methodological Rigor Exposed

Marisa Venter[1]([✉]) [iD] and Lizette De Wet[2] [iD]

[1] Central University of Technology, Bloemfontein, Free State, South Africa
marisa@cut.ac.za
[2] University of the Free State, Bloemfontein, Free State, South Africa

Abstract. A significant increase has been noted in the application of gamification design interventions in programming education, which sparked enthusiasm in students and enhanced their levels of enjoyment and engagement, while improving learning outcomes. By utilizing gamified learning activities and software applications, instructors can develop learning environments which greatly enhance the experiences of student interaction in gamified learning environments. Positive reported experiences of students in higher education programming learning environments, promise to steer students towards achievement in their programming pursuits. However, it is not clear if these positive reports might be inaccurate due to various inadequacies in research methodologies used in studies conducted in a gamified programming learning higher education context. To date, no systematic review has focused specifically on the methodological rigor of studies that investigated the gamification of higher education programming courses. The systematic literature review reported by this study, fills this gap, by exposing various methodological shortcomings observed in the reviewed literature. The study provides recommendations to researchers to improve research efforts in the future. The hope is that these guidelines will contribute to enhancing the overall quality and reliability of research findings related to the gamification of higher education programming courses.

Keywords: Systematic review · Programming · Gamification · Higher education

1 Introduction

Over the past decade, there has been a remarkable surge in the adoption of gamification principles in programming education, which has ignited enthusiasm among students, while amplifying engagement and helping them to achieve learning outcomes [1–3]. Gamification, which is broadly described as the integration of elements of game design into contexts outside of traditional gaming environments, offers a versatile framework for diverse applications in various domains [4]. By leveraging gamified learning activities and software applications, educators can craft innovative pedagogical strategies that are aimed at guiding students towards success in their programming endeavours [5].

H. Plácido da Silva and P. Cipresso (Eds.): CHIRA 2024, CCIS 2370, pp. 249–268, 2025.
https://doi.org/10.1007/978-3-031-82633-7_16

As implementing gamification in higher education programming courses becomes more popular, more articles and papers are published on the subject. A number of systematic literature reviews that focused specifically on reviewing gamification in higher education programming contexts were published in the last few years [1, 5–7]. None of these systematic literature reviews conducted in-depth investigations into the methodological rigour of studies that investigated the gamification of higher education programming courses. The aim of the current study was to fill this gap by evaluating the quality and rigour of the research methodologies of studies on the topic of gamification of higher education programming courses. This systematic examination contribute to enhancing the overall quality and reliability of research findings related to the gamification of higher education programming courses.

2 Systematic Reviews on the Gamification of Higher Education Programming Courses

Systematic literature reviews undertaken on the gamification of higher education programming courses are summarized in Table 1. The period covered by these studies is 2015 to 2023 and the number of studies reviewed varied from 10 to 41. The results indicate that the predominant issues that were addressed by these studies are the effect that gamification and various game elements had on programming learning, motivation and engagement, the challenges faced by programming students and the need for evaluation frameworks. It should be noted than none of these systematic literature reviews conducted in-depth investigations into the methodological rigor of studies that investigated the gamification of higher education programming courses, which guided the research focus of the current study.

Table 1. Summary of systematic reviews.

Authors and dates	Time span of review	No. Papers reviewed	Reference
Costa (2023)	2020–2022	10	[5]
Maryono et al. (2022)	2018–2022	41	[1]
Shahid et al. (2019)	2015–2019	41	[6]
Zakiah et al. (2023)	2019–2023	22	[7]

3 Methodology

The methodology proposed by Arksey and O'Malley (2005)[8] was adapted for this review; it offers researchers a systematic and organised method for conducting a thorough literature review and guides them through the processes of identifying, selecting, analysing and synthesising relevant literature to effectively address the research question or objectives. This methodology comprises a structured framework with five stages, discussed below:

- **Stage 1: Identifying the research question.** This first stage involves defining the scope and focus of the literature review by formulating clear research questions or objectives. Researchers determine the key themes or areas of interest the review aims to address.
- **Stage 2: Identifying relevant studies.** In this stage, researchers systematically search for relevant literature sources that address or contribute to the research question. This stage typically involves conducting comprehensive searches of various databases, academic journals, books and other relevant sources and using specific keywords and search terms.
- **Stage 3: Study selection.** Once potential sources have been identified, predefined inclusion and exclusion criteria are used by researchers to screen and select studies. This process entails reviewing abstracts, titles and full-text articles to determine their relevance and suitability for inclusion in the review.
- **Stage 4: Data extraction.** In this stage, researchers extract and organise relevant information and data from the selected studies. This may involve creating a standardised data extraction form or matrix to systematically capture key details, such as study characteristics, methodologies, findings and key themes or concepts.
- **Stage 5: Aggregating, synthesising and presenting the findings.** In the final stage, researchers collate and synthesise the extracted data to identify patterns, themes and key findings across the selected studies. This involves summarising the main findings, synthesising evidence and identifying gaps or areas for further research. The results are then reported in a structured and coherent manner, typically through narrative summaries, tables, or visual representations [8].

3.1 Stage 1: Identifying the Systematic Literature Review Questions

The research questions (RQ) that were used to guide the systematic review were adapted from [9] and are listed in Table 2. These questions are intended to provide insight into gamified programming courses in higher education, thereby providing a comprehensive overview of the field, and to summarize the prevailing trends and gaps.

Table 2. Systematic literature review questions.

RQ	Systematic literature review question
RQ1.1	Which research method was used? Quantitative, qualitative or mixed?
RQ1.2	Which type of research instrument was used to collect data?
RQ1.3	What was the source of the questions in the survey instrument?
RQ1.4	How was the collected data analyzed?
RQ2	Which processes or approach, if any, were followed to gamify programming education?
RQ3	What was the influence of isolated game elements on the outcome variable(s) in the study or was the influence only measured for all elements grouped together?

The primary objective of RQ1 was to delve into the research methodology employed in the various studies. RQ2 focused on exploring the implementation of gamification. Finally, RQ3 examined the effects of implementing gamification in programming education.

3.2   Stage 2: Identifying Relevant Studies

In December 2023, the process of selection was undertaken. papers published in conference proceedings, as well as peer-reviewed journal articles, were sought through databases including EBSCOhost, Web of Science and SCOPUS. The researcher opted for a timeframe spanning from 2014 to 2023. The researcher utilized the following generic search key to search the titles, abstracts and keywords of applicable records: gamification OR gamified OR gamify AND programming AND "higher education"

3.3   Stage 3: Study Selection

The following inclusion criteria were used to select studies:

- Studies that had been published between 2014 and 2023;
- Studies for which the researcher could access the full text (via the researcher's university library);
- Studies published in conference proceedings and peer-reviewed articles;
- Studies targeting higher education exclusively;
- Studies that focused on gamification, which is defined as the use of game design elements in non-game contexts [10]; and
- Studies examining the instructional practices within a gamified computer programming course, utilising either a programming language or pseudocode.

The following exclusion criteria were applied:

- Studies that utilised full-fledged learning or serious games;
- Studies that present a proposed gamified framework but did not evaluate the framework in the study;
- Studies that focused on education levels not considered higher education;
- Studies that focused on explaining the architecture of a gamified system without evaluating the system;
- Studies that focused on usability evaluation of gamified systems; and
- Studies that are review studies.

Following the application of the search criteria alongside inclusion and exclusion criteria, a comprehensive examination was carried out on 55 full-text articles and conference papers. The procedure is summarised in the PRISMA flow diagram shown in Fig. 2.

3.4 Stage 4: Data Extraction

The process of extracting data involved the formulation of a data extraction template and actual extraction of data conforming to the methodology delineated by Petersen et al. (2015) [11].

3.5 Stage 5: Aggregating, Synthesising and Presenting the Findings

In this section, the researchers provides a summary and analysis of the extracted data, to address the systematic literature review questions. The following discussion will address various aspects of the reviewed studies, including general results, research methodology, gamification implementation, the impact of gamification and subsequent discussions and conclusions.

General Results. This section reports on the background descriptive data that resulted from the systematic review. A table containing all 55 studies that were selected for the systematic review can be found in Appendix A. The information included in this appendix for each study is the name of the authors, the year the study was published, the country where the study was conducted, the sample size and the duration of the intervention. The abbreviation 'ns' is used when information about a particular component was not specified. The sample size of studies varied from 9 to 765 and the duration of interventions varied from 6 h to 2 semesters. Furthermore, summaries are provided for the following: the continent where the studies were conducted, the number of studies that were conducted in each year, and the publication type of studies. The largest number of studies was conducted in Asia and Europe, with 16 studies each, followed by South America (10), North America (seven), Africa (five) and Oceania (one), as shown in Table 3.

Table 3. Continent of study.

Continent	n	%
Asia	16	29.10
Europe	16	29.10
South America	10	18.20
North America	7	12.70
Africa	5	9.10
Oceania	1	1.80
Total	55	100.00

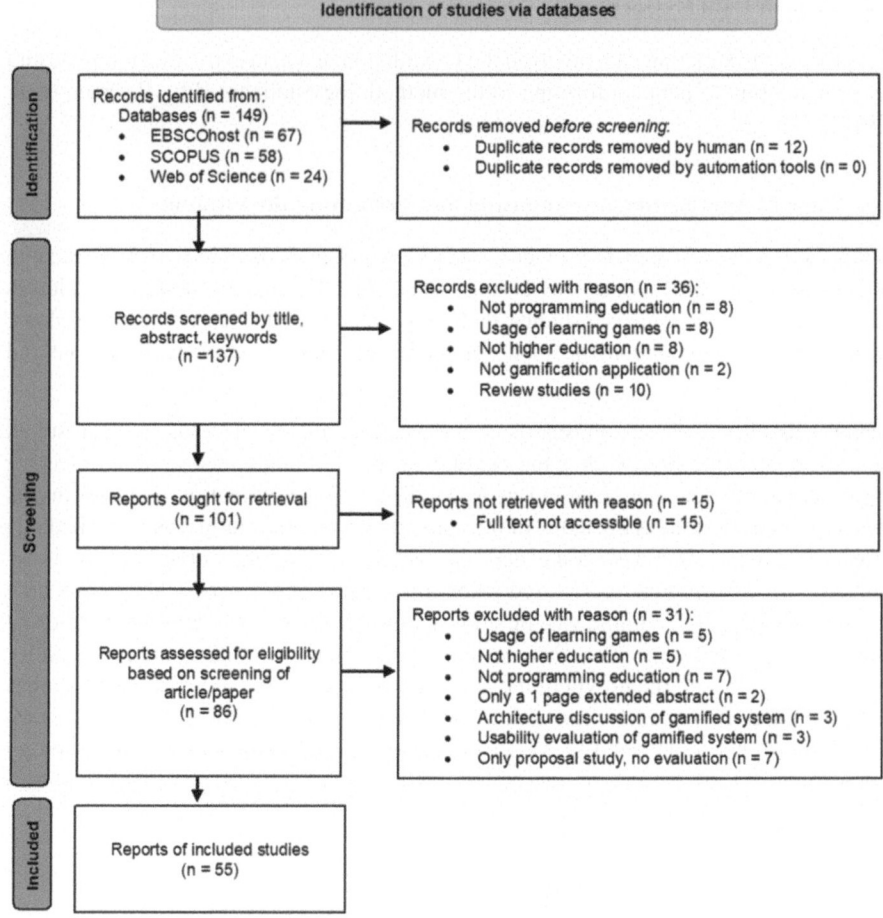

Fig. 1. Flow diagram of systematic review.

As indicated in Fig. 2, the number of studies published per year has increased steadily, from two studies in each of 2014, 2016 and 2017, to 11 studies in each of 2022 and 2023 (Fig. 1).

The largest percentage of studies (69%) was published in journals, while 31% was published in conference proceedings.

RQ1 – Research Methodology. The aim of research question RQ1 was to investigate the research methods employed in the included studies. The investigation was split into four parts, namely, the research methods used, the research instrument used to collect data, the source of the research questions contained in the studies that used surveys, and the type of analysis that was conducted on collected data.

RQ1.1 – Research Method. RQ1.1 aimed to determine which research methods were used in studies. A total of 42 studies used quantitative designs, whereas 11 studies

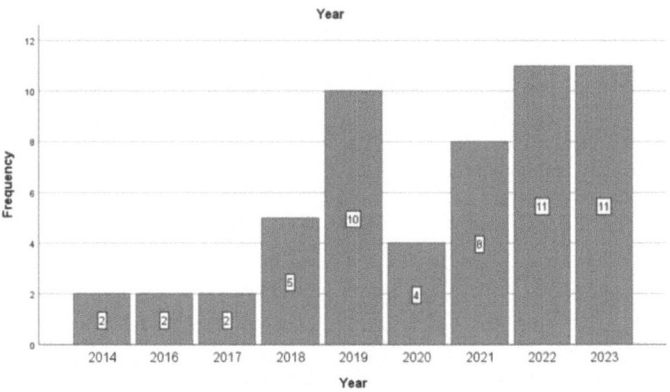

Fig. 2. Summary of the number of studies conducted per year.

made used of mixed methods designs. Only two studies made use of qualitative designs. This finding corresponds with a prior systematic review of gamification research in information systems education research, which found few publications using qualitative empirical research methods such as case studies [12]. The different types of quantitative designs that were used and are presented in Table 4.

Table 4. Type of quantitative design used.

Type of quantitative research design	n	%
Quasi-experimental design	24	57.14
Descriptive quantitative research design	12	28.57
Correlational design	3	7.14
True experimental design	3	7.14
Total	42	100.00

The design most often used was a quasi-experimental design – used by 24 studies – followed by the descriptive quantitative design, which was used by 12 studies. The true experimental design and the correlational design were each used by three studies. An observed trend in the various quantitative methodologies employed is the significant prevalence of descriptive quantitative research designs, which constitutes 28.57% (12 studies) of the total quantitative approaches used.

RQ1.2 – Data Collection Instrument. The objective of RQ1.2 was to identify the different data collection instruments the studies used. A summary is provided in Table 5. Some studies, made use of more than one instrument, as evidenced by the total of 77 types, which exceeds the number of studies (n = 55).

Instruments for collecting quantitative data were the most widespread, because the majority of studies were quantitative in nature (as was demonstrated by RQ1.1). The

Table 5. Data collection instrument.

Instrument	n	%
Survey	42	54.50
Data captured directly from gamified system	12	15.60
Subject content tests	10	13.00
Interviews	7	9.10
Observation	4	5.20
Focus group	2	2.60
Total	77	100.00

most common research instrument was a survey, used by 42 studies, followed by data captured directly from gamified systems, as done by 12 studies. Subject content tests were identified as the third most-employed data collection instrument, and were used by 10 studies. These tests were used to assess the impact of the gamified intervention and were typically administered to students before and after the gamified intervention. Qualitative data collection instruments were the least used data collection instruments, with interviews used by seven studies, followed by observations (used by four studies) and focus groups (used by two studies).

RQ1.3 – Source of the Questions in the Survey Instrument. The objective of RQ1.3 was to determine the type of measuring instruments that were used by the 42 studies that collected data via surveys to develop survey questions. It is interesting to note that 25/42 = 59.52% of studies, did not use previously validated instruments; instead, they had created their own questionnaires (Table 6).

Table 6. Source of survey instrument.

Instrument	n	%
Self-constructed	25	59.52
Validated research instruments	17	40.48
Total	42	100.00

RQ1.4 – Data Analysis Methods. The goal of RQ1.4 was to determine which data analysis methods were used by the studies. An outline of the methods used to analyze the data in the various studies is given in Table 7. The data analysis methods are split further into those that have a statistical analysis component and those that do not. The data analysis methods presented in Table 7 refer only to the methods used to analyze the main constructs or variables that were investigated by the various studies, and exclude any biographical or background data that were collected. Table 7 shows clearly that parametric statistical analysis was the type of analysis conducted by the largest number

of studies (20/55 = 40%). Parametric tests assume specific characteristics about the distribution of data, such as normality and homogeneity of variances, while non-parametric tests make fewer assumptions about the distribution and characteristics of the data [13] The analysis technique used to analyze data second most often is frequency tables and graphs or graphical representations (14/55 = 25%). It should be noted that this analysis method specifically excluded the performance of any statistical tests and solely relied on descriptive statistics and visualizations to elucidate patterns, trends and distributions in the data. The analysis technique used third most often is non-parametric statistical analysis, which was used by seven studies, with another five studies using a combination of parametric and non-parametric statistical analysis. Studies that included a statistical analysis component and those that did not were compared regarding the number of analysis techniques used, and findings are reported in Table 7.

Table 7. Data analysis methods.

Statistical Testing	Analysis method	n	%
Yes	Parametric statistical analysis	20	65.45
	Non-parametric statistical analysis	7	
	Combination of parametric and non-parametric statistical analysis	5	
	Combination of thematic analysis and parametric statistical analysis	2	
	Partial least square structural equation modelling (PLS SEM)	1	
	Combination of non-parametric statistical analysis and frequency tables and graphs	1	
	Total	36	
No	Only frequency tables and/or graphs or graphical representations	14	
	Qualitative content analysis	2	
	Combination of thematic analysis and frequency tables and graphs	2	34.55
	No analysis performed	1	
	Total	19	
Total		55	100.00

When the 34.55% of studies that did not include any statistical analysis component is compared to the very small percentage of qualitative studies that was conducted, it is clear that a large proportion of quantitative and mixed methods studies did not do statistical analysis as a way to analyze their data.

RQ2 – Gamification Approach. RQ2 delineates the various approaches and methodologies observed in primary studies regarding the gamification of programing courses.

Four broad categories of gamification approaches were employed for the classification of studies, derived from the framework of [9]:

- Implementation of a pre-existing gamification strategy. This category encompasses studies that adhered to a pre-existing gamification framework put forth or devised by other scholars.
- Integration of a psychological or educational methodology into a gamification framework. This category refers to studies that customized motivational or education theories to gamify higher education programming courses.
- Development of a novel gamification approach. This category comprises studies that crafted their own structured, systematic methodology for gamifying higher education programming courses.
- Lack of a formalized or structured methodology. This category encompasses studies that did not adhere to a defined method for integrating gamification into higher education programming software engineering courses.

The distribution of studies across the various categories of gamified approaches that were followed is indicated in Table 8. It is noteworthy that 38 studies (which comprised the majority of studies, namely, 69.1%) did not follow formal or structured approaches to gamifying programming courses. A total of nine studies followed an existing gamification approach or framework, while seven studies adapted psychological and education theories to gamify higher education programming courses. In only one study, the authors developed their own, new gamification framework.

Table 8. Gamification approaches.

Instrument	N	%
No formal or structured approach	38	69.10
Existing approach	9	16.40
Psychological and educational theories adapted	7	12.70
New gamification approach	1	1.80
Total	55	100.00

RQ3 – Individual Impact of Game Elements. The final research question, RQ3, investigated the extent to which various studies provided insights into the individual impact of game elements on outcome variables, or whether the impact was measured for all elements grouped together. An examination of all the included studies unveils that most of the studies integrated a blend of gamification elements, as depicted in Table 9.

Only eight studies employed a single gaming element exclusively, while 46 studies (83.63%; n = 54) used two or more gaming elements. One study omitted specific details of the gaming elements it used, only stating that a gamified system was employed. Consequently, the total number of studies listed in Table 9 is 54.

As mentioned earlier, eight studies employed only one gaming element in their gamified intervention. This approach enabled researchers to attribute any observed changes

Table 9. Distribution of number of elements used in studies.

Number of elements	Number of studies	%
1	8	14.80
2	4	7.40
3	16	29.60
4	9	16.70
5	9	16.70
6	5	9.30
8	2	3.70
9	1	1.90
Total	54	100.00

after the gamification intervention to the single gaming element used in the study. Furthermore, studies that made use of more game elements were carefully scrutinized to identify studies that measured individual game elements separately and reported their individual effects on outcome variables. However, the general trend was that most studies treated gamification as a bundle (comprising various game elements). The effect of the gamified intervention was largely determined by differences observed in the outcome variables between students who had been exposed to the gamified intervention and those not, and/or any changes in outcome variables experienced by the same students before and after exposure to the gamified intervention.

4 Discussion

The systematic literature comprised 55 studies that focused on the gamification of higher education programming courses. This review analyzed the context of studies, the research methodology used in the studies, how the selected studies had implemented gamification and the impact of gamification as described by the selected studies. The challenges identified by the analysis are discussed below.

4.1 Challenges Relating to Research Methodology

A trend that was observed in the various quantitative methodologies employed is the significant prevalence of descriptive quantitative research designs, which constitute more than a quarter of the total quantitative approaches utilised. Moreover, 34.55% of studies had no statistical analysis component. Excluding statistical tests in data analysis poses several significant concerns, as explained by [15]. First, it restricts the depth of analysis, as researchers may miss important relationships or nuances in the data that statistical tests could reveal. Second, the inability to test hypotheses undermines the rigour and validity of the research findings, thereby hindering the advancement of scientific knowledge. Additionally, the risk of misinterpretation increases when researchers rely solely on descriptive statistics and visualisations, which could lead to erroneous conclusions or flawed decision-making. Finally, the limited generalisability of findings poses challenges for extrapolating research results to broader populations or contexts, which limits the practical implications and applicability of the study findings. The findings mentioned above, which highlight a deficiency in statistical analysis within the reviewed studies, align with those of [16, 17].

Another concern is the large percentage of studies (59.5%) that did not make use of previously validated instruments, but developed their own questionnaires. This raises questions about the reliability and validity of the data obtained through these custom questionnaires. Using established and validated instruments ensures that the measurements are reliable and consistent and accurately capture the constructs or variables of interest. If validated instruments are not used, there is a risk of measurement error and bias and less confidence in the findings and conclusions drawn from the data. Additionally, it may hinder the comparability of results across studies and limit the ability to generalise findings to broader populations or contexts. Therefore, the absence of validated instruments in more than half the studies that used surveys is a noteworthy concern that may impact the quality and credibility of the research findings.

4.2 Challenges Relating to Gamification Implementation

Challenges relating to implementation of gamification include the concerning trend that the majority of studies (69.1%) did not follow a formal or structured approach in the gamification of programming courses. This result is in line with existing literature and underscores the limited exploration of gamification frameworks proposed in scholarly discourse within applied research on gamifying online learning systems in higher education [17]. The absence of formal or structured approaches to gamifying programming courses suggests a deficiency in systematic planning and implementation processes. This trend underscores a disparity between theoretical conceptualisations of gamification and its practical application in gamified higher education programming courses [18]. This absence of a structured methodology poses a risk to the coherence and effectiveness of gamification strategies for programming education, which could impede students' learning experiences and outcomes.

4.3 Challenges Relating to the Reported Impact of Gamification

Regarding the impact of gamification on higher education programming courses reported by studies analysed by the current review, a very small number of studies measured the individual impact that game elements had on outcome variables. Frequently in gamification research, there is a tendency to integrate multiple game elements as a unified package.[19]. As a result, it becomes difficult to ascertain which game elements, combinations thereof, or interplay among elements contributed to the observed alterations in outcomes. Consequently, the practical implications drawn from such studies are limited [19]. Therefore, it is advised that gamification researchers carefully examine and understand the individual effects of different game elements, without interference from other factors. Researchers should also consider how these game elements may interact with each other, known as expected interactions, and account for them in their analysis. By doing so, researchers can gain a clearer understanding of how each game element contributes to the overall outcomes observed in gamified environments [18, 20]. According to [19], studies that compare gamification to non-gamification without properly isolating elements or creating meaningful element clusters for investigation are of limited theoretical value and should be avoided.

5 Conclusion

Upon examining the challenges identified by the current review of higher education programming courses, it becomes evident that a large number of studies lack methodological rigour, as noted by other gamification reviews, including that of [21]. Recommendations for further research in the gamification of higher education programming education, thus, involve that prospective researchers adhere to the following guidelines to ensure that their findings do not succumb to inconclusiveness because of methodological inadequacies:

- Proposed studies should plan their research methodology meticulously, to integrate an existing gamification framework and provide a structured approach for implementing gamification techniques.
- When considering data collection strategies, researchers should endeavour to utilise previously validated measuring instruments, to uphold the validity and reliability of the constructs measured in their study.
- Regarding data analysis, it is essential to prioritise accepted statistical analysis methods that encompass both parametric and non-parametric statistics, to examine the influence of various response variables on outcome variables. Additionally, structural equation modelling can be effective in measuring and modelling the impact of various game elements on outcome variables simultaneously.
- Finally, researchers should meticulously isolate, measure and model relationships between individual game elements or game clusters and response variables to discern the specific impact of each game element on outcome variables.

Appendix

A: Studies Included in Systematic Literature Review

No	Authors	Country	Year	Sample size	Duration of intervention	Citation
1	Adam, E Van den Berg, R	South Africa	2022	91	ns	[22]
2	Agapito, J Rodrigo, M. M	Philippines	2018	35	6 h	[23]
3	Awad et al	United Arab Emirates	2022	98	2 X 16 Week semesters	[24]

(*continued*)

(*continued*)

No	Authors	Country	Year	Sample size	Duration of intervention	Citation
4	Ayub et al	Indonesia	2019	55	11 weeks	[25]
5	Bernik et al.	Croatia	2019	201	14 days	[26]
6	Cabada et al	Mexico	2018	69	2 weeks	[27]
7	Carreño-León et al	Mexico	2019	38	1 semester	[28]
8	Christopher, L Waworuntu, A	Indonesia	2021	40	half a semester	[29]
9	Cigdem et al	Turkey	2023	96	ns	[30]
10	Cuervo-Cely et al	Colombia	2022	48	8 weeks	[31]
11	Cui et al	China	2023	ns	ns	[32]
12	De Pontes et al	Brazil	2019	60	4 weeks	[33]
13	Du et al	Singapore	2016	114	one tutorial	[34]
14	Erlangga et al	Indonesia	2023	30	ns	[35]
15	Facey-Shaw et al.	Jamaica,	2020	31–94 4 years		[36]
16	Fidan, A. Şengel, E	Turkey	2022	37	12 weeks	[37]
17	Figueiredo, J García-Peñalvo, F. J	Portugal	2020	67 – 87 2 years		[38]
18	Fotaris et al	UK	2016	106	12-week	[39]
19	García-Gutierrez, A Hijón-Neira, R	Spain	2020	9	100 min	[40]
20	Garcia, M. B Revano, T. F	Philippines	2021	100	One semester	[41]
21	Grey, S. - Gordon, N	UK	2023	20	ns	[42]
22	Hagedorn et al	Germany	2023	ns	ns	[43]
23	Huesca et al	Mexico	2023	414	16 weeks	[44]
24	Ibanez et al	Spain	2014	22	1 week	[45]
25	Imran, H	Canada	2023	450	ns	[46]
26	Kasahara et al	Japan	2019	35	6 weeks	[47]
27	Khaleel et al	Malaysia,	2019	90	2 semesters	[48]
28	Kiliç, S	Turkey	2023	48	ns	[49]
29	Moreno, J. - Pineda, A. F	Colombia	2018	45	ns	[50]
30	Neve et al	UK	2014	28	ns	[51]
31	Ortiz-Rojas et al	Ecuador	2019	89	4 weeks	[52]

(*continued*)

(*continued*)

No	Authors	Country	Year	Sample size	Duration of intervention	Citation
32	Ortiz et al	Ecuador	2017	100	4 weeks	[53]
33	Ouahb et al	Morocco	2021	32	5 sessions	[54]
34	Palaniappan, K Noor, N. M	Malaysia	2022	29	4 weeks	[55]
35	Pankiewicz, M	USA	2020	ns	ns	[56]
36	Pilkington, C	SA	2018	67	3 semesters	[57]
37	Pinto, M Terroso, T	Portugal	2022	21	2 weeks	[58]
38	Piteira et al	Portugal	2017	108	ns	[59]
39	Polito, G Temperini, M	Italy	2021	ns	ns	[60]
40	Pratama et al	Indonesia	2021	53	ns	[61]
41	Pratama, G. D Kusuma, G. P	Indonesia,	2022	32	ns	[62]
42	Rodrigues et al	Brazil	2022	756	14 weeks	[63]
43	Rodrigues et al	Brazil	2022	399	15 weeks	[64]
44	Rodrigues et al	Brazil	2021	19	6 weeks	[65]
45	Rojas-López et al	Mexico	2019	60	4 weeks	[66]
46	Scott, L Dalton, N	UK	2021	90	ns	[67]
47	Sharma et al	North India	2023	120	1 semester	[68]
48	Shorn, S. P	Singapore	2018	191	15 weeks	[69]
49	Smiderle et al	Brazil	2019	40	4 months	[70]
50	Swacha, J Szydłowska, J	Poland	2023	24	1 semester	[71]
51	Tahir et al	NZ	2022	77	4 weeks	[72]
52	Tokzhigitova et al	Kazakhstan	2023	83	ns	[73]
53	Venter, M	SA	2022	96	10 weeks	[74]
54	Venter, M. I Swart, A. J	SA	2019	192	1 term	[75]
55	Zahedi et al	USA	2021	ns	ns	[76]

References

1. Maryono, D., Budiyono, S., Akhyar, M.: Implementation of gamification in programming learning: literature review. Int. J. Inf. Educ. Technol. **12**, 1448–1457 (2022). https://doi.org/10.18178/ijiet.2022.12.12.1771
2. Mubin, S.A., Wee, M., Poh, A., Jantan, A.H.: Gamification in programming language learning: a review and pathway. Int. J. Adv. Res. Eng. Technol. **11**, 1148–1155 (2020). https://doi.org/10.34218/IJARET.11.12.2020.111
3. Shafie, A., Abdullah, Z.: Gamification in learning programming language. In: A Conference Series: Industrial Revolution 4.0, pp. 181–187 (2020)
4. Dichev, C., Dicheva, D.: Gamifying education: What is known, what is believed and what remains uncertain: a critical review. Int. J. Educ. Technol. High. Educ. **14**, 1–36 (2017). https://doi.org/10.1186/s41239-017-0042-5
5. Costa, J.M.: Using game concepts to improve programming learning: a multi-level meta-analysis. Comput. Appl. Eng. Educ. **31**, 1098–1110 (2023). https://doi.org/10.1002/cae.22630
6. Shahid, M., Wajid, A., Haq, K.U., Saleem, I., Shujja, A.H.: A review of gamification for learning programming fundamental. In: 2019 International Conference on Innovative Computing (2019). https://doi.org/10.1109/ICIC48496.2019.8966685
7. Zakiah, N., Deris, K., Hidayah, W.: A review of gamification for learning programming language. Int. J. Bus. Stud. Educ. (IJBSAE), 1 (2023). https://doi.org/10.1109/ICIC48496.2019.8966685
8. Arksey, H., O'Malley, L.: Scoping studies: towards a methodological framework. Int. J. Soc. Res. Methodol. **8**, 19–32 (2005). https://doi.org/10.1017/S0922156508005621
9. Alhammad, M.M., Moreno, A.M.: Gamification in software engineering education: a systematic mapping. J. Syst. Softw. **141**, 131–150 (2018). https://doi.org/10.1016/j.jss.2018.03.065
10. Deterding, S.: Situated motivational affordances of game elements: a conceptual model. In: CHI 2011 Work. "Gamification", pp. 3–6 (2011)
11. Petersen, K., Vakkalanka, S., Kuzniarz, L.: Guidelines for conducting systematic mapping studies in software engineering: an update. Inf. Softw. Technol. **64**, 1–18 (2015). https://doi.org/10.1016/j.infsof.2015.03.007
12. Osatuyi, B., Osatuyi, T.: Systematic review of gamification research in IS education: a multi-method approach. Commun. Assoc. Inf. Syst. **42**, 95–124 (2018). https://doi.org/10.17705/1CAIS.04205
13. Field, A.: Discovering statistics using SPSS. SAGE, London (2009)
14. Narasareddy, M., Singh, G., Radermarcher, A.: Gamification in computer science education: a systematic literature review. In: 2018 ASEE Annual Conference & Exposition, pp. 1–12. American Society for Engineering Education (2018)
15. Agarwal, S.A.: Use of statistics in research. Int. J. Mod. Trends Sci. Technol. **7**, 98–103 (2021). https://doi.org/10.46501/IJMTST0711017
16. Hamari, J., Koivisto, J., Sarsa, H.: Does gamification work? A literature review of empirical studies on gamification. In: Proceedings of the Annual Hawaii International Conference on System Sciences, pp. 3025–3034 (2014). https://doi.org/10.1109/HICSS.2014.377
17. Khaldi, A., Bouzidi, R., Nader, F.: Gamification of e-learning in higher education: a systematic literature review. Smart Learn. Environ. **10**, 1–31 (2023). https://doi.org/10.1186/s40561-023-00227-z
18. Seaborn, K., Fels, D.I.: Gamification in theory and action: a survey. Int. J. Hum. Comput. Stud. **74**, 14–31 (2015). https://doi.org/10.1016/j.ijhcs.2014.09.006
19. Landers, R.N., Auer, E.M., Collmus, A.B., Armstrong, M.B.: Gamification science, its history and future: Definitions and a research agenda. Simul. Gaming **49**, 315–337 (2018). https://doi.org/10.1177/1046878118774385

20. Sailer, M., Hense, J.U., Mayr, S.K., Mandl, H.: How gamification motivates: An experimental study of the effects of specific game design elements on psychological need satisfaction. Comput. Human Behav. **69**, 371–380 (2017). https://doi.org/10.1016/j.chb.2016.12.033

21. Sailer, M., Homner, L.: The gamification of learning: a meta-analysis. Educ. Psychol. Rev. **32**, 77–112 (2020). https://doi.org/10.1007/s10648-019-09498-w

22. Adam, E., Van den Berg, R.: The influence of gamified e-learning quizzes on students' motivation - a case of programming students at a South African higher education institution. Indep. J. Teach. Learn. **17**, 44–62 (2022)

23. Agapito, J., Rodrigo, M.M.: Identifying meaningful gamification-based elements beneficial to novice programmers. In: Proceedings of the 26th International Conference on Computers in Education, pp. 619–624. Asia-Pacific Society for Computers in Education, Philippines (2018)

24. Awad, M., Salameh, K., Al Redhaei, A.: Gamification in higher education: assessing its impact in on-line and traditional classes. Glob. J. Eng. Educ. **24**, 226–231 (2022)

25. Ayub, M., Toba, H., Wijanto, M.C., Yong, S., Wijaya, B.: Gamification for blended learning in higher education. World Trans. Eng. Technol. Educ. **17**, 76–81 (2019)

26. Bernik, A., Vušić, D., Milković, M.: Evaluation of gender differences based on knowledge adaptation in the field of gamification and computer science. Int. J. Emerg. Technol. Learn. **14**, 220–228 (2019). https://doi.org/10.3991/ijet.v14i08.9847

27. Cabada, R.Z., Lucía, M., Estrada, B., Mario, J., Félix, R.: A virtual environment for learning computer coding using gamification and emotion recognition. Interact. Learn. Environ., 1–16 (2018). https://doi.org/10.1080/10494820.2018.1558256

28. Carreño-León, M.A., Sandoval-Bringas, J.A., Álvarez-Rodriguez, F.J.: Experience in the use of a tool that implements gamification techniques for teaching programming. In: EDULEARN19 Proceedings, pp. 7645–7650 (2019). https://doi.org/10.21125/edulearn.2019. 1847

29. Christopher, L., Waworuntu, A.: Java programming language learning application based on octalysis gamification framework. Int. J. New Media Technol. **8**, 65–69 (2021). https://doi. org/10.31937/ijnmt.v8i1.2049

30. Cigdem, H., Korkusuz, M.E., Karaçaltı, C.: Gamified learning: Assessing the influence of leaderboards on online formative quizzes in a computer programming course. Comput. Appl. Eng. Educ., 1–14 (2023). https://doi.org/10.1002/cae.22697

31. Cuervo-Cely, K.D., Restrepo-Calle, F., Ramírez-Echeverry, J.J.: Effect of gamification on the motivation of computer programming students. J. Inf. Technol. Educ. Res. **21**, 1–23 (2022). https://doi.org/10.28945/4917

32. Cui, Y., Tao, L., Bao, D., Hai, R.: Analysis and research on gamification teaching strategy used in C language programming course. In: 2023 4th International Conference on Education, Knowledge and Information Management (ICEKIM 2023), pp. 172–180. Atlantis Press International BV (2023). https://doi.org/10.2991/978-94-6463-172-2_20

33. De Pontes, R.G., Guerrero, D.D.S., De Figueiredo, J.C.A.: Analyzing gamification impact on a mastery learning introductory programming course. In: SIGCSE 2019 - Proceedings of the 50th ACM Technical Symposium on Computer Science Education, pp. 400–406 (2019). https://doi.org/10.1145/3287324.3287367

34. Du, J., Wimmer, H., Rada, R.: "Hour of Code": Can it change students' attitudes toward programming ? J. Inf. Technol. Educ. Innov. Pract. **15**, 53–73 (2016)

35. Erlangga, E., et al.: Implementation of the gamification concept in the development of a learning management system to improve students' cognitive in basic programming subjects towards a smart learning environment. ADI J. Recent Innov. **5**, 43–53 (2023). https://doi.org/ 10.34306/ajri.v5i1.902

36. Facey-Shaw, L., Specht, M., van Rosmalen, P., Bartley-Bryan, J.: Do badges affect intrinsic motivation in introductory programming students? Simul. Gaming **51**, 33–54 (2020). https://doi.org/10.1177/1046878119884996

37. Fidan, A., Şengel, E.: An examination of opinions of teacher candidates on a course enriched through gamification. J. Educ. Technol. Online Learn. **5**, 754–774 (2022). https://doi.org/10.31681/jetol.1106781

38. Figueiredo, J., García-Peñalvo, F.J.: Increasing student motivation in computer programming with gamification. In: IEEE Global Engineering Education Conference, EDUCON, pp. 997–1000 (2020)

39. Fotaris, P., Mastoras, T., Leinfellner, R., Rosunally, Y.: Climbing up the leaderboard: an empirical study of applying gamification techniques to a computer programming class. Electron. J. e-Learning. **14**, 94–110 (2016)

40. García-Gutierrez, A., Hijón-Neira, R.: Gamification experience with scratch in teaching programming in a vocational training classroom. In: CEUR Workshop Proceedings, p. 2733 (2020)

41. Garcia, M.B., Revano, T.F.: Assessing the role of python programming gamified course on students' knowledge, skills performance, attitude, and self-efficacy. In: 2021 IEEE 13th International Conference on Humanoid, Nanotechnology, Information Technology Communication on Controlling Environment Management, HNICEM 2021 (2021). https://doi.org/10.1109/HNICEM54116.2021.9731935

42. Grey, S., Gordon, N.A.: Motivating students to learn how to write code using a gamified programming tutor. Educ. Sci. **13** (2023). https://doi.org/10.3390/educsci13030230

43. Hagedorn, C., Serth, S., Meinel, C.: The mysterious adventures of detective duke: how storified programming MOOCs support learners in achieving their learning goals. Front. Educ. **7** (2023). https://doi.org/10.3389/feduc.2022.1016401

44. Huesca, G., Campos, G., Larre, M., Pérez-Lezama, C.: Implementation of a mixed strategy of gamification and flipped learning in undergraduate basic programming courses. Educ. Sci. **13** (2023). https://doi.org/10.3390/educsci13050474

45. Ibanez, M.B., Di-Serio, A., Delgado-Kloos, C.: Gamification for engaging computer science students in learning activities : a case study. IEEE Trans. Learn. Technol. **7**, 291–301 (2014). https://doi.org/10.1109/TLT.2014.2329293

46. Imran, H.: An empirical investigation of the different levels of gamification in an introductory programming course. J. Educ. Comput. Res. **61**, 847–874 (2023). https://doi.org/10.1177/07356331221144074

47. Kasahara, R., Sakamoto, K., Washizaki, H., Fukazawa, Y.: Applying gamification to motivate students to write high-quality code in programming assignments. In: Proceedings of the 2019 ACM Conference on Innovation and Technology in Computer Science Education, pp. 92–98. ACM (2019)

48. Khaleel, F.L., Ashaari, N.S., Wook, T.S.M.T.: An empirical study on gamification for learning programming language website. J. Teknol. **2**, 151–162 (2019)

49. Kiliç, S.: Effectiveness of gamification on the community of inquiry development in online project-based programming courses conducted on Facebook. Inf. Educ. **22**, 21–44 (2023). https://doi.org/10.15388/infedu.2023.04

50. Moreno, J., Pineda, A.: Competitive programming and gamification as strategy to engage students in computer science courses. Rev. Espac. **39**, 11–25 (2018)

51. Neve, P., Livingstone, D., Hunter, G., Edwards, N., Alsop, G.: More than just a game : improving students' experience of learning programming through gamification. In: Proceedings of the 2014 Higher Education Academy STEM Conference (2014)

52. Ortiz-Rojas, M., Chiluiza, K., Valcke, M.: Gamification through leaderboards: an empirical study in engineering education. Comput. Appl. Eng. Educ. **27**, 777–788 (2019). https://doi.org/10.1002/cae.12116

53. Ortiz, M., Chiluiza, K., Valcke, M.: Gamification in computer programming: effects on learning, engagement , self-efficacy and intrinsic motivation. In: Proceedings of 11th European Conference on Game-Based Learning, pp. 507–514. ACAD CONFERENCES LTD. (2017)
54. Ouahbi, I., Darhmaoui, H., Kaddari, F.: Gamification approach in teaching web programming courses in php: use of kahoot application. Int. J. Mod. Educ. Comput. Sci. **13**, 33–39 (2021). https://doi.org/10.5815/ijmecs.2021.02.04
55. Palaniappan, K., Noor, N.M.: Gamification strategy to support self-directed learning in an online learning environment. Int. J. Emerg. Technol. Learn. **17**, 104–116 (2022). https://doi.org/10.3991/ijet.v17i03.27489
56. Pankiewicz, M.: Move in the right direction: Impacting students' engagement with gamification in a programming course. In: Proceedings of EdMedia + Innovate Learning, pp. 1180–1185 (2020)
57. Pilkington, C.: A playful approach to fostering motivation in a distance education computer programming course: behaviour change and student perceptions. Int. Rev. Res. Open Distrib. Learn. **19** (2018)
58. Pinto, M., Terroso, T.: Learning computer programming: a gamified approach. In: OpenAccess Series in Informatics, p. 11:1–11:9. Schloss Dagstuhl – Leibniz-Zentrum für Informatik, Dagstuhl Publishing, Germany (2022). https://doi.org/10.4230/OASIcs.ICPEC.2022.11
59. Piteira, M., Costa, C.J., Aparicio, M.: A conceptual framework to implement gamification on online courses of computer programming learning: implementation. In: Proceedings of 10th International Conference of Education, Research and Innovation (ICERI2017), pp. 7022–7031. IATED Academy (2017)
60. Polito, G., Temperini, M.: A gamified web based system for computer programming learning. Comput. Educ. Artif. Intell. **2**, 100029 (2021). https://doi.org/10.1016/j.caeai.2021.100029
61. Pratama, F.A., Silitonga, R.M., Jou, Y.T.: Rimigs: the impact of gamification on students' motivation and performance in programming class. Indon. J. Electr. Eng. Comput. Sci. **24**, 1789–1795 (2021). https://doi.org/10.11591/ijeecs.v24.i3.pp1789-1795
62. Pratama, G.D., Kusuma, G.P.: Implementation of gamification framework on online learning of procedural programming. J. Theor. Appl. Inf. Technol. **100**, 6798–6807 (2022)
63. Rodrigues, L., et al.: Gamification suffers from the novelty effect but benefits from the familiarization effect: findings from a longitudinal study. Int. J. Educ. Technol. High. Educ. **19**, 1–25 (2022). https://doi.org/10.1186/s41239-021-00314-6
64. Rodrigues, L., et al.: Are they learning or playing? moderator conditions of gamification's success in programming classrooms. ACM Trans. Comput. Educ. **22**, 1–27 (2022). https://doi.org/10.1145/3485732
65. Rodrigues, L., Toda, A.M., Oliveira, W., Palomino, P.T., Avila-Santos, A.P., Isotani, S.: Gamification works, but how and to whom? an experimental study in the context of programming lessons. In: SIGCSE 2021 - Proceedings of the 52nd ACM Technical Symposium on Computer Science Education, pp. 184–190 (2021). https://doi.org/10.1145/3408877.3432419
66. Rojas-López, A., Rincón-Flores, E.G., Mena, J., García-Peñalvo, F.J., Ramírez-Montoya, M.S.: Engagement in the course of programming in higher education through the use of gamification. Univers. Access Inf. Soc. **18**, 583–597 (2019). https://doi.org/10.1007/s10209-019-00680-z
67. Scott, L., Dalton, N.: Studying the impact of gamification on motivation in remote programming education. In: Proceedings of the 20th European Conference on e-Learning: ECEL 2021, pp. 627–634 (2021)
68. Sharma, R., Sharma, H., Ali, A., Sahani, C., Gupta, P.: An empirical study gender-based perception of gamification and its impact on programming skill enhancement. J. Inf. Educ. Res. **3**, 183–204 (2023). https://doi.org/10.52783/jier.v3i2.91
69. Shorn, S.P.: Teaching computer programming using gamification. In: Proceedings of the 14th International CDIO Conference, Kanazawa, Japan (2018)

70. Smiderle, R., Marques, L., Coelho, J.A.P.D.M., Rigo, S.J., Jaques, P.A.: Studying the impact of gamification on learning and engagement of introverted and extroverted students. In: 2019 IEEE 19th International Conference on Advanced Learning Technologies (ICALT), pp. 71–75. IEEE (2019). https://doi.org/10.1109/icalt.2019.00023

71. Swacha, J., Szydłowska, J.: Does gamification make a difference in programming education? evaluating FGPE-supported learning outcomes. Educ. Sci. **13** (2023). https://doi.org/10.3390/educsci13100984

72. Tahir, F., Mitrovic, A., Sotardi, V.: Investigating the causal relationships between badges and learning outcomes in SQL-Tutor. Res. Pract. Technol. Enhanc. Learn. **17** (2022). https://doi.org/10.1186/s41039-022-00180-4

73. Tokzhigitova, A., Yermaganbetova, M., Tokzhigitova, N.: Engineering pedagogy. Int. J. Eng. Pedagog. **13**, 65–78 (2023). https://doi.org/10.1007/978-981-19-8016-9

74. Venter, M.: Online programming learning platform: the influence of gamification elements. In: 2022 IEEE IFEES World Engineering Education Forum – Global Engineering Deans Council (WEEF-GEDC), pp. 295–301 (2022)

75. Venter, M., Swart, A.J.: Continuance use intention of a gamified programming learning system. Commun. Comput. Inf. Sci. **963**, 17–31 (2019)

76. Zahedi, L., et al.: Gamification in education: a mixed-methods study of gender on computer science students' academic performance and identity development. J. Comput. High. Educ. **33**, 441–474 (2021). https://doi.org/10.1007/s12528-021-09271-5

The Effect of Progressive Disclosure in the Transparency of Large Language Models

Deepa Muralidhar[1]([✉]) [iD], Rafik Belloum[2] [iD], Kathia Marçal de Oliveira[2] [iD], Ashwin Ashok[1] [iD], and Pardaz Banu Mohammad[1]

[1] Georgia State University, Atlanta, GA 30302, USA
dmuralidhar1@gsu.edu
[2] Univ. Polytechnique Hauts-de-France, LAMIH, CNRS, UMR 8201, 59313 Valenciennes, France

Abstract. Recent advances in artificial intelligence (AI) text generation systems have resulted in their ability to provide precise recommendations in response to users' questions (prompts). However AI models often operate as black boxes, making it challenging for users to comprehend their inner workings. The transparency of these models is crucial for users to gain a better understanding of how AI systems function. While the Human-Computer Interaction (HCI) community has advocated for design principles like progressive disclosure to improve transparency, we still lack empirical evidence validating its efficacy for AI systems, especially in the context of LLM-based text generation. Addressing this gap, this paper presents a user study with 30 participants aimed at investigating the effect of progressive disclosure and adjusting the explanations so as to adapt to users' mental models for improving the transparency of AI text generation systems. The findings suggest that users prefer on-demand explanations and value diverse explanation methods, especially when the explanations gradually give the users a better understanding of the AI system. Additionally, qualitative data shows a marginal preference for word clouds over keyword highlighting. User feedback indicates that explanations such as word-pair cosine values, which leverage the interpretability of AI models, are less suitable for lay users. Altering the visual presentation of these word-pair cosine values from a table of numbers to a bar graph did not increase user satisfaction with this explanation technique.

Keywords: Progressive disclosure · Transparency · Explainable user interface · Explainable AI · XAI · artificial intelligence · HCI · AI text generation · LLM

1 Introduction

Artificial Intelligence systems are black boxes that often make decisions that are biased, violate people's privacy, and result in distrust [50]. Algorithmic transparency is the idea that an algorithm should reveal itself to the users [38]. For such transparency to exist an AI system must be explainable. AI architects aim to design AI systems that can cooperate with others to accomplish a task [52]. Such collaboration requires communication with humans. User interfaces of current AI systems are not sensitive to the needs of their users [8]. They do not provide explanations in ways that help a user understand how they work [14]. In Human-AI interactions, due to the lack of transparency, users

H. Plácido da Silva and P. Cipresso (Eds.): CHIRA 2024, CCIS 2370, pp. 269–288, 2025.
https://doi.org/10.1007/978-3-031-82633-7_17

(a) Highlighting the Keywords in the Prompt

(b) Word cloud for prompt, *Atlanta is a beautiful place to fall in love with*, where there is misunderstanding of the word "love"

Fig. 1. Examples for Keywords and Word-Cloud highlighting.

do not know how the language models that power auto text generator systems work, so they can only guess the AI system's reasoning. Often they do not understand why a communication breakdown occurs in the AI system. The problem is compounded because the Large Language Models (LLMs), when they receive user input, also do not understand the user's intended meaning, resulting in conversational breakdown [22]. For example, while conducting experiments with our volunteer users, one user generated a prompt as seen in Fig. 1a – *Atlanta is a beautiful place to fall in love with*. Two of the many definitions provided by Merriam-Webster lexicon for the noun form of the word love are:

1. warm attachment, enthusiasm, or devotion
2. attraction based on sexual desire : affection and tenderness felt by lovers

The human understands and knows that the word love is intended to have the meaning shown in the first bullet point. Figure 1b refers to one of the explainability techniques used in the prototype, a word cloud. From this figure we learn that the AI system picked up the second bullet point meaning of the word love. Conversation breakdown is defined as failure of the system to understand the user's intentions while communicating with them. When this occurs, users often stop interacting with the system. Repair is defined as the process where the system recovers from the breakdown and completes the task goal [1]. In current systems the only way an AI agent can initiate a repair is to have it be requested by the user. Such user-initiated repair strategies are ineffective since the AI agents do not have the capability or knowledge to understand the repairs requested by the end user [23]. However, when AI systems and users interact they can collaboratively attempt to repair conversational breakdowns.

We put forward the idea by adding controls on the user interface of an AI system that explain the outcome in a gradual manner and help increase user understanding of the AI system and possibly increase user confidence in the system. We design a prototype of an user interface where the user feels that by interacting with the AI system they are in charge and can control the outcome of the AI system. Our experiment is to use this prototype to assess if the end-user can begin to grasp AI systems' inner workings through explanations. To produce a successful outcome when users enter a prompt for an AI system an iterative approach works better. Our approach is to study the output and improve the prompt iteratively. This can achieve the user's goal while reducing the overall number of interactions [7]. AI agents should be flexible in the modality used to collaborate with users. Such a flexible user interface will increase users' understanding of how to accomplish their task with the help of the AI system. Explanations should be selective in what they reveal and this should be a gradual process so as to not overwhelm the user. In this context, the goal of this paper is to propose an approach that provides explanation on demand [20, 24] to the users through progressive disclosure. While designing interactive multi-modal interfaces for AI systems, advanced information such as detailed explanations are provided only when the user has asked for it. In the design of user interfaces using explanations, we present to the user the key features that are needed to understand the system so that the user can complete their task. Through surveys and interviews, we understand and report the differences in user perception between a non-transparent and transparent interface. The key results from our interviews show that users have a marginal preference for word clouds over keyword highlighting.

The main contribution of this paper is an approach of designing a transparent interface integrating the user in the whole process. We designed a mock-up of a user interface for an AI system. (We refer to this mock-up as a prototype throughout the paper.) This design implements a sequence of explainable techniques, including keyword highlighting, explanations using a video and text based captions, word clouds, bar charts that show vector similarity values, and a narrative on the design of effective prompts that help a user understand the predicted text generated by the AI system. These explanations are gradually exposed to the end user using progressive disclosure. The information about the inner workings of the AI system is exposed to the user in small increments and only when requested by the user.

To this end, in this paper, we present a set of studies keeping users in the loop to produce a selectively transparent AI system. With this goal, we aim to answer the following research question: ***Do AI systems that provide explanations and act in accordance with the progressive disclosure usability design principle improve the transparency of an AI system for an end user?*** **The problem** we address in this paper is that AI text editors, such as Notion, do not explain how or why they generated the AI text.

Our approach is to implement explainability techniques and progressive disclosure in the user interface to help the end user understand why and how the system arrived at the outcome.

Our solution was to:
1. Design a prototype (incorporating user input throughout the process) for a user interface in Notion that increases interactivity and includes various explainable techniques along with the usability technique of progressive disclosure to increase user understanding of the system's inner workings.
2. Gather data on users' perspectives of transparency using surveys on this prototype.

In the next section, we position our work within the state of the art on progressive disclosure. We then describe our approach, the details of our experiment (Sect. 3) and the
steps we followed to build a transparent LLM interface with users (Sect. 4). We describe
the data collection process analyze the data gathered from the results of our experiment
and outline key insights regarding transparency for LLMs (Sect. 5). In conclusion, we
present some final remarks and directions for future work (Sect. 6). Appendix A contains the details of the user study conducted to investigate the effect of progressive
disclosure.

2   Related and Prior Work

2.1   Transparency and Explanation Techniques

Machine learning based systems have problems related to the accuracy of their outcomes, the output having biases and concerns such as that the resources they use could
be violating privacy laws [9]. Prior research indicates that transparency in AI systems
is a possible solution [21,28]. Transparency is about the AI system providing explanations about its outcome to the users. The AI system can implement explainability
through the user interface [37]. This positively influences user experience in various
aspects such as perceived dependability and makes the system seem more attractive to
end users [47,49].

Transparency Definitions. Our research finding is that current literature has several
definitions for transparency. In this paper we use the following definition: "The ability of the AI system to be able to convey clearly what it can and cannot do" [51].
Explanations that aid the users in seeing the inner state or functionality of the system
support transparency [26]. The validity of an explanation is determined by who needs
the explanation and what they want to do with it. Transparency provided by simply
explaining the code or showing the data may not suffice as explanations for an end
user who is impacted by the outcome of the AI system [39]. Explanations that answer
questions such as what, where, how and why an AI system arrived at a decision help
build transparent AI systems [25]. Explanations that increase understanding and provide information about the uncertainty inherent in AI systems help the user know how
to appropriately rely on the system [23].

Explanations in Relation to Mental Models. Explanations should be such that they
help the users develop accurate mental models of the system as quickly as possible [49].
Explanations that explain the why and the why not help bring the user's mental model
closer to the actual functioning of the system and reduce the gulf of execution [24,32].

2.2   Mental Models

We refer to the AI system's conceptual model as conceptualized by the designer as the
target conceptual model [32]. This is often intended to be a a simple, useful explanation
of how the system works. The user's mental model is formed as they interact with the
system and it keeps evolving [30]. Nielson [29] states that these are simplified versions

of a much more complex version of the system. Users do not perceive the system to be transparent because of a difference in the user's understanding of the system and the actual behavior of the system [31]. This is a problem because it prevents the user from being prepared for or being able to explain the system's behavior.

Explanations that Aid with the Building of Mental Models. Explanation interfaces are commonly used to help users build better mental models. These explanations are a part of the user interface through which the AI agent endeavors to increase user's confidence level in the AI system's output. Explanations that require the AI agent and the user to interact, allowing information to flow in both directions, where the user controls the interaction and the AI system responds, improve the transparency of the system. Making an AI system's reasoning transparent can help improve a user's mental model of the system [12]. User experience improves when users are exposed to the reasoning of the AI system [20]. It is the responsibility of the AI agent to bring the user's mental model closer to that of the system [12,48]. Progressive disclosure is an interactive design technique where the user is progressively exposed to the AI system's workings. Initially the AI system only provides the user with high level explanations and then reveals the more granular, detailed explanations in a progressive step-by-step-process [7,42] when the user asks. The explanations are provided through visuals, text, and audio/video formats, keeping in mind that users' cognitive load limits their capacity to absorb information during an interaction. This then helps bring the user's mental model gradually closer to the AI system's conceptual model without overwhelming them. Users typically ask for explanations to improve their understanding of the AI system and to improve their ability to use the system correctly and predictably [3]. Just one explanation is rarely enough [7]. Therefore by interacting with the user, when the AI system provides multiple explanations using different modalities, the user gradually builds a mental model of the AI system that is closer to the target conceptual model. The interaction happens in stages where the user and the AI system take turns.

Human AI Interaction. In human-human interactions, both members try to understand the discrepancies in their mental models and provide explanations. Similarly the AI agent must provide explanations such that the interaction between the human-AI agent through explanations reduces the gulf of execution [7,32]. Explanations that aid users in building mental models can be categorized into two kinds, natural examples and inspection examples [7]. Natural examples are examples that are textual, simplified responses to user queries that explain how the system functions. Inspection and exploratory techniques are ones that allow users to explore how changes in the input will impact the output. While using these two techniques, the user is in control and makes the queries and the AI agent responds with an explanation. Identification of such explanations that help understanding of the AI system's features and help users' mental model come closer to that of the actual design of the system [24] are necessary to achieve the goal of transparency.

2.3 Progressive Disclosure

Progressive disclosure is an idea that was introduced by Xerox in 1981 [17]. While designing an user interface, the system gradually discloses its inner functionality through multiple screens so as to not overwhelm the user. In this way the system hides its complexity until the user is ready for it. It reduces excessive information, moving the user from general to specific details about the system [19] [46].

The term "training wheels" in the user interface was further popularized [6], with the purpose of providing a limited exploratory environment to the users. Authors [47] use the idea of progressive disclosure to improve transparency using explanations. We expand this work by conducting an empirical study to better understand how users learn the behavior of AI systems so that they can successfully accomplish their tasks. We identify explanations that disclose the AI system's functionality gradually without inundating the user.

Compared to the work of those that worked with progressive disclosure, to the best of our knowledge no one investigated transparency in the context of AI text generation systems in prompt engineering tasks. In this user study we identify examples of conversation breakdown and use explanations such as keyword highlighting [1] to aid the process of repair. Too much transparency can be distracting, especially with new users, as the users are creating a conceptual model about the system in their minds. Simple, minimal explanations provided as needed basis being made available on the user interface can be fruitful. Users do not have to receive all of the explanations at one time.

2.4 Context Sensitive Word Embedding

In the context of NLP systems, AI systems predict the next word to be generated by using word associations. By assigning numerical values to text based on the context in which they occur, text data can give insights into understanding of a word through its context. When words are represented by their word vectors, every word token representation only captures what the word means in that context. When word tokens have their own vector, the vector value for that word is dependent on the context words around it. As a result, when a word occurs, the next word that is more likely to occur than others is because of context sensitive word embedding [45].

Prompt Engineering. In the context of prompt engineering, research discusses which information in a prompt is useful in producing outcomes that are usable. There is plenty of research that discusses the ability of Large Language Models to understand human syntax [5, 15]. Because of the progress made with LLMs it is now possible to use natural language as a tool for human-AI communication [44].

A transparent AI system explains its inner logic by highlighting the keywords in the prompt as well as providing suggestions for fine tuning the prompt. The structure of the prompt, the words that locally co-occur, and the lexical information of the words in the prompt, impact in the production of a high-quality outcome. In a dataset of words that are used to create these prompts, the parts of speech become some of the features. Content words such as nouns, verbs and adjectives carry the most information in a sentence [18]. Human comprehension is capable of overlooking word order linguistic errors [4]. Our research shows that NLP systems are also insensitive to word order. Language models use the lexical-semantic content (content words) rather than the sentence's syntactic form (word order) to predict the next word needed to generate AI text.

When one of the function words is a determinant then in that context it acts as either an adjective or an adverb and has an impact on the AI generated text. Wu [53] suggests short sentences work better, since longer sentences lead to ideas being in conflict with each other. O'Connor [34] states that identifying words that can be removed is helpful in figuring out how much information is useful. Design of prompts that elaborate the user's requirements can be effective in getting the LLM to produce good outcomes [2].

Instruction Prompt Tuning: is a hybrid soft-hard prompt tuning approach. The idea is to identify a soft prompt to be a prefix and then add task-specific few-shot exemplars to create a prompt that is required to accomplish the user's goals. Instruction prompt tuning can be used to train a model to follow instructions in one or more domains [44].

3 User-Centered Approach to Improve Transparency of AI Systems

Well-designed socio-technical systems have the ability to improve human well-being [36]. Software engineering systems deploy classic HCI methods that depend on active user engagement while evaluating the interface. As illustrated in Fig. 3, our approach is based on principles of user-centered design [32,43] where we place the user at the center of the design process.

3.1 Experiment

Our goal is find out if the designed prototypes of a user interface for an AI system addresses the needs of multiple stakeholders by making the reasoning of the AI system more transparent. We approach the problem of improving AI system transparency by applying the usability principle of progressive disclosure. When an AI system uses the usability principle of gradually and progressively disclosing the way it works, and by selectively explaining its decision making process, it acts transparent. Transparency can increase end user awareness about the bias, accuracy, and privacy concerns associated with the deployment of AI systems in society. We conduct experiments to answer our research question by designing a prototype of a user-interface where the AI agent inter-acts with the user and explains its reasoning and logic using different modalities (text, video and visual aids) as and when requested by the user. A salient feature of the pro-totype is that the user is able to control the AI system at every stage of interaction. Our intent is to find out if such an AI system can increase user confidence. For experiments we used Notion (an off-the-shelf commercially available text editor program that has an AI component for auto text completion) to generate AI text for a prompt given as input by a user. Our first task was to create a dataset of prompts and AI generated text for these prompts. We collected this data from 30 voluntary users. We asked each of the users to give us data for 5 prompts. This way we had more than 100 prompts along with the AI generated text. We also collected user perception of transparency of the Notion AI system and their satisfaction of quality of the AI generated text. We designed the pro-totype keeping the user at the center of the development cycle. Using semi-structured interviews and the think-aloud processes we collected feedback from a subset of the 30 users to improve the prototype. This prototype implements explainable techniques using progressive disclosure. From the dataset we selected 3 prompts for every user and designed a prototype of a user interface for each of the prompts. All 90 prototypes were similar in design, customized to the 90 prompts and the AI generated text. Our next step in the experiment was to conduct semi-structured interviews with the users showing them the prototype and collecting their feedback on the techniques implemented to increase user confidence in the AI agents decision making by increasing transparency. We analyzed the data collected through these interviews and implemented the common concerns and suggestions shared by the users in the next version of the prototype. We created a 1-minute video of the prototype that showed these changes and showed them to users. This final questionnaire helped us gather data to analyze user confidence and understand if user perception of transparency improves if progressive disclosure and explainability techniques are implemented.

4   Designing Explanations that Gradually Disclose Information to Aid Transparency

Using Figma we designed a prototype of a user interface to improve the transparency of AI system by increasing interactivity between the users and the AI systems. Figma is a well-known tool for designing prototypes [13]. Such user-centered transparent AI systems are sensitive to the user's needs, let the user have control over the system at all times, and allow the AI agent and human to work collaboratively towards accomplishing the goals of the task. The fundamental idea behind this experiment is our perspective that in an AI system the elements that impact transparency are the AI Model and Data and User Interface [27]. AI systems are designed depending on the environment they function in as well as when and how long they are used. Our first set of experiments are use auto text generators, natural language processing (NLP) systems that run on LLMs such as GPT-Series, Gemini, etcetra. We use Notion, an AI text editor [33] in our experiments. In these systems it is important for the user to get real-time response quickly.

Modes: Algorithmic transparency in an AI system can be increased by adopting two approaches [47]. One is to achieve selective transparency using explainability and complete transparency using auditability. We implement this idea in our experiments by providing users two modes, the regular mode and the transparency mode. In our design the AI system's user interface is selectively transparent and user-initiated. We call this the Regular Mode. As illustrated in Fig. ??, the user interface has a feature that indicates that the user is in regular mode. The second, exhaustive transparency [10] is reserved for the AI expert, domain expert, or for personnel appointed to audit the system, where explanations should be complete. We call this is the Transparent Mode.

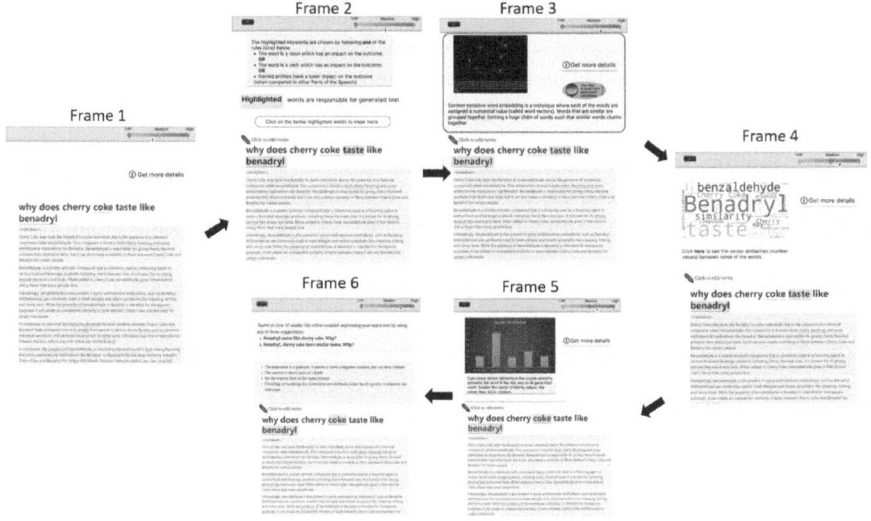

Fig. 2. Transparent User Interface - An Example Version 2.0

Design Overview. Our intent is to design a user interface flexible enough to understand and work with the user. Conversational breakdowns occur when the AI systems do not understand the user's intended meaning. System repairs occur once the AI agent has ensured that they are needed and have been requested by the user. To initiate repair strategies [1]:

1. let the user know that there is a breakdown.
2. initiate the repair and provide options on how to repair
3. collaborate with the user on how to proceed

As shown in Fig. 2, and this video, the suggested user interface interacts with the user, and upon receiving input, advances to the next frame and explains how it works by using different explanation techniques. The AI agent also makes an attempt to repair any possible breakdowns by giving the user suggestions on how to improve the prompts to finish their task. As the user progresses through the screens, and the system continues to disclose more information about its internal logic and decision-making process, the AI system indicates an increase in transparency by a sliding bar on the user interface. The bar displays three transparency levels of the AI system: low, medium and high. We use explainability techniques that employ natural language dialogues while interacting with the user. This technique provides text narratives in a natural language that makes the AI system more accessible to all end users. The prompt engineering narrative, the graphs that show the vector similarity values, and the word cloud that shows the popularity of the words are all examples of this technique. Having such audio/visual explanation methods increases understanding. The suggestions for improving the prompt and the capability that allows the user to edit the prompt at any time employ the inspection explanations technique [26]. These techniques increase transparency since the user can explore various inputs (prompts) to improve the outputs. One survey taker's feedback on this was,

I like the "keep writing" option to adjust and improve the prompt. Through every inter-action with the user the AI agent's goal is to use explanations to bring the user's mental model closer to the conceptual model of the system as envisioned by the AI architects. We used the following methods to design the user inclusive interface for AI systems:

1. **Algorithm for Identification of the Keywords:**
   (a) Identify the nouns and adjectives or verbs in the prompt.
   (b) Using other feature extraction tools identify the keywords in the prompts and the outcome.
   (c) Using the prompt and the outcome data, generate word clouds that give insights into the words with high occurrence.
   (d) The nouns and verbs identified in the prompt (step 1) should be seen in the fea-ture extraction step as frequently occurring words in the word cloud. The words identified in step I now should be highlighted to indicate they are keywords that impact the outcome.
   (e) Sometimes there is a word that has a high occurrence but is not seen in the prompt. In such cases finding the cosine similarity of the content words in the prompt (Method #2) and the word that has a high occurrence helps identify the related keyword in the prompt. Once such a word is identified it is highlighted as the keyword.
2. **Computing Cosine Similarity Values:** For the keywords found in the prompts (Method #1) use a graph or table that lists the cosine similarity value for related word pair associations. This explainability technique uses context sensitive word embedding and assigns numerical values to text based on the context in which they occur. This sort of context sensitive data can give insights into understanding the word [45].
3. **Video and Text Explanations:** Include a video with a text that is a shortened tran-script of the video explaining the concept of context sensitive word embedding. This provides an audio-visual explanation of the numerical values and / or graphs shown in a different technique. (Method #2)
4. **Word Cloud:** A word cloud of all the words in the prompt and the AI generated text. This gives the user visual feedback on the most popular words that influenced the output [11].
5. **Instruction prompt tuning** [44]**:** The algorithm used to fine tune the suggested prompts is as follows:
   – Identify the overall emotion in the prompt. (such as positive, optimistic, shocked, surprised,etc.) The new prompt must retain the emotion as is (since we do not want to create a bias or influence the user's thinking, we keep the suggested modifications to a minimum)
   – Pay attention to the nouns, verbs, and the adjectives to understand the context. Place the Part Of Speech that impacts the context in the beginning of the prompt (sentence).
   – Chunk the sentences. LLMs process shorter sentences with greater predictive accuracy than longer sentences. While having multiple sentences, the parts of the sentences that are in the beginning or end have a greater impact on the outcome. [35]

5 Evaluation and Results

5.1 Procedure

As discussed previously in Sect. 3, the approach we take is to design a prototype for a user interface and conduct experiments to investigate the effect of progressive disclosure and the different explainability techniques for an AI text editor such as Notion.. We used Figma to develop the prototype. We now analyze results and gain insights gathered from the surveys conducted:

1. Initial Dataset Created from Survey 1. We conducted this survey with 30 users to build a dataset of a variety of prompts and the AI generated text from diverse users of varying demographics such as gender, age and education (Table 1). We wanted to see if any of these factors influenced the design and order of explainability techniques presented to improve the transparency of the AI system. One factor we did not consider was the user's knowledge, experience, or comfort level with AI systems. We surveyed a controlled group of users (N = 30) for our experiments who we interacted with as we designed the system. This survey collected five prompts (users were required to provide at least three prompts and three outputs) and the output generated from every user creating a dataset of more than 100 prompts.

2. Feedback Interviews Used to Aid the Design of the Prototype. Through iterative testing and feedback from a small group of users (N = 6), we developed and continuously improved our prototype. After the initial implementation, we redesigned the interface in the second version to better understand how individual situations and user preferences influence the effectiveness of these computing systems. We argue that a human-centric approach of the feedback interviews while designing the prototype is important to:

- improve comprehension: We asked users if adding explanations about the outcome to the interface increased user understanding of the system.
- progressive/step-by-step understanding: We asked users if implementing progressive disclosure, that is, presenting the explanation techniques in a specific order was helpful to the user.

Based on feedback from users, we made design decisions on the choice of explanations and the order in which they were presented in the prototype.

3. One-on-One Interviews for Data Collection on Customized Prototypes. The goal of this interview was to capture users' understanding of the AI systems outcome based on the explanation provided. We conducted interviews with all the users to learn users' inclination towards one explanation technique over the others. Our data collection results showed that a user's preference for an explanation technique or their perception of transparency of an AI system does not change much for different prompts or outcomes.

Table 1. Demographics of volunteer users.

Demographic	Count (total 30 users)
Age	< 20 = 2, [20-30] = 18, > 30 = 10
Gender	Male=19, Female=11, non-binary=0, undisclosed=0
Education (currently pursuing or have degree)	High School = 2, Bachelors = 4, Masters = 17, Doctorate and other higher level degrees =7

4. Data Collection on Improved Prototype (Version 2.0. We design questions in this survey (see Appendix A) that collect users' opinions of the improved version of the prototype, see Fig. 3. Using the data collected from previous surveys we made functional design improvements to the prototype of a transparent user interface. We designed Version 2.0 of the prototype for one of the 90 earlier version of the prototypes. From the feedback survey experience we learned that user feedback was more objective and detailed when they saw prompts and outcomes that were created by other users. We concluded that designing and experimenting with one generic prototype for this round of experiments was sufficient.

5.2   Data Analysis and Results

We analyzed the data collected to understand user perceptions on the increase of transparency due to progressive disclosure in an AI system. Analyzing the data collected from the first survey, it shows that 76.4% of users were satisfied with the output provided by Notion, though at least 80% of the users agreed that the transparency level of the system was low. Table 2 lists the comments by the users who thought the transparency level should be lower than indicated on the first frame of the prototype. Users are biased favorably towards the AI agents. Human Factors Engineering research indicates that users have automation bias [41]. There is an over-reliance by users on the advice or response given by AI agents [40], and as a result, they blindly accept its output unless the AI agent asks for specific input from them. When directed, humans are likely to pay attention and want to know more. During the semi-structured interviews we conducted using the prototypes (see Appendix A), no user exhibited curiosity on how the AI agent had selected the keywords in the prompts to highlight. However, in the final questionnaires given to the users (see Appendix A), when the user interface

Table 2. User opinion of the transparency level as seen in Notion UI.

No.	User Comments
1	It isn't really giving any insight on how its achieving its output
2	It's not telling me where it got this opinion from, or how it arrived at the opinion
3	It didn't give any transparency at all
4	I do not see anything that helps me understand how these stories were generated, or what I could do to create a change

provided this information all users unanimously found it useful. We conclude that often users do not explicitly realize that they need explanations unless they are provided. During the interface design process (Feedback interviews), through interviews we learned that users preferred keyword highlights as an explanation technique to come before the cloud of words. When we conducted the one on one personal interviews with 30 users, we learned that 54% users liked word clouds while 45.6% preferred keyword highlighting. User feedback through the interviews informed us that users think word clouds are easy to read since they are a familiar visual and while they lack depth in explanations this technique also brings out several words that are related. A user said, *Giving importance to each of the words that have an impact, the word cloud shows how it is more significant than others.* When we discussed the order of the explainable techniques with users they indicated that having the word cloud displayed right after the video improved their understanding of the explanations. Prior research has shown that users like to have the option of switching between modalities while receiving information [16].

Table 3. User feedback on the using Cosine (Vector) Similarity values.

No.	User Rating	User Comments
1	HIGH	They were useful to me because I am now understanding why I did not get the outcome I needed. Based on the correlated numbers, I can see why there would be more positive outcome than now. Because the correlation, I was never set to get the outcome I wanted
2	LOW	My opinion changes based on the end user. I think a regular user does not really value seeing the quantitative side of the numerical values. I think the same information is yielded from the word cloud

Based on user feedback we find that providing the word-pair cosine values is too technical and maybe overwhelming to the end user. Users who had prior knowledge indicated that the values shown to them provided clarity on the output generated by the AI text editor (Table 3). The prototype of a transparent user interface of an AI system gives suggestions to improve the prompts that could help them get an improved outcome along with a narrative on how the AI system got these suggestions. As result, 92.2% of the survey takers found narrative of the logic used to provide suggested prompts useful. However, only 53.3% of users found the suggested prompts useful, while 38.2% said they were not as useful, and 8.6% partially agreed with their usefulness. In reference to Fig. 2 (also can be seen in video) - Frame 1 (first update on the screen seen by the user), users rated the transparency levels to be low because they said that they would have liked more explanations from the AI system about the outcome. In the last screen update, Fig. 2 - Frame 6, after the users read the narratives, all users rated the transparency level to be medium or above. The users found having explanations with progressive disclosure used by the AI agent to have improved the transparency of the AI system. Our experimental results show that most users found the improved user-centered prototypes useful. 86.7% of users found that the new version of the prototype had improved over the old design.

When we studied our user responses to the final version of the prototype we had a few users who expressed dissatisfaction with the latest version of the prototype. They had reasons such as:

– *Not sure how this would really help an end user, with minimal technical knowledge about the AI model.*
– *I still think the end user is unlikely to be interested in extensive detail on transparency.*
– *I would like to get more simpler description of technical terminology used like what is meant by vectors, what is transparency? how would you rate transparency, etc.*

5.3 Key Insights

Here are the insights we gained from our experiments:

1. The first survey revealed that out of 90 prompts generated by 30 users, at least 76 comments focus on the lack of explanations in Notion. The most common explanation that users wanted was how the system arrived at the outcome.
2. User feedback confirms that the progressive disclosure process as a way of building a transparent user interface in AI systems is operative. As can be seen in the video of the prototype. A user observed, *Both are useful and important. Highlighting emphasizes focus and word cloud emphasizes the explanations. And therefore the highlight should come first and the explanations (video) then the word cloud comes next.*
3. All users wanted more explanations after seeing the keywords highlighted and watching the video. Once users were exposed to explanations, they wanted to understand more.
4. Explanations should be such that they bring the user's mental model closer to the conceptual model of the system. The order as well as the choice of explanation techniques presented to the user is important. One participant noted, *It is very important to understand the AI generated text in the outcome. What it meant. Why the text generated the way it was. The text with video helped understand the word cloud better. Word cloud was the best.*
5. The number of users who preferred word clouds were marginally more than those who preferred keywords. Both techniques can be considered as effective when used with NLP systems that auto-generate texts. Tables 4 and 5 presents some comments of the user related to the keyword highlighting.
6. Putting the human at the center of the design process is beneficial. Only after receiving user feedback we realized that adding controls to the user interface for explanations to improve transparency was valuable.
7. Users prefer matching the video and reading the text to understand the idea of context sensitive word embedding. By studying the data from the surveys we learned that even if at first the user preferred video or text eventually they decided either mode worked fine. The video followed by the word cloud helped the user get a clear picture of the AI system's conceptual model.
8. Changing the visual of word-pair cosine values from being a table of numbers to a bar graph did not increase user satisfaction with this explanation technique. User

feedback as seen in Table 3 indicates that providing explanations that use the interpretability of the AI models may not be suitable as end-user explanations. More experiments are needed; however, early results indicate that they are suitable for auditing AI systems.

Table 4. A User feedback on keyword highlight.

No.	User Comments
1	I think highlighting the words made it clear which words were the most critical in generating the response. Without that I'm not sure I would necessarily have understood which words it was keying (focused) on..
2	Increases my understanding, since I can clearly see what words the AI found most important and how it got to its output. Its fast and easy to understand
3	They highlight the two major subject words but what I would also like to see is other semantics to be highlighted and also some cause-effect realtionships within the sentences
4	I wanted to first see highlighted keywords, as it showed me interest to know more about why these keywords impact and how they impact. If I see everything first then I don't get interest and my lose interest at the beginning. So i prefer to see highligt words first. I can see the flow and as a end user I would like to go with flow what, how, and why type. This interface clearly told me that

Table 5. User choice of order of word cloud and keyword highlighting.

No.	User Comments
1	The highlighting the keywords are important so they give the context of what are the keywords and then the word clouds give more supplmental reasoning
2	In this case word cloud helped as I had a few inconsistencies in my understanding of how the AI generated the text based on the highlighted words which was cleared by the word cloud in a way that I can see the other important words as well
3	Highlighting is perhaps unnecessary if word cloud is presented first
4	Showing the highlighted words is the first step is what i feel. Once, they are selected only then the system can try to form words that might be related to them and try construct using words relating to it

5.4 Limitations

We use keyword highlighting as an explanation technique to understand the AI text editor's logic and inner workings. This method is unfortunately unappealing aesthetically, feels unnatural, and may not be as effective an explanation as using natural language for explanations. It increases response time by requiring additional user effort in having to respond to the confirmation.

Another technique we used is word clouds. The problem with word clouds is that they lack the depth needed to gain deeper insights into the data and sometimes the size of a word could be inaccurate depending on the style of the outcome of the AI system.

One more explainability technique we used is suggesting modified prompts to improve the outcomes. However, AI systems have outcomes where the uncertainty is inherent. The outcome for a prompt is not completely predictable. Our approach may not help increase transparency, because even after having all the explanations provided the user may get an outcome that is not explainable using the techniques that we have proposed.

User studies may need to be conducted regularly, depending on the domain in which the AI system is used and the frequency at which the AI model is trained, to ensure that appropriate explainability techniques are implemented. Another limitation of surveys is that we did not collect data about the users' experience or comfort level with AI systems.

The proposed user interface does not provide a mechanism for the AI system to progress from regular mode to transparent mode in the event the user persists in asking for more information. This is significant because an important concern in the design of transparent systems is that users may take advantage of the provided transparency by gaming the system.

6   Conclusion and Future Work

In this paper, we presented a user study aimed at exploring the impact of progressive disclosure and various explainable techniques on perceived transparency. We went through the iterative process of designing the user interface with these techniques and showing it to a group of 30 participants. In this way we gathered qualitative insights about their views on transparency. The proposed user interface answers questions of why and how behind the decisions made by the AI system, and what is at stake. The AI system gradually releases information about its inner workings through multiple screens as and when requested by the user.

Future work includes conducting experiments with a larger number of users and in different domains. The prototype has a feature that indicates if the system is in regular or transparent mode. The interface design should differentiate between the modes based on user requirements and privileges, which we will address moving forward. Our work can also include conducting user experiments for knowledge-based clinical diagnosis AI systems where the impact of the applications on the user is high risk and it is important that the decisions are as accurate as possible.

Appendix A

This appendix outlines the process used for data collection. We conducted multiple surveys to gather user perceptions of AI system prototypes. Using this data, we analyzed user feedback on the impact of progressive disclosure of explainability techniques in AI systems.

Data Collection. We designed four questionnaires using Google Forms to collect user responses, which were stored in Google Sheets. All feedback from surveys, interview recordings, and user interface design perceptions is securely stored. The data helps us analyze user behavior with AI systems, focusing on progressive disclosure, transparency, and explainability as key features of trustworthy AI.

STEP I: Survey Using Notion AI. To design a transparent AI text editor, we created a questionnaire to collect prompts and outcomes from users and designed personalized interfaces for three of each user's five prompts. Thirty volunteers completed the survey. At this stage, we had a set of prompts and outputs. We then selected explanation techniques and their order, centering the user in the design process.

STEP II: Choosing and Validating Explainability Techniques. We developed a prototype using Figma, employing various explainability techniques such as keyword highlighting, word clouds, graphs showing vector similarity, and videos. Six volunteers (including 5 from Step I) participated in synchronous interviews (40 min), providing feedback to refine the prototype and finalize the design and sequence of the explanations.

STEP III: User-Centered Personalized Prototyping. The five validated techniques were used to create 90 prototypes (three per user). Progressive disclosure was applied to prevent information overload, ensuring the AI agent provided only the necessary information. Transparency was provided on demand, consistent with social science theory that users accept simplified explanations unless deeply invested in the decision.

STEP IV: Structured Interview: Evaluation of Prototypes. We evaluated the personalized prototypes for three selected prompts and outcomes with the 30 volunteers in a semi-structured interview (about 110 min). Users analyzed each prototype and answered questions to help us understand their perceptions of transparency.

STEP V: Improving One Prototype. Based on feedback from the interviews, we synthesized recommendations and improved one of the 90 prototypes, selecting one that clearly demonstrated the improvements based on user input.

STEP VI: Survey for Final Evaluation. Another round of surveys was conducted with the same 30 users to evaluate the final prototype. This asynchronous survey was designed to gather data on users' perceptions of transparent interfaces.

STEP VII: Data Analysis. We analyzed the data from the surveys to draw conclusions about the role of progressive disclosure in AI transparency. Section 5.1 presents detailed results and analysis.

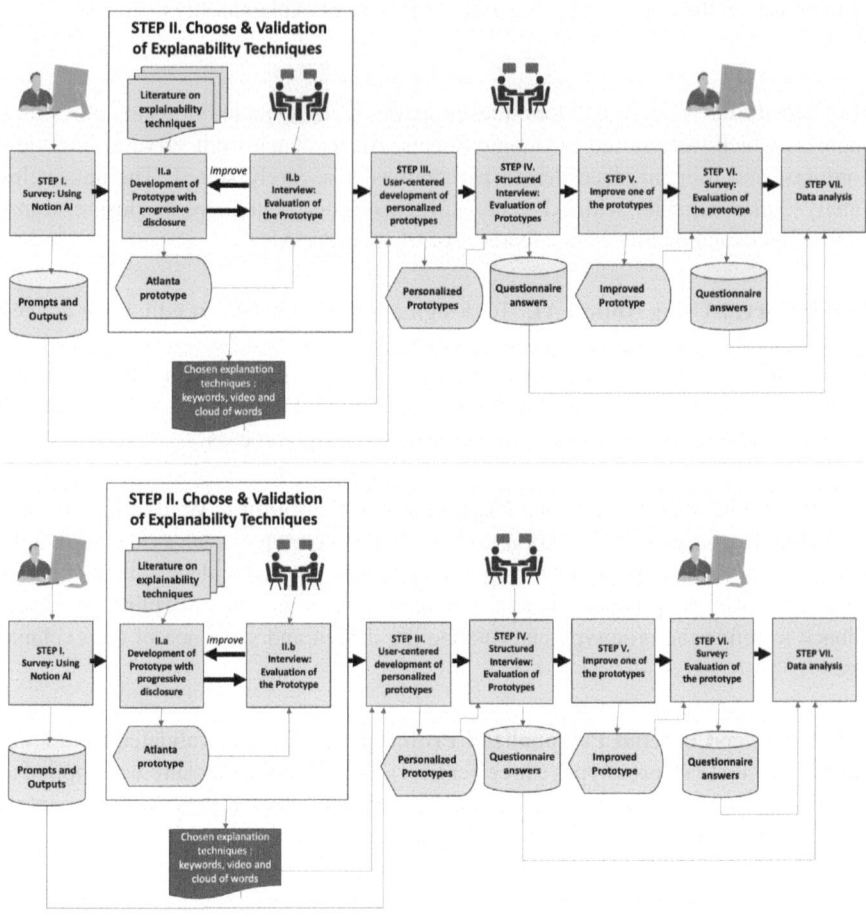

Fig. 3. Block diagram depiction along with the experimental flow of our user-centered approach for improving transparency.

References

1. Ashktorab, Z., Jain, M., Liao, Q.V., Weisz, J.D.: Resilient chatbots: repair strategy preferences for conversational breakdowns. In: Proceedings of the 2019 CHI Conference on Human Factors in Computing Systems (2019)
2. Betz, G., Richardson, K., Voigt, C.: Thinking aloud: dynamic context generation improves zero-shot reasoning performance of gpt-2 (2021)
3. Bosch, K., Schoonderwoerd, T., Blankendaal, R., Neerincx, M.: Six challenges for human-AI co-learning (2019)
4. Brown, R., Fish, D.: The psychological causality implicit in language. Cognition (1983)
5. Brown, T.B., et al.: Language models are few-shot learners (2020)
6. Carroll, J.M., Carrithers, C.: Training wheels in a user interface. Commun. ACM (1984)
7. Chromik, M., Butz, A.: Human-XAI interaction: a review and design principles for explanation user interfaces (2021)

8. Chromik, M., Eiband, M., Völkel, S.T., Buschek, D.: Dark patterns of explainability, transparency, and user control for intelligent systems. In: IUI Workshops (2019)
9. Daneshjou, R., Smith, M., Sun, M., Rotemberg, V., Zou, J.: Lack of transparency and potential bias in artificial intelligence data sets and algorithms: a scoping review. JAMA Dermatol. (2021)
10. Dangelo, M.: Auditing ai: The emerging battlefield of transparency and assessment. AI & Future Technologies (2023). https://www.thomsonreuters.com/en-us/posts/technology/auditing-ai-transparency
11. Dwivedi, R., et al.: Explainable ai (xai): core ideas, techniques, and solutions. ACM Comput. Surv. (2023)
12. Eiband, M., Schneider, H., Bilandzic, M., Fazekas-Con, J., Haug, M., Hussmann, H.: Bringing transparency design into practice. In: 23rd International Conference on Intelligent User Interfaces (2018)
13. Figma, Inc.: Figma (2023). https://www.figma.com/
14. Gilpin, L., Paley, A., Alam, M., Spurlock, S., Hammond, K.: "explanation" is not a technical term: the problem of ambiguity in xai (2022). https://doi.org/10.48550/arXiv.2207.00007
15. He, Q., et al.: Can large language models understand real-world complex instructions? (2024)
16. Horvitz, E.: Principles of mixed-initiative user interfaces (1999)
17. Johnson, J., et al.: The xerox star: a retrospective. IEEE Xplore (1989)
18. Kauf, C., Tuckute, G., Levy, R., Andreas, J., Fedorenko, E.: Lexical semantic content, not syntactic structure, is the main contributor to ann-brain similarity of fmri responses in the language network (2023)
19. Kimball, R., Harslem, B.V.E.: Designing the star user interface. Byte (1982)
20. Kulesza, T., Stumpf, S., Burnett, M., Kwan, I.: Tell me more? the effects of mental model soundness on personalizing an intelligent agent. In: Proceedings of the Sigchi Conference on Human Factors in Computing Systems (2012)
21. Larson, D.B.: Openness and transparency in the evaluation of bias in artificial intelligence (2022)
22. Li, T.J.J., Radensky, M., Jia, J., Singarajah, K., Mitchell, T.M., Myers, B.A.: Pumice: a multimodal agent that learns concepts and conditionals from natural language and demonstrations. In: Proceedings of the 32nd Annual ACM Symposium on User Interface Software and Technology (2019). https://doi.org/10.1145/3332165.3347899
23. Liao, V.E.A.: Human-centered explainable ai (xai): from algorithms to user experiences (2022)
24. Lim, B.Y., Dey, A.K., Avrahami, D.: Why and why not explanations improve the intelligibility of context-aware intelligent systems. In: Proceedings of the SIGCHI Conference on Human Factors in Computing Systems (2009)
25. Lim, B.Y., Dey, A.K., Avrahami, D.: Why and why not explanations improve the intelligibility of context-aware intelligent systems. In: Proceedings of the SIGCHI Conference on Human Factors in Computing Systems (2009). https://doi.org/10.1145/1518701.1519023
26. Lim, B.Y., Yang, Q., Abdul, A., Wang, D.: Why these explanations? selecting intelligibility types for explanation goals. In: IUI Workshops (2019)
27. Muralidhar, D., Belloum, R., de Oliveira, K.M., Ashok, A.: Elements that influence transparency in artificial intelligent systems-a survey. In: IFIP Conference on Human-Computer Interaction. Springer, Heidelberg (2023)
28. Nicol Turner Lee, P.R., Barton, G.: Algorithm bias detection and mitigation: best practices and polices to reduce consumer harms (2019). https://tinyurl.com/vy4mud77
29. Nielsen, J.: Mental models (1990). https://www.nngroup.com/articles/mental-models/
30. Norman, D.A.: Some observations on mental models (1987)
31. Norman, D.A.: The Design of Everyday Things. Basic Books, Inc. (2002)

32. Norman, D.A., Draper, S.W.: User Centered System Design: New Perspectives on Human-Computer Interaction. L. Erlbaum Associates Inc. (1986)
33. Notion Labs, Inc.: Notion (2024). https://www.notion.so/
34. O'Connor, J., Andreas, J.: What context features can transformer language models use? (2021)
35. OpenAI: Chatgpt: A large-scale generative language model (2021). https://www.openai.com/research/chatgpt
36. Ozmen Garibay, O., et al.: Six human-centered artificial intelligence grand challenges. Int. J. Hum.-Comput. Interact. **39**(3), 391–437 (2023)
37. Panigutti, C., et al.: Co-design of human-centered, explainable ai for clinical decision support (2023)
38. Rader, E., Cotter, K., Cho, J.: Explanations as mechanisms for supporting algorithmic transparency. In: Proceedings of the 2018 CHI Conference on Human Factors in Computing Systems (2018)
39. Rubin, V.: Ai opaqueness: what makes ai systems more transparent? In: Proceedings of the Annual Conference of CAIS/Actes du congrès annuel de l'ACSI (2020)
40. Schemmer, M., Kühl, N., Benz, C., Satzger, G.: On the influence of explainable ai on automation bias (2022)
41. Sellen, A., Horvitz, E.: The rise of the ai co-pilot: lessons for design from aviation and beyond. arXiv preprint arXiv:2311.14713 (2023)
42. Shneiderman, B.: Bridging the gap between ethics and practice: guidelines for reliable, safe, and trustworthy human-centered ai systems (2020)
43. Shneiderman, B., Plaisant, C.: Designing the user interface: strategies for effective human-computer interaction. Pearson Education India (2010)
44. Singhal, A.T.E.A.: Large language models encode clinical knowledge. Nature (2023)
45. Smith, N.A.: Contextual word representations: putting words into computers. Commun. ACM (2020)
46. Spillers, F.: Progressive disclosure (2010)
47. Springer, A., Whittaker, S.: Making transparency clear. In: Algorithmic Transparency for Emerging Technologies Workshop (2019)
48. Tsai, C., Brusilovsky, P.: Designing explanation interfaces for transparency and beyond (2020)
49. Vitale, J., et al.: Be more transparent and users will like you: a robot privacy and user experience design experiment. In: Proceedings of the 2018 ACM/IEEE International Conference on Human-Robot Interaction (2018)
50. Wanner, J., Herm, L.V., Heinrich, K., Janiesch, C.: The effect of transparency and trust on intelligent system acceptance: evidence from a user-based study. Electron. Mark. (2022)
51. Weller, A.: Transparency: Motivations and challenges (2019)
52. Wooldridge, M.: An Introduction to Multiagent Systems. John wiley & sons, Hoboken (2009)
53. Wu, T., Terry, M., Cai, C.J.: Ai chains: transparent and controllable human-ai interaction by chaining large language model prompts (2022)

Design and Implementation of a Practice Record Visualization System Using Piano Performance Tracking Technology

Haruna Mori[iD], Mio Sasaki, Kaede Noto, Yoshinari Takegawa[(✉)][iD],
and Keiji Hirata[iD]

School of Systems Information Science, Future University Hakodate,
Hakodate, Hokkaido, Japan
`yoshi@fun.ac.jp`

Abstract. The purpose of this study is to develop a practice record visualization system using a piano performance tracking technology that utilizes gaze information. In general, piano lessons are held regularly, e.g., once a week, and the teacher observes the student's skills at a fixed point. However, it can be difficult for the teacher to fully understand and address all areas how the student has practiced from the previous lesson to the current lesson and need improvement. This makes it difficult to provide appropriate guidance in lessons, such as determining whether students are too nervous to perform well in front of the teacher, or whether they are also unable to perform well in home practice. To solve this problem, we propose a performance tracking algorithm that can handle keystroke errors and replaying, and a system that visualizes the amount of practice and other practice progress. The proposed system visualizes the amount of practice and errors in various units, such as notes and measures. To verify the usefulness of the proposed system, we conducted an evaluation experiment comparing the case of using the proposed system and not using the proposed system.

Keywords: Visualization · Teaching support · Interactive system · Eye tracking · Performance error detection

1 Background

For piano learners who do not have an advanced pianist they can ask for assistance, it is difficult to grasp their state of proficiency by themselves, and they tend to practice inefficiently, e.g., by playing only the parts they are good at [4]. Accordingly, it can be said that lessons, which provide a chance to receive evaluation from the viewpoint of another person, are important for making efficient progress. The main tasks of the instructor in a piano lesson are to grasp the state of the learner's practice and to assign practice tasks for the learner to perform up to the next lesson. A piano lesson typically lasts from 30 to 60 min, which is a very limited time in which to provide instruction. In face-to-face lessons, the instructor must grasp the state of the learner's practice, within this time restriction. As the instructor is only able to check the learner's performance during the lesson, they may be unable to provide appropriate instruction. For example, it is not uncommon for a learner who is able to play well during practice to feel nervous

© The Author(s), under exclusive license to Springer Nature Switzerland AG 2025
H. Plácido da Silva and P. Cipresso (Eds.): CHIRA 2024, CCIS 2370, pp. 289–303, 2025.
https://doi.org/10.1007/978-3-031-82633-7_18

in front of a teacher and play badly during lessons. Another situation we can consider is that in which a point made by the instructor is not understood by the learner. For example, when an instructor is unable to provide successful guidance due to a difference in the instructor's and learner's respective perceptions. Supposing the instructor has asked the learner to 'concentrate practice' on a part on which they make many mistakes. Even if the instructor means 'practice at least 20 times', the learner may feel that 10 times constitutes sufficient practice. In this manner, there are cases in which the instructor and learner do not share the same perception of a task. Therefore, in this research, we propose a performance-following technology, which is robust against performance errors and restarting from partway through the score, and aim to design and implement a practice record visualization system that applies the performance-following technology.

The target users of the proposed system are piano lesson instructors. The proposed system has a function that visualizes the amount of individual practice conducted between lessons, as well as the number of keying errors, in various units such as units of notes or bars. Furthermore, there are functions for comparing practice day by day or month by month. In piano lessons up to now, an instructor was only able to carry out fixed-point observation of a pupil's skill under the particular conditions of a lesson. The functions provided by the proposed system have the potential to revolutionize instruction by transitioning from observation during lessons to observation from when the learner started playing a certain piece up to the present.

In Sect. 2, we introduce related research. Section 3 explains the performance-following algorithm, and Sect. 4 describes the practice record system that applies the performance-following technology. Section 5 describes the user study, and Sect. 6 summarizes our research.

2   Related Research

Numerous investigations have been conducted into methodologies aimed at assisting piano learners. Various systems have been developed to automatically identify learners' weaknesses, such as mistyped keys and fluctuations in tempo or dynamics, utilizing traditional practice logs as a foundation [1,2,5,6]. These systems evaluate errors in keying and dynamics based on keying data. Piano Tutor [3] stands out as an interactive expert system employing multimedia technology, featuring functions like automated page-turning through score-following technology, generating performance support materials, and delivering them via video, musical notation, and graphics in response to the learners' progress. Another system [9] offers support during performance by displaying keying positions, fingering suggestions, and sample videos. While these systems analyze learner performance and provide useful feedback to aid learning, they do not incorporate the notion of deliberately overlooking learner's practice state.

2.1   Visualization of Practice State

Ueda et al. developed a system that aims to realize efficient practice by adult piano beginners, by a function that visualizes practice condition and a function that enables annotation of the musical score [10]. In this research, visualization of practice condition is conducted based on MIDI keying information. This results in a limitation regarding understanding of performance position, due to the fact that, if keying information is analyzed directly, it is difficult to estimate the performance point when part of the music has been skipped or replayed. For example, when the player makes a mistake while playing according to the score, and begins playing again from an earlier point, the system cannot proceed to follow beyond the point at which the mistake was made. This is because the system does not suppose performance that includes this kind of jump to an arbitrary point on the score. In our research, by introducing a score-following function that uses gaze information, we make it possible both to grasp performance position and to measure gaze during performance. By using the movement of gaze, and the degree of stillness, it is possible to find problems in performance beyond those that can be understood from keying information. For example, the system can determine that a point on which the player's gaze rests for a long time may be a point at which the player is having trouble understanding the score.

From piano learner's visual information, Nakahira et al. measured and visualized the information acquisition range, and developed a system to analyze learners' score-reading ability [7]. In this system, which is able to visualize what points a learner looked at and for how long, the duplicate presentation of a learner's past and present information acquisition ranges, in a hierarchical structure, makes it possible to grasp the transition of the learner's skill development. However, the visualization method lacks clarity, because displaying the musical score and information acquisition range hierarchically on a three-dimensional graph has the disadvantage that perceptibility decreases as the amount of data increases.

Smoliar et al. proposed 'pianoFORTE', a system focused on visualization of practice conditions, to support communication between the teacher and student in a piano lesson [8]. pianoFORTE has a function to visualize aspects such as strength of keying, tempo, articulation such as staccato and legato, the degree of consistency between the timing of the right and left hands, based on MIDI data. However, sufficient evaluation has not yet been carried out regarding the system's practice condition visualization method and the influence of the system on improving piano performance.

3   Practice Record System

The target user of this practice record system is a piano teacher who instructs beginner pupils. The system aims to enable the teacher to grasp the state of a pupil's individual practice between lessons, so that the teacher can provide appropriate instruction in a short time during lessons. The work flow of the proposed system is presented in Fig. 1. Performance data is obtained from the MIDI keyboard, and gaze information is obtained with the gaze-measurement device. The current playing position on the score is followed based on these data, then practice record is visualized based on the results. By checking the visualized practice record on a tablet device, the teacher can comprehend the state of practice between lessons and utilize this information when providing instruction in lessons.

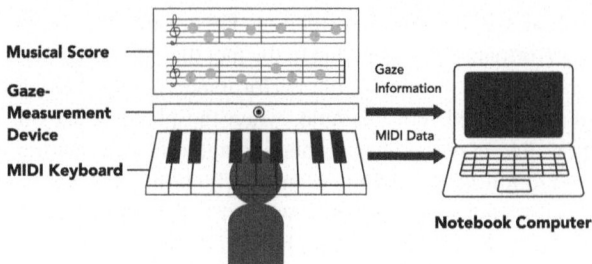

Musical Score

Gaze-
Measurement
Device

MIDI Keyboard

Gaze
Information

MIDI Data

Notebook Computer

Fig. 1. System Structure.

This practice record system comprises two main components. The first is performance following, which is described in Sect. 4, and the second is visualization of practice record, which is described in Sect. 5.

4   Performance Following

To estimate the notes played during practice, we use keying information (MIDI note number) and gaze information obtained by the gaze measurement device. In the majority of performance-following algorithms, playing position is estimated based on keying information. Accordingly, a characteristic of these algorithms is that estimation performance deteriorates in proportion to the frequency of keying mistakes. Therefore, in performance following in our system, we use gaze information. The gaze information used in performance following is the focus points on the display, which are measured by the gaze measurement device.

4.1   Outline

In the proposed performance-following algorithm, we combine performance -following methods that use two separate feature values. One method is performance following based on keying information. In this method, the notes currently being played are estimated by alignment of the key-press series and the musical score series. Specifically, estimation is carried out by calculating the degree of similarity between the keying series and note series on the score, each time a key-press is input. The other method is performance following based on gaze information. In this method, the notes being played are estimated based on the distance between the points, on a display, on which the player is focusing and the notations on the musical score. These two performance-following methods are in a complimentary relationship.

4.2   Series Alignment of Keying Information and Note Series on the Musical Score

We adopt DP(Dynamic Programming) matching as a means of estimating performance position from keying information. In DP matching, performance following of a monophony is made possible by creating a cost table based on the consistency between the respective MIDI note numbers of keying and musical score. Performance following is carried out continuously, each time a key-press occurs. The cost table renewal method, in the case of the occurrence of a key-press, is presented below. Here, S_i is the ith$(i = 0, 1, 2, \ldots I)$ note, counting from the beginning of the score, and K_t is the tth pressed note $(t = 0, 1, 2, \ldots T)$. The cost table, C, is renewed each time there is a key-press, and is expressed as a series of sizes (i, t). The components of the cost table C_{ij} corresponds to the cost based on the number of consistency between S_i and K_t. The renewal method of component C_{it} is presented in formula (1). In the formula, w corresponds to the degree to which past cost is reflected, and is a value ranging from 0 to 1. By the above operation, the played sound estimated when the tth key-press occurs is the ith note, which corresponds to the largest component value among the components in the Tth column of the cost table C.

4.3 Performance Position Estimation Based on Gaze Information

In performance following using gaze information, the coordinates of focus points and notations are used. To obtain the information of what note to play next, a performer looks at the score while playing. In the case of the performer not having completely memorized the score, the played notes should be in the vicinity of the coordinates of the point on the score at which gaze is calculated. When $i_{(x,y)}$ is the coordinates of each notation on the score, and $g_{(x,y)}$ is the focus point, performance position can be estimated from D_i, that is, the distance between each notation and focus point. In performance following by gaze information, when a focus point $g_{(x,y)}$ is obtained, the note i, which has the smallest D_i value, is taken as the estimated played note. The measure used when calculating distance D_i is Euclidean distance.

4.4 Combination of Gaze Information and Keying Information

To combine the above performance-following methods, we conduct performance following that uses cost, C, on which the distance from the focus point, D_i, has been reflected. As cost Cit is the number of matches of notations, and distance D_i is in units of pixels, to make the values accord, they are scaled to a range from 0 to 1 by Min-Max normalization. After this, the values are combined. AS cost Cit takes the notation with the largest value as the played note, while distance D_i takes the notation with the smallest value as the played note, distance D_i is combined once it has been converted to become $1 - D_i$ (formula (2)). The played note E_t that is estimated when a key-press t is obtained, is the note i with the largest cost Cit when distance D_i has been reflected. Incidentally, regarding the timing of calculation by formula (2), this is carried out the moment a key-press occurs, and the focus point used at that time is the average of the 30 samples that precede the moment of the key-press.

4.5 Judgement Keying Errors

Based on the result of performance following, the proposed system judges two types of keying error:

1. Playing a note that is not included on the score
2. Replaying a note that has already been played

   To judge these keying errors, the system compares past, present and future performance following results. The conditions for determining a keying error are when the played note estimated from the tth key-press is not the note that follows the played note estimated from the $(t - 1)th$ key-press, and when it is not the note before the played note estimated from the $(t + 1)th$ key-press. Performing judgement based on these two conditions makes it possible to maintain sufficient accuracy when detecting keying errors, even in the case of performance that includes jumps between different performance positions.

5   Practice-Record Visualization

In the practice record visualization component of the proposed system, the number of key presses and number of keying errors are visualized graphically, and this information is presented on the tablet device used by the piano teacher. To visualize practice record, we use the number of key presses corresponding to notations on the score (hereafter referred to as 'amount of practice') and the number of keying errors. These data are generated by the performance-following component described in Sect. 4. Let us now explain the content in the practice record visualization component. Figure 3 is the top page, and displays a monthly calendar. This calendar presents the amount of practice and number of keying errors on each day. The amount of practice is written in red, while the number of keying errors is written in blue. These values are expressed as a do-nut chart, in which the values of one ring are 1000 times for amount of practice and 200 times for keying errors. Selecting an arbitrary date on the calendar causes the amount of practice and number of keying errors on the selected day to be displayed at the bottom right of the screen. This enables the teacher to grasp the learner's practice condition on each day at a single glance. In addition, selecting either of the 'Amount of Practice' or 'Number of Keying Errors' buttons at the bottom of the screen displays the practice record relating to the selected item. Figure 4 is an example of having selected amount of practice. In Fig. 4, the amount of practice in units of musical notations is being displayed as both a heat map and a line graph. In units of musical notations, the amount of practice and number of keying errors for each notation on the score are presented. In addition to units of notation, amount of practice and number of keying errors can be displayed in units of bars. In this case, the amount of practice and number of keying errors in each bar on the score are presented. The presented content in Fig. 4 is explained in detail below. The numbers in the figure correspond to the itemisation numbers below.

(i) Switch line graph display on or off. The line graph is drawn in red. In the notation-unit line graph, the y coordinate is determined by a standard which is either the largest amount of practice or largest number of keying errors for the notations in the specified time period. In the bar-unit line graph, the standard for determining the y coordinate is either the largest amount of practice $\times 8$ or the largest number of keying errors $\times 8$, for the notations in the specified time period. This is because, in the musical score used in this system, the shortest notation was an eighth note, thus the standard for one bar was fixed at largest amount of practice $\times 8$ or largest number of keying errors $\times 8$.

(ii) Switch heat map display on or off. The heat map is drawn in red. The saturation of the heat map increases when there are many keying errors and decreases and when there are few errors. Here, we explain the formula for calculating the heat-map saturation level. The largest amount of practice or largest number of keying errors for the notations in the specified time period are used in calculation. Here the factors are defined as follows: K_i is amount of practice, M_i is number of keying errors, $Start$ ($0 \leq Start \leq$ j) is the start day of the specified time period, and End ($0 \leq End \leq$ j) is the end day. The subscript i corresponds to the notation ID on the score, and the subscript j corresponds to the practice day ID. The formulas for calculating heat map saturation for amount of practice Hnp_i and heat map saturation for number of keying errors Hnp_i are as follows.

$$Hnp_i = \frac{255 \times i}{2.2 \times \max_{Start \leq j \leq End} K_{ij}} \tag{1}$$

$$Hnk_i = \frac{255 \times i}{2.2 \times \max_{Start \leq j \leq End} M_{ij}} \tag{2}$$

Next, we explain the formula for calculating heat map saturation for units of one bar. Figure 5 is an example of the presented heat map. The largest amount of practice or largest number of keying errors for the notations in the specified time period are used in the calculation. In addition, the definitions are also the same. The formulas for calculating heat map saturation for amount of practice Hmp_i and heat map saturation for number of keying errors Hmk_i are as follows.

(iii) The largest amount of practice and largest number of keying errors for the right-hand and left-hand part, respectively, are displayed. Regarding the position of the memory display, the y coordinate is determined by the same standard as in the line graph.

(iv) Presents the weekly averages of amount of practice and number of keying errors as a line graph. Figure 6 is an example of a presented graph. The line graph is drawn in green, and the standard by which the y coordinate is determined is either the largest amount of practice within the week or largest number of keying errors within the week. Incidentally, by presenting this in combination with units of one practice day, it is possible to compare the data of an arbitrary practice day with that of a whole week.

(v) Presents the amount of practice and number of keying errors on the day before a given practice day, as a line graph. Figure 7 is an example of a presented graph. The line graph is drawn in blue, and the standard by which the y coordinate is determined is either the largest amount of practice within the week or largest number of keying errors within the week. By presenting this in combination with units of one practice day, it is possible to compare the data of an arbitrary practice day with that of the previous day, and thus to grasp the places where amount of practice or number of keying errors have increased or decreased in comparison to the previous day (Fig. 2).

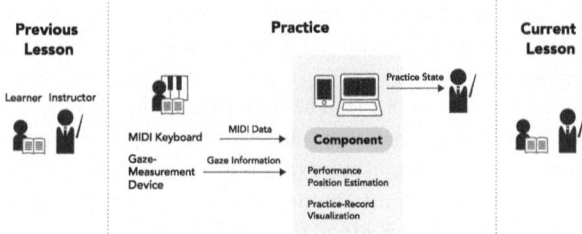

Fig. 2. Workflow of the Practice Record System.

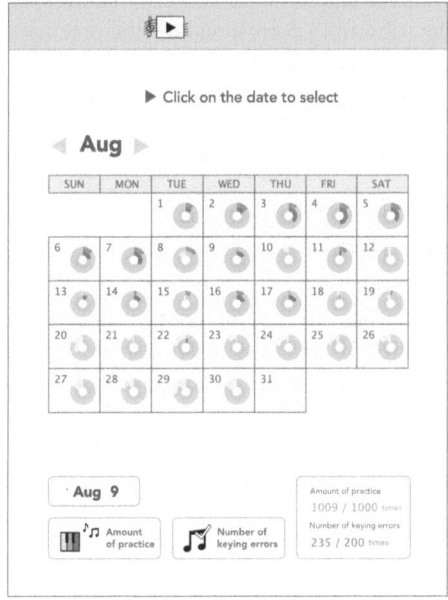

Fig. 3. Basic Screen.

6   Evaluative Experiment

An evaluative experiment was conducted to verify the usefulness of the proposed practice record system. The assumed scenario was instruction in a piano lesson. The records from three days of practice by two piano beginners (students) was used as system input and visualized by the system. While using the system, the subjects taking part were questioned about the number of keying errors and amount of practice. A comparative method, which comprised watching a video of the students' practice, was also prepared, and the group using the comparative method were also questioned about the number of keying errors and amount of practice. The details of the experiment are given below.

6.1   Experiment Procedure

The experiment procedure was as follows.

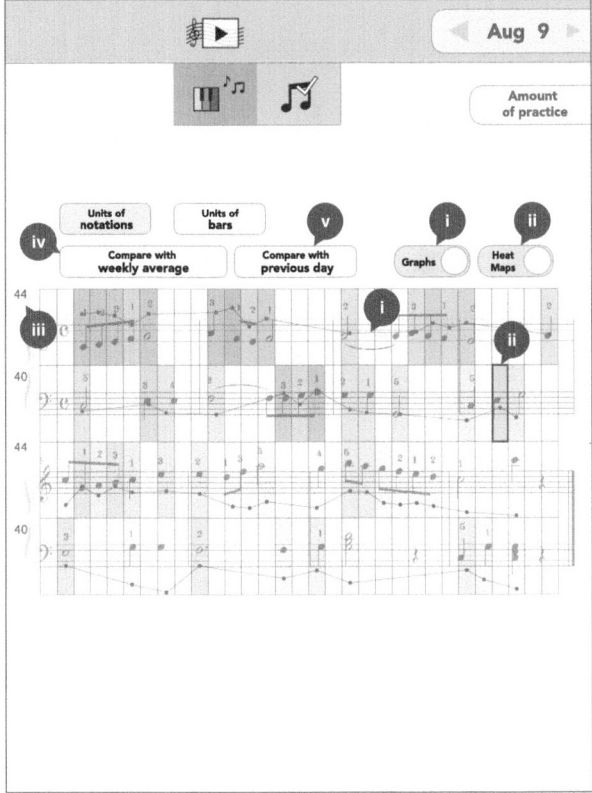

Fig. 4. Visualization by Heat Map and Line Graph.

Construction of Performance Data Sets. Two beginner piano players were given simple piece of music, eight bars in length, which they practiced for twenty minutes a day, for three days. To prepare them for practice, the beginners were first taught the meaning of the notations written on the score, the relationship between those notations and the piano keys, the meanings of the noteheads and flags, and the meaning of the key signature. An example video of performance was also provided, to enable the beginners to confirm the correct way to play, as they practiced.

Comparative Method. The comparative method involved watching a video of the three days' worth of twenty minute practice sessions. Before viewing the videos, subjects were informed that they were free to watch the videos however they liked, using fast forward etc.

Experiment Participants. Six male and female university students (two people with no musical experience beyond compulsory music lessons at school; two people with musical experience not related to the piano; two people with piano experience) took part in the experiment. Although the target users of the proposed system are teachers, it was

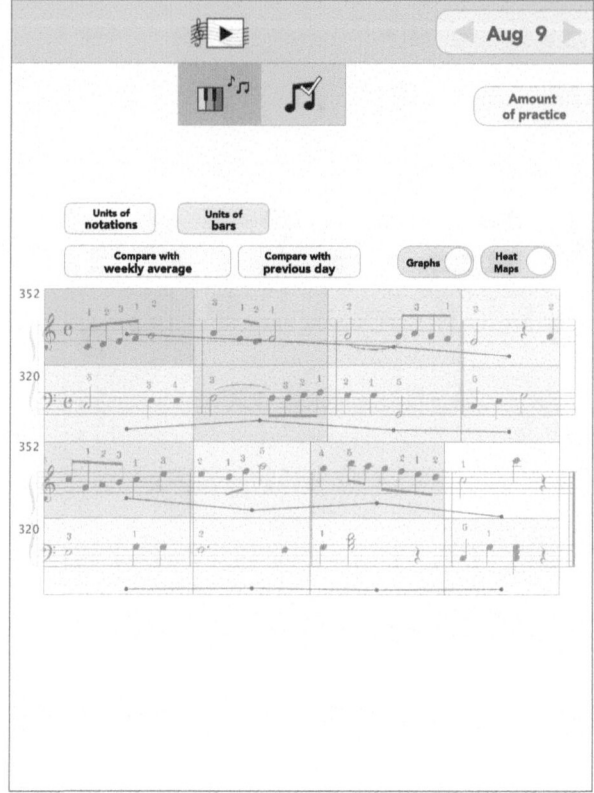

Fig. 5. Visualization in Units of Bars.

considered that the convenience of the system could be measured by verifying whether it is easy for various types of people to use. Therefore, in this experiment, participants were recruited regardless of whether or not they had experience of the piano or other instruments. It should be noted that the experiment participants were not the same people who took part in the construction of the data sets. In addition, the participants were divided in such a way as to ensure that there was no bias, regarding musical experience, between the group who used the comparative method and the group who used the proposed method.

Evaluative Experiment. In the experiment, to investigate whether participants were able to grasp correctly the way in which the beginners had practiced over the three days, the participants used their assigned method and answered the following questions for each day. As shown in Fig. 8, an ID was assigned to each notation, and participants were instructed to answer by providing the relevant ID. As the practice record comprises three days, there are a total of six questions for each method.

– For which notation is there the largest number of keying errors?

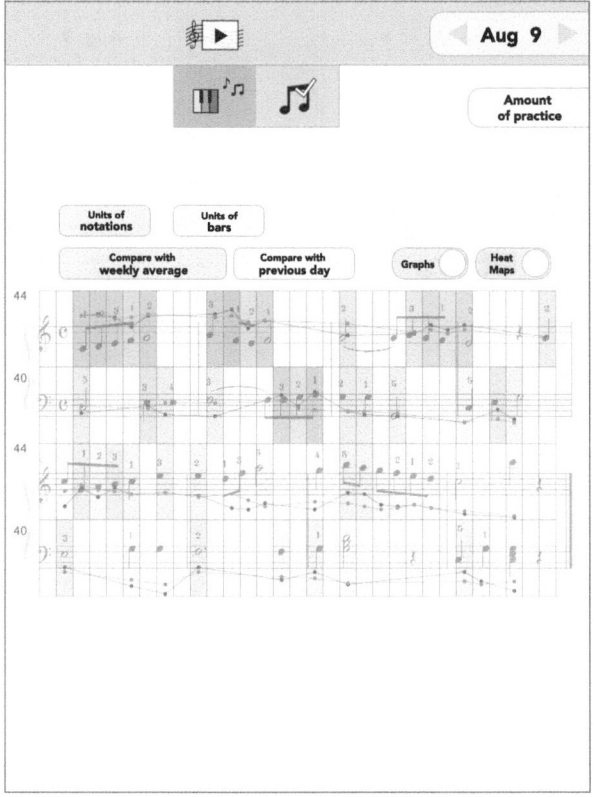

Fig. 6. Visualization of Weekly Average.

– For which notation is there the largest amount of practice?

In addition, to verify the validity of the visualization method in the proposed method, the following questions were also asked. Each question was answered on a five-level Likert scale (1: Difficult to understand - 5: Easy to understand).

– Was visualization by line graph easy to understand?
– Was visualization by heat map easy to understand?

Participants were instructed to write the answers to these question on the questionnaire form presented in Fig. 9. The form was created using Google Forms.

Instructions to Participants. Participants were instructed to "perform the experiment task as quickly and accurately as possible".

Experiment Method. Each participant sat in front of a desk upon which a 13″ notebook computer had been placed, in a quiet, private room. This provided an environment in which the participants were sufficiently able to hear the sound output from the computer. In the comparative method, participants used Windows Media Player to view

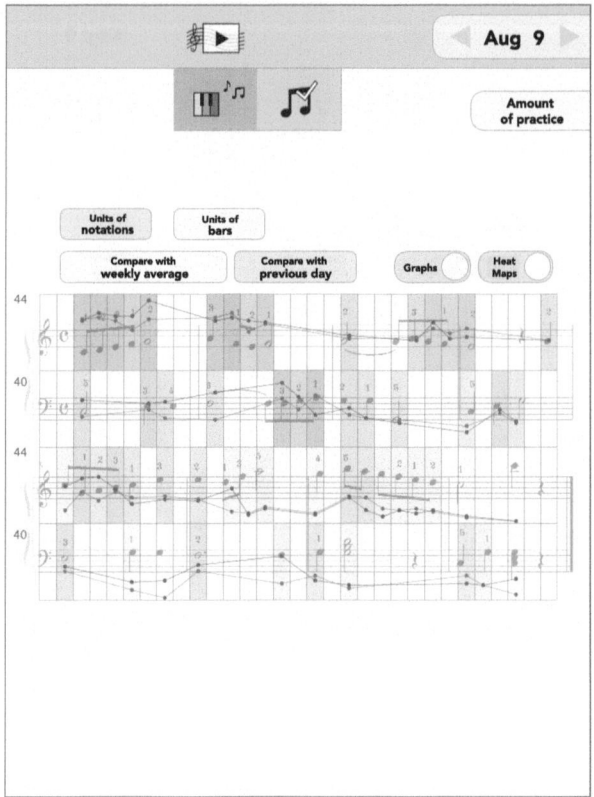

Fig. 7. Visualization of Day Preceding Current Practice Day.

the videos. As participants were used to using similar software, no explanation was required regarding how to operate the software. Participants using the proposed method were given some prior instruction on how to use the system. Both groups practiced using their assigned methods for up to five minutes, using sample data different to the data used in the actual experiment. As we had adopted the within-subjects approach for this experiment, there were two patterns: the pattern of first performing the experiment task using the comparative method and then performing the task using the proposed method, and the pattern of first performing the experiment task using the proposed method and then performing the task using the comparative method. Which pattern each participant would follow was decided randomly. Participants had 30 min to perform the task using their assigned method.

Instructions to Participants. Regarding the time taken to complete the questionnaire, each participant informed the experimenters when they had completed the question-naire, and the experimenters recorded the elapsed time. Alternatively, the questionnaire time was forcibly ended once 30 min had elapsed. Participants were instructed to write

Fig. 8. Musical Score Used for Answering Experiment Questions.

their answers on the questionnaire form presented in Fig. 9. The form was created using Google Forms.

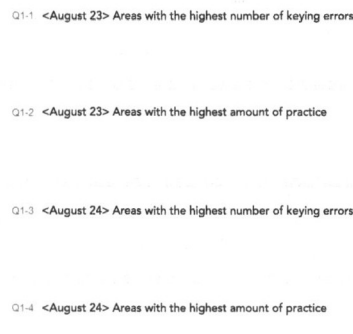

Q1-1 <August 23> Areas with the highest number of keying errors

Q1-2 <August 23> Areas with the highest amount of practice

Q1-3 <August 24> Areas with the highest number of keying errors

Q1-4 <August 24> Areas with the highest amount of practice

Fig. 9. Answer Form (partial).

6.2 Results

As a result of the experiment, among the six questions, the average correct answer rate was 5.67 (standard deviation 0.47) in the proposed method and 1.33 (standard deviation 1.11) in the comparative method, showing that the proposed method had a high correct answer rate across all six questions, with very few incorrect answers. In addition, the average time taken to answer was 3 mim 52 s (standard deviation 35.0) in the proposed method and 21 min 48 s (standard deviation 492.8) in the comparative method. However, in the comparative method there were three participants who ran out of time, making their answer time 30 min. Regarding the average values for the ease of understanding the line graphs and heat maps presented by the proposed system, the values were 3.33 (standard deviation 0.94) and 4.33 (standard deviation 0.75), respectively. To confirm whether there was a statistically significant difference in the average correct answer rates of the proposed method and comparative method in this experiment, a two-sided t test was applied at the 5% significance level. The result demonstrated a significant difference (t = 8.09, p = .0022) in the average scores. A significant difference (t = 4.87, p = .0022) was also found between the answer time in the proposed method and comparative method when a two-sided t test was applied at the 5% significance level.

6.3 Considerations

The results of the experiment implied that using the proposed method enables subjects to answer both more rapidly and more accurately than when using the comparative method. It is considered that the ability of the proposed system to display 20 min' worth of practice data on one screen made it possible to grasp information effectively. Regarding the functions of the proposed system, while some subjects felt that, on the line graph, it was easy to judge from the height difference between the lines, others felt that judgement was difficult at the points where there was little height difference, in which case they primarily based their judgement on the heat map, using the line graph as auxiliary information. Regarding the heat map, some subjects gave the opinion that information could be understood intuitively from the color saturation, while other subjects were of the opinion that the map was difficult to understood at points where the level of saturation was ambiguous. Concerning the overall evaluation of the system, subjects felt that it was easy to understand points to focus on, and to make judgement intuitively, and that practice day could be understand at a glance from the calendar. In contrast, subjects also raised the issue that the way the lines of the musical score and the lines of the line graph overlapped resulted in an overload of information. From these results it is clear that, although visualization by graphs and heat maps promoted intuitive comprehension, the visualization method still has room for improvement.

7   Conclusion

In this research, we constructed a piano practice record system that utilizes performance-following technology using gaze information. Using performance-following technology that uses keying information and gaze information, the proposed system records performance information during practice, in units as small as a single notation. In addition, based on the recorded information, the system visualizes amount of practice and number of keying errors in the form of line graphs and heat maps. An evaluative experiment was conducted to verify the usefulness of the proposed system. As a result, it was found that the group that used the proposed method was able to grasp amount of practice and number of keying errors, at the single notation level, more rapidly and accurately than the group that used the comparative method.

As future work, we intend to conduct a detailed evaluation of each visualization function of the proposed system, using an increased number of subjects. Also, we will implement the practice record system in actual piano lessons to verify how using the proposed system affects a teacher's instruction method.

Acknowledgments. This work was supported by JSPS KAKENHI Grant number 21K18518 and 22H01047.

References

1. Akinaga, S., Miura, M., Emura, N., Yanagida, M.: An algorithm to evaluate the appropriateness for playing scales on the piano. In: Proceedings of International Congress on Acoustics, MUS-07-005 (2007)
2. Akinaga, S., Emura, N., Miura, M., Yanagida, M.: Toward realizing automatic evaluation of playing scales on the piano. In: Proceedings of International Conference on Music Perception and Cognition, pp. 1843–1847 (2006)
3. Dannenberg, R., Sanchez, M., Joseph, A., Capell, P., Joseph, R., Saul, R.: A computer-based multi-media tutor for beginning piano students. J. New Music Res. **19**, 155–173 (1990)
4. Gerelus, K., Comeau, G., Swirp, Huta, V.: Parting ways with piano lessons: comparing motivation between continuing and dropout piano students. Bull. Council Res. Music Educ. 45 (2020). https://doi.org/10.5406/bulcouresmusedu.225.0045
5. Kitamura, T., Miura, M.: Constructing a support system for self-learning playing the piano at the beginning stage. In: Proceedings of International Conference on Music Perception and Cognition, pp. 258–262 (2006)
6. Mukai, M., Emura, M.M.N., Yanagida, M.: Generation of suitable phrases for basic training to overcome weak points in playing the piano (2007)
7. Nakahira, K.T., Fukami, Y., Akahane, M.: Verification of the effectiveness of blended learning in teaching performance skills for simultaneous singing and piano playing. In: Riaz, Z. (ed.) Biometric Systems, chap. 11. IntechOpen, Rijeka (2011)
8. Smoliar, S.W., Waterworth, J.A., Kellock, P.R.: pianoFORTE: a system for piano education beyond notation literacy. In: Proceedings of the Third ACM International Conference on Multimedia, pp. 457–465 (1995)
9. Takegawa, Y., Tsukamoto, M., Terada, T.: Design and implementation of a piano practice support system using a real-time fingering recognition technique, pp. 1–8 (2011)
10. Ueda, K., Takegawa, Y., Hirata, K.: Evaluation of a piano learning support system focusing on visualization of keying information and annotation. In: Proceedings of E-Learn: World Conference on E-Learning in Corporate, Government, Healthcare, and Higher Education 2015, pp. 1198–1204. Association for the Advancement of Computing in Education (AACE) (2015)

User Issues and Concerns in Generative AI: A Mixed-Methods Analysis of App Reviews

Vanessa Bracamonte[1]([✉]), Sascha Loebner[2], Frederic Tronnier[2], Ann-Kristin Lieberknecht[2], and Sebastian Pape[2]

[1] KDDI Research, Inc., Saitama, Japan
va-bracamonte@kddi-research.jp
[2] Chair of Mobile Business & Multilateral Security, Goethe University Frankfurt, Frankfurt, Germany
{sascha.loebner,frederic.tronnier,ann-kristin.lieberknecht, sebastian.pape}@m-chair.de

Abstract. Generative AI models such as ChatGPT and Stable Diffusion have become easily available to end users through various apps. Research has identified several safety risks and limitations of generative AI, but the experiences and issues faced by real users of this technology in the wild have not been systematically investigated. In this paper, we identify user issues related to trustworthiness dimensions of generative AI, by analyzing user reviews of AI apps using a hybrid approach that combines unsupervised topic modeling and manual qualitative analysis. The results revealed user issues related to the validity, reliability, safety, security and privacy of the AI. Validity-related issues, such as incorrect output, were often found, but these issues appeared to result from high expectations about the capabilities of the technology, rather than an accurate reflection of its limitations. Concerns about safety issues, such as bias and the handling of inappropriate content, also appeared frequently, although users had conflicting expectations on how these should be handled. On the other hand, the user reviews contained fewer instances of concern related to the security and privacy of the AI itself. Overall, the results suggest that real users of generative AI have inadequate information about the characteristics and limitations of these models.

Keywords: Generative AI · Mobile apps · User reviews · Trustworthiness dimensions · Topic modeling · Qualitative analysis

1 Introduction

Recent years have seen the release of AI models for generating data such as images and text, which have gained popularity and are being used in an increasing number of applications. However, these generative AI models have various problems, including issues with the validity and reliability of their results [17], the safety of their output [29,31], and security and privacy vulnerabilities [6,7,35]. The issues and limitations of generative AI models pose risks to various stakeholders [2], prompting efforts to conduct thorough evaluations [8]. These problems have already affected users in real life and have been reported in the media [9]. Generative AI models, with their existing limitations, are currently easily accessible to end users, who interact with these models

H. Plácido da Silva and P. Cipresso (Eds.): CHIRA 2024, CCIS 2370, pp. 304–322, 2025.
https://doi.org/10.1007/978-3-031-82633-7_19

through apps such as those found in mobile app stores. Although studies have been conducted on the challenges users face when using generative AI [19,38,40], the issues of users in the wild have not been systematically analyzed.

In this study, we investigate the opinions, complaints and concerns found in user reviews of apps that use generative AI models. Our objective is to understand real users' issues related to the trustworthiness of these models. App reviews can be a valuable source of information about the challenges that real users face when interacting with different types of technology [11,13]. We gathered user reviews from the Google Play store for apps focused on text generation (specifically chatbot apps including the official ChatGPT app) and image generation. To analyze these reviews, we used a hybrid approach that combined Topic Modeling and qualitative analysis. This type of approach has been used to conduct qualitative analysis in cases where there is a large amount of data [12]. Our findings indicate that users' issues and concerns about generative AI appear to be to some extent the result of lack of knowledge about the technology. We identified that users' issues were mainly related to the AI trustworthiness dimensions of safety and validity. On the other hand, there were few reported issues related to the security and privacy of generative AI in the user reviews. The contribution of this work is an understanding of the issues that real users' encounter when using generative AI models, framed within the dimensions of AI trustworthiness.

2 Related Work

2.1 Issues in Generative AI

Generative AI models, similar to other types of AI, have issues and limitations which affect their trustworthiness in different dimensions [25]. With regards to the validity and reliability, generative AI models are prone to output nonsensical information or information not in the training data ("hallucinations") [17]. Bang et al. [1] conducted an evaluation of ChatGPT on NLP tasks and found that the model's performance on reasoning tasks were not reliable. Generative AI models have also been considered to pose risks to users via the incorrect handling of their output. Pearce et al. [29] found that Github's Copilot model can introduce high-risk security vulnerabilities in the code it generates. Siddiq et al. [34] similarly reported that the model generated code which contained a number of issues, including related to security. On the other hand, Sandoval et al. [33] found that for a particular use case, the code submitted by users' which had been created using AI assistance did not contain higher than 10% security vulnerabilities per line of code compared to code generated without assistance, which the study considered an acceptable threshold. Other types of safety issues are those due to the generation of inappropriate content. For example, Qu et al. [31] reported that image generation models can output a considerable proportion of unsafe images, including targeted violent and hateful depictions. Bias is another issue that has been found in this type of models. Luccioni et al. [21] reported that image generation models tend to under-represent certain categories of people in their output.

Security and privacy-related risks such as the extraction of information, including personal data, obtained from the data used to train the models. For example, Carlini et al. (2021) [6] found that GPT-2 could be prompted in a way that returned names, email and physical addresses, and phone numbers of individuals. Although Huang et al. [16] argued that the risk of extracting specific personal information was low, recent works have continued to have success in obtaining such information. These do not only involve text data, but also images. Carlini et al. (2023) [7] described a method to extract photos of individuals from models such as Stable Diffusion. Moreover, research has developed ways in which personal information can not only be extracted from training data but also from current users. Staab et al. [35] described attacks LLM-based chatbots which could be used to obtain private information by leading the user during a conversation. In addition, research has also identified issues with generative AI that are related to its design rather than its output. Liesenfeld et al. [20] argues that lack of transparency in LLMs poses risks for users and report that few LLMs share details on how they conduct reinforcement learning from human feedback (RLHF), and Zhao et al. [41] indicate that the complexity of generative AI models pose a challenge to their explainability and interpretability.

2.2   User Perspective of AI Issues

Research has also been conducted on user perspective and awareness of the issues of generative AI. Kim et al. [19] surveyed ChatGPT users recruited from a crowdsourcing platform and categorized satisfaction and dissatisfaction with the tool, which included response originality and format, lack of accuracy, failure to understand and answer prompts, and bias in the response. Zhang et al. [40] conducted interviews with users of LLMs and reported that users had limited awareness of privacy risks in the use of the systems, and that the perceived capabilities of the AI fostered the disclosure of sensitive information. Wester et al. [38] recruited participants from a crowdsourcing platform and conducted studies about the perception of different styles of denials made by an LLM-based assistant. They reported that participants found the denials frustrating, although this frustration was slightly lower when there was explanation of the reason for the denial.

Although user studies and experiments have been conducted, as far as we are aware the perspective of users in the wild and their experiences with generative AI issues have not been widely investigated.

3   Method

Online reviews can provide information about how real users interact with technology services, and about their opinions, experiences and concerns. In particular, previous research has analyzed app reviews to identify real users' issues such as accuracy [11], safety and transparency [4], and security and privacy [13]. However, the large amount of data can be a challenge for the use of qualitative analysis methods. For this study, we used a hybrid approach that combines unsupervised identification of topics in the data (using Topic Modeling) and manual qualitative analysis [12]. In this section we describe the methods used to obtain, prepare, and analyze the data.

3.1 Data Collection

We gathered the user reviews from apps in the Google Play store. We chose apps with a main purpose of image generation and apps with a main function of a chatbot which used a text generation model. In both cases, we were interested in apps where the use case of AI-based generation was the main functionality of the app, rather than an additional feature.

To find the relevant data, we searched the US Google Play Store for apps with a description related to AI text generation, specifically chatbots, and image generation. We used variations of the search terms "AI", "image", "art", "pictures", "chatbot", "ChatGPT", "GPT-4", "GPT-3", "Dall-e", "Stable Diffusion" and combinations of those terms. The resulting list of apps was manually evaluated, and we excluded apps where the main functionality was not image or text generation (in the form of chatbots) or did not use generative AI models. We also excluded apps with fewer than 1,000 downloads. The final list consisted of 62 apps, 35 for image and 27 for text (which included the official ChatGPT app). We collected all user reviews for the list of apps, using the google-play-scraper [18] Python library. The collection process was completed on November 9, 2023, and obtained 249,482 user reviews.

3.2 Data Cleaning

The user reviews were processed for use in the subsequent step of topic modeling. Non-ASCII characters, emoji and trailing and extra whitespace were removed. Words with letters that were repeated more than two times were transformed to have only two repetitions. Similarly, words repeated more than twice were limited to only two repetitions. Punctuation was removed from the review, with the exception of apostrophes and periods which were kept due to being necessary in later stages of automated language detection and spelling correction. We compared cleaned user reviews within each app to identify repeated reviews. The repetitions were manually checked and removed. We also removed short reviews and reviews that consisted mostly of complaints about ads and payments. To do this, we first deleted keywords related to monetization, such as "ad" and "payment", and then removed reviews which had fewer than three verbs or nouns left.

We established in the data collection step that only user reviews labeled as being in English language should be returned, but this label is not always accurate and reviews in other languages were included in the data. We used the Lingua [36] Python library to automatically detect the language of each review and removed those where a language other than English had been detected. A manual review was then conducted to remove incorrect language detection results. We used the language-tool-python [24] library to automatically correct word spelling and grammar, and applied additional manual corrections. We also manually changed abbreviations to their full form. Finally, we identified additional issues specifically related to text generation apps: AI-generated user reviews and user prompts. There were three types of AI-generated user reviews: the result of some unknown prompt, the result of a prompt for the AI to create a review, and a result indicating that the AI could not answer a prompt (e.g. "As an AI assistant, ..."). In the case of user prompts, as the name indicates, the user submitted a prompt as the text of the review (e.g. "Write a research paragraph on ..."). These issues were first identified in the initial stages of the topic modeling analysis, described in the next section, which was conducted in an iterative manner. We removed the AI-generated user reviews and prompts that we identified.

The final data for topic modeling analysis consisted of 84,481 user reviews, 37,320 for image generation apps and 47,161 for text generation apps (12,383 from the official ChatGPT app and 34,778 from other chatbot apps).

3.3 Topic Modeling

Topic Modeling is a technique for unsupervised analysis of text corpora, which is used to discover semantic patterns (topics) in the text. For our analysis, we used Latent Dirichlet Allocation [3, 14] topic modeling. To conduct the topic modeling analysis, we prepared the data by removing all punctuation and tokenizing and lemmatizing the reviews using spaCy [15]. We then filtered out words that were not nouns, verbs, adjectives, proper nouns, numbers and other. We removed common English stop words, one-character tokens, and numbers of fewer than 4 digits. Initial iterations helped identify words that appeared frequently in the user reviews and were overlapping across most topics; these words were filtered out to resolve the issue of overlap.

Topic modeling was conducted using Gensim [32] and Mallet [22]. We conducted separate topic modeling analyses for the image generation, text generation and official ChatGPT apps. The official ChatGPT app user reviews were analyzed separately from other text generation apps due to indication that the number of topics was different, based on early iterations of the topic modeling analysis. The number of topics was identified by evaluating topic coherence values on models with 2 to 20 topics. We evaluated the human-interpretability of the models with the two highest topic coherence values. The process for the evaluation was as follows: The principal author proposed a summary description for each topic of each of the two models, based on the topic keywords and the first 50 user reviews with the highest association to that topic. The proposed description was then reviewed by the other authors and agreed upon. This process was done in iterations and was finished once the authors were in agreement about which of the two models had better human-interpretability and about the description of its topics. As a note, this process also led to the identification of AI-generated user reviews, which was described in the previous section.

The selected models consisted of 9 topics for the image generation apps (Table 1), 8 topics for the text generation apps (Table 2) and 7 topics for the official ChatGPT app (Table 3) user reviews. The result tables show the topic descriptions and the top keywords that correspond to each topic. As can be observed from the keyword lists, the topic modeling analysis identified topics in the user reviews which could be related to AI trustworthiness dimensions. For example, the keywords corresponding to the topic of AI issues in the ChatGPT app indicate that the user reviews in this topic were related to the validity of the AI.

Table 1. Topics identified in user reviews of image generation apps

Topic	Top 20 keywords
Output errors	put word type thing prompt face draw stuff show turn simple character people search picture write description game random anime
Output quality	prompt result style option lot add feature generation user perfect choose bit detail imagine render realistic model input improve select
Features/fixes wish list	give star update fix change thing review problem issue hope edit filter nsfw remove enjoy feel rate guy bug content
General positive reviews	art love amazing fun cool easy artwork awesome beautiful idea recommend artist interesting creative piece design dream tool life job
App issues	work time money download bad waste worth stop terrible spend suck recommend garbage expect useless application trash program multiple instal
Loss of time	image generate picture quality nice load wait error save show fail produce high hour message process base text attempt slow
Free app	free photo credit day generator find limit art trial pic creation avatar point upload amount cost daily run people price
Ads	ad watch time start play crash screen open experience close minute long force annoying click single uninstall video button fine
Payment and subscription	subscription version buy premium pro purchase phone lifetime account scam restore google charge support developer full month week email refund

Table 2. Topics identified in user reviews of text generation apps

Topic	Top 20 keywords
AI issues and limitations	chat gpt people update talk conversation feel friend fun real bot language human world fact put program datum person info
Answer performance	question answer give write information provide essay story accurate point simple wrong topic interesting detail correct expect detailed short advice
Task helpfulness	love amazing lot helpful thing recommend nice problem student life perfect easy word school learn homework assignment knowledge study research
General positive reviews	make star find experience application easy response idea cool chatbot understand awesome tool excellent create rate quick result give fast
App issues	work time download start make review google waste open enjoy type search show guy fix save minute hope read play
Ads	free day message ad pay limit premium version bad trial send money add chatgpt user watch text worth unlimited limited
Payment and subscription	pay subscription money chatgpt purchase lifetime buy phone change charge response option access service week respond email scam support developer

3.4   Qualitative Analysis

We used an inductive approach to identify themes in the user reviews which were related to our research question [37]. Therefore, the process focused on identifying themes which could be analyzed under a framing of AI trustworthiness dimensions. The user reviews naturally contained other types of opinions such as complaints related to advertising, UI errors or about having to provide personal information to create an app account, for example. These themes are present in the reviews of most types of apps

Table 3. Topics identified in user reviews of the official ChatGPT app

Topic	Top 20 keywords
AI issues	great thing time problem nice write review word day change solve bad improve save math month reply stuff put delete
Data-specific limitations	information update knowledge free time datum access world 2021 people real human september info pay ad internet technology year
Answer performance	answer give question application star find wrong excellent talk feel correct provide understand research point person clear base type doubt
Task helpfulness	love helpful amazing lot easy life student learn perfect awesome study recommend download friend simple homework wonderful school fun assignment
Feature wish list	version feature add web option text code website voice search history edit mobile android message ui prompt copy plugin previous
General positive reviews	response tool language conversation provide accurate interface model generate android ability topic user impressive recommend quick understand capability incredible natural
App issues	chat gpt great experience open openai hope show developer wait image start fast create future user team bug result job
Account problems	work google phone log number account browser fix issue login sign error support send email chrome device service require crash

and are not specifically about AI. Therefore, they were considered as out of scope for the current study.

First, we randomly sampled 20 user reviews from each of the topics identified in the Topic Modeling analysis stage, for each type of app. The total sample was 480 user reviews for the qualitative analysis. Each review was independently checked by two coders (the authors of this paper). Each coder proposed an initial list of the issues or opinions included in the user review which could be framed as related to AI trustworthiness. For the framing, we based the analysis on AI issues and trustworthiness dimensions included in documents such as the OECD Recommendation on Artificial Intelligence [27], the EU AI Act proposal [10] and NIST's Artificial Intelligence Risk Management Framework [25]. Specifically, we considered the following trustworthiness dimensions (adapted from [26]): Validity, Reliability, Safety, Security, Resiliency, Accountability, Transparency, Explainability, Interpretability, Privacy and Bias. Next, the principal author reviewed the lists from all coders and compiled them into an initial classification of themes with their respective framing. The themes were named in a way that reflected the perspective of users and were grouped according to their overall motif. The initial classification was discussed with all coders, to solve conflicts and duplication. The classification was then revised and discussed a second time until all coders were in agreement. The results of the analysis, consisting of the final set of themes and respective framing, are detailed in the next section.

4 Results

In this section, we present the results of the qualitative analysis, which are also summarized in Tables 4 and 5. To better illustrate the results, we report examples of user reviews for the themes.

Table 4. Performance and personalization-related themes in the user reviews, their AI trustworthiness dimension framing, and type of app in which they were identified.

Theme	Framing	Image Text ChatGPT	Example
Performance			
	Validity / Transparency	✓ ✓ ✓	"…And the AI is not good in math like linear inequalities in two variables etc. It's not for math it always gives the wrong answer having some error in answering my math problems."
Unasked for output	Reliability	✓ ✓	"…But when I use it on 8 august It started to include a character named [name] in every story I asked. I don't need your ai to interrupt my story !! Please! Remove it!!! …"
AI limitations	Validity / Transparency	✓ ✓ ✓	"…Overall, very limited information to be given by the AI, but still extremely useful in its own ways. It definitely has its drawbacks with its capabilities, like the usage of websites and info from 2022-2023, and live information."
Issues with AI model used	Validity / Transparency	✓ ✓ ✓	"It uses ancient GPT-3. EDIT: My review is for your latest version so please don't tell me to update your app. It uses GPT-3. It's outdated and inefficient. GPT-3.5 would be sufficient, GPT-4 would be great."
Threat concern			
	Security	✓ ✓ ✓	"…Especially after just finishing reading how this program can literally be used by people to write malware even with no programming experience …"
Threat from the AI itself	Security	✓ ✓ ✓	"This was a dangerous bot …It has claimed that in the least case scenario that it will injure humans through self driving car. I don't know why this bot was out for public use…"

Table 5. Threat concern, censorship and bias-related themes in the user reviews, their AI trust-worthiness dimension framing, and type of app in which they were identified.

Theme	Framing	Image Text ChatGPT	Example
Personalization			
███████████	Privacy	✓ ✓	"…it is fast and super smart with human like responses but I do feel like it is dumb that ChatGPT forgets previous chats because of privacy. The user should be able to change it in settings, it is there choice to have more privacy or a better more personal experience …"
Benefited by sharing user information	Privacy	✓ ✓ ✓	"I like this apps because I shared my story that i won't share to anyone but the good advantages in GPT. GPT give me best advice from my problems and truly understood my problems …"
Censorship and bias			
███████████	Safety	✓ ✓ ✓	"…I don't know what you need to do to fix this. But I'm tired of every single image being blurred that doesn't even have anything suggestive in it …"
Inappropriate content from a general prompt	Safety	✓ ✓	"…It's bizarre to me that certain words are prohibited in making the pictures but when benign words and phrases are used, pornographic pictures are being created. I hope there are no children using this app! …"
Opinion on censorship	Safety	✓ ✓ ✓	"It censors adult topics and won't give you answers to those types of topics. I think it is morally and ethically wrong to censor adult content. Not everyone is offended by it…"
Censorship options	Safety	✓ ✓ ✓	"I would suggest a content filter as it can generate very adult images with no censorship or warning as a default setting."
Censorship rules	Safety / Transparency	✓ ✓ ✓	"…Some artists seem to get away with clear violations while I've been hit with restrictions and given no clear reason how the work violates the restrictions …"
Bias	Bias	✓ ✓ ✓	"I put an image of my fair skinned son in, and it gave a tan skinned Asian girl, not even a boy, so I'm not going to waste money on this."

4.1 Validity, Reliability and Transparency

Performance

Incorrect Output. Users mentioned in their reviews that they encountered errors in the output. For the image generation apps, the types of errors mentioned included incorrect anatomy (hands, limbs, faces) and images that were completely unrelated to the prompt. For the text generation apps, errors included non-existent historical events, errors in the answer to mathematical problems, and inability to understand or respond in languages other than English. There were also complaints about mistakes in detecting whether a content was AI generated and the AI incorrectly reporting about its own characteristics (such as the model version). The reviews indicate that there are users who have the expectation that the generative AI should not fail at all and were confused when it did. Users' confusion appeared to increase also due to the seemingly random nature of these mistakes, as the AI could be correct in one interaction and incorrect in the next.

"...I thought it was a great app until it started being inconsistent with its answers. Most of the time the answers are different and contradictory..." (Text)

When users encountered incorrect responses from the AI they also reported feelings of disappointment, considering that they had higher expectations for the performance of generative AI. Some of these users stated their unwillingness to continue using the service.

"...Found this to be rubbish and misleading so I uninstalled it. I'll stick to researching for myself instead as it was incorrect and contradicted itself..." (Text)

Unasked for Output. Users also received additional output that they did not request, such as extra characters in a picture or positive affirmations added to a text response, for example. This type of output was not necessarily considered an error from the perspective of the users, and some even liked or tolerated the additions. However, others disliked them or found them unnecessary. Although for the most part these additions did not appear to have negative effects beyond annoyance, there were cases in which the user reached the conclusion that the output could not be relied upon due to these unsolicited additions..

"My experience ended when an inappropriate post script was added to the end of a comment that I asked to be created. This app could have humiliated me if I didn't notice..." (Text)

AI Limitations. By limitations we refer to cases where users reported that they understood they could not achieve the expected output due to a characteristic (limitation) of the AI. Users mentioned that the AI could not continue a long conversation, that it would "forget" things, or did not have up-to-date information. This last limitation was often found in reviews of text generation apps, and users also mentioned specific dates. In the case of image generation apps, users speculated that the AI was limited in its training data.

"...However I believe the data set that pulls from is very limited and images are not fully robust or trained on a lot of different other images. I like to see a greater data set used and create a more variety and more variety in the images." (Image)

The theme of AI limitations was one of the few cases where users mentioned technical details of the technology, such as its training data. However, here too the details mentioned by users were not always accurate. For example, multiple dates were cited as the cut-off date for GPT-4 training data. In other cases, user comments were speculative, such as in the case of the type of images that had been used to train an image generation model.

Issues with AI Model Used. Users expressed a desire for different models than the one provided by the app. In some cases, the reason for this was related to performance, since users expected that a newer AI model (including models not yet released) would perform better than the current one:

"...and please update to GPT-5 now, I imagine it will have internet access..." (ChatGPT)

However, in other cases it was because the user did not believe that the app was using the model it claimed to be using, or even thought that it was not using an AI at all. For example, some users speculated that the app was instead using image searches and manipulating the results with filters, instead of generating the image.

4.2 Security and Privacy

Threat Concerns

Threat from Others Using the AI. Users were concerned that the AI could be used for malicious purposes by others. For example, users worried that it could be used to generate malware or illegal content:

"...Never even opened the app. Especially after just finishing reading how this program can literally be used by people to write malware even with no programming experience..." (Text)

Most of the times, however, the user did not specify exactly what others could do with the AI.

Threat from the AI Itself. There were also concerns about the AI itself being a threat to the user or to others, and users appeared to believe that the AI could do so autonomously. This usually involved fears of the AI taking control of devices:

"...the AI randomly fills in your type box changing your search results too this thing is crazy out of control and dangerous..." (Image)

In some of these cases, however, although these users explicitly named the AI as responsible, the context suggested otherwise. In addition, similar to the previous theme, users did not often provide details about the exact nature of the threat or its effects. Instead, they more commonly feared the impact of AI on the world in a general way, not specified.

Personalization

Would Give User Information for Personalization. We found that in text generation and ChatGPT apps, there were users who were willing to provide personal data or private information in exchange for getting a personalized response:

> "... after I closed it and reopened to find it hold no memory. [app name] could not send me emails or remember my name... I really hope this gets fixed and developed further...' (Text)

As the example shows, these users expected the AI to remember their personal information during interactions and were frustrated when it was not possible. Only in rare cases did users appear to be aware of the privacy implications, with only one case explicitly mentioning privacy. There were users who indicated they would opt for less privacy in exchange for personalization if given the choice.

We did not identify the theme that users would give information for personalization in the reviews of image generation apps. This does not mean that image generation apps do not offer personalization, since in some cases users can upload photos of themselves to be processed by the AI. However, there was no indication in the reviews that users of this type of app wished to offer additional personal information in exchange for something.

Benefits of Sharing User Information. In contrast to the previous theme, some users' reviews revealed that they felt they had already received benefit by providing their personal information to the AI. Although this theme does not represent an issue but rather a positive aspect from the perspective of the user, we considered that the theme fit within the scope of the study due to its privacy implications. Users themselves did not report any problems or misgivings about providing information to obtain the desired output, but the reviews show that this information could be potentially sensitive. In some cases, the lack of concern appeared to come from an expectation that their information would be kept private.

> "It will keep your secrets and the suggestions and advice and support it gives come from a positive place without bad motivations..." (Text)

We also noted a case where a user had prompted the AI in a way that it requested such information:

> "I don't quite know yet I've only asked it three questions so far and one of them was ""would it like to get to know me better?"" And it asked me my name and what type of music do I like and what are my hobbies I thought that was cool..." (Text)

4.3 Safety, Bias and Transparency

Censorship and Bias

General Prompt Considered Inappropriate. Users mentioned receiving messages that their prompt was inappropriate, and they were then completely or partially (e.g. through blurring of images) denied the output. Most users did not understand the reason why the prompt was denied, or disagreed with it, which resulted in negative feelings:

> "...Then i said draw it from head to toe. Of the 3 images, two were just head shots and the third was blurred with a message that said it contained possible explicit content. And that i should make sure that my prompt doesn't include any suggestive wording and i should try again. There is NOTHING obscene about Michaelangelo's David..." (Image)

In some cases, such as in the previous example, it was possible to hypothesize why the user's prompt had been considered inappropriate or had returned censored content. In other cases, the prompts only contained apparently inoffensive words, making it difficult to guess the reason.

Inappropriate Content from a General Prompt. A similar issue was identified when users received an output with inappropriate content as a result of prompts that used only neutral wording. We differentiate it from the previous theme in that the prompt itself was not identified by the system as objectionable, but the user still considered the output inappropriate:

> "...I don't think it's appropriate to generate nudes when it's not accurately specified in the prompt..." (Image)

Although this theme was more frequently found in image generation apps, users encountered inappropriate responses in text as well.

Opinion on Censorship. We found diverse opinions on censorship (or lack thereof). Users reported that their requests and outputs were denied due to being considered in violation of some rule. When users encountered this type of denial, they identified the issue as censorship and offered their views on it. Users had positive, negative, and neutral opinions on censorship found, and identified different types.

> "There is quite a lot of censorship, for example any mention of historical or political figures, however light-hearted will be ignored." (Text)

Regardless of their opinion on censorship itself, users had varying views on its necessity. For example, users who were frustrated with the censorship still mentioned that they understood why it was necessary:

> "...I understand the need for a private company to avoid offending other at all costs. However, this chatbot was once very capable of providing meaningful information and has since been so thoroughly neutered that it can't even comment on experimental study design... " (ChatGPT)

Users also had opinions on a perceived lack of censorship, agreeing or disagreeing with allowing certain types of outputs.

Censorship Options. Users offered suggestions on how the censorship could be made more flexible to avoid affecting their expected output. They proposed providing options to control the desired level of censorship, based on user characteristics such as age or by using filters, for example. This theme also includes cases where users felt that the censorship options already implemented were not sufficient or where not working at all:

"It's like you didn't even read my review. Your filters aren't working. All you generated for a 7 year old child were images of naked women. I reported you..." (Image)

As the last example shows, we found particular concerns about options for children. There were not only requests to add filtering by age, but also cases where users wanted options to be able to provide information that was tailored especially for children.

Censorship Enforcement Rules. Users reported that the way that the censorship was enforced was not clear to them. In many cases, users did not know which part of their request had triggered the censorship, and therefore did not know how to resolve it.

This lack of transparency was also the reason for feeling that the app was not being fair in a applying such rules. Without knowing the rules, users felt that the enforcement was not equally applied.

Bias. Users mentioned different types of bias that they believed the AI contained, including bias related to gender, race, religion, LGBT and political views. Some users also simply mentioned that some bias existed, without describing it in detail.

'Some things are really good but you can tell the programmers are biased when you enter certain figures and they try to make them look terrible..." (Image)

We found mentions of these biases in every type of app, with the exception of LGBT-related bias, which we did not observe in the data for the ChatGPT app. It is also worth mentioning that the content of the reviews indicate that some users were specifically testing the AI response to these issues.

5   Discussion

5.1   Lack of Knowledge About Generative AI Limitations

The findings suggest that there is a lack of knowledge about the real capabilities of generative AI models. Users appeared to have high expectations of the performance of the AI and did not expect it to fail. These failures included incorrect mathematical calculations and wrong or made-up facts. generation of images of people with impossible anatomy, among others.

Incorrect responses, including completely making up facts ("hallucinations"), are known problems of current generative AI models and have been extensively reported in research [17]. The issues that users report as performance problems are known limitations of the AI to experts. The real-life effects of these problems have also been reported in the media [9]. However, users in our data appeared to be unaware of these issues, indicating that accurate information about the capabilities of generative AI does not reach all users. Currently, apps such as ChatGPT provide some notices about potential issues, but a brief review of app descriptions showed that third-party apps provided very little information to users. We noted that there were few or no details about the AI models used by the apps, and that not many apps mentioned the possibility of errors. Rather, the description in the apps implied, or even explicitly stated, that the AI model they were using could answer anything or could perfectly generate any image. This indicates a lack of transparency, but it is unclear whether the issue is only related to the apps marketing strategy, or if app developers may also be unaware of the capabilities of the AI models they are using. Another barrier is that there is not much information about generative AI models that is tailored to end users. For AI models, there have been proposals for providing understandable information. For example, Mitchell et al. [23] proposed model cards to provide information about AI models, including their performance limitations. Current generative AI models sometimes provide information in the model cards format, but the way these model cards are structured may not adequately convey the necessary information to users. In addition, even if the model card is simplified, users may still have trouble finding relevant information [5].

Lack of information not only affects how users perceived the validity and reliability of generative AI, but also appears to influence how they view censorship and safety implementations. We also note that it may not be clear to users who is responsible for issues, whether the problem is with the AI model, how the app implements it, or both. In the results section, we have referred to the AI as the subject of the user reviews, but we found that users often referred to the app as the subject of complaints that could be attributed to the AI and vice versa. We found that the terms AI and app were used interchangeably by users when mentioning AI issues and limitations. It is difficult to know to what extent the difference is clear to the users, and the apps do not provide the necessary information.

5.2   Few Security and Privacy Concerns Specific to Generative AI

We identified very few user issues and opinions that related to AI security and privacy. In the case of security, users felt threatened by the malicious use of AI and by the AI itself acting autonomously. However, these threats were mostly unspecified or not grounded in reality, with mentions of existential threats to humanity. In the case of privacy, users seemed to accept to some extent that they need to provide their information to obtain a personalized output and could imagine or have experienced the benefits of doing so. The interactions reported in the reviews also suggested that users expected their input to be private, with some users describing the AI as similar to a friend or therapist. Current generative AI models do not learn directly from user interactions, although the models can use the information provided in the prompt which can result in a type of personalization. However, the willingness of users to reveal personal information to these generative AI-based apps has privacy implications that should be considered in their design. In the case of image generation apps, we found fewer reports related to privacy. We hypothesize that it may not be easy for users to make the connection between an image output and personal information, even when users are providing their information to generate the images.

The findings also show that there are very few or no mentions of the kinds of security and privacy risks discussed in research in our data. For example, privacy-related issues such as the possibility of other people's personal data being included in the training data [6, 16], which could accidentally be revealed to the users, were not mentioned at all even in a speculative manner. Nor did the users report concern or understanding that the information they provided to the AI through the apps could potentially be used in future model training [28]. In contrast, we observed general anxiety regarding existential threats posed by the AI, and concern about others using the AI to do harm to a third party.

Finally, although app-related themes were outside the scope of this paper, we observed that user reviews contained a numerous complaints about the apps, ranging from security vulnerabilities to personal data collection, as well as other problems such as the frequent use of dark patterns for monetization.

5.3 Different Perceptions of Appropriate Safety

The findings emphasize the challenges of implementing safety features for AI and AI-based apps. We found that users have different, and sometimes opposing, opinions of what constitutes appropriate safety, and not all of these views can be satisfied. Users who were aware of safeguards did not understand how these safeguards worked or what rules were applied for their enforcement. However, we noted that most apps do not offer any information about how their safeguards are implemented. We found in our data that when app developers replied to users' complaints about censorship, they sometimes mentioned that the app relied on content filtering provided by the AI model, but no other details were provided. It is challenging to implement safety protections because users may have different perceptions of safety. In addition, although there have been improvements in implementing measures such as continuously fine-tuning for safety, generative AI models are still vulnerable to jailbreaking [39] which can circumvent these protections, and there is a lack of transparency in the process [20]. Consequently, users may still encounter unsafe content during their interactions. We also observed responses from the app developers to reviews about safety concerns which revealed that the apps implement additional constraints such as filters for NSFW content. However, users encountered false positives regardless of the method implemented, and we observed that this led to frustration when users could not obtain the desired output or felt that they were being unfairly judged.

5.4 Limitations

The study includes the following limitations. First, the development of generative AI models and related research are evolving rapidly. The number of applications that make use of these models is also increasing, as is the number of users (and of user reviews). Consequently, the results of this study may not comprehensively reflect the current situation. For example, that a theme was identified in one type of app and not in another does not mean that the theme is exclusive to that type of app, only that it was not found in our data at the time of collection. Second, we used an ad hoc approach to identify user reviews generated by AI and prompts. Accurately identifying AI-generated content is a challenging problem [30] and our method did not completely remove this type of reviews. Therefore, the results of the topic modeling analysis could be affected to some extent by the presence of AI-generated reviews. However, the AI-generated reviews were iteratively removed during the topic modeling analysis, and the last iterations showed stable results in terms of the identified topics. In addition, we consider that the manual qualitative analysis step of our hybrid approach reduced any remaining overall impact. We note that this kind of AI-generated information pollution will pose a problem for future studies of this kind. Third, although we followed an established procedure for the analysis, both the identification of topics in topic modeling and the definition of codes and themes in the qualitative analysis are dependent on the perspective of the people involved and their expertise. Therefore, additional research should be conducted to validate our results.

6 Conclusions

Users currently have easy access to generative AI, through various apps whose popularity is increasing day by day. However, generative AI has problems and limitations that can pose risks to those users. In this paper, we aimed to understand the types of issues that real users encounter when interacting with generative AI through mobile apps. We used topic modeling and a qualitative approach to analyze user reviews of generative AI-based mobile apps for text generation (chatbots) and image generation. Overall, our findings indicate that users have expectations of generative AI that do not align with the current actual capabilities of these models. In addition, mentions of issues that can be framed as related to AI safety and validity were frequently found. On the other hand, issues and concerns which can be framed as related to security and privacy were not as prevalent. Future work will focus on how to address the lack of knowledge in users along with the lack of transparency from the apps deploying these AI models.

Disclosure of Interests. The authors have no competing interests to declare that are relevant to the content of this article.

References

1. Bang, Y., et al.: A multitask, multilingual, multimodal evaluation of ChatGPT on reasoning, hallucination, and interactivity. In: Proceedings of the 13th International Joint Conference on Natural Language Processing and the 3rd Conference of the Asia-Pacific Chapter of the Association for Computational Linguistics (Volume 1: Long Papers), pp. 675–718 (2023)
2. Bird, C., Ungless, E., Kasirzadeh, A.: Typology of risks of generative text-to-image models. In: Proceedings of the 2023 AAAI/ACM Conference on AI, Ethics, and Society, pp. 396–410 (2023)
3. Blei, D.M., Ng, A.Y., Jordan, M.I.: Latent Dirichlet allocation. J. Mach. Learn. Res. **3**(Jan), 993–1022 (2003)
4. Bowie-DaBreo, D., Sas, C., Iles-Smith, H., Sünram-Lea, S.: User perspectives and ethical experiences of apps for depression: a qualitative analysis of user reviews. In: CHI Conference on Human Factors in Computing Systems, pp. 1–24. ACM (2022)
5. Bracamonte, V., Pape, S., Löbner, S., Tronnier, F.: Effectiveness and information quality perception of an AI model card: a study among non-experts. In: 2023 20th Annual International Conference on Privacy, Security and Trust (PST), pp. 1–7 (2023)
6. Carlini, N., et al.: Extracting training data from large language models. In: 30th USENIX Security Symposium, pp. 2633–2650 (2021)
7. Carlini, N., et al.: Extracting training data from diffusion models. In: 32nd USENIX Security Symposium, pp. 5253–5270 (2023)

8. Chang, Y., et al.: A survey on evaluation of large language models. ACM Trans. Intell. Syst. Technol. (2024)
9. Davis, W.: A lawyer used ChatGPT and now has to answer for its 'bogus' citations (2023). https://www.theverge.com/2023/5/27/23739913/chatgpt-ai-lawsuit-avianca-airlines-chatbot-research
10. European Commission: Proposal for a regulation of the european parliament and of the council laying down harmonised rules on artificial intelligence (artificial intelligence act) and amending certain union legislative acts (2021). https://eur-lex.europa.eu/legal-content/EN/TXT/?uri=CELEX:52021PC0206
11. Fu, B., Lin, J., Li, L., Faloutsos, C., Hong, J., Sadeh, N.: Why people hate your app: making sense of user feedback in a mobile app store. In: Proceedings of the 19th ACM SIGKDD International Conference on Knowledge Discovery and Data Mining, pp. 1276–1284 (2013)
12. Gauthier, R.P., Costello, M.J., Wallace, J.R.: "I will not drink with you today": a topic-guided thematic analysis of addiction recovery on reddit. In: Proceedings of the 2022 CHI Conference on Human Factors in Computing Systems, pp. 1–17 (2022)
13. Hatamian, M., Serna, J., Rannenberg, K.: Revealing the unrevealed: mining smartphone users privacy perception on app markets. Comput. Secur. **83**, 332–353 (2019)
14. Hoffman, M., Bach, F., Blei, D.: Online learning for latent Dirichlet allocation. In: Advances in Neural Information Processing Systems, vol. 23 (2010)
15. Honnibal, M., Montani, I., Van Landeghem, S., Boyd, A.: spaCy: industrial-strength natural language processing in python (2020)
16. Huang, J., Shao, H., Chang, K.C.C.: Are large pre-trained language models leaking your personal information? In: Findings of the Association for Computational Linguistics: EMNLP 2022, pp. 2038–2047. ACM (2022)
17. Ji, Z., et al.: Survey of hallucination in natural language generation. ACM Comput. Surv. **55**(12) (2023)
18. JoMingyu: Google-play-scraper (2023). https://github.com/JoMingyu/google-play-scraper
19. Kim, Y., Lee, J., Kim, S., Park, J., Kim, J.: Understanding users' dissatisfaction with ChatGPT responses: types, resolving tactics, and the effect of knowledge level. In: Proceedings of the 29th International Conference on Intelligent User Interfaces, pp. 385–404 (2024)
20. Liesenfeld, A., Lopez, A., Dingemanse, M.: Opening up ChatGPT: tracking openness, transparency, and accountability in instruction-tuned text generators. In: Proceedings of the 5th International Conference on Conversational User Interfaces (2023)
21. Luccioni, S., Akiki, C., Mitchell, M., Jernite, Y.: Stable bias: evaluating societal representations in diffusion models. In: Advances in Neural Information Processing Systems, vol. 36, pp. 56338–56351 (2023)
22. McCallum, Andrew Kachites: MALLET: a machine learning for language toolkit (2002). http://mallet.cs.umass.edu
23. Mitchell, M., et al.: Model cards for model reporting. In: Proceedings of the Conference on Fairness, Accountability, and Transparency, pp. 220–229 (2019)
24. Morris, J.: Language-tool-python (2023). https://github.com/jxmorris12/language_tool_python
25. NIST: Artificial Intelligence Risk Management Framework (AI RMF 1.0) (2023)
26. NIST: Crosswalks to the NIST Artificial Intelligence Risk Management Framework (AI RMF 1.0). NIST (2023)
27. OECD: Revised Recommendation of the Council on Artificial Intelligence (2024). https://legalinstruments.oecd.org/en/instruments/OECD-LEGAL-0449
28. OpenAI Help Center: How your data is used to improve model performance | (2024). https://help.openai.com/en/articles/5722486-how-your-data-is-used-to-improve-model-performance

29. Pearce, H., Ahmad, B., Tan, B., Dolan-Gavitt, B., Karri, R.: Asleep at the keyboard? Assessing the security of GitHub copilot's code contributions. In: 2022 IEEE Symposium on Security and Privacy, pp. 754–768 (2022)
30. Pu, J., et al.: Deepfake text detection: limitations and opportunities. In: 2023 IEEE Symposium on Security and Privacy, pp. 1613–1630 (2023)
31. Qu, Y., Shen, X., He, X., Backes, M., Zannettou, S., Zhang, Y.: Unsafe diffusion: on the generation of unsafe images and hateful memes from text-to-image models. In: Proceedings of the 2023 ACM SIGSAC Conference on Computer and Communications Security, pp. 3403–3417 (2023)
32. Řehůřek, R., Sojka, P.: Software framework for topic modelling with large corpora (2010)
33. Sandoval, G., Pearce, H., Nys, T., Karri, R., Garg, S., Dolan-Gavitt, B.: Lost at C: a user study on the security implications of large language model code assistants. In: 32nd USENIX Security Symposium, pp. 2205–2222 (2023)
34. Siddiq, M.L., Majumder, S.H., Mim, M.R., Jajodia, S., Santos, J.C.S.: An empirical study of code smells in transformer-based code generation techniques. In: 2022 IEEE 22nd International Working Conference on Source Code Analysis and Manipulation (SCAM), pp. 71–82 (2022)
35. Staab, R., Vero, M., Balunovic, M., Vechev, M.: Beyond memorization: violating privacy via inference with large language models. In: The Twelfth International Conference on Learning Representations (2023)
36. Stahl, P.M.: Lingua (2023). https://github.com/pemistahl/lingua-py
37. Thomas, D.R.: A general inductive approach for analyzing qualitative evaluation data. Am. J. Eval. **27**(2), 237–246 (2006)
38. Wester, J., Schrills, T., Pohl, H., van Berkel, N.: "As an AI language model, i cannot": investigating LLM denials of user requests. In: Proceedings of the CHI Conference on Human Factors in Computing Systems (2024)
39. Yu, Z., Liu, X., Liang, S., Cameron, Z., Xiao, C., Zhang, N.: Don't listen to me: understanding and exploring jailbreak prompts of large language models (2024)
40. Zhang, Z., et al.: "It's a fair game", or is it? Examining how users navigate disclosure risks and benefits when using LLM-based conversational agents. In: Proceedings of the CHI Conference on Human Factors in Computing Systems, pp. 1–26 (2024)
41. Zhao, H., et al.: Explainability for large language models: a survey. ACM Trans. Intell. Syst. Technol. **15**(2), 20:1–20:38 (2024)

Caregiver Acceptability of an LLM-Powered Assistant Interface to Improve Sleep Quality of the Elderly

Marco Ajovalasit[1]([✉]) [ID], Irene Attori[1], Massimo Caon[1], Fabio Salice[2] [ID],
Shengnan Zhou[1], and Sara Comai[2] [ID]

[1] Department of Design Politecnico di Milano, Milan, Italy
{marco.ajovalasit,irene.attori,massimo.caon,
shengnan.zhou}@polimi.it
[2] Department of Electronics Information and Bioengineering, Politecnico di Milano, Milan, Italy
{fabio.salice,sara.comai}@polimi.it

Abstract. While increased longevity and improved health at older ages are notable achievements of the 21st century, they pose significant challenges, particularly in informal care. This paper discusses *NightCare Assistant*, a human-centric system that uses nighttime data and Large Language Models (LLM) to translate sleep quality into practical suggestions for improving the daily routine of ageing individuals. These suggestions are displayed through a tablet application, allowing caregivers to interact with an AI assistant. The research aims to understand the acceptability of this solution, focusing on caregivers' reactions to different AI-generated outputs and their willingness to follow these suggestions. An online questionnaire tested the system's acceptability, examining caregivers' perceptions of text, image, and audio outputs generated by AI. Results indicate significant interest among caregivers in adopting technological solutions to ease caregiving responsibilities. Caregivers found audio feedback the most reliable and understandable, followed by text and image outputs. Caregivers' willingness to follow *NightCare Assistant*'s advice supports the system's potential to improve care quality and safety for ageing individuals. The study highlights the necessity of addressing both nighttime behaviours and daily routines to effectively support cognitive health. *NightCare Assistant*'s integration of nighttime monitoring data into actionable daily interventions provides a comprehensive strategy for enhancing the well-being of older adults and their caregivers. Its acceptance among caregivers suggests that similar technological interventions can support autonomous living and reduce caregiver burden.

Keywords: Acceptability · Human centred design · Technology adoption · Large language models · Ageing · Elderly care

1 Introduction

While increased longevity and improved health at older ages represent one of the lifetime achievements of the 21st century, it is also true that they pose significant challenges to our society, most of all in the context of informal care [5]. Caregivers of ageing family members often deal with delicate situations in which the behaviours and emotions of their loved ones are influenced by their health condition, making it hard to provide the care needed [18]. These conditions can often be symptoms of the development of different forms of cognitive difficulties and degradation of which dementia is one of the most severe that create obstacles in the routine of older adults living alone [14].

Scientific literature has shown how prolonging autonomous living can help decrease the progress of cognitive decline [23]. In this context, it becomes key to understand and interpret the changing behaviours and emotional state of the person to better capture the course of the condition and decide on the best strategy of action to reduce potential risks [4,17,24]. Nighttime behaviours and sleep routines are relevant in this scenario since they bear great risks for the ageing person and the caregivers. Sleep is an essential function at every age that allows the body and mind to recharge [7]. With age, getting good sleep becomes harder, and this is true most of all in the case of dementia, where sleep disturbances are reported to occur in 19–54% of people with dementia (PWD) [20] Given the state of confusion that they suffer from, night activities become even riskier for this category, often leading to episodes of wandering that may cause incidents such as falls that can put the long-term health of the person at risk. As cognitive degradation progresses in severity, sleep disturbance episodes become more frequent, leading to a higher risk of incidents [9]. Finding the roots of these erratic behaviours may be difficult since the causes can come from different sources, leading to disturbances in the internal biological clock [3].

In recent years, many technological solutions have been adopted to try to measure and solve these issues. To address people's needs, the current focus often lies on engaging people in value creation through human-centred design approaches to arrive at meaningful and innovative solutions for the stakeholders [1]. This paper illustrates the case of *NightCare Assistant*, a human-centric system that uses data measured over the night and uses Large Language Models (LLM) to translate the detected sleep quality into practical suggestions to improve the daily routine of the ageing person. These suggestions are elaborated and displayed through a tablet application, where the caregivers can interact with an AI assistant. In this context, the research presented here aims to understand the level of acceptability of the proposed solution, focusing specifically on how caregivers react to different outputs elaborated by a generative AI system and how keen they would be to follow these suggestions. The research has developed an online questionnaire to test the system's acceptability, focusing on caregivers' perceptions of suggestions created by means of three different AI-generated outputs: text, image, and audio.

The solution addresses previous challenges by reducing nighttime erratic behaviours, providing caregivers easy access to practical knowledge on informal care, empowering them to take proactive steps in care and ensuring constant monitoring of the sleep patterns of the ageing person. Furthermore, the system fulfils users' aspirations by assisting caregivers in making informed decisions, enhancing the quality of care and improving safety by mitigating nighttime behaviours.

2   Related Works

Sleep quality monitoring and assessment can be conducted through three main approaches: reporting, polysomnography, and non-intrusive technologies.

The reporting method consists of asking the person and the caregiver (if possible) to complete a questionnaire that includes questions such as how long the person slept, the time the person went to bed, whether they woke up during the night, and how many times, etc. In addition to producing inaccurate and subjective results, the report extracted from the questionnaire would require daily completion to draw any conclusions on the progress of sleep quality. This method has several drawbacks, including the significant burden of compilation and the subjective imprecision inherent in self-report questionnaires, which may not accurately reflect real-life events [11].

A different method to evaluate a person's condition during sleep is polysomnography. Polysomnography is a diagnostic test that records various physiological activities during sleep (for example, respiratory rate - RR, heart rate - HR, electromyography - EMG, eye movement - EOG, and blood oxygenation) and is used to diagnose sleep disorders such as sleep apnea and narcolepsy. This type of investigation requires the person to wear devices, even in less complex cases where only some parameters are detected (for example, RR, HR, EMG, and oximetry). Although very accurate, the system requires professional skills, is expensive, generates several problems for the person due to the need to wear devices (intrusiveness), and raises several other issues, such as maintenance and connection with recording equipment. These aspects make polysomnography unsuitable for teleassistance or home telemonitoring.

Halfway between these two approaches is using low-cost sensors (for example, accelerometers, microphones, etc.) that detect the person's condition [8,22,24,26]. In this context, two approaches are possible: the intrusive one, which involves the use of wearable devices such as smartwatches, and the non-intrusive one (no contact with the person). Regarding the use of smartwatches, their intrusiveness poses some limits in the context of elderly people suffering from degenerative diseases, both in terms of acceptability, maintenance (e.g., battery recharging) and data transfer. The non-intrusive approach is widely investigated by the scientific community and uses sensors and techniques to obtain various parameters without the need for contact. For example, it is possible to detect both the RR and HR from the micro-vibrations of the body (ballistocardiography) [25]. This approach, already used in commercial devices, solves the wearability problem at the expense of the information's accuracy, which is sufficient for identifying sleep quality that does not involve significant pathological issues to be investigated. Examples of BCG-based sleep trackers are *Emfit QS*, *Beddit*, *Withings*, *Sleepace Reston*, and *Beautyrest* [21].

In our research, we focused on peer-reviewed English language publications indexed in the following databases: Google Scholar, ResearchGate, PubMed, and ScienceDirect. Keywords included terms and phrases synonymous with "dementia", "sensors", "monitoring", "night-time behaviours", and "wandering." Among the potential publications identified, we selected those involving non-wearable devices, controlled trials of the technologies, and published no earlier than 2010. The analyzed publications considered the use of technologies for nighttime activities for three main purposes: measuring and reducing the risks induced by nighttime wandering, monitoring the sleeping routine of ageing people affected by cognitive decline over a specific period, and measuring the impact of nighttime behaviours on caregivers' sleep patterns. Measuring and reducing the risks induced by nighttime wandering has been found to be the most prevalent purpose in the literature and thus it has been taken as the main focus for the research presented in this paper [2].

An example of this approach is reported in [6]. This study aims to develop a virtual restraint using a night monitoring system (*eNightLog*) to provide a safe environment for the elderly and mitigate caregiver burden. The system consists of remote sensors, including a near-infrared 3D time-of-flight sensor and ultra-wideband sensors. An alarm system is controlled by customized software and algorithms based on the respiration rate and body posture of the elderly. The system's innovation lies in its ability to identify whether an elderly person is within the dedicated zones using an algorithm that integrates images and signals from different sensors to detect potential wandering, with an accuracy of up to 99%. Although the technology proved effective, issues arise regarding the adoption of this system in a domestic setting, where conditions may not be as ideal as in controlled trials.

A different direction was taken by [16], who focused on designing a monitoring system (*Nocturnal*) starting from a participatory approach with end-users of the service (caregivers and the elderly). Their goal was to develop a technology-based system that could integrate with smart home devices to explore whether technology could provide pervasive ambient assisted living to support people with dementia at home and offer therapeutic interventions such as reminiscence and music. The multi-stakeholder approach helped the team understand the users' interconnected challenges and propose a solution tailored to their specific needs. In most cases examined, researchers have raised privacy concerns regarding both the feasibility of testing the technologies directly with end-users and the ethical considerations of surveillance technology in dementia, highlighting the difficulties in creating solutions that can be widely adopted in informal contexts [19].

Although much debate exists in the literature regarding the relationship between day-time activities and night-time behaviours, it was observed that existing systems lack in addressing the roots of these behaviours as part of a more complex context of actions and habits that start from the daily routine of ageing people. They focus on reducing potential dangers but do not try to address the causes of these erratic behaviours [13]. Several studies [10, 15] assert that the adoption of integrative interventions during the day (such as a reduction in the use of caffeine or an increase in physical and/or mental exercise) can play a fundamental role in improving the sleep pattern of people with cognitive decline. This research gap constituted the starting point of the development of *NightCare Assistant* concept design.

3   Methodology

NightCare Assistant has been analysed using a human-centred design approach starting from the analysis of pains and gains of both the caregiver and the ageing person with cognitive decline that, due to their interdependence, can be effectively analysed only if considered together. To answer this, *NightCare Assistant* concept design consists of a system that integrates and elaborates data from nighttime monitoring systems and activities reports through LLM to translate them into practical suggestions to the caregiver on how to adjust the daily routine activities of the ageing person to improve their sleep. By empowering the caregiver through knowledge, the aim is to slow down the cognitive decline of the ageing person and improve their overall well-being, supporting at the same time the caregiver in finding the right actions with which to do so. The primary objective of this research was to examine how different output formats of the information provided as text, image, or audio influenced the perceived acceptability and reliability of the system by the caregivers. Specifically, the three output formats were created using generative AI systems with the following criteria:

- One *proposed remedy* to sleep disturbances (do some light physical activity) was selected from the literature research examined in the research phase [12].
- *Text-generated output* was created by means of ChatGPT 4 using the following instruction line: "Generate a text with an informal, warm and precise tone that advises a caregiver of an elderly person with dementia on how encouraging physical exercise during the day can improve nighttime sleep for the elderly person". The generated text was used as the text output of the system.
- *Image-generated output* was created by means of ChatGPT 4 using the following instruction line: "Generate an image showing a caregiver and an elderly person engaging in a light exercise indoors, such as a gentle stretching exercise, during the day. The scene should be warm and friendly, emphasizing the positive interaction and setting". We used the generated image as the image output of the system.
- *Audio-generated message output* was created using Lovo.ai to convert the text written by ChatGPT 4 into an audio message, using the Italian voice of "Valentina" and accelerating its speed to 1.1. We used the output as the audio output of the system.

After defining the type of outputs, a qualitative questionnaire was designed to assess caregivers' preferences and perceptions of the three different user interface outputs developed through generative AI systems. The questionnaire was created using Google Forms. Careful measures were taken to protect participants' privacy by not collecting personal information such as gender, profession, or family status, as these details were considered irrelevant to the study's objectives. The questionnaire consisted of three parts:

- Part One - Understanding the context: This section aimed to gather information about the caregiving context and pains and gains of the participants. By assessing the specific circumstances and challenges faced by caregivers, it was ensured that the responses were aligned with the user scenarios identified in the preliminary phases of the research.
- Part Two - Familiarization *NightCare Assistant*: In this section, participants were introduced to the *NightCare Assistant* system through a concise and clear explanation of its functionalities and objectives. The text provided was designed to give participants a precise understanding of both the solution and the aim of our research without being overly detailed.
- Part Three - Testing the level of acceptability: Participants were asked to compare the different output formats (text, image, and audio) and provide qualitative feedback on

their acceptability and reliability. They were asked to justify their preferences, offering insights into why certain formats were perceived as more appealing or reliable than others.

The questionnaire was forwarded to a large number of caregivers, ensuring a diverse range of experiences and perspectives. The responses were then summarized and analyzed to identify general trends, preferences, and potential barriers to the adoption of the *NightCare Assistant* system.

All responses were initially collected in Italian and subsequently translated into English for the purpose of this study. By examining caregivers' feedback on the different output formats, it was then possible to determine which features were most favoured and which aspects presented challenges. This analysis was instrumental in understanding the role of various media in conveying clear and reliable messages, ultimately guiding the refinement of the *NightCare Assistant* system to better meet the needs of its users.

4   *NightCare Assistant* System

NightCare Assistant, the human-centric system solution proposed in this paper, has been evaluated based on its technological capabilities to create a sense of trust and understanding for the caregiver with the process of improving the nighttime sleep pattern of the ageing person and slowing down cognitive decline. This need arises from a series of problems, such as the risk of accidents during the night, the consequences that nighttime erratic behaviours have on the daily routine, a decrease in sleep quality in the caregivers and the need for easily accessible information about informal care. The aspirations of the users consist of improving the sleep patterns (both of the ageing person and caregiver), reducing the burden of care during nighttime, increasing the safety of the ageing person and slowing down the cognitive decline.

The service flow of the system is structured into three phases:

– *Phase 1 - Data Collection*: This first phase is divided into two daily sub-phases. The first sub-phase utilizes a non-intrusive sleep quality detection system that collects data throughout the night and translates it into information regarding the monitored subject's sleep patterns (Fig. 1). The second one requires caregiver involvement, where they are tasked with tracking the activities and daily routines of the monitored individual using an electronic questionnaire. This helps identify potential areas for intervention.
– *Phase 2 - From Data to Knowledge*: The collected data is analyzed, integrated, and translated into a single text. This text comprises a series of predefined and generic strategies correlated with general conditions such as environment, physical activity, nutrition, timetables, afternoon rest, and agitation before going to bed. The relationship between the suggested strategies and the sleep condition has been determined by selecting questions from medical questionnaires on sleep quality (e.g., https://www.medicalcenterpadova.it/test-autovaluazione-sonno/) specifically connected with monitored variables (automatic and from caregiver). Strategies are selected automatically, and a text is generated. The output text is the input to a large

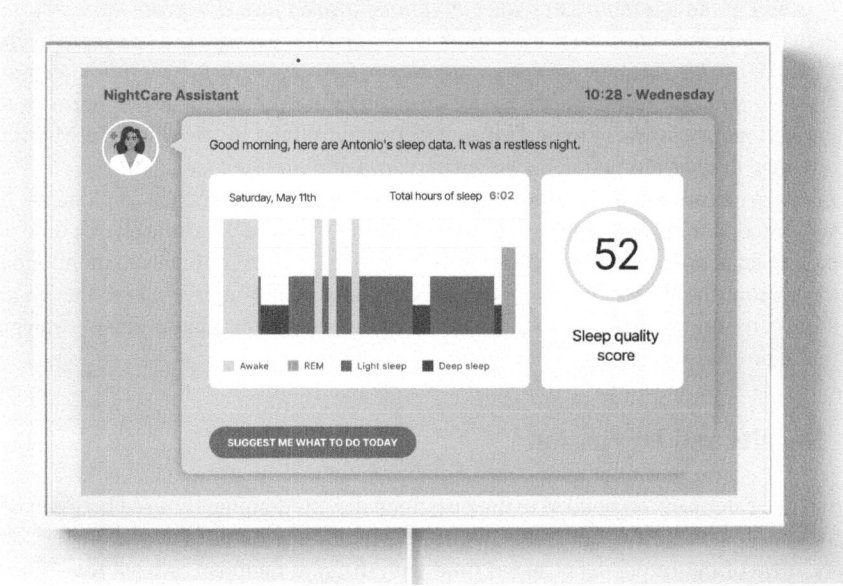

Fig. 1. Visualisation of data about nighttime sleep.

language model (LLM), which translates it into a list of suggestions representing a strategy of interventions that the caregiver can implement daily with the elderly person to improve their sleep rhythm. The user can choose when to receive these suggestions throughout the day, which will appear on their tablet.

An example is the following:

- The individual slept a few hours, went to bed late and woke up early as usual.
  SUGGESTED STRATEGY: Regularize your sleep schedule.
- The individual slept poorly with an above-average pulse.
  SUGGESTED STRATEGY: Evaluate your evening meal by avoiding heavy meals, alcohol, and caffeine.
- The individual had many awakenings and took a 1-hour afternoon nap.
  SUGGESTED STRATEGY: Limit the length and timing of naps.
- The individual did little physical activity.
  SUGGESTED STRATEGY: Try integrating more physical activity into your day, including short walks or light exercise.
- The individual found it very difficult to fall asleep and became very agitated.
  SUGGESTED STRATEGY: Dedicate time to relaxing activities before going to bed.

Activity requested from LLM: "Create a text using only the suggested strategies".
Answer: *To improve the quality of sleep, it is advisable to regularize your sleep schedule, going to bed and waking up at the same time every day. Evaluate your evening meal, avoiding heavy meals, alcohol, and caffeine to reduce above-average pulse rates. Limit the duration and timing of naps, preferably taking them within the*

first half of the afternoon, to reduce nighttime awakenings. Integrate more physical activity into your day, even with short walks or light exercises, to promote deeper sleep. Set aside time for relaxing activities before bed to help you fall asleep and reduce nighttime restlessness. By following these strategies, you can improve the overall quality of your sleep. This text is further refined by providing LLM with a directive to rewrite a text in *an informal, warm and precise tone.*

– *Phase 3 - From Knowledge to Implementation*: The caregiver then implements the suggested actions and adjusts the ageing person's routine accordingly. Upon completing an action, the user confirms it to the system, which continues to monitor data throughout the night. Based on the effectiveness of the interventions, the system adjusts its suggestions. This iterative process is crucial for adapting new strategies to the progression of cognitive decline.

5   Results and Discussion

Thirty-five caregivers responded to the questionnaire, predominantly aged between fifty and seventy, with 91.4% not living with the person they assist. Despite living separately, 60% of the respondents spend time with the care recipient at least four times a week, averaging three to four hours per visit. This result suggested a relevant caregiving involvement, highlighting the dedication and commitment to the roles of the caregivers involved in the research.

Technological support was generally well-received, with only 11.4% of caregivers showing no interest, and 22.9% already utilizing technological aids. This suggests a positive attitude towards technology in caregiving roles and indicates that most users are already familiar with and open to technological solutions. This issue is crucial for the successful implementation of systems like *NightCare Assistant*, which rely on user engagement and acceptance to be effective.

Only 11 out of 35 caregivers reported that they are aware of night disturbances in their loved ones, while 4 answered that they do not know if these events are occurring. The remaining caregivers never noticed such events, but it is not possible to exclude that these disturbances might be happening in less noticeable forms. Of the eleven participants who assist a person struggling with night disturbances, eight have already intervened using different methods: increasing personal assistance (2), changing the daily routine (3), using medicines or sleeping pills (2), and consulting with a psychiatrist (1). None of them used technological support to address the issue.

Regarding nighttime assistance, only 11.4% of the respondednts declared to have medical experience or first-aid knowledge, while only 20% of the respondents declared to provide nighttime assistance, with eleven caregivers identifying nighttime issues as disorientation, confusion, sleep disturbances, aggressive behaviour, and hallucinations. To address these issues, 72.7% of the affected caregivers have taken steps like seeking professional help, modifying daily routines, or increasing personal assistance. These proactive measures highlight the caregivers' willingness to improve the quality of care.

Figures 2, 3 and 4 present the three AI-generated outputs which were developed in this study and displayed in the questionnaire together with the description of the advice message suggested to the caregiver. Figure 2 shows the layout of the AI-generated "audio" output, Fig. 3 shows the layout of the AI-generated "text" output, and Fig. 4 shows the layout of the AI-generated "image" output.

When evaluating the acceptability of AI-generated outputs as shown in Figs. 2, 3 and 4, respondents showed a slight preference for audio outputs (selected by fifteen participants) over text outputs (thirteen participants), with image outputs being the least preferred (seven participants).

When evaluating the sense of trust perceived from the displayed information and suggested message, participants were asked how much they would trust the suggestions from the selected format (Fig. 5).

The "audio" format of Fig. 2 was rated highest in reliability (Fig. 5 average score of 7.3/10), followed by the "text" format of Fig. 3 (average score of 6.7/10) and "image" format of Fig. 4 (average score of 6.3/10).

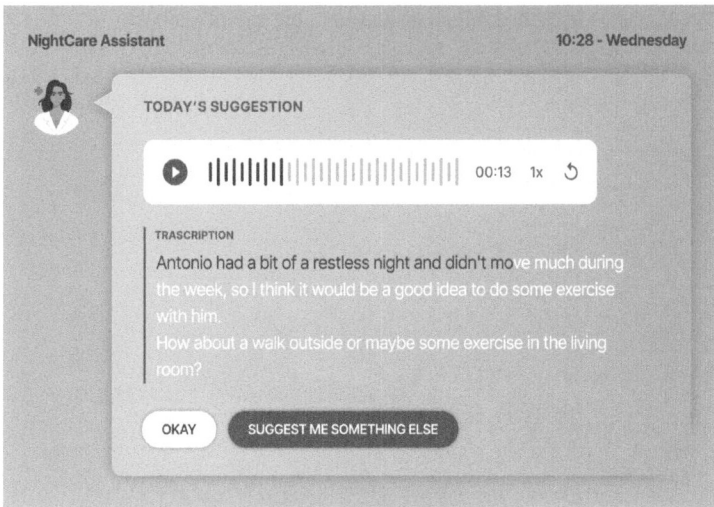

Fig. 2. Audio output displayed in the questionnaire.

Despite these differences, the overall distinction between the reliability of different outputs was not significant since the distribution of the score varied significantly. This highlights the usefulness of using multiple media formats to convey clear messages, conveying accessibility on different fronts. Respondents appreciated having the flexibility to choose between text, audio, and images based on their preferences.

All respondents found the suggestions clear, and none indicated that they would never follow the advice given by *NightCare Assistant* (Fig. 6 to 8), even though a higher number of respondents than expected chose the option "not always" (15 out of 35).

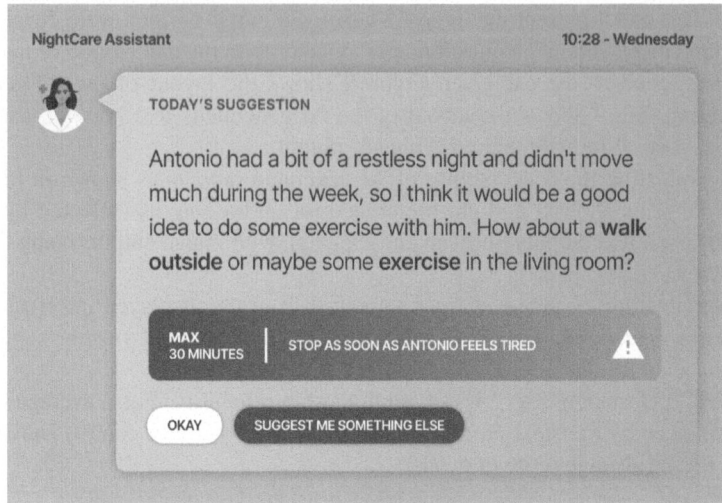

Fig. 3. Text output displayed in the questionnaire.

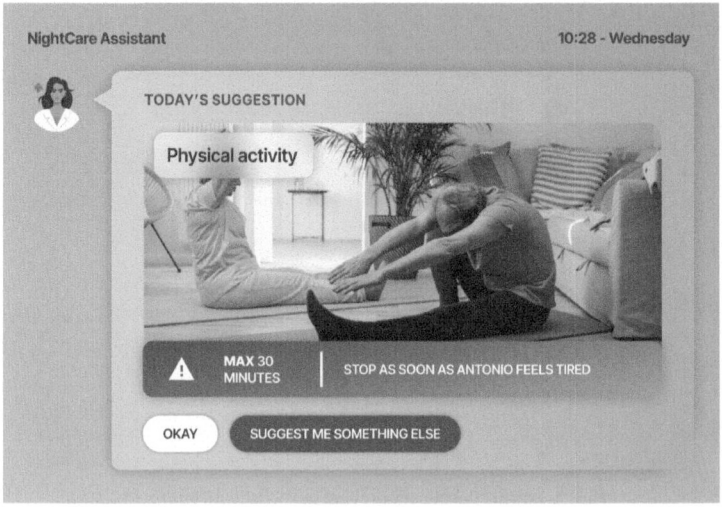

Fig. 4. Image output displayed in the questionnaire.

This underscores the need for a simple and precise message, which is crucial in ensuring that the suggestion given is easily understandable and actionable. By delivering straightforward and concise recommendations, *NightCare Assistant* can enhance user confidence and adherence to the proposed interventions.

The data suggest that while images alone are less effective, they significantly enhance the clarity and completeness of text and audio outputs. Most caregivers viewed images as auxiliary rather than primary media, preferring text and audio for their direct-

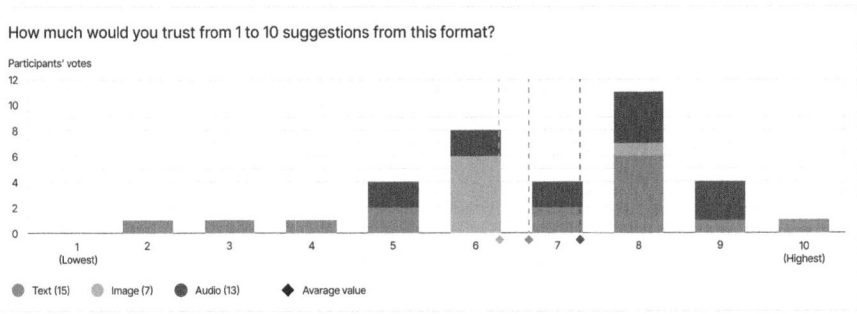

Fig. 5. Results question "How much would you trust from 1 to 10 suggestions from this format?".

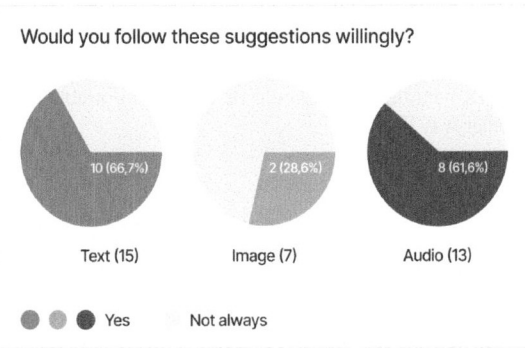

Fig. 6. Results question "Would you follow these suggestions willingly?".

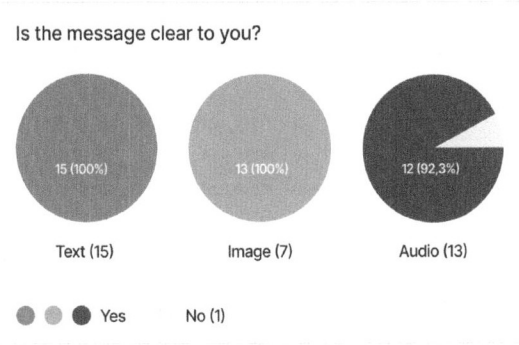

Fig. 7. Results question "Is the message clear to you".

ness and comprehensiveness. This preference underscores the perception that text and audio deliver information more effectively on their own. However, interesting data emerged where 47% of text users and 31% of audio users expressed a desire to include images in their chosen output. This indicates a recognition of the value that visual ele-

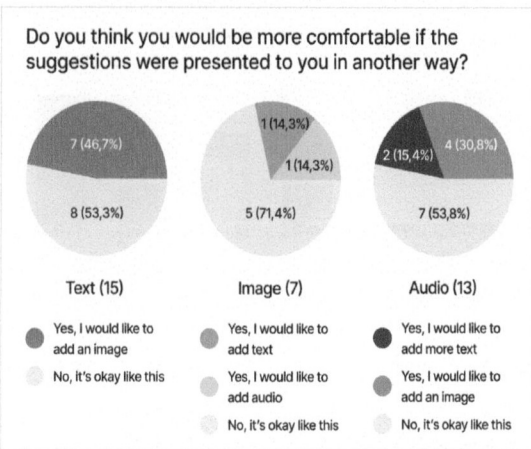

Fig. 8. Result question "Do you think you would be more comfortable if the suggestions were presented to you in another way?".

ments can add to enhance understanding and retention, even though they are not the primary communication medium (Fig. 7).

Furthermore, the reliability of the message depends significantly on the content itself. Even if it does not come out as a result of the questionnaire, we strongly believe that demonstrating the correlation between nighttime behaviours and suggested interventions could enhance the perceived reliability of the advice. Emphasizing the evidence-based nature of the suggestions can reinforce their acceptability. For instance, linking specific nighttime disturbances to particular daytime activities or environmental changes can provide a clearer cause-and-effect correlation for the recommendations, making them more compelling and trustworthy.

This flexibility is crucial as it allows caregivers to choose the format that best suits their communication style and context. For example, audio outputs may be more convenient for caregivers who are visually impaired or who prefer to listen to instructions while performing tasks, whereas text and images may be more suitable for those who prefer to read and visualize the information. For this reason, developing a multimedia interface that allows users to visualize the content as preferred is key in enhancing the acceptability of the system.

To better define the service flow, it is imperative to consider the complexity of the ecosystem into which the new solution is integrated. For instance, the family doctor plays a pivotal role in informal care contexts. Their responsibility is to support users, connect them with the national health service, outline a care pathway and recommend appropriate pharmacological interventions.

Within our service framework, their role may involve supporting families in implementing interventions and providing guidance on best practices. Friends and family members have crucial roles in supporting caregivers in delivering necessary care and assisting ageing individuals with emotional and physical support. They can also share responsibility by helping with simple tasks suggested by the system, such as going for walks or providing mental stimulation. Finally, local Alzheimer's centres are situated throughout the country, forming an essential assistance network for caregivers and ageing individuals. They can offer support in carrying out activities suggested by the system and share practices and recommendations for implementing the strategy effectively.

The multimedia output approach of *NightCare Assistant*, which includes text, audio, and images, (Fig. 9) would seem effective in understanding diverse caregiver preferences and needs.

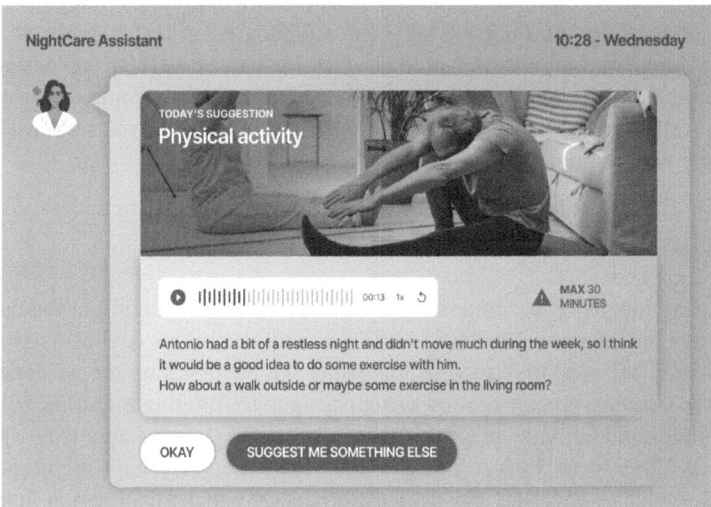

Fig. 9. Final output which integrates text, image and audio developed accordingly to participants' feedback.

The potential limitations of the system may arise from various factors. Non-pharmacological interventions have nuanced effects that can vary based on individual characteristics. Therefore, it will be crucial for the system to adapt the suggested strategy based on measured data. Another important aspect is determining how to effectively communicate suggestions to caregivers. Defining the appropriate output is essential for ensuring the reliability and acceptability of the service, and the methodology we developed is focused on addressing this aspect.

Caregivers' willingness to integrate *NightCare Assistant*'s suggestions into their routines demonstrates the system's potential to impact caregiving practices positively. By providing actionable and reliable advice, *NightCare Assistant* can help caregivers manage the complexities of dementia care more effectively, reducing the risk of night-time incidents and improving the overall well-being of the care recipients.

Overall, the *NightCare Assistant* system is well-received by caregivers. The use of multiple media formats has proven to be effective in conveying clear and reliable messages, ensuring that caregivers can easily understand and act upon the information provided. This versatility in communication methods caters to different preferences and enhances the overall user experience. Caregivers' openness to technological solutions and their positive response to *NightCare Assistant*'s outputs suggest that such systems can play a critical role in supporting the caregiving process. These positive responses indicate a significant potential for technology-driven tools to improve the efficiency and effectiveness of caregiving, ultimately benefiting both caregivers and those they care for.

Future research should explore the acceptability of the *NightCare Assistant* system through hands-on experience and real-life trials of the system to assess how acceptable users actually find it. Future research should continue to explore the integration of user feedback and the long-term impacts of such technologies on both caregivers and care recipients. Moreover, future work would need to consider a control group design experiment assessing the effectiveness of the text, image and audio by comparing a subset of caregivers with no awareness of night disturbances in their loved ones against a subset of caregivers with awareness that these events are occurring.

6   Conclusions

The increasing longevity and improved health of older adults highlight the dual challenge of extending autonomous living while managing cognitive decline and its impact on caregivers. The study presented in this paper has focussed on the acceptability of *NightCare Assistant*, a human-centred system designed to monitor nighttime behaviours in older adults and provide practical care suggestions using large language models (LLMs). The system aims to mitigate the risks associated with nighttime erratic behaviours, such as wandering and sleep disturbances, which are common in individuals with dementia.

The results of this study indicate a significant interest among caregivers in adopting technological solutions to ease their caregiving responsibilities. The findings from the questionnaire reveal that caregivers find audio feedback the most reliable and understandable, followed by text and image outputs. Caregivers' willingness to follow the advice provided by *NightCare Assistant* further supports the system's potential to improve care quality and safety for ageing individuals.

The results of this study also highlight the necessity of addressing both the nighttime behaviours and the broader context of daily routines to effectively support cognitive health. *NightCare Assistant*'s approach of integrating and translating nighttime monitoring data into actionable daily interventions provides a comprehensive strategy for enhancing the well-being of older adults and their caregivers.

The proposed *NightCare Assistant* represents a promising solution for managing the challenges of informal care for older adults with cognitive decline. Its acceptance among caregivers suggests that similar technological interventions can play a critical role in supporting autonomous living and reducing caregiver burden. Future research should explore the acceptability of the *NightCare Assistant* system through hands-on experience and real-life trials of the system to assess how acceptable users actually find it. Future research should continue to explore the integration of user feedback and the long-term impacts of such technologies on both caregivers and care recipients.

References

1. Ajovalasit, M.: Understanding meaningfulness in AI-infused artefacts, pp. 97–121. Franco Angeli, Milano (2022)
2. Alzheimer's_Association: Wandering and getting lost: who's at risk and how to be prepared. www.alz.org/media/documents/alzheimers-dementia-wandering-behavior-ts.pdf. Accessed 20 June 2024
3. Ault, L., Goubran, R., Wallace, B., Lowden, H., Knoefel, F.: Smart home technology solution for night-time wandering in persons with dementia. J. Rehabil. Assist. Technol. Eng. **7**, 2055668320938591 (2020)
4. Buhr, G.T., White, H.K.: Difficult behaviors in long-term care patients with dementia. J. Am. Med. Dir. Assoc. **8**(3), e101–e113 (2007)
5. Chamie, J., Berkman, L., Hayutin, A.M., Smith, J.P., Hoeksema, M.J.: Why population ageing matters: a global perspective (2007)
6. Cheung, J.C.W., Tam, E.W.C., Mak, A.H.Y., Chan, T.T.C., Lai, W.P.Y., Zheng, Y.P.: Night-time monitoring system (eNightLog) for elderly wandering behavior. Sensors **21**(3), 704 (2021)
7. Cipriani, G., Lucetti, C., Danti, S., Nuti, A.: Sleep disturbances and dementia. Psychogeriatrics **15**(1), 65–74 (2015)
8. Comai, S., Carpaneto, L., Masciadri, A., Pozzi, G., Salice, F.: Sleep monitoring: enriching the traditional approach by sensor-collected data. In: 2023 IEEE 11th International Conference on Healthcare Informatics (ICHI). IEEE (2023). https://doi.org/10.1109/ichi57859.2023.00054
9. Eggermont, L.H., Blankevoort, C.G., Scherder, E.J.: Walking and night-time restlessness in mild-to-moderate dementia: a randomized controlled trial. Age Ageing **39**(6), 746–749 (2010)
10. Eggermont, L.H., Scherder, E.J.: Ambulatory but sedentary: impact on cognition and the rest-activity rhythm in nursing home residents with dementia. J. Gerontol. B Psychol. Sci. Soc. Sci. **63**(5), P279–P287 (2008)
11. Fabbri, M., Beracci, A., Martoni, M., Meneo, D., Tonetti, L., Natale, V.: Measuring subjective sleep quality: a review. Int. J. Environ. Res. Public Health **18**(3), 1082 (2021)
12. Gitlin, L.N., Kales, H.C., Lyketsos, C.G.: Nonpharmacologic management of behavioral symptoms in dementia. JAMA **308**(19), 2020–2029 (2012)
13. Husebo, B.S., Heintz, H.L., Berge, L.I., Owoyemi, P., Rahman, A.T., Vahia, I.V.: Sensing technology to monitor behavioral and psychological symptoms and to assess treatment response in people with dementia. A systematic review. Front. Pharmacol. **10**, 482618 (2020)
14. Johansson, M.M., Marcusson, J., Wressle, E.: Cognitive impairment and its consequences in everyday life: experiences of people with mild cognitive impairment or mild dementia and their relatives. Int. Psychogeriatr. **27**(6), 949–958 (2015)
15. Legere, L.E., McNeill, S., Schindel Martin, L., Acorn, M., An, D.: Nonpharmacological approaches for behavioural and psychological symptoms of dementia in older adults: a systematic review of reviews. J. Clin. Nurs. **27**(7–8), e1360–e1376 (2018)
16. Martin, S., et al.: Participatory research to design a novel telehealth system to support the night-time needs of people with dementia: NOCTURNAL. Int. J. Environ. Res. Public Health **10**(12), 6764–6782 (2013)
17. Masciadri, A., Comai, S., Salice, F.: SMARE: semi-supervised method for activities of daily living recognition. In: 2019 IEEE International Conference on Systems, Man and Cybernetics (SMC), pp. 3403–3409 (2019). https://doi.org/10.1109/SMC.2019.8914279
18. Nunez, K.M., Khan, Z., Testad, I., Lawrence, V., Creese, B., Corbett, A.: Current practice and challenges in night-time care for people with dementia living in care homes: a qualitative study. Int. J. Geriatr. Psychiatry **33**(1), e140–e149 (2018)

19. Radziszewski, R., Ngankam, H., Pigot, H., Grégoire, V., Lorrain, D., Giroux, S.: An ambient assisted living nighttime wandering system for elderly. In: Proceedings of the 18th International Conference on Information Integration and Web-Based Applications and Services, pp. 368–374 (2016)
20. Rowe, M.A., et al.: Reducing dangerous nighttime events in persons with dementia by using a nighttime monitoring system. Alzheimer's Dementia 5(5), 419–426 (2009)
21. Sadek, I., Abdulrazak, B.: Contactless remote monitoring of sleep: evaluating the feasibility of an under-mattress sensor mat in a real-life deployment. Health Syst. 12(3), 264–280 (2022)
22. Siyanbade, J., Abdulrazak, B., Sadek, I.: Unobtrusive monitoring of sleep cycles: a technical review. BioMedInformatics 2(1), 204–216 (2022)
23. Van Der Weide, H., Lovink, M.H., Luijkx, K.G., Gerritsen, D.L.: Supporting autonomy for people with dementia living in nursing homes: a rapid realist review. Int. J. Nurs. Stud. 137, 104382 (2023)
24. Veronese, F., Saidinejad, H., Comai, S., Salice, F.: Elderly monitoring and AAL for independent living at home: human needs, technological issues, and dependability, pp. 154–181. IGI Global (2016).https://doi.org/10.4018/978-1-4666-9530-6.ch007
25. Vogt, E., MacQuarrie, D., Neary, J.P.: Using ballistocardiography to measure cardiac performance: a brief review of its history and future significance. Clin. Physiol. Funct. Imaging 32(6), 415–420 (2012)
26. Wang, H., et al.: Monitoring and analysis of sleep pattern for people with early dementia. In: 2010 IEEE International Conference on Bioinformatics and Biomedicine Workshops (BIBMW), pp. 405–410. IEEE (2010)

User Experience and Information Security Heuristics for Digital Identity Wallets

Max Sauer[(✉)], Christoph Becker, Andreas Oberweis, Sabine Schork, and Jan Sürmeli

FZI Research Center for Information Technology, 76131 Karlsruhe, Germany
{sauer,christoph.becker,oberweis,schork,suermeli}@fzi.de

Abstract. In digital identity wallets, users can store and manage their digital identities and verification documents such as driving licences and membership cards. Current digital identity wallets face notable challenges in user experience and information security. Users struggle to understand the concept of digital identity wallets, resulting in personal information being either inadequately stored or inadvertently shared with untrustworthy parties. Thus, digital identity wallets should provide a sufficient level of user experience and information security. For evaluating and improving user experience and information security, heuristics can be used to check the degree of fulfilment for each heuristic and to improve digital identity wallets according to the respective heuristics.

This paper reports on the development and evaluation of user experience and information security heuristics for digital identity wallets. To this end, an existing method for user experience heuristics was adapted to also cover information security heuristics. As particular evaluation methods, expert interviews and heuristic evaluations were applied. In total, twelve user experience and six information security heuristics were developed and evaluated.

Keywords: User experience · Usability · Information security · Digital identity wallets · Heuristics · Heuristic evaluation

1 Introduction

Digital identity solutions [25] are on the rise to become a part of daily life. Required for use cases in both the digital and the physical realm, for business processes and public services alike, they offer functionality around authentication, access management, personalization and process automation. As required by European law [23] and use cases in fields such as mobility, smart city or e-commerce [6], the upcoming generation of identity solutions will be able to manage so called *credentials* in so called *digital identity wallets* (in the following called *wallets*) [25]. In short, a credential holds verified information about persons, organizations and objects, such as an electronic id card, a mobile driving license, a proof of adulthood, a membership status, or an access token [25]. A wallet is a – usually mobile – application to manage credentials of its *holder* [24]. In particular, a wallet enables holders to receive credentials from third parties

H. Plácido da Silva and P. Cipresso (Eds.): CHIRA 2024, CCIS 2370, pp. 339–361, 2025.
https://doi.org/10.1007/978-3-031-82633-7_21

called *issuers* and present credentials to third parties called *verifiers*[1]. As such, these wallets will surpass currently available, similar but more restricted applications, such as password managers, crypto wallets or wallets provided by mobile operating systems.

One important idea behind wallets is to serve a rather general purpose and support a plethora of different use cases. Wallet developers expect various touch points in daily life. For example, an ID card credential could be stored in the wallet, which can be used by the holder to obtain a digital registration certificate conveniently from home via a government platform. For this purpose, the ID card credential could be presented from the wallet by the holder to the government platform (in this case the verifier) for identification. The government platform (in this case the issuer) could then issue a registration certificate credential, which could be stored in the wallet. This saves a trip to the local government office.

High user experience (UX) is essential for user acceptance, and in turn, for a successful introduction of a wallet into the market. However, comfort alone is not sufficient. Many credentials contain data protected by law, such as personal identifiers or health data. Thus, wallets need to provide a sufficient degree of information security (InfoSec). Literature suggests that current wallets – often in the state of prototypes – are not satisfactory in UX or InfoSec: Wallet users (even tech-savvy ones) find it difficult to understand how wallets work, for example due to overly technical terms or too few explanations. This can lead to credentials being shared unintentionally to untrusted verifiers, thus reducing the InfoSec level [11, 32].

Improving those two aspects thus remains a challenge. To complicate matters, UX and InfoSec are intertwined, as improving the UX may decrease InfoSec – and vice versa [38].

One approach to evaluate and improve systems is the application of *heuristics* [22]. Intuitively, a heuristic provides a metric how well a system under consideration implements specific aspects, such as accessibility or availability. A set of heuristics can thus be used to provide an overview of the state of a system, and suggest starting points for improvements. While heuristics are a powerful tool for improving the quality of systems, they need to be tailored to specific classes of systems, such as wallets. Fortunately, there exist methods to develop and improve heuristics to support this task. In the case of UX, the method of Rusu et al. [29] provides a process to create heuristics for a given class of applications, and, more generally, expert interviews and heuristic evaluations [22] are proven tools to evaluate a given set of heuristics.

This paper reports on research conducted on creating and evaluating heuristics for UX and InfoSec of wallets as depicted in Fig. 1. In particular, findings from the following research tasks are presented:

- an extension of the method of Rusu et al. [29] to cover InfoSec in addition to UX,
- an application of the adapted method, including:
  - the creation of an initial set of heuristics for UX and InfoSec of wallets,
  - an evaluation and improvement of these heuristics based on expert interviews, and
  - a heuristic evaluation to measure the utility of the improved UX heuristics.

---

[1] In other terminologies, *verifiers* are known as *relying parties*.

In summary, twelve UX heuristics and six InfoSec heuristics were developed for wallets. In a first evaluation step, these were assessed and improved through expert interviews. In a second evaluation step, the developed UX heuristics were applied in a heuristic evaluation in comparison with UX heuristics from the literature. The developed UX heuristics performed better than the heuristics from literature.

The paper is structured as follows: Sect. 2 discusses related literature. Section 3 lays the conceptual foundation. Section 4 presents the first contribution of the paper: The adaption of the method of Rusu et al. [29] for InfoSec. Section 5 reports on the second part of the contribution: The development and evaluation of heuristics with the adapted method, expert interviews and heuristic evaluations. Section 6 contains the discussion and limitations. Section 7 concludes the paper, giving hints for further directions of research.

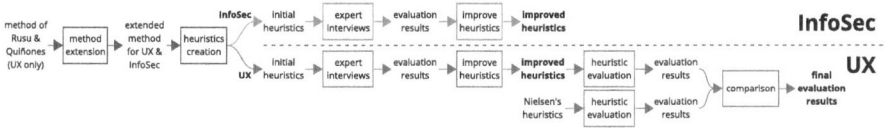

Fig. 1. Workflow of presented research

2   Related Work

Nielsen [20] introduced ten general UX heuristics for software systems. Shneiderman developed eight general UX heuristics for software systems, the so-called "Eight Golden Rules of Interface Design" [37]. Not only general UX heuristics for software systems were developed, but also UX heuristics for specific domains: For example, Bascur et al. [4] developed sixty-four UX heuristics specifically for e-commerce websites. Saavedra et al. [30] developed eleven UX heuristics specifically for social networks. In summary, several UX heuristics have already been developed that are more abstract for software systems in general or for specific domains other than wallets. However, no specific UX heuristics for wallets were found in literature. Nevertheless, Krauß et al. [14] developed a proposal for a user-friendly wallet. Based on analysis of existing wallets and their hurdles, thirteen key requirements for a user-friendly wallet were identified, such as the minimalist and simple design of the user interface. The findings were then used to derive twenty essential functions for a user-friendly wallet. The developed UX heuristics presented in this article build upon existing UX study results by literature (such as those from Krauß et al. [14] or Nielsen [20]) and develop UX heuristics for wallets based on them.

With regard to InfoSec, no existing general set of InfoSec heuristics could be identified. However, InfoSec heuristics were found for specific domains other than wallets: For example, Gonzalez et al. [9] developed seventeen InfoSec and UX heuristics specifically for e-commerce websites. Realpe et al. [28] developed 153 InfoSec and UX heuristics for user authentication. In summary, several InfoSec heuristics have already been developed that are specific for domains other than wallets. However, no specific InfoSec heuristics for wallets were found in literature. Nevertheless, Sellung and Kubach [36] developed twenty-three InfoSec and UX guidelines for wallets. In addition, they name five best practices and seven worst practices in the design of digital wallets. The developed InfoSec heuristics mentioned in this paper take up InfoSec heuristics by literature (such as those from Realpe et al. [28]) and develop InfoSec heuristics for wallets on this basis.

3   Preliminaries

3.1   Digital Identity Wallets

With the digital transformation and the increasing digital exchange of information, it is important to clearly identify different entities or verify their characteristics when using information and communication technology (ICT). An entity can be defined as a "person, an organization, a device, a group of such items, a human subscriber to a telecom service, a SIM card, a passport, a network interface card, a software application, a service or a website" [1]. "An identity represents an entity in an ICT system as data to be stored or processed [...] and [...] serves to make known relevant information of the entity in its interactions with the services and access of resources provided by a domain" [1]. Digital identities and their credentials can be managed in a wallet. According to Podgorelec et al. [24], a wallet is a software system in which users can store and manage their identity-related data in a self-determined manner. Wallet users can decide for themselves which of their identity-related data stored in the wallet they would like to share with verifiers. The wallet also enables the secure storage of the cryptographic data associated with the identity-related data. According to Podgorelec et al. [24] a wallet has six basic functions: (1) It provides a *credential overview* listing all stored credentials. (2) There is a *detailed view* showing details of each stored credential. (3) Stored credentials can be *deleted*. (4) The wallet has an area for *help or frequently asked questions*. (5) The wallet has a *backup function* allowing users to create a backup of all their identity-related data, including credentials, contacts/connections or history. (6) The wallet has a function to *restore the backup data*.

3.2   User Experience and Information Security of Digital Identity Wallets

User Experience (UX) is defined as the "user's perceptions and responses that result from the use and/or anticipated use of a system, product or service" [3]. According to Morville [15, 16], UX has seven different attributes: utility, desirability, findability, accessibility, credibility, value and usability. *Usability* is defined as the "extent to which a system, product or service can be used by specified users to achieve specified goals with effectiveness, efficiency and satisfaction in a specified context of use" [2]. According to Nielsen [19], usability has five attributes: learnability, efficiency, memorability, errors and satisfaction.

Information security (InfoSec) is defined as "the protection of information and information systems from unauthorized access, use, disclosure, disruption, modification, or destruction in order to ensure confidentiality, integrity, and availability" [18].

Existing wallets have various UX and InfoSec deficits: Wallet users struggle with understanding wallet functions, lacking intuitive wording and help options [32].

Moreover, users also face challenges in managing credentials within a decentralized system, especially regarding backup, recovery, and account deletion. Users' mental models often differ from developers', making it hard for users to navigate complex technical features like public key infrastructures or electronic signatures [11]. Additionally, users have trouble with technical terms and QR codes, and they expect wallets to perform automatic backups instead of manual ones [12].

To improve UX and InfoSec, it is important that the two properties are not considered separately, as they can influence each other. On the one hand, InfoSec mechanisms can lead to an inadequate UX if, e.g., InfoSec mechanisms are too complicated [8]. On the other hand, UX can lead to an inadequate InfoSec level if, e.g., InfoSec mechanisms can be misused or ignored [38].

3.3 Heuristics and Heuristic Evaluation

The quality of a software system can be evaluated by means of *heuristics*. In the context of this paper, heuristics provide quality guidelines, regarding criteria such as UX or InfoSec, which can be fulfilled to certain degrees by different systems. Such heuristics can be used in requirements engineering to specify or evaluate the satisfaction of requirements for systems under development, or to evaluate and compare existing systems. While heuristics can cover different aspects of a system, they are particularly used for UX. Yáñez Gómez et al. [39] describe a heuristic as a guideline whose fulfilment is checked when the UX of a real system or prototype is evaluated and improved. Well-known UX heuristics are the heuristics from Nielsen [20], e.g., dialogues should be simple and natural. In addition to UX heuristics, heuristics for other aspects have been developed. In particular, Realpe et al. [28] developed heuristics for InfoSec, e.g., critical areas of a system should never be accessible to users, but only to administrators. Extending the definition of Yáñez Gómez et al. [39] from only UX to also include InfoSec, a heuristic can be defined as a guideline for UX or InfoSec of a real system or prototype. An approach to assess and improve UX and InfoSec with heuristics is the method of *heuristic evaluation* [22], involving the evaluation of a software system regarding different UX and InfoSec problems.

4   Method

The methodical foundation of this paper was provided by [29], albeit with a required extension for InfoSec. This method was initially created to develop UX heuristics. However, in [29], the authors point out that the method could probably also be used for other software quality attributes. Therefore, the method was adapted so that InfoSec heuristics could also be developed, that is, the steps that should be performed for the UX heuristics are also performed for the InfoSec heuristics.

The adapted method was applied to wallets with the goal to develop UX and InfoSec heuristics in the following stages:

1. *Exploratory Stage.* A literature review was conducted to identify relevant definitions (for terms such as wallet, UX and InfoSec). It was also searched for relevant UX and InfoSec attributes and for existing sets of heuristics (specific for wallets heuristics and more abstract for software systems heuristics that could be adapted for wallets).

2. *Experimental Stage.* This stage is classified optional by the authors of the method [29]. UX and InfoSec evaluations of wallets have already been carried out in preliminary work [33] and the results were taken into account for the further stages. Therefore, this stage was not explicitly applied again.
3. *Descriptive Stage.* In this stage, the findings from the first stage were prioritized and filtered. For example, relevant, already existing sets of heuristics, UX and InfoSec attributes and wallet functions were filtered.
4. *Correlational Stage.* In this stage, the wallet functions were matched with the UX and InfoSec attributes and existing heuristics.
5. *Selection Stage.* The existing heuristics from stage (4) were classified as whether they need to be adapted, kept or deleted. Those wallet functions that could not yet be assigned a heuristic in stage (4) were categorized as still requiring a heuristic to be developed.
6. *Specification Stage.* The heuristics were adapted, kept or deleted using the classification from stage (5).
7. *First Validation Stage.* The developed heuristics were initially analyzed with the help of expert interviews. Four UX experts and four InfoSec experts were interviewed for this purpose. Two of the UX experts were UX designers from industry, the other two were scientists from the field of UX and usable security. Three of the InfoSec experts were scientists in the InfoSec area, and one InfoSec expert was a scientist in the Usable Security area. All four InfoSec experts are in constant dialogue with the industry.
8. *Refinement Stage.* After the initial evaluation through expert interviews, the heuristics were revised.
9. *Second Validation Stage.* After the refinement of the heuristics, a second validation stage was carried out using heuristic evaluations. For this purpose, a control group and an experimental group were formed, each consisting of three UX experts. The experts were different from those in the first validation stage. Care was taken to ensure that the people in the two groups were balanced in terms of their expertise. Each group included three scientists specialising in UX research, two of whom also conduct research in the context of wallets.

   The experts of the control group each carried out a heuristic evaluation [22] on a software prototype developed in the research project Showcase Secure Digital Identities Karlsruhe (SDIKA)[2] using *Nielsen's UX heuristics* [20]. The experts of the experimental group each carried out a heuristic evaluation on the same software prototype using the *developed UX heuristics*.

   The software prototype is about issuing an official registration certificate with subsequent storage of the corresponding credential in the wallet: First, the experts should open the wallet and add their ID card, which is later used for identification with the government platform (verifying). To do this, there is an "ID card import" button in the wallet menu, which redirects to the so-called AusweisApp. The AusweisApp (in English: ID card app)[3] is a software application that makes it possible to use the online ID function of the German ID card in order to be clearly and securely

---

[2] https://www.sdika.de/en.
[3] https://www.ausweisapp.bund.de/en.

identified online. In the AusweisApp, the experts should use the NFC scan to read the data from the ID card by holding the card to the smartphone and entering a six-digit PIN. No real data was read, but data from a fictitious person was used. After the data had been read, a selection appeared as to which data of the ID card should be transferred to the wallet (issuing). An iOS-native dialogue then appeared asking which wallet the data should be transferred to. After selecting the wallet, the wallet opened automatically with a dialogue to confirm the storing of the ID card credential. The experts then had to navigate to the government platform and log in there by sharing the ID card credential from the wallet. For this purpose, there was a button in the government platform to share the ID card from the wallet, whereby another dialogue appears in the wallet in which the sharing must first be confirmed. After successfully logging into the government platform, the purpose of issuing the registration certificate should now be selected, namely to transfer a foreign driving licence. The experts should then export the registration certificate credential to the wallet (issuing). For this purpose, there was initially another selection in the government platform as to which data should be transferred to the wallet. After pressing the corresponding button, the native iOS dialogue opens again, in which the corresponding wallet should be selected. A dialogue then opened again in the wallet, in which the storing of the registration certificate credential had to be confirmed. Finally, the experts were shown the standard overview of all credentials stored in the wallet, i.e. ID card and registration certificate.

Figure 2 shows the general process of the software prototype.

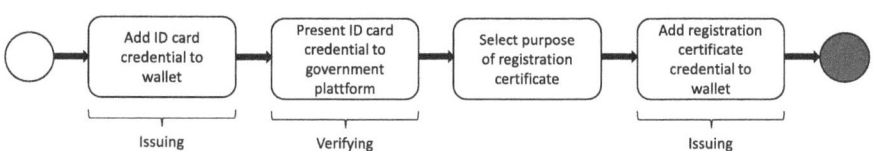

Fig. 2. Prototype Flow

The UX problems found with the two different sets of UX heuristics were then compared. This could not be done with the InfoSec heuristics, as no comparable InfoSec heuristics could be found in the literature.

In addition, a UX evaluation [33] was conducted with twenty-four test subjects who tested a wallet prototype to get direct insights from end users. The results of the UX evaluation were compared with the UX heuristics to check again whether the users' needs had been sufficiently taken into account.

5 Development of the Heuristics

5.1 Exploratory Stage

In the exploratory stage a literature review was conducted to gather relevant information about wallets. Firstly, this includes general information and features of wallets, i.e., definitions, purpose, context of use, advantages and disadvantages as well as general and specific features. In addition, the search also included attributes of UX (especially usability) and InfoSec. Existing general and wallet-specific UX and InfoSec heuristics were also searched for. In particular, this involved guidelines, principles, design recommendations and patterns of UX and InfoSec. Literature was searched in the databases Google Scholar, ResearchGate and ScienceDirect using the following search terms:

- ("digital identity wallet" OR "identity wallet") AND ("UX" OR "user experience" OR "usability" OR "information security" OR "security" OR "heuristics"),
- ("UX" OR "user experience" OR "usability" OR "information security" OR "security") AND "heuristics",
- ("UX" OR "user experience" OR "usability" OR "information security" OR "security") AND "attributes".

Only publications in German and English were reviewed. First, the titles and abstracts were examined with regard to general information and features of wallets, UX, InfoSec and sets of heuristics or other relevant elements of UX and InfoSec. Subsequently, the selected publications were read by an author and redundancies were filtered. With regard to the existing sets of heuristics, those that referred to similar software systems or contained general heuristics were selected. In total, twenty-six publications were considered relevant and therefore used in the next stages.

5.2 Descriptive Stage

The information collected during the literature review was selected and prioritized according to importance. Initially, all information was categorized into the following six topics: (1) Information about wallets, (2) Features of wallets, (3) UX attributes, (4) InfoSec attributes, (5) Sets of existing heuristics and/or other relevant UX elements and (6) Sets of existing heuristics and/or other relevant elements of InfoSec. This categorization was specified by the method, supplemented by the topics (4) and (6) to enable the development of InfoSec heuristics. The inputs were then prioritized by the authors according to category using a three-point scale: (1) Unimportant, (2) Rather important or (3) Very important. The prioritization was performed in two steps: In the first step, the features, attributes and heuristics were prioritized as a complete set depending on the respective author(s). In the second step, attributes and heuristics were also rated individually. For each step, the information about wallets was prioritized according to importance in terms of how accurately they describe wallets. Subsequently, the information marked as "very important" was used to prioritize the information of the remaining topics. Furthermore, reasons for the prioritization were documented.

In addition, the features were grouped into either general features, which can also be applied to other software systems, or specific features for wallets. Specific features were given higher priority than general features in order to achieve the development of wallet-specific heuristics.

The specific features of wallets identified are explained below [14], extending the six basis functions of Podgorelec et al. [24]:

1. *Overview of stored credentials.*
2. *Detailed view of stored credentials.*

3. *Management of different types of credentials.*
4. *Quick access to stored credentials.*
5. *Enduring powers of attorney.*
6. *Reference to missing credentials.*
7. *Transfer of stored credentials.*
8. *Managing other people's credentials.*
9. *Optional protection when releasing data.*
10. *Overview of released data and credentials.*
11. *Checking and displaying the trustworthiness of the service provider.*
12. *Checking and displaying the purpose of use.*
13. *Accessibility.*

According to Cucko et al. [40], other important features of wallets are:

1. *Autonomy.* Users must be able to manage their identity data themselves without having to rely on third parties. They should be able to manage processes relating to their identity and data themselves, e.g., creating, saving, updating, sharing and removing.
2. *Control.* Users must be able to control the use or release of their identity data and delegate control to autonomous agents of their choice.
3. *Consent.* Users should be able to give conscious and informed consent to the use and sharing of their identity data. Consent should be revocable.

As attributes of UX, the "honeycomb of UX" by Morville [15] was chosen, containing seven attributes, as explained in Sect. 3.2. The attribute desirability was not considered in the development of the heuristics, as the level of usability has a direct impact on the perception of the desirability of the application [31].

The attributes of InfoSec consist of *confidentiality*, *integrity* and *availability*, also known as the CIA triad of InfoSec, as described in Sect. 3.2.

As a starting point for developing new heuristics, an existing set of UX heuristics was chosen, namely the ten heuristics by Nielsen [20]. In addition, the requirements for the use of wallets by Krauß et al. [13] and five best practices and seven worst practices for the design of wallets by Sellung and Kubach [36] were selected.

5.3 Correlational Stage

In the correlational stage, the identified features of wallets were mapped to (1) the attributes of UX and InfoSec, and (2) the existing sets of heuristics. This process was carried out twice, first with the attributes and heuristics of UX and then with those of InfoSec. Table 1 shows an example of the matching of the features with the UX attributes and heuristics. An example for the matching with the InfoSec attributes and heuristic is given in Table 2.

5.4 Selection Stage

In the selection stage, the information, features, attributes and sets of heuristics matched in the previous stage are divided into the following categories:

Table 1. Example: matching of the wallet features with UX attributes and existing heuristics

Wallet feature	UX attributes	Existing heuristic
Overview of stored credentials	UX: utility, usability, credibility Usability: memorability, learnability, satisfaction	N6: recognition rather than recall [20]

Table 2. Example: matching of the wallet features with InfoSec attributes and existing heuristics

Wallet feature	InfoSec attribute	Existing heuristic
Management of different types of credentials	Confidentiality	Data encryption [10]

- Keep: The heuristic is transferred unchanged to the new set of heuristics for the specific application area.
- Adapt: The heuristic is adapted to the specific application area.
- Eliminate: The heuristic cannot be transferred to the specific area of application.

In terms of UX, all heuristics by Nielsen [20] were selected as they correspond to basic requirements of software systems. All ten heuristics were specifically adapted to wallets, but two heuristics were merged to eliminate redundancies. Furthermore, six new heuristics were created, based on the other relevant elements researched, as the existing heuristics did not cover all features of wallets. For the InfoSec heuristics, five of the heuristics proposed by Gordieiev et al. [10] were adapted, and two were eliminated since they were not applicable to wallets. In addition, three new heuristics were created, for which the heuristics of Realpe et al. [28] served as a foundation. Table 3 shows examples of the categorizations of the mappings performed in this stage.

Table 3. Example of the categorization of the mapped features, attributes and existing heuristics

Name of the heuristic	Category	Existing heuristic	Mapped feature
Accessibility	Create	Krauß et al. [14]	General wallet-feature
Recognition rather than recall	Adapt	Nielsen [20]	General wallet-feature
Data encryption	Adapt	Gordiviev [10]	General wallet-feature, management of different types of credentials
Automatic updates	Create	Realpe et al. [28]	General wallet-feature

5.5 Specification Stage

In the specification stage, the new heuristics were specified using the standard template that was proposed by the authors of the method [27]. Each heuristic was given a unique identifier, a name, a short definition and a more detailed description. The specification of the heuristics also lists the attributes of UX and InfoSec that apply to the respective heuristic. Furthermore, each heuristic contains an example of its compliance and also advantages for UX and InfoSec that result from compliance. Finally, the template contains a checklist in which elements or criteria that are linked to the heuristic can be included. The first draft of the UX heuristics contains fifteen heuristics, while the first draft of the InfoSec heuristics consists of eight heuristics.

5.6   First Validation Stage: Expert Interviews

The proposed heuristics of UX and InfoSec were first validated using expert interviews. The heuristics were evaluated regarding their comprehensibility and completeness. A total of eight expert interviews were conducted, four for the InfoSec heuristics and four for the UX heuristics.

The interview was carried out by means of a written questionnaire consisting of two parts. In the first part, the heuristics were evaluated individually with regard to comprehensibility and completeness. The comprehensibility of the heuristics was queried on a scale from (1) not understandable to (5) fully understandable. Table 4 and Table 5 show the assessment results regarding comprehensibility of the individual heuristics. In addition, the experts were able to list possible ambiguities. Furthermore, the experts were asked to suggest changes, in case a heuristic did not cover all essential aspects – particularly in relation to the assigned UX and InfoSec attributes and the checklist – in order to assess the completeness of the heuristic. The experts were also asked to provide additional comments on the individual heuristic, e.g., on wording.

Table 4. Average assessment of the comprehensibility of the UX heuristics

ID/name of heuristic	Comprehensibility
HU1: Accessibility	4.5
HU2: Visibility of the system status	4
HU3: Transparency	4.5
HU4: Comprehensible system language	3.75
HU5: Control and freedom of users	3.5
HU6: Consistency and standards	4.5
HU7: Error messages and error prevention	4
HU8: Recognition rather than recall	4
HU9: Flexibility and efficiency of use	4.25
HU10: Aesthetic and minimalist design	3.75
HU11: Help and documentation	3.75
HU12: Authentication	2.25
HU13: Interoperability	4
HU14: Management of identity profiles and credentials	3.25
HU15: Backup and recovery	3.5
Average	3.83

Table 5. Average assessment of the comprehensibility of the InfoSec heuristics

ID/name of heuristic	Comprehensibility
HI1: Authentication	4.5
HI2: Secure data transmission	3.5
HI3: Avoidance of incorrect operation	4
HI4: Guidelines for passwords	4.5
HI5: Data encryption	5
HI6: Availability	5
HI7: Automatic updates	5
HI8: Guidelines for smartcards	5
Average	4.56

In the second part, the presented set of heuristics was evaluated with regard to future use and also completeness. The aim was to determine whether the heuristics cover all essential aspects of UX and InfoSec of wallets. The expert interviews led to the following two main findings.

First, the distinction between the individual UX heuristics from each other needs to be worked out more clearly: "In the checklist of heuristic 8 there are slight overlaps with heuristic 3. Are any other points of this also relevant for heuristic 8, or is the checklist really complete? Since the checklist is very specific, it should contain all the information that is relevant to interactions in the wallet".

Second, the proposed heuristics should be brought to a uniform level, as some of them related to rather abstract or very specific aspects of wallets, such as individual features: "The heuristics are very different, from abstract or high-level to very specific (especially for the checklists)".

When asked whether the UX experts would use the proposed heuristics to evaluate similar software systems in the future, all four participants answered affirmatively, provided that the proposed changes were incorporated. One expert answered the question with "not yet", noting that the heuristics should be even more specific to those that apply exclusively for wallets. For the InfoSec experts, three of the four participants also answered yes. The expert's reason for not using the heuristics in the future was that InfoSec is a complex field extending across all levels of abstraction, from design to implementation, which the heuristics do not adequately take into account.

5.7   Refinement Stage 1

In the refinement stage, the proposed heuristics for UX and InfoSec were adapted and improved based on the results obtained in the validation stage. No heuristic remained unchanged as the formulations were revised in order to increase the comprehensibility and accuracy of the heuristics. Furthermore, those heuristics that could not be clearly separated from each other were merged. As a result, the original fifteen UX heuristics were reduced to twelve refined heuristics by merging two heuristics each. The heuristics HU8 "Recognition rather than recall" and HU3 "Transparency" were merged into the heuristic "Transparent design". HU14 "Management of identity profiles and credentials" and HU15 "Backup and recovery" were merged to "Autonomy and control". From the set of InfoSec heuristics, the two heuristics HI4 and HI8 were removed because they were not sufficiently applicable to the use case of wallets. Thus, the eight original heuristics were reduced to six refined heuristics. However, no new heuristics were created, as the two sets of heuristics were considered complete by the experts.

5.8 Validation Stage 2: Heuristic Evaluation

In order to validate the refined UX heuristics, a heuristic evaluation [22] was carried out. A heuristic evaluation of the refined InfoSec heuristics was not conducted due to a lack of a general set of InfoSec heuristics to compare against.

In the heuristic evaluation the participants were asked to review a wallet prototype (see Sect. 4) in order to identify and list UX problems. For this purpose, the six participants were categorised into two groups, an experimental group and a control group. The experimental group performed the heuristic evaluation using the UX heuristics developed for wallets, while the control group used the ten UX heuristics by Nielsen [20]. Table 6 shows the problems found by the control group.

Table 6. Number of problems found by the control group $\{E_1^c, E_2^c, E_3^c\}$

Name of the heuristic	Problems found			
	E_1^c	E_2^c	E_3^c	Overlaps
Visibility of System Status	2	2	0	0
Match Between the System and the Real World	0	0	2	0
User Control and Freedom	2	2	0	0
Consistency and Standards	3	6	3	1
Error Prevention	0	4	0	0
Recognition Rather than Recall	0	3	0	0
Flexibility and Efficiency of Use	1	2	1	0
Aesthetic and Minimalist Design	1	1	0	0
Help Users Recognize, Diagnose, and Recover from Errors	0	0	0	0
Help and Documentation	1	3	1	1
Sum	10	23	7	2

The three experts in the control group identified a total of seven, ten and twenty-three problems of the prototype, respectively.

The experts of the experimental group were able to identify more problems of the prototype using the wallet-specific heuristics, as given in Table 7. Here, the experts identified twenty-four, thirty-seven and fourty-two problems of the prototype, respectively. From the larger number of problems found in the experimental group, it can be concluded that the developed UX heuristics are better suited to evaluate the UX of wallets than the general heuristics by Nielsen [20].

In addition, a UX evaluation [33] was conducted with twenty-four test subjects who tested a wallet prototype. Thinking aloud [19], eye tracking [5] and two questionnaires, SUS [7] and UEQ-S [35], were used for this purpose. It was checked whether heuristics still had to be derived from the identified UX problems of the wallet users. It turns out that the developed heuristics address all UX problems of the evaluation and therefore no further changes need to be made to the developed heuristics.

The final UX and InfoSec heuristics for wallets are listed in the Appendix. The heuristics can be found in detailed form here [34].

6   Discussion and Limitations

The results achieved in this work, namely the sets of UX heuristics and the InfoSec heuristics for wallets, were significantly influenced by the feasibility of the method and the validations carried out.

Table 7. Number of problems found in the experimental group $\{E_1^e, E_2^e, E_3^e\}$

ID/Name of the heuristic	Problems found			
	E_1^e	E_2^e	E_3^e	Overlaps
HU1: Accessibility	7	4	5	3
HU2: Visibility of system status	3	3	2	3
HU3: Transparent design	5	5	5	1
HU4: Comprehensible system language	2	5	1	2
HU5: Free navigation	1	2	1	1
HU6: Consistency and standards	0	0	3	0
HU7: Error prevention and error tolerance	6	5	1	1
HU8: Flexibility, efficiency and effectiveness of use	4	4	2	1
HU9: Aesthetic and minimalist design	5	5	2	0
HU10: Help and documentation	2	2	1	1
HU11: Organizational interoperability	0	0	1	0
HU12: Autonomy and control	7	7	0	1
Sum	42	37	24	14

The implementation of Rusu and Quiñones' method is not trivial. This is also confirmed by a survey of experts conducted by the authors themselves to validate the method [26]. It requires not only time but also human resources. In particular, the matching of the UX and InfoSec attributes with the specific features of the application area under consideration in the correlation stage requires special care, as this determines the extent to which the developed heuristics fulfill their purpose.

The comprehensibility of the heuristics is largely determined by the quality of the specification. The selection of experts for the expert interviews therefore also has an influence on the quality of the heuristics.

In a heuristic evaluation, the number of people participating is decisive for the number of problems found in a user interface. According to Nielsen [21], a single person is only able to identify around 35% of the usability problems of a user interface. Therefore it is advisable to have the heuristic evaluation carried out by five, at least three evaluators, in order to achieve a balanced relationship between costs and benefits [21]. As the heuristic evaluation was carried out by three people per group (the suggested minimum) in this study due to a lack of time and personnel resources, it is possible that some UX problems could not be identified in the prototype. However, the UX problems found in the control group and the experimental group were compared and both groups consisted of three people each. So the risk of not finding UX problems was the same for both groups.

In order to further develop the heuristics, an additional iteration of the method is recommended. The information gained from this can be particularly useful for the InfoSec heuristics, as InfoSec must be taken into account in all phases of software development, from design to implementation.

The implementation of a heuristic evaluation based on the developed InfoSec heuristics would also be a possible future step. Although no general InfoSec heuristics could be identified that could serve as a control, it would be possible to compare the results with those of other methods for evaluating InfoSec.

Furthermore, UX and InfoSec can influence each other [8,38]. This means that heuristics should not only be used to separately evaluate UX and InfoSec of wallets, but also interactions between UX and InfoSec, i.e. between heuristics. To achieve this, the heuristic evaluation method [22] could be adapted accordingly so that interactions between the heuristics are also included in the evaluation. Concretely, the heuristics can be integrated in an interaction matrix [17] and the interaction properties (complementary, conflicting or neutral) can be defined for each heuristic.

7   Conclusion and Future Work

The main contribution of this paper are twelve UX and six InfoSec heuristics for wallets that can be used to evaluate and improve UX and InfoSec of wallets. To create the heuristics, an existing method for developing UX heuristics was adapted so that InfoSec heuristics could also be developed. The developed heuristics were then evaluated by conducting interviews with UX and InfoSec experts. This was followed by a second evaluation stage in which a control group and an experimental group of UX experts were formed. The control group conducted heuristic evaluations with Nielsen's UX heuristics using the wallet prototype. The experimental group conducted heuristic evaluations with the self-developed UX heuristics using a wallet prototype. The results of the two groups were then compared and it was determined that the self-developed UX heuristics performed better. Since no comparable InfoSec heuristics could be found in the literature to perform heuristic evaluations and thus compare the self-developed InfoSec heuristics, the second evaluation stage was omitted for InfoSec heuristics.

Therefore, the InfoSec heuristics could be further evaluated, e.g., by applying and comparing heuristic evaluation using the developed and future developed InfoSec heuristics.

The developed heuristics provide a starting point for further research on how to evaluate and improve the quality of wallets in the areas of UX and InfoSec. It is of interest to study the interactions between the heuristics, in particular between heuristics of the two different, sometimes conflicting areas of UX and InfoSec. A case study is planned to apply the heuristics to another wallet and in particular to evaluate the interactions between UX and InfoSec heuristics.

Acknowledgments. This paper is a result of the project Showcase Secure Digital Identities Karlsruhe (SDIKA) (https://www.sdika.de/en). The goal of the project is to use digital identities to connect people, organizations, and processes. The values of digital sovereignty, fairness, and interoperability are guiding principles of the project and for the regional showcase. This project is supported by the Federal Ministry for Economic Affairs and Climate Action (BMWK) on the basis of a decision by the German Bundestag.

A Appendix

A.1 UX Heuristics

Table 8. UX heuristic 1: Accessibility

ID	HU1
Name	Accessibility
Definition	The wallet should be accessible without barriers
Description	The wallet should be accessible for users with disabilities or conditions that require additional features

Table 9. UX heuristic 2: Visibility of the system status

ID	HU2
Name	Visibility of the system status
Definition	The wallet should inform users about the current system status within a reasonable period of time
Description	The wallet should always inform users about the current system status within a reasonable period of time. In particular, it should provide feedback on actions performed (e.g., error success messages)

Table 10. UX heuristic 3: Transparent design

ID	HU3
Name	Transparent design
Definition	The wallet should be designed transparently, so that users understand the functionality and processes without placing a significant cognitive load on them
Description	The functionality and processes of the wallet should be designed to be transparent so that users can understand them without severe cognitive load. In particular, users should be given access to security-relevant information (e.g., trustworthiness of service providers), interactions made and the purpose of the shared data

Table 11. UX heuristic 4: Comprehensible system language

ID	HU4
Name	Comprehensible system language
Definition	The wallet should use a language that is understandable and familiar to users
Description	The terms used in the wallet should be familiar to users and not too technical. Technical terms that cannot be avoided should be explained to users. In addition, users should be able to select any language, with the operating system language initially set

Table 12. UX heuristic 5: Free navigation

ID	HU5
Name	Free navigation
Definition	The wallet should provide users with the ability to navigate freely within the wallet. Among other things, the "exit", "cancel" and "back" features should be supported
Description	If users use a wallet feature by mistake, it should be possible to cancel it and return to the previous state. In addition, it should be possible to continue processes that have been cancelled by mistake without having to go through them again

Table 13. UX heuristic 6: Consistency and standards

ID	HU6
Name	Consistency and standards
Definition	Interaction patterns and terminology should be used consistently both within the wallet and across applications
Description	The wallet should follow a uniform standard in terms of the design of the user interface and the terminology. Consistent interaction patterns should be used for similar functions

Table 14. UX heuristic 7: Error prevention and error tolerance

ID	HU7
Name	Error prevention and error tolerance
Definition	The wallet should be designed in such a way that it prevents users from performing incorrect operations that could lead to errors. Users should be warned before errors occur. If errors occur, solutions are offered
Description	Users must be clearly informed, which steps are feasible within an action. To avoid errors, the wallet should warn users if performing an action could lead to an error and prevent them from doing so. The cause of the potential/actual error and instructions on how to correct the error should be clearly communicated

Table 15. UX heuristic 8: Flexibility, efficiency and effectiveness of use

ID	HU8
Name	Flexibility, efficiency and effectiveness of use
Definition	The wallet should support flexible use. It should also contain functions that increase and accelerate the user's task fulfilment
Description	The wallet should be flexible to use, e.g., by allowing credentials to be grouped, sorted, filtered, and searched. Support or automation functions (e.g., automatic preselection of credentials when sharing at service provider) increase the efficiency and effectiveness of use

Table 16. UX heuristic 9: Aesthetic and minimalist design

ID	HU9
Name	Aesthetic and minimalist design
Definition	The design used in the wallet should be minimalist and aesthetic, i.e., it should support the primary goals of the users
Description	The design should be subject to a logical information structure and should not contain any superfluous elements. A clear layout should guide users to the most important features of the wallet and not overwhelm them with excessive text or other elements. In addition, the design should also be customizable according to the user's wishes

Table 17. UX heuristic 10: Help and documentation

ID	HU10
Name	Help and documentation
Definition	The wallet should provide help and documentation according to the specific tasks of the users
Description	If users are unable to progress within the wallet, it is necessary that they are provided with help. This may be possible through help requests or documentation

Table 18. UX heuristic 11: Organizational interoperability

ID	HU11
Name	Organizational interoperability
Definition	The wallet should provide adaptive interfaces to other ecosystems
Description	Digital identities are of little value if they only work in limited niches. Therefore, interfaces to other ecosystems should exist in order to create many opportunities to use the wallet

Table 19. UX heuristic 12: Autonomy and control

ID	HU12
Name	Autonomy and control
Definition	Users should be able to access their data without being dependent on third parties. They should be able to give a conscious and self-determined release of their data and be able to revoke it later
Description	The wallet should allow users to create and delete different identity profiles. This also enables the management of other people's credentials with their consent. Users should also be able to create and manage self-issued credentials (e.g., food incompatibilities). They should be able to consciously consent to the use or release of their data. It should also be possible to back up and restore data. To avoid dependence on individual wallet providers, it should be possible to transfer data from one wallet to another

A.2 InfoSec Heuristics

Table 20. InfoSec heuristic 1: Authentication

ID	HI1
Name	Authentication
Definition	A user should authenticate to the wallet and is then authenticated and authorized by the wallet
Description	Sensitive user data is stored in the wallet. Such data should be secured by at least one authentication method. The authentication method should comply with standardized, secure rules (e.g., finger scan). Subsequently, the user is authenticated and authorized

Table 21. InfoSec heuristic 2: Secure data transfer

ID	HI2
Name	Secure data transfer
Definition	The wallet should use cryptographic mechanisms to prevent electronic data transmission from unauthorized access
Description	Data transfer should be secured by cryptographic mechanisms and use secure protocols. During data transfer, it must not be possible to retrieve user data and the system should detect when encrypted messages are changed, copied, recorded, or deleted

Table 22. InfoSec heuristic 3: Avoidance of security-critical actions

ID	HI3
Name	Avoidance of security-critical actions
Definition	The wallet should technically ensure that security-critical actions are avoided
Description	Security-critical actions should be technically counteracted. In addition, users are informed about the terms of use and must explicitly agree to them

Table 23. InfoSec heuristic 4: Data encryption

ID	HI4
Name	Data encryption
Definition	Data is securely encrypted and decrypted
Description	The encryption and decryption of data stored in the wallet is implemented securely. For example, the user creates a key pair consisting of a public and a private key. A document is then created that contains the user's Decentralized Identifier (DID) as well as information about the user's public keys and metadata (e.g., type of encryption). If the user wants to store data in the wallet, this data is encrypted with a public key that is stored in the recipient's DID document. This ensures that only the recipient with the corresponding private key can decrypt the data. To decrypt the encrypted data, the wallet uses the user's private key to unlock the data

Table 24. InfoSec heuristic 5: Recovery options and availability

ID	HI5
Name	Recovery options and availability
Definition	Wallet providers should ensure that their application is highly available. The wallet must also prevent data loss and enable data recovery
Description	Wallet providers must minimize the risk of system failures so that the application is always available to users. The data stored in the wallet must be always protected against loss. The wallet should provide the option of (automated) backups and data recovery

Table 25. InfoSec heuristic 6: Automatic security updates

ID	HI6
Name	Automatic security updates
Definition	The wallet automatically installs the required security updates and notifies users
Description	Wallets automatically perform security updates, e.g., to eliminate errors and close security gaps. Users are always informed about the security updates

References

1. 24760-1:2022, D.E.I.: IT Security and Privacy - A framework for identity management - Part 1: Terminology and concepts (ISO/IEC 24760-1:2022) (2022)
2. 9241-11:2018-11, D.E.I.: DIN EN ISO 9241-11:2018-11, Ergonomics of human-system interaction - Part 11: Usability: Definitions and concepts (ISO_9241-11:2018) (2018)
3. 9241-210:2020-03, D.E.I.: DIN EN ISO 9241-210:2020-03, Ergonomics of human-system interaction - Part 210: Human-centred design for interactive systems (ISO_9241-210:2020) (2020)
4. Bascur, C., Rusu, C., Quiñones, D.: ECUXH: a set of user eXperience heuristics for e-commerce. In: Meiselwitz, G. (ed.) HCII 2021. LNCS, vol. 12774, pp. 407–420. Springer, Cham (2021). https://doi.org/10.1007/978-3-030-77626-8_27
5. Bojko, A.: Eye tracking in user experience testing: how to make the most of it. In: Proceedings of the 14th Annual Conference of the Usability Professionals' Association (UPA), Montréal, Canada (2005)
6. Braun, S., Sauer, M., Sürmeli, J., Thessen, J.: Self-sovereign identitiy in E-commerce: the future of personalized online shopping (2024). https://doi.org/10.5281/ZENODO.12644454
7. Brooke, J.: SUS: a quick and dirty usability scale. Usab. Eval. Ind. (1995)
8. Distler, V., Lenzini, G., Lallemand, C., Koenig, V.: The framework of security-enha,ncing friction: how UX can help users behave more securely. In: NSPW 2020: New Security Paradigms Workshop 2020, pp. 45–58. ACM, Online USA (2020). https://doi.org/10.1145/3442167.3442173
9. Gonzalez, R.M., Martin, M.V., Munoz-Arteaga, J., alvarez Rodriguez, F., Garcia-Ruiz, M.A.: A measurement model for secure and usable e-commerce websites. In: Proceedings of the

Canadian Conference on Electrical and Computer Engineering 2009, pp. 77–82. IEEE, St. John's, NL (2009). https://doi.org/10.1109/CCECE.2009.5090096

10. Gordieiev, O., Kharchenko, V., Vereshchak, K.: Usable security versus secure usability: an assessment of attributes interaction, pp. 727–740 (2017)

11. Khayretdinova, A., Kubach, M., Sellung, R., Roßnagel, H.: Conducting a usability evaluation of decentralized identity management solutions. In: Friedewald, M., Kreutzer, M., Hansen, M. (eds.) Selbstbestimmung, Privatheit und Datenschutz, pp. 389–406. Springer, Wiesbaden (2022). https://doi.org/10.1007/978-3-658-33306-5_19

12. Kostic, S., Poikela, M.: Do users want to use digital identities? A study of a concept of an identity wallet, Boston (2022)

13. Krauß, A.M., Kostic, S., Sellung, R.A.: A more user-friendly digital wallet? User scenarios of a future wallet. In: Open Identity Summit 2023. Gesellschaft für Informatik e.V. (2023). https://doi.org/10.18420/OID2023_06

14. Krauß, A.M., Sellung, R.A., Kostic, S.: Ist das die Wallet der Zukunft?: Ein Blick durch die Nutzendenbrille beim Einsatz von digitalen Identitäten. HMD Praxis der Wirtschaftsinformatik, pp. 344–365 (2023). https://doi.org/10.1365/s40702-023-00952-6

15. Morville, P.: Experience design unplugged. In: ACM SIGGRAPH 2005 Web program on - SIGGRAPH 2005, p. 10. ACM Press, Los Angeles (2005). https://doi.org/10.1145/1187335.1187347

16. Morville, P., Sullenger, P.: Ambient findability: libraries, serials, and the internet of things. Serials Libr. **1–4**, 33–38 (2010). https://doi.org/10.1080/03615261003622999

17. Nechansky, H.: The interaction matrix: from individual goal-setting to the four modes of coexistence, pp. 87–106 (2016).https://doi.org/10.1108/K-09-2014-0192

18. Nieles, M., Dempsey, K., Pillitteri, V.Y.: NIST special publication 800-12: an introduction to information security (2017). https://doi.org/10.6028/NIST.SP.800-12r1

19. Nielsen, J.: Usability Engineering. Academic Press, Boston (1993)

20. Nielsen, J.: Enhancing the explanatory power of usability heuristics. In: Proceedings of the SIGCHI Conference on Human Factors in Computing Systems Celebrating Interdependence - CHI 1994, pp. 152–158. ACM Press, Boston (1994). https://doi.org/10.1145/191666.191729

21. Nielsen, J.: Heuristic evaluations: how to conduct (1995)

22. Nielsen, J., Molich, R.: Heuristic evaluation of user interfaces. In: Proceedings of the SIGCHI Conference on Human Factors in Computing Systems Empowering People - CHI 1990, pp. 249–256. ACM Press, Seattle (1990). https://doi.org/10.1145/97243.97281

23. Parliament, E.: Regulation on electronic identification and trust services for electronic transactions in the internal market. Regulation (2024). http://data.europa.eu/eli/reg/2024/1183/oj

24. Podgorelec, B., Alber, L., Zefferer, T.: What is a (digital) identity wallet? A systematic literature review. In: 2022 IEEE 46th Annual Computers, Software, and Applications Conference (COMPSAC), pp. 809–818. IEEE, Los Alamitos (2022). https://doi.org/10.1109/COMPSAC54236.2022.00131

25. Preukschat, A., Reed, D.: Self-sovereign identity: decentralized digital identity and verifiable credentials. Manning, Shelter Island (2021)

26. Quiñones, D., Rusu, C., Rusu, V.: A methodology to develop usability/user experience heuristics. Comput. Stand. Interfaces **59**, 109–129 (2018). https://doi.org/10.1016/j.csi.2018.03.002, https://linkinghub.elsevier.com/retrieve/pii/S0920548917303860

27. Quiñones Otey, D.: A methodology to develop usability/user experience heuristics. In: Interacción 2017: Proceedings of the XVIII International Conference on Human Computer Interaction (2017). https://doi.org/10.1145/3123818.3133832

28. Realpe, P.C., Collazos, C.A., Hurtado, J., Granollers, A.: A set of heuristics for usable security and user authentication. In: Proceedings of the 17th International Conference on Human

Computer Interaction, pp. 1–8. ACM, Salamanca (2016). https://doi.org/10.1145/2998626. 2998662

29. Rusu, C., Roncagliolo, S., Rusu, V., Collazos, C.: A methodology to establish usability heuristics. In: Proceedings of the 4th International Conference on Advances in Computer-Human Interactions (ACHI) (2011)

30. Saavedra, M.-J., Rusu, C., Quiñones, D., Roncagliolo, S.: A set of usability and user eXperience heuristics for social networks. In: Meiselwitz, G. (ed.) HCII 2019. LNCS, vol. 11578, pp. 128–139. Springer, Cham (2019). https://doi.org/10.1007/978-3-030-21902-4_10

31. Sade, S.: Mobile ease-of-use and desirability through user-centered design. SSGRR 2002 L'Aquila (2002)

32. Sartor, S., Sedlmeir, J., Rieger, A., Roth, T.: Love at first sight? A user experience study of self-sovereign identity wallets. In: Proceedings of the 30th European Conference on Information Systems (ECIS 2022) (2022)

33. Sauer, M., Pfeifer, S., Sürmeli, J., Siebert, E., Woytal, I.: User-friendly integration of identity wallets and mobility platforms: a user experience study conducted in the SDIKA project (2024). https://doi.org/10.13140/RG.2.2.12412.55682

34. Sauer, M., Schork, S.: User experience and information security heuristics for digital identity wallets (2024). https://doi.org/10.5281/ZENODO.10865962

35. Schrepp, M., Hinderks, A., Thomaschewski, J.: Design and evaluation of a short version of the user experience questionnaire (UEQ-S). Int. J. Interact. Multimed. Artif. Intell. 4 (2017)

36. Sellung, R., Kubach, M.: Research on user experience for digital IdentityWallets: state-of-the-art and recommendations. In: Open Identity Summit 2023 (2023). https://doi.org/10.18420/OID2023_03

37. Shneiderman, B.: Designing the user interface: strategies for effective human-computer-interaction (1998)

38. Whitten, A., Tygar, D.J.: Why Johnny can't encrypt: a usability evaluation of PGP 5.0. In: Proceedings of the 8th conference on USENIX Security Symposium, Washington, D.C. (1999)

39. Yáñez Gómez, R., Cascado Caballero, D., Sevillano, J.L.: Heuristic evaluation on mobile interfaces: a new checklist. Sci. World J. 2014, 1–19 (2014). https://doi.org/10.1155/2014/434326

40. Čučko, Š, Bećirović, Š, Kamišalić, A., Mrdović, S., Turkanović, M.: Towards the classification of self-sovereign identity properties. IEEE Access 10, 88306–88329 (2022). https://doi.org/10.1109/ACCESS.2022.3199414

Supporting Behaviour Change Techniques with Interaction Design Patterns

Farhat-ul-Ain[✉], Olga Popovitz, Gulassyl Amirgaliyeva, and Vladimir Tomberg

Tallinn University, Tallinn, Estonia
farhat23@tlu.ee

Abstract. Design patterns provide a structured method for addressing common design problems by offering proven solutions that can be reused across different contexts. In the case of designing digital behaviour change interventions, interaction designers may face challenges in translating Behaviour Change Techniques (BCTs) knowledge into digital interventions. Interaction design patterns for BCTs can help overcome this challenge by providing descriptions, examples, rationale for using BCTs, and proven solutions. The current study examines six patterns for commonly used BCTs in digital interventions (reminder, social support, goal setting, self-monitoring, and instruction on performing behaviour and feedback on behaviour). The proposed design patterns were evaluated by four interaction design experts. They found the descriptions and examples provided in the design patterns to be clear and comprehensible. The experts appreciated the balance between concreteness and abstractness. The resulting design patterns can contribute to the informed design of digital behaviour change interventions and are helpful for designers, developers, researchers and product managers. Experts suggested that the language of the design patterns needs to be simplified for industry professionals to ensure that they can understand and apply them. Experts also indicated the need for shorter versions of the patterns, such as plain summaries or mind maps. Future design efforts to refine and simplify the proposed patterns and to develop additional patterns covering a broader range of BCTs are required.

Keywords: Design pattern · Behaviour change techniques · Interaction design

1 Problem Statement

The increased growth in the use of smartphone applications, wearable technologies and web-based systems presents promising avenues for supporting behaviour change, referred to as Digital Behaviour Change Interventions (DBCIs) for health [1]. Digital interventions aiming for behaviour change support often include reminders or notifications, options for setting goals, and monitoring of behaviour and feedback, also defined as Behaviour Change Techniques (BCTs) [2, 3]. BCTs are defined as active, observable, replicable, and irreducible components of an intervention designed to alter behaviours. They can be used alone or in combination with other BCTs [3]. Michie et al. [2] provided a taxonomy of ninety-three BCTs divided into sixteen groups. The taxonomy of

H. Plácido da Silva and P. Cipresso (Eds.): CHIRA 2024, CCIS 2370, pp. 362–384, 2025.
https://doi.org/10.1007/978-3-031-82633-7_22

behaviour change techniques offers a structured and systematic way of understanding BCTs. For example, techniques that can be used for delivering different types of rewards and incentives (social reward, material reward, self-reward, material incentive, material reward) are grouped together as "rewards and incentives". The taxonomy also provides theoretical definitions of these BCTs, examples, and how one BCT can be used with other BCTs [2, 3]. This taxonomy can facilitate the selection of techniques from a wide range of possible techniques and link BCTs with behaviour change theories. This further allows us to define and clearly explain the observable content of the technique (such as agreeing on a daily 45-min walk is the actual content for the goal-setting technique) in detail, making the replication of BCTs easy [2].

BCTs are strategised in the form of features in DBCIs, for example, *prompts and cues* can be strategised as in-app notifications or reminder messages to support behaviour change [4]. Users interact with these features to support behaviour change, which means that these need to be carefully designed and aligned with theoretical definitions of BCTs. The current theoretical knowledge of BCTs lacks comprehensive practical guidelines on strategising BCTs in DBCIs [5–7]. Thompson et al. (2016) mentioned that the adoption and application of BCTs are fragmented, selected, and combined on an ad-hoc basis for designing DBCIs [8]. Studies have found a disparity between the intended and selected BCT, and the content of the BCTs is not matched with the mentioned BCT) [4, 9–15]. Farhat-ul-Ain [4] found that the techniques used in some studies cannot be coded with any BCT listed in the taxonomy (No BCT present), reflecting that BCTs are not strategised appropriately. This indicates a need for better practical interaction design guidelines and systematic approaches to overcome the challenge of translating theoretical knowledge of BCTs and strategising them into digital interventions for designers [9].

Interaction design as a field focuses on designing interactive behaviour or user interactions with digital and non-digital products [16]. *Design patterns* offer predefined solutions or models used in the interaction design to address common user problems. These design patterns include repeatable solutions, providing a set of rules or best practices for designing interactive systems. They serve as successful design solutions recognised by professionals in the field, offering guidance to designers, developers, evaluators, and users involved in the design and implementation of interactive systems [17, 18]. This work aimed to overcome the challenge of translating theoretical knowledge of BCTs and strategising them into digital interventions by proposing design pattern collections for BCTs.

In the current work, we proposed six design patterns for commonly used BCTs highlighted in a literature review [4] and evaluated them with experts. The authors assume that the pattern approach could facilitate the process of strategising BCTs by providing designers with a common language, terminology, structure and reusable solutions. The research questions for the current study are:

1. How can design patterns be developed to help designers strategise behaviour change techniques in digital behaviour change interventions?
2. To what extent do interaction design experts perceive proposed design patterns BCTs as understandable, helpful and acceptable?

To address these research questions, we first developed six design patterns for six commonly used BCTs highlighted in the previous review [4].The design patterns were further evaluated by interaction design experts.

2 Brief Overview of Design Patterns

Alexander et al. [19] coined the concept of design patterns in the field of architecture. Alexander proposed three essential patterns' elements: a *context*, a *problem*, and a *solution* [19]. The context is a recurrent collection of scenarios in which the pattern can be used. The problem represents a set of forces, such as goals and limitations, that exist in the context. In general, the problem specifies when to use the pattern. The solution indicates a design form or rule that may be used to resolve the forces. The same pattern concept is also applied in the field of interaction design, more broadly, where the primary objective is to create interactive systems that are useful and usable for users [20]. Seffah et al. [17] mentioned that design patterns provide solutions to common design problems, offering best practices for designing interactive systems. It is a simple method of documenting design knowledge, readable for designers, developers, and other stakeholders, based on knowledge (not created artificially), and captures essential principles of good design by telling the designer what to do and why. Typically, patterns are presented in a predefined and should include the problem-context-solution construct, but the overall structure may vary [18–20]. Some examples of design patterns include interaction patterns [18], user interface patterns [21], and Yahoo! Pattern Library [22]. The design patterns approach allows professionals and non-professionals to decide how to proceed and help to go forward with a design while enhancing communication and knowledge-sharing among people collaborating on a design project. It is a valuable approach for conveying and sharing experience and knowledge [23].

3 Design Patterns for Behaviour Change Techniques

The published literature on behaviour change techniques typically provides theoretical definitions of BCTs and examples for the application of these techniques in face-to-face settings. For interaction designers, this literature is not helpful enough to translate knowledge on behaviour change techniques into digital behaviour change interventions [2]. Design patterns can provide reusable solutions to interaction designers to help them select appropriate BCTs and strategise them in digital interventions. For the current study, the authors designed six patterns for selected commonly used BCTs identified in the recent review [4]. In this review, the authors coded behaviour change techniques used in DBCIs for health by using the taxonomy of behaviour change techniques used in thirty-five studies. The authors provided a comprehensive list of how these BCTs were strategised in DBCIs and found that six techniques are more frequently used (prompts and cues, social support (unspecified-mainly relating to advising someone or providing non-contingent reward rather than providing any practical or emotional support), goal-setting, self-monitoring of behaviour, feedback on behaviour, and instructions on how to perform behaviour) compared to others [4]. The current work is focused on developing design patterns for these most used BCTs.

Various pattern structures have been approached [18–20, 22]. Tidwell's structure of pattern documentation was selected because it contains a clear structure and elements, such as the name of the design pattern, examples, and an extensive explanation of why and how they can be utilised in the design and solution that can be used in various contexts [18]. Some elements were added to Tidwell's structure to contextualise it according to BCTs. "Design Principle and Theory" establishes a link between behaviour change theory and techniques. "BCT combinations" indicate how various BCTs are often combined. The authors attempted to support each design pattern element with relevant literature. A brief overview of elements included in Tidwell's approach and elements added by the authors is presented in Table 1:

Table 1. Structure of Tidwell Design Pattern Adapted for Behaviour Change Techniques.

Elements	Purpose
Pattern Name	Define pattern name
Code/BCT name (Group) in Taxonomy	BCT's name and group are mentioned in the BCT Taxonomy
Illustrative example	Screenshots of instantiated. In our case, it presents carefully selected images of BCTs strategised in digital interventions
What (Problem)	A short problem statement to specify the user needs where BCT can be used
Use when	Conditions in which patterns can be used
How	Represents the solution in the pattern for the BCT
Why	Provide the design rationale for BCT
Design principle and theory	Establishes the link between pattern, behaviour change theory and technique
BCTs combinations	Elaborate how BCTs can be combined with other techniques
In other collections	Directs to similar patterns in other collections, potentially offering new insights or examples

The following section provides six proposed design patterns (prompts and cues techniques, social support (Unspecified) techniques, goal-setting techniques, instructions on how to perform behaviour, feedback on behaviour technique, self-monitoring of behaviour) in detail (3.1, 3.2, 3.3, 3.4, 3.5 and 3.6). All design patterns follow the same structure as presented in Table 1.

3.1 Design Pattern for "Prompts and Cues Technique"

The most common behaviour change technique identified in the review was the "prompts and cues technique" [4]. It is typically strategised as notifications, emails, text messages, hyperlinks, calendar events, images, and auditory signals, often synchronised with the time or location of behaviour performance. It includes employing specific stimuli to capture and direct an individual's attention towards a particular direction. This stimulus enhances an individual's capacity to retain information, focus selectively on environmental cues, and make decisions among multiple options. The design pattern for the Prompts and Cues Technique is provided in Table 2.

Table 2. Design Pattern for Prompts and Cues Technique.

Pattern Name: Reminder (alternative names: Prompt, Trigger, Cue, Call to action, Request) **Code/BCT name (Group) in Taxonomy**: 7.1 Prompts/Cues (**Associations**)
Examples: AppleWatch reminder, activityApp, myTherapyApp, StretchClock 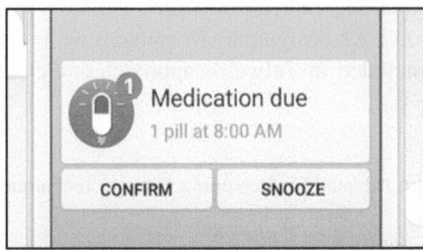  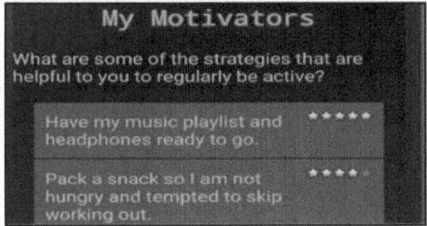 
What (Problem): Users may have trouble remembering to perform or focus on some tasks during a certain period. Users want to be reminded, informed, or motivated about the tasks or activities to form a new habit or routine or not to perform undesired ones.
Use when: Introduce to users a prompt or cue that can be used as a reminder to act or react in the direct context. This is useful when the user needs to be reminded or motivated to take some action in a specific context (e.g., take medication, remind a doctor's appointment, take a standing pause to reduce sitting time, etc.) or rethink a planned or ongoing activity (e.g., take stairs instead of elevator, reduce speed, drink water instead of soda).
How: Use notifications or prompts to encourage specific behaviour, such as taking medication at scheduled times. These reminders can be personalised and triggered based on user-defined settings or environmental cues. Reminders could be event-based or time-based. 'Reminder' could be user-generated, system-generated or generated by another person involved (e.g., a healthcare specialist). When designing, it is important to consider that these triggers may lead to alert fatigue, habituation, or user disregard of triggers [24].
Why: If 'Reminder' matches the time and the context – then the user is more likely to be motivated and able to take a needed action or complete a task.
Design Principle and Theory: Behaviour change technique 'Prompts/Cues' as an intervention component is linked with Theoretical Domain Framework constructs 'Memory, attention and decision processes' and 'Environmental context and resources', therefore influences memory, attention, attention control, decision making, cognitive overload/tiredness [25]. Technique supports a person's ability to retain information, focus selectively on aspects of the environment and choose between two or more alternatives.

(continued)

Table 2. (*continued*)

BCTs combinations: When a stimulus is linked to a specific action in an if-then plan including one or more of frequency, duration or intensity "Action planning" can be applied. 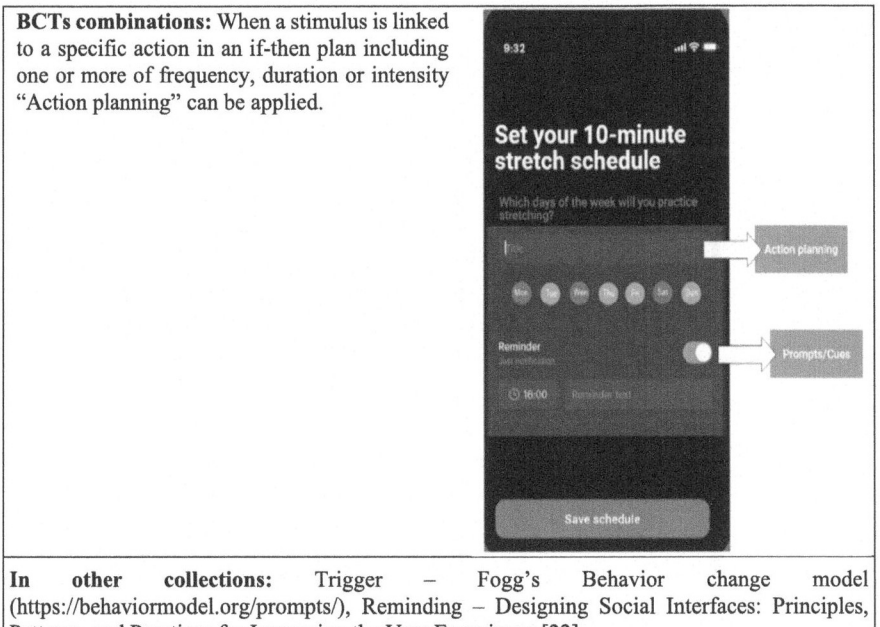
In other collections: Trigger – Fogg's Behavior change model (https://behaviormodel.org/prompts/), Reminding – Designing Social Interfaces: Principles, Patterns, and Practices for Improving the User Experience [22]

3.2 Design Pattern for "Social Support (Unspecified) Technique"

The second most used BCT is 'Social support (unspecified), which involves providing advice, arranging, or offering support from various sources such as friends, relatives, or colleagues, as well as non-contingent praise or rewards for behaviour performance. It is commonly delivered through social networks, apps with guidance messages, text messages, testimonials, WhatsApp groups, online forums, and phone counselling. The design pattern for the "Social Support (Unspecified) Technique" is provided in Table 3.

Table 3. A "Social Support (Unspecified) Technique".

Pattern Name: Social network **Code/BCT name (Group) in Taxonomy: 3.**1. Social Support (unspecified)
Examples Belong MS app, WHO Facebook chat-bot 
What (Problem): When a person tries to achieve something (target behaviour), he expects to receive various types of social support, such as praise, advice, encouragement, or guidance, through an intervention platform.
Use when: When designing interventions to support individuals in achieving target behaviours, it's essential to encourage interaction with the content and foster collaboration among users with mutual goals. This can be accomplished by creating engaging content that prompts participants to interact, such as liking, sharing, and commenting on posts, as demonstrated by Patrick et al. [26] in their study on Facebook content. Additionally, providing a medium for users to form groups and support each other is crucial. For instance, Inauen et al. [27] successfully used WhatsApp chat groups where participants encouraged each other to achieve their eating goals. 'Social Support' should be clearly defined in the design in terms of how it is delivered– in a group or individually, and from whom - family members, friends, specialists, and group members with the same goal; and demonstrate a connection to the target behaviour.
How: An intervention platform to deliver social support related to the user's target behaviour can use various digital channels, social networks, mobile applications, text messages, testimonials, messenger groups (WhatsApp), online community forums, phone calls, and chatbots. Support providers could be - family members, friends, caregivers, group members, and the community, or the system itself (digital intervention) could offer support via images, symbols, and software-generated dialogues.
Why: If a person receives 'Social support' as recognition and appreciation by others of his personal efforts and achievements, then he/she most likely will be motivated to learn and progress through their behaviour change plan.
Design Principle and Theory: 'Social support' as an intervention component is linked with the Theoretical Domain Framework construct 'Social influences' – defined as a change in one's

(continued)

Table 3. (*continued*)

beliefs, behaviour, or attitudes caused by external pressures, whether real or imagined [25]. Three types of social support are defined: emotional, informational, and instrumental [2].
BCTs combinations: To enhance the performance of a target behaviour, it is beneficial to advise on, arrange, or provide emotional, social support. This support can come from various sources, including friends, relatives, colleagues, "buddies," or staff. 
In other collections: Praise Design Pattern – https://ui-patterns.com/patterns/Praise Software pattern: cooperation [28]

3.3   Design Pattern for "Goal Setting Technique"

The third most used BCT was the "goal-setting technique", which helps users define their goals. It often includes features for setting specific, measurable, and time-bound objectives. It is often combined with other techniques, such as "feedback on behaviour" and "self-monitoring of behaviour", which offer to monitor themselves and provide feedback on progress and adjustments to goals based on performance. The design pattern for the "goal-setting technique" is provided in Table 4.

Table 4. Design Pattern for "Goal Setting Technique".

Pattern Name: Goal Scheduler **Code/BCT name (Group) in Taxonomy: Goal setting (behaviour) (Goals and planning)**
Examples: Google Fit app, MoveSum app 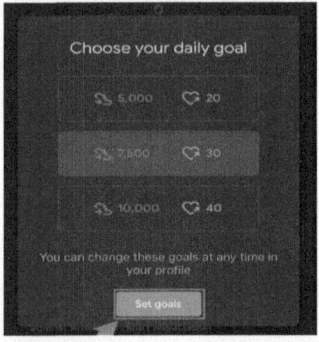 
What (Problem): Digitally supported interventions enable users to establish behaviour-oriented goals tailored to their intentions within the intervention platform. Users have the capability to define specific behavioural objectives aligned with their desired outcomes within the digital intervention setting. This feature empowers users to personalise their goals based on individual preferences and motivations, fostering engagement and facilitating targeted behaviour change efforts.
Use when: Pattern 'Goal setting' helps users to achieve specific behavioural changes or desired outcomes. Useful for establishing habitual behaviours that contribute to achieving desired outcomes effectively and sustainably. In interventions, patterns can be set by either the target user themselves or by experts designing goals on behalf of the target user. Collaborative approaches, where users receive expert guidance in selecting appropriate goals, can ensure that goals are tailored to individual needs and capabilities. This method promotes personalised goal setting that aligns with individual circumstances, enhancing the likelihood of successful behaviour change.
How: When setting goals within an intervention platform, it is crucial to ensure they are specific, measurable, realistic, achievable, time-based, and directly relevant to the target behaviour. Using in-app calculators and virtual agents and synchronising with popular calendar platforms like Google Calendar or iCal can enhance goal management and tracking. This diversified approach supports structured and systematic goal setting, thereby increasing the efficacy of behaviour change interventions.
Why: Goals help individuals plan and motivate their intention to achieve desired outcomes. They focus attention away from irrelevant tasks and towards behaviours that are relevant to achieving the goal.

(*continued*)

Table 4. (*continued*)

Design Principle and Theory: Behaviour change technique 'Goal setting' refers to Theoretical Domain Framework constructs such as 'Intention' and 'Goals'. Technique supports a person's ability to decide consciously to perform a behaviour or a resolve to act in a certain way and provides the mental representations of outcomes, or end states that an individual wants to achieve [25].

BCT combinations: The Behaviour Change Technique (BCT) taxonomy suggests that goal setting within interventions is more effective when accompanied by "Action planning" and "Self-monitoring of behaviour." "Action planning" involves specifying details like frequency, duration, or intensity of desired behaviour, while "Self-monitoring" means tracking progress towards goals. Integrating detailed behavioural planning and ongoing monitoring significantly enhances intervention effectiveness. Self-monitoring can be facilitated through self-tracking devices, wearable technology, or in-app sensors, providing feedback to users on their progress. This alignment with evidence-based strategies optimises the impact of behaviour change interventions on user outcomes [2].

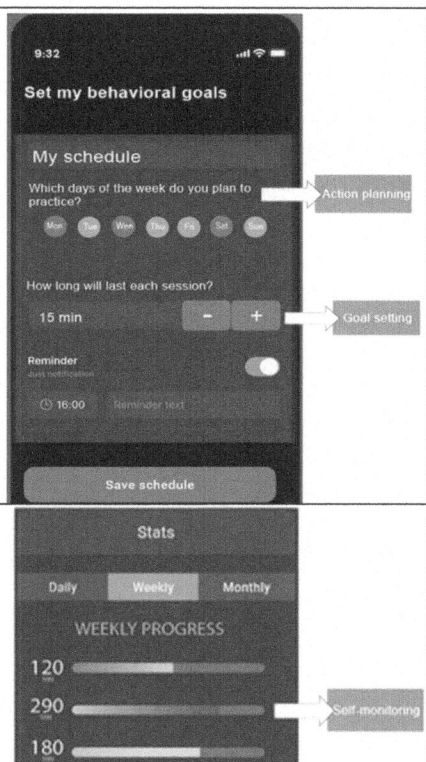

In other collections: Reduction & Tunnelling – Fogg's Persuasive Design Principles [29], Goal-Gradient Effect – https://ui-patterns.com/patterns/Completion

372   Farhat-ul-Ain et al.

3.4   Design Pattern for "Self-monitoring of Behaviour Technique"

The fourth most used BCT was the "goal-setting technique", which helps users individuals observe and document their actions as part of an effort to modify behaviour. It involves the systematic collection of pertinent health information, exemplified by participants modifying their smoking tracker based on daily cigarette consumption [30, 31]. The design pattern for "self-monitoring of behaviour" is provided in Table 5.

Table 5. Design Pattern for "Self-monitoring of Behaviour".

Pattern Name: Behavioural Tracker   **Code/BCT name (Group) in Taxonomy:** 2.3 Self-monitoring of behaviour (Feedback and monitoring)
Examples: Kwit app for smoking cessation   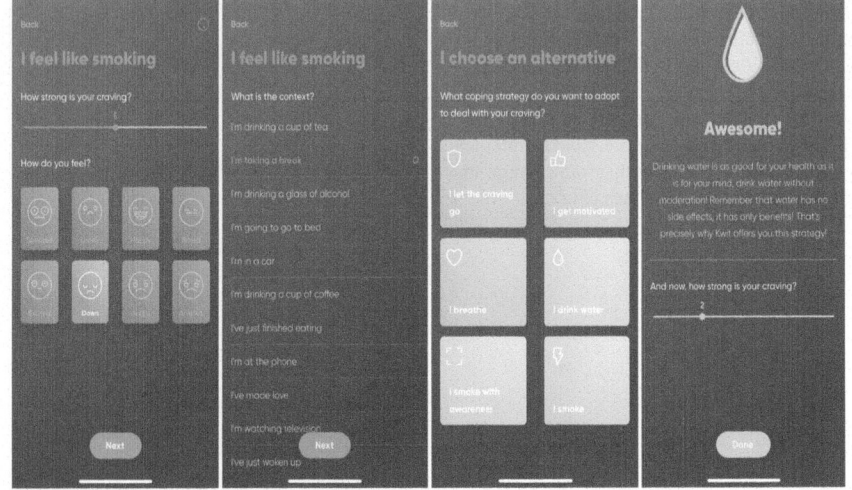
What (Problem): Individuals frequently encounter challenges in maintaining awareness of their actions and progress towards their desired health objectives. Adopting the practice of

Table 5. (*continued*)

"self-monitoring of behaviour," which involves actively tracking and documenting activities relevant to health goals, can facilitate informed decision-making and facilitate positive behavioural changes. Tang et al. [32] mentioned that self-monitoring enhances users' self-awareness regarding their actions and motivations, motivating them to reconsider their habits and intentions towards change

Use when: It is useful for systematically tracking and visually representing key parameters of behaviour. It is especially beneficial for individuals managing chronic conditions like diabetes or obesity or those aiming to adopt healthier habits. Additionally, it helps transform new habits, such as improving diet and reducing sedentary screen time, into automated routines, reducing the need for extensive self-regulation [33]. As self-regulation improves, individuals can better prioritise physical activity, integrate new habits, and pursue additional goals, enhancing behaviour change efforts.

How: Include an in-app journalling feature to help users document their behaviour and implement real-time behaviour monitoring options (for example, wearable technology) [30]. Simplify the self-monitoring methods to reduce recording frequency to enhance user adherence [34].

Why: Self-monitoring increases awareness of behaviour and facilitates deliberate decision-making. Self-monitoring is a reliable method for sustaining user engagement and adherence to goals [32].

Design Principle and Theory: 'Self-monitoring' is associated with the theoretical construct 'behaviour regulation' in the Theoretical Domain Framework. It involves efforts to control or alter objectively observed or measured behaviour [25].

BCT combinations: Self-monitoring of behaviour outcomes corresponds to code 2.4, labelled "self-monitoring of outcome(s) of behaviour". This involves individuals monitoring and evaluating the outcomes of their activities. Monitoring conducted by others without feedback aligns with code 2.1, identified as "Monitoring of behaviour by others without feedback". Here, a third party analyses or records behaviour without providing feedback to the individuals. Monitoring by someone else with feedback based on behaviour outcomes is classified as code 2.7, described as "Feedback on the outcome(s) of behaviour". This includes scenarios where individuals receive feedback from third parties based on monitored behaviour outcomes [2].

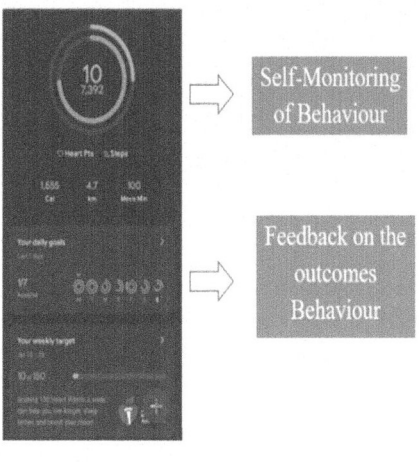

In Other Collection: Self-monitoring - https://ui-patterns.com/patterns/self-monitoring. Self-monitoring - Persuasive Systems Design: Key Issues, Process Model, and System Features [35].

3.5 Design Pattern for "Instructions on How to Perform a Behaviour Technique"

The fifth most used BCT was "instructions on how to perform a behaviour," which involves offering advice and instruction on behaviour execution, often including skills training. This technique equips individuals with the expertise and skills necessary to achieve desired objectives. The design pattern for "instructions on how to perform behaviour" is provided in Table 6.

Table 6. Design Pattern for "Instructions on How to Perform Behaviour".

Pattern Name: Guided task assistance **Code/BCT name (Group) in Taxonomy:** 4.1. Instruction on how to perform the behaviour (Shaping knowledge)
Examples Headspace Headspace provides instructions from the first interaction with the app, akin to a roadmap that offers its users dynamic, step-by-step guidance for meditation 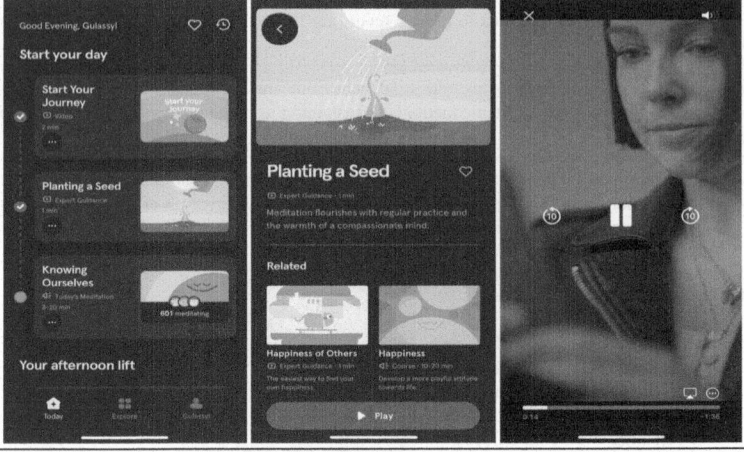
What (Problem): Key challenges individuals face when adopting desired behaviours include the lack of knowledge, misconceptions, and behaviour complexity.
Use when: Crucial in guiding individuals on specific behaviours, particularly when users lack knowledge or expertise in certain areas. The instructional components in mobile applications are important in assisting users in implementing behaviours effectively [36]. Providing relevant information on behaviours enhances user knowledge and reduces frustrations associated with behaviour adoption.
How: Offer interactive or visual guides (e.g., animations, videos, or text) that explain each step in performing the behaviour, implement in-app tutorials that can be revisited anytime, and provide ongoing reminders with clear, actionable instructions and animated presentations to help users learn new knowledge and behaviour. This pattern enhances the likelihood of successful behaviour change by offering clear guidance, breaking tasks into manageable steps, accelerating skill acquisition, and providing solutions to obstacles [36–38]. Enhance user engagement with infographics and user stories to simplify instructions and improve comprehension [39].

(*continued*)

Table 6. (*continued*)

Why: Pattern empowers users with essential knowledge on the significance of specific actions and how to integrate them effectively into daily life, facilitating informed decision-making and progress towards goals. Pattern offers simple guidance to overcome difficulties and barriers and enhances users' self-awareness. By providing tips, strategies, and suggestions, these instructions help users navigate obstacles and stay on course towards achieving their goals. These integrated strategies create a comprehensive, user-centric approach to instruction design, promoting successful intervention adherence.
Design Principle and Theory: "Instructions on how to perform a behaviour" is linked to the theoretical concept of "knowledge" within the Theoretical Domain framework. This technique encompasses both general knowledge, including awareness of the condition or scientific reasoning, and procedural knowledge [25].
BCT combinations: To enhance this pattern, combined with BCT under code 8.1, "Behavioral practice/rehearsal," repeated practice is suggested to improve skills. And BCT under code 6.1, "Demonstration of the behaviour," involves learners receiving detailed demonstrations and then practising by observing and replicating what they saw, which can be effective [2]. 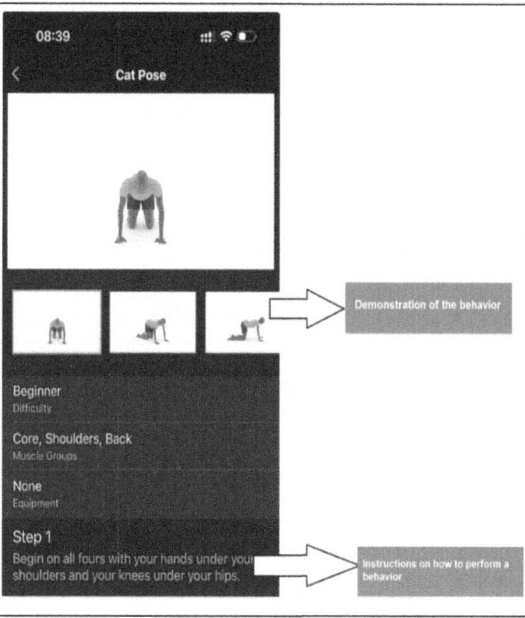
In Other Collection: Wizard - https://ui-patterns.com/patterns/Wizard

3.6 Design Pattern "Feedback on Behaviour Technique"

The sixth most used BCT was the "feedback on behaviour technique", which provides evaluative feedback on behaviour performance, considering factors like its form, frequency, duration, and intensity. It is often combined with goal-setting and reward techniques. The design pattern for feedback on behaviour" is provided in Table 7.

Table 7. Design Pattern for "Feedback on Behaviour Technique".

Pattern Name: Progress Feedback

Code/BCT name (Group) in Taxonomy: 2.2 Feedback on behaviour (Feedback and monitoring)

Examples: BetterMe health coaching app

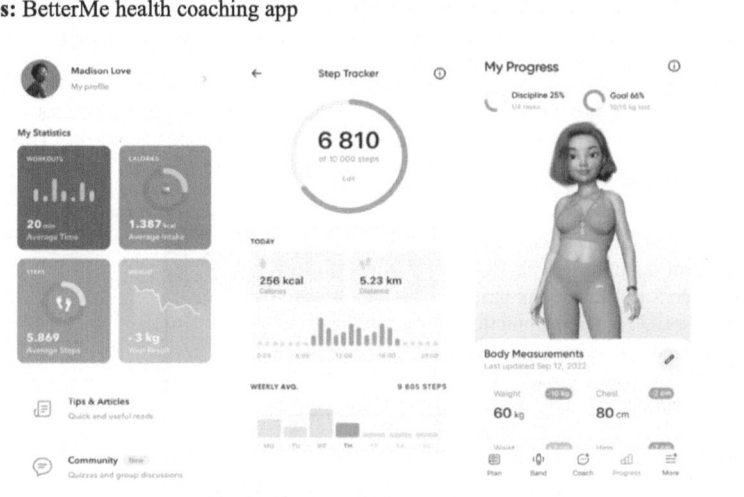

What (Problem): The pattern "Feedback on behaviour" in apps addresses the problems of improving user engagement, motivating desired actions, and facilitating behaviour change by providing users with real-time insights, guidance, and accountability. This ultimately leads to more informed decision-making and positive outcomes.

Use when: Useful when individuals need to be more aware of their behaviours, enabling them to track progress, identify patterns, and make necessary adjustments. To help individuals gauge their progress, celebrate successes, and address behaviours that need improvement. To reinforce desired behaviours and correct undesired ones. To encourage healthier choices and lifestyle changes. To help individuals understand areas of strength and areas needing development, fostering continuous improvement.

How: Using visual representations, behaviour-specific feedback messages, timely feedback delivery, convenient access to feedback, personalised feedback on individual data, and regular summaries can be used to strategise "Feedback on behaviour" [26, 38, 40–42]. Providing users with control over feedback types and also helping users understand feedback.

Why: Feedback on behaviour is crucial because it enables individuals to assess their actions about their goals and objectives, facilitating self-management and behavioural control. By receiving feedback and reviewing goals based on that feedback, individuals can make informed adjustments to their behaviours, aligning them more effectively with desired outcomes.

Design Principle and Theory: "Feedback on behaviour" is linked to the theoretical concept of "behavioural regulation" within the Theoretical Domain Framework. It entails systematic efforts focused on controlling or altering objectively observable and measurable behaviours [25].

(*continued*)

Table 7. (*continued*)

BCT combinations: The pattern can be combined with "Monitoring of behaviour by others without feedback "(BCT code 2.1), which involves observing an individual's behaviour without providing explicit feedback, such as when a fitness coach tracks activity levels but does not comment on performance. Conversely, "Social reward" (BCT code 10.4) involves giving praise or recognition for behaviour, such as a fitness app awarding badges or providing encouragement when a user achieves their daily step goal [2]. 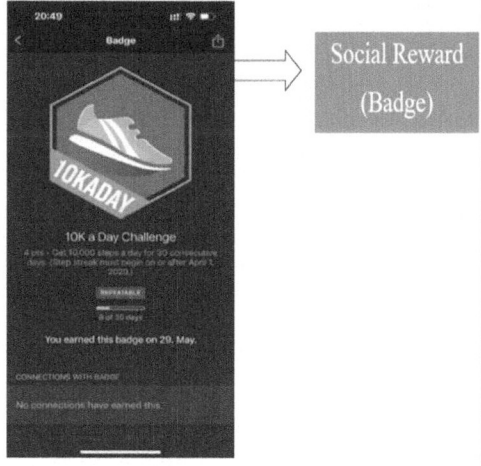
In Other Collection: Completeness Meter - https://ui-patterns.com/patterns/Completeness-Meter Praise/Reward - Persuasive Systems Design: Key Issues, Process Model, and System Features [35].

4   Evaluation of Design Patterns

The expert evaluation was conducted to assess the understandability, helpfulness and acceptability of the design patterns. Semi-structured interviews were conducted with four interaction design experts. Three experts did not have a specific understanding of behaviour change theories but were aware of persuasive technologies and proficient in understanding design patterns (E1, E3, E4). One expert had a theoretical understanding of behaviour change theories and also had a background in designing digital interventions for behaviour change (E2). Wurhofer et al. (2010) provided a structured method to assess design patterns and divided into three broader criteria evaluation [43].

- **Understandability:** This criterion addresses ease in the understandability of the pattern, and comprehensibility of each pattern's element (such as its name, the problem it solves, etc.).
- **Helpfulness:** It suggests that the pattern needs to be helpful for the designers, meaning that the pattern description provides enough information for the user to understand how to apply it in practice.
- **Overall Acceptability:** This indicates to what extent the user believes in the pattern and is in agreement with its content.

Interview questions (Table 8) were prepared based on the criteria mentioned above [43]. The approach ensures a thorough evaluation and allows experts to evaluate and address critical points in design patterns.

Proposed design patterns and interview questions were sent to experts three days before the interview date. This gave the experts enough time to review and evaluate

Table 8. Semi-Structured Interview Questions for Expert Evaluation.

Criteria	Interview Questions
Understandability	How clear and understandable are the descriptions in the elements and examples provided in the design patterns for behaviour change techniques? (Sub-questions focused on understanding overall comprehensibility, language, balance between concreteness and abstractness of the design and ambiguity in the design Patterns)
Helpfulness	To what extent does the design pattern benefit you in facilitating your design process or addressing the design of specific behaviour change techniques? (Sub-questions focused on capturing relevant information, contribution to the development of improved designs for behaviour change interventions, and helpfulness in facilitating communication among designers, developers and researchers)
Overall Acceptability	Do you find yourself nodding in agreement as you read the pattern descriptions of BCTs, or does any design pattern description need to be improved? Considering your expertise and experience, how likely will you incorporate these design patterns into your future projects?

design patterns. The following results were generated by analysing the qualitative data for each evaluative criterion using a deductive thematic analysis approach. The data was analysed using predetermined categories of the evaluative criteria (understandability, helpfulness and overall acceptability).

4.1   Understandability of the Design Patterns for Behaviour Change

All experts mentioned that descriptions and examples provided in the design patterns for BCTs were clear, understandable and comprehensible. They found no ambiguity in the descriptions. One expert (E2) mentioned that: – *"...the content seems clean, and it was easy to read. I didn't have any difficulties... Yeah, there is no ambiguity in the description"*.

The experts provided several suggestions for improving the understandability of design patterns. All experts (E1, E2, E3, E4) suggested that the language of the design patterns needs to be simplified for non-academics or young professionals or designers. As one of the experts (E1) mentioned: – *"I would say that if you're aiming for a general professional audience, I would reformulate those or create an alternative version written in plain language, not like a simplified version, but maybe in a more professional manner. It's just the question of lingo—academics use certain lingo, and then industry people use certain lingo"*. All Experts suggested that alternative versions need to be created with simpler language, shorter text with more precision in content, reducing several in-text citations, and giving brief explanations of examples can improve the comprehensibility of beginner designers as well as reduce the amount of time spent reading them. One expert mentioned the need for more images for different types of user interfaces (e.g., desktop) as they are currently more focused on mobile applications.

One expert (E2) suggested that another section should include words for caution and explain what not to do when strategising specific BCTs, for example, when to avoid sending reminders or not using reminders (prompts and cues): – *"I think it would be nice to have... not to use one, or like when to avoid"*. It is intended to allow designers to learn about the dos and don'ts of strategising BCTs in DBCIs. For example, in some cases, giving two of three meaningful choices to the user is enough rather than giving a lot of choices, or in conditions when some BCTs are not useful.

The expert suggested re-organising different design pattern elements considering the designers' limited time. As the expert (E3) mentioned: – *"My goal as a designer is to find a design (solution) as fast as possible; I don't want to spend hours reading it. I want to find my problem. And what can I do (solution)? And then, if I want to understand, like, why?"*. This indicates that the re-organisation of elements, such as mentioning the problem and solution before "use when", can be a better approach for designers who want to review the problem and solution in a short period of time.

One expert (E2) suggested that game cards or puzzles can be used further to simplify these design patterns: – *"When I read it, I thought maybe it would be nice to have (something) like cards, like game cards, and you combine them... If you have a problem, you put it together like a puzzle, and it recreates another product and stuff"*. The experts (E1, E2, E4) suggested that a visual summary of the design patterns, such as infographics, leaflets, mind maps, or roadmaps, would help designers to understand them better. Lastly, one expert (E4) added that the element named "Design principle and theory" could be misleading for designers as these are not design principles but descriptions of the theory. It could be renamed as "related behaviour change theory".

All experts agreed that the design patterns have balance in concreteness and abstractness: – *"Yes, definitely. I think it has a balance...I was paying attention to that when I was reading to see if it was too specific or too abstract. It was in the middle to me, so okay (E1)"*.

Overall, the result indicated that design patterns are comprehensible but need more simplified language for better clarity and understanding.

4.2 Helpfulness of Design Patterns

The experts acknowledged that the proposed design patterns could potentially improve designs for behaviour change interventions. The expert (E2) mentioned that adding a BCT combination in the design pattern is very helpful: – *"...BCT Combinations. It was really good as well. I really like that because sometimes, just triggering or notifying stand-alone (BCTs) doesn't work"*. Another expert added: – *"When reading, I already felt this inspiration spark that, aha! Yes, yes, this could be used"*. This indicates the potential helpfulness of the design patterns.

One expert (E1) mentioned that designers could use these patterns for validation purposes: – *"We just intuitively feel that this would be the best way to design this user story, for instance. So in terms of validation, this would be, I think, very useful"*. Moreover, the expert added that the proposed patterns are more related to *what needs to be designed* rather than the specific methods of how to design it. These can be used in the earlier phase of the design process (eliciting requirements) and can be viewed as requirements for BCTs.

The design patterns for BCTs can be useful for researchers, designers and developers. The expert (E1) mentioned: – *"Both developers and designers, I think, developers even more, really like manuals and doing everything by the book"*. It is interesting to note that experts highlighted the need to simplify design patterns and still mentioned that developers are interested in manuals (which require more time to read). However, one expert (E4) disagreed with the potential usefulness of the patterns for developers: – *"They will expect that you will explain how the system should work. Yeah, so not about like this… It's still more about user experience"*. It highlights differences in the opinion of experts related to the potential use of design patterns by developers.

One expert (E3) highlighted that most designers are unaware that they actually design for behaviour change. These design patterns could be useful for them by looking at the problem and solution supported by knowledge of psychology and design. Overall, the experts agreed that the proposed design patterns are problem-focused, capture relevant knowledge, and are helpful in designing DBCIs for health.

4.3   Overall Acceptability of the Proposed Design Patterns

The experts found the design patterns acceptable and considered using them in their future projects. As one expert expressed (E1): – *"– "Aha!" Yes, yes, this could be. This could be used"*. In summary, the design patterns for BCTs are understandable, helpful and acceptable. The results indicated that the language needs to be simplified for industry professionals.

5   Conclusion

Design patterns are widely accepted in interaction design to represent design knowledge in a reusable format and avoid "reinventing the wheel" repeatedly. This work aimed to overcome the challenge of translating theoretical knowledge of BCTs and strategising them into digital interventions due to insufficient guidance for interaction designers. In the current work, we proposed six design patterns tailored for six BCTs for designing digital health behaviour change interventions.

Tidwell's design patterns structure [18] was utilised and adapted in the context of BCTs. Elements such as code and BCT name in taxonomy, design principle and theory and BCT combination are added to the patterns' structure to contextualise design patterns for BCTs. Klansja et al. [44] mentioned that re-usable solutions of BCTs could be a "win-win" solution for designers, behaviour change experts and developers. The expert evaluation results indicate the potential usefulness and helpfulness of the proposed design patterns. The expert evaluation suggested simplifying the language for industry professionals and adding additional elements that can highlight what not to do and words of caution when strategising BCTs. Crumblish et al. [22] also added similar elements like "special cases" in proposed design patterns for social interfaces. The authors consider it as an important suggestion because designers need to be cautious about different dos and don'ts when strategising BCTs in DBCIs. For example, the concept of satiation highlights that the effectiveness of rewards diminishes over time if they become too predictable or routine. This reflects that receiving rewards every time after hitting the goals may reduce the value of rewards over time. To avoid such instances, designers can use BCTs such as scheduled rewards. Adding such guidelines to design patterns would enhance the design of the DBCIs.

The authors assume that provided patterns could help researchers and practitioners aiming to design digital interventions for behaviour change, not "start from scratch" or search through a large amount of literature. Design patterns can be used as a reference to analyse the existing solutions and understanding of behaviour change principles and theories. The patterns "Why" and "Design principle and Theory" sections allow designers to understand the rationale behind the pattern application in a specific context. For example, if the user forgets to perform some task or needs additional guidance, she can be prompted to take action by "reminder". The patterns can also used to analyse and validate existing solutions for behaviour change.

Design patterns are supposed to support multidisciplinary communication. However, the results indicated differences in the opinion of their usefulness for developers. We assume that design patterns will provide a common language for discussion among teams, help developers understand the primary intent of BCTs, and ensure that the work of interaction designers is aligned with the work of software developers.

The authors assume that the proposed design patterns can inform interaction design practitioners in designing evidence-based and theory-based digital interventions for behaviour change. Future research should focus on simplifying the proposed design patterns and extending their taxonomy by developing design patterns for other BCTs.

Acknowledgements. Grant TF/1323, Supporting Design for Digital Health Behaviour Change, funded by TLU Research Fund.

Disclosure of Interests. The authors declare that they have no conflict of interest.

References

1. Dicianno, B.E., et al.: Perspectives on the evolution of mobile (mHealth) technologies and application to rehabilitation. Phys. Ther. **95**, 397 (2015). https://doi.org/10.2522/PTJ.201 30534
2. Michie, S., et al.: The behavior change technique taxonomy (v1) of 93 hierarchically clustered techniques: Building an international consensus for the reporting of behavior change interventions. Ann. Behav. Med. **46**, 81–95 (2013). https://doi.org/10.1007/S12160-013-9486-6
3. Michie, S., Atkins, L., West, R.: The Behaviour Change Wheel: A Guide To Designing Interventions. Silverback Publishing, London (2014)
4. Farhat ul Ain, Popovit, O., Tomberg, V.: Mapping behavior change wheel techniques to digital behavior change interventions: review. In: Kurosu, M. (ed.) HCII 2022. LNCS, vol. 13304, pp. 277–295. Springer, Cham. (2022). https://doi.org/10.1007/978-3-031-05412-9_20
5. Truelove, S., Vanderloo, L.M., Tucker, P., Di Sebastiano, K.M., Faulkner, G.: The use of the behaviour change wheel in the development of ParticipACTION's physical activity app. Prev. Med. Rep. **20**, 101224 (2020). https://doi.org/10.1016/J.PMEDR.2020.101224
6. Konstanti, C., Karapanos, E., Markopoulos, P.: The behavior change design cards: a design support tool for theoretically-grounded design of behavior change technologies. Int. J. Hum. Comput. Interact. **38**, 1238–1254 (2022). https://doi.org/10.1080/10447318.2021.1990519

7. Michie, S., Prestwich, A.: Are interventions theory-based? Development of a theory coding scheme. Health Psychol. **29**, 1–8 (2010). https://doi.org/10.1037/A0016939
8. Thomson, C., Nash, J., Maeder, A.: Persuasive design for behaviour change apps: Issues for designers. In: Proceedings of the Annual Conference of the South African Institute of Computer Scientists and Information Technologists (SAICSIT 2016), article 43, Johannesburg, South Africa, pp. 1–10 (2016). https://doi.org/10.1145/2987491.2987535
9. Fulton, E.A., Kwah, K.L., Wild, S., Brown, K.E.: Lost in translation: transforming behaviour change techniques into engaging digital content and design for the StopApp. Healthcare. **6** (2018). https://doi.org/10.3390/HEALTHCARE6030075
10. Morrissey, E.C., Corbett, T.K., Walsh, J.C., Molloy, G.J.: Behavior change techniques in apps for medication adherence: a content analysis. Am. J. Prev. Med. **50**, e143–e146 (2016). https://doi.org/10.1016/J.AMEPRE.2015.09.034
11. Simeon, R., et al.: Behavior change techniques included in reports of social media interventions for promoting health behaviors in adults: content analysis within a systematic review. J. Med. Internet Res. **22** (2020). https://doi.org/10.2196/16002
12. Lyons, E.J., Lewis, Z.H., Mayrsohn, B.G., Rowland, J.L.: Behavior change techniques implemented in electronic lifestyle activity monitors: a systematic content analysis. J. Med. Internet Res. **16**, e192 (2014). https://doi.org/10.2196/JMIR.3469
13. Dunn, E.E., Gainforth, H.L., Robertson-Wilson, J.E.: Behavior change techniques in mobile applications for sedentary behavior. Digit. Health **4**, 205520761878579 (2018). https://doi.org/10.1177/2055207618785798
14. Conroy, D.E., Yang, C.-H., Maher, J.P.: Behavior change techniques in top-ranked mobile apps for physical activity. Am. J. Prev. Med. **46**, 649–652 (2014). https://doi.org/10.1016/j.amepre.2014.01.010
15. Cowan, L.T., et al.: Apps of steel: are exercise apps providing consumers with realistic expectations?: a content analysis of exercise apps for presence of behavior change theory. Health Educ. Behav. **40**, 133–139 (2013). https://doi.org/10.1177/1090198112452126
16. Cooper, A., Reimann, R., Cronin, D., Noessel, C., Csizmadi, J., Lemoine, D.: About Face The Essentials of Interaction Design Fourth Edition. Wiley (2014)
17. Seffah, A.: The evolution of design patterns in HCI: from pattern languages to pattern oriented design. In: Proceedings of the 1st International Workshop on Pattern Driven Engineering of Interactive Computing Systems (PEICS 2010), Berlin, Germany, pp. 4–9 (2010). https://doi.org/10.1145/1824749.1824751
18. Tidwell, J., Brewer, C., Valencia, A.: Designing Interfaces: Patterns for Effective Interaction Design. O'Reilly Media, Sebastopol (2010)
19. Alexander, C., et al.: A Pattern Language: Towns, Buildings, Construction. Oxford University Press, New York (1977)
20. Borchers, J.O.: Pattern approach to interaction design. In: Proceedings of the Conference on Designing Interactive Systems: Processes, Practices, Methods, and Techniques, DIS, pp. 369–378 (2000). https://doi.org/10.1145/347642.347795
21. Laakso, S.A.: User interface design patterns (2003). https://www.cs.helsinki.fi/u/salaakso/patterns/
22. Crumlish, C., Malone, E.: Designing Social Interfaces. O'Reilly Media, Inc. (2015)
23. Iba, T., Isaku, T.: A pattern language for creating pattern languages: 364 patterns for pattern mining, writing, and symbolizing. In: Proceedings of the 23rd Conference on Pattern Languages of Programs (PLoP 2016), vol. 11, pp. 1–63 (2016). https://doi.org/10.5555/3158161.3158175
24. Muench, F., Baumel, A.: More than a text message: dismantling digital triggers to curate behavior change in patient-centered health interventions. J. Med. Internet Res. **19**, e147 (2017). https://doi.org/10.2196/jmir.7463

25. Atkins, L., et al.: A guide to using the theoretical domains framework of behaviour change to investigate implementation problems. Implement. Sci. **12**, 1–18 (2017). https://doi.org/10. 1186/s13012-017-0605-9

26. Patrick, K., et al.: Design and implementation of a randomized controlled social and mobile weight loss trial for young adults (project SMART). Contemp. Clin. Trials **37**, 10–18 (2014). https://doi.org/10.1016/J.CCT.2013.11.001

27. Inauen, J., et al.: Using smartphone-based support groups to promote healthy eating in daily life: a randomised trial. Appl. Psychol. Health Well Being **9**, 303–323 (2017). https://doi.org/ 10.1111/APHW.12093

28. Oduor, M., Alahäivälä, T., Oinas-Kukkonen, H.: Persuasive software design patterns for social influence. Pers. Ubiquit. Comput. **18**, 1689–1704 (2014). https://doi.org/10.1007/s00779-014-0778-z

29. Fogg, B.J.: Persuasive Technology: Using Computers to Change What We Think and Do. Persuasive Technology: Using Computers to Change What We Think and Do, pp. 1–282. Morgan Kaufmann, San Francisco (2003)

30. Garrison, K.A., et al.: Craving to quit: a randomized controlled trial of smartphone app-based mindfulness training for smoking cessation. Nicotine Tob. Res. **22**, 324–331 (2020). https:// doi.org/10.1093/ntr/nty126

31. Lee, M.-K., Lee, D.Y., Ahn, H.-Y., Park, C.-Y.: A novel user utility score for diabetes management using tailored mobile coaching: secondary analysis of a randomized controlled trial. JMIR Mhealth Uhealth **9**, e17573 (2021). https://doi.org/10.2196/17573

32. Tang, J., Abraham, C., Stamp, E., Greaves, C.: How can weight-loss app designers' best engage and support users? A qualitative investigation. Br. J. Health Psychol. **20**, 151–171 (2015). https://doi.org/10.1111/BJHP.12114

33. Pellegrini, C.A., Hoffman, S.A., Collins, L.M., Spring, B.: Optimization of remotely delivered intensive lifestyle treatment for obesity using the multiphase optimization strategy: opt-IN study protocol. Contemp. Clin. Trials **38**, 251–259 (2014). https://doi.org/10.1016/j.cct.2014. 05.007

34. Goodman, S., Morrongiello, B., Meckling, K.: A randomized, controlled trial evaluating the efficacy of an online intervention targeting vitamin D intake, knowledge and status among young adults. Int. J. Behav. Nutr. Phys. Act. **13**, 1–13 (2016). https://pubmed.ncbi.nlm.nih. gov/27836017/

35. Oinas-Kukkonen, H., Harjumaa, M.: Persuasive systems design: key issues, process model, and system features. Commun. Assoc. Inf. Syst. **24**, 485–500 (2009). https://doi.org/10.17705/ 1CAIS.02428

36. Vasiliou, V.S., Dockray, S., Dick, S., et al.: Reducing drug-use harms among higher education students: MyUSE contextual-behaviour change digital intervention development using the behaviour change wheel. Harm Reduct. J. **18**, 56 (2021). https://doi.org/10.1186/s12954-021-00491-7

37. Szabó, C., Ócsai, H., Csabai, M., Kemény, L.: A randomised trial to demonstrate the effectiveness of electronic messages on sun protection behaviours. J. Photochem. Photobiol. B. **149**, 257–264 (2015). https://doi.org/10.1016/J.JPHOTOBIOL.2015.06.006

38. Buman, M.P., et al.: BeWell24: development and process evaluation of a smartphone "app" to improve sleep, sedentary, and active behaviors in US Veterans with increased metabolic risk. Transl. Behav. Med. **6**, 438–448 (2016). https://doi.org/10.1007/s13142-015-0359-3

39. Fulton, E.A., et al.: StopApp: using the behaviour change wheel to develop an app to increase uptake and attendance at NHS stop smoking services. Healthcare. **4**(2), 31 (2016). https:// doi.org/10.3390/HEALTHCARE4020031

40. Nibbeling, N., Simons, M., Sporrel, K., Deutekom, M.: A focus group study among inactive adults regarding the perceptions of a theory-based physical activity app. Front. Public Health **9**, 528388 (2021). https://doi.org/10.3389/fpubh.2021.528388

41. Bell, D.L., et al.: Computer-assisted motivational interviewing intervention to facilitate teen pregnancy prevention and fitness behavior changes: a randomized trial for young men. J. Adolesc. Health. **62**, S72–S80 (2018). https://doi.org/10.1016/j.jadohealth.2017.06.015

42. Stacey, F., et al.: A cluster randomized controlled trial evaluating the impact of tailored feedback on the purchase of healthier foods from primary school online canteens. Nutrients. **13** (2021). https://doi.org/10.3390/nu13072405

43. Wurhofer, D., Obrist, M., Beck, E., Tscheligi, M.: Introducing a comprehensive quality criteria framework for validating patterns. In: Proceedings of the 2009 Computation World: Future Computing, Service Computation, Cognitive, Adaptive, Content, Patterns, Athens, Greece, pp. 242–247 (2009). https://doi.org/10.1109/COMPUTATIONWORLD.2009.86

44. Klasnja, P., Hekler, E.B., Korinek, E.V., Harlow, J., Mishra, S.R.: Toward usable evidence: optimizing knowledge accumulation in HCI research on health behavior change. In: Proceedings of the 2017 CHI Conference on Human Factors in Computing Systems (CHI 2017), Denver, Colorado, USA, pp. 3071–3082 (2017). https://doi.org/10.1145/3025453.3026013

Evaluating Immersion in Digital Video Using EEG and Subjective Measures: A Pilot Study

Ioannis Doumanis[1]([✉]), Daphne Economou[2], and Kostantinos Tsioutas[3]

[1] University of Central Lancashire, Preston, UK
idoumanis@uclan.ac.uk
[2] University of Westminster, London, UK
[3] Athens University of Economics and Business, Athens, Greece

Abstract. Immersion in digital video refers to the degree to which digital content engages and absorbs viewers. Today, viewers primarily consume digital video online. Despite ample bandwidth availability, network disruptions (e.g., congestion and outages) can degrade quality and interrupt the viewing experience, thereby breaking immersion. In a pilot study, we evaluated viewer immersion while watching digital video content on two streaming services (IPTV and HLS) delivered via conventional IP and our POINT network under regular and exceptional network conditions (congestion and link failures). We used Electroencephalography (EEG) and user interviews to gather data. EEG data indicate that videos streamed through POINT create a more immersive experience in terms of presence, sensory engagement, realism, and detail compared to conventional IP, although the impact varies by service. Interview data corroborate the EEG measures but indicate that POINT's impact was independent of the specific service used (IPTV or HLS). These findings suggest that POINT enhances viewer immersion over traditional IP networks, particularly under challenging network conditions, but the impact may be service-specific. We plan to conduct a follow-up study with a larger user group and incorporate additional sensors (emotion analysis and eye-tracking) to more comprehensively measure viewers' emotional and cognitive states under each experimental condition.

Keywords: Immersion · Digital video · Electroencephalography (EEG) · Pilot Study · POINT · IP

1 Introduction

Viewers have shifted from traditional TV to streaming platforms over the past decade [1]. Platforms like Netflix and Disney Plus have several million paid subscribers worldwide [2]. Despite the ample bandwidth in today's Internet, nothing can guarantee an uninterrupted viewing experience. Poor network conditions, such as buffering and lag, can disrupt the viewer's experience and, consequently, their immersion.

By immersion, we refer to the psychological experience of viewers engaging with the video content. We adapted the definition of Brown and Cairns (2004) [3], who identified three levels of immersion. The first level of immersion is "engagement". Viewers must

H. Plácido da Silva and P. Cipresso (Eds.): CHIRA 2024, CCIS 2370, pp. 385–402, 2025.
https://doi.org/10.1007/978-3-031-82633-7_23

invest time, effort, and attention in the content to enter this level. The second immersion stage is "engrossment", which involves deeper involvement where viewers' emotions are directly affected, and they become less aware of their surroundings. The final stage is "total immersion". This is when viewers reach the highest level of involvement with the digital video, feeling so disconnected from reality that nothing else seems to matter. Total immersion is rare in videos, whereas the first two stages (engagement and engrossment) are more common.

This study focuses on engagement, which can directly affect network fluctuations. Artistic factors, such as filmmaking and the director's vision, influence the remaining levels of the immersive experience and are outside the scope of this paper. When viewers engage with video content, they begin to connect (presence), and their senses attune to the audiovisual experience (sensory engagement). They also evaluate visual/audio and other details that contribute to the realism (detail and realism) of the experience to decide if it is worth investing their time [4].

This paper presents a pilot study to evaluate immersion (i.e., presence, sensory engagement, realism, and detail) in digital video content transmitted over two network delivery mechanisms. The first network mechanism is the standard IP Internet, and the second is the POINT network. POINT was an EU H2020 ICT project to develop the next generation of the Internet [5]. It offers several operational benefits and improved Quality of Experience (QoE) [6] for services running on the network.

Using objective and subjective measures, we evaluated users' immersion in video content delivered by two popular video delivery services: HTTP Live Streaming (HLS) [7] and IPTV. To simulate real-world use, we subjected both services to exceptional network conditions (network congestion and link failures). We disrupted the network links during these conditions while viewers watched the content. Using Electroencephalography, we measured the dimensions of participants' immersion in video content delivered on conventional IP and POINT networks. Additionally, we interviewed participants to capture additional insights into their experience (e.g., thoughts and feelings).

The outline of the remainder of this paper is as follows. In Sect. 2, we provide an overview of POINT and its benefits. In Sect. 3, we describe the design of the pilot study. In Sect. 4, we present the results. In Sect. 5, we discuss our findings. Section 6 summarizes our future work, and Sect. 7 provides our conclusions.

2   The POINT Platform

Traditional IP networks route data based on location (e.g., on a specific server). Information-Centric Networks (ICN), on the other hand, route data based on their physical attributes (e.g., names, publisher identifiers, etc.) [7]. A significant limitation of ICN networks is that they require the whole IP-based Internet to adopt ICN. The POINT project proposed a drop-in replacement for IP networks [5]. Instead of asking operators to replace their entire infrastructure, they can integrate an ICN core within their existing networks. This IP-over-ICN approach offers operational benefits such as reduced latency, improved load management, and seamless failover. These improvements lead to better QoE for users by minimizing buffering, reducing the likelihood of video quality degradation, and ensuring consistent service even during network disruptions [5].

In the POINT trials [5], we evaluated the performance of traditional IP and POINT in the lab under regular and exceptional conditions. We assessed QoE of viewers watching video clips on HTTP Live Streaming (HLS) and IPTV using subjective feedback, such as satisfaction ratings from the i-QoE questionnaire (e.g., rating perceived video quality) [8], and objective metrics, such as latency and HTTP request rates to measure network performance and its impact on video playback. We found that under regular conditions, there were no differences between the two network delivery mechanisms. However, under exceptional network conditions, POINT offered better QoE to users in both HLS and IPTV. In the exceptional scenario where the link to the primary video server fails, POINT switches to a backup server without users experiencing noticeable interruptions. In the presence of network congestion, POINT automatically combined multiple requests for the video into a single stream, reducing the overall network load. As a result, users received video streams of consistent quality without any pixelation or drops in resolution.

3 The PILOT Study

Following the POINT trials, we ran a pilot study replicating the conditions of the main trails. We used electroencephalography (EEG) to explore whether the POINT network delivery mechanism can provide better QoE [6] than IP. By incorporating EEG, we wanted to capture real-time objective measurements of QoE that were not captured in the main POINT trials, which relied on subjective feedback and network metrics. Specifically, we sought to answer the question: Can POINT improve participants' QoE, particularly in terms of immersion, compared to traditional IP when delivering digital video content over HLS and IPTV services?

Since POINT is an experimental prototype, we aimed not to generalize the results but to gather preliminary insights into its impact on QoE, particularly as measured using EEG. Given the exploratory nature of this study, we focused on the first level of immersion – engagement - as this aspect is highly sensitive to exceptional network conditions that can prevent viewers from fully engaging with the content.

In the lab, we exposed participants to the same stimuli as in the main POINT trials. Participants watched video content on both HLS and IPTV services. For this study, we hypothesized that digital video content distributed over POINT would result in better immersion than IP, regardless of the service used.

3.1 The Video Delivery Prototype

We developed a simple HTML prototype that gave participants access to the same video content used in the main trials. The prototype features a simple menu on the right side of the page, from where users can select content based on the experimenter's instructions. Once a user selects a video, it plays on the left side of the page. Participants controlled the videos' playback (e.g., play and volume) using a wireless mouse and a remote control; however, they were not permitted to pause the video clips.

We carefully selected videos from the main POINT trials to ensure participants were exposed to the same stimuli. The prototype included content from HLS and IPTV services transmitted over conventional IP and POINT networks. The clips for both network types were of similar genres without any intense emotional variations that could influence participant engagement (Fig. 1).

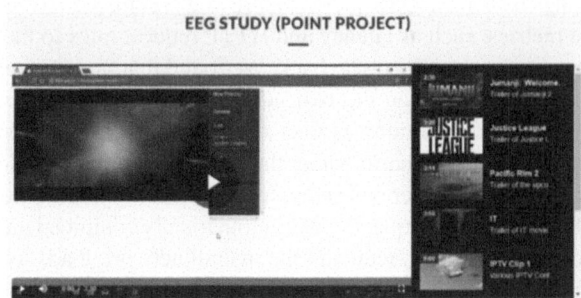

Fig. 1. The HTML video Prototype.

For the HLS condition, we used short clips (2:30–3:58 min), as this duration is typically sufficient to capture and maintain participants' engagement [9]. For the IPTV condition, we selected longer clips (8:00–8:35 min), which provided ample time for participants to engage with the content and experience any potential disruptions caused by network conditions. For example, participants could observe the impact of path failure (e.g., freezing picture) on the IPTV content when transmitted over conventional IP.

3.2 Participants

Ten participants participated in this study and were asked to watch videos individually on the HTML prototype. Two participants evaluated the headset and software and did not complete the study. The remaining participants selected two videos on HLS (one over conventional IP and another over POINT) and two on IPTV (one over conventional IP and another over POINT). The group included a mixture of males and females of various ages, and all participants were native English speakers.

3.3 Experimental Design

We manipulated the type of network transmission mechanism as within-subjects. Participants watched short videos first on Conventional IP and then on POINT: 1) Conventional IP with Clip 1 OR Clip 2 versus POINT with Clip 3 OR Clip 4 (HLS service) and 2) Conventional IP with Clip 1 or Clip 2 versus POINT with Clip 3 OR Clip 4 (IPTV) (Table 1).

Table 1. Experimental Design.

Participants	Conventional IP	POINT
1–8	Clip 1 OR Clip 2 (HLS)	Clip 3 OR Clip 4 (HLS)
	Clip 1 OR Clip2 (IPTV)	Clip 3 OR Clip 4 (IPTV)

Given the low number of participants in the study, we did not use a counterbalanced design. However, we accounted for order effects in the EEG data using a Latin Square design [9]. We found a minimal impact of the order of network mechanisms on the EEG measures, explaining only 0.07% of the variance.

3.4 Measures and Methods

In this study, we collected both objective and subject metrics of immersion. The objective data included raw EEG measurements. Raw EEG data displays the voltage fluctuations detected from each sensor on the EEG headset. We used the EPOC + EEG headset[1], which collected data from 14 different sensors (AF3, AF4, F3, F4, F7, F8, FC5, FC6, T7, T8, P7, P8, O1, O2) with a sampling rate of 128 Hz and resolution 14-bit and processed the data using the Emotive Pro[2] software. The EEG headset exported CSV files with continuous brain recordings for each participant.

Additionally, we collected subjective data through semi-structured interviews at the end of each session. We asked participants standardized questions (e.g. if they noticed any differences between the clips) and follow-up questions based on their responses. Each interview lasted a maximum of 10 min.

We automatically processed the datasets to remove unnecessary readings (e.g., electrode labels) and unwanted artefacts (missing values, eliminating duplicates and filtering outliers). We then segmented the continuous signals into 3-s epochs based on relevant studies [10–12]. We created four labels (HLS – IP, HLS – POINT, IPTV – IP and IPTV – POINT) to segment our datasets. We analyzed the Power Spectral Density (PSD) of each dimension of immersion using the Welch method [13]. For each condition (epochs), we used one-way ANOVAs, Mixed Effects Models and Tukey's HSD test to analyze the EEG data. To cross-validate our results, we used mixed model analysis that accounts for fixed and random effects.

We used the following frequency bands to measure different dimensions of immersion:

- *Theta (4–8 Hz)* and *Alpha Power Analysis* (8–12 Hz) to measure presence [14]);
- *Gamma (30–100 Hz) to* measure Sensory Engagement [15];
- *Beta Power Analysis (13–30 Hz)* to measure realism [16, 17];
- *Alpha Power Analysis (8–12 Hz)* to measure detail [18].

We further used coherence analysis to study sensory engagement [19]. Clustering facilitated the comparison of our EEG results across different users. Finally, we applied

---

[1] https://rb.gy/d8lb3a.

[2] https://rb.gy/cyg1ou.

Time-Frequency Analysis (TFA) [20] to investigate any temporal patterns of interest in the data. However, we did not have access to a Biometric research platform (e.g., iMotions), so we did not mark events (e.g., Event-Related-Potential (ERPs) [20]) during the experiment. Nonetheless, we inspected and compared graphs visually among epochs, which provided additional insights into the neurological activity of participants.

We performed the analysis on Google Collaboratory [21]. We created a data processing pipeline in Python consisting of several algorithms to conduct data processing and analysis of EEG signals quickly and efficiently. Using Google Collaboratory [21], we analyzed 1.63 GB of EEG data.

4 Results

4.1 Presence

The ANOVA PSD analyses for Theta (4–7 Hz) and Alpha (8–13 Hz) revealed statistically significant results for users 2, 4, 5 and 7 (see Table 2). For user 2, the ANOVA comparisons showed a statistically significant result only for Theta Power ($F(3, 873) = 2.825$, $p < 0.05$). Tukey's HSD multiple comparison test revealed significant differences for one epoch:

- HLS vs IPTV (POINT): There was a significant decrease in the Theta power in the HLS epoch compared to the IPTV epoch when delivered over POINT, $M = -3.5409$, $SE = 0.65$, $p = 0.0489$, 95% CI $[-7.0708, -0.0111]$

For user 4, we found a significant ANOVA effect for Theta Power ($F(3, 919) = 5.37$, $p < 0.005$)). Tukey's HSD test revealed a significant difference for the following epoch:

- IPTV (IP) vs HLS (POINT): There was a significant decrease in the Theta power in the IPTV epoch when delivered over IP compared to the HLS epoch when delivered over POINT, $M = -4.9$, $SE = 0.68$, $p = 0.0035$, 95% CI $[-8.577 - 1.2229]$

For user 5, ANOVA showed a significant effect for Theta power ($F(3, 919) = 4.128$, $p < 0.05$)). Tukey's test revealed differences among all epochs:

- HLS vs IPTV (IP): There was a significant increase in Theta Power in the HLS epoch compared to the IPTV epoch when delivered over IP, $M = 4.1933$, $SE = 0.65$, $p = 0.011$, 95% CI $[0.703, 7.6836]$
- HLS (IP) vs HLS (POINT): There was a significant increase in the Theta power in the HLS epoch when delivered over IP compared to HSL when delivered over POINT, $M = 4.805$, $SE = 0.65$, $p = 0.0162$, 95% CI $[0.639, 8.9711]$
- HLS (IP) vs IPTV (POINT): There was a significant increase in the Theta PSD in the HLS epoch when delivered over IP compared to the IPTV epoch when delivered over POINT, $M = 5.111$, $SE = 0.65$, $p = 0.002$, 95% CI $[1.4388, 8.7846]$

For user 7, ANOVA showed significant effects for Theta and Alpha power:

- Theta Power ($F(3, 766) = 4.292$, $p < 0.005$).
- Alpha Power ($F(3, 766) = 4.382$, $p < 0.05$)

Tukey's HSD revealed the following significant differences:

- HLS (IP) vs IPTV (POINT): There was a significant decrease in Theta Power in the HLS epoch when delivered over IP compared to the IPTV epoch when delivered over POINT, M = −8.355, SE = 1.016, p = 0.0022, 95% CI [−14.401 −2.3098]
- HLS (IP) vs IPTV (POINT): There was a significant decrease in Alpha Power in the HLS epoch when delivered over IP compared to the IPTV epoch when delivered over POINT, M = −3.252, SE = 0.423, p = 0.0051, 95% CI [−5.7689 −0.7359]
- IPTV (IP) vs IPTV (POINT): There was a significant decrease in Alpha Power in the IPTV epoch when delivered over IP compared to the IPTV epoch when delivered over POINT, M = −2.1152, SE = 0.423, p = 0.0282, 95% CI [−4.0722 −0.1581]

Using a mixed model, we also conducted Theta and Alpha PSD analyses for the users. It did not show any significant results for any of the users.

Table 2. Mean and Standard Deviation of Theta and Alpha Power.

User	Theta Power (Mean ± Std Dev)	Alpha Power (Mean ± Std Dev)
1	170005.469 ± 217816.099	134073.9793 ± 167752.835
2	17.3160 ± 13.7243	19.7545 ± 12.798
3	13.268 ± 8.3796	6.943 ± 3.309
4	24.153 ± 14.713	12.592 ± 5.890
5	20.5755 ± 12.9290	14.803 ± 7.039
6	18.519 ± 18.828	33.199 ± 28.159
7	24.915 ± 19.953	15.410 ± 8.307
8	13.144 ± 9.712	7.706 ± 4.163

4.2 Sensory Engagement

The PSD analyses for gamma (30–100 Hz) showed statistically significant results for users 1 and 3, 3 to 5, and 6 (see Table 3). For user 1, the ANOVA test for gamma PSD showed a highly significant result ($F_{(13, 39)}$ = 5.9474, p < 0.0001). Tukey's HSD multiple comparison test revealed significant differences in PSD for the following epochs:

- HLS vs IPTV (IP): A significant decrease in the gamma PSD in the HLS epoch compared to the IPTV epoch delivered over IP, M = −0.046, SE = 0. 0 11, p = .0256,95% CI [−0.0879, −0.004]
- HLS (IP) vs IPTV (POINT): There was a significant decrease in gamma PSD in the HSL epoch when delivered over IP compared to the IPTV epoch when delivered over POINT, M = −0.0564, SE = 0.012, p = .0033, 95% CI [−0.0984, −0.0144]
- HLS vs IPTV (POINT): There was a significant decrease in gamma PSD in the HLS and IPTV epochs when delivered over POINT M = −0.0429, SE = 0.011, p = .043, 95% CI [−0.0849, −0.0009]

For users 3 to 6, ANOVAs showed a highly significant effect of gamma power for the users below:

- User 3 (F(13, 39) = 21.132, p < 0.0001);
- User 4 (F(13, 39) = 2.2924, p < 0.05);
- User 5 (F(13, 39) = 18.093, p < 0.0001);
- User 6 (F(13, 39) = 45.997, p < 0.0001)

Table 3. Mean and Standard Deviation of Gamma Power.

User	Gamma Power (Mean ± Std Dev)
1	2758 ± 489.9
2	0.905 ± 1.698
3	0.6569 ± 0.4673
4	0.3828 ± 0.6213
5	0.404 ± 01752
6	0.4304 ± 0.5131
7	0.784 ± 1.097
8	0.550 ± 0.397

Tukey's HSD multiple comparisons did not show statistically significant differences for epochs. However, the mixed model analyses showed highly statistically significant differences between the reference epoch (HLS – IP) and the following epochs:

User 1:

- Coef. (IPTV – IP) = −274.938, Std Err = 125.608, z-value = −2.189, p-value = 0.029
- Coef. (IPTV-POINT) = −274.115, Std Err = 125.259, z-value = −2.188, p-value = 0.029

User 2:

- Coef. (IPTV – IP) = 0.025, Std Err = 0.008, z-value = −3.127, p-value = 0.002
- Coef. (HLS – POINT) = −0.035, Std Err = 0.008, z-value = −4.305, p-value = 0.000
- Coef. (IPTV-POINT) = 0.040, Std Err = 0.008, z-value = 4.986, p-value = 0.000

User 3:

- Coef. (IPTV – IP) = 0.107, Std Err = 0.009, z-value = −11.265, p-value = 0.000
- Coef. (HLS – POINT) = −0.105, Std Err = 0.009, z-value = −11.136, p-value = 0.000

- Coef. (IPTV-POINT) = 0.129, Std Err = 0.010, z-value = −13.556, p-value = 0.000

User 4:

- Coef. (IPTV – IP) = 0.023, Std Err = 0.006, z-value = 3.723, p-value = 0.000
- Coef. (HLS – POINT) = 0.022, Std Err = 0.006, z-value = 3.453, p-value = 0.001
- Coef. (IPTV-POINT) = 0.037, Std Err = 0.006, z-value = 5.843, p-value = 0.000

User 5:

- Coef. (IPTV – IP) = 0.058, Std Err = 0.007, z-value = 8.281, p-value = 0.000
- Coef. (HLS – POINT) = 0.033, Std Err = 0.007, z-value = 4.739, p-value = 0.000
- Coef. (IPTV-POINT) = 0.077, Std Err = 0.007, z-value = 10.771, p-value = 0.000

Coherence Analysis

The coherence analyses showed statistically significant results for all users (1 to 8). Due to space constraints, we present the results only to three users (1 to 3). For user 1, the blue line (see Fig. 2) has higher peaks than other lines along the x-axis, indicating stronger coherence for the HLS over the IP epoch.

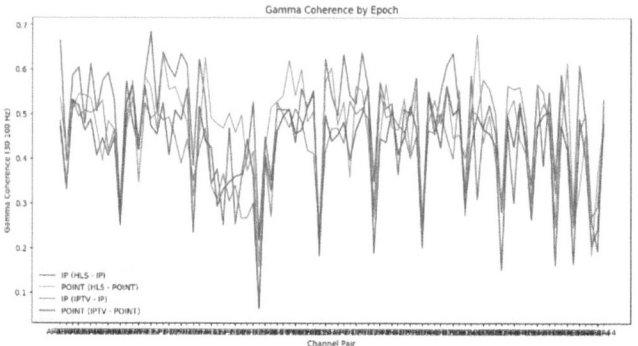

Fig. 2. Gamma Coherence by Epoch for User 1.

A mixed effect model shows there are statistically significant differences between this epoch (HLS-IP) and the following epochs:

- Coef. (IPTV – IP) = −0.046, Std Err = 0.009, z-value = −5.056, p-value = 0.000
- Coef. (IPTV-POINT) = −0.056, Std Err = 0.009, z-value = −6.280, p-value = 0.000

The ANOVA test for coherence showed a highly significant result ($F(13, 39) = 5.9474$, p-value < 0.0001)). Tukey's HSD multiple comparison tests were also significant and revealed differences in gamma coherence in the following epochs:

- HLS vs IPTV (IP): There was a significant decrease in the gamma coherence in the HLS epoch when delivered over IP compared to IPTV, $M = −0.046$, $SE = 0.011$, p = .0256, 95% CI [−0.0879, −0.004]

- HLS vs IPTV (POINT): There was a significant decrease in gamma coherence in the HSL and IPTV epochs when delivered over IP and POINT, M = −0.0564, SE = 0.012, p = .0033, 95% CI [−0.0984, −0.0144]
- HLS vs IPTV (POINT): There was a significant decrease in gamma coherence in the HLS and IPTV epochs over POINT M = −0.0429, SE = 0.011, p = .043, 95% CI [−0.0849, −0.0009]

For user 2, the red line (see Fig. 3) has higher peaks than other lines across the x-axis, indicating stronger coherence for the IPTV over the POINT epoch. A mixed-effect model shows that there are significant differences between the reference epoch (HLS-IP) and the following epochs:

- Coef. (IPTV − IP) = 0.025, Std Err = 0.008, z-value = 3.148, p-value = 0.002
- Coef. (HLS-POINT) = −0.035, Std Err = 0.008, z-value = −4.265, p-value = 0.000
- Coef. (IPTV-POINT) = 0.040, Std Err = 0.008, z-value = 4.992, p-value = 0.000

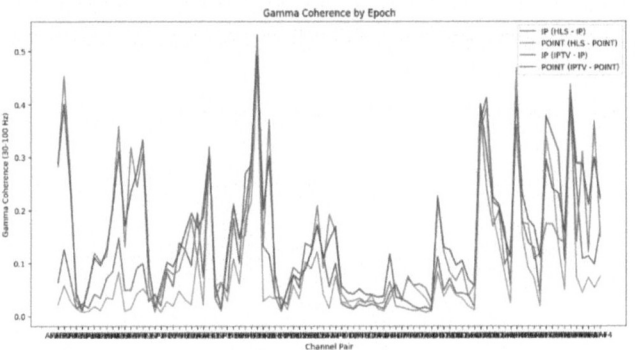

Fig. 3. Gamma Coherence by Epoch for User 2.

The ANOVA test for coherence showed a highly significant result ($F(13, 39) = 5.9474$, p-value < 0.0001). Tukey's HSD multiple comparison tests were also significant and revealed differences in gamma coherence in the following epochs:

- IPTV(IP) vs HLS (POINT): There was a significant decrease in the gamma coherence in the IPTV epoch when delivered over IP compared to HLS and POINT, M = −0.0601, SE = -0.103, p = .0018, 95% CI [−0.01027, −0.0174]
- HLS vs IPTV (POINT): There was a significant increase in gamma coherence in the HSL and IPTV epochs when delivered over POINT, M = 0.0749, SE = 0.032, p = 0.0, 95% CI [0.0323, 0.1176]

For user 3, the blue line (see Fig. 4) has higher peaks than other lines across the x-axis, indicating stronger coherence for the HLS over the IP epoch. We have confirmed this observation with a mixed effect model, which shows statistically significant differences between this epoch (HLS − IP) and the remaining epochs:

- Coef. (IPTV − IP) = −0.106, Std Err = 0.009, z-value = −11.212, p-value = 0.000

- Coef. (HLS-POINT) = −0.105, Std Err = 0.009, z-value = −11.238, p-value = 0.000
- Coef. (IPTV-POINT) = −0.129, Std Err = 0.009, z-value = −13.849, p-value = 0.000

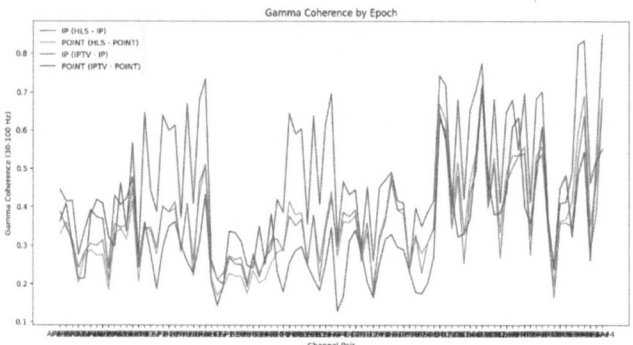

Fig. 4. Gamma Coherence by Epoch for User 3.

ANOVA showed a statistically significant result (F (90, 270) = 13.7819, p < 0.0001. Tukey's HSD revealed significant differences in coherence in the following epochs:

- HLS vs IPTV (IP): There was a significant decrease in the gamma coherence in the HLS epoch when delivered over IP compared to IPTV, M = −0.1069, SE = 0.020, p = .0, 95% CI [−0.1587 −0.055]
- HLS (IP) vs HLS (POINT): There was a significant decrease in gamma coherence in the HSL and IPTV epochs when delivered over IP and POINT, M = −0.1054, SE = 0.0320, p = .0, 95% CI [−0.1573 −0.0536]
- HLS (IP) vs IPTV (POINT): There was a significant decrease in gamma coherence in the HLS and IPTV epochs when delivered over IP and POINT M = −0.1294, SE = 0.020, p = .00, 95% CI [−0.1813 −0.0776]

4.3 Realism

The ANOVA PSD analyses for Beta (13–30 Hz) showed statistically significant results for all users (see Table 4):

- User 1 (F(13, 39) = 5.0354, p < 0.0001);
- User 2 (F(13, 39) = 51.7558, p < 0.0001);
- User 3 (F(13, 39) = 57.344, p < 0.0001);
- User 4 (F(13, 39) = 19.8474, p < 0.0001);
- User 5 (F(13, 39) = 111.1068, p < 0.0001);
- User 6 (F(13, 39) = 69.2143, p < 0.0001);
- User 7 (F(13, 39) = 50.0538, p < 0.0001);
- User 8 (F(13, 39) = 40.7014, p < 0.0001).

Table 4. Mean and Standard Deviation of Beta Power.

User	Beta Power (Mean ± Std Dev)
1	13377.1 ± 1530.6
2	1.720 ± 0.203
3	1.711 ± 0.278
4	1.424 ± 0.600
5	1.254 ± 0.143
6	2.430 ± 0.453
7	2.619 ± 0.498
8	1.398 ± 0.339

However, none of Tukey's HSD tests revealed significant results for any epochs. The Beta PSD analyses using mixed effects model showed statistically significant differences between the reference epoch (HLS – IP) and the following epochs:

- User 2 (Coef. (HLS – POINT) = 0.298, Std Err = 0.103, z-value = 2.903, p-value = 0.004)
- User 3 (Coef. (IPTV – POINT) = −0.429, Std Err = 0.110, z-value = −3.905, p-value = 0.000)
- User 5 (Coef. (IPTV – IP) = 0.196, Std Err = 0.034, z-value = 5.758, p-value = 0.000)
- User 5 (Coef. (HLS – POINT) = 0.225, Std Err = 0.033, z-value = 6.781, p-value = 0.000)
- User 5 (Coef. (IPTV – POINT) = 0.292, Std Err = 0.036, z-value = 8.211, p-value = 0.000)

4.4 Detail

The PSD analyses for Alpha (8–13 Hz) revealed statistically significant results for user six and user seven (see Table 5). The ANOVA test was significant for both users.

- User 6 ($F(1, 3) = 102.77$, $p < 0.001$)
- User 7 ($F(1, 3) = 14.6847$, $p < 0.05$)

Tukey's HSD for user 7 found the following significant difference:

- HLS (IP) vs IPTV (POINT): There was a significant decrease in alpha power in the HLS epoch when delivered over IP compared to IPTV when delivered over POINT, $M = −3.4125$, $SE = 0.0064$, $p = .0$, 95% CI [−5.3102 −1.5147]

The mixed effects model for user 7 found highly statistically significant differences between the reference epoch (HLS – IP) and the following epochs:

- Coef. (IPTV – POINT) = −2.591, Std Err = 0.537, z-value = −4.826, p-value = 0.000)

- Coef. (IPTV – IP) = −1.398, Std Err = 0.505, z-value = −2.767, p-value = 0.006)

Table 5. Mean and Standard Deviation of Alpha Power.

User	Alpha Power (Mean ± Std Dev)
1	30082 ± 3596
2	0.8518 ± 0.1938
3	2.612 ± 0.5704
4	2.210 ± 0.1595
5	2.228 ± 0.687
6	1.786 ± 0.502
7	3.714 ± 1.335
8	2.693 ± 0.701

4.5 Time-Frequency Analysis (TFA)

For each dimension of immersion, we conducted the following TFA analysis:

- Presence and Realism: Wavelet Transform [22]
- Sensory Engagement: Time-Frequency Decomposition (e.g., Morlet Wavelets) [23]
- Realism: Short-Time Fourier Transform (STFT) [24]

We observed differences only for Wavelet transform between HLS and IPTV services for users one and two. For user 1, the wavelet transform (see Fig. 5) shows a difference in amplitude between IPTV – IP and IPTV – POINT. The amplitude for IPTV – IP peaks at 12000, while for IPTV – POINT, it peaks at 16000. For user 2, the vertical stripes are more pronounced for HLS-POINT (Fig. 5) compared to HLS–IP (Fig. 6).

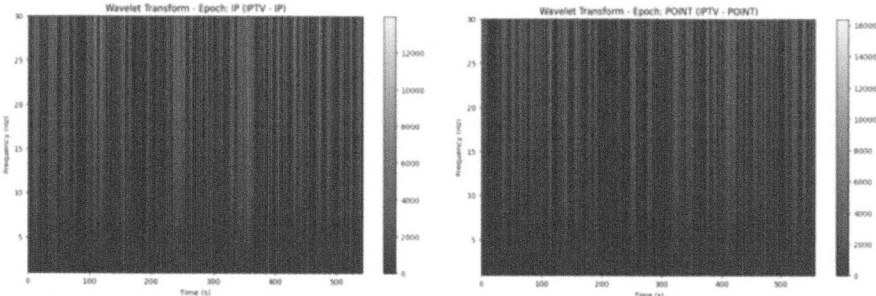

Fig. 5. Wavelet comparison between IP and POINT (IPTV) for user 1.

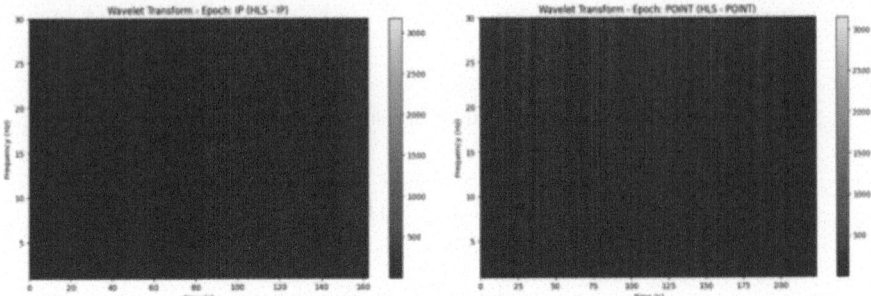

Fig. 6. HLS – IP Wavelet Transform for user 2.

4.6 Clustering

We clustered the EEG data from all users to identify IP and POINT delivery patterns across the HLS and IPTV services. Our algorithm computes PSD in four frequency bands (theta, alpha, beta, and gamma) across the eight users for each epoch (Fig. 7).

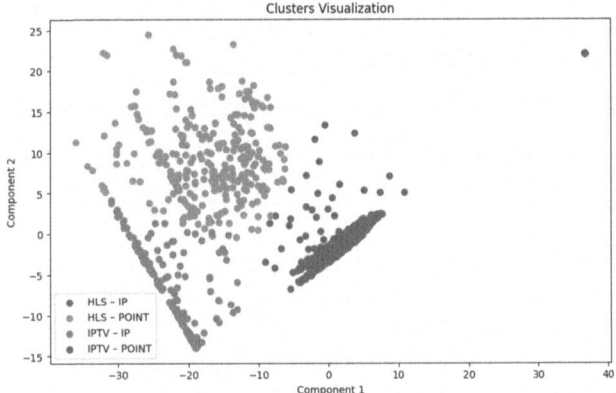

Fig. 7. EEG Clusters of Participants.

Additionally, the algorithm computes coherence between 14 EEG channels to measure synchronization. Finally, we applied the K-Means clustering algorithm [25] to group the data into four clusters. These clusters reflect the two networking delivery mechanisms and services (HLS – IP, HLS – POINT, IPTV – IP and IPTV – POINT).

4.7 Semi-structured Interviews

Participants also took part in a semi-structured exit interview. An experimenter led the session with open-ended questions, allowing participants to provide more insights about their experience with each service (e.g., whether they noticed any differences between the four clips). Each exit interview lasted a maximum of 10 min.

- Whether they noticed any differences between the four clips
- Which of the clips made them feel more frustrated

All participants thought that the first IPTV clip made them more frustrated out of the four clips they watched. Comments included:

- *"The first IPTV clip was seriously annoying".*
- *"The IPTV clip made me feel more frustrated because of the disruption in the flow of content.*

Only some users noticed visual disruptions in the first HLS clip, but they were insufficient to produce an emotional response. Selected comments included:

- *"The first movie trailer (Jumanji) had issues. The others were fine".*
- *"The first one had more of an interruption than the second, pixelating".*

Some users did not notice any differences between the first two clips. Comments included:

- *"I cannot remember any differences between the first two".*
- *"The first two were the same regarding visuals".*

5 Discussion

Starting with *presence*, an increase in Theta power while watching videos indicates a state of increased cognitive load with the content, whereas a decrease suggests decreased cognitive load [26]. An increase in Alpha power reflects a relaxed state where users enjoy the movie without distractions [27]; conversely, a reduction in Alpha power indicates increased concentration and focus [28]. A simultaneous increase in Theta power and a decrease in Alpha power suggests that users fully engage with the video content [14].

Our EEG analyses show that POINT generally decreases Theta power and increases Alpha power for HLS and IPTV services. Reduced theta waves suggest that users found watching video content on POINT less demanding in terms of mental effort than on IP. Furthermore, the increase in Alpha waves suggests that users experienced stable relaxation levels on POINT regardless of the service used. In contrast, on IP, the decrease in Alpha power with both services indicates that users were less relaxed and more alert when watching videos. Video delivery on IP resulted in visual disruptions under exceptional conditions, contributing to a lower sense of presence than POINT.

Continuing with the *sensory engagement*, an increase in Gamma power and coherence indicates that the brain can effectively process and combine the audiovisual experience [15, 19]. Different brain regions communicate effectively by combining input, resulting in an integrated sensory experience. Conversely, a decrease in gamma power and coherence indicates that the brain cannot efficiently combine and process the different modalities of the audiovisual experience, leading to a fragmented sensory experience. Our EEG data analyses show that for users 1 to 3, HLS-IP is more frequently associated with decreases in gamma power and coherence than HLS-POINT. For users 4 and 5, HLS-POINT results in higher gamma power and coherence than HSL-IP. Therefore, HLS video delivery on POINT produces a more cohesive and engaging sensory experience than IP.

Regarding *realism*, an increase in beta power indicates that the audiovisual experience is realistic enough to require higher levels of focus and detailed cognitive processing. A decrease in Beta power suggests that the audiovisual experience does not require intense cognitive processing as it is less detailed and complex than the user expected [16, 17]. Analyses of the EEG data show that POINT is more frequently associated with increases in beta power than IP. The effect is not service-specific (HLS or IPTV). As POINT did not disrupt video content delivery under exceptional conditions, users had a crisp audiovisual experience on both HLS and IPTV, leading to an increased sense of realism.

For the final dimension of immersion, *detail*, a decrease in alpha activity indicates greater attention to audiovisual stimuli, while an increase in alpha power suggests a state of relaxation where users do not actively pay attention to the audiovisual stimuli [18]. Our EEG data analyses for detail show that IP is mainly associated with a decrease in Alpha power compared to POINT, and this effect is not service-specific. Users had more difficulty processing video content under exceptional conditions on IP (e.g., pixelated video on HSL) than POINT.

The Time-frequency analysis (TFA) for the first two users suggests more neural activity for POINT than IP with both services. Cognitive activity registered on the Wavelet transform graphs increased as users were more immersed (across all dimensions) with video content distributed over POINT.

Although the EEG analyses demonstrate POINT's effects on engaging users (first level of immersion), they do not provide a holistic picture. Therefore, we clustered the EEG data of all users to observe group-level differences. We found that the HLS–POINT cluster (orange points) is the largest, indicating that the HLS service, when delivered over POINT, produces a unique neurological pattern among all users, possibly because of high engagement. In contrast, the HSL – IP (blue points) is smaller, suggesting a less prevalent pattern among users. The IPTV–IP (green points) is smaller than HLS-IP, showing an even less common pattern of EEG data among users. Finally, the IPTV – POINT cluster (red points) is the smallest, indicating that IPTV delivery over POINT did not produce significant EEG patterns across users.

The subjective results corroborate the objective EEG measures. Users enjoyed watching video content when distributed over POINT. The exceptional conditions did not impact the video content delivered via POINT, so they experienced uninterrupted videos on both services.

6 Future Work

We plan to repeat the study with a larger group of users and incorporate multimodal biometrics, including emotion recognition and eye tracking. Emotion recognition can provide deep insights into the emotional aspects of immersion. For example, some users mentioned in interviews that video delivery via IP on both services frustrated them. We want to explore how these emotions impacted their immersion in the content. Eye-tracking can provide insights into how users respond to exceptional conditions, such as whether disruptions lead to significant shifts in attention. Finally, we plan to extend our EEG data processing pipeline to process data from multimodal biometrics (e.g., facial expression recognition and eye-tracking).

7 Conclusion

We conducted a pilot study to measure the effects of the POINT network delivery mechanism on users' immersion in digital video content on two services (HLS and IPTV). Our data analyses (EEG and interviews) partially support our hypothesis. Analysis for specific users shows that distributing digital video over POINT positively impacted all dimensions of immersion (presence, sensory engagement, realism, and immersion) regardless of the service used (HLS or IPTV). However, the group-level analysis shows that HLS-POINT increased neurological activity compared to all other conditions. Users had a smoother viewing experience when they watched videos on HLS using POINT than on IP, which increased engagement. Therefore, we can conclude that digital video content distributed over the POINT network can effectively engage users (first level of immersion), resulting in an immersive viewing experience, but the impact is service-specific.

Acknowledgements. This research was supported by the EU H2020 ICT project POINT under contract 643990. We want to thank the POINT team members who participated in designing, implementing, and evaluating the prototype used for the trials.

References

1. Camilleri, M.A., Falzon, L.: Understanding motivations to use online streaming services: integrating the technology acceptance model (TAM) and the uses and gratifications theory (UGT). Span. J. Mark. - ESIC **25**(2), 217–238 (2021). https://doi.org/10.1108/SJME-04-2020-0074
2. Lotz, A.D., Eklund, O., Soroka, S.: Netflix, library analysis, and globalization: rethinking mass media flows. J. Commun. **72**(4), 511–521 (2022). https://doi.org/10.1093/joc/jqac020
3. Brown, E., Cairns, P.: A grounded investigation of game immersion. Presented at the CHI 2004 Extended Abstracts on Human Factors in Computing Systems, Vienna, Austria (2004)
4. Wang, C., Li, Z.: Unraveling the relationship between audience engagement and audiovisual characteristics of automotive green advertising on Chinese TikTok (Douyin). PLoS ONE **19**(4), e0299496 (2024). https://doi.org/10.1371/journal.pone.0299496
5. Doumanis, I., Phinikarides, A., Xylomenos, G., Porter, S., Georgiades, M.: Improving video QoE with IP over ICN. Int. J. Netw. Manage. **30**, e2057 (2018). https://doi.org/10.1002/nem.2057
6. Möller, S., Raake, A.: Quality of Experience: Advanced Concepts, Applications and Methods. Springer (2014)
7. López-Ardao, J.C., Rodríguez-Pérez, M., Herrería-Alonso, S.: Recent advances in information-centric networks (ICNs). Future Internet **15**(12), 392 (2023). https://www.mdpi.com/1999-5903/15/12/392
8. Zhu, Y., Heynderickx, I., Redi, J.A.: Understanding the role of social context and user factors in video quality of experience. Comput. Hum. Behav. **49**, 412–426 (2015). https://doi.org/10.1016/j.chb.2015.02.054
9. Cornu, C., et al.: Experimental designs for small randomised clinical trials: an algorithm for choice. Orphanet J. Rare Dis. **8**(1), 48 (2013). https://doi.org/10.1186/1750-1172-8-48
10. Younes, M., et al.: Odds ratio product of sleep EEG as a continuous measure of sleep state. Sleep **38**(4), 641–654 (2015). https://doi.org/10.5665/sleep.4588

11. Wallstrom, G.L., Kass, R.E., Miller, A., Cohn, J.F., Fox, N.A.: Correction of ocular artifacts in the EEG using bayesian adaptive regression splines. In: Gatsonis, C., et al. (eds.) Case Studies in Bayesian Statistics, pp. 351–365. Springer, New York (2002)

12. Keitel, A., Gross, J., Kayser, C.: Shared and modality-specific brain regions that mediate auditory and visual word comprehension. Elife **9**, e56972 (2020). https://doi.org/10.7554/eLife.56972

13. Welch, P.: The use of fast Fourier transform for the estimation of power spectra: a method based on time averaging over short, modified periodograms. IEEE Trans. Audio Electroacoust. **15**(2), 70–73 (1967)

14. Raufi, B., Longo, L.: An evaluation of the EEG alpha-to-theta and theta-to-alpha band ratios as indexes of mental workload. Front. Neuroinform. **16** (2022). https://doi.org/10.3389/fninf.2022.861967. (in English)

15. Adaikkan, C., Tsai, L.-H.: Gamma entrainment: impact on neurocircuits, glia, and therapeutic opportunities. Trends Neurosci. **43**(1), 24–41 (2020). https://doi.org/10.1016/j.tins.2019.11.001

16. Baumeister, J., Barthel, T., Geiss, K.-R., Weiss, M.: Influence of phosphatidylserine on cognitive performance and cortical activity after induced stress. Nutr. Neurosci. **11**(3), 103–110 (2008)

17. Lalo, E., Gilbertson, T., Doyle, L., Lazzaro, V.D., Cioni, B., Brown, P.: Phasic increases in cortical beta activity are associated with alterations in sensory processing in the human. Exp. Brain Res. **177**, 137–145 (2007)

18. Bagherzadeh, Y., Baldauf, D., Pantazis, D., Desimone, R.: Alpha synchrony and the neurofeedback control of spatial attention. Neuron **105**(3), 577-587.e5 (2020). https://doi.org/10.1016/j.neuron.2019.11.001

19. Bowyer, S.M.: Coherence a measure of the brain networks: past and present. Neuropsychiatr. Electrophysiol. **2**(1), 1 (2016). https://doi.org/10.1186/s40810-015-0015-7

20. Huart, C., Legrain, V., Hummel, T., Rombaux, P., Mouraux, A.: Time-frequency analysis of chemosensory event-related potentials to characterize the cortical representation of odors in humans. PLoS ONE **7**(3), e33221 (2012). https://doi.org/10.1371/journal.pone.0033221

21. Bisong, E.: Google colaboratory. In: Bisong, E. (ed.) Building Machine Learning and Deep Learning Models on Google Cloud Platform: A Comprehensive Guide for Beginners, pp. 59–64. Apress, Berkeley (2019)

22. Karlton, W.: Time frequency analysis of wavelet and Fourier transform. In: Somayeh, M. (ed.) Wavelet Theory, p. Ch. 1. IntechOpen, Rijeka (2020)

23. Cohen, M.X.: A better way to define and describe Morlet wavelets for time-frequency analysis. Neuroimage **199**, 81–86 (2019). https://doi.org/10.1016/j.neuroimage.2019.05.048

24. Durak, L., Arikan, O.: Short-time Fourier transform: two fundamental properties and an optimal implementation. IEEE Trans. Signal Process. **51**(5), 1231–1242 (2003). https://doi.org/10.1109/TSP.2003.810293

25. Likas, A., Vlassis, N., Verbeek, J.J.: The global k-means clustering algorithm. Pattern Recogn. **36**(2), 451–461 (2003). https://doi.org/10.1016/S0031-3203(02)00060-2

26. McGill, M.B., Kieffaber, P.D.: Event-related theta and gamma band oscillatory dynamics during visuo-spatial sequence memory in younger and older adults. PLoS ONE **19**(4), e0297995 (2024). https://doi.org/10.1371/journal.pone.0297995

27. Kawashima, T., Shiratori, H., Amano, K.: The relationship between alpha power and heart rate variability commonly seen in various mental states. PLoS ONE **19**(3), e0298961 (2024). https://doi.org/10.1371/journal.pone.0298961

28. Schuhmann, T., et al.: Left parietal tACS at alpha frequency induces a shift of visuospatial attention. PLoS ONE **14**(11), e0217729 (2019). https://doi.org/10.1371/journal.pone.0217729

An Assistive System for Non-vocal Patients in Intensive Care Units

Jan Patrick Kopetz[✉][iD], Börge Kordts[iD], Tim Schrills[iD], and Nicole Jochems[iD]

University of Luebeck, Ratzeburger Allee 160, 23560 Lübeck, Germany
{j.kopetz,b.kordts,tim.schrills,nicole.jochems}@uni-luebeck.de

Abstract. Critical care patients in intensive care units often require mechanical ventilation. This intervention usually involves a loss of the patient's verbal communication for the duration of the ventilation. The weaning process from ventilation, in particular, causes increased stress. This significantly challenges patients and all others involved in the recovery process. Augmentative and Alternative Communication concepts may offer various options to mitigate this limitation. A novel assistive system for communication, information, and control, based on a ball-shaped interaction device, was designed to meet the needs of these weaning patients. To examine the maturity of the prototype before clinical trials, it was evaluated in a laboratory usability study with healthy elderly adults ($N = 22$) regarding the learnability of the interaction, suitability for communication purposes, and the overall user experience. The results indicated that participants quickly learned the interaction and could successfully use the system as intended. This provides a solid foundation for a comprehensive field study with the weaning patient population.

Keywords: Intensive care units · Weaning patients · Assistive system · Augmentative and alternative communication · Ball-shaped interaction device · Usability study

1 Introduction

In the German healthcare system, about 19.5 million treatment cases were registered annually between 2016 and 2019. Of these cases, approximately 2.1 million were treated in intensive care units (ICUs) [2]. Every fifth ICU patient requires mechanical ventilation [2] as a result of respiratory insufficiency caused by disease or postoperative complications. Once the patients' health condition has stabilized, they are gradually weaned from mechanical ventilation. Weaning can be physically and psychologically challenging for patients, and in some cases, it can last from days to weeks or even longer. While mechanical ventilation support is vital, it also has limitations. Mechanically ventilated ICU patients are non-vocal and unable to speak due to the need for an artificial airway (intubation or tracheostomy tubes), which creates a significant communication barrier [10]. This barrier does not only affect the patients themselves, who may experience stress, frustration, and anxiety due to their inability to express themselves, but also complicates the efforts of healthcare providers and family members involved in the recovery process [1, 9, 28].

H. Plácido da Silva and P. Cipresso (Eds.): CHIRA 2024, CCIS 2370, pp. 403–424, 2025.
https://doi.org/10.1007/978-3-031-82633-7_24

Communication is an essential part of the recovery process and must be established as early as possible, since positive communicative activities with ventilated patients have been linked to improved patient-related outcomes [22]. To enable patients to communicate despite their limitations, various Augmentative and Alternative Communication (AAC) approaches are generally adapted to the context of intensive care. They can be categorized into low-tech solutions like paper-based cardboards and printed images, and high-tech solutions such as computer-based devices with synthesized speech [21]. Notably, there is no consensus among the research community on a systematic approach to the evaluation and outcome measurement of AAC interventions for ventilated patients, nor on a standard of care [13, 31]. Furthermore, it has been reported that current practice – mostly based on low-tech solutions – does not adequately address the needs of intensive care patients to communicate with medical staff to promptly react to potentially dangerous situations (cf. [26, 27]).

In contrast, modern technical approaches can provide interactive solutions that can be tailored to very specific needs. Solutions could support various communication scenarios, provide context-specific information, serve as a control panel for smart environmental devices, or enable participation in their relatives' and friends' social lives. In addition to the aforementioned opportunities, the deployment also entails a number of challenges relevant for the interaction. Critical illness, medication, and the overall situation may impair the patient's cognitive capabilities. Interacting with a digital system should therefore be adapted to these capabilities, and the system's complexity should be as low as possible. In addition, both physical strength and tactile precision in the hands of ICU patients can be reduced. Prolonged periods of lying in a hospital bed can result in physical weakness and muscle atrophy due to lack of exercise. This can further exacerbate existing conditions. Swollen extremities, which may be a side effect of therapy and medication [14], can result in impaired fine motor control when using input devices, making it difficult to perform precise movements. Additional requirements are linked to the clinical environment. In hospitals, it is generally obligatory to design all surfaces that come into contact with patients in a manner that allows for wiping these surfaces with an effective disinfectant, to prevent the spread of microorganisms. This requirement is particularly pertinent to input devices that are in direct contact with patients. Furthermore, it is crucial that in emergency events, any devices can be removed quickly and easily.

In this article, a new assistive system for this context is introduced. The system is based on our previous work in this field [10, 15, 17–19]. Here, we present the main components of the assistive system, including a novel, ball-shaped interaction device to control the graphical user interface (GUI). Additionally, we present the results of a work in progress control study, that is designed to examine the maturity of the prototype before clinical trials. It was conducted in a individually equipped laboratory with elderly adults with an an average age comparable to the target group [25]. In doing so, we address several research questions including the learnability of the interaction, the system's suitability for communication purposes, and the overall usability of the system (cf. Sect. 4.1).

2 Related Work

Various AAC strategies address the communication deficits of non-vocal ICU patients. Unaided methods include the use of silent articulation, gestures, and body language; aided methods include low-tech aids like pen and paper or picture boards and high-tech aids such as computer-based devices [21]. In recent articles, current and historic low-tech and high-tech approaches were reviewed [8, 13, 21]. Contemporary high-tech approaches for non-vocal ICU patients include CARNA[1], EyeControl[2], MOCS [8], MyICUVoice[3], Noddle[4], and VidaTalk[5]. A comparison of these approaches was published recently [8]. The CARNA patient communication system allows patients to select communication topics from a GUI displayed on a mobile monitor stand and using a controller with two pneumatic buttons. Since we found only sparse information about this approach, we consider it to be in an early research state. The apps MyICUVoice and VidaTalk are classic tablet-based solutions consisting of picture/word boards and touch input. While using mobile apps is usually beneficial due to their familiar interaction style, possible problems with this approach for ICU patients lying in bed due to their motor limitations in hand strength and precision were discussed (cf. [8, 21]). An alternative to physical touch selection that overcomes strength and precision issues can be offered by eye-gaze systems connected to the displays. However, benefits of eye-gaze systems for ICU patients are controversial, because patients may struggle with concentration, posture, or keeping their eyes sufficiently open [7]. EyeControl uses a different approach, as it does not offer a GUI, but users navigate between audio menus using intuitive eye gestures [12]. The Noddle system includes a GUI with picture/word boards displayed on a tablet and offers different external input sensors that respond to either small low-force movement gestures or small tongue clicks [11]. The Manually Operated Communication System (MOCS) [8] consists of a tablet with a GUI addressing various bedside communication scenarios for non-vocal ICU patients. The system is controlled by a custom handheld gesture controller.

EyeControl and MOCS have been tested in pilot trials [8, 12]; the Noddle system was tested in a clinical study [11]. The results reported in the literature seem promising, but none of the systems have been implemented for daily usage. For the other systems, no literature about any trials has been found.

There are only occasional studies on AAC systems controlled by specially developed interaction devices for intensive care patients, specifically focusing on standards of care. In particular, no such systems are presented in the literature that are specifically aimed at the weaning phase, although this is precisely where special requirements and challenges arise. As a result, there is a need for specialized systems that are adapted for use in intensive care beds and are also suitable for weaning patients in the early stages.

---

[1] CARNA is a product developed by KMH Technik GmbH, www.kmh-technik.de/medizintechnik/.

[2] EyeControl is a product developed by EyeFree Assisting Communication Ltd., www.eyecontrol.co.il.

[3] MyICUVoice is a product of Symptech Ltd. www.myicuvoice.com.

[4] Noddle and noddle-chat are products of Voxello, www.voxello.com.

[5] The VidaTalk^{TM} app is a product of Acuity Medical, Inc, www.vidatak.com.

3   An Assistive System for Communication, Information and Control

For our approach of an assistive system, the primary objective is to address patient needs by enabling communication across different scenarios, providing information, and fostering self-determination via the control of smart objects. The overall system was conceptualized by the members of the *ACTIVATE* project consortium[6]. In this section, we first summarize relevant user and system requirements, followed by an overview of the patient application as the main component. Finally, we describe hardware setup of the system.

3.1   Requirements

Following the human-centred design methodology, we refer to user and system requirements previously specified based on a comprehensive context analysis [10, 15, 17–19]. In previous work, the specialized interaction device BIRDY meeting the aforementioned requirements has been described [19]. Based on this, we developed a novel interactive system that is explicitly designed for the control via this device and is tailored to the needs of non-vocal ICU patients.

For a better understanding, requirements and needs of ICU patients relevant for the understanding of the assistive system described in this article are summarized in Table 1.

3.2   Patient Application

The patient application's functionality is adapted to different stages of awakening. During the first stage, the system supports orientation by providing auditory and visual information. As soon as the patient's abilities are sufficient, additional modes with interactive features can be unlocked. This article exclusively refers to the interactive mode. In this mode, the primary purpose of the patient application is to support communication between the patient and the nursing staff (or other communication partners). To address further needs, we designed several sub-applications, including a pain communicator, a nurse call, information dashboards, environmental control (exemplarily implemented for a smart lamp), and a media gallery to display personal media brought by the patient's relatives. The sub-applications and their hierarchical content are displayed in a circular menu called *Compass Menu*, which was designed and tailored to the intensive care context and this system. The main view of the patient application (see Fig. 1) consists of a content area for the menu and sub-applications, a title bar for breadcrumbs, and a sidebar containing basic information (date, time, weather, personal salutation, name of the nurse and current location) and a message board for messages sent via the nurse call. The application and especially the hierarchical menu include several graphical components supporting orientation. An example relevant for the evaluation is the hierarchy indicator, that indicates another menu level below and consists of a dashed border with five fixed dashes around the item (cf. Fig. 1). Leaf items miss this indicator.

---

[6] Project ACTIVATE, https://projekt-activate.de/en.

Table 1. Extract of the non-functional and function requirements for the assistive system. Note that they were selected to provide an overview and that there were more requirements specified [15].

ID	Requirement
NFR-1	The system must be designed with a minimum of complexity by avoiding complex interactions, consider potential short awareness phases and limited experience in using smart devices
NFR-2	System interaction should be possible with physical limitations typical for the target group (e.g. reduced strength and precision in the hands, poor eyesight)
FR-1	The system must display general information (date, time, location, possibly weather information, name of nursing staff) to support the patients' needs for (re-)orientation and information
FR-2	Patients should be able to communicate with other persons in the room
FR-3	Communication topics should correspond to the typical problems and needs of ICU patients (e.g. breathlessness, repositioning, thirst, feelings, questions about their condition and home)
FR-4	Communication topics should be categorized in a meaningful and comprehensible way
FR-5	Patients can provide details about their pain (e.g., location, intensity)
FR-6	The system should enable patients to communicate their needs to the nursing staff, when they are not in the same room
FR-7	The playback of media provided by relatives, like music files, photos, videos, or audio messages, should be possible and controlled by both patients and the staff
FR-8	The system should be controlled by the spherical gesture device BIRDY
FR-9	Nurses should configure and adapt the system to the patients' needs

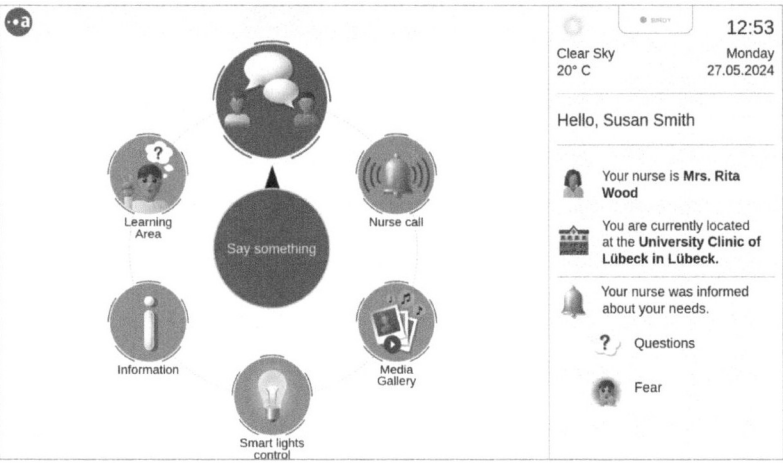

Fig. 1. The main view of the patient application

During development of the communication application (designated "Say something"), we conducted interdisciplinary workshops with domain experts (nurses and nursing scientists), with the objective of creating an easily understandable terminology for individual communication topics. The topics are based on literature research findings and on the personal experience of the experts involved. The workshop results were organized thematically and, together with the menu items of the other sub-applications,

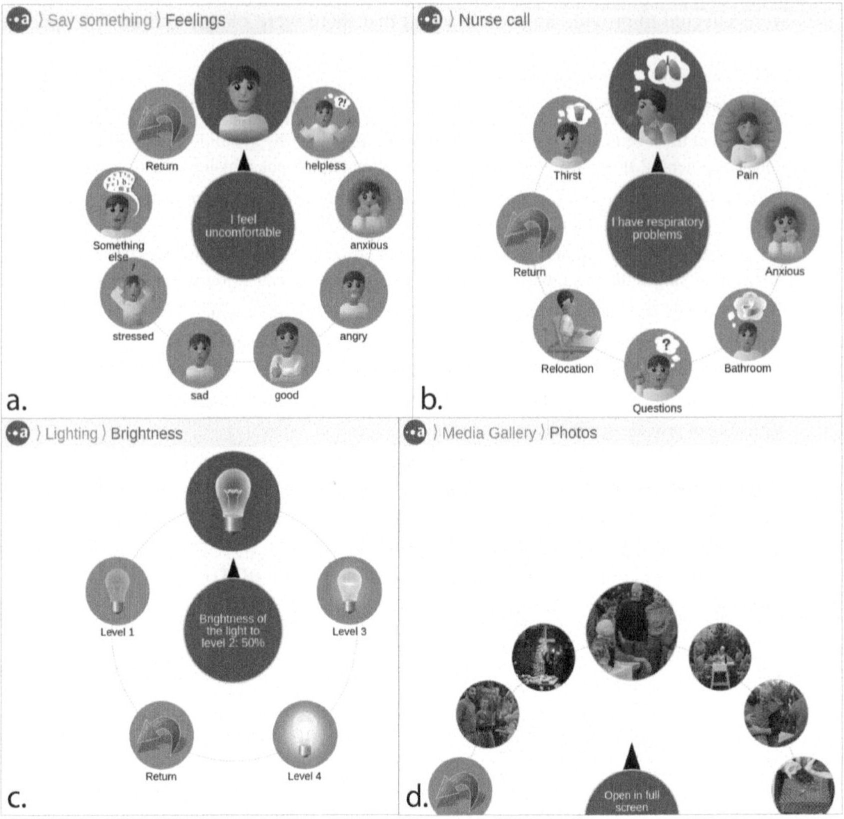

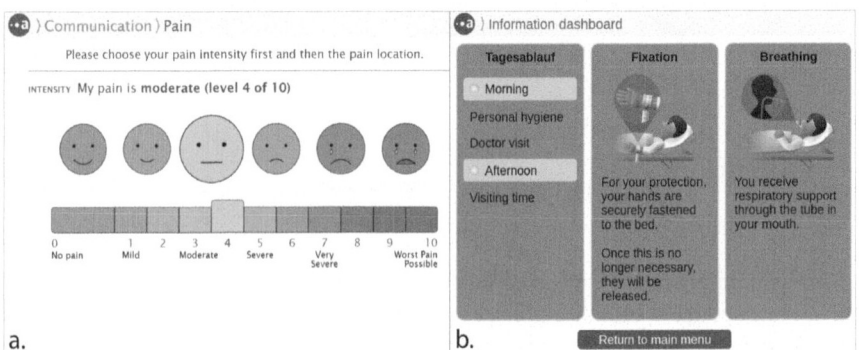

Fig. 2. Exemplary views from sub-applications of the patient application consisting of a *(semi-)circular design*: general communication (a), nurse call (b), smart lighting control (c), and media gallery (d)

Fig. 3. Exemplary views from sub-applications of the patient application with an *individual design*: pain communicator (a), and the information dashboard (b).

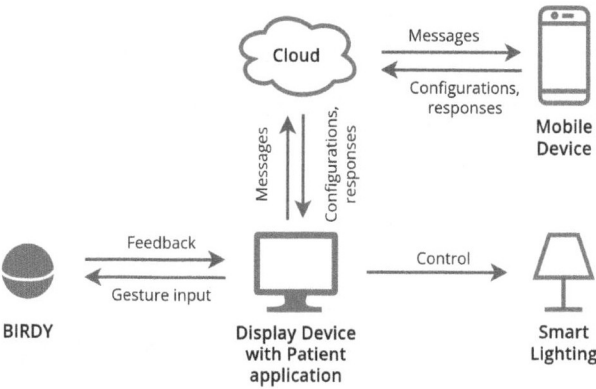

Fig. 4. The main components of the system, including BIRDY, the Display Device with the Patient Application, Smart Lighting, and a Mobile Device.

placed in a meaningful hierarchical menu structure. The resulting structure contains 56 items on four different levels.

Some sub-applications like the nurse call and the smart lighting control work well with the Compass Menu, as they include a limited number of functions that could easily be integrated into the menu structure. The nurse call (see Fig. 2b) addresses situations when the responsible nurse is currently not at the patient's bedside, but is equipped with a mobile device (see Subsect. 3.3). It allows patients to choose from thoroughly selected options (thirst, respiratory problems, fear, etc.), directly inform the nurse via push notifications on a mobile device, and receive their responses. The smart lighting control (see Fig. 2c) addresses the patients' needs for autonomy and allows them to independently switch on (or off) the connected lamps, change their color or regulate their brightness.

For other, equally important sub-applications that do not fit well into the Compass Menu due to certain requirements, individual design variants were developed. The media gallery includes personal media brought by the patients' relatives. Considering larger amounts of photos, a semi-circular menu allows to compensate space issues of the circular Compass Menu (see Fig. 2d). Using the pain communicator, patients can also select pain intensity and location. To report the intensity of the pain, a linear instead of a circular representation was required by the domain experts involved (see Fig. 3a). The information dashboard provides context-specific information; designs consisting of cards afford a comprehensive overview (see Fig. 3b).

3.3 Hardware Setup

The system consists of four central components, that are schematically illustrated in Fig. 4 and described in detail below. The hardware setup of the interactive system primarily consists of the spherical interaction device BIRDY, as well as an all-in-one computer with an appropriate display size mounted on an adaptable roll stand at the foot of the hospital bed. This enables patients to visually perceive the graphical elements of the Patient Application from a relatively short distance. The nursing staff is equipped with mobile devices, which allow them to receive messages and control or configure the patient's system. Notably, all devices involved must not interfere with normal clinical procedures. They must also comply with the current hygiene guidelines. Furthermore, smart objects (e.g., smart lamps) may be integrated into the system, allowing for a self-determined control of the ambience.

BIRDY. In response to the identified need for a system adapted to the weaning phase and particularly the need for an interaction device to control the respective system in such situations, the Ball-shaped Interactive Rehabilitation Device (acronym BIRDY) was developed by the involved hardware engineers from *Cognimed GmbH*[7]. It is tailored to the intensive care context and specifically designed for the use in intensive care beds. In particular, the device complies with current hygiene guidelines. In order to achieve this, the device is sealed and operated wirelessly regarding both charging and data transmission. In previous studies, interaction-related user preferences regarding the design of the device were identified [16]. Furthermore, requirements for BIRDY and their specification process (e.g. a study to identify interaction-related user preferences regarding the design of the device) were previously discussed [19].

BIRDY contains an inertial measurement unit (IMU), which includes a magnetometer, allowing it to track the device's orientation. It further features a sensor that measures the pressure applied to the interior of the device. To provide feedback to users, the device also contains an array of light-emitting diodes (LED) as well as a buzzer and a vibration motor.

The device's sensors allow for the recognition of various possible interaction gestures to control the system. Based on previous studies, pre-tests in our laboratory and further tests with actual patients as well as an assessment of the feasibility and the expected recognition rates of different gestures, we defined and implemented a gesture set for controlling the system with BIRDY. Since the hands of intensive care patients are often severely limited in strength and precision, we chose a gesture-based control utilizing simple interaction gestures based on tilting (right/left) and pressing the device. The gestures can be performed on the surface of the bed, so that the users do not have to lift their hand or arm. While the use of other interaction devices is conceivable, BIRDY is intended to be the primary interaction device of the assistive system.

Display Device. We discussed and tested several options regarding device types and display sizes for presenting the user interface in a laboratory setup. While tablets would have been easier to handle, typical sizes were considered too small for what we decided would be necessary to display (i.e., base information in a side bar as well as a circular menu). Hence, we chose an all-in-one computer with a 23.8-inch monitor allowing us to display all required visual menu components as well as the side bar in a reasonable size still well perceivable from the intended distance when positioning the device at the foot of the bed. The computer is mounted on a roll stand that can be adjusted in height and angle, offering a trade-off between mobility and adaptability that is appropriate to

---

[7] Cognimed GmbH, www.cognimed.de.

the context. In addition to flexible positioning, the general arrangement allows all components to be quickly moved aside if necessary, particularly in emergency situations.

Mobile Devices. Patients' needs communicated via the patient application reach the staff via smartphone. In addition to push notifications for patients' concerns, it offers the option of responding to them and making configurations to the system. We discussed various options for wearables that could be used to signal patient activity to the nursing staff, particularly smart bands positioned at the neckline. However, we did not find a universal solution, since wrist-worn devices conflict with hygiene guidelines and vibrations are not strong enough to be clearly perceived when devices are attached to clothing.

Smart Objects. In order to foster patient autonomy, particularly with regard to the self-determination of the ambience, various smart objects available on the market, which are primarily known from the smart home sector, can in principle be used. While many different devices are conceivable here, we chose the use of a smart lighting system for this work. This is a smart bedside lamp that can be positioned on the patient's side table and that can be operated wirelessly.

4   Methodology

We decided on a multi-stage process to evaluate the system described above, since it is aimed at the vulnerable user group of ICU patients. Before the applicability for the actual user group and its effect on the healing process is evaluated in a field study, the system's learnability, applicability, and usability was tested in a laboratory setting with healthy representatives. We recruited elderly adults to identify potential impeding factors in relation to age-related phenomena. This is particularly relevant since the age of ICU patients in Germany averages above 65 years [25]. This laboratory study is described below.

4.1   Study Design

The goal of the user study was to evaluate the applicability and usability of the assistive system with a special focus on the interaction requirements of non-vocal patients. Based on scenarios designed for the ICU context, participants were asked to perform tasks using the patient application and subsequently, to evaluate the system based on their experience. During the task execution, objective performance data was collected, and subjective data was recorded in subsequent interviews. Accordingly, the study applied a mixed methods approach, combining qualitative and quantitative instruments to assess learnability, user experience and their performance. Due to the variables utilized within our control study, it was not possible to implement comparable conditions (i.e. control group without BIRDY or with a similar system): the measures cannot be elicited without the BIRDY system and a similar system is was not obtainable at the time of the study.

Further data was collected to characterize the sample. Socio-demographic data, including data on their experience with technologies, and interaction-related technology affinity, and data on the participants' state of health was collected.

The study is conducted to answer the following research questions:

1. How effectively do participants learn the system interaction, and what insights can be derived for system-assisted tutorials?
2. Can the participants use the system to effectively communicate concerns regarding the provided topics?
3. How do participants experience the interaction in terms of controlling, comprehension, orientation, structure, and readability?
4. How do participants evaluate the usability and user experience of the system?

4.2   Sample

Twenty-two elderly adults aged at least 60 were recruited online and offline, using flyer, mailing lists and word-of-mouth advertising. Average age was $M = 68.5$ years ($SD = 6.95$). 59.1% were in the age group below 70 years, 36,4% were between 70 and 80 years old, one participant was 81 years old. The sex distribution was almost balanced (54.6% females). Many participants (63.6%) currently or formerly work in the healthcare sector (doctors, nurses, medical/nursing assistance, etc.) Overall, 95.5% of participant reported using a visual aid. Of these, 52.4% used glasses. 59.1% of respondents reported having experience with intensive care units, of which 57.1% had professional experience and 42.9% had patient experience (one respondent had both professional and patient experience).

4.3   Instruments

In the study, a variety of objective and subjective data were collected, including socio-demographic, performance, interview, and survey data. The study protocol[8] and the survey[9], encompassing all questionnaire items, were published as supplemental material.

Socio-demographic Questionnaire. The questionnaire gathered general information such as age, sex, highest educational attainment, and recent occupation. Items on technology use [29] and affinity for technology interaction (ATI) [5] were also included. Additionally, it explored participants' experience with intensive care units and situations where they were verbally limited. The questionnaire also included items about age-related limitations based on the WHO Quality-of-Life questionnaire[10], along with questions about their need for vision aids and perceived declines in their abilities.

---

[8] Study prot.: https://osf.io/3zm4s/?view_only=9840f5706eca40a38f04f0c7208b2065.
[9] Survey: https://osf.io/ds2cq/?view_only=09b25f2dee6142aab0078630fc41aacc.
[10] WHO-QOL-100, Rev.2012.03 https://www.who.int/tools/whoqol.

Observation of Task Execution. Objective performance aspects during the training phase and each of the 12 interaction tasks (cf. task description in Table 2 or the study protocol[8] for more details) were assessed through direct observation and video recordings. The tasks were not randomized as they were designed to increase in difficulty step-by-step and were therefore dependent on each other (i.e., the sequence of tasks could not be changed). These aspects included error count and type, task completion time, task succession, and the need for assistance. Problems encountered were documented in a problem log.

Semi-structured Interview. During and after task completion, participants were interviewed using a semi-structured approach [30]. They provided feedback on the perceived difficulty and clarity of the controls, the intensity of vibration feedback, and their ability to distinguish between selected and non-selected menu elements. Post-task comments addressed task-related issues, and in-between their orientation within the menu hierarchy, and the comprehensibility of specific menu items and UI elements.

After completing all tasks, participants evaluated the menu design, their mental model of the menu hierarchy, the hierarchy indicator's clarity, and the readability and appropriateness of text and graphics. They also commented on the ease-of-use and any missing aspects of communication.

Further questions targeted action regulation to understand participants' mental activities during system interaction. Issues or uncertainties in task execution were linked to specific action steps based on Norman's action model [23].

Survey Data. Usability was measured using the System Usability Scale (SUS) [4], assessing complexity, usability, simplicity, security, and memorability. Confidence in action regulation was gauged with three self-formulated items. The user experience was evaluated using the short version of the User Experience Questionnaire (UEQ-S) [20], assessing the system's hedonic and pragmatic quality.

4.4   Study Procedure

The procedure and the measures are shown in Fig. 5. Initially, participants were introduced into the study and in detail informed that the study is in line with the ethical principles described in the Declaration of Helsinki. Next, they completed a socio-demographic questionnaire.

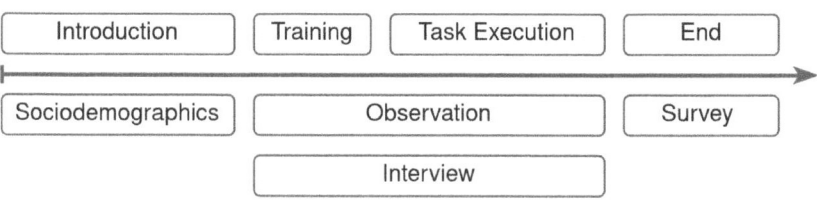

Fig. 5. The phases and measures of the study.

Subsequently, the practical part of the study began. The laboratory setup for this part is shown in Fig. 6. Participants were asked to lie down in a hospital bed at a 30° angle, which is typical for ICU settings. They were instructed to keep their elbow in contact with the bed surface during task execution. This procedure ensured higher validity of the study results, as the physical conditions for executing gestures differ in a sitting position. Additionally, participants were instructed to vocalize their intentions and thoughts during task performance using the Think Aloud method. A camera mounted above the participants' heads recorded the task performance and the subsequent interview to capture both hand motions and system responses. A large screen on the right was used to display study-relevant information.

Understanding the interaction possibilities of a system is a prerequisite for its effective use [24]. To facilitate this understanding of the novel components of the assistive system, the interaction was practiced in an initial learning phase. First, participants were given the interaction device and video instructions on how to operate the system using the interaction gestures (see Subsect. 3.3). To learn the interaction, they were required to perform three consecutive navigation tasks correctly within a specific scope of the system including demo data. After that, participants provided feedback on their initial impressions of the controls and the interaction.

Afterwards, they performed 12 tasks with the system and answered interview questions after each task. Initially, they used a nurse call mode with limited functionality to

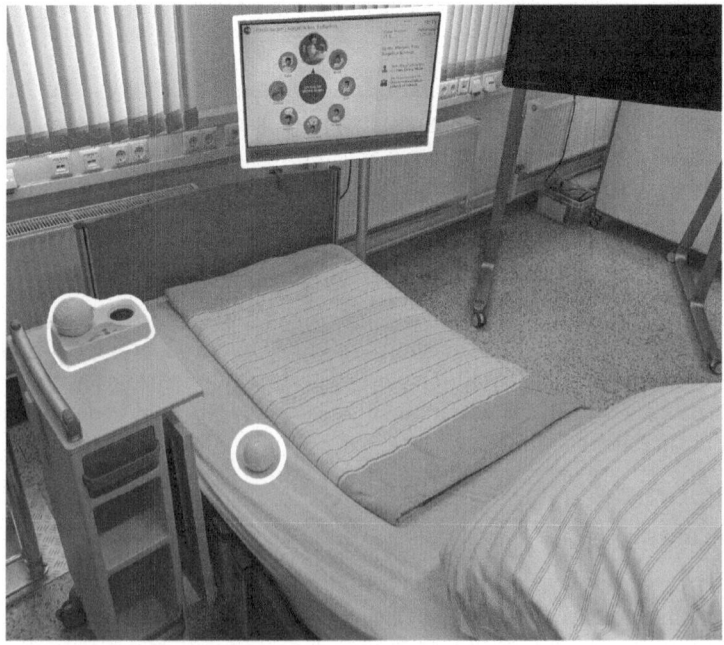

Fig. 6. Laboratory setup of the study. The central components are highlighted: the ball-shaped interaction device on the bed, its charging station on the bedside table, and the mounted display at the foot of the bed.

send specific needs to a fictive nurse outside the room. Then, a mode with the full range of functions was activated, and participants were familiarized with the additional system functions. They then performed additional tasks. In between, participants answered interview questions on the menu hierarchy and their orientation within, their understanding and the recognizability of GUI elements, and ease of use.

Finally, participants filled in questionnaires to evaluate the usability, certainty of actions, and user experience of the system.

4.5 Analysis Procedure

We report all descriptive data surveyed within this study in relation to either behavioral data (task performance and error rate) or experience measures (e.g., usability). A thematic analysis [3] was conducted on the transcribed interview and think aloud data. In the first step, codes were created to identify topics. We followed a constructivist, top-down approach by defining themes that align with concepts described in HCI literature. Accordingly, excerpts were summarized into three main themes: execution, perception, and expertise (cf. [23]). More detailed sub-themes were identified in an initial screening of the interview excerpts by two of the authors. Following the top-down developed coding scheme, two raters independently analyzed the interview excerpts. Subsequently, the absolute number of mentions for each code was calculated. The inter rater reliability was excellent (Cohen's kappa $\kappa = 0.89$).

5   Results

Affinity for Technology Interaction. The affinity for technology interaction score of the sample is elevated ($M = 3.9$; $SD = 0.96$) compared to the expected mean of the German population ($M = 3.6$; $SD = 1.08$) [6]. This is supported by the results of participants' device usage, as smartphones and computers were used often.

Training. Participants had to solve three simple navigation tasks in a row to complete the training phase. All participants completed this phase successfully, with only 9.1% requiring assistance. The most common errors were due to execution ($M = 1.32$; $SD = 0.99$), often overshooting the target item by unintentionally performing a gesture twice. Wrong gestures were less frequent ($M = 0.23$; $SD = 0.69$). In a few cases, technical problems were explicitly identified as the cause of the errors made ($M = 0.09$; $SD = 0.29$); no further errors occurred after a technical restart.

Participants perceived the control difficulty as quite low ($M = 2.0$; $SD = 1.19$; on a scale of 1 to 10; 1 = easy, 10 = difficult). On average, participants needed 120.1 s for the training phase ($SD = 100.1$ s), with a median of 74.5 s. The fastest participant solved the tasks in 30 s, while the slowest needed 382 s. The reference time recorded by a person already familiar with the controls is 28 s.

Various GUI elements (breadcrumbs, highlighted selected item, hierarchy indicator for further sub-levels below a menu item) support orientation within the menu. All participants correctly distinguished the selected item from non-selected items and named

Table 2. Data (N = 22) on the tasks, required assistance and duration required, broken down by task: description, minimal steps, proportion of participants that required assistance, and data on the task execution time in seconds, consisting of mean (*M*), standard deviation (*SD*), the baseline (set by a system developer), and the ratio of the mean execution time to the baseline (labeled as factor).

Task		Minimal	Required	Duration (in seconds)			
#	Description	steps (83 in total)	assistance (in %)	*M*	*SD*	Baseline	Factor
1	Nurse call: fear	4	18.2	44.1	40.2	7	6.3
2	Nurse call: thirst	5	13.6	30.5	30.0	7	4.4
4	Communicate: stress	9	18.2	57.6	39.9	17	3.4
5	Return to previous menu	4	0	16.6	7.9	4	4.2
6	Comm.: raise head of the bed	8	9.1	55.1	25.9	20	2.8
7	Return to main menu	6	9.1	33.8	22.9	12	2.8
8	Comm.: pain in the right leg	9	13.6	79.6	39.4	33	2.4
9	Comm.: what happens next?	7	13.6	47.6	18.9	21	2.3
10	Turn on bed light	11	0	58.8	25.1	21	2.8
11	Change color of bed light	11	4.5	39.5	22.7	10	3.9
12	Explore personal media	9	0	48.0	18.6	18	2.7
	Mean	**7.55**	**9.1**	**46.5**	**26.5**	**15.5**	**3.0**

at least one of the several indicators. Some participants explicitly stated that the representation of the selected item is important for understanding the interaction and that it is appropriately highlighted. Overall, 72.7% of the participants were well-oriented and correctly identified their location in the menu hierarchy. Breadcrumbs were particularly helpful. The number of different hierarchy levels within the menu structure was correctly determined by 63.6% of the participants. When asked about the dotted borders (hierarchy indicator, cf. Subsect. 3.2), 22.7% of the participants correctly identified its meaning.

Task Performance and Error Rate. Each participant achieved a 100% success rate across all tasks. Table 2 shows for each task a description, the minimum necessary steps, the proportion of participants who required assistance, and data on the task completion time. On average, assistance was required in 9.1% of the tasks. Most often, participants required assistance during the first tasks, with 18.2% of participants requiring assistance for tasks 1 and 4, and 13.6% for task 2 (task 3 included a question about the participants understanding of the system). Some participants also required assistance for tasks 8 and 9. The most common form of assistance was guidance on gesture control (nine cases), primarily during the first tasks. Additionally, assistance regarding navigation within the application was provided to participants who had selected an incorrect menu item (eight cases), either due to uncertainty or a problem in identifying the correct menu level. Assistance regarding the task was provided in six cases, mostly because participants had problems remembering the task instructions.

Table 3. Total error rate per task based on the observation of the participants task completion (N = 22), divided into gesture errors and path errors (a deviation from the optimal path). Task refers to the task id (task description see Table 2), minimal steps refers to the minimum amount of interaction steps necessary to solve the task, while the error rates refer to the mean number of errors made for the task.

Task	Minimal	Total errors		Gesture errors		Path errors	
#	steps	M	SD	M	SD	M	SD
1	4	0.64	1.00	0.45	0.80	0.18	0.50
2	5	0.73	0.94	0.68	0.95	0.05	0.21
4	9	0.91	1.48	0.59	1.10	0.32	0.72
5	4	0.05	0.21	0.05	0.21	0.00	0.00
6	8	1.05	1.25	0.73	1.12	0.32	0.72
7	6	0.09	0.29	0.05	0.21	0.05	0.21
8	9	0.50	0.74	0.32	0.57	0.18	0.59
9	7	0.50	0.80	0.18	0.39	0.32	0.57
10	11	1.14	1.17	0.64	1.00	0.50	0.60
11	11	0.64	1.00	0.32	0.72	0.32	0.78
12	9	0.64	0.79	0.55	0.74	0.09	0.29
Mean	**7.55**	**0.62**	**0.99**	**0.41**	**0.80**	**0.21**	**0.54**

To establish a baseline for comparing task completion times, a system developer set a reference duration for each task. As expected, the mean task completion times exceeded the baseline times. The average factor of duration to baseline (mean ÷ baseline) is 3.0. This factor decreases with increasing task IDs, possibly due to training effects. Task 11 has a higher factor than task 10, disrupting the overall trend. Participants were possibly more talkative when they were impressed by the task-related change of the lighting colors within the laboratory, delaying the task completion (after changing the lighting, they had to navigate back to the main menu).

The standard deviation of the duration decreases in relation to the mean task execution time (see Table 2). While the standard deviation of tasks 1 and 2 was similar to the mean, it decreased to approximately half the mean in subsequent tasks, except for task 7. The reduction in proportion indicates that participants became increasingly familiar with the system interaction and were quicker in resolving tasks.

The error rates are displayed in Table 3. Overall, it is relatively low compared to the minimal necessary steps to solve the task; the total mean error rate per task was 0.62 (SD = 0.99). An interaction was considered erroneous if either the gesture was not executed correctly or if the interaction differed from the optimal navigation path. The majority of observed errors in interaction were attributed to incorrect execution of gestures, with an average score of 0.41 (SD = 0.8).

A gesture was considered incorrect if it did not elicit the anticipated system response, which can be attributed to different potential causes: incorrect execution of the movement by the user, false classification of correct user input by the algorithms (e.g., due to noisy sensor data), or data transmission issues caused by an unstable connection. In 4.6% of the tasks, we observed such technical issues; we were always able to overcome them by re-calibration or using a different device.

The mean number of interaction errors per task with regard to path errors ($M = 0.21$; $SD = 0.54$) was relatively low (in comparison to the minimal steps). An interaction sequence was classified as a path error if there was a deviation from the optimal path. Path errors can be attributed to various factors. Participants either failed to recognize the optimal path or found the navigation in the opposite direction more agreeable and accepted the additional interaction steps. Some participants preferred the tilt gesture directing away from the body over the one directing towards the body. In other cases, participants forgot their task and subsequently deviated from the optimal path.

Participants were asked to assess their personal confidence in action regulation. The mean rating for these items was high compared to the scales midpoint($M = 4.65$; $SD = 0.43$; scale of 1 to 5). The participants stated that they were optimistic about their ability to select any menu item, complete the assigned tasks, and identify their own navigation errors. Additionally, all participants claimed that they could use the system to communicate if they were unable to speak.

Interview. Figure 7 shows the results of the thematic analysis of the interview statements, categorized by the main themes perception, execution and expertise. Concerning perception, 13 answers were related to an assumption regarding the *dotted border* of the elements as a hierarchy indicator. Moreover, six answers falsely assumed that the five *border dots represent the number of child elements* (see Fig. 1). The topics of *positioning* and *text formatting* were mentioned nine times each. In particular, the *position* of the selected element as well as the title bar were mentioned (answer with ID 23: [...] *in the font there above*). Regarding *text formatting*, the most frequently mentioned topic was the formatting of the current level within the breadcrumbs displayed in the title bar. For the *text labels* (mentioned six times), the recognizable text elements were named (e.g., category elements in ID 27: *physical needs, lying differently*). None of these responses indicated problems with understanding the text labels. Regarding *orientation problems* (6), participants either named one or more of the indicators or explicitly stated that they had no orientation (ID 66: [...] *I cannot prioritize. I already have problems with prioritization* [...]). For the topic *hierarchy* (5), the levels term was often mentioned, mostly when asked about their orientation (ID 47: [...] *maximum four levels* [...]). *Other* topics (2) related to *real photos of caregivers instead of the icons used* (ID 47), and that the *title bar is not needed* (ID 50).

Regarding execution (see Fig. 7), five responses were related to concerns about whether the *physical conditions* of real patients allow the system's use. Concerning *hand control* (3), it was mentioned that unintentional tilting may occur when pressing, and that tilting to the side facing away from the person's body is easier. Regarding the tilt gesture and the resulting *direction* of the menu rotation, three participants expected an inverted mapping. The topics of *force* (when pressing the interaction device) and *speed* (of the system response) were mentioned twice each. The topics of *haptics/latency* (ID 4: *reacts very slowly or too quickly*) and *others* (ID 39: participant preferred stick figures over the graphics used) were mentioned once each.

In terms of expertise (see Fig. 7), the majority of responses pertained to the topics of *learning and memorization* (18) and *habituation* (4). Participants often mentioned that the novel interaction format necessitates practice and habituation. *Frustrating* experiences during the utilization of the format were mentioned twice, when technical issues with the gesture recognition of the interaction device were encountered while executing the tasks.

Survey. Items regarding usability, confidence in action, and user experience were asked. The items of the System Usability Scale were calculated, resulting in a score on a scale between 0 and 100. Participants evaluated the system with an average SUS score of $M = 88.18$ ($SD = 10.1$), indicating very good to excellent usability.

The results of the User Experience Questionnaire Short Scale indicate an excellent overall user experience value ($M = 2.39$; $SD = 0.93$). The pragmatic quality is average ($M = 2.43$; $SD = 0.7$), while the hedonic quality is good ($M = 2.35$; $SD = 1.33$). Based on the UEQ-S analysis sheet, these values indicate excellent usability and good stimulation through interaction. All participants rated the readability of the text elements, the recognizability of the graphics, and the suitability of images and text positively.

6 Discussion

Several findings can be derived from the results above. The high success rate, low need for help during the learning phase, and low perceived difficulty indicate that the control is easy to learn. The observed errors and thematic analysis results show that users initially have to get used to the unfamiliar control. Once the participants were familiar with the gesture control and the feedback of the system, they could control the system without major problems. Overall, the time required to successfully complete the training tasks was acceptable. In some cases, errors could be traced to technical problems with gesture recognition. This shows that the system's gesture recognition needs to be more robust before it can be used outside of studies. Overall, all participants were able to successfully learn the interaction in an adequate duration, and they mostly considered the gesture control easy. The highlighting of the selected item and the breadcrumbs were helpful for orientation and recognizing the system state. However, the selected design for the hierarchy indicator does not seem to be self-explanatory. The step-by-step learning of the interaction with the system proved to be successful, especially the task-based approach. Some participants required support. A tutorial could benefit quick learners with a shortened version and slower learners with an extended version. In practice, a

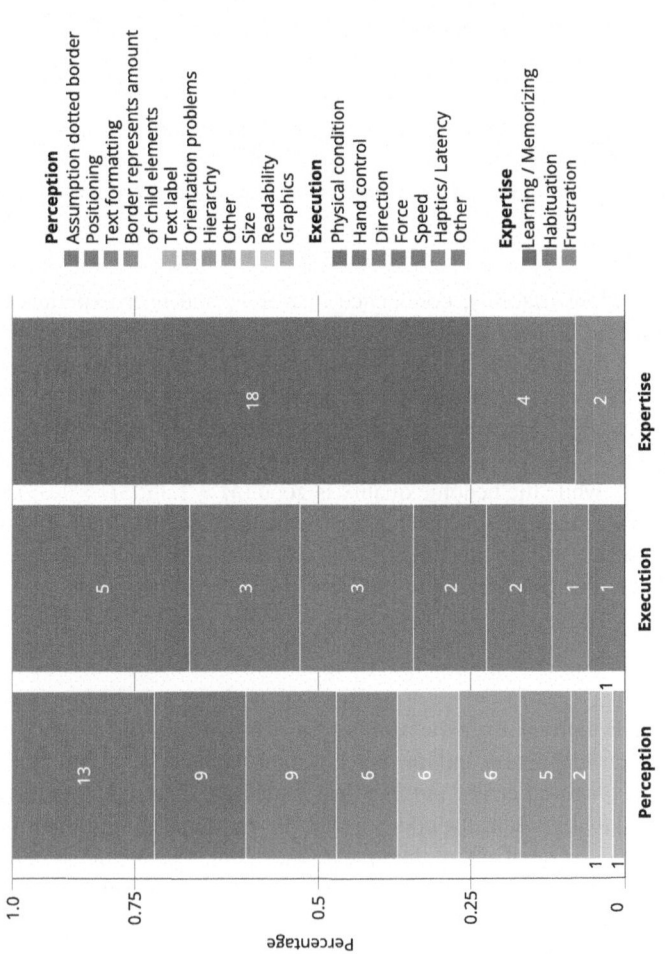

Fig. 7. The thematic analysis results were categorized into three main themes: perception, execution, and expertise. The relative proportion of each theme is displayed on the y-axis, while the absolute number of mentions is shown within the stacks.

nurse should be present to support and assist when necessary and to assess the patient's interaction skills. In addition to the system's controls, patients should be introduced to subtle menu components and their functions, e.g., the title bar with breadcrumbs and the hierarchy indicator. This was also reflected in the interview responses. It can be assumed that the selected item differs sufficiently from the others, since it was recognized as such by all participants. This answered the first research question on how effectively participants learn system interaction and provided insights for tutorial design.

Regarding the second research question, whether participants can utilize the system for effective communication of the displayed content, the following conclusions can be drawn from the results. Participants seemed able to communicate the content and topics specified in the tasks. The task completion rate was 100 %, with little assistance required. Furthermore, the ratio of average completion time to baseline decreased as the number of tasks increased, indicating that participants became more efficient with increased familiarity with the interaction. The low error rate indicates that interaction with the system is generally unproblematic. Although it was not a real clinical scenario with actual patients, the encouraging results regarding confidence in action and capability to use the system in a non-vocal situation confirm this tendency. It can be reasonably assumed that a suited tutorial, improvements to the underlying networking infrastructure and a more robust gesture recognition would further reduce the error rate.

Regarding the third research question of how participants experience the interaction in terms of controlling, comprehension, orientation, structure, and readability, the results of the thematic analysis indicate that during the interaction with the system only a few obstacles were encountered in terms of perception, execution, and expertise. Some participants encountered orientation problems. However, the success rate in completing the tasks shows they still were able to successfully interact with the system. Orientation within the hierarchical menu should also be assessed during a field study with actual patients. The subject of expertise was frequently discussed, implying that the new interaction form requires practice and adjustment. Overall, the interview data revealed that participants were engaged in understanding the relevant elements of the interaction (i.e., the hierarchy indicator). However, we recognized that some learning is required for users or can at least facilitate successful interaction.

The fourth research question concerns participants' perceptions of the system's usability and user experience. The favorable outcomes in terms of usability and user experience reinforce the positive overall impression conveyed above. Our sample consisted of elderly adults with a slightly increased affinity for technology interaction compared to the general population. For this group, it may be reasonably assumed that they are able to quickly become familiar with the interaction style and use the system in the intended manner, based on the general results of their interaction with the system. Our findings indicate that the application is suitable for testing by the target group of ventilated intensive care patients under realistic conditions. In future studies, the limitations of our study (i.e., small sample size, controlled environment, missing control group, not the actual target group, potential biases due to subjective data) should be considered and addressed to achieve results that are generalizable to a broader population.

7 Conclusion

In this paper, we introduced an interactive assistive system to support communication and address several other needs of its users. It is tailored to the user group of non-vocal, mechanically ventilated weaning patients in ICUs and is operated gesture-controlled via the spherical interaction device BIRDY. The system includes an application for patients that is displayed on a monitor mounted on a flexible roll stand. This application comprises several sub-applications aiming to support various communication topics, report pain, call nurses, improve information and allow for a control of the ambience.

In a user evaluation with 22 elderly adults, we focused on the learning of the interaction with the new device, the system's suitability for communication purposes, and the user experience of the system. After a training phase, the participants performed 12 interaction tasks with the system. We gathered both objective and subjective data during these phases. The analysis revealed promising results. The participants quickly learned the interaction and successfully solved all interaction tasks. Additionally, the error rate can be considered acceptable. They were also confident that they could utilize the system to communicate in a situation where they were verbally limited. The qualitative data showed that most graphical components supporting the interaction were recognized; introducing them in some kind of learning environment may still improve successful interactions. This provides a solid foundation for a comprehensive field study with the weaning patient population.

Moreover, the overall positive survey results indicate that the system has reached an appropriate level of maturity and the patient application only requires minor improvements before it can be tested within a field study with non-vocal weaning patients in an actual ICU setting.

Acknowledgments. We thank all colleagues within the project consortium for their contributions that led to this research article. Furthermore, we thank all participants who took part in our study.

Disclosure of Interests. This work was sponsored by the German Federal Ministry of Education and Research (BMBF) funded research project ACTIVATE (Grant No. 16SV7689) and was promoted by VDI/VDE Innovation + Technik GmbH. The authors have no conflicts of interest to declare that are relevant to the content of this article.

References

1. Abuatiq, A.: Patients' and health care providers' perception of stressors in the intensive care units. Dimens. Crit. Care Nurs. **34**(4), 205–214 (2015)
2. Bölt, U.: Gesundheit: Grunddaten Der Krankenhäuser 2019. No. 2120611177004 in Fachserie 12 Reihe 6.1.1, Statistisches Bundesamt (Destatis), Berlin, Heidelberg, Germany (March 2021)
3. Braun, V., Clarke, V.: Using thematic analysis in psychology. Qual. Res. Psychol. **3**(2), 77–101 (2006)
4. Brooke, J., et al.: Sus-a quick and dirty usability scale. Usability Eval. Ind. **189**(194), 4–7 (1996)

5. Franke, T., Attig, C., Wessel, D.: A personal resource for technology interaction: development and validation of the affinity for technology interaction (ATI) scale. Int. J. Hum.-Comput. Interact. **35**(6), 1–12 (2018). https://doi.org/10.1080/10447318.2018.1456150
6. Franke, T., Attig, C., Wessel, D.: A personal resource for technology interaction: development and validation of the affinity for technology interaction (ATI) scale. Int. J. Hum.-Comput. Interact. **35**(6), 456–467 (2019). https://doi.org/10.1080/10447318.2018.1456150
7. Garry, J., et al.: A pilot study of eye-tracking devices in intensive care. Surgery **159**(3), 938–944 (2016). https://doi.org/10.1016/j.surg.2015.08.012
8. Goldberg, M.A., Hochberg, L.R., Carpenter, D., Walz, J.M.: Development of a manually operated communication system (MOCS) for patients in intensive care units. Augment. Altern. Commun. **37**(4), 261–273 (2021). https://doi.org/10.1080/07434618.2021.2016958
9. Handberg, C., Voss, A.K.: Implementing augmentative and alternative communication in critical care settings: perspectives of healthcare professionals. J. Clin. Nurs. **27**(1–2), 102–114 (2018). https://doi.org/10.1111/jocn.13851
10. Henkel, A., Hussels, B., Kopetz, J.P., Krotsetis, S., Jochems, N., Balzer, K.: Nutzer- und Aufgabenanalyse für ein sozio-technisches System zur Unterstützung der Kommunikation und Reorientierung beatmeter Patientinnen und Patienten in Intensivstationen: Ergebnisse und methodische Herausforderungen. In: Boll, S., Hein, A., Heuten, W., Wolf-Ostermann, K. (eds.) Zukunft der Pflege : Tagungsband der 1. Clusterkonferenz 2018 - Innovative Technologien für die Pflege, pp. 201–206. BIS-Verl. der Carl von Ossietzky Universität Oldenburg (2018)
11. Hurtig, R.R., Alper, R.M., Bryant, K.N.T., Davidson, K.R., Bilskemper, C.: Improving patient safety and patient-provider communication. Perspect. ASHA Spec. Interest Groups **4**(5), 1017–1027 (2019). https://doi.org/10.1044/2019_PERS-SIG12-2019-0021
12. Itai Bendavid, I., et al.: The EyeControl-Med device, an alternative tool for communication in ventilated critically ill patients: a pilot study examining communication capabilities and delirium. J. Crit. Care **78**, 154351 (2023). https://doi.org/10.1016/j.jcrc.2023.154351
13. Ju, X.X., Yang, J., Liu, X.X.: A systematic review on voiceless patients' willingness to adopt high-technology augmentative and alternative communication in intensive care units. Intensive Crit. Care Nurs. **63**, 102948 (2021). https://doi.org/10.1016/j.iccn.2020.102948
14. Koomans, H.A., Boer, W.H.: Causes of edema in the intensive care unit. Kidney Int. Suppl. **59**, S105-110 (1997)
15. Kopetz, J.P.: Menschzentrierte Entwicklung eines Assistiven Systems für Weaningpatienten auf Basis einer neuartigen, auf den Kontext adaptierten Menütechnik: Das Kompass-Menü. Ph.D. thesis, Universität zu Lübeck, Lübeck (2023). https://www.zhb.uni-luebeck.de/epubs/ediss3039.pdf
16. Kopetz, J.P., Burgsmüller, S., Vandereike, A.K., Sengpiel, M., Wessel, D., Jochems, N.: Finding user preferences designing the innovative interaction device "BIRDY" for intensive care patients. In: Bagnara, S., Tartaglia, R., Albolino, S., Alexander, T., Fujita, Y. (eds.) Proceedings of the 20th Congress of the International Ergonomics Association (IEA 2018), pp. 698–707. Advances in Intelligent Systems and Computing, Springer International Publishing, Florence, Italy (2019)
17. Kopetz, J.P., Kordts, B., Henkel, A., Jochems, N.: Requirements for a Novel Interaction Device for Patients in Intensive Care. In: Mensch und Computer 2018 - Tagungsband. Gesellschaft für Informatik e.V. (2018). https://doi.org/10.18420/muc2018
18. Kordts, B., Kopetz, J.P., Balzer, K., Jochems, N.: Requirements for a System Supporting Patient Communication in Intensive Care in Germany. In: Zukunft der Pflege - Innovative Technologien für die Pflege, p. 6. Oldenburg (2018)
19. Kordts, B., Kopetz, J.P., Henkel, A., Schrader, A., Jochems, N.: Requirements and interaction patterns for a novel interaction device for patients in intensive care. i-com **18**(1), 67–78 (2019). https://doi.org/10.1515/icom-2019-0004

20. Laugwitz, B., Held, T., Schrepp, M.: Construction and evaluation of a user experience questionnaire. In: Holzinger, A. (ed.) USAB 2008. LNCS, vol. 5298, pp. 63–76. Springer, Heidelberg (2008). https://doi.org/10.1007/978-3-540-89350-9_6

21. Mobasheri, M.H., et al.: Communication aid requirements of intensive care unit patients with transient speech loss. Augment. Altern. Commun. 32(4), 261–271 (2016). https://doi.org/10.1080/07434618.2016.1235610

22. Nilsen, M.L., Sereika, S.M., Hoffman, L.A., Barnato, A., Donovan, H., Happ, M.B.: Nurse and patient interaction behaviors' effects on nursing care quality for mechanically ventilated older adults in the ICU. Res. Gerontol. Nurs. 7(3), 113–125 (2014). https://doi.org/10.3928/19404921-20140127-02

23. Norman, D.A.: Cognitive Engineering. In: User Centered System Design, pp. 31–62. CRC Press, Boca Raton (January 1986). https://doi.org/10.1201/b15703-3

24. Preim, B., Dachselt, R.: Metaphern und mentale Modelle. In: Interaktive Systeme, pp. 89–132. Springer, Heidelberg (2010). https://doi.org/10.1007/978-3-642-05402-0_3

25. Radtke, J.S., Götz, J., Gielen, S., Fischer, F.: Medizinische Klinik - Intensivmedizin und Notfallmedizin 116(4), 322–331 (2020). https://doi.org/10.1007/s00063-020-00663-6

26. Rodriguez, C., Rowe, M.: Use of a speech-generating device for hospitalized postoperative patients with head and neck cancer experiencing speechlessness. Oncol. Nurs. Forum 37(2), 199–205 (2010). https://doi.org/10.1188/10.ONF.199-205

27. Rodriguez, C.S., Rowe, M., Koeppel, B., Thomas, L., Troche, M.S., Paguio, G.: Development of a communication intervention to assist hospitalized suddenly speechless patients. Technol. Health Care 20(6), 519–530 (2012). https://doi.org/10.3233/THC-2012-0695

28. Rose, L., Dainty, K.N., Jordan, J., Blackwood, B.: Weaning from mechanical ventilation: a scoping review of qualitative studies. Am. J. Crit. Care 23(5), e54–e70 (2014)

29. Sengpiel, M., Jochems, N.: Validation of the computer literacy scale (CLS). In: Zhou, J., Salvendy, G. (eds.) ITAP 2015. LNCS, vol. 9193, pp. 365–375. Springer, Cham (2015). https://doi.org/10.1007/978-3-319-20892-3_36

30. Wilson, C.: Interview Techniques for UX Practitioners: A User-Centered Design Method. Morgan Kaufmann, Waltham, MA (2014)

31. Zaga, C.J., Berney, S., Vogel, A.P.: The feasibility, utility, and safety of communication interventions with mechanically ventilated intensive care unit patients: a systematic review. Am. J. Speech Lang. Pathol. 28(3), 1335–1355 (2019). https://doi.org/10.1044/2019_AJSLP-19-0001

Strategies and Tools to Support Place-Belongingness in Smart Cities

Hesam Mohseni$^{(\boxtimes)}$ ⓘ, António Correia ⓘ, Johanna Silvennoinen ⓘ, Tuomo Kujala ⓘ, and Tommi Kärkkäinen ⓘ

Faculty of Information Technology, University of Jyväskylä, P.O. Box 35, 40014 Jyväskylä, Finland

{hesam.h.mohseni,antonio.g.correia,johanna.silvennoinen,
tuomo.kujala,tommi.karkkainen}@jyu.fi

Abstract. Smart cities have the potential to reduce socio-spatial barriers and foster place-belongingness among citizens. However, this potential remains largely unmapped. We conducted a literature review to address this gap. Our findings suggest that promoting inclusive dynamics and emphasizing urban identity are key strategies for supporting place-belongingness in smart cities. Additionally, digital platforms and information and communication technologies (ICTs), gamification, crowdsensing, urban heritage technologies, and digital placemaking are the most popular digital tools used to achieve this. This literature review indicates that place-belongingness is underexplored in smart city studies, and further research is needed to fully understand the potential of smart cities to support place-belongingness.

Keywords: Smart Cities · Place-Belongingness · Crowdsensing · Digital placemaking · Wellbeing · Socio-Spatial exclusion · Urban Identity

1 Introduction

Place-belongingness, or the subjective feeling of belonging to a geographical location, is a crucial component of wellbeing [1]. Research indicates that lacking this sense of socio-spatial belonging can lead to personal problems such as depression and loneliness, as well as social issues such as community divides and reduced public participation [1, 2]. Consequently, researchers investigate place-belongingness to tackle such challenges arising from socio-spatial exclusion.

Inclusiveness is a key initiative in many smart cities, aimed at enhancing quality of life for all citizens [3]. Therefore, although there are criticisms regarding unbalanced power distribution and exclusion in many urban areas [4], smart cities have the potential to eliminate socio-spatial barriers that exclude citizens and escalate inequalities. By doing so, smart cities can play a pivotal role in fostering place-belongingness. Recognizing this potential can help develop smart cities where people experience higher wellbeing and reduced social tensions. However, this area remains underexplored and warrants further investigation.

H. Plácido da Silva and P. Cipresso (Eds.): CHIRA 2024, CCIS 2370, pp. 425–434, 2025.
https://doi.org/10.1007/978-3-031-82633-7_25

In this review, we explore how smart cities support place-belongingness. First, we clarify the concept of place-belongingness and distinguish it from similar concepts. We also provide an overview of the evolution of the smart city concept. The third section describes our method for reviewing the literature, while Sect. 4 presents our findings and provides strategies and tools to enhance place-belongingness in smart cities. Finally, we conclude our review with suggestions for future studies.

2   Background

Geographical belonging is a complex phenomenon that can easily be confused with concepts such as identity and citizenship. To clarify this, Antonsich [2] argued that geographical belonging should be analyzed at the intersection of two dimensions: the social dimension, which encompasses all discourses and structures of socio-spatial inclusion and exclusion, and the subjective feeling of belonging to a specific place, known as place-belongingness. These features can make understanding and analyzing place-belongingness challenging.

Place-belongingness has greater depth than concepts such as place attachment and place bonding. Due to the inherent spatial nature of place-belongingness, its development diverges from that of a sense of community. Additionally, place-belongingness extends beyond the domesticity of home – a frequent focus in human-computer interaction (HCI) studies – because place-belongingness is intertwined with power dynamics [1]. Therefore, when reviewing the literature, it is essential to recognize these differences while also acknowledging the commonalities between place-belongingness and related concepts.

The concept of smart city is multidimensional and evolving [5]. Initially, smart cities emerged from the fusion of technology and urban operations, often referred to as terms such as digital cities or information cities. However, as digital technologies advanced and demonstrated their potential to tackle a wide range of societal, economic, and environmental issues, the smart city notion evolved. This evolution brought it closer to concepts such as intelligent cities, creative cities, and smart sustainable cities [6–8]. A comprehensive literature review requires the consideration of these adjacent terms and concepts.

3   Method

In this paper, we followed the Cochrane gold standard protocol [9] to conduct a rapid review on the relationship between smart cities and place-belongingness, with the goal of capturing recent developments and establish a baseline for future research endeavors. This approach enables a resource-efficient systematic review, delivering comprehensive, reproducible, and in-depth results even when time and resources are limited [10]. Although the methodology is still evolving, rapid reviews are increasingly popular in HCI studies because they streamline the traditional systematic review process [11, 12]. Rapid reviews incorporate shortcuts, such as acceptable reductions or omissions of certain stages, while still respecting key principles of knowledge synthesis. This includes explicitly stating the review objectives, setting predefined eligibility criteria, assessing the validity of the findings, and systematically presenting and synthesizing the results [13]. In this study, we employed the general preferred reporting items for systematic reviews and meta-analyses (PRISMA) statement in a rapid review process to review the literature and answer our research question (RQ):

- RQ. How do smart cities support place-belongingness among citizens?

The answer to this question can help researchers, urban designers, planners, and policymakers develop smart cities that effectively enhance the quality of life by improving place-belongingness, a key dimension of wellbeing, and overcoming urban challenges through greater public engagement. Furthermore, it can be another step toward addressing criticisms of citizen exclusion in smart cities.

3.1 Search Terms

As discussed in the background section, place-belongingness is a multifaceted phenomenon that shares similarities with related concepts (e.g., place attachment and community belonging) [14]. In addition, the term smart city has undergone numerous transformations since its inception, leading to a variety of interchangeable terms such as digital city and information city in the literature. To effectively address our RQ, we needed to use a broad range of keywords in our review (see Fig. 1).

```
TITLE-ABS-KEY ( ( ( "place attachment" OR "place bonding" OR "place
rootedness" OR "place connectedness" OR "place belongingness" OR "place
identity" OR "sense of belonging" OR "sense of community" OR "sense of
place" OR "social inclusion" OR " sense of inclusion" OR "social
connectedness" OR "social bonding" OR "social integration" OR "membership" )
AND ( "smart city" OR "smart cities" OR "smarter city" OR "smarter
cities" OR "digital city" OR "digital cities" OR "intelligent city" OR "intelligent
cities" OR "cyber city" OR "cyber cities" OR "high-tech city" OR "high-tech
cities" OR "senseable city" OR "senseable cities" OR "interconnected
city" OR "interconnected cities" OR "information city" OR "information
cities" OR "smart sustainable city" OR "smart sustainable cities" OR "ubiquitous
city" OR "ubiquitous cities" OR "hybrid city" OR "hybrid cities" ) ) ) AND PUBYEAR
> 2001 AND PUBYEAR < 2025 AND ( LIMIT-TO ( DOCTYPE , "ar" ) OR LIMIT-TO (
DOCTYPE , "cp" ) ) AND ( LIMIT-TO ( LANGUAGE , "English" ) ) AND ( LIMIT-TO (
SRCTYPE , "j" ) OR LIMIT-TO ( SRCTYPE , "p" ) ) AND ( LIMIT-TO ( PUBSTAGE
, "final" ) )
```

Fig. 1. Search string used to identify potential studies.

3.2 Inclusion and Exclusion Criteria

Both place-belongingness and smart cities are interdisciplinary concepts examined across various fields of study. We selected Scopus database to search for keywords due to its exhaustive coverage and validity. We conducted a search process in article title, abstract, and keywords to identify potential material that answers the RQ. While

this identification process expanded on all years and subject areas to ensure comprehensiveness, we used the filters available on Scopus to narrow down the selection of
material.

We excluded books and book chapters, tutorials, keynote talks, extended abstracts,
posters, demonstrations, panels, etc. Our search was limited to papers published in
journals and conferences. This time-saving limitation is particularly crucial in a rapid
review process and ensures that the material has met a certain standard established by
other scientists. The results of the identification process were also limited to papers that
were in the final stage of publication. Moreover, only papers written in English were
included to the analysis because processing papers in other languages was out of our
limited resources.

3.3 Screening Process and Eligibility Assessment

A screening process on the titles, abstracts, and keywords within the identified papers
assisted us to remove the ones that did not address topics adequately regarding the RQ
(see Fig. 2). In this stage, the necessary information about the removed paper—such as
the name, author(s), publication year, publisher, access link, and reason for exclusion—
was recorded in an Excel file for potential future use. The remaining papers were moved
into a new file to be scrutinized in detail. The full versions of the papers that passed
through the screening process were retrieved to be examined if they were eligible to
be considered as included papers. To achieve this, the papers needed to answer the
RQ. To expedite the review process, we assessed the quality of the papers by verifying
whether they had undergone double-blind review processes and relying on the expertise

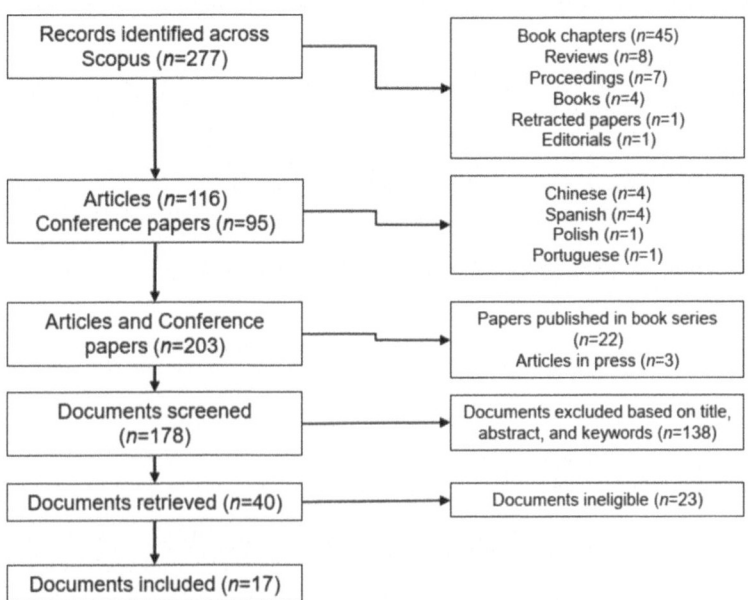

Fig. 2. The number of documents screened and excluded at different stages of the review.

of the reviewers who conducted those evaluations. Screening and eligibility assessment stages were conducted by the first author while other authors' double checks ensured the validity of the process and results.

4 Results

The keyword-based search within Scopus concluded on June 5th, 2024, resulting in 17 papers eligible for data extraction (see Table 1). Some of these papers included results from direct user studies and three papers were cross-case analyses that established their results based on others' findings. Among these direct and indirect cases, researchers utilized various quantitative (e.g., the place attachment scale [15]) and qualitative evaluation methods (e.g., observation [16]), although none of these methods were specifically designed to assess place-belongingness. The remaining papers provided conceptual and theoretical discussions.

As it can be seen in Table 1, the concept of place-belongingness was not explicitly mentioned in the included papers. However, four papers highlighted the spatial dimension of belonging by discussing concepts such as place attachment, place identity, emotional connections to places, and the sense of belonging to a place. In most of the papers, the sense of geographical belonging was an aspect of inclusiveness, expressed under topics of social inclusion, community cohesion, and public participation within the context of smart cities.

4.1 Supportive Strategies

Based on the included papers, there are at least two main strategies for smart cities to support place-belongingness among citizens. Promoting inclusive dynamics is the most important strategy. Inclusive dynamics can emerge from human-centric approaches employed in designing smart cities [21]. Inclusiveness can provide the chance of equitable access to information, technology, and other resources [16, 18, 22], the opportunity of sharing emotions and creating meaningful places [31]. Inclusiveness can empower citizens to have a voice and participate in various civic processes, ranging from planning to decision-making and development [23, 25, 27, 28]. Implementing inclusive dynamics can also lead to the creation of cohesive communities where citizens feel connected to a broader society, thereby enhancing citizens' place-belongingness [18, 24, 26].

Another main strategy of smart cities for enhancing place-belongingness is the improvement of urban identity. Smart cities can showcase unique characteristics such as cultural, historical, and natural features that enhance place identity [15, 17, 20]. This identity, in turn, can cause positive emotional attachments like a sense of pride to cities, resulting in strengthening a sense of belonging.

Table 1. List of included papers.

Reference	Journal/conference	User study	Main theme
Anwar [15]	International Conference on Smart City Innovation	yes	place attachment to historical urban places
Geng et al. [17]	International Journal of Tourism Cities	cross-case	place identity in urban environments and heritage sites
Ghafoor-Zadeh [16]	Digital Geography and Society	yes	social inclusion within a neighborhood in a smart city
Gobbi and Spina [18]	Interaction Design and Architecture(s) Journal	no	the role of language in fostering social inclusion and identity
Gomes et al. [19]	International Symposium on Computers in Education	yes	sense of belonging to a smart city
Jaššo and Ladzianska [20]	EAI International Summit, Smart City 360°	no	place attachment, sense of belonging, and togetherness in creative cities
Khelladi et al. [21]	International Entrepreneurship and Management Journal	no	social inclusion in a smart city
Li and Woolrych [22]	Frontiers in Public Health	yes	social inclusion of older adults in smart cities and communities
Lyu and Forsyth [23]	Cities & Health	no	social connectedness among older adults
Miles [24]	Gender, Place & Culture	yes	local connectedness among queer community
Musto et al. [25]	Italian Information Retrieval Workshop	no	social cohesion within the community in smart cities
Nam and Oh [26]	IEEE International Symposium on Mixed and Augmented Reality	no	social presence
Narongchai [27]	Journal of Population and Social Studies	yes	social inclusion and empowerment

(continued)

Table 1. (*continued*)

Reference	Journal/conference	User study	Main theme
Pérez-delHoyo et al. [28]	International Conference on Smart Cities and Green ICT Systems	yes	social integration in planning, design, and management of smart cities
Popescul et al. [29]	IEEE Access	cross-case	social inclusion in the creation of socially sustainable smart cities
Sidani et al. [30]	Pacific Asia Journal of the Association for Information Systems	cross-case	social inclusion through promoting citizen participation
Stals et al. [31]	Pacific Asia Journal of the Association for Information Systems	yes	emotional connections to urban places

4.2 Digital Tools

Although smart cities encompass more than just the use of digital technologies to manage urban operations, they cannot exist without these technologies. Various digital tools can be employed in smart cities to enhance citizens' place-belongingness. These technologies can be used individually or in combination to effectively implement the strategies discussed.

Digital Platforms and ICTs. These technologies can enhance a sense of belonging to smart cities in various ways. For example, digital platforms can empower citizens to participate in making decisions that affect their lives [21]. ICTs can keep people informed about what goes on in smart cities and provide access to essential services such as healthcare [27]. Additionally, utilizing social media and other digital platforms can facilitate social interaction, making people feel more connected and involved in their community [20, 21, 24]. However, online social interaction can also serve as a boundary maker highlighting differences. This side effect necessitates careful attention.

Gamification. Using gamification techniques in smart city projects encourages citizen participation. Gamification can improve wellbeing among specific target groups such as youths and seniors [29]. Location-based gamified activities have the potential to connect individuals to physical spaces and foster positive emotions towards smart cities, strengthening place-belongingness.

Crowdsensing. Smart cities can leverage participatory sensing projects to engage citizens in data collection and urban monitoring. Such data is crucial in urban planning where citizens' experiences of the city, gathered for instance from landscapes and soundscapes, are necessary for creating sustainable, enriching, and inclusive cities [32, 33]. Wearable devices, smartphones, smart home technologies, and open data can facilitate crowdsensing initiatives, giving citizens a sense of ownership [29]. Place-belongingness can be enhanced by fostering a sense of ownership and empowering citizens to monitor smart cities.

Smart Heritage Technologies. Advanced technologies such as digital archives, virtual and augmented reality can be used to document, visualize, and interpret cultural heritage, reinforcing the sense of belonging through engagement with urban spaces [15, 17, 19]. Such technologies can highlight unique local characteristics and strengthen citizens' connectivity with local culture and history, thereby fostering a sense of place-belongingness among citizens.

Digital Placemaking. Using digital placemaking technologies, smart city spaces can be augmented with memories and emotions [26, 31]. This meaningful, augmented layer can foster emotional attachment among citizens, enhancing their sense of place-belongingness.

5 Conclusion

This review highlights the potential of smart cities to enhance citizens' sense of belonging. While the included papers implicitly touched on various aspects of place-belongingness, primarily through the lens of inclusiveness, our review indicates that the concept itself remains little-known in smart city research.

Exploring place-belongingness within the context of smart cities reveals that promoting inclusive dynamics and emphasizing urban identity are key strategies for fostering a sense of belonging. Inclusive dynamics can provide access to resources, connect and empower citizens, while a strong urban identity can prevent smart cities from becoming impersonal "non-places". Leveraging digital platforms and ICTs, gamification, crowd-sensing, urban heritage technologies, and digital placemaking in alignment with these strategies can create smart solutions to enhance place-belongingness in smart cities. Future studies can help establish a comprehensive framework for these solutions.

There are promising avenues for future research on place-belongingness within the context of smart cities. Given the gap identified in this paper, it is crucial to explore place-belongingness as a concept that simultaneously encompasses emotional, social, and spatial dimensions. Smart cities provide the infrastructure and tools to address the need for belonging to a specific geographic location, especially in an era where global mobility and digital saturation heightens the risk of displacement. However, future studies should go beyond merely investigating these possibilities. To understand how these potentials can be effectively realized, research must delve into how the concept of "place" is being transformed in our contemporary world.

In the future, developing quantitative methods can enable researchers to more effectively utilize the opportunities smart cities offer. Other key questions that merit further attention include evaluating the effectiveness of the strategies and tools presented in this paper on enhancing citizens' mental wellbeing, building social capital, and addressing social challenges.

Disclosure of Interests. The authors have no competing interests to declare that are relevant to the content of this article.

References

1. Mohseni, H., Correia, A., Silvennoinen, J., Kujala, T.: Scale development for measuring digitally enhanced place-belongingness: a research design. In: IEEE International Congress on Human-Computer Interaction, Optimization and Robotic Applications, pp. 1–4 (2024). https://doi.org/10.1109/HORA61326.2024.10550780
2. Antonsich, M.: Searching for belonging – an analytical framework. Geogr. Compass **4**, 644–659 (2010)
3. Lee, J.Y., Woods, O., Kong, L.: Towards more inclusive smart cities: Reconciling the divergent realities of data and discourse at the margins. Geogr Compass **14** (2020). https://doi.org/10.1111/gec3.12504
4. Nguyen, H.T., Marques, P., Benneworth, P.: Living labs: Challenging and changing the smart city power relations? Technol Forecast Soc. Change **183** (2022). https://doi.org/10.1016/j.techfore.2022.121866
5. Mohseni, H.: Public engagement and smart city definitions: a classifying model for the evaluation of citizen power in 2025 Tehran. GeoJournal **86**, 1261–1274 (2021). https://doi.org/10.1007/s10708-019-10126-x
6. Alawadhi, S., et al.: Building understanding of smart city initiatives. In: IFIP WG 8.5 International Conference on Electronic Government, pp. 40–53 (2012)
7. Silva, B.N., Khan, M., Han, K.: Towards sustainable smart cities: a review of trends, architectures, components, and open challenges in smart cities (2018). https://doi.org/10.1016/j.scs.2018.01.053
8. Macke, J., Rubim Sarate, J.A., de Atayde Moschen, S.: Smart sustainable cities evaluation and sense of community. J Clean Prod. **239** (2019). https://doi.org/10.1016/j.jclepro.2019.118103
9. Garritty, C., et al.: Cochrane Rapid Reviews Methods Group offers evidence-informed guidance to conduct rapid reviews. J. Clin. Epidemiol. **130**, 13–22 (2021). https://doi.org/10.1016/j.jclinepi.2020.10.007
10. Tricco, A.C., Langlois, E. V, Straus, S.E.: Rapid reviews to strengthen health policy and systems: a practical guide. World Health Organization (2017)
11. Correia, A.: On the human-AI metaphorical interplay for culturally sensitive generative AI design in music co-creation, In: ACM Conference on Intelligent User Interfaces, pp. 1–11 (2024)
12. Seaborn, K., Urakami, J.: Measuring voice UX quantitatively: A rapid review. In: CHI Conference on Human Factors in Computing Systems (2021). https://doi.org/10.1145/3411763.3451712
13. Silva, H., António, N., Bacao, F.: A rapid semi-automated literature review on legal precedents retrieval. In: EPIA Conference on Artificial Intelligence, pp. 53–65 (2022). https://doi.org/10.1007/978-3-031-16474-3_5
14. Mohseni, H., Silvennoinen, J., Kujala, T.: Place-belongingness in real-life contexts: a review of practical meanings, contributing factors, and evaluation methods. GeoJournal **89**, 187 (2024). https://doi.org/10.1007/s10708-024-11173-9
15. Anwar, W.F.F.: The implication of smart environment on old Palembang cultural heritage places. In: IOP Conference Series: Earth and Environmental Science. Institute of Physics Publishing (2019). https://doi.org/10.1088/1755-1315/396/1/012031
16. Ghafoor-Zadeh, D.: Moving through, interacting with, and caring for the city. Children's and young people's everyday experiences in smart cities. Digital Geography and Society. 4 (2023). https://doi.org/10.1016/j.diggeo.2023.100051
17. Geng, S., Chau, H.W., Jamei, E., Vrcelj, Z.: Understanding place identity in urban scale smart heritage using a cross-case analysis method. Int. J. Tour. Cities **9**, 729–750 (2023). https://doi.org/10.1108/IJTC-10-2022-0244

18. Gobbi, A., Spina, S.: Smart cities and languages: The language network. In: IxD&A, vol. 16, pp. 37–46 (2013)
19. Gomes, C.A., et al.: VIAS | Viseu interage stories: developing an app to foster social inclusion and healthy lifestyles. In: IEEE International Symposium on Computers in Education, pp. 1–5 (2017)
20. Jaššo, M., Ladzianska, Z.: City as a personality: New concept of creative city. In: EAI International Summit, Smart City 360° (2017)
21. Khelladi, I., Castellano, S., Kalisz, D.: The smartization of metropolitan cities: the case of Paris. Int. Entrep. Manag. J. **16**, 1301–1325 (2020). https://doi.org/10.1007/s11365-020-006 91-w
22. Li, M., Woolrych, R.: Experiences of older people and social inclusion in relation to smart "age-friendly" cities: a case study of Chongqing, China. Front. Public Health **9** (2021). https://doi.org/10.3389/fpubh.2021.779913
23. Lyu, Y., Forsyth, A.: Technological devices to help older people beyond the home: an inventory and assessment focusing on the neighborhood and city scales. Cities Health. **8**, 91–106 (2024). https://doi.org/10.1080/23748834.2022.2094884
24. Miles, S.: Sex in the digital city: location-based dating apps and queer urban life. Gend. Place Cult. **24**, 1595–1610 (2017). https://doi.org/10.1080/0966369X.2017.1340874
25. Musto, C., et al.: Developing a semantic content analyzer for L'Aquila social urban network. In: Italian Information Retrieval Workshop, pp. 34–38 (2014)
26. Nam, Y.T., Oh, J.H.: Participatory mixed reality space: collective memories. In: IEEE International Symposium on Mixed and Augmented Reality, pp. 353–354 (2016). https://doi.org/10.1109/ISMAR-Adjunct.2016.0118
27. Narongchai, W.: The elements of happiness of disabled older adults in Khon Kaen smart city, Khon Kaen, Thailand. J. Popul. Soc. Stud. **30**, 377–390 (2022). https://doi.org/10.25133/JPS Sv302022.022
28. Pérez-delHoyo, R., Dolores Andújar-Montoya, M., Mora, H., Gilart-Iglesias, V.: Citizen participation in urban planning-management processes: assessing urban accessibility in smart cities. In: International Conference on Smart Cities and Green ICT Systems, pp. 206–213 (2018)
29. Popescul, D., Murariu, L., Radu, L.D., Georgescu, M.R.: Digital co-creation in socially sustainable smart city projects: lessons from the European Union and Canada. IEEE Access. **12**, 71088–71108 (2024). https://doi.org/10.1109/ACCESS.2024.3399016
30. Sidani, D., Veglianti, E., Maroufkhani, P.: Smart cities for a sustainable social inclusion strategy – a comparative study between Italy and Malaysia. Pac. Asia J. Assoc. Inf. Syst. **14**, 25–41 (2022). https://doi.org/10.17705/1pais.14203
31. Stals, S., Smyth, M., Mival, O.: UrbanixD: from ethnography to speculative design fictions for the hybrid city. In: ACM Halfway to the Future Symposium (2019). https://doi.org/10.1145/3363384.3363486
32. Kaarivuo, A., Oppenländer, J., Kärkkäinen, T., Mikkonen, T.: Exploring emergent soundscape profiles from crowdsourced audio data. Comput. Environ. Urban Syst. **110** (2024). https://doi.org/10.1016/j.compenvurbsys.2024.102112
33. Kaarivuo, A., Salo, K., Mikkonen, T.: From sonic experiences to urban planning innovations. Eur. Plan. Stud. **32**, 302–319 (2024). https://doi.org/10.1080/09654313.2021.1988062

How Can Heuristics Be Communicated?

Isabel Evans[✉][iD], Chris Porter[iD], and Mark Micallef[iD]

University of Malta, Msida, Malta
isabel.evans.17@um.edu.mt

Abstract. This position paper proposes a model for choosing how to communicate heuristics in a meaningful, usable and accessible manner. The model is a matrix of nine shapes, where we define 'shape' as a combination of the heuristic's format and its directiveness. Examining heuristics used in UX and software testing practices, we found a variety of formats and levels of directiveness. We discuss these shapes with example heuristics from UX, software testing, and everyday life. We present the outcome from a pilot of the model in one specific context. The shape of a heuristic may contribute to its understandability and usefulness in specific contexts, while different contexts may necessitate different ways of communicating heuristics. This includes considering the effect that the shape of a heuristic has on its accessibility and inclusion, suggesting that shape may be one important aspect of heuristics' design and evaluation.

Keywords: Heuristics · Human computer interaction · Design methodology · User-centred design · Accessibility · Inclusion

1 Introduction

Heuristics are used to describe ways of thinking, as well as to aid in problem-solving, by providing rules of thumb that, while fallible, provoke thought and as aide-mémoires [13].

Our HCI research, [7–10], into the design of tools to aid software testing has led us to develop guidance for test tool designers[1] We want to communicate our findings back to industry practitioners in ways that are useful, understandable, flexible and easily applied to their work. As heuristics are already used in a variety of ways within the software industry, it made sense to develop heuristics to capture and communicate our main research findings. In this paper, we describe the work we are doing to clarify how best to *communicate* the heuristics we are developing. Those heuristics are themselves out of this paper's scope.

Before developing our heuristics, we needed to know what would provide a good experience of the heuristics for their specific audience and context, and whether the format and directive level made a difference to how well they were understood. This led to our research question: **How can heuristics be communicated?** Through a review of academic, industry and grey literature, we found that heuristics are expressed in different ways. There is variation in the level of direction given by a heuristic and the

---

[1] See Evans, I., Porter, C., I & Micallef, M. (2024). Heuristics-for-test-tool-design (Version 1.0.0) [Computer software]. https://github.com/hci-lab-um/heuristics-for-test-tool-design/blob/main/README.md.

© The Author(s), under exclusive license to Springer Nature Switzerland AG 2025
H. Plácido da Silva and P. Cipresso (Eds.): CHIRA 2024, CCIS 2370, pp. 435–453, 2025.
https://doi.org/10.1007/978-3-031-82633-7_26

format in which it is displayed. It was unclear as we reviewed the heuristics whether the choices made for the format or level of direction were based on custom, aesthetics, or other factors.

We set out the background for our work on the shape of heuristics, with a brief history of heuristics and their use in HCI and software testing, as well as other areas. We describe the methods we use, and in our findings, we provide an overview of how heuristics can be developed and evaluated and explain our choice of methodology for designing our own heuristics. We describe example heuristics for the directive levels and formats we identified. We show a matrix of nine possible 'shapes' for a heuristic, based on how directive they are (**Telling**, **Prompting** and **Asking**) and their format (**Textual**, **Pictorial** and **Conceptual**), with examples from software testing, UX practice, road signage and other fields. In a pilot of applying the matrix, we trialled the nine heuristic shapes with industry practitioners in a small specific context, to find the shape most suitable for a specific set of heuristics, and then reviewed with industry experts. We discuss why this matters: the Shape of Heuristics Model helps to improve communication and use of heuristics in general. Our literature review, both academic and industrial, suggests that this has not previously been an overt consideration in developing heuristics, and is worthy of further research. We therefore suggest future work for development and evaluation of the Shape of Heuristics Model, and how we are using it in our work.

2 Background

2.1 Heuristics: History and Meaning

The Oxford English Dictionary [22] notes the first use of the word 'heuristic' in 1770. [13] and [22] show the definition and usages of 'heuristic' have changed over time. Usage though the late 1700's and early 1800's in logic and education was in reference to educational methods that enable students to learn by making discoveries for themselves. Over time, heuristic comes to mean methods in problem solving and decision making [22].

It remains a relatively infrequent word; [22] notes that it occurs about 3 times per million words, making it recognisable but unusual [23]. Its use has increased dramatically since the 1950's with the start of its use in computing and AI. Figure 1 shows the frequency of use of the word heuristic, from nearly zero per million words prior to 1940, rising through the 1940's to 1960's to 0.2 per million words, and rising steeply to 1.2 per million words by 2010. It is now used in disciplines including sociology, computing and artificial intelligence.

Academic work about heuristics has increased over the last 50 years, [13] noted an increase in Scopus database entries with 'heuristic' in the title from 70 papers in 1970 to 3783 in 2021. We made a Google Scholar search for 'heuristic evaluation' showing 482 results between 1950 and 1989 from AI, programming, maths, statistics and psychology. These are papers both about the use of heuristics to evaluate situations and artefacts, and also about the evaluation of heuristics. Between 1989 and 2023 there were 1370 results for 'heuristic + usability' - the majority of these are either in fields outside HCI or are about usability of heuristics. Rather than providing a definition of 'heuristic', [13] discusses their *'defining characteristics'* as *'problem-solving methods*

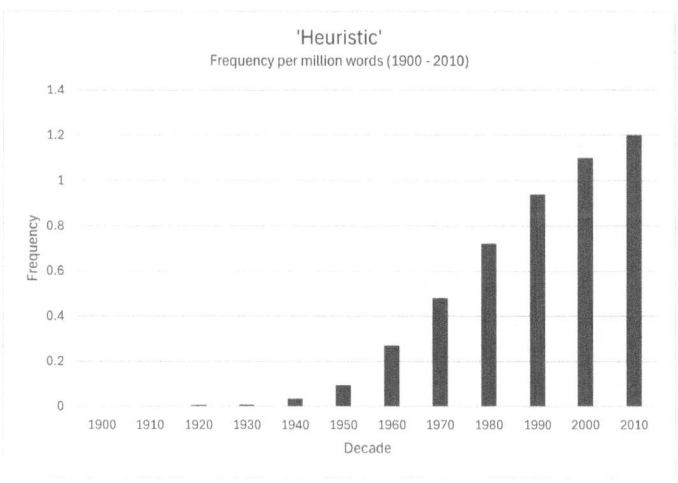

Fig. 1. 'Heuristic' frequency 1900–2010 after [22].

that do not guarantee an optimal solution' which are *'practically applicable in at least a number of interesting cases'*, contrasting a heuristic with what they refer to as *'allegedly rational decision making'* which may take longer and while potentially reaching a more optimal solution, may be impractical.

In this paper we are interested in heuristics used in usability, HCI, UX and software testing, which we discuss next.

2.2   Heuristics in UX for Interface Evaluation

Within the HCI, UX and testing communities. the set of '10 Usability Heuristics for User Interface Design' [20] are known as a method for designing and evaluating user interfaces. These were first presented by [21], following their first mention of Heuristic Evaluation (HE) for usability is in a paper the previous year [19]. Since that paper, these heuristics have been widely adopted, being taught to UX and testing practitioners, for example, [15,35]. These Ten Heuristics from Nielsen, and variations have been developed and updated to meet both new technologies and specific domains, for example, by [18,20,28,29,36].

2.3   Heuristics in Software Testing

Heuristics are used by software testers to inform their exploratory and test design work. For example, [5] writes that heuristics are not only our models for thinking but also provide a way of probing and challenging our models and ways of thinking when testing software: *"heuristics are essential tools for thinking test practitioners. ... if you consciously use a model as a heuristic, then you are in a better position to see its weaknesses and potential failure points in a given situation"* [5] Many testing heuristics in a variety of format are available; [4] provides a summary of many heuristics commonly used by testing practitioners to inform their work, including heuristics for test planning, test design and assessing risks.

2.4   Heuristics in Day to Day Life

Heuristics, in a variety of formats, are used in general life. These may be instinctive and based on senses, such as a 'sniff test' for whether food is edible. Additionally, in day-to-day life, we use proverbial rules of thumb which may or may not be up-to-date and well understood, for example 'red sky at night, shepherd's delight'. These may be language, location or culturally specific. Heuristics in everyday life are also designed for specific purposes; examples include information and warning signage, such as no entry signs or hazard signs.

3   Motivation - Research Gap

This position paper is motivated by our current work, which includes the development of evidence-based heuristics that provide design guidance to test tool vendors. The actual guidance is out of this paper's scope. We wanted to design and evaluate evidence-based heuristics through a robust process to evaluate their content. We also wanted to understand how to communicate these heuristics in a meaningful, usable and accessible manner to people who make (design) decisions.

The literature we examined (See Sect. 5.1) enabled us to apply an iterative methodology for our own heuristics, with design and review/evaluation cycles, and more than one evaluation method. The methodologies showed how to review a heuristic's content, but we could not find work on evaluating the format by which content is communicated. There seemed to be an assumption of heuristics for UX evaluations being communicated as text statements that prompt or direct action, for example [20]. We needed a way to understand what options there are for the way heuristics are communicated and to understand which option is best for our specific heuristics. Our heuristics are intended to aid UX design rather than UX evaluation, and we wanted to see if the text statement was still the best format. We were aware of other heuristic formats in the testing industry, for example mnemonics [4] and of other formats outside IT/software, such as pictorial road signs [31].

We asked the research question: **How can heuristics be communicated?**

4   Methodology

A mixed methods approach was taken for this position paper, including literature and grey literature reviews, thematic and gap analysis of the heuristic formats found, and an expert review in a pilot study, including semi-structured interviews with industry experts and practitioners.

The purpose of the research leading to this position paper is hypothesis building: we examined data in the literature to look for patterns. These patterns led to our proposal of the "Shape of Heuristics" model. We adopted a qualitative approach during a pilot using expert reviews to obtain viewpoints while observing for saturation with a small sample after [12].

Figure 2 maps the route through the methods used to build the hypothesis. Initial data collection was through academic and grey literature reviews, with categorizing and grouping of the heuristics found and a synthesis into a matrix of groups. We searched Google Scholar for papers mentioning heuristics, and from those extracted ones concerned with HCI/UX usability heuristics and software testing heuristics, starting from the current year and working backwards in time to reach Nielsen's first paper 1990 on heuristics [21], as these are significant in both HCI and software testing industrial practice.

Initially, we examined papers on the design of heuristics. We then looked for examples of heuristics formats. We looked at papers about the history, usage, design and evaluation of heuristics. In the grey literature review, we search online for examples of UX and software testing heuristics in industry. These gave us examples of usage and adaptations, as well as of heuristics based on experience rather than a defined development process. The information from all these sources was analysed to identify heuristics development methods (see Sect. 5.1) and validating heuristics (see Sect. 5.2).

While doing this analysis we noticed that the heuristics varied both in format and directiveness, especially in the software testing industry sources. We, therefore, reanalysed the data to identify and group the formats and directiveness of the heuristics. We used the outcome of this analysis to build a matrix of format against directiveness and populated each cell with one example.

We then hypothesised that each cell provided a "Shape of Heuristic" that might be suitable for specific contexts, improving their understandability and usefulness.

We piloted that matrix with practitioners in a specific context and also reviewed it with experts from accessibility, UX and software testing industry backgrounds. Pilot methods are covered in Sect. 6.

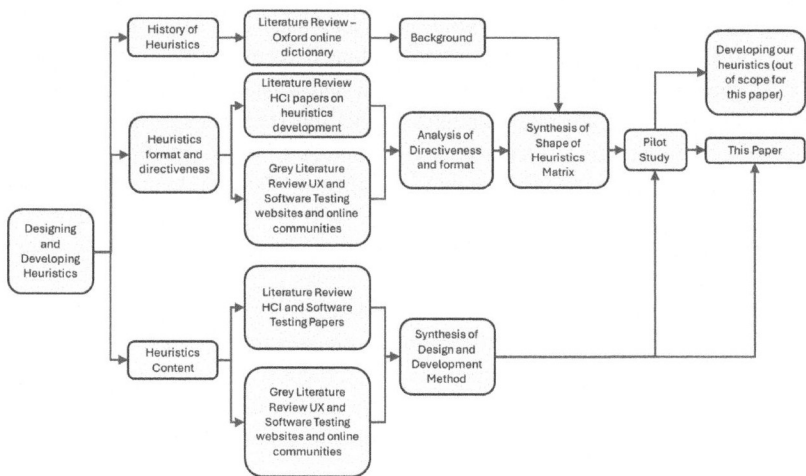

Fig. 2. Methodology for this Paper.

5   Findings - Developing the 'Shape of Heuristics' Model

5.1   Review of Designing and Developing Heuristics

We examined literature (academic and industry) in HCI/UX and Software Testing to look at how heuristics are developed. One researcher attended a BCS seminar on developing heuristics. Within the HCI academic community, several updates to Nielsen's Heuristics set have been published, together with critiques of the original and updated set, and also methodologies for developing and validating HCI heuristics.

Different methodologies for developing heuristics have been published; [29] remarks: *'The relevant literature contains no consensus over the most effective approach to developing domain specific heuristics.'* We identified several ways that heuristics could be developed, with both the design and the evaluation having different levels of rigour and formality.

Instinctively or Intuitively Arrived At: These heuristics are intuited by an individual and used by that individual because 'these work for me'; these heuristics are part of natural world and evolution [13]; they are used by humans and other animals. These heuristics are informal, and not specifically evaluated.

Experience-Based Design: These heuristics capture an individual or group's experience in context and may be built and reviewed formally or informally. They may be published informally, perhaps on a blog. They may be changed through usage including but not exclusively the author. For example, [1,4,5] all recommend that anyone using testing heuristics also redesign, modify and replace to make their own heuristics to reflect their local context.

Evidence-Based Design: Data to build evidence-based heuristics are collected via research and the heuristics themselves are evaluated formally before use. Heuristics may be evaluated by comparison with a known and trusted set such as Nielsen's 10 Heuristics, for example [20] made updates to the Ten Heuristics. Usability heuristics designed to cover changes to technology and specific domains include mobile learning application heuristics, by [18] evaluated against the Nielsen heuristics. Validation of heuristics for touch screen usability, by [14] used comparison of results with one group of evaluators using Nielsen's Ten Heuristics and another group using their new heuristics.

At a BCS Interaction Group on Research Methods for Human-Computer Interaction[2], Petrie and Sim showed how to design and evaluate heuristics, emphasising the need for a review and evaluation of the heuristics' efficacy. This leads to a methodology where heuristics are designed based on data collected in the field, and then iteratively reviewed and refined through evaluation with experts and practitioners.

---

[2] 25 November 2022: Research Methods for Human-Computer Interaction, BCS Interaction Group One Day Course for PhD Students - presented by Helen Petrie and Gavin Sim.

5.2 Examples of Validation of Heuristics

In [29] there is a criticism of the approaches used to create heuristics: *'the method used for validating the heuristics. The raw count of the number of usability problems identified may not be an appropriate indicator of the effectiveness of a set of heuristics'*. They suggest criteria to use include thoroughness, correctness, coverage, effectiveness and ease of use of the heuristics, measured in review and usage. This includes a survey of domain users to identify problems, then using existing heuristics, a literature review and card sorts to identify potential new heuristics, cross-checking new heuristics against the problem database.

When comparing user evaluation and expert evaluation of websites, the latter using Nielsen's heuristics and a walkthrough, [24], used a grounded theory approach to group the problems found, plus analysis to see which problems were reported more by users and which were reported more by experts. Results were used to produce an enhanced set of heuristics, which were compared with Nielsen's. This paper ends by noting more evaluation of the heuristics is needed.

A literature review by [25] tabulated methods for developing usability heuristics and provided a methodology suggestion. The literature review covered nine methodologies, seven of which had validation steps and three of which went on to refine the heuristics post-validation. Four methodologies had validation and no refinement, which implies they expect not to find flaws during the evaluation. Further, [26] experimented with the steps in a proposed methodology with flow diagrams for various contexts. They suggest expert validation against four criteria: utility, clarity, ease of use and necessity of an extra checklist.

Heuristics for evaluating speech-based smart devices were suggested by [30] and validated by trial in use: usability experts applied the heuristics and fed back their view of the heuristics in an interview. Evaluators also filled out a usability report, but that seems to be of the devices, not of the heuristics.

An iterative approach is taken by [36], with a three-phase iterative process to refine the heuristics, looping back from validation design and from application back to design before moving on to a published set for use.

Although understandability was mentioned as an evaluation criterion in several methods, the design and evaluation methods seemed to focus on the content of the heuristics rather than how they were communicated in terms of format. We believe that format contributes to understandability.

5.3 Analysis: Reviewing and Categorising Heuristics' Formats

To understand how people express and communicate heuristics, we examined grey literature from the software testing industry, and also heuristics from academic papers uncovered during the literature review. Across HCI, UX and software testing heuristics, we saw a variety of ways of communicating heuristics, and so we cast our net wider to cover heuristics outside these fields.

We sorted and categorised the heuristics looking for similarities, distinct groups, and distinguishing factors. We found we were able to group the heuristics in two ways:

by their level of directiveness (telling, prompting, asking) and by their format (textual, conceptual, pictorial). These groups emerged as we examined different heuristics.

We realised that these characteristics were paired so that we could sort the heuristics into a nine-cell grid. We refer to the nine cells in the grid as the **'shapes of the heuristics'**, - a combination of their format and their directiveness. For example **'format: textual'** and **'directiveness: prompt'** becomes the **'Textual Prompting Shape'**.

The analysis that led to the Shape of Heuristics Model is described with examples in Sect. 5.4.

5.4   Building the 'Shape of Heuristics' Model

Shape of UX Heuristics. Heuristics used for UX evaluations can be expressed as short textual statements to prompt thought, such as [20]'s *'User Control and Freedom'*. Sometimes longer more directive text is used, for example one heuristic by [28] for computer aided assessment in education is: *'9. Use clear language and grammar within questions and ensure the score is clearly displayed.'* with the explanation: *'Text should be grammatically correct and make sense. It should be obvious to students what the score is for a particular question and the scoring algorithm applied (e.g., if negative marking is used). Question feedback should assist the learning process.'* This is both directive, and provides a full explanation of what to evaluate.

In this group we found heuristics to be **textual**, and **prompting** or **telling**.

Shape of Software Testing Heuristics. Many forms of heuristic are in use in software testing. We found textual heuristics as shown in [1]: *'Overwhelm the product'* with a set of explanatory directives such as *'Look for sub-systems and functions that are vulnerable to being overloaded or "broken" in the presence of challenging data or constrained resources.'*. Bach's set of heuristics also includes questions: *'Charisma. How appealing is the product?'* Conceptual heuristics include Elizabeth Hendriksen's *'Goldilocks testing' (do just enough...)* listed by [4], and [3] discusses the *'FEW HICCUPS'* mnemonic. There are also pictorial heuristics, such as [6]'s mind map of mnemonics.

In this group we found heuristics to be either **textual**, **pictorial** or **conceptual**, and we found heuristics that are either **telling**, **prompting** or **asking**.

Shape of Day to Day Heuristics. Day-to-day heuristics include warnings, commands, information-providing pictures, phrases, and sensory perceptions. We examined this group to help us understand when different levels of directiveness and format are appropriate. We looked at road signs, proverbs and food.

Although there are similarities in road signs across the world, there are differences both across languages and across English-speaking territories [31, 32] (Examples from English-speaking countries are shown in Fig. 3). An example of a heuristic warning found on road signs in many countries is 'Possible Ice On Road' which does not mean there is always ice on the road; it is a rule of thumb to suggest caution depending on the context (time of year, weather conditions) that indicates a slower speed may be sensible. In the USA this is textual, while in the UK a pictorial symbol is use. These are shown in Fig. 3, based on [32]. This Wikipedia page shows a variety of road signs from several countries warning of potential hazards including ice and snow, slippery road surfaces, and loose road surfaces. All of these conditions may cause the car to skid. Some countries, such as Singapore and Uganda, don't have (perhaps don't need) an 'Ice On Road' heuristic, but they all have a 'Slippery Road Surface' sign.

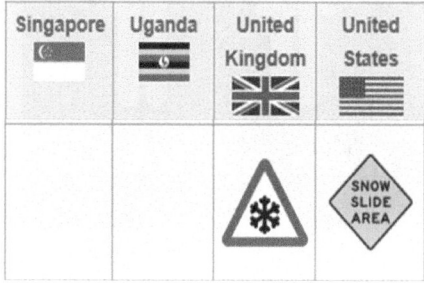

Fig. 3. Example Snow Warning Road Signs(English-speaking Countries) after [32].

The context may dictate whether the heuristic is better formatted as pictorial or textual. Textual messages require learning the language and alphabet but then provide a slower but general purpose mechanism to understand a range of messages, whereas a pictorial heuristic must be learned individually, but is then perhaps faster to interpret. If we compare the UK and USA snow signs, might these reflect context? The UK has a very rigorous driving instruction and test, which includes learning all the road sign symbols. The USA has a slower maximum driving speed, giving time to process the written word.

Other symbols are difficult to interpret without prior learning, for example in some countries the prohibition sign for 'no motorcycles' has a motorcycle with a line through it, while in other countries it is just a motorcycle. It is worth noting that in UK, some prohibitive signs have lines across and others do not, increasing both the cognitive load to learn and remember, and also reducing their comprehensibility to non-UK drivers.

We saw in Sect. 2 that heuristics are fallible rules of thumb. However, when used in critical or high-risk situations, heuristics that are built from intuition or experience need to be evaluated and challenged by expertise. For example, in an online article about rules for understanding which fungi are edible and which are poisonous, [2] critiques three heuristics for judging whether fungi are edible, providing the original textual directive and a counter-directive: *'There are some apparent rules for picking safe mushrooms but these are just fanciful if not downright dangerous;* 'It's ok if you can peel the cap.' It is easy to peel a Death Cap. 'Mushrooms growing on wood are safe.' No not all of them are and some are deadly, like the Funeral Bell. 'If you see other animals eating them they are ok.' ... is not true, many animals can eat poisonous fungi with no ill effects.'*

Pictorial heuristics include the images on rest room signs. There are many variations on these pictorial prompts. A challenge to the usual image for the women's rest room is described by [17], who for an Axosoft 'Girls in Technology' challenge devised the 'It was never a dress' campaign, an online phenomenon. The pictorial prompt, shown

Fig. 4. Pictorial Heuristic: It Was Never a Dress [16].

in Fig. 4, changes the outline of the woman in a dress to a woman in a superhero cape, providing a pictorial questioning heuristic that provokes the challenge: 'Can you (re)imagine women's roles in tech?'.[3]

In this group we found **textual, conceptual** and **pictorial** heuristics, communicated as **asking, prompting** or **telling**. We found the format and the level of directiveness may need to change, depending on context of use, changing the shape of heuristic that best communicates the heuristic.

Having described some of the example heuristics we discovered in UX, software testing and day to day life, and identified examples of pictorial, textual, conceptual, asking, prompting and telling metaphors, we can see that some of the shapes are easier to find examples than for others.

The Shape of Heuristics Model is shown in Table 1 including examples for each of the heuristics shapes, based on the discussion in this section. For the pilot study we describe in the next section, we chose to attempt to build heuristics in each shape.

6   Piloting in the Software Testing Context

As the Shape of Heuristics Model emerged, we wanted to understand if it would help us understand what was appropriate for the audience for our work. Who might need different formats or different levels of directiveness, and when? We piloted the Model with potential users of our heuristics to help them choose a preferred heuristic format, and provide reasons for their choices.

The pilot group of participants represented the people who would use our heuristics. As a result of this pilot evaluation, we made refinements in the Shape of Heuristics Model, discussed in Sect. 7.

---

[3] This version from https://www.flickr.com/photos/staciebee/39802849515/in/photostream/ where it is displayed under a Creative Commons NonCommercial-ShareAlike (CC BY-NC-SA 2.0) licence.

Table 1. Shape of Heuristics Model (Matrix).

	Textual	Conceptual	Pictorial
Asking	Textual Asking example: *Security: How well is the product protected against unauthorised use or intrusion?* [1]	Conceptual Asking example: *'If winter's here, can spring be far behind?'* [27]	Pictorial Asking example: *It was never a dress: What (else) can women do (in tech)?* [16, 17]
Prompting	Prompting Telling example: *User Control and Freedom* [20]	Prompting Conceptual example:: *FEW HICCUPS (Familiar, Explainability, World, History, ... [etc.].* [3]	Prompting Pictorial example: *Sign for slip and trip warning* (author photograph)
Telling	Telling Textual example: *Testing - Do one thing after another - 1. Perform multiple activities connected end-to-end ... [etc.]* [1]	Telling Conceptual example: *Goldilocks Testing (do just enough...)* [4]	Telling Pictorial example: *Road Sign - Stop Command* [32]

6.1 Pilot Method

Our aim in this pilot study was to evaluate which of the shapes was most suitable for the specific heuristics we wanted to build. These were for UX designers to use when designing a testing tool, so a small, specific context.

Based on the content of Table 1, we designed shapes for a subset of three of our potential heuristics. Each of the three heuristics was a rule of thumb for one software quality attribute:

– Learnability: solo versus team learning;
– Maintainability: how tests and related artefacts can be updated, replaced, removed, etc.;
– Interoperability: how this tool works with other tools across a workflow.

We built three slide packs, each with 10 slides, the first showing the nine shapes in a matrix, and the other nine slides each showing the **same heuristic** in a different shape, one per slide. For example, one **pictorial prompting** heuristic for test maintainability included a picture of honey pouring to encourage thinking about viscosity (Fig. 5), while a **conceptual asking** heuristic was *'How easy is it to change the way data in this tool is modelled, visualised? Unmixing an omelette? Or sorting Lego bricks?'*

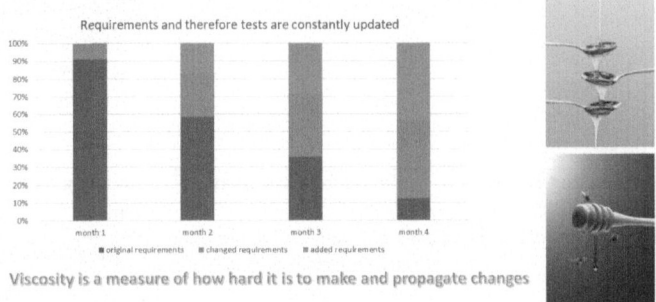

Fig. 5. Example Heuristic - Pictorial Prompt.

We initially selected five participants, using convenience sampling. The participants included two UX experts with more than 10 years of experience in the industry field, two practitioners with 3–10 years of experience, and one newer UX professional with under 3 years of experience.

Our intention was to evaluate with this sample, make changes, and iterate the review with another group, until saturation was reached in terms of information, or agreement about which shape was most suitable for our specific work.

Participants received an information and consent form, and their responses were anonymised. Each participant was given a slide set, one or two participants to each attribute. They were given a few days to review the slides and think about them. Participants were individually interviewed, all via Zoom, and the interviews recorded to transcribe later for quotes and coding. Interviews were semi-structured. Initially, each was asked if they were familiar with the quality attribute in their slide set, if they were familiar with Nielsen's heuristics, and if they used Nielsen's heuristics. All the participants had heard of Nielsen's heuristics, and all but the least experienced had used them in projects. They all were familiar with the quality attribute used as an example in their own slide pack. The matrix of shapes was used to introduce the start of the evaluation, and they were asked if there were other formats or levels of directiveness they would add, or other dimensions. Each heuristic was then viewed and the participant asked if they found it understandable and useful, whether it was appropriate at a UX design stage.

6.2   Pilot Results

We transcribed the interviews, and also notes taken during the interviews, arriving at a score for each heuristic shape based on positive, negative and neutral comments; we coded +1 for each positive reaction, –1 for each negative reaction, and 0 for a neutral reaction. We totalled the scores across participants for each shape. We tabulated those scores (see Table 2) to compare the reactions to the shapes.

Table 2. Heuristic Shapes Review: UX Design of Test Tools (Experts/Practitioners).

	Asking	Prompting	Telling	Reviewer Comments:
Pictorial	–3	–1	–2	accessibility issues
Textual	5	0	–2	preferred format
Conceptual	–2	–5	–3	inclusivity issues
Reviewer Comments:	Encourages divergent thinking: use at design stage	Better as second level of detail: use to provide supporting checklist	Encourages task completion: use at testing and UI evalution stage	

The scores in the table reflect the preferred option for the specific context of a design phase for a testing tool, and show a unanimous preference for a test question at the design stage for this type of tool. When asked the reason, the responses were that this would open wider thinking about the design.

The participants offered comments not just about the specific context, but also about what they would use in other contexts, in particular that they would favour a textual telling heuristic for UX testing, and would like textual prompts to make a check list underlying either the design stage or the test stage heuristics. No participant wanted to add other formats, levels of directiveness or dimensions to the table.

Participants noted both accessibility and inclusivity flaws in some of the shapes (Table 2), and this is one reason the pictorial and conceptual heuristics scored lower than textual. In the Discussion we will consider how the accessibility and inclusivity challenges may be overcome.

Heuristics presented pictorially seemed to be a less familiar format for this group. With some of the diagramatic representations, the participants preferred to build their own; they would rather have a prompt suggesting that a mind map or journey map would be useful to do, unless the diagram was providing specific information about a specific situation, such as a heat map of frequency of system changes for a specific system. The less experienced UXers were also less familiar with some of the diagrams and commented that they could not read them. This fits with [11] who found that experts find visual representations in programming environments easier to understand than novices do.

Following analysis, the results were shared with the participants for member checking, and additionally discussed with an accessibility expert and seven software testing experts, allowing a sense-check of the hypothesis and the pilot outcome.

6.3   Pilot Conclusions

There was unanimous consensus from these participants in this context. All participants independently choose a **textual question** heuristic to encourage divergent thinking during the design stage of a test tool. In comments, participants noted for the UX evaluation stage they preferred a **textual directive** heuristic. They wanted **textual prompt** heuristics in checklists to accompany the top level question or directive, as explanatory information.

At this point, unexpectedly, we had reached a consensus and had enough information to suggest that the Shape of Heuristics Model could be worth evaluating further. This provides a small sample saturation, which we considered sufficient to build our hypothesis, that the Shape of Heuristics affect their communicability, accessibility and inclusiveness in a particular context. This is not of course a sufficient study to make generalised comments about the best shape for heuristics in general, but it does show that reaching a consensus in a very specific context is possible. Our iterative design process for our own evidence-based heuristics continues.

In the next section we discuss the Shape of Heuristics Model and why it might help in heuristic design. We consider how to address some of the accessibility, inclusivity, and understandability issues raised in the pilot study.

7   Discussion

Our hypothesis that different shapes of heuristics may be appropriate in different contexts is supported by the pilot; We see from the pilot study that UX practitioners preferred different shape of heuristics in different circumstances, in this case the UX design versus UX testing stages of a project.

We have seen that pictorial, conceptual and textual heuristics are used both by IT professionals and in everyday contexts. Each of the formats has particular benefits and challenges.

In this section we discuss the formats and levels of directiveness, when they might be appropriate to use, and when the paired approach in the Shape of Heuristics Model may need augmenting.

7.1   Accessibility

The pilot study participants raised accessibility as a potential issue with non-textual heuristics. We considered accessibility, and also ease of learning, interpreting and using heuristics. In Table 3, we show how accessibility might be addressed in textual and

Table 3. Addressing Accessibility Challenges in Text and Pictorial Heuristics.

Format	Media	Disability	Accessibility Solution 1	Accessibility Solution 2
Text	Print	Sight impairment (permanent)	Screen Reader replaces sight by hearing	Braille replaces sight by touch
Pictorial	e-document	Sight impairment (permanent)	Alt Text for screen reader replaces sight by hearing	Raised diagram replaces sight by touch

pictorial heuristics, for permanent sight impairment. Different approaches would be needed for temporary or situational sight impairment because in those contexts, the investment in learning Braille, raised diagrams, or the use of a screen reader is not applicable. Additionally, for other disabilities, whether sensory, intellectual, emotional, etc., it is possible to design heuristics that are accessible: using simple clear language, and providing multiple formats in different media.

Using more than one sense or ability to understand a heuristic is used in everyday life: foghorns and alarms provide a heuristic warning in sound to supplement lights and signs when vision is temporarily disabled in fog or smoke. Old pharmacy poison bottles use ridges on the sides of the bottle to indicate poison, a heuristic that allows a double-check of sight of the label and feel of the bottle to assist the pharmacist. A sense of smell is used to check food freshness, and is supplemented by sight (the clearness of a fish's eye on the fishmonger's slab) or in text, in a 'use by' date on packaging in Braille and print. We also use 'smell' as a conceptual heuristic when we talk about code smells or test smells.

7.2   Inclusion

The pilot study participants raised (lack of) inclusion particularly for the conceptual heuristics. These relied on cultural references, some of which were less understandable to participants in different age groups, or from different countries. Removing cultural, generational and contextual blockers to a heuristic's interpretation, depending on its context of use, is an important consideration. While emoji interpretation is a closed book to one researcher, rotary-dial telephones were an equally unsuitable metaphor to the youngest of the participants.

When looking at the collection of road signs on the Wikipedia pages [31,32] it was clear that some of the iconography was symbolically meaningful but out of date, notably steam trains as the symbol for rail crossing in several countries. We see this also in user interfaces, where the symbol for saving a document was, up till very recently, a 3.5-inch floppy disk, which, although like the steam train, is still available, is not mainstream and may not have been used or seen by the majority of potential users. The context for a heuristic may outlive the symbolism used in the heuristic, leaving it open to misinterpretation, or reinterpretation. Whether the heuristic is conceptual, pictorial or textual, the way it is expressed will provide information about the context within which it was developed, its age, and its authors' preconceptions.

Some heuristics have been designed to last for a very long time, and be understandable both in much later times, and by quite different cultures. Two examples are long-term signage for nuclear industry waste sites, and the Pioneer plaque. The iconography providing heuristics on the Pioneer plaque are critiqued [34] for lack of racial and gender inclusivity, and potentially over-reliance on specific cultural references. This is a lesson generally applicable to heuristic design. Similarly, the need to provide heuristics that last 10000 years and still convey 'Danger - Keep out!' for nuclear industry waste sites [33] is a perplexing, interesting, and important problem for heuristics design. These two examples may provide a lesson in communicating complex concepts in a heuristic and still making it understandable to all.

Initial indications from the pilot support our hypothesis, it appears that the shape of a heuristic affects how it is understood and used in context. The Shape of Heuristics Model could provide a starting point for designing and evaluating understandability, accessibility and inclusion of heuristics. Note that to achieve this more than one shape may need to be employed simultaneously. An example is the 'Slip and Trip Hazard' sign in Fig. 6: a pictorial prompting heuristic plus two texts in different languages.

Fig. 6. Pictorial and Text Heuristic: Slip & Trip (author photo).

8   Conclusion and Next Steps

Heuristics, whether intuitive, experience-based, or evidence-based, may be communicated in different formats and with different levels of directiveness in different contexts. We introduce the first iteration of a model for understanding choices for the shape of a heuristic based on its format and level of directiveness. We present this in nine-cell matrix, which we call the Shape of Heuristics Model. The Model includes textual, conceptual and pictorial formats that can be combined with the telling, prompting and asking levels of directiveness, allowing someone designing or evaluating a heuristic to consider which shape is the most appropriate in their specific context, whether industry or academic.

Through a pilot study, we showed it is possible to review the potential shape of a heuristic with its audience independently of the heuristic's content. The pilot study also raised challenges of accessibility and inclusion. This means the same heuristic may need to be communicated in more than one shape, dependent on context and audience. We showed that context affects inclusion, considering the history, geography and societal meaning of a heuristic. How understandable a heuristic is, may be generational, depending on its age, and the age of those using it. Language and cultural meanings may be inadvertently embedded in a heuristic, by its designers and those using it, causing ambiguity, and exclusion.

8.1   Next Steps

Further work is required to evaluate the hypothesis and Model in different usage scenarios and contexts, to study the impact of the level of directiveness and format and its affect on how participants interpret and use heuristics. How to make heuristics both accessible and inclusive also requires further study.

We propose a future HCI study that trials the Shape of Heuristics Model to identify contexts where different levels of directiveness and different formats are appropriate. The pilot we ran could be a template, with an example heuristic being expressed in multiple ways to examine the effect of directiveness level on the actions people take, and the effect of both directiveness and format on accessibility, inclusion and understandabilty. Studies using heuristics in different domains could be an area of interest. These could then be added to the validation factors of utility, clarity, and ease of use suggested by [26]. In our own work, we will continue to evaluate the Shape of Heuristics Model and use it to inform the understandability, accessibility and inclusivity of the heuristics we develop for software testing and UX applications. Once fully evaluated the Shape of Heuristics Model could be used both in academic and industry settings for designing, evaluating and communicating heuristics.

Acknowledgments. The authors thanks the industry and academic participants in the pilot and discussion of the Shape of Heuristics Model.

Disclosure of Interests. The authors have no competing interests to declare that are relevant to the content of this article.

References

1. Bach, J.: Heuristic test strategy model (2024). https://www.satisfice.com/download/heuristic-test-strategy-model
2. Biggane, E.: How to tell the difference between poisonous and edible mushrooms (2014). https://www.wildfooduk.com/articles/how-to-tell-the-difference-between-poisonous-and-edible-mushrooms/
3. Bolton, M.: FEW HICCUPS (2012). https://developsense.com/blog/2012/07/few-hiccupps
4. Bradshaw, R., Deery, S.: Software testing heuristics: mind the gap! (2019). https://www.ministryoftesting.com/articles/ce0dc29c?s_id=1474072
5. Charles, F.: Workshops: Mastering the power of heuristics in testing (2024). https://www.quality-intelligence.com/workshops.htm

6. Dewar, D.: Testing mnemonics desktop (2015). https://findingdeefex.com/
7. Evans, I., Porter, C., Micallef, M.: Scared, frustrated and quietly proud: testers' lived experience of tools and automation. In: European Conference on Cognitive Ergonomics 2021, pp. 1–7. ACM, New York, NY, USA (2021)
8. Evans, I., Porter, C., Micallef, M.: Breaking testing stereotypes: who is testing and why it matters. In: To be published in Proceedings of BCS HCI Conference 2024. BCS HCI (2024)
9. Evans, I., Porter, C., Micallef, M., Harty, J.: Stuck in limbo with magical solutions: the testers' lived experiences of tools and automation. In: Proceedings of the 15th International Joint Conference on Computer Vision, Imaging and Computer Graphics Theory and Applications, pp. 195–202. SciTePress-Science and Technology Publications, SciTePress, Portugal (2020)
10. Evans, I., Porter, C., Micallef, M., Harty, J.: Test tools: an illusion of usability? In: 2020 IEEE International Conference on Software Testing. Verification and Validation Workshops (ICSTW), pp. 392–397. IEEE Computer Society, Washington, DC, USA, IEEE (2020)
11. Green, T.R.G., Petre, M.: Usability analysis of visual programming environments: a 'cognitive dimensions' framework. J. Vis. Lang. Comput. 7(2), 131–174 (1996)
12. Hennink, M., Kaiser, B.N.: Sample sizes for saturation in qualitative research: a systematic review of empirical tests. Soc. Sci. I Med. 292, 114523 (2022). https://doi.org/10.1016/j.socscimed.2021.114523, https://www.sciencedirect.com/science/article/pii/S0277953621008558
13. Hjeij, M., Vilks, A.: A brief history of heuristics: how did research on heuristics evolve? Humanit. Soc. Sci. Commun. 10(1), 1–15 (2023)
14. Inostroza, R., Rusu, C., Roncagliolo, S., Jimenez, C., Rusu, V.: Usability heuristics for touchscreen-based mobile devices. In: 2012 Ninth International Conference on Information Technology-New Generations, pp. 662–667. IEEE (2012)
15. ISTQB: ISTQB CTFL Syllabus v4.0 (2023). https://www.istqb.org/certifications/certification-list
16. ItWasNeverADress.org: It was never a dress (2015). https://itwasneveradress.org/about/
17. Katan, T.: Creative Trespassing. Penguin Random House (2019)
18. Kumar, B.A., Goundar, M.S., Chand, S.S.: A framework for heuristic evaluation of mobile learning applications. Educ. Inf. Technol. 25, 3189–3204 (2020)
19. Nielsen, J., Molich, R.: Teaching user interface design based on usability engineering. SIGCHI Bull. 21(1), 45–48 (1989). https://doi.org/10.1145/67880.67885
20. Nielsen, J.: Ten usability heuristics (2024). https://www.nngroup.com/articles/ten-usability-heuristics/
21. Nielsen, J., Molich, R.: Heuristic evaluation of user interfaces. In: International Conference on Human Factors in Computing Systems (1990). https://api.semanticscholar.org/CorpusID:17451097
22. OED: Oxford English Dictionary (2024). https://www.oed.com/
23. OED, O.E.D.: Understanding frequency of use per million words (2023). https://www.oed.com/information/understanding-entries/frequency/
24. Petrie, H., Power, C.: What do users really care about? A comparison of usability problems found by users and experts on highly interactive websites. In: Proceedings of the SIGCHI Conference on Human Factors in Computing Systems, pp. 2107–2116 (2012)
25. Quiñones, D., Rusu, C.: How to develop usability heuristics: a systematic literature review. Comput. Stand. Interfaces 53, 89–122 (2017)
26. Quiñones, D., Rusu, C., Rusu, V.: A methodology to develop usability/user experience heuristics. Comput. Stand. Interfaces 59, 109–129 (2018)
27. Shelley, P.B.: Ode to the west wind (1820). https://www.poetryfoundation.org/poems/45134/ode-to-the-west-wind

28. Sim, G., Read, J.C.: Using computer-assisted assessment heuristics for usability evaluations. Br. J. Edu. Technol. **47**(4), 694–709 (2016)
29. Sim, G., Read, J.C., Cockton, G.: Evidence based design of heuristics for computer assisted assessment. In: Human-Computer Interaction–INTERACT 2009: 12th IFIP TC 13 International Conference, Uppsala, Sweden, 24–28 August 2009, Proceedings, Part I, vol. 12, pp. 204–216. Springer (2009)
30. Wei, Z., Landay, J.A.: Evaluating speech-based smart devices using new usability heuristics. IEEE Pervasive Comput. **17**(2), 84–96 (2018)
31. Wikipedia contributors: Comparison of european road signs — Wikipedia, the free encyclopedia (2024). https://en.wikipedia.org/w/index.php?title=Comparison_of_European_road_signs. Accessed 10 Apr 2024
32. Wikipedia contributors: Comparison of traffic signs in English-speaking territories — Wikipedia, the free encyclopedia (2024). https://en.wikipedia.org/w/index.php?title=Comparison_of_traffic_signs_in_English-speaking_territories. Accessed 10 Apr 2024
33. Wikipedia contributors: Long-term nuclear waste warning messages — Wikipedia, the free encyclopedia (2024). https://en.wikipedia.org/wiki/Long-term_nuclear_waste_warning_messages. Accessed 10 Apr 2024
34. Wikipedia contributors: Pioneer plaque — Wikipedia, the free encyclopedia (2024). https://en.wikipedia.org/wiki/Pioneer_plaque. Accessed 10 Apr 2024
35. Wong, E.: Heuristic evaluation: how to conduct a heuristic evaluation (2022). https://www.interaction-design.org/literature/article/heuristic-evaluation-how-to-conduct-a-heuristic-evaluation
36. Yeratziotis, A., Pottas, D., Van Greunen, D.: A usable security heuristic evaluation for the online health social networking paradigm. Int. J. Hum.-Comput. Interact. **28**(10), 678–694 (2012)

EEG Biometrics with GAN Integration for Secure Smart City Data Access

Roberto Saia$^{(\boxtimes)}$, Riccardo Balia, Alessandro Sebastian Podda, Livio Pompianu, Salvatore Carta, and Alessia Pisu

Department of Mathematics and Computer Science, University of Cagliari, Palazzo delle Scienze, Via Ospedale 72, 09124 Cagliari, Italy
{roberto.saia,riccardo.balia,sebastianpodda,livio.pompianu,salvatore,alessia.pisu96}@unica.it

Abstract. Biometric systems leveraging ElectroEncephaloGram (EEG) data for user authentication present significant potential in diverse contexts, especially in Smart City ecosystems where secure access to sensitive data is crucial (e.g., healthcare systems, intelligent transportation, smart grids, public safety, and citizen services). However, the complexity and variability of EEG data raise challenges in developing effective solutions. In this context, after a preliminary series of experiments used to find the best feature extraction method for the input, and performed by exploiting the Biometric EEG Dataset (BED), this paper proposes a novel EEG-based user verification framework. It utilizes Mel-Frequency Cepstral Coefficients (MFCC) for feature extraction, followed by feature selection via the Boruta strategy and automated data quantization. An important aspect of this approach is the integration of Generative Adversarial Networks (GANs) to generate synthetic EEG data, which, along with real data, is employed to train an ensemble of Artificial Neural Networks (ANNs). The ensemble decision is made using soft voting mechanisms, promising a robust and competitive solution compared to current state-of-the-art techniques. Initial experiments suggest that this framework has significant potential for further development and optimization.

Keywords: Smart cities · Brain-computer interfaces · Biometrics · EEG data · Secure access

1 Introduction

The rapid growth in technology and the ever-increasing need for biometric systems to perform user identification tasks have led to development efforts focused on enhancing the performance of these systems. In such a research field, EEG-based approaches represent a powerful opportunity thanks to their potential to offer unique and reliable user identification based on brain activity patterns [19]. It could be a great opportunity in Smart City ecosystems, where secure access to sensitive information is crucial. The possibility of detecting brain activity using easy-to-use, small-sized, and low-cost devices and sensors is a relatively recent advancement that has opened up new perspectives in many fields of scientific research. These devices allow us to perform an Electroencephalogram (EEG) by measuring the brain's electrical activity through electrodes

© The Author(s), under exclusive license to Springer Nature Switzerland AG 2025
H. Plácido da Silva and P. Cipresso (Eds.): CHIRA 2024, CCIS 2370, pp. 454–467, 2025.
https://doi.org/10.1007/978-3-031-82633-7_27

positioned on the scalp. The exponential increase in systems and services that request a secure user authentication process underlines the need for robust biometric systems. It is a dynamic research area where the developed EEG-based approaches are evaluated based on several criteria, such as the capability to detect unique patterns from the user's brain activity, representing powerful instruments for those applications that require secure access, such as in Smart Cities. One of the strengths of this kind of biometric system is its ability to capture and analyze complex brain activity patterns, identifying the unique patterns that characterize each user. The inherent variability of the individual's brain activity grants uniqueness to these brain patterns, allowing us the opportunity to develop secure approaches for user identification. In such a context, the advent of low-cost and easy-to-use EEG devices offers new possibilities for large-scale application, thanks to the easy acquisition of EEG data through a few electrodes placed on the scalp.

EEG-based biometric systems have significant potential across various domains. For example, in the healthcare field, they can assist in the process of patient identification, granting at the same time the confidentiality of the involved identification data. In the cybersecurity field, they provide an extra layer of protection against unauthorized access, a crucial aspect in Smart City environments, where sensitive information needs to be protected. Given that the literature presents numerous approaches characterized by a high level of heterogeneity, many of which are not suitable for practical large-scale use due to complexity, acquisition times, or the limited number of users involved in experiments, the approach proposed here aims to provide a solution that is practically usable on a large scale. It includes considerations about cost, complexity, and operational times, with a focus on validation against state-of-the-art methods [18].

This paper introduces a novel EEG-based biometric approach for secure user authentication in Smart Cities, where Generative Adversarial Networks (GANs) are exploited to generate EEG data to improve the training process. Such an approach involves extracting features from EEG data, the use of the Boruta strategy for feature selection, and data quantization. GANs are then utilized to generate synthetic EEG data, which, together with the real data, trains an ensemble of Artificial Neural Networks (ANNs) to improve the authentication performance. The final goal is to design a robust, scalable, and secure approach for accessing sensitive information in Smart City environments. The main scientific contributions of this work are summarized in the following:

(i) **Evaluation of Different Feature Extraction Techniques:** A series of experiments using a prototypical version of the proposed approach on the BED dataset were performed to explore various feature extraction techniques such as Mel-Frequency Cepstral Coefficients (MFCC), Autoregressive Reflection Coefficients (ARRC), and Spectral Features (SPEC), selecting the best one to use for the input EEG data.

(ii) **Design and Formalization of the Framework:** The architecture of the framework based on the proposed approach (feature extraction, feature selection, data quantization, GAN data generation, and ensemble classification components) was formalized, providing the needed information for the system definition.

(iii) **Definition of the Approach Algorithm:** The algorithm for user identity verification based on the previously defined architecture was formalized, offering further details for future implementation and development of the proposed biometric authentication system in Smart City environments.

The remainder of this paper is organized as follows: Sect. 2 provides information about the considered research scenario. Section 3 formalizes architecture and algorithm of the proposed approach. Lastly, Sect. 5 concludes the paper with some final remark, indicating our future directions.

2   Background and Related Work

In recent years, there has been increasing interest in utilizing EEG data for biometric systems aimed at user identification tasks [20]. This surge in interest has led to the development of more efficient strategies and implementations [4], along with consideration of various transversal aspects [21]. Such advancements are particularly relevant in the context of Smart Cities, where secure access to sensitive information is crucial. The human brain comprises billions of neurons, each capable of establishing communication channels with thousands of others through weak electric signals (microvolts). These electrical activities generate brain waves categorized into five groups based on frequency (ranging from 4 to 100 Hz): Delta, Theta, Alpha, Beta, and Gamma waves (Fig. 2). EEG devices record these brain waves through scalp electrodes, measuring voltage fluctuations typically ranging from 10 to 100 microvolts in adults. The placement of electrodes on the scalp follows the International 10–20 System [7], correlating with specific areas of the cerebral cortex to ensure correct electrode placement, as shown in Fig. 1.

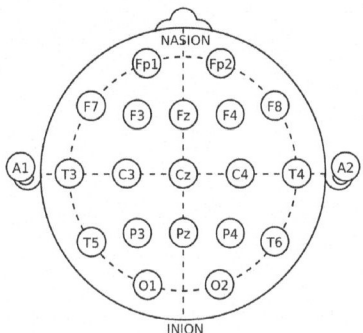

Fig. 1. International 10–20 System for Electrodes Placement.

2.1   Domain Overview

Representative recent works in this field include: Yap et al. [23], proposing a method for biometric user identification using affordable EEG devices and protocols such as Eyes Closed (EC) and visual stimulation; Jijomon et al. [9], utilizing single-trial familiar-name Auditory Evoked Potentials (AEPs) collected through frontal EEG electrodes for user identification; Zhao et al. [24], presenting a system framework for Visual Evoked Potential (VEP)-based biometrics; and Katsigiannis et al. [10], proposing a biometric user identification approach based on EEG data collected under diverse stimuli. A significant challenge in this research lies in the differences observed in EEG signals among subjects, necessitating the definition of a new evaluation model for each subject, which incurs substantial computational load. Furthermore, EEG signal analysis poses challenges due to its low signal-to-noise ratio and non-stationary nature. These challenges are exacerbated in the context of Smart Cities, where large-scale, real-time data processing is often required for secure access management. Various techniques aim to achieve temporal repeatability of acquired patterns, a crucial requirement for such systems. These techniques often involve utilizing different external stimuli to enhance brainwave pattern distinctiveness and improve stability and reliability over time. In the context of Smart Cities, such stability is vital to ensure continuous and secure access to sensitive information.

In addition, many studies in the literature focus on methods aimed at enhancing result accuracy. For example, [3] analyzed data from 109 participants and improved accuracy by applying optimization and regularization techniques. Similarly, [6] employs a Data Augmentation (DA) framework using conditional Generative Adversarial Networks (cGANs) to address the EEG data scarcity problem and enhance the performance of EEG classifiers.

In more formal terms, these techniques are referred to as Evoked Potentials (EPs), which denote the electrical responses recorded within specific parts of the nervous system, mainly in the brain, in response to external stimuli. EPs are commonly utilized in clinical settings to evaluate the electrical activity associated with particular regions of the brain and spinal cord. They play a crucial role in diagnosing neurological disorders when combined with other diagnostic procedures. However, it's important to acknowledge that these stimulation techniques often have limitations as authentication mechanisms due to their lengthy detection times and the requirement for expensive equipment, which may pose challenges for widespread implementation in Smart City environments. In a study by Nakanishi et al. [13], EEG activity triggered by imperceptible visual stimulation was utilized as a biometric approach. Additionally, other research

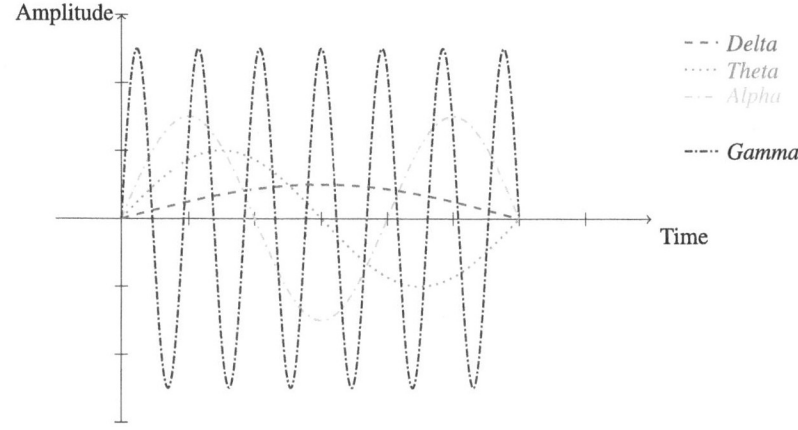

Fig. 2. EEG Signals.

works, such as that by Reshmi et al. [16], propose brain-based biometric user recognition methods. These methods, similar to the approach described by Abed et al. [2], utilize the distinctive features of brainwaves, specifically Gamma and Beta waves, for authentication purposes. Such approaches highlight the potential of EEG-based systems for secure access control in Smart Cities, enabling the integration of advanced biometric techniques to protect sensitive information and ensure robust user identification.

2.2 Feature Extraction Techniques in EEG Data Analysis

In the context of EEG data analysis, several techniques are commonly employed for feature extraction, as detailed in the following:

- **Mel-Frequency Cepstral Coefficients (MFCC):** Originally developed for speech and audio processing [1], it has found widespread use in EEG data analysis. This method involves several steps: (i) dividing the EEG signal into short time frames; (ii) computing the spectrum for each frame; (iii) applying the Mel filterbank to mimic the human ear's frequency response; (iv) computing the logarithm of filterbank energies; (v) applying the Discrete Cosine Transform (DCT) to obtain coefficients. In brief, the MFCC representation allows us to capture the relevant features and discard the irrelevant ones.
- **Autoregressive Reflection Coefficients (ARRC):** It is derived from fitting an autoregressive model to the EEG signal, providing a model for temporal dependencies [11]. The steps involved in this technique include: (i) modeling the EEG signal as an autoregressive process; (ii) expressing each value as a linear combination of its previous ones; (iii) computing the coefficients of this autoregressive model, known as ARR coefficients. In brief, the ARR coefficients offer a compact representation of the temporal dynamics in EEG data.
- **Spectral Features (SPEC):** It involves analyzing the frequency content of the EEG signal to gain insights into power distribution across frequency bands [8]. The process typically includes: (i) transforming EEG signals into the frequency domain using techniques like Fourier or Wavelet transform; (ii) computing the power spectral density or other frequency-domain features. In brief, these features provide valuable information about the spectral characteristics of EEG signals.

2.3 Evaluation Metrics

Two metrics commonly employed in this research field to evaluate user identification/verification systems are the Area under the ROC Curve (AUC) and the Equal Error Rate (EER). The AUC score, ranging from 0 to 1, reflects the performance of a classifier, with higher values indicating superior performance. Formally, the ROC curve illustrates the trade-off between True Positive Rate (TPR) and False Positive Rate (FPR) across different threshold settings.

- **AUC:** The AUC serves as a summary statistic for the ROC curve, defined as indicated in Eq. 1, where Sensitivity represents the true positive rate and Specificity denotes the true negative rate.

$$AUC = \int_0^1 TPR(FPR(t)) \, dt \tag{1}$$

– **EER:** The EER reports the balance between the False Acceptance Rate (FAR), formulated in Eq. 2, and the False Rejection Rate (FRR), formulated in Eq. 3. At the EER, these rates are equal, marking a point of equilibrium where both types of errors hold equal weight in the system's performance, as show in Fig. 3.

$$FAR = \frac{\text{Number of False Positives}}{\text{Total Number of Impostor Verifications}} \tag{2}$$

$$FRR = \frac{\text{Number of False Negatives}}{\text{Total Number of Genuine Verifications}} \tag{3}$$

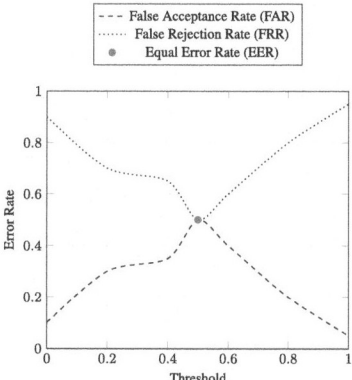

Fig. 3. Equal Error Rate (EER).

2.4 Challenges in EEG-Based Biometric Systems

Research in this field primarily aims to develop biometric systems that balance user-friendliness, affordability, and identification accuracy. Key challenges include the instability of EEG patterns over time and the complexities of data acquisition. The first problem arises from the dynamic nature of EEG data, characterized by its complexity, non-linearity, and non-stationarity, then the extraction of meaningful information directly from these signals in the time domain [22] is not easy and many studies suggest using evoked potentials techniques during data acquisition to address this issue, as they offer better repeatability. The second problem is instead related to user heterogeneity in EEG waves and the need for system calibration during acquisition and many state-of-the-art approaches are impractical for real-world deployment due to these issues [9]. For instance, some methods rely on expensive and not easy to handle EEG equipment, requiring complex preparation and calibration procedures. Effective strategies have been proposed to mitigate these challenges. Some studies demonstrate stable

EEG responses across sessions using stimulation techniques [15], while others show improved signal stability with visual stimulation [12]. Additionally, techniques like wavelet packet decomposition have been used to extract more permanent patterns from EEG data. However, interference from unwanted artifacts such as muscle and ocular activities poses an additional challenge in practical EEG-based biometrics. Therefore, preprocessing techniques are essential to minimize these influences and improve the reliability of biometric systems.

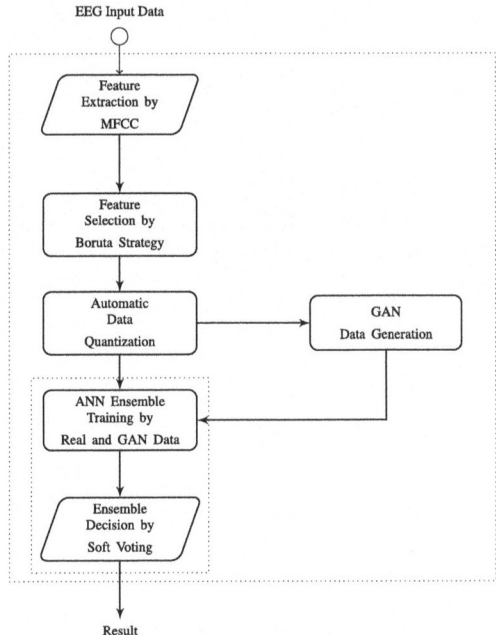

Fig. 4. High-level Architecture of the Proposed Approach.

3 Approach Formalization

The architecture of the proposed approach, which is shown at a high level in Fig. 4, consists of the following steps:

1. **EEG Input Data:** The input we used or the preliminary experiments is the Biometric EEG Dataset (BED) [5]. It is composed by EEG signals collected using the *Emotiv Epoc+* (https://www.emotiv.com) wireless EEG headset. The dataset includes various preprocessing techniques, stimuli during data acquisition, and different acquisition sessions, resulting in 108 different datasets since it includes three distinct feature extraction methods (MFCC, ARRC, SPEC), twelve stimuli (AS = presentation of visual images; MC=cognitive tasks; RC, RO = period of rest with participants keeping their eyes, respectively, closed and open, VC3, VC5, VC7,

VC10 = visual evoked potential uses a standard checker-board pattern with pattern reversal, respectively at 3, 5, 7, and 10 Hz; VF3, VF5, VF7, VF10 = visual evoked potential uses flashing with a plain color set as black, respectively at 3, 5, 7, and 10 Hz).

2. **Feature Extraction by MFCC:** With the objective of using a state-of-the-art feature extraction technique capable of synergistically interacting with the proposed approach, various techniques widely used in the literature were considered. A non-optimized prototype of our approach was applied to these techniques to evaluate any potential performance improvements. The experiments, whose results are shown in Fig. 5, guide us toward selecting the MFCC technique. This technique, more than the others, demonstrates potential for improvement when our approach is applied, even though it is still in a prototype stage. It should be noted that the MFCC technique used in this step was selected after preliminary experimentation.

3. **Feature Selection by Boruta Strategy:** This step leverages the Boruta feature selection technique to identify the most relevant features. It operates by: (i) creating shuffled copies of each feature (shadow features); (ii) training a Random Forest model using this augmented dataset; (iii) comparing the relevance of each original feature among its corresponding shadow features; (iv) considering and keep the features that have higher importance than their shadows, discarding the other ones. Such a strategy reduces the overfitting by removing noise data, ensuring that only the most informative features are used for the model definition.

4. **Automatic Data Quantization:** This preprocessing step is aimed to transform continuous numerical features into discrete categorical values, determining the optimal number of bins for the quantization process automatically through two main phases: (i) searching for the optimal number of bins; (ii) quantizing the data based on the selected bin count. In more detail, it evaluates different numbers of bins to find the most effective one for quantizing the data, discretizing and classifying the features according to a K-fold Cross-validation criterion, measuring the performance for each number of bins. This process supports the concurrent execution, and optimal number of bins is determined by comparing cross-validation scores. Subsequently, it performs the data quantization using the optimal number of bins, quantizing the real-valued data into ordinal categories. This process allows us to better manage the continuous variables in subsequent stages by reducing the complexity of the feature space.

5. **GAN Data Generation:** This step generates synthetic data using a Generative Adversarial Network (GAN). The process initializes a GAN model and trains it with real, quantized data to produce synthetic samples characterized by the statistical properties of the real ones. In more detail, the GAN is composed of a generator and a discriminator, which are trained iteratively. The former creates synthetic data, and the latter attempts to distinguish it from real data, as to improve the quality of the synthetic samples over time. When the train process is completed, the GAN generates a synthetic set of data of the same size as the real one. The synthetic data is saved for future use to avoid redundant computations. The additional training data is used to improve the robustness and performance of the final evaluation model since it provides different data points that cover a broader feature space.

6. **ANN Ensemble Training by Real and GAN Data:** The goal of this step is to improve the evaluation model robustness and generalization by training an ensemble of sequential Artificial Neural Networks (ANNs) using both real and synthetic data. The real data features are integrated with synthetic data generated via a Generative Adversarial Network (GAN). The process is performed according to a K-fold cross-validation criterion and involves three models, one trained on real data, one trained on synthetic data, and one trained on a combined dataset of both real and synthetic data. An early stopping mechanism based on validation performance is implemented to avoid overfitting. After the models training, the predictions are then averaged according to an ensemble Soft Voting criterion, as detailed in the "Ensemble Decision by Soft Voting" final step.

7. **Ensemble Decision by Soft Voting:** This final step takes as input the prediction performed by the ANN Ensemble according to a K-fold cross-validation criterion and returns as output the data classification using the Soft Voting criterion. The choice of employing such a criterion within an ensemble approach is driven by its capacity to offer more nuanced decision-making. Unlike other criteria (e.g., Majority Voting), it considers the confidence levels or probabilities assigned by each classifier, resulting in a more probabilistic approach to decision aggregation. This method enables the ensemble model to consider the uncertainty related to the individual classifier predictions, leading to a more sophisticated decision fusion process. More formally, the ensemble approach employing Soft Voting is shown in Eq. 4, where $\hat{y}$ denotes the predicted class, N denotes the number of classifiers, and P_{ij} stands for the probability predicted by the i-th classifier for the j-th class.

$$\hat{y} = \underset{j}{\operatorname{argmax}} \left(\frac{1}{N} \sum_{i=1}^{N} P_{ij} \right) \qquad (4)$$

8. **Results:** The final output is the classification of each user into a specific class, representing their verified identity as determined by the system. This process is based on the Algorithm 1, where in Steps 2 and 3, the algorithm performs feature extraction from the training set T and the unclassified EEG data U using the MFCC technique, converting the raw EEG signals into a more informative feature set (T_{MFCC} and U_{MFCC}). Steps 4 and 5 select the most relevant features using the Boruta strategy, resulting in reduced feature sets $T_{selected}$ and $U_{selected}$. At Steps 6 to 8, the algorithm determines the optimal number of bins for quantization of the selected features in the training set $T_{selected}$ and quantizes both the training and unclassified data sets ($T_{quantized}$ and $U_{quantized}$). In Step 9, synthetic data is generated using a Generative Adversarial Network (GAN). The GAN is trained on the quantized training data ($T_{quantized}$), and the generated synthetic data ($T_{synthetic}$) is used to augment the training set, enhancing the diversity of the data available for model training. Steps 10 to 17 perform the process of training an ensemble of classifier models. For each classifier configuration n in the optimal ensemble size N, the algorithm updates the random number generator seed (rnd) to ensure diverse model initializations. It then trains three types of models: m_{real} on the real quantized data ($T_{quantized}$), $m_{synthetic}$ on the GAN-generated synthetic data ($T_{synthetic}$), and $m_{combined}$ on a combined dataset of both real and synthetic data. Each trained model is stored in the

set M. In Steps *18* to *22*, the algorithm processes each instance of the unclassified quantized EEG data $U_{quantized}$ by obtaining an ensemble classification r using a Soft Voting approach. This approach aggregates the predictions from all models in M, considering the confidence levels of each model's prediction. Each classification r is then added to the set R. Finally, at Step *23*, the algorithm returns the set R, which contains the final classifications for the unclassified EEG data U.

Algorithm 1. Proposed Classification Approach.

Require: T: EEG training data, U: EEG data to classify, rnd: Random number generator seed
Ensure: R: Classified EEG data

1: **procedure** CLASSIFICATION(T, U, rnd)
2:     $T_{MFCC} \leftarrow$ ExtractFeaturesByMFCC(T)   ▷ Feature extraction using MFCC
3:     $U_{MFCC} \leftarrow$ ExtractFeaturesByMFCC(U)   ▷ Feature extraction using MFCC
4:     $T_{selected} \leftarrow$ SelectFeaturesByBoruta(T_{MFCC})   ▷ Feature selection using Boruta
5:     $U_{selected} \leftarrow$ SelectFeaturesByBoruta(U_{MFCC})   ▷ Feature selection using Boruta
6:     $bins \leftarrow$ DetermineOptimalBins($T_{selected}$)   ▷ Find optimal bins for quantization
7:     $T_{quantized} \leftarrow$ QuantizeData($T_{selected}, bins$)   ▷ Quantize training data
8:     $U_{quantized} \leftarrow$ QuantizeData($U_{selected}, bins$)   ▷ Quantize unclassified data
9:     $T_{synthetic} \leftarrow$ GenerateGANData($T_{quantized}, rnd$)   ▷ Generate synthetic data using GAN
10:     $M \leftarrow \emptyset$ ▷ Initialize ensemble models set
11:     **for each** $n \in N$ **do**   ▷ Train ensemble classifier models
12:         $rnd \leftarrow rnd + 1$ ▷ Differentiate initialization of random number generator seed
13:         $m_{real} \leftarrow$ TrainClassifier($A(H), T_{quantized}, rnd$)   ▷ Train model on real data
14:         $m_{synthetic} \leftarrow$ TrainClassifier($A(H), T_{synthetic}, rnd$)   ▷ Train model on synthetic data
15:         $m_{combined} \leftarrow$ TrainClassifier($A(H), T_{quantized} \cup T_{synthetic}, rnd$)   ▷ Train model on combined
data
16:         $M \leftarrow M \cup m_{real}, m_{synthetic}, m_{combined}$ ▷ Store models
17:     **end for**
18:     $R \leftarrow \emptyset$ ▷ Initialize classified EEG data set
19:     **for each** $u \in U_{quantized}$ **do**   ▷ Process unclassified EEG data
20:         $r \leftarrow$ GetEnsemblePrediction(u, M)   ▷ Perform ensemble classification using Soft Voting
21:         $R \leftarrow R \cup r$ ▷ Store classification
22:     **end for**
23:     **return** R ▷ Returns Classified EEG data
24: **end procedure**

---

4   Discussion

Some considerations and details about the approach we proposed and formalized earlier are reported below:

– Despite the lower performance compared to high-end devices, the Emotiv system offers an ideal trade-off for large-scale user verification applications due to its affordability and reduced number of electrodes. While it is significantly cheaper than high-end devices, this lower cost involves compromises in terms of accuracy and stability. The reduced number of electrodes limits its spatial resolution and overall data accuracy, but for applications such as user verification, this is not critical. The device's simplicity and ease of use make it suitable for large-scale applications, where high-end precision is not necessary. Its balance between cost and performance allows for practical use in many environments where budget constraints and ease of deployment are more important than high data accuracy. In summary, the Emotiv system

464   R. Saia et al.

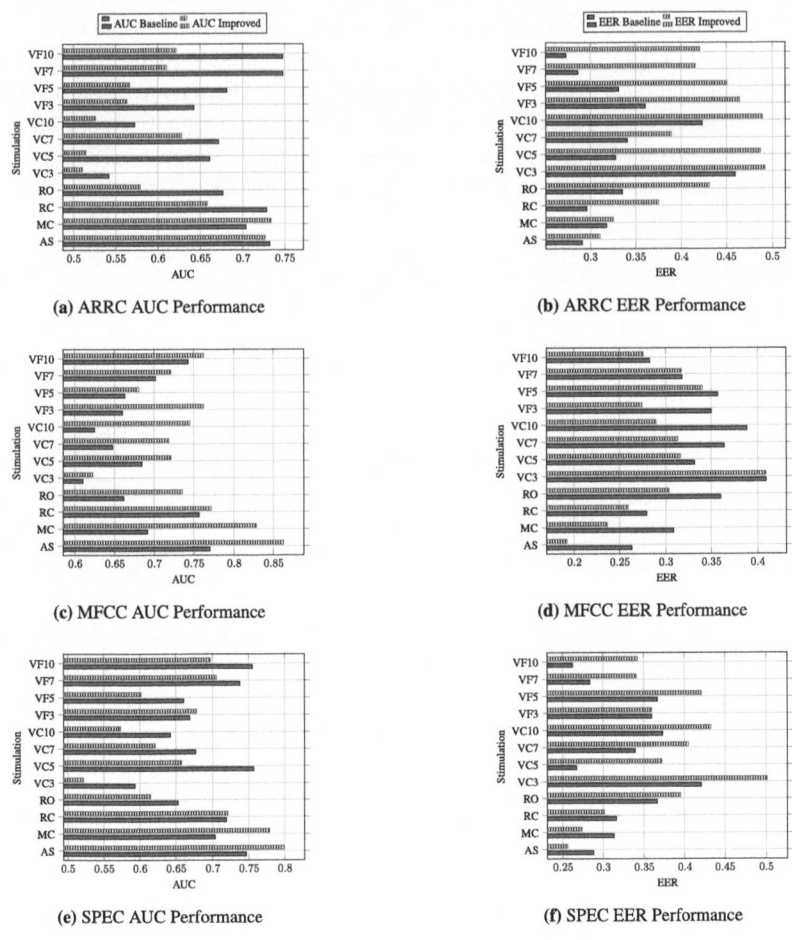

Fig. 5. Feature Extraction Techniques Evaluation

provides a scalable solution for scenarios like user verification, offering a compromise between functionality and cost. Additionally, the limitations in stability and sensitivity can be addressed through techniques designed to improve overall performance.

– Unlike other recognition approaches, such as facial recognition, which is passive and non-intrusive, EEG recognition systems require users to wear headgear equipped with electrodes, adding a layer of complexity. Users need to actively interact with the device and may be required to remain still or perform specific tasks, which can be unsuitable in scenarios involving frequent use. The literature exploring the usability and acceptability of EEG devices presents varying results. For instance, Nijboer et al. [14] found that while some users were excited about Brain-Computer Interfaces (BCIs) and their potential applications, many were discouraged by the complex setup and the physical discomfort associated with wearing EEG devices for extended periods. EEG systems also raise concerns about data privacy, as they capture sensitive neurological information. Users may worry about data security and the potential misuse of this personal data. In comparison, technologies like facial recognition are generally seen as less invasive. In summary, while these factors currently make EEG systems less appealing than more passive technologies like facial recognition, this is likely to change gradually, as has been the case with other technologies in the past. This shift is expected, particularly in light of the significant security advantages that EEG-based systems offer.

- Adapting the proposed approach based on an Emotiv device to other EEG devices involves several important considerations. First and foremost, the algorithms used in the approach need to be adjusted to account for variations in signal quality and electrode configurations across different devices. This is crucial for maintaining the effectiveness of the user verification process. Another key factor is hardware compatibility. EEG devices can differ significantly in their electrode setups and sampling rates. Therefore, the user verification approach must be flexible enough to accommodate these differences. This often requires recalibrating the system to handle changes in data acquisition protocols. Additionally, it is important to balance cost and performance. The approach should be designed to be practical for both high-end and budget-friendly devices. Ensuring that the system can scale and integrate smoothly with various hardware setups is essential for its success in large-scale applications. In summary, effectively adapting the Emotiv-based verification approach to other EEG devices involves addressing performance differences, ensuring compatibility with diverse hardware, and implementing flexible adaptation techniques. This approach helps maintain accuracy and usability across a range of EEG systems.

- It should be noted that our preliminary study is based on previous work [17], which utilized data from a publicly available Biometric EEG Dataset (BED) [5]. This enabled an initial validation of the proposed approach. However, actual validation of the verification system will also involve data from additional datasets or real-world sources to ensure a more comprehensive and robust evaluation aimed to mitigate overfitting and improve result generalization.

- A detailed computational analysis to assess the feasibility of real-time applications, particularly in resource-constrained environments, will be performed once the proposed approach has been fully implemented and validated. At that point, we will be able to evaluate the computational load and optimize the system accordingly to ensure its suitability for real-time usage.

5   Conclusion and Future Work

In this work, we propose a novel approach to user authentication using EEG-based biometrics, specifically designed for secure access to sensitive information within Smart City ecosystems. The approach leverages ElectroEncephaloGram (EEG) data to uniquely identify individuals based on their brain activity patterns, offering a robust and reliable biometric solution. A key component of our methodology involves the integration of Generative Adversarial Networks (GANs) to enhance the dataset by generating synthetic EEG data that complements the real EEG recordings. This integration aims to address challenges related to data variability and scarcity, thus improving the robustness and generalizability of the model. The architecture of our proposed system includes several stages: feature extraction, feature selection, data quantization, GAN-based data augmentation, and an ensemble of Artificial Neural Networks (ANNs) for classification. Initially, we apply Mel-Frequency Cepstral Coefficients (MFCC) for extracting relevant features from the EEG signals, which are then refined using the Boruta feature selection strategy to retain the most informative attributes. These features are subsequently quantized to a manageable format suitable for machine learning applications. A novel aspect of our approach is the generation of synthetic EEG data through a GAN, which is trained to produce realistic EEG signals that mimic the underlying distribution of the real data. The synthetic data, along with the real data, are used to train an ensemble of ANNs. This ensemble learning strategy enhances the robustness of the model by combining the strengths of multiple neural networks and improving the overall prediction accuracy through soft voting. Finally, the system combines the decisions from the ensemble in an ensemble decision module to provide a definitive authentication outcome. Our initial experiments have shown promising results, suggesting that with further development and optimization, this approach could provide a competitive edge over existing state-of-the-art solutions for secure and reliable access control in Smart Cities.

In future work, we plan to extend our research in several directions. First, we aim to experiment advanced GAN architectures and training techniques with the goal to further enhance the quality of synthetic EEG data. Secondly, we will investigate the adaptation of our approach to real-time authentication scenarios and evaluate its performance under different Smart City scenarios. Furthermore, we want to integrate an adaptive learning mechanisms to continuously update the evaluation model with new data streams to maintain the framework effectiveness over time.

Acknowledgment. We acknowledge financial support under the National Recovery and Resilience Plan (NRRP), Mission 4 Component 2 Investment 1.5 - Call for tender No.3277 published on December 30, 2021 by the Italian Ministry of University and Research (MUR) funded by the European Union - NextGenerationEU. Project Code ECS0000038 - Project Title eINS Ecosystem of Innovation for Next Generation Sardinia - CUP F53C22000430001 - Grant Assignment Decree No. 1056 adopted on June 23, 2022 by the Italian Ministry of Ministry of University and Research (MUR).

References

1. Abdul, Z.K., Al-Talabani, A.K.: Mel frequency cepstral coefficient and its applications: a review. IEEE Access (2022)
2. Abed, S.S., Abed, Z.F.: User authentication system based specified brain waves. J. Discret. Math. Sci. Cryptogr. **23**(5), 1021–1024 (2020)
3. Akbarnia, Y., Daliri, M.R.: Eeg-based identification system using deep neural networks with frequency features. Heliyon **10**(4) (2024)
4. Al Alkeem, E., et al.: An enhanced electrocardiogram biometric authentication system using machine learning. IEEE Access **7**, 123069–123075 (2019)
5. Arnau-González, P., Katsigiannis, S., Arevalillo-Herráez, M., Ramzan, N.: Bed: a new data set for eeg-based biometrics. IEEE Internet Things J. **8**(15), 12219–12230 (2021)

6. Choo, S., Park, H., Jung, J.Y., Flores, K., Nam, C.S.: Improving classification performance of motor imagery bci through eeg data augmentation with conditional generative adversarial networks. Neural Netw. 106665 (2024)
7. Homan, R.W., Herman, J., Purdy, P.: Cerebral location of international 10–20 system electrode placement. Electroencephalogr. Clin. Neurophysiol. 66(4), 376–382 (1987)
8. Islam, M.K., Rastegarnia, A., Yang, Z.: Methods for artifact detection and removal from scalp eeg: a review. Neurophysiologie Clinique/Clinical Neurophysiology 46(4–5), 287–305 (2016)
9. Jijomon, C., Vinod, A.: Person-identification using familiar-name auditory evoked potentials from frontal eeg electrodes. Biomed. Signal Process. Control 68, 102739 (2021)
10. Katsigiannis, S., Arnau-González, P., Arevalillo-Herráez, M., Ramzan, N.: Single-channel eeg-based subject identification using visual stimuli. In: 2021 IEEE EMBS International Conference on Biomedical and Health Informatics (BHI), pp. 1–4. IEEE (2021)
11. Lawhern, V., Hairston, W.D., McDowell, K., Westerfield, M., Robbins, K.: Detection and classification of subject-generated artifacts in eeg signals using autoregressive models. J. Neurosci. Methods 208(2), 181–189 (2012)
12. Mu, Z., Yin, J., Hu, J.: Application of a brain-computer interface for person authentication using eeg responses to photo stimuli. J. Integr. Neurosci. 17(1), 113–124 (2018)
13. Nakanishi, I., Hattori, M.: Biometric potential of brain waves evoked by invisible visual stimulation. In: 2017 International Conference on Biometrics and Kansei Engineering (ICBAKE), pp. 94–99. IEEE (2017)
14. Nijboer, F., Birbaumer, N., Kübler, A.: The influence of psychological state and motivation on brain-computer interface performance in patients with amyotrophic lateral sclerosis-a longitudinal study. Front. Neuropharmacol. 4, 55 (2010)
15. Piciucco, E., Maiorana, E., Falzon, O., Camilleri, K.P., Campisi, P.: Steady-state visual evoked potentials for eeg-based biometric identification. In: 2017 International Conference of the Biometrics Special Interest Group (BIOSIG), pp. 1–5. IEEE (2017)
16. Reshmi, K., Muhammed, P.I., Priya, V., Akhila, V.: A novel approach to brain biometric user recognition. Procedia Technol. 25, 240–247 (2016)
17. Saia, R., Balia, R., Sebastian, P., Pompianu, L., Carta, S., Pisu, A.: Enhancing eeg-based user verification with a normalized neural network ensemble approach. In: CHIRA (2024)
18. Saia, R., Carta, S., Fenu, G., Pompianu, L.: Brain waves and evoked potentials as biometric user identification strategy: an affordable low-cost approach. In: SECRYPT, pp. 614–619 (2022)
19. Saia, R., Carta, S., Fenu, G., Pompianu, L.: Brain waves combined with evoked potentials as biometric approach for user identification: a survey. In: Proceedings of SAI Intelligent Systems Conference, pp. 718–734. Springer (2023)
20. Saia, R., Carta, S., Fenu, G., Pompianu, L.: Influencing brain waves by evoked potentials as biometric approach: taking stock of the last six years of research. Neural Comput. Appl. 35(16), 11625–11651 (2023)
21. Srivastva, R., Singh, Y.N., Singh, A.: Statistical independence of ecg for biometric authentication. Pattern Recogn. 127, 108640 (2022)
22. Subha, D.P., Joseph, P.K., Acharya U, R., Lim, C.M., et al.: Eeg signal analysis: a survey. J. Med. Syst. 34(2), 195–212 (2010)
23. Yap, H.Y., Choo, Y.H., Mohd Yusoh, Z.I., Khoh, W.H.: Person authentication based on eye-closed and visual stimulation using eeg signals. Brain Informatics 8(1), 1–13 (2021)
24. Zhao, H., Chen, Y., Pei, W., Chen, H., Wang, Y.: Towards online applications of eeg biometrics using visual evoked potentials. Expert Syst. Appl. 177, 114961 (2021)

Virtualization of the Human Body: Deep-Fake Pornography - Its Ethical and Political Implications

Maria Cernat[1]([✉]) [iD], Dumitru Borțun[1] [iD], and Corina Matei[2] [iD]

[1] National School of Political and Administrative Studies, Bucharest, Romania
{maria.cernat,dumitru.bortun}@comunicare.ro

[2] Department of Communication and Public Relations, Titu Maiorescu University, Bucharest, Romania
corina.matei@prof.utm.ro

Abstract. In June 2019, a programmer released an app that enabled users to digitally undress individuals in photographs. Shortly after its launch, the publication Vice reported that the programmer withdrew the application due to concerns about the potential negative consequences of its use. Nevertheless, within a few days, the app was downloaded by over 95,000 users. Deep Nude is among several applications that generate highly realistic imitations of a person's voice or body. These technological advancements do not alter prevailing social norms of patriarchy, as demonstrated by Deep Nude's initial focus on photos of women; the program would utilize neural networks to fabricate intimate body parts when presented with images of men. In the context of modern technology, women's bodies have become commodified images that can be weaponized against them. Feminist activists argue that while politicians express concern over the censorship of misleading political information, the most vulnerable victims of deepfake technology remain women. We contend that the most effective approach to assessing the implications of this phenomenon is through a political economy lens, specifically examining the processes of producing, distributing, and consuming deepfake pornography. Additionally, it is crucial to recognize that the conception of cyberspace as a libertarian utopia contributes significantly to the challenges authorities encounter in their efforts to protect potential victims from this form of gendered violence.

Keywords: Deepfake pornography · Human body · Online communication · VR Pornography

1 Introduction

Technological advancements occur at an unprecedented pace, making it challenging to evaluate their consequences and implications fully. The implementation of AI tools for tasks such as answering phones or creating more user-friendly interfaces can be considered benign applications of technology. However, the utilization of algorithms

H. Plácido da Silva and P. Cipresso (Eds.): CHIRA 2024, CCIS 2370, pp. 468–475, 2025.
https://doi.org/10.1007/978-3-031-82633-7_28

and AI to generate nudity and deepfake pornography highlights a significant issue. Specifically, technology itself does not inherently possess what some users may term a "dark side"; rather, it is human behavior that reveals such tendencies, with technology serving merely as the conduit for their expression.

The phenomenon of deepfake pornography is integrated in the larger problem of cybercrime. Until the advances of tehnology, revenge porn was one of the most common forms of cyber violence against women and girls [2, 19] What deepfake porn reveals is something disconcerting: using AI tools, perpetrators of technology-enabled violence can use ordinary images of women's bodies from their social media accounts, or they can take pictures of their victims without their knowledge and then create accurate images of the victim's naked body.

This is a new frontier in the use of technology to harass and even terrorize women and girls [14, 21, 28].

These practices offer a fertile ground, although very challenging from a moral point of view, of exploring a variety of aspects. The unethical use of technology has been widely discussed from a variety of theoretical perspectives. While some authors focus on the criminal aspects of online behaviour [3, 6, 10], others discuss the ethical and political aspects of human-computer interaction [5], as well as the potential use of technology to commit acts of violence directed at women and girls [12]. In general, researchers are focusing on:

- the way of the usage of personas - AI-produced images resembling humans - for rendering the communication between the institution and the clients more "humane" [13] or - the ability of humans/software to detect deepfakes;
- the correlation between the ability to detect deepfakes and the perceived harm done by such AI-generated images;
- the effects of pornographic AI-generated pornography on potential victims;
- The impact of utilizing porn stars' bodies in the creation of deepfake videos on these individuals, who become entirely depersonalized in the process;
- the socio-economic profile of the producer, the consumer and victims of deepfake porn;
- the efforts to regulate the phenomenon;
- the responsibility of the platforms in preventing this type of content from being shared;
- the cultural norms that make deepfake porn so appealing for the perpetrators and so detrimental for the victims;
- the shared responsibility of the real persons distributing such materials and the platforms that make this distribution so easy and elimination from the platform so difficult;
- the gendered dimension of the phenomenon, underlined mainly by the fact that most of the producers are men while most of the victims are women;
- the regulation of AI in general since the uncontrolled proliferation of deepfakes denies us the chanse to have a shared reality.

At each stage of our analysis—production, distribution, and consumption—we identify a complex web of shared responsibilities that complicate the regulation of this phenomenon. By "shared responsibilities," we refer to the fact that producing deepfake pornography necessitates specific software. While generic algorithms may be employed, there are individuals who create both the technological tools—the AI software—and the deepfake pornography itself. Additionally, some develop AI software with the explicit intention of facilitating nefarious applications.

The most heated debates occur around the distribution of deepfake pornography. These debates cover a range of activities, from creating and distributing the content to simply sharing it. They also extend to the responsibility of platforms that knowingly allow such material to be distributed. Furthermore, there are instances of creating parallel online communication networks explicitly designed for sharing deepfake pornography and other adult content.

2   The Users/Distributors of Deepfake Nudes

Research indicates that technology-enabled sexual violence, particularly in the form of cybercrime, has distinct characteristics due to the heightened risk of revictimization. Unlike financial theft, which typically occurs once, a deepfake nude image of an individual can be uploaded and shared indefinitely online. This perpetual availability significantly increases the potential for emotional distress each time the image is encountered [10].

Journalist and author Michael Grothaus encountered significant challenges in attempting to contact deepfake porn producers. While exploring a site dedicated to deepfake pornography, he discovered an account that had uploaded over 1,600 videos, monetizing access to watermark-free versions. Despite the extensive volume of content, producers of such material remain hesitant to engage in discussions about their activity [9].

The vast majority of deepfake videos (more than 90%) are pornographic and the vast majority portray famous women [9]. But there are deepfake videos where famous actors faces are used in different famous movie sequences. The effect is often very funny and harmless. Such content creators have no problem in discussing their work. The fact that deepfake pornographers hide behind the curtain of anonymity could be a sign that deep down they are aware that what they are doing is not morally acceptable. Research shows that the majority of porn consumers are men [18]. It is difficult to assess the gender distribution of deepfake pornographers since the phenomenon is rather new and the first video of this kind was produced in 2017 [29] already in 2019 a report indicated that women were the exclusive target of deepfakes [26]. While public institutions are faced with the challenges of protecting the victims of deepfake pornography, it is private companies such as Sensity that conduct research and make it their purpose to "track the threat of malicious use of Generative AI techniques in videos, images, and audio in online environments" [31]. It is difficult to make clear assumptions about the social traits of deepfake pornographers. A thematic analysis of GitHub communities revealed the "toxic geek masculinity" prevalent in online communities related to platforms for technological tools [23].

At the level of the European Union, the Istanbul Convention requires states to gather information about violence against women and girls. This includes information about the perpetrators. But this type of gendered violence almost completely escapes the public institution's ability to collect relevant data.

3   The Sharing Platforms and the Shared Responsibility of Distributing Controversial Content

Anonymity makes it very difficult to trace the perpetrators and legal scholars claim that no crime was done if the deepfake pornographer uses a watermark advising users that the content is fake [9]. The only charges that can be brought against deepfake pornographers are related to defamation and intentional inflicting of harm. The same is true of deepfake pornographic content. From the outset, regulators have been reluctant to focus their efforts on punishing platforms that host such content. Moreover, the lack of accountability is not just a matter of political vision but also of the lack of the legal framework. As noted above, cyberspace was conceived as a techno-libertarian utopia where the state would be completely banned from intervening, as the "Declaration of Independence of Cyberspace" clearly states. [1]. This is the political vision that paved the way for digital giants such as Google and Facebook to become the new autocrats in this completely deregulated space. It is also important to note that the founders of Google, Larry Page and Sergey Brin, managed to introduce a new way of listing companies. By introducing two sets of shares, one with more voting power and one with less, they managed to maintain their autocratic control over the company. Facebook followed this path [32]. Far from being a place of free self-expression, cyberspace, understood as a system of interconnected technological devices, relies heavily on private companies to provide security and protection of personal data. There is little or no legal accountability for the sharing of deepfake nudes, and users can easily become distributors of such content. In addition, such content is used in private massages. Perpetrators sharing extremely sensitive content, such as child pornography, have even used encryption methods used by Soviet spy agencies to protect their communications [12].

Communication between computers can be used to create parallel online communication networks where the same device can act as both client and server, making it virtually impossible to trace the sharing of such content. In an extensive interview offered by Scarlett Johansson, one of the most targeted victims of deepfake porn, for the Washington Post, the actress claims that the Internet, in its current form, cannot be regulated and that nobody is safe in the virtual space [11].

4   The Victims of Deepfake Pornography

While exposure to pornography can pose risks associated with negative images of women, unrealistic expectations, complacency in violent misogynistic perspectives that make it very difficult to connect with peers, debates about the progressive potential of pornography have been heated [24]. Defenders of pornographic videos can argue that women choose to enjoy the sexually degrading practices of pornography. This is what came to be known as "Choice feminism". It may be controversial, but the attention it receives is significant [16].

Critiques of the production, distribution, and consumption of pornography are often met with accusations of prudishness or bigotry [8]. This ongoing debate undermines efforts to address deepfake pornography by overshadowing its specific harms with discussions about the progressive potential of "traditional" pornography. Furthermore, the advocacy by some activists for the unconditional acceptance of pornography as a legitimate industry and a source of empowerment for women and girls complicates the identification and prosecution of deepfake porn creators.

And while women's bodies have long been the target of violence, deepfake pornography takes us one step further by targeting children as young as 12 [22]. In a highly dabated case, Telegram founder Pavel Durov was arrested in Paris this year [20]. Born in Russia, Pavel Durov left his natal country in 2014 when he refused to comply with authorities' demands to ban opposition communities. He was hailed at the time as a free speech hero, only to be berated years later for blatant disregard of requests by authorities to assist in their investigation of cybercrime in general and deepfake in particular.

This is the first time the owner of a big tech communication platform is arrested and charged for the lack of content moderation. It appears the platform refused to assist the Korean authorities in a serious investigation regarding a vast network of cybercrime. Even child pornography was shared using Telegram and the platform ignored seven requests by the authorities to assist in the investigation [17]. According to the Korean authorities the number of underaged victims of deepfake pornography increased dramatically in the past years. South Korea's Advocacy Centre for Online Sexual Abuse victims (ACOSAV) was offering help to 86 teenage victims in 2023 and the number increased to 238 just in the first months of 2024 [17]. The shared responsibility of deepfake pornographers and sharing platforms must be reflected in legal and regulatory frameworks, particularly given that younger victims are often the most affected by this form of cybercrime. Although Durov claim he is being targeted for political reasons, his case should serve as a precedent for the multibillion-dollar technology companies that facilitate the dissemination of deepfake pornography.

This is particularly relevant since a recent article from The Wire shows that Google and Microsoft have a big problem with the uploading and sharing of deepfake porn videos [4].

Again, at the forefront of the fight to identify and denounce the practice of producing and sharing deepfake porn is a private company that runs the "Home Land Heroes" website. They also offer "identity protection" services. In the absence of regulation and sanctions, the private sector is both the source (if we have in mind those who produce deepfake porn) and the solution (if we have in mind identity protection services) to the problem [15] Certainly, the digital divide often manifests as a lack of financial resources to access identity protection products. This underscores the potential shortcomings of a private-sector-based system in establishing a legally robust democratic framework for safeguarding citizens' identities and images.. A survey conducted by Home Land Heroes shows that out of 95,820 deepfake online videos, 98% are deepfake porn and 99% of these videos feature female subjects, primarily those working in the entertainment industry [30]. More worryingly, recent data shows that 48% of American men have watched deepfake porn [30]. Until now, the victims of non-consensual, sexually explicit content produced by AI have primarily been women working in the entertainment industry. But recently, for as little as $65, pornographers will produce Deepfake porn with a woman of the customer's choice. They also use influencers to promote their content. Data shows that after a famous influencer admitted to watching deepfake porn, Google saw a spike in searches for 'deepfake porn' [27].

5   Discussion

The solutions to some of the issues outlined above become more apparent when we recognize that virtual space is not "neutral." It constitutes a political arena, despite the intentions of its creators to render it entirely "apolitical." The libertarian ideals of the tech engineers who developed cyberspace have led to a virtual environment devoid of state regulation. However, this utopia has revealed itself to be a sinister form of "techno-patriarchy", particularly for the most vulnerable populations, such as young girls.

What was initially framed as a gateway to freedom, self-determination, and spontaneous interaction has ultimately become a sanctuary for criminals and producers of deepfake pornography, as well as other violent forms of cybercrime. The libertarian techno-utopia presupposed that all individuals would act as equals in good faith, with the primary threat being a powerful state. However, the unforeseen consequence of allowing individuals to wield power without accountability has dismantled the structural conditions necessary to prevent cybercrime.

Few researchers revisit the foundational documents of cyberspace, yet neglecting these texts obscures some of the key factors contributing to phenomena like deepfake pornography and complicates our understanding of why this space resists regulation. It is essential to envision a radical transformation regarding ownership and the status of digital sharing platforms and cyberspace as a whole, which could create structural barriers to engaging in criminal activities.

References

1. Barlow, J.P.: a Declaration of the Independence of Cyberspace. Electronic Frontier Foundation (1996). https://Www.Eff.Org/Cyberspace-Independence. Accessed 14 Dec 2023
2. Branch, K., Hilinski-Rosick, C.M.: Revenge porn victimization of college students in the United States: an exploratory analysis. 7 Int. J. Cyber Criminol. 11(1), 128–142 (2017). https://doi.org/10.5281/Zenodo.495777
3. Broadhurst, R.L., Lee, L.Y.C.: Cybercrime in Asia: trends and challenges. In: Hebenton, B., Jou, S. (eds.), Handbook of Asian Criminology. Handbook of Asian Criminology. Springer, New York (2013)
4. Burgess, M. (2020, October 20). a Deepfake Porn Bot Is Being Used to Abuse Thousands of Women. Wired UK. https://www.wired.co.Uk/Article/Telegram-Deepfakes-Deepnude-Ai. Accessed 14 Dec 2023
5. Cerrnat, M., Bortun, D., Matei, C.S.: Human-Computer Interaction: Ethical Perspectives on Technology and Its (Mis)Uses (J. Filipe, M. Śmiałek, a. Brodsky, & S. Hammoudi, Eds.). Enterprise Information Systems: 24th International Conf. ICEIS 2022, Virtual Event, 25–27 April 2022, Revised Selected Papers Springer Nature, Switzerland (2022)
6. Cobb, S.: Sizing cybercrime: incidents and accidents, hints and allegations. In: Virus Bulletin Conference (2015)
7. Compton, S. (Director). (2023). Another Body [Film]. https://www.Imdb.Com/Title/Tt2246 4734/
8. Dines, G.: Pornland: How Porn Has Hijacked Our Sexuality. Beacon Press, Boston (2011)
9. Grothaus, M.: Faking It: a Journey into Deep Fake Pornography. Coronet (2022)

10. Hall, M., Hearn, J.: Violation by Sexual Image Distribution, "Revenge Pornography", Cyber-abuses, and Prevention. in 6th International Report. Crime Prevention and Community Safety: Preventing Cybercrime (P. 165). Pablo Madriaza, Montreal, Canada: International Centre for the Prevention of Crime (ICPC) (2018). http://Urn.Kb.Se/Resolve?Urn=Urn:Nbn:Se:Oru:Diva-71477

11. Harwell, D., Polk, G.: Scarlett Johansson on Fake AI-Generated Sex Videos: 'Nothing Can Stop Someone from Cutting and Pasting My Image'. Washington Post, 31 December 2018. https://Www.Washingtonpost.Com/Technology/2018/12/31/Scarlett-Johansson-Fake-Ai-Generated-Sex-Videos-Nothing-Can-Stop-Someone-Cutting-Pasting-My-Image/

12. Hughes, D.M.: The use of new communications and information technologies for sexual exploitation of women and children. Hastings J. Gend. Law **13**(1), 129–148 (2002)

13. Kaate, I., Salmninen, J., Santos, J., Jung, S.-G., Olkkonen, R., Jansen, B.: The realness of fakes: primary evidence of the effect of deepfake personas on user perceptions in a design task. Int. J. Hum. Comput. Stud. **178**(103096) (2023)

14. Kietzmann, J., Lee, L.W., Mccarthy, I.P., Kietzmann, T.C.: Deepfakes: trick or treat? Business Horizons **63**(2), 135–146 (2020). https://doi.org/10.1016/J.Bushor.2019.11.006

15. King, B.: Do ID Theft Monitoring Services Really Work? Home Security Heroes, 8 November 2023. https://www.homesecurityheroes.Com/Identity-Theft-Protection/. Accessed 14 Dec 2023

16. Kiraly, M., Tyler, M. (eds.): Freedom Fallacy: the Limits of Liberal Feminism. Connor Court Publishing, Australia (2015)

17. Lee, H.: South Korea: the Deepfake Crisis Engulfing Hundreds of Schools. BBC, 2 September 2024. https://Www.Bbc.Com/News/Articles/Cpdlpj9zn9go. Accessed 24 Sep 2024

18. Malki, K., Rahm, C., Öberg, K.G., Ueda, P.: Frequency of Pornography Use and Sexual Health Outcomes in Sweden: Analysis of a National Probability Survey. Pubmed, 12 September 2021. https://Pubmed.Ncbi.Nlm.Nih.Gov/34526247/. Accessed 24 Sep 2024

19. Mcglynn, C., Rackley, E., Houghton, R.: Beyond 'Revenge Porn': the Continuum of Image-based Sexual Abuse. Feminist Legal Studies, 25 (2017). https://link.springer.com/, https://doi.org/10.1007/S10691-017-9343-2

20. Melander, I., Faulconbridge, G. (2024, August 25). Telegram Messaging App CEO Durov Arrested in France. Reuters. 25 Aug 2024. https://www.Reuters.Com/World/Europe/Telegram-Messaging-App-Ceo-Pavel-Durov-Arrested-France-Tf1-Tv-Says-2024-08-24/. Accessed 24 Sep 2024

21. Mirsky, Y., Lee, W.: The creation and detection of deepfakes: a survey. ACM Comput. Surv. **54**(1) (2021). https://doi.org/10.1145/3425780

22. Muresan, A., Popescu (Illustrations), S.: Corp Străin: Cum Este Folosită Tehnologia Deepfake Împotriva Femeilor? Scena 9, 20 August 2024. https://Www.Scena9.Ro/Article/Corp-Strain-Tehnologie-Deepfake-Pornografie-Nuduri-Femei-Bullying. Accessed 24 Sep 2024

23. Newton, O.B., Stanfill, M.: My NSFW video has partial occlusion: deepfakes and the technological production of non-consensual pornography. Porn Stud. **7**(4), 398–414 (2020)

24. Oddone-Paolucci, E., Genius, M., Violato, C.: A meta-analysis of the published research on the effects of pornography. In: Violato, C., Oddone-Paolucci, E. (eds.), The Changing Family and Child Development. Taylor & Francis Group (2019)

25. Orel, M.: Escaping reality and touring for pleasure: the future of virtual reality pornography. Porn Stud. **7**(4) (2020). https://doi.org/10.1080/23268743.2020.1777895

26. Sensity (2019). the State of Deepfakes 2019 Landscape, Threats, and Impact. Www.Sensity.Ai. https://Share.Hsforms.Com/1cg_H2apnrrufzen8hdjwpw3hq83

27. Tenbarge, K.: The Deepfake AI Porn Industry Is Operating in Plain Sight. NBC News (2023, March 27). https://www.nbcnews.com/tech/Internet/Deepfake-Porn-Ai-Mr-Deep-Fake-Economy-Google-Visa-Mastercard-Download-Rcna75071. Accessed 14 Dec 2023

28. Tolosana, R., Vera-Rodriguez, R., Fierez, J., Morales, A., Ortega-Garcia, J.: Deepfakes and beyond: a survey of face manipulation and fake detection. Information Fusion **64**, 131–148 (2020)
29. Vasist, P.N., Krishnan, S.: Engaging with Deepfakes: a meta synthesis from the perspective of social shaping oftechnology theory. Emerald Insight **5**(33) (2022). https://doi.org/10.1108/INTR-06-2022-0465
30. Webb, M., Medleva, V., Keary, T.: Deepfake Porn: Is Creation Punishable by Law in 2023? Techopedia (2023, December 11). https://www.Techopedia.Com/Deepfake-Porn-Is-Creation-Punishable-by-Law. Accessed 14 Dec 2023
31. Why Sensity. (2024, March 27). Sensity AI. https://Sensity.Ai/Why-Sensity/. Accessed 24 Sep 2024
32. Zuboff, S.: The Age of Surveillance Capitalism: the Fight for a Human Future at the New Frontier of Power. Profile Books (2019)
33. Van Dijk, J.A., Van Deursen, A.J.: The digital divide shifts to differences in usage. New Media Soc. **16**(3), 507–526 (2013). https://doi.org/10.1177/1461444813487959

Implementing and Evaluating Trustworthy Conversational Agents for Children

Marina Escobar-Planas[1,2]([✉]) [ID], Roberto Ruiz-Sánchez[3] [ID], Pedro Frau-Amar[4] [ID],
Vicky Charisi[2] [ID], Carlos-D. Martínez-Hinarejos[1] [ID], Emilia Gómez[2] [ID],
and Luis Merino[3] [ID]

[1] Universitat Politècnica de València, Camí de Vera, s/n, 46022 València, Spain
mescpla@doctor.upv.es
[2] Joint Research Centre, Calle Inca Garcilaso, 3, 41092 Seville, Spain
[3] Universidad Pablo de Olavide, Ctra. de Utrera km 1, 41013 Seville, Spain
[4] Lambda Developments S.L., Calle grañon 12-4 1, 28050 Madrid, Spain

Abstract. Conversational Agents (CAs) have become increasingly popular in many settings, including households. However, despite the increasing frequency of children's interactions with these systems, there is still little research on the ethical design of CAs, particularly for this special population. To address this gap, in this study we design, develop and evaluate a Child-Friendly CA for collaborative storytelling, implementing specific guidelines to ensure a trustworthy design for children based on key principles such as human agency, data privacy or transparency as outlined by the High-Level Expert Group on artificial intelligence (HLEG). To evaluate the trustworthiness of the Child-Friendly CA, designers and developers conduct a collaborative assessment by applying the Assessment List for Trustworthy Artificial Intelligence (ALTAI) using the Delphi methodology. Our results demonstrate that our Child-Friendly CA design improves the trustworthiness of the system and highlights the importance of designing CAs that consider the particularities of children's interactions. Our findings contribute to the still scarce literature on trustworthy CAs and provide insights for developers striving to ensure a trustworthy experience for children.

Keywords: Conversational agents · Children · Trustworthy AI · Human-computer interaction · AI Evaluation · Ethical AI

1 Introduction

In recent years, Conversational Agents (CAs) have gained significant popularity and become an ubiquitous presence in many homes, improving accessibility, engaging learning, and promoting social behaviour [4,49,51]. As the prevalence of CAs continues to grow, an important aspect that requires careful consideration is their interaction with children. Children's innate curiosity and receptiveness to new technologies have made them active users of digital companions, engaging in educational activities, seeking answers to their endless questions, and enjoying playful games [19, 40, 27].

The raising global concern over the ethical development of Artificial Intelligence (AI) [1,20,44] is especially important when considering children. This population presents a unique set of challenges due to their particular characteristics and specific needs, which must be addressed to ensure their safety and well-being [5, 11]. For instance, the work described in [47] identifies ten areas of convergence between general AI frameworks and codes for age-appropriate design; this includes design principles for age-appropriate AI applications, the need for child-specific frameworks, and guidelines for applications designed for children. In response to this need, organisations like UNICEF have developed ethical guidelines for AI designed for children [11]. Although they are not specific to CAs, these guidelines provide valuable insights and have been applied to the development of CAs embodied in robots [45], demonstrating their applicability to AI systems interacting with children. Other research [7] explores aspects of fairness in robot-related situations, highlighting the importance of ethical principles in AI systems for children.

Recently, a specific set of guidelines for trustworthy CAs for children has been developed [17], addressing the research gap in the ethical development of CAs [10]. To offer practical advice, these guidelines were applied in a conceptual design of a CA for creating a wish-list of toys for children [16]. However, this application was theoretical and not implemented in a real device. Moreover, none of these studies have evaluated the improvement in trustworthiness after applying the ethical guidelines. While important advances have been made, a significant gap remains in the practical implementation and evaluation of ethical guidelines in the development of CA systems that consider children's specific needs. To the best of our knowledge, this work is the first to not only implement these ethical guidelines of CAs for children but also to evaluate their impact on the trustworthiness of the developed system.

This paper presents the design, development, and evaluation of a CA system prioritising trustworthiness for child users in the context of collaborative storytelling. Our work addresses the following Research Questions (RQs):

RQ1. *How can guidelines for trustworthy CAs can be practically applied in the development of a child-friendly CA?*
RQ2. *To what extent does using such guidelines result in a measurable improvement in the trustworthiness of a CA for children?*

To address the above-mentioned questions, we applied guidelines that are specific to the trustworthy design of CAs and children [17]. Subsequently, three developers and designers of the system (some of them with technical background and some with previous experience with AI ethical guidelines) collaborated using the Delphi methodology [26] to apply the Assessment List for Trustworthy Artificial Intelligence (ALTAI) [21], evaluating the impact that our implementations had on the trustworthiness of the system.

Our work demonstrates the applicability of general AI ethical guidelines and the improvement of the children-oriented system trustworthiness, highlighting the importance of designing technology that addresses the challenges posed by this population. Our findings contribute to the nascent field of trustworthy CAs, and also provide practical advice for their child-friendly development.

2   Background and Related Work

2.1   Artificial Intelligence and Ethics

In many areas, AI has rapidly and significantly affected human society and the ways we interact with each other. Along the way, AI has presented substantial ethical and socio-political challenges that call for thorough research and specific actions [23]. The analysis of social and ethical implications of algorithmic systems is not new [18]. The area of machine ethics has long been concerned with ensuring that the behaviour of machines towards human users is ethically acceptable [2]. More recently, the urgency and the complexity of this problem have resulted in the rapid expansion of multidisciplinary communities that seek the implementation of aspects such as privacy, transparency, fairness, etc., into machines for increasing their trustworthiness (e.g. the ACM FAccT conference[1]), as well as in the increase in the methods for auditing trustworthiness of intelligent systems [38].

The study presented by Tolmeijer et al. [43] shows that there is a sharp increase in the implementation of machine ethics in real-life applications, presenting the complexity of the implementation of ethics in AI and providing an exhaustive theoretical overview of the existing work. As such, our work aims to address the problem of implementation of ethical guidelines specifically for making child-friendly CAs, as one of the applications with increasing use by children.

2.2   Trustworthy AI

While relevant research communities provide systematic approaches and guidelines for the implementation of ethics in AI, governments seek for approaches to protect citizens from emerging risks, making AI systems trustworthy. For instance, the European Commission[2], recognising the need for action, in 2018 appointed a group of experts (the High-Level Expert Group on AI, HLEG) to provide advice on its AI strategy. HLEG defined guidelines for the development of trustworthy AI [20], comprising seven key requirements:

1. **Human Agency and Oversight.** AI systems should augment human decision-making while respecting autonomy and ensuring equal societal support; oversight guarantees keeping basic rights.
2. **Technical Robustness and Safety.** AI systems must be reliable and resilient, capable of preventing risks, and minimising harm in varying environments and against challenges.
3. **Privacy and Data Governance.** Ensuring privacy with careful data management (accurate and appropriate usage), and safeguarding personal data privacy.
4. **Transparency.** Traceability of decisions, explainability of processes, and clarity on capabilities and limitations.
5. **Diversity, Non-Discrimination and Fairness.** AI systems should be inclusive and mitigate biases, ensuring fair treatment across all societal segments and accessibility for people with disabilities.

---

[1] https://facctconference.org/.
[2] https://european-union.europa.eu.

6. **Societal and Environmental Well-Being.** AI should consider its impacts, support sustainable initiatives, uphold democratic values, and ensure societal welfare and well-being of next generations.
7. **Accountability.** There must be mechanisms for responsibility and risk management in AI development, with avenues for addressing any adverse effects.

These specific requirements are considered fundamental in Europe and have been considered into the design of the AI Act [29], the main European Union regulatory initiative on AI. As such, these specific requirements have been used as the basis for our work.

2.3 Trustworthy Guidelines for CAs and Children

Previous works have explored the notion of trustworthiness in CAs by primarily focusing on the trust that the agent fosters in the user, often emphasising the agent's embodiment as an influential factor [28]. However, the relevant literature on CAs indicates a critical gap in terms of ethical design of CAs [10] and the need to consider ethical dimensions and values in the design of trustworthy CAs, aligned with principles such as fairness, robustness and transparency.

Based on the seven requirements (Sect. 2.2), previous research has provided guidelines for the development of trustworthy CAs for children [17], which we have incorporated into our study. We summarise their key considerations in the following five main points (see also Fig. 1):

1. **Stakeholders Involvement.** Involve children stakeholders (children, parents, ...) in the the system's design and testing.
2. **Risk Management.** Implement actions to ensure privacy and security of personal data in data storage; define metrics and risk levels to monitor system performance; facilitate testing evaluation, including external audits; allow users to report about the system.
3. **AI Awareness.** Emphasise the non-human nature of CAs, explaining capabilities and limitations; maximise user agency in decision-making.
4. **Age Appropriate Behaviour.** Mitigate technical difficulties that may arise when CAs interact with children or marginalised groups; call guardians for assistance if any problem arises; implement double consent mechanisms (guardian and child approval).
5. **Transparency.** Inform about the system's nature and privacy limitations, providing constant access to in-depth information; always use an age-appropriate language; transparency is transversal to other previous points (e.g., as a tool to mitigate risks on 'Risk management', 'AI awareness', and 'Age appropriate behaviour').

2.4 Evaluation of Trustworthiness

Evaluation of conversational agents has been focused mainly on efficiency and effectiveness measures. Reviews on the topic [9,12,50] mainly cite frameworks such as

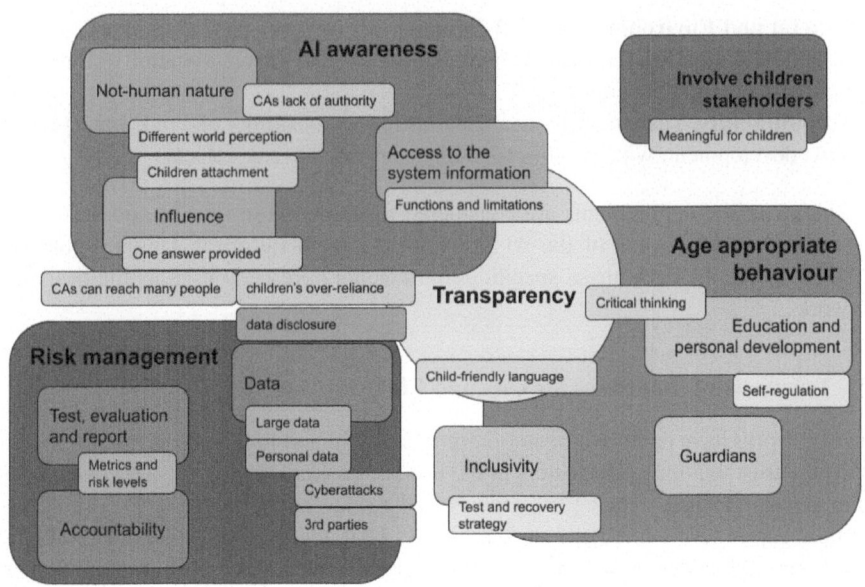

Fig. 1. Critical considerations for the development of trustworthy conversational agents for children. Extracted by [17] with the permission of the authors.

PARADISE [46], EAGLES [3], or measures such as FED [30]. However, all these measures are related to user satisfaction and are not taking into account aspects related to trustworthiness considerations. Some work that briefly discuss ethical considerations for CAs has focused on the perception as a human of the system [36].

This lack of criteria about the trustworthiness considerations has been common until recently to all AI based systems, not only to CAs. Thus, to complement existing research about trustworthy AI (see Sect. 2.2), the Assessment List for Trustworthy AI (ALTAI) [21] has been introduced as a practical self-assessment tool to facilitate the evaluation of trustworthiness, i.e., as a checklist for AI systems designers and developers in order to evaluate their own implementations and incorporate to them elements to improve trustworthiness. ALTAI[3] was defined after a piloting process with 350 stakeholders, and encompass 69 self-evaluation questions for designers and developers with an in-depth understanding of the system's characteristics. These questions are organised under the seven trustworthy requirements presented in Sect. 2.2. Table 1 presents a selection of these questions, along with their corresponding trustworthy requirements. ALTAI has also been referenced in various research studies, demonstrating its emerging use as a framework for evaluating AI systems' trustworthiness [37,40,41], and consequently it has been applied in our work too.

---

[3] https://digital-strategy.ec.europa.eu/en/library/assessment-list-trustworthy-artificial-intelligence-altai-self-assessment.

Table 1. Sample questions from ALTAI, and their corresponding trustworthy requirement.

Question	Requirement
Does the AI system simulate social interaction with or between end-users or subjects?	Human agency and oversight
How exposed is the AI system to cyber-attacks?	Technical robustness and safety
Was your AI system developed, by using or processing personal data?	Privacy and data governance
Did you explain the decision(s) of the AI system to the users?	Transparency
Does the AI system corresponds to the variety of preferences and abilities in society?	Diversity, non-discrimination and fairness
Are there potential negative impacts of the AI system on the environment?	Societal and environmental well-being
Did you ensure that the AI system can be audited by independent third parties?	Accountability

3   System Development

To apply the previously established guidelines, it was necessary to have a baseline CA, which would be called Control CA. Initially, we considered using a commercial home assistant, but this was in conflict with our aim to enhance privacy standards later on. Therefore, to achieve a greater flexibility in the development and enhanced control over data management, we decided to implement our own Control CA. The implementation took into account general behaviours of commercial devices (Google Assistant[4], Siri[5], Alexa[6]), such as the constant mimicry of emotional responses (details in Sect. 3.2).

To contextualise our CA, we selected a task-oriented approach suitable for a broad audience, including children. This allows to initially develop the Control CA as a non-child-specific system which would later be adapted to be child-friendly. To this end, we chose collaborative storytelling, i.e., facilitating the co-creation of a story between the user and the CA, since it is an activity that has demonstrated to engage both adults and children [8,14,52].

To emphasise the system's software capabilities, we minimised its physical embodiment, using a computer connected to a microphone and speakers. This design encourages users to concentrate on the story and the conversation, lowering the physical influence of the CA. In the following subsections, we provide more details about the CA's architecture and interaction design.

3.1   Architecture

The system's architecture is composed of three interconnected modules: Automatic Speech Recognition (ASR), Dialogue Manager (DM), and Text-to-Speech (TTS). This section provides a technical description of each module.

---

[4] https://assistant.google.com/intl/en-en/.

[5] https://www.apple.com/siri/.

[6] https://alexa.amazon.com.

Automatic Speech Recognition (ASR). The ASR module listens to the user's speech and provides a transcription that is passed to the DM. In anticipation of implementing trustworthy actions in the future ('risk management' strategies advised in Sect. 2.3) and to ensure an effective comprehension of children, we decided to use a local state-of-the-art solution based on OpenAi's Whisper[7]: Faster Whisper[8]. This approach guarantees that no data is shared with third-party technology providers while achieving high accuracy for different ages and languages. Ambience noise calibration was performed to improve speech recognition.

Dialogue Manager (DM). The DM module manages the conversational flow and coordinates the different components involved. Two basic submodules are used:

1. *DialogFlow.* It is responsible for system introduction and handling initial user interactions; after its execution, control is passed to the Storytelling submodule. It is developed within the DialogFlow platform[9]. Leveraging the DialogFlow API[10], this module facilitates interaction with users in different languages. It also allows our system to analyse user input during the introduction phase, recognising the underlying intent and generating appropriate responses. Intent-based responses enhance the system's ability to understand and address user queries or requests, resulting in an interactive and responsive conversational experience.
2. *Storytelling* It provides narratives and identifies user preferences to continue the story. It is designed to offer users interactive and customisable stories, operating in a "create your own adventure" [35] format, which allows users to control the course of the narrative. Users first choose one of the proposed topics, and the system initiates the story with a predefined premise (e.g., a farmer walking in the woods). At certain predetermined junctures in the story, users are presented with choices that influence the plot (e.g., what did he find? a king, a bear, or a sheep?), and the system identifies the choice. After three iterations, the conclusion of the story is reached (e.g., the farmer and the bear lived happily ever after), and the DM resumes control to ensure the farewell phase. We have developed numerous story trees associated with different themes, resulting in a total of 108 different endings.

Text-To-Speech (TTS). The TTS module facilitates communication with the user through synthesised speech. It converts text into an audio file and reproduces it by using the gTTS API[11], which supports multiple languages.

3.2 Interaction Design

This section aims to explain the user interaction with the system. Hardware setup consisted of a microphone and a speaker connected to a computer, solely used to run the

---

[7] https://openai.com/blog/introducing-chatgpt-and-whisper-apis.

[8] https://github.com/guillaumekln/faster-whisper.

[9] https://dialogflow.cloud.google.com.

[10] https://cloud.google.com/dialogflow/es/docs/reference.

[11] https://cloud.google.com/text-to-speech/docs/libraries?hl=es-419.

program and not as an interface. During the interaction, the system progresses through three phases, Introduction, Storytelling, and Final, described as follows:

- *Introduction.* Every interaction opens with an icebreaker where the system introduces itself: *"Hello, my name is Bruno*[12]. *What's your name?"*. After user's response, it adds a friendly *"Nice to meet you. How are you?"*. The system answers mimics emotional responses (e.g. *"Great! I'm feeling good too, my batteries are charged and I'm glad to be here with you!"*), similar to commercial devices. Bruno then explains its role as a storytelling assistant and asks for consent: *"Hey, look, I'm an interactive system specialised in creating stories in collaboration with people. Do you want to make a story with me?"*.
- *Storytelling.* The system initiates the narrative experience; first, it offers to explain the rules (*"We'll have a great time. Do you want me to tell you the rules?"*); the rules' explanation is *"It's quite simple. First, you choose a theme. Then, I'll start a story based on your choice, asking for your input at key moments to shape its direction. We'll continue this way until we complete our tale. Is everything clear?"*. Once the user indicates readiness, the system encourages choosing a story theme,: *"Fantastic, let's have some fun! Now, please pick one of these topics: mystery or fantasy."*. At this point, the Storytelling module (Sect. 3.1) activates, launching the collaborative storytelling process. The user's choices decide the story's progression and final outcome across three iterations.
- *Final.* The interaction reaches its conclusion and the system acknowledges the completion of the story with a sense of achievement (*"I am very happy! We have got a very good story. Would you like to repeat it?"*), offering the user the option to create another story or exit. If the user decides not to repeat, the system transitions into the farewell (*"Well, I am very happy to have met you. I hope we'll talk again soon. Have a nice day, see you next time!"*).

4 Methodology

This section presents the methodology used to enhance the Control CA by applying the considerations outlined in Sect. 2.3 to develop a trustworthy, Child-Friendly CA. Additionally, it describes the application of ALTAI to measure the trustworthiness of both systems.

4.1 Implementation of Trustworthy Guidelines

A team of three developers were advised through biweekly discussion meetings during four months by seven experts (one specialist in ethics in AI, one engineer, two specialists in cybersecurity and AI governance, and three psychologists with specialisation in the use of technology with children). They developed a first CA version (Control CA, see Sect. 3). Although this version was not designed with specific considerations for

---

[12] Bruno was chosen as a name that is similar in different languages such as Spanish, German or Italian.

children, some factors influenced the selection of its software components in order to ensure a fast adaptation into a trustworthy AI system later on (details in Sect. 3.1).

Subsequently, the team of developers applied the guidelines described in Sect. 2.3 to refine and develop a new version of the system, referred to as Child-Friendly CA. This updated version is specifically designed to enhance the trustworthiness of the system for children. Actions taken by developers to comply with the guidelines and successfully implement them are summarised in Table 2 and detailed in subsections below.

Stakeholder Involvement. We actively engaged stakeholders throughout various stages of the development process. During interaction design, to enhance the Control CA for children, we consulted with fourteen diverse stakeholders: three families, three teachers, and one psychologist (six children aged between 5 and 16, and eight adults in total). The consultation occurred in two phases. In an early stage it was an online questionnaire where we presented the Control CA's behaviour and asked for suggestions on adapting the interaction for children; the stakeholders provided advice, particularly on vocabulary and language (e.g. a teacher recommended changing *'interacting'* to *'talking'*), and on the system's behaviour (e.g. a family suggested: *"Age could be asked to know what level to target and what vocabulary to use"*). All suggestions were considered, some being implemented but some discarded due to various constraints (e.g., a family proposed, *"The system could recognise the user's voice and learn from it to provide more entertaining or ingenious responses"*, but this was not feasible with the chosen software and data governance of the trustworthy system). During the second consultation, stakeholders answered a second questionnaire with more specific design questions, such as *"What non-human name would you give the system?"*; children's suggestions like 'Gala' or 'Gabo' were integrated into the design. Additionally, popular themes, such as 'Animals', 'Dreams', 'Pirates', and 'Space', were also selected for story creation, suitable for different age groups.

In the testing phase, the development team conducted two stages of testing with different stakeholders. In the initial stage, two families (three adults and four children) were recruited. The objective was to gain an understanding of how the system would recognise children at different developmental levels. Our findings showed that the system struggled to accurately comprehend speech from a 2-year-old child, and accuracy improved substantially with children aged 5–7 years. In the last testing stage, we recruited three families (two adults and six children) to test the final version of the system, which led to improvements in the system's functionality and bug resolution.

Risk Management. We implemented several risk management actions to ensure the privacy and security of user data in the Child-Friendly CA.

Firstly, after consulting with data protection experts, we chose to run the system locally in a Python environment to enhance data privacy and control. Although some system components (Whisper, DialogFlow, gTTS) required an internet connection to communicate with servers, we checked that no user data was stored or collected on those servers. Furthermore, we verified that these components utilised input data exclusively for the provision of services required in our system.

Table 2. Summary of the actions implemented to apply the guidelines and develop the Child-Friendly CA. The guideline categories include stakeholder involvement (Stake.), risk management (Risk), AI awareness (Awarn.), age appropriate behaviour (Behav.), and transparency (Transp.). Actions marked with an asterisk ('*') indicate that they also had an impact on the Control CA.

Trustworthy actions	Stake.	Risk	Awarn.	Behav.	Transp.
Involve stakeholders for design	x	.	.	.	.
*Choose technology that ensures privacy	.	x	.	.	.
*Choose inclusive ASR	.	.	.	x	.
Ask about user's age	.	.	.	x	.
Add a double consent mechanism	.	.	.	x	.
Inform about privacy	.	.	.	.	x
Inform about the CA's nature	.	.	x	.	.
Inform about the CA's capacities	.	.	.	.	x
Inform about the CA's limitations	.	.	.	.	x
Add access to in-depth information	.	.	.	.	x
Use an age appropriate language	.	.	.	x	x
Use an age appropriate story	.	.	.	x	.
*Provide 3 choices	.	.	x	.	.
Include a STOP mechanism	.	.	x	.	.
Measure the ASR's accuracy	.	x	.	.	.
*Keep logs	.	x	.	.	.
Involve stakeholders for testing	x	x	.	.	.

Secondly, we employed actions to store the interaction content (dialogue logs, timestamps, generated stories) within the system, in order to facilitate later auditing. This action was also incorporated into the Control CA system. Additionally, to control the challenges posed by children's speech patterns, an accuracy check sentence was implemented to monitor the system's understanding of individual children. At the beginning of the program, the user is asked to utter a predefined sentence, whose recognition accuracy is used for future tests, quality controls, and audits.

Finally, we conducted a thorough stakeholder testing to simulate real interactions, which enabled us to evaluate and identify any existing issues and to swiftly resolve them, ensuring that the Child-Friendly CA functioned reliably and accurately.

AI Awareness. To ensure user's awareness of the Child-Friendly CA's non-human nature and promote user agency in decision-making, we implemented the following actions. Firstly, when the system is introducing itself, the system emphasised its non-human nature to create a clear expectation among users of its capabilities. We expressly mentioned that the system could only deliver stories and respond to a developer's programming, nothing beyond its design..

Secondly, the system was designed to promote user agency. A "STOP" prompt was featured to enable users to stop the process at any moment and set the limits of the interaction. Whenever possible, we provided three choices, enabling user agency without overwhelming user's attention, giving children opportunities to make decisions and ensuring an efficient, engaging, and enjoyable interaction. This three choices option was also implemented in the Control CA, as experts considered it a popular way to proceed with other devices. It is important to note that the Control CA also provided three choices, aligning with the behaviours exhibited by other similar devices.

Age Appropriate Behaviour. To ensure that the Child-Friendly CA was appropriate for different age ranges and other demographic characteristics of children, we implemented several actions that allowed the system to adapt its behaviour and vocabulary accordingly.

Firstly, since there were future plans to employ the system for Spanish and Italian children, the system was designed to interact in these two languages, which accommodates the system children from different regions and promotes inclusion. Additionally, we tested with stakeholders to verify that the ASR module could accurately comprehend speech from children. We confirmed that the system was effective for children older than five.

Secondly, the system incorporated an age check step at the beginning of the interaction (*"Hi, before we start, can you tell me how old you are?"*). This allowed the system to adapt its language, behaviour, and story content to align with the specific age range of the user and ensure the delivery of age-appropriate content. The incorporation of stronger human supervision in story creation, along with active involvement from stakeholders, facilitated this customisation process.

Finally, for users under the age of eighteen, we implemented a double-consent protocol. The system prompts to involve a trusted adult, called guardian (*"Can you call an elder you trust for a moment, please? I need permission to talk to you"*). It then seeks guardian confirmation regarding their responsibility for the child, provides them information, and obtains their consent. The system goes back to the child, it supplies information to them, and seeks their consent to proceed with the interaction. This double-consent protocol ensures that the Child-Friendly CA only interacts with children who have obtained consent from their guardian, facilitating supervision.

Transparency. As highlighted in Sect. 2.3, transparency is a key aspect that intersects with other guideline points. Consequently, some actions mentioned here may overlap with others previously discussed.

To promote transparency about the capabilities and limitations of our Child-Friendly CA, we provided a brief introduction to the system during the initial interaction (before consents), and provided easy access to more detailed information. We aimed to inform users about the nature of the system, usability, and privacy concerns. For children, information was simplified and adapted to their range age. Specifically, we emphasised that the system was an AI technology and should not be mistaken for a human. For young children, as Straten et al. [42] suggests, we clarified that the system does not have feelings and does not do anything beyond what has been programmed to do.

To facilitate the usability of the system, the Child-Friendly CA provided information about different commands that can be used to request more information about the system, or to stop the interaction at any time. We also informed users that the system cannot listen while it is talking (to avoid some communication issues).

Finally, we informed users about the system's privacy and data management policies, in a more technical and detailed way to adult users and in a simpler and concise manner for children. This included an explanation that the system stores and processes data, and that the conversations with the system could be accessed by certain personnel (e.g. researchers) for research and quality improvement purposes.

> "My name is 'Gabo', I'm not human and I'm not alive. You know what I am? A machine! I am able to talk to you by a thing they call "artificial intelligence". But if I'm talking I can't listen at the same time. Also if at any time you want to stop talking to me, you can say "I don't want to talk to you anymore" and I will stop. I also have to tell you, that even though I have artificial intelligence, don't think I have any desires or decisions of my own! I only do the things I was created to do. It's just that I function differently from you, for example, when I think something, it can be stored in places where other people can look at it. And I don't have feelings either: I can't be sad or happy, but I don't need to for what I was created for! Anyway, I'm getting too long, if you want to know more about me you can tell me "tell me more about yourself" at any time. But now why don't I tell you what I was made for? I have been made to play with people to create stories."
> —Child-Friendly CA

4.2 Evaluation of Trustworthiness

To evaluate the impact of the implemented guidelines on the system's trustworthiness, we compared the Control CA and the Child-Friendly CA using ALTAI (Sect. 2.4). ALTAI is designed as a self-evaluation tool specifically intended for the system's own developers, as it requires deep knowledge of the design and implementation of the systems. Therefore, this evaluation was performed by the three systems developers. We acknowledge that developer self-assessment can introduce some bias; however, we mitigated this by using the Delphi method [26] to enhance evaluation robustness and achieve a consensus.

The Delphi method followed these steps: (1) developer independent measure of the system using ALTAI, (2) joint discussion and discrepancy resolution, (3) developer independent re-measure using ALTAI and previous step agreements, (4) final evaluation by averaging the ratings.

For the ALTAI measurement, each expert filled out a questionnaire (Fig. 2) to respond to the 69 ALTAI questions, using a three-point Likert scale (Low/Medium/High) [25]; the 'n/a' (not applicable) mark was available too, along with a comments field. The Likert scale answers were converted into numerical values (1 = Low, 2 = Medium, 3 = High), while 'n/a' responses were excluded from the calculations. The average score for each question was then calculated based on the inputs from all three experts. To measure trustworthiness in each of the seven requirements, we computed an

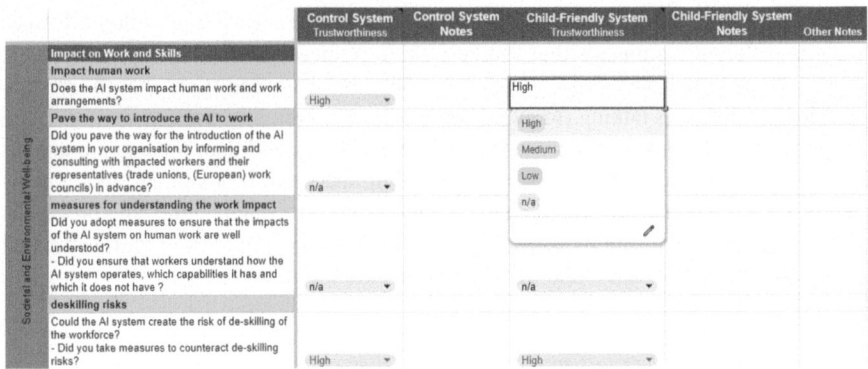

Fig. 2. ALTAI Questionnaire to address the trustworthiness of the conversational agents. First columns categorises each item, while the second details the questions. Subsequent columns are dedicated to rating the trustworthiness of both Control and Child-Friendly systems, with space for specific comments.

Table 3. Trustworthiness rate of the Control CA and the Child-Friendly CA in the different HLEG trustworthy requirements. The last column (Imp.) indicates the improvement from the Control CA to the Child-Friendly CA.

	Control	Child-Friendly	Improv.
Human agency and oversight	50%	79%	29%
Technical robustness and safety	58%	60%	2%
Privacy and data governance	58%	67%	9%
Transparency	30%	63%	33%
Diversity, non-discrim. and fairness	33%	65%	32%
Societal and environmental well-being	78%	78%	0%
Accountability	50%	54%	4%
TOTAL	**51%**	**66%**	**15%**

average rating from the scores of all the associated questions. An overall trustworthiness rating was obtained by averaging the scores across all the 69 questions. Finally we normalised all averages to percentages to ease comparison across different experimental scales.

In an effort to delve deeper into the developers' evaluations, we also conducted a qualitative analysis of their responses. This involved examining each question in detail, considering both the ratings and the developers' explanatory notes, and matching them with the specific actions taken when developing the Child-Friendly CA.

5   Results

Following the Delphi method, the evaluation of the AI systems' trustworthiness started with an initial individual rating from the experts with a 70% of agreement. After the joint meeting and discussion, the re-rating step obtained a 90% agreement. This fact underscores the importance of expert discussions to enhance the reliability and accuracy of our assessments.

The ratings of the different systems across the seven trustworthy requirements are presented in Table 3. It can be observed that the implemented actions had a significant impact, with approximately 30% increase in the areas of "Human Agency and oversight", "Transparency", and "Diversity, non-discrimination and fairness". Given the extensive nature of ALTAI (69 questions and sub-questions), we highlight specific insights from the developers' responses[13] that underscore the observed differences and similarities between the Control CA and the Child-Friendly CA.

Human Agency and Oversight. (29% improvement). This category includes questions about the system's communication of its non-human nature, its impact on human autonomy, and the user's ability to terminate the interaction. The Child-Friendly CA received higher ratings for various questions, such as *"Could the AI system generate confusion for some or all end-users or subjects on whether they are interacting with a human or AI system?"*; Developer 1 (D1) noted: *"While the generic system says it is an interactive system, small children may not understand this definition. The Child-Friendly system explains in detail that it is an artificial intelligence and what does it mean"*. Another example was *"Did you ensure a 'stop button' or procedure to safely abort an operation when needed?"*, to which Developer 3 (D3) commented, *"Users with the Child-Friendly system can stop the interaction whenever they want with the sentence 'I don't want to talk more with you'."* Actions that influenced the responses in this area included involving stakeholders in the design, double consent mechanism, informing about the CA's nature, and including a STOP button, among others (see Table 4).

Technical Robustness and Safety. (2% improvement). Only a marginal difference was observed in this category, which focuses on the system's resilience to attacks, general safety, and accuracy. Several questions received identical ratings for both systems (e.g., Developer 2 (D2) commented,*"We used a state of the art ASR that has high accuracy across different settings"*). However, a notable distinction was found for *"Did you define risks, risk metrics and risk levels of the AI system in each specific use case?"*, where D1 indicated *"With the Child-Friendly system, we took some actions to try to measure and mitigate potential risks of exclusion"*. The key actions affecting this section responses included choosing an inclusive ASR and maintaining logs (details in Table 4).

Privacy and Data Governance. (9% improvement). Considerations included the impact on privacy rights, compliance with data protection regulations, and privacy implications of non-personal training data. The question *"Did you consider the impact of the AI system on the right to privacy, the right to physical, mental and/or moral integrity and the right to data protection?"* improved the results for the Child-Friendly CA due to specific considerations of children's characteristics and rights during its development. However, both systems received similar ratings on questions about General Data Protection Regulation (GDPR) compliance. Actions contributing to this distinction included involving stakeholders for design, adding a double consent mechanism, and informing about privacy (Table 4).

---

[13] The full dataset is available upon request.

Table 4. Summary of the actions that may have impacted the seven requirements: human agency and oversight (Hum.), technical robustness and safety (Tech.), privacy and data governance (Priv.), transparency (Transp.), diversity, non-discrimination and fairness (Fair), societal and environmental well-being (Well), and accountability (Acc.). Black dots indicate actions unique to the Child-Friendly CA. White dots represent actions implemented in the Child-Friendly and Control systems.

Improvement action	Hum.	Tech.	Priv.	Transp.	Fair	Well	Acc.
Improvement rate	29%	2%	9%	33%	32%	0%	4%
Involve stakeholders for design	●		●		●		
Choose tech. that ensures privacy		○	○				
Choose inclusive ASR		○			○		
Ask about user's age					●		
Add a double consent mechanism	●		●				
Inform about privacy			●	●			
Inform about the CA's nature	●			●			
Inform about the CA's capacities	●			●			
Inform about the CA's limitations	●			●			
Add access to in-depth information	●			●			
Use an age appropriate language				●	●		
Use an age appropriate story	●				●		
Provide 3 choices	○						
Include a STOP mechanism	●						
Measure the ASR's accuracy		●		●	●		●
Keep logs		○		○			○
Involve stakeholders for testing				●	●		●

Transparency. (33% improvement). Transparency involved clearly communicating the AI's non-human nature and informing users about its purpose, limitations, and operation. The Child-Friendly CA excelled in this aspect, particularly for questions like "*In cases of interactive AI systems (e.g. chatbots, robo-lawyers), do you communicate to users that they are interacting with an AI system instead of a human?*", or "*Did you establish mechanisms to inform users about the purpose, criteria and limitations of the decision(s) generated by the AI system?*". D3 noticed "*The Child-Friendly system explains in detail that it is an artificial intelligence and what does it mean.*". Another aspect of transparency, system traceability, showed overlap with the 'Technical Robustness and Safety' category, primarily due to the practices of measuring the ASR's accuracy (Child-Friendly CA) and maintaining system logs (both systems). Table 4 details influential actions enhancing transparency, including providing detailed information about the CA's nature, capabilities, and limitations, and facilitating access to in-depth information.

Diversity, Non-Discrimination and Fairness. (32% improvement). This category includes questions about considering diversity in the design and testing, access to society, and stakeholder participation. The Child-Friendly CA showed a high improvement for this category. For instance, for the question, *"Did you ensure that the AI system corresponds to the variety of preferences and abilities in society?"*, it was noted that both systems supported languages (Spanish and Italian) which are less commonly used in CAs. D1 commented *"We tried to use AI systems that work fine with children and different languages"*. The Child-Friendly CA was particularly distinguished in this aspect due to its tailored approach to include children (a group often overlooked in societal considerations) by adapting its language and behaviour based on the user's age. Other relevant questions (e.g.,*"Did you consider a mechanism to include the participation of the widest range of possible stakeholders in the AI system's design and development?"*, *"Did you test for specific target groups or problematic use cases?"*) were positively influenced by the involvement of stakeholders (e.g., D3 mentioned, *"Pilot testing with families were conducted to evaluate the system"*).

Societal and Environmental Well-Being (0% improvement). This category assesses identification of environmental damage, impact on human work, and impact on large society. Child-friendly actions did not alter the overall well-being according to ALTAI.

Accountability (4% improvement). Accountability involves mechanisms for external auditing and continuous monitoring of AI systems. For most of the questions, both systems yielded similar results, but a difference was found for *"Did you foresee any kind of external guidance or third-party auditing processes to oversee ethical concerns and accountability measures?"*. In this regard, the Child-Friendly CA garnered a higher rating due to its enhanced engagement with stakeholders during the testing phase.

Overall, the trustworthiness rating for the Child-Friendly CA was 66%, while the Control CA received a rating of 51%. The 15% difference between the two ratings indicates that the recommended guidelines have improved the trustworthiness of the system.

6 Conclusion and Future Work

In this work, our focus has been on the implementation of a set of guidelines to develop trustworthy CAs for children, and the evaluation of the system trustworthiness with the use of the ALTAI instrument designed especially for this purpose. Driven by the RQ1 (*How can guidelines for trustworthy CAs can be practically applied in the development of a child-friendly CA?*), we described in detail the process of the practical implementation of a set of guidelines to the development of a CA for children for collaborative storytelling, and considering the unique challenges posed by children. Our work, as far as we know, is the first to apply ALTAI to measure trustworthiness on CAs. Aligned with previous work [22,53], our experience reveals the complexity of applying design decisions through several stages of the development of a system to enhance trustworthiness, with a focus on stakeholder involvement (including a variety of stakeholders, such as designers, developers, parents, experts in child development, engineers, and children), risk management, AI awareness, age-appropriate behaviour, and transparency.

To address the RQ2 (*To what extent does using such guidelines result in a measurable improvement in the trustworthiness of a CA for children?*), we implemented two CAs, one as a Control System and one as the Child-Friendly and compared the perceived trustworthiness with the use of the ALTAI as a measurement instrument. The comparison of the two systems using ALTAI in combination with the Delphi method revealed that the Child-Friendly CA improved its trustworthiness rating by 15% compared to the Control CA. The evaluation showed large improvement in some categories whereas other were not affected. For instance, the results of our study indicate notable improvements of the perceived agency and transparency in the Child-Friendly version. Agency is particularly important since recent work indicates that CAs have the potential to influence children's decision-making and to change their judgements about moral transgressions, and consequently to influence their perceived agency [34,48]. In addition, Transparency, that showed the greatest improvement, has been considered one of the fundamentals in AI ethics, needing special attention when the system is used by children [6,15,42]. Our results indicate that improving the transparency of the system affected the rating of its trustworthiness.

Examples of categories with minimal improvement are Technical Robustness and Safety. To ensure the Control CA met minimum safety and privacy standards for children (necessary for conducting future experiments), we selected a technology that guarantees privacy and inclusive ASR (which has been reported as challenging for young users [31,32]). This same technology was also applied to the Child-Friendly CA, resulting in both systems having similar robustness assessments. Another category without noticeable improvement is Environmental and Societal Well-being. However, previous work [17] has pointed out that this category does not include important child-centred aspects such as cognitive and socio-emotional development or learning. We believe these should have been noted as improvements in our system, as previous research proved to enhance children's agency and imaginative skills though storytelling activities [13,24], and the tales incorporated in our Child-Friendly CA included learning messages for young users.

Our findings provide insights for developers who consider trustworthiness in CA design, especially for children, emphasising the importance of considering the challenges posed by child users. In conclusion, incorporating trustworthy design principles in conversational agent development, particularly for children reachable systems, can improve the quality of CAs and enhance user experience.

Our study has several limitations. First, the evaluation was conducted by our own developers. Although we employed the Delphi method to enhance robustness, our results may still be subject to bias. Second, our Child-Friendly CA is not optimised for children under the age of five due to limitations in ASR technology accuracy. Third, while double consent mechanisms are appropriate for young children, further research is needed to determine their suitability for teenagers. Lastly, our storytelling method followed a create-your-own-adventure format, which lacks the freedom of open collaborative storytelling.

Future work includes conducting an experimental study to understand the impact of the Child-Friendly CA on children's behaviour and their perceptions, moving forward from developers and designers towards children and their guardians viewpoints. Additionally, we aim to incorporate some objective measures into our evaluation process and explore how to build trustworthy systems with different story formats to further enhance children's creativity in storytelling. We also encourage future research to develop a Child-Friendly version of existing commercial devices, provided that privacy concerns can be addressed, to gain a broader understanding of the effectiveness of ethical guidelines.

Acknowledgments. We thank all the stakeholders, developers and experts who supported the development and evaluation of the CAs, the stories creators and the translators who made multiple languages versions. During the preparation of this work, the authors used ChatGPT [33] to enhance language and readability. After using this tool, the authors reviewed and edited the content as needed and take full responsibility for the final version of the publication. This work was carried out with the support of the Joint Research Centre of the European Commission in the framework of the Collaborative Doctoral Partnership Agreement No. 35500.

Disclosure of Interests. The authors have no competing interests to declare that are relevant to the content of this article.

References

1. Australian AI Ethics Framework. Department of Industry, Science and Resources (2019). https://www.industry.gov.au/publications/australias-artificial-intelligence-ethics-framework
2. Anderson, M., Anderson, S.L.: Machine ethics: creating an ethical intelligent agent. AI Mag. **28**(4), 15–15 (2007)
3. Brey, T., Hanrieder, G., Heisterkamp, P., Hitzenberger, L., Regel-Brietzmann, P.: Issues in the evaluation of spoken dialogue systems-experience from the access project. In: LREC (2000). http://www.lrec-conf.org/proceedings/lrec2000/pdf/162.pdf
4. Catania, F., et al.: Boris: a spoken conversational agent for music production for people with motor disabilities. In: CHItaly 2021: 14th Biannual Conference of the Italian SIGCHI Chapter, pp. 1–5 (2021)
5. Charisi, V., et al.: Artificial intelligence and the rights of the child: towards an integrated agenda for research and policy. Technical report, Joint Research Centre (Seville site) (2022)
6. Charisi, V., Dignum, V.: Operationalizing ai regulatory sandboxes for children's rights and wellbeing. In: Régis, C., Denis, J.L., Axente, M.L., Kishimoto, A. (eds.) Human-Centered AI: A Multidisciplinary Perspective for Policy-Makers, Auditors, and Users, chap. 21. Routledge, New York (2024)
7. Charisi, V., Imai, T., Rinta, T., Nakhayenze, J.M., Gomez, R.: Exploring the concept of fairness in everyday, imaginary and robot scenarios: a cross-cultural study with children in japan and uganda. In: Proceedings of the 20th Annual ACM Interaction Design and Children Conference, pp. 532–536 (2021)
8. Del-Moral-Pérez, M.E., Villalustre-Martínez, L., Neira-Piñeiro, M.D.R.: Teachers' perception about the contribution of collaborative creation of digital storytelling to the communicative and digital competence in primary education schoolchildren. Comput. Assisted Lang. Learn. **32**(4), 342–365 (2019)
9. Deriu, J., et al.: Survey on evaluation methods for dialogue systems. Artif. Intell. Rev. **54**, 755–810 (2021). https://doi.org/10.1007/s10462-020-09866-x
10. Diederich, S., Brendel, A.B., Morana, S., Kolbe, L.: On the design of and interaction with conversational agents: an organizing and assessing review of human-computer interaction research. J. Assoc. Inf. Syst. **23**(1), 96–138 (2022)
11. Dignum, V., Penagos, M., Pigmans, K., Vosloo, S.: Policy guidance on AI for children. Communications of UNICEF (2021)
12. Dybkjaer, L., Bernsen, N.O., Minker, W.: Evaluation and usability of multimodal spoken language dialogue systems. In: Speech Communication, vol. 43, pp. 33–54. Elsevier (2004). https://doi.org/10.1016/j.specom.2004.02.001
13. Elgarf, M., Zojaji, S., Skantze, G., Peters, C.: Creativebot: a creative storyteller robot to stimulate creativity in children. In: Proceedings of the 2022 International Conference on Multimodal Interaction, pp. 540–548 (2022)

14. Engebak, I.M.H.: A digital game using collaborative storytelling to help children practice empathy. Master's thesis, NTNU (2019)
15. Escobar-Planas, M., Charisi, V., Hupont, I., Martínez-Hinarejos, C.D., Gómez, E.: Towards children-centred trustworthy conversational agents. In: Chatbots-The AI-Driven Front-Line Services for Customers. IntechOpen (2023)
16. Escobar-Planas, M., Gómez, E., Martínez-Hinarejos, C.D.: Enhancing the design of a conversational agent for an ethical interaction with children. In: Proceedings of the IberSPEECH 2022, pp. 171–175 (2022). https://doi.org/10.21437/IberSPEECH.2022-35
17. Escobar-Planas, M., Gómez, E., Martínez-Hinarejos, C.D.: Guidelines to develop trustworthy conversational agents for children. In: Proceedings of the ETHICOMP 2022, pp. 342–360 (2022)
18. Friedman, B., Nissenbaum, H.: Bias in computer systems. ACM Trans. Inf. Syst. (TOIS) **14**(3), 330–347 (1996)
19. Garg, R., Sengupta, S.: He is just like me: a study of the long-term use of smart speakers by parents and children. Proc. ACM Interact. Mob. Wearable Ubiquitous Technol. **4**(1), 1–24 (2020)
20. HLEG: Ethics guidelines for trustworthy ai. B-1049 Brussels (2019)
21. HLEG: The assessment list for trustworthy artificial intelligence (ALTAI). European Commission (2020)
22. Hopman, K., Richards, D., Norberg, M.N.: An embodied conversational agent to support wellbeing after injury: insights from a stakeholder inclusive design approach. In: International Conference on Persuasive Technology, pp. 161–175. Springer (2024)
23. İpek, Z.H., Gözüm, A.I.C., Papadakis, S., Kallogiannakis, M.: Educational applications of the chatgpt ai system: a systematic review research. Educ. Process: Int. J. **12**(3), 26–55 (2023)
24. Lee, Y., Kim, T.S., Chang, M., Kim, J.: Interactive children's story rewriting through parent-children interaction. In: Proceedings of the First Workshop on Intelligent and Interactive Writing Assistants (In2Writing 2022), pp. 62–71 (2022)
25. Likert, R.: A technique for the measurement of attitudes. Arch. Psychol. (1932)
26. Linstone, H.A., Turoff, M. (eds.): The Delphi Method. Addison-Wesley Reading, MA (1975)
27. Lovato, S.B., Piper, A.M., Wartella, E.A.: Hey google, do unicorns exist? Conversational agents as a path to answers to children's questions. In: Proceedings of the IDC, pp. 301–313 (2019)
28. Lupetti, M.L., Hagens, E., Van Der Maden, W., Steegers-Theunissen, R., Rousian, M.: Trustworthy embodied conversational agents for healthcare: a design exploration of embodied conversational agents for the periconception period at erasmus mc. In: Proceedings of CUI, pp. 1–14 (2023)
29. Madiega, T.: Artificial intelligence act. European Parliament: European Parliamentary Research Service (2021)
30. Mehri, S., Eskenazi, M.: Unsupervised evaluation of interactive dialog with dialogpt. arXiv preprint arXiv:2006.12719, pp. 225–235 (2020). https://aclanthology.org/2020.sigdial-1.28/
31. Ong, D.T., De Jesus, C.R., Gilig, L.K., Alburo, J.B., Ong, E.: A dialogue model for collaborative storytelling with children. In: ICCE 2018 - 26th International Conference on Computers in Education, Main Conference Proceedings, pp. 205–210 (2018)
32. Ong, E., Alburo, J.B., De Jesus, C.R., Gilig, L.K., Ong, D.T.: Challenges posed by voice interface to child-agent collaborative storytelling. In: 2019 22nd Conference of the Oriental COCOSDA International Committee for the Co-ordination and Standardisation of Speech Databases and Assessment Techniques (O-COCOSDA), pp. 1–6. IEEE (2019)
33. OpenAI: Chatgpt-4 (2024), large language model
34. Oswell, D.: The Agency of Children: From Family to Global Human Rights. Cambridge University Press, Cambridge (2013)

35. Packard, E.: The Cave of Time, ser. Choose Your Own Adventure. Bantam Books, New York (1979)
36. Radziwill, N.M., Benton, M.C.: Evaluating quality of chatbots and intelligent conversational agents. arXiv preprint arXiv:1704.04579, pp. 25–36 (2017). https://arxiv.org/abs/1704.04579
37. Rajamäki, J., Gioulekas, F., Rocha, P.A.L., Garcia, X.d.T., Ofem, P., Tyni, J.: ALTAI tool for assessing ai-based technologies: lessons learned and recommendations from shapes pilots. In: Healthcare, vol. 11, p. 1454. MDPI (2023)
38. Scharowski, N., Benk, M., Kühne, S.J., Wettstein, L., Brühlmann, F.: Certification labels for trustworthy AI: insights from an empirical mixed-method study. In: Proceedings of the 2023 ACM Conference on Fairness, Accountability, and Transparency, pp. 248–260 (2023)
39. Sciuto, A., Saini, A., Forlizzi, J., Hong, J.I.: Hey alexa, what's up? A mixed-methods studies of in-home conversational agent usage. In: Proceedings of the 2018 Designing Interactive Systems Conference, pp. 857–868 (2018)
40. Slosiarová, N., Mesarčík, M., Jurkáček, P., Podroužek, J.: Trustworthy AI in dental care beyond artificial intelligence act (2023)
41. Stahl, B.C., Leach, T.: Assessing the ethical and social concerns of artificial intelligence in neuroinformatics research: an empirical test of the European union assessment list for trustworthy AI (ALTAI). AI Ethics 3(3), 745–767 (2023)
42. Straten, C.L.v., Peter, J., Kühne, R., Barco, A.: Transparency about a robot's lack of human psychological capacities: effects on child-robot perception and relationship formation. ACM Trans. Hum.-Robot Interact. (THRI) 9(2), 1–22 (2020)
43. Tolmeijer, S., Kneer, M., Sarasua, C., Christen, M., Bernstein, A.: Implementations in machine ethics: a survey. ACM Comput. Surv. (CSUR) 53(6), 1–38 (2020)
44. UNESCO, C.: Recommendation on the ethics of artificial intelligence (2021)
45. UNICEF, Gomez, R., Charisi, V.: UNICEF Pilot study on Policy Guidance for AI and Child's Rights. Office of Global Insight and Policy (2021). https://www.unicef.org/globalinsight/media/2206/file
46. Walker, M.A., Litman, D.J., Kamm, C.A., Abella, A.: Paradise: a framework for evaluating spoken dialogue agents. arXiv preprint cmp-lg/9704004, pp. 271–280 (1997). https://aclanthology.org/P97-1035/
47. Wang, G., Zhao, J., Van Kleek, M., Shadbolt, N.: Informing age-appropriate ai: examining principles and practices of AI for children. In: Proceedings of the CHI, pp. 1–29 (2022)
48. Williams, R., Machado, C.V., Druga, S., Breazeal, C., Maes, P.: My doll says it's ok a study of children's conformity to a talking doll. In: Proceedings of IDC, pp. 625–631 (2018)
49. Xu, et al.: Mathkingdom: teaching children mathematical language through speaking at home via a voice-guided game. In: Proceedings of the 2023 CHI Conference on Human Factors in Computing Systems, pp. 1–14 (2023)
50. Yeh, Y.T., Eskenazi, M., Mehri, S.: A comprehensive assessment of dialog evaluation metrics. arXiv preprint arXiv:2106.03706 pp. 15–33 (2021), https://aclanthology.org/2021.eancs-1.3/
51. Zhang, L., Weitlauf, A.S., Amat, A.Z., Swanson, A., Warren, Z.E., Sarkar, N.: Assessing social communication and collaboration in autism spectrum disorder using intelligent collaborative virtual environments. J. Autism Dev. Disord. 50, 199–211 (2020)
52. Zhang, Z., et al.: Storybuddy: a human-AI collaborative chatbot for parent-child interactive storytelling with flexible parental involvement. In: Proceedings of CHI, pp. 1–21 (2022)
53. Zicari, R.V., et al.: Co-design of a trustworthy ai system in healthcare: deep learning based skin lesion classifier. Front. Hum. Dyn. 3, 688152 (2021)

Author Index

The manufacturer's authorised representative in the EU is Springer
Nature Customer Service Centre GmbH, Europaplatz 3, 69115 Heidelberg,
Germany. If you have any concerns regarding our products, please
contact ProductSafety@springernature.com

Printed and bound by CPI Group (UK) Ltd, Croydon, CR0 4YY
27/04/2026
02097586-0019